Rocky Hill Sep 7 1783

Sir,

I have carefully perused the
Papers which you put into my hands
relative to Indian Affairs.

My Sentiments with respect to
the proper line of Conduct to be observed
towards these people coincides precisely with those
delivered by Genl Schuyler, so far as he has gone in his Letter
of the 29th July to Congress (which with
the Paper alluded to is herewith returned) — & for the rea:
:sons there he has assigned; a repetition
of them therefore by me would be unnecessary. — But
independant of the following
considerations have, as well, weight in my Mind.

To suffer a wide extended Country
to be over run with Land Jobbers — the
over run with scattered settlers, in my opinion, is
culators & Monopolizers is inconsistant
with that wisdom & policy which our true interest
dictates, or an enlightned People ought to
adopt, and besides is pregnant of
disputes both with the Savages, evils which
are easier to be conceived than described
and for the sake of aggrandizing a few avaricious men
to the prejudice of many & the embarrass:
ment of Government. — for the People
without contributing in the smallest
degree to the support of Government or
considering themselves as amenable
to its Laws, will involve it by their un
restrained conduct, in inextricable per
plexities, more than probable in Blood

My ideas therefore of the
line of Conduct proper to be observed not only to
wards the Indians, but for the government
of the Citizens of America, in their settle
=ment

BURT FRANKLIN: BIBLIOGRAPHY & REFERENCE SERIES 339
American Classics in History & Social Science 129

CALENDAR OF

THE CORRESPONDENCE OF

GEORGE WASHINGTON

CALENDAR OF

THE CORRESPONDENCE OF

GEORGE WASHINGTON

COMMANDER IN CHIEF OF THE CONTINENTAL ARMY

WITH THE CONTINENTAL CONGRESS

PREPARED FROM THE ORIGINAL MANUSCRIPTS
IN THE LIBRARY OF CONGRESS BY JOHN C.
FITZPATRICK, DIVISION OF MANUSCRIPTS

Fitzpatrick, John Clement 1876-1940

Burt
Franklin
New York

1. Washington, George, Pres. U.S. 1732-
1799

I.t

MAKE a
NOTE →

Published by BURT FRANKLIN
235 East 44th St., New York, N.Y. 10017
Originally Published: 1906
Reprinted: 1970
Printed in the U.S.A.

Library of Congress Card Catalog No.: 72-124310
Burt Franklin: Bibliography and Reference Series 339
American Classics in History and Social Science 129

CONTENTS

3

PREFATORY NOTE

Under an Executive order of March 9, 1903, the Washington Papers were transferred from the Department of State to the Library of Congress. Long as the manuscripts had been in the possession of the Government, no list of the letters of Washington had ever been so much as attempted; and the letters written to him had been but imperfectly listed by Jared Sparks when engaged in preparing his "Writings of George Washington" first published in 1833–37. The great size and historical importance of the collection demand a closer study, and a series of calendars generally descriptive of its contents. The first of these calendars deals only with the correspondence between the General and the Continental Congress.

The segregation in the Library of Congress of other collections offered an unusual opportunity to make the calendar complete so far as concerned the materials for the period covered. So that while the Washington Papers forms the basis of the calendar, related material is drawn from other sources, wherever the original is found in the Library of Congress. The various sources are the Washington Papers, the papers of the Continental Congress, and the papers of Robert Morris.

I. THE WASHINGTON PAPERS.

The arrangement of the Washington Papers is peculiar, and was due to the ingenuity of Jared Sparks. They are divided into two great series. The letters from and the letters to the General; and the letters from him during the Revolutionary War are subdivided into subseries as follows:

A. Letters to the President, Committees, and individual members of the Continental Congress.

B. Letters and orders to officers of the Continental Army.

C. Letters to the Governors and other civil officers of the States.

D. Letters to foreign ministers, officers or individuals.

E. Letters to officers in the service of the British Crown.

F. Records of the Councils of War and opinions of the general officers on military affairs.

P. Private letters.

Before this division, which appears to have been due to the secretaries and aids of the General, had been perfected, copies of letters were kept in books irrespective of a distribution according to addressee. Four volumes of such letters exist and the contents have been drawn upon as needed for this calendar.

The entire contents of Series A appear in this calendar as well as such letters and papers in the other series as were pertinent to the purpose. These letters are the first drafts, either in the writing of Washington or his aids, and are, for the most part, not signed. As the idea and not the language of the letter, when written by an aid, was Washington's, some effort has been made to identify the writer of the draft. The success is greater than was anticipated, and it is for the first time possible to measure the confidence reposed in his aids by the Commander-in-chief. It was a surprise to find some drafts or copies in the writing of Martha Washington; it was quite as surprising to learn the great number of papers in the writing of Alexander Hamilton, John Laurens and Tench Tilghman. It is still more surprising to find elaborate drafts entirely in the writing of Washington himself, and often prepared in the most critical periods of the war. As a general and useful guide to the writers of these drafts a list of those serving as aids and secretaries to Washington, with a page of their writing, is added (p. 9). Outside of Series A a few letters have been drawn from Series P, and from the four combined volumes. Of these two series there exist transcripts prepared by Richard Varick in 1781–3. A few missing originals have been made good from these transcripts.

The Letters to Washington, comprising 117 volumes, form the second great source of materials listed in this calendar. Some attempt had been made by Mr. Sparks to bind in separate volumes what papers had been received from the Continental Congress; but the attempt was imperfectly planned and very imperfectly carried into effect. The result has been that not only were those Congress volumes calendared (Vols. 89–98) but the entire collection has been examined for papers that had been misplaced.

II. PAPERS OF THE CONTINENTAL CONGRESS.

The third great source of papers were the Papers of the Continental Congress. A rough list of these papers was prepared when Peter Force was compiling the "American Archives," but it is a list useless for historical purposes, conveying no idea of the contents of the different papers or of the relations of one to another. Crudely planned, it was still more crudely prepared, and it is impossible to trace even the location of a single letter and the response made, or of a single paper and its enclosures. The letters of Washington to the Congress fill eleven volumes, and transcripts were made of them in nine volumes under the direction of the Secretary, Charles Thomson. This series, undoubtedly the finest series of Washington letters in existence, contains many holographs of Washington, and many written by his aids, with a large number of enclosures relating to civil and military affairs. The writer of the body of the papers has in each case been identified, so far as was possible. The letter books of the Presidents of Congress (those of John Hancock are not in the collection), and the Dispatch and Committee books gave much additional material. Of high importance was the series of reports of committees of Congress on letters of Washington. The letter books of Robert Morris, while Superintendent of Finance, were searched and whatever was written to Washington was inserted in this calendar.

In the preparation of so extensive a list certain details were omitted which might seem of importance. The same letter may exist in four forms: 1, the draft; 2, the Varick transcript of the draft; 3, the letter sent to the President, and 4, the Thomson transcript of this letter. It has not been thought necessary to mention the letter in more than one of its forms. Should a closer study of a letter be desirable the investigator can easily learn whether the other forms are in the Library. Series A, of the drafts forms the basis of the list, and is the more interesting as being the form of paper nearest to headquarters and while in process of composition. The changes and additions clearly show this process. The dates of replies to letters are noted in the calendar wherever they are to be found endorsed on the original letter (an asterisk [*] denotes that the reply is in the Library of Congress); but no attempt had been made to insert such information when not so noted as the chronological arrangement of this calendar readily lends itself to the uses of the investigator. The number of pages occupied by a paper in a book of transcripts is not given, as the information would convey no true conception of the length of the original paper.

While it would be useful to indicate where each document could be found in print (if it has been printed), the task would be greater than the value of the results. References have been confined to the Sparks and the Ford editions of the " Writings of Washington," and to the "Journals of the Continental Congress."

The true first document of the calendar is Washington's paper read in Congress June 16, 1775, accepting the command of the Continental army. The last document was properly the resignation of his commission in 1783. Two entries of 1784 were added to complete the story of incidents occurring before the resignation; and one of 1789, announcing the election of Washington to the Presidency under the Federal Constitution, fittingly closed his connection with the Continental Congress, and marked his re-entrance into public life under the new political conditions which put an end to the existence of that revolutionary, but then almost powerless, legislative body.

It would be useless to undertake to summarize the nature of this collection or to dwell upon its importance to history and biography. It is enough to say that it is unique, most notable and of imperishable interest, embodying the history of the Revolution and the acts of the leading men of that time.

The calendar has been prepared by Mr. John C. Fitzpatrick, of the Division of Manuscripts.

WORTHINGTON CHAUNCEY FORD
Chief Division of Manuscripts

HERBERT PUTNAM
    Librarian of Congress
        Washington, April, 1906

LIST AND WRITING OF WASHINGTON'S AIDS-DE-CAMP AND SECRETARIES

This comprises all of the regularly appointed aids and secretaries, the General Orders, a resolution of the Continental Congress, or a definite statement from the Commander-in-Chief being the authority. It does not include the many individuals who were transiently at Headquarters and occasionally pressed into service as amanuenses:

SOURCES AND REFERENCES

I. Papers of George Washington: [by series and volume.]

Series A: (7 vols.) Drafts of Washington's letters to the Presidents of Congress, Committees, Board of War, etc. Designation: **A.**

Series P: (3 vols.) Drafts of private letters to the Presidents, Members of Congress, etc. Designation: **P.**

Miscellaneous: (4 vols.) Letter books covering in the main the years 1775–1776. Designation: **M.**

Letters to Washington: (117 vols.) Volumes 89–98 comprize the larger part of the letters received from Congress. Designation: (volume number of the series) e. g. **89.**

From the Force Collection: (7 vols.) Drafts and letters from and to Washington. (Calendar of these was issued by the Library in 1901.) Designation: **W.**

Miscellany: Some hundred loose, unbound, and unindexed material from various sources, the larger part from the Department of State. Designation: **Miscel.**

II. Papers of the Continental Congress: [**C. C.** and volume number.]

Nos. 13, 14, 15, 16, 18: (5 vols.) Letter books of the Presidents of Congress.

No. 33: (2 vols.) Reports of Committees.

No. 133: (1 vol.) Letter book of the Committee left in charge at Philadelphia. 1776–7.

No. 152: (11 vols.) Washington's letters to Congress. This supplements and is supplemented by Series A above, the gaps in each being in great measure filled by the other.

No. 169: (9 vols.) Transcript made in the Office of the Secretary of Congress of 152, supplying many deficiencies.

Nos. 185, 186, 191: (6 vols. in all.) Despatch and Committee Books, which for the period covered (1779 and on), traces the history of the various documents received in their course through Congress.

III. Papers of Robert Morris: [**Morris.**]

Official letter books: (7 vols.) Correspondence while Superintendent of Finance.

CALENDAR

1775
MAY 12

Massachusetts, Provincial Congress. Watertown. Establishment of ten companies of matrosses. Transcript. Enclosed in Washington to the President of Congress, 1775, Sept. 21. C. C. 169, 1, 400

1775
MAY

Connecticut, General Assembly. Order establishing daily allowance of a soldier. Contemporary copy. 1 p. In handwriting of Thomas Mifflin. Enclosed in Washington to the President of Congress, 1775, Aug. 4. C. C. 152 ,1, 69

1775
JUNE 10

Massachusetts, Provincial Congress. Watertown. Resolve establishing daily allowance of a soldier. Contemporary copy. 1 p. In handwriting of Thomas Mifflin. Enclosed in Washington to the President of Congress, 1775, Aug. 4. C. C. 152, 1, 67

[1775]
[JUNE 16]

Washington, George. [Philadelphia.] To the President [of Congress, Philadelphia]. Acceptance of commission as Commander-in-chief of the army. Contemporary copy. 1 p. In handwriting of Edmund Pendleton. Endorsed by Charles Thomson: "Genl. Washington's answer to the Congress upon his Accepting the Office." C. C. 152, 1, 1
Printed: Writings of Washington (Ford) N. Y. 1889. 2, 477.

1775
JUNE 16

Continental Congress, Resolve. Chief of Engineers and assistants. A. D. S. of Charles Thomson, with autograph initialed note of John Hancock. Transmitted to Washington. 89, 167

1775
JUNE 17

British Army, Officers. Return of killed and wounded at battle of Charlestown [Bunker Hill]. Names of officers; general account of a Boston citizen. 3 pp. In handwriting of Horatio Gates? Enclosed in Washington to the President of Congress, 1775, July 14. C. C. 152, 1, 31

1775
JUNE 19

Continental Congress. Commission to George Washington as General and Commander-in-chief of the army of the United Colonies and of all forces raised or to be raised by them. D. S. of John Hancock, countersigned by Charles Thomson. Parchment. 1 p. In handwriting of Timothy Matlack.

1775
JUNE 22

Hancock, John, Thomas **Cushing**, Samuel **Adams**, John **Adams**, and Robert Treat **Paine**. Philadelphia. To Gen. [George] Washington [Cambridge, Massachusetts]. Authorities of Massachusetts; men of influence. A. L. S. of John Adams, signed also by the others. 1 p.   **89, 12**

1775
JUNE 24

Washington, George. New York. To [the President of] Congress, Philadelphia. Journey to Boston; scarcity of powder. Unsigned. 1 p. In handwriting of Thomas Mifflin.   **C. C.** 152, 1, 3
Printed: Writings of Washington (Ford), N. Y. 1889. 2, 493.

1775
JUNE 24

Washington, George. New York. To the President of Congress, Philadelphia. Scarcity of powder. L. S. 1 p. In handwriting of Thomas Mifflin.   **C. C.** 152, 1, 5
Printed: Writings of Washington (Ford) N. Y. 1889. 2, 496.

1775
JUNE 27

Continental Congress. Resolves. Maj. Gen. P[hilip John] Schuyler and an attempt on Canada. Contemporary copy. 1 p. In handwriting of Timothy Matlack, attested by Charles Thomson. Enclosed in President of Congress to Washington, 1775, June 28.   **89, 1**

1775
JUNE 28

Continental Congress, President. Philadelphia. To [George] Washington [Cambridge]. Maj. Gen. [Philip John] Schuyler's instructions respecting Canada; commissions. A. L. S. of John Hancock. 2 pp. "Answered July 11." [10]*   **89, 2**

1775
JUNE 29

Rodney, Caesar and Thomas **McKean**. Philadelphia. To [George] Washington [Cambridge]. Recommending Ensign John Parke. L. S. of McKean and Rodney. 1 p.   **6, 111**

1775
JULY 5

Continental Congress, President. Philadelphia. To [George] Washington [Cambridge]. Forwarding regulations for government of troops. A. L. S. of John Hancock. 1 p. "Answered July 11." [10]*   **89, 4**

1775
JULY 9

Continental Army, Council of War. Cambridge. Strength of enemy; recruiting the army; rendezvous in case of retreat; defense of Dorchester Point. 3 pp. In handwriting of Joseph Reed. Read in Congress July 19. Enclosed in Washington to the President of Congress, 1775, July 10. **C. C.** 152, 1, 21

1775
JULY 10

Washington, George. Cambridge. To the President [of Congress, Philadelphia]. Organization and disciplining of the army; officers; clothing, etc.,

L. S. 10 pp. In handwriting of Joseph Reed.
Read in Congress July 19.

C. C. 152, 1, 9

Printed: Writings of Washington (Ford) N. Y. 1889. 3, 8.

1775
[July 10?]
    Continental Army. [Cambridge.] Return of killed, wounded and missing in battle of Bunker Hill. 1 p. Read in Congress July 19. Enclosed in Washington to the President of Congress, 1775, July 10.

C. C. 152, 1

1775
July 10
    Hancock, John. Philadelphia. To [George] Washington [Cambridge]. Intention to serve in army. A. L. S. 1 p. Answered July 21.*   **89, 6**

Printed in part: Writings of Washington (Ford) N. Y. 1889. 3, 39, note.

1775
July 12
    Pendleton, Edmund. Philadelphia. To [George] Washington [Cambridge]. Introducing George Baylor; Rifle and German companies raised in Pennsylvania. A. L. S. 1 p.   **6, 130**

1775
July 14
    Washington, George. Cambridge. To [the President of Congress, Philadelphia]. Recruiting; enemy's loss at Bunker Hill; scarcity of provisions in Boston; minor matters. L. S. 2 pp. In handwriting of Joseph Reed.   C. C. 152, 1, 27

Printed in part: Writings of Washington (Ford) N. Y. 1889. 3, 24, note.

1775
July 17
    Trumbull, Jonathan. Lebanon [Connecticut]. To [George] Washington [Cambridge]. Raising of two regiments; flour; prize brig *Nancy*. Transcript. Enclosed in Washington to the President of Congress, 1775, July 21.

C. C. 169, 1, 391

1775
July 19
    Hancock, John. Philadelphia. To [George] Washington, Cambridge. Introducing [Matthew] Ogden and [Aaron] Burr. A. L. S. 1 p. Answered Feb. 9*.

6, 150

1775
July 20
    Continental Congress, Resolve. Command of troops on Northern frontier. Contemporary copy. 1 p. In handwriting of Charles Thomson. Enclosed in President of Congress to Washington, 1775, July 24.   **89, 10**

1775
July 21
    Washington, George. Cambridge. To [the President of Congress, Philadelphia]. Progress of the siege; organizing the army, etc. L. S. 8 pp. In handwriting of Joseph Reed.   C. C. 152, 1, 35

Printed: Writings of Washington (Ford), N. Y. 1889. 3, 28.

1775
July 21
    Washington, George. Cambridge. To [John] Hancock [Philadelphia]. His intention to join the Army.

Letter-book copy.   In handwriting of Joseph
Reed.   M. I, 26

1775
JULY 21

Heath, William.   Roxbury.   To [George] Washington
[Cambridge].   Burning of the light house.   Transcript.   Enclosed in Washington to the President
of Congress, 1775, July 21.   C. C.   169, 1, 396

1775
JULY 24

Continental Congress, President.   To [George] Washington
[Cambridge].   Proceedings of Congress in Army
matters; Indians on northern frontier; arming of
tories; advices from Georgia.   L. S. 4 pp.
In handwriting of Timothy Matlack.   Answered
Aug. 4*.   89, 18

1775
JULY 26

Lee, Richard Henry, P[atrick] **Henry**, jr., and Th[omas]
Jefferson.   Philadelphia.   To [George] Washington [Cambridge].   Recommending Edmund Randolph.   A. L. S. of Lee, signed also by Henry
and Jefferson.   2 pp.   6, 157

1775
JULY 27

Washington, George.   Cambridge.   To [the President of
Congress, Philadelphia].   Sailing of transports
from Boston.   L. S.   2 pp.   In handwriting of
Joseph Reed.   C. C.   152, 1, 47
<small>Printed: Writings of Washington (Ford), N. Y. 1889. 3, 47, note.</small>

1775
JULY 27

Continental Congress, Resolve.   Appropriating money for
powder.   A. D. S. of John Hancock.   1 p.
Transmitted to Washington.   89, 14

1775
JULY 27

Continental Congress, Resolves.   Establishing hospital for
Army.   Contemporary copy.   2 pp.   Trans-
mitted to Washington.   89, 8
<small>Dated in error July 17.</small>

1775
JULY 29

Continental Army, General return [Cambridge].   State-
ment of numbers.   Transcript.   Enclosed in
Washington to the President of Congress, 1775,
Aug. 4.   C. C.   169, 1, 398

1775
JULY 29

Massachusetts. House of Representatives.   Resolve requesting a detachment to protect the Eastern
coast.   Contemporary copy attested.   1 p.   In
handwriting of Horatio Gates.   Enclosed in
Washington to the President of Congress, 1775,
Aug. 4.   C. C.   152, 1, 77
<small>Printed: Writings of Washington (Ford) N. Y. 1889. 3, 51, note.</small>

1775
JULY 31

Washington, George.   Cambridge.   To the General Court
of Massachusetts Bay [Watertown].   Inability
to make detachment requested.   Contemporary
copy.   2 pp.   In handwriting of Thomas Mifflin.
Enclosed in Washington to the President of Congress, 1775, Aug. 4.   C. C.   152, 1, 79
<small>Printed: Writings of Washington (Ford) N. Y. 1889. 3, 53.</small>

1775
JULY 31

Henry, P[atrick] jr. Philadelphia. To [George] Washington [Cambridge]. Recommending [Maj. John Gizzard] Frazer. A. L. S. 1 p. **6, 164**

1775
[JULY]

Continental Congress. Establishment of state of appointments and pay of officers from Commander in chief down; memorandum of certain staff appointments. A. D. S. of John Hancock. 3 pp. Transmitted to Washington. **89, 23**

See: Journals of Congress, 1775, July 29. Resolves on report of a Committee of the Whole.

1775
AUG. 1

Continental Congress, Resolve. Appropriating money for use of army. A. D. S. of John Hancock. 1 p. Transmitted to Washington. **89, 16**

1775
AUG. 1

Lee, Richard Henry. Philadelphia. To [George Washington, Cambridge]. Efforts of Congress to lighten Washington's burdens; adjournment; powder; blockade of Boston harbor; friendship of Indians; lack of news from England. A. L. S. 3 pp. **6, 175**

1775
AUG. 1

[Noyes, Belcher.] Boston. To his son. The situation in Boston; sickness; mortality among troops. Contemporary copy. 3 pp. In handwriting of Thomas Mifflin. Enclosed in Washington to the President of Congress, 1775, Aug. 4.

C. C. **152, 1, 83**

1775
AUG. 4

Washington, George. Cambridge. To [the President of Congress, Philadelphia]. Commissions; recruiting; powder, etc. L. S. 14 pp. In handwriting of Joseph Reed. Read in Congress Sep. 13.

C. C. **152, 1, 51**

Printed: Writings of Washington (Ford) N. Y. 1889. 3, 58.

1775
AUG. 11

Washington, George. Cambridge. To [Maj.] Gen. [Thomas] Gage [Boston]. Treatment of American prisoners. Contemporary copy. 1 p. In handwriting of Edmund Randolph. Enclosed in in Washington to the President of Congress, 1775, Aug. 23. C. C. **152, 1, 87**

Printed: Writings of Washington (Ford) N. Y. 1889. 3, 79.

1775
AUG. 13

Gage, Thomas. Boston. To George Washington [Cambridge]. Treatment of American prisoners; justification. Contemporary copy. 1 p. In handwriting of Edmund Randolph. Enclosed in Washington to the President of Congress, 1775, Aug. 23. C. C. **152, 1, 103**

Printed: Writings of Washington (Ford) N. Y. 1889. 3, 79, note.

1775
AUG. 19

Washington, George. Cambridge. To [Maj.] Gen. [Thomas] Gage [Boston]. Irrelevancy of his answer to complaint of treatment of prisoners. Contemporary copy. 2 pp. In handwriting of Edmund Randolph. Enclosed in Washington to the President of Congress, 1775, Aug. 23.

C. C. **152**, 1, 91

Printed: Writings of Washington (Ford) N. Y. 1889. 3, 90.

1775
AUG. 23

Great Britain, Royal Proclamation for suppressing rebellion and sedition. Broadside. 2 pp. London. Printed by Charles Eyre and William Strahan. Enclosed in Washington to the President of Congress, 1775, Nov. 2. C. C. **152**, 1, 271

1775
AUG. 23

Tudor, William. [Cambridge.] To George Washington [Cambridge]. Arduous nature of his duties; pay and assistants. A. L. S. 3 pp. Enclosed in Washington to the President of Congress, 1775, Aug. 23. C. C. **152**, 1, 99

1775
AUG. 25

Griffin, Peter. Ticonderoga. Examination of. Report of his scout around St. Johns. Contemporary copy. 2 pp. In handwriting of Charles Thomson. Enclosed in President of Congress to Washington, 1775, Sep. 26. 89,·28

1775
AUG. 30

Washington, George. Cambridge. To the President of the New York Convention [New York]. Want of powder. Contemporary copy made and attested by John McKesson. 1 p. Endorsed by Charles Thomson: "* * * transmitted from the com^{tt} of N. Y. & read before Congress 14 Septr. 1775" "Mr. Chase Mr. Nelson Mr. Crane Mr. Jay Mr. Duane Mr. Dyer Mr. Lynch, Jay J. Adams, Lewis. The Delegates from Pensyl. having informed the Congress that from sundry occurrences they had not pd. any of the expenses &c recommended to be pd. by them & desiring that some members be added from other Colonies as sundry debts have been incurred in other colonies.

Resolvd. that Mr Chase &c. be added to the delegates from Pen. & that any five of them be a quorum to settle the accots. of Expresses riffle men & the Hussars, &c.——" C. C. **152**, 1, 107

[1775]
[AUG. 31]

Washington, George. [Cambridge.] To [the President of Congress, Philadelphia]. Appointments; new fortifications etc. L. S. 4 pp. In handwriting of Joseph Reed. C. C. **152**, 1, 95

Printed: Writings of Washington (Ford) N. Y. 1889. 3, 104.

[1775]   **Boston.** Fortifications in and around. Sketch plan of
[Aug.]   American and British intrenchments [by John
         Trumbull]. 2 pp. Enclosed in Washington to
         the President of Congress, 1775, Aug. 4.
                                        C. C. 152, 1, 75

[1775]   **Roxbury.** American intrenchments. Sketch plan [by
[Aug.]   John Trumbull]. 2 pp. Enclosed in Washing-
         ton to the President of Congress, 1775, Aug. 4.
                                        C. C. 152, 1, 71

1775   **[Lee Arthur?]** [London?] To [R. H. Lee?] The situation
Sep. 4. in Great Britain; arming all classes; injury to com-
         merce; correspondence, seizures and retaliation in
         America; forces preparing to go to America; peti-
         tion of Congress; free trade intention of America.
         Contemporary copy. 2 pp. Enclosed in Lee,
         Richard Henry to Washington, 1775, Nov. 13.
                                              7, 186

1775   **Douw,** Volckert P[ieterse] and Oliver **Wolcott.** Albany
Sep. 5. [New York]. Certificate respecting Rev. [Samuel]
         Kirkland's expenses. D. S. 1 p. Enclosed in
         Washington to the President of Congress, 1775,
         Sep. 30.   C. C. 152, 1, 179

1775   **Schuyler,** [Philip John]. Isle aux Noix [Canada]. Proc-
Sep. 5. lamation to the Inhabitants of Canada. Purpose
         of the invasion. Contemporary copy. 2 pp. In
         handwriting of Charles Thomson. Enclosed in
         President of Congress to Washington, 1775,
         Sep. 26.   89, 25

1775   **Gamble,** Thomas. Quebec. To [Maj.] Gen. [Thomas] Gage
Sep. 6. [Boston]. Forwarding cattle to Boston; situation
         on the frontier; sympathies of the Canadians.
         L. S. 4 pp. Enclosed in Washington to Con-
         gress, 1775, Oct. 5.   C. C. 152, 1, 209
         Printed in part: Writings of Washington (Ford), N.Y. 1889. 3,167,
         note.

1775   **Gamble,** Thomas. Quebec. To Maj. [William] Sheriff
Sep. 6. [Boston]. Personal mercantile matters; disposi-
         tion of the Canadians; private affairs. L. S.
         4 pp.   C. C. 152, 1, 213
         Printed in part: Writings of Washington (Ford), N.Y. 1889. 3, 167,
         note.

1775   **[Trumbull,** Joseph.] Cambridge. To [George] Washing-
Sep. 6. ton [Cambridge]. Purchase of flour and pork.
         A. D. 2 pp.   C. C. 152, 1, 113

1775
SEP. 7.

Washington, George. Cambridge. To [the President of Congress, Philadelphia]. Supplies for the winter; salt and powder. L. S. 2 pp. In handwriting of Joseph Reed. Read in Congress Sep. 21.

C. C. 152, 1, 109.

1775
SEP. 7.

Continental Army. Council of War. Near St. Johns, Canada. Fortifying Isle aux Noix. Contemporary copy. 1 p. In handwriting of Charles Thomson. Enclosed in President of Congress to Washington, 1775, Sep. 26. **89, 27**

1775
SEP. 8.

Washington, George. Cambridge. To the general officers of the Army. Requesting opinion as to attack on Boston. Contemporary copy. In handwriting of Joseph Reed. Enclosed in Washington to the President of Congress, 1775, Sep. 14. Read in Congress Sep. 29. C. C. 152, 1, 141

Printed: Writings of Washington (Ford), N. Y. 1889. 3, 114.

1775
SEP. 8

Schuyler, Ph[ilip John]. Isle aux Noix. To [the President of Congress, Philadelphia]. Attack on St. Johns and subsequent movements. Contemporary copy. 4 pp. In handwriting of Charles Thomson. Enclosed in President of Congress to Washington, 1775, Sept. 26. **89, 31**

1775
SEP. 11

Continental Army, Council of War. Cambridge. Minutes. Deciding against an attack on Boston. Contemporary copy. In handwriting of Joseph Reed. Enclosed in Washington to the President of Congress, 1775, Sept. 14. Read in Congress, Sept. 29. C. C. 152, 1, 141

Printed: Writings of Washington (Ford) N. Y. 1889. 3, 114.

1775
SEP. 13

Continental Congress, Resolve. Pay of troops in Massachusetts. A. D. S. of Charles Thomson. 1 p. Enclosed in President of Congress to Washington, 1775, Sep. 19. **89, 310**

1775
SEP. 13

Getchell, Dennis and Samuel **Berry**. Vassalboro [12 miles above Augusta, Maine]. To Reuben Colburn. Account of their journey into Canada. Contemporary copy. 3 pp. In handwriting of Horatio Gates with note by Joseph Reed respecting Colburn. Enclosed in Washington to the President of Congress, 1775, Oct. 5. C. C. 152, 1, 205

1775
SEP. 14

Washington, George. [Cambridge.] To Col. Benedict Arnold [Cambridge]. Instructions for the Canadian Expedition. Conciliation of inhabitants;

plundering, etc.   D. S.   4 pp.   In handwriting
of Joseph Reed.   Enclosed in Washington to the
President of Congress, 1775, Sept. 21.

C. C.   152, 1, 137

Printed: Writings of Washington (Ford) N. Y. 1889. 3, 121.

1775
SEP. 19

Continental Congress, President. To [George] Washington,
Cambridge. Money for army. L. S. of John
Hancock. 1 p. In handwriting of Charles
Thomson.   **89, 21**

1775
SEP. 19

Continental Congress, Resolve. Case of Col. John Fenton.
A. D. S. of Charles Thomson, countersigned by
John Hancock. 1 p. Transmitted to Washing-
ton.   **89, 316**

1775
SEP. 20

Continental Congress, President. [Philadelphia.] To [Maj.
Gen. Philip John Schuyler, Isle aux Noix]. Sense
of Congress respecting his operations in Canada.
Contemporary copy. 2 pp. In handwriting of
Charles Thomson. Enclosed in President of Con-
gress, to Washington, 1775, Sept. 26.   **89, 33**

1775
SEP. 21

Washington, George. Cambridge. To [the President of
Congress, Philadelphia]. Articles of war; pay
of officers; clothing; lack of money; subsistence,
etc. L. S. 11 pp. In handwriting of Joseph
Reed. Read in Congress Sept. 29.

C. C.   152, 1, 119

Printed: Writings of Washington (Ford) N. Y. 1889. 3, 137.

1775
[SEP. 21]

Canada, Expedition against. Route to Quebec from the
Kennebec River. 2 pp. In handwriting of
Joseph Reed. Enclosed in Washington to the
President of Congress, 1775, Sept. 21. Read in
Congress Sept. 29.   C. C.   152, 1, 135

1775
SEP. 25

Arnold, Benedict. Fort Weston [Augusta, Maine]. To
[George] Washington [Cambridge]. March
toward Canada; disputes of rank and other matters. Contemporary copy. 4 pp. In handwriting of Horatio Gates. Enclosed in Washington to the President of Congress, 1775, Oct. 5.

C. C.   152, 1, 201

1775
SEP. 26

Washington, George. Cambridge. To [the Hartford Com-
mittee of Safety, Hartford, Connecticut]. Treat-
ment of Maj. [Christopher] French and other
British officers; privilege of wearing their swords.
Contemporary copy. 1 p. In handwriting of
George Baylor?.   C. C.   152, 1, 117

Printed: Writings of Washington (Ford) N. Y. 1889. 3, 150, note.

1775 SEP. 26	**Continental Congress**, President. Philadelphia. To [George] Washington [Cambridge]. Arrangement and organization of army and miscellaneous military matters. A. L. S. of John Hancock. 3 pp. Answered Oct. 12.* **89, 35**
1775 SEP. 26	**Lee**, Richard Henry. Philadelphia. To [George] Washington [Cambridge]. Personal mentions from Virginia; disciplining the army; appointment of [Maj. Thomas] Mifflin, Quartermaster General; feeling in England and her difficulty in raising men. A. L. S. 4 pp. **6, 357**
1775 SEP. 29–30	**Continental Congress**, Resolves. Appointing committee, Lynch, Franklin and Harrison, to confer with the Commander in Chief. D. S. of John Hancock. 1 p. In handwriting of Charles Thomson. Enclosed in Washington to the President of Congress, 1775, Sept. 30. **89, 37**
1775 SEP. 30	**Washington**, George. Cambridge. To the President of Congress [Philadelphia]. Introducing Rev. [Samuel] Kirkland to Congress. L. S. 2 pp. In handwriting of Joseph Reed. Read in Congress Oct. 25. **C. C. 152, 1, 175** Printed: Writings of Washington (Ford) N. Y. 1889. 3, 153.
1775 SEP. 30	**Continental Congress**, President. Philadelphia. To [George] Washington [Cambridge]. Appointment of Committee of Conference. A. L. S. 2 pp. Answered Oct. 12.* **89, 39**
[1775] [SEP. 30]	**Continental Congress**, Instructions to the Committee of Conference. Reorganization and pay of army; supplies, recruiting. Contemporary copy. 3 pp. In handwriting of Joseph Reed. **89, 41**
[1775] [SEP. 30?]	**Continental Congress**, President. Philadelphia. To [George Washington, Cambridge]. Intelligence of British forces destined for America; Hessians. A. L. S. of John Hancock. 3 pp. **89, 49**
[1775] [SEP.]	**Washington**, George. [Cambridge.] Address to the Inhabitants of Canada. Transcript. Enclosed in Washington to the President of Congress, 1775, Sept. 21. **C. C. 169, 1, 52** Printed: Writings of Washington (Ford) N. Y. 1891. 3, 126.
[1775] [SEP.]	**Continental Army**. Subalterns. Petition to George Washington for increase of pay. 2 pp. A. D. S. of John Smith. Enclosed in Washington to the President of Congress, 1775, Sept. 21. Read in Congress Sept. 29. **C. C. 152, 1, 131**

Head Quarters 16: Aug.ᵗ 1775

Sir

You are to proceed with the Detachment of Rifle Men under your Command
to Cape Ann, where you are to endeavour, not
only to protect the Inhabitants from all attempts of the Enemy, but to do your utmost
to Distress, & annoy, any Detachments from the
Ministerial Army, that may be sent from
Boston, to plunder, or Destroy that Settlement,
upon your March, and during your Residence
at Cape Ann, As well as upon your March back
to Camp, you will Observe strict Discipline,
& on no Account Suffer any under your Command
to Pillage, or Marraud — upon your Arrival
at Cape Ann you will dispatch a Messenger
to acquaint the General with the State you
find things in there. And you will frequent-
:ly report to the General, all extraordinary
Occurrences that may happen — I am Sir

Your most Obedient
Humble Servant —

WRITING OF THOMAS MIFFLIN.

[1775]
[SEP.?]
[Church, Benjamin] [Cambridge.] To Maj. [Edward?] Cane [Boston]. Losses at Bunker Hill; sentiment of liberty; strength of Continental Army; personal matters. Contemporary copy of translation of an intercepted letter. 3 pp. In handwriting of Elisha Porter. Enclosed in Washington to the President of Congress, 1775, Oct. 5.
C. C. 152, 1, 193

[1775]
[SEP.?]
Thompson, William. [Cambridge.] Voucher for expenditure of $5,000 in the service. Itemized account. D. S. 2 pp. Enclosed in Washington to the President of Congress, 1775, Oct. 12.
C. C. 152, 1, 233

1775
OCT. 2
Continental Congress, Resolves. Pay of troops; salt provisions; rewards in event of attack on Boston. D. S. of John Hancock. 1 p. In handwriting of Charles Thomson. Enclosed in President of Congress to Washington, 1775, Oct. 3. 89, 43

1775
OCT. 2
Portsmouth, Committee of Safety. To [George] Washington [Cambridge]. Capture of British ship with flour. L. S.: H. Wentworth, Chairman. 2 pp. Enclosed in Washington to the President of Congress, 1775, Oct. 5. C. C. 152, 1, 197

1775
OCT. 3
Continental Congress, President. To [George] Washington [Cambridge]. Money for pay of army. A. L. S. of John Hancock. 1 p. 89, 45

1775
OCT. 3
Continental Army, Council of War. Cambridge. Charges against Dr. [Benjamin] Church for holding correspondence with enemy. 3 pp. In handwriting of Stephen Moylan. Enclosed in Washington to President of Congress, 1775, Oct. 5.
C. C. 152, 1, 189

1775
OCT. 5
Washington, George. Cambridge. To [the President of Congress, Philadelphia]. Fuel, etc., for army; Dr. [Benjamin] Church; captured vessels; Canadians. D. S. 7 pp. In handwriting of Joseph Reed. Read in Congress, Oct. 13.
C. C. 152, 1, 181
Printed: Writings of Washington (Ford) N. Y. 1889. 3, 162.

1775
OCT. 5
Continental Congress, President. Philadelphia. To [George] Washington [Cambridge]. Armed vessels to intercept British storeships. A. L. S. of John Hancock. 3 pp. Answered Oct. 12.* 89, 46

1775
Oct. 5
Continental Congress, President. To [George Washington,
Cambridge]. Intelligence from London; plans of
the Ministry; military preparations. A. L. S.
of John Hancock. 3 pp.   89, 48

1775
Oct. 5
Mifflin, Thomas. Cambridge. Estimate of cost of bar-
racks for 100 men. A. D. S. 1 p. Read in
Congress Oct. 21. Enclosed in Washington to
the President of Congress 1775, Oct. 12.
C. C.   152, 1, 229

1775
Oct. 8
Lee, Richard Henry. Philadelphia. To [George Washington, Cambridge]. British designs. A. L. S. 1 p.
7, 16

1775
Oct. 9
Trumbull, Jonathan. Lebanon. To Matthew Griswold.
Commission to attend the Committee of Confer-
ence at Camp. A. D. S. 1 p. Seal of Connec-
ticut. Transmitted to Washington.   89, 51

[1775]
[Oct. 10]
Trumbull, Joseph. [Cambridge.] Estimate of cost of
supplies for army of 22,000 from Oct. 10, 1775
to May 10, 1776. D. S. 1 p. In handwriting
of Horatio Gates. Enclosed in Washington to
the President of Congress, 1775, Oct. 12. Read
in Congress Oct. 24.   C. C.   152, 1, 225

1775
Oct. 12
Washington, George. Cambridge. To [the President of
Congress, Philadelphia]. The Committee from
Congress; hospital directorship; armed vessels;
Arnold's expedition. L. S. 6 pp. In hand-
writing of Joseph Reed. Read in Congress, Oct.
21.   C. C.   152, 1, 217
Printed: Writings of Washington (Ford) N. Y. 1889. 3, 172.

1775
Oct. 12
Continental Congress, Resolve. Subsistence allowances for
recruiting service. Contemporary copy. 1 p.
Enclosed in Board of War to Washington 1777,
May 20.   95, 320

1775
Oct. 12
Cowley, William. Middlesex [Massachusetts]. Deposi-
tion respecting Maj. John Connolly. D. S. 3 pp.
In handwriting of Horatio Gates. Record of oath
to above taken before Abraham Fuller. Enclosed
in Washington to the President of Congress 1775,
Oct. 12. Read before Congress Oct. 21.
C. C.   152, 1, 237

1775
Oct. 12
Trumbull, Jonathan. Lebanon. To Nathanael Wales.
Commission to attend the Committee of Confer-
ence at Camp. D. S. 1 p. Seal of Connecticut.
Transmitted to Washington.   89, 53

1775
Oct. 16

Jones, Pearson. Falmouth [Massachusetts]. Account of the destruction of Falmouth. Contemporary copy. (Made at Cambridge Oct. 24 by Horatio Gates). 3 pp. Enclosed in Washington to the President of Congress, 1775, Oct. 24.

C. C.   152, 1, 247

1775
Oct. 18–22

Continental Congress, Committee of Conference. Cambridge. Minutes of proceedings. Organization of army; pay, clothing, arms, supplies, recruiting, etc. A. D. S. of Joseph Reed. 28 pp.   **89, 54**

Committee: Matthew Griswold, Nathanael Wales from Connecticut; Nicholas Cooke from Rhode Island; Thomas Lynch, Benjamin Franklin, Benjamin Harrison from Congress; James Bowdoin, James Otis, William Sever and Walter Spooner from Massachusetts.

1775
Oct. 20

Gridley, Richard. Cambridge. To [George] Washington [Cambridge]. Inventory of ordnance stores necessary for the army. Transcript. Transmitted to Congress.   C. C.   169, 1, 103

1775
Oct. 20

Continental Congress, President. Philadelphia. To [George] Washington [Cambridge]. Scheme for destruction of British fleet in Boston harbor. L. S. of John Hancock. 1 p. In handwriting of Charles Thomson. Answered Nov. 8.*   **89, 72**

1775
Oct. 22

Lee, Richard Henry. Philadelphia. To [George] Washington [Cambridge]. News from Virginia; news from Canada; importance of that country; powder; death of Peyton Randolph. A. L. S. 2 pp. Answered Nov. 8.   **7, 68**

1775
Oct. 23

Parsons, Samuel H[olden]. Roxbury [Massachusetts]. To [George] Washington [Cambridge]. Number of officers and men willing to continue in the service. A. L. S. 1 p. Enclosed in Washington to the President of Congress, 1775, Oct. 30.

C. C.   152, 1, 263

1775
Oct. 23

Storrs, Experience. Cambridge. To G[eorge] Washington [Cambridge]. Officers and men willing to continue in the service. A. L. S. 1 p. Enclosed in Washington to the President of Congress, 1775, Oct. 30.   C. C.   152, 1, 265

1775
Oct. 23

Webb, Charles. Winter Hill [near Boston]. To George Washington, Cambridge. Officers and men willing to continue in the service. A. L. S. 1 p. Enclosed in Washington to the President of Congress, 1775, Oct. 30.   C. C.   152, 1, 269

1775
OCT. 24

Washington, George. Cambridge. To the President of Congress [Philadelphia]. Destruction of Falmouth. L. S. 2 pp. In handwriting of Joseph Reed. Read in Congress Nov. 1.

C. C. 152, 1, 241

Printed: Writings of Washington (Ford) N. Y. 1889. 3, 181.

1775
OCT. 25

Washington, George. [Cambridge.] To Maj. [Christopher] French [Hartford]. Right to wear his sword. Contemporary copy. In handwriting of Jonathan Trumbull, jr.   C. C. 152, 1, 251

Printed: Writings of Washington (Ford) N. Y. 1889. 3, 151, note.

1775
OCT. 26

Reed, Joseph. Cambridge. To Thomas Seymour, Hartford. Dispute over Maj. [Christopher] French's claim to right to wear his sword. Contemporary copy. In handwriting of Jonathan Trumbull, jr.

C. C. 152, 1, 251

1775
OCT. 27

Arnold, Benedict. Chaudière Pond [Canada]. To [George] Washington [Cambridge]. Account of his march. Contemporary copy. In handwriting of Robert Hanson Harrison. Enclosed in Washington to the President of Congress, 1775, Nov. 19.

C. C. 152, 1, 287

1775
OCT. 28

Continental Congress, Resolve. Ordering raising of a company of matrosses in New York. Contemporary copy. 1 p. In handwriting of and attested by Robert Benson. Transmitted to Washington.

89, 74

[1775]
OCT. 28

Virginia Gazette (The). Williamsburg. Clipping of account of Lord Dunmore's attack on Hampton and consequent order of the Virginia Committee of Safety. Enclosed in Lee, Richard Henry to Washington, 1775, Nov. 13.   7, 186

1775
OCT. 30

Washington, George. Cambridge. To [the President of Congress, Philadelphia]. Resignation of officers. L. S. 2 pp. In handwriting of Joseph Reed. Read in Congress Nov. 7.   C. C. 152, 1, 255

Printed: Writings of Washington (Ford) N. Y. 1889. 3, 190.

[1775]
[OCT.]

Washington, George. [Cambridge.] To Capt. Nicholas Broughton [Cambridge]. Instructions for cruising in the schooner *Hannah*. Contemporary copy. 3 pp. In handwriting of Horatio Gates. Read in Congress Oct. 21. Enclosed in Washington to the President of Congress, 1775, Oct. 12.

C. C. 152, 1, 235

[1775]
[OCT.]

Continental Congress, Committee of Conference. Memorandum of Washington's instructions to Capt. [Nicholas] Broughton and arrangements of Congress respecting prizes taken by armed vessels. 1 p. In handwriting of Robert Hanson Harrison.
89, 71

1775
Nov. 2

Washington, George. Cambridge. To [the President of Congress, Philadelphia]. Recruiting orders; British proclamations. A. L. S. 2 pp. Read in Congress Nov. 13. C. C. 152, 1, 259
Printed: Writings of Washington (Ford) N. Y. 1889. 3, 193.

1775
Nov. 3

Massachusetts, House of Representatives.' Resolves respecting muster rolls of Massachusetts troops. Contemporary copy, attested by Perez Morton. 3 pp. In handwriting of Charles Morse. Transmitted to Washington. 89, 75

1775
Nov. 6

Continental Congress, Resolves. Pay, rations, clothing, etc. of army; regulations for government; duties of officers, etc. D. S. of John Hancock. 8 pp. In handwriting of Timothy Matlack, attested by Charles Thomson. Enclosed in President of Congress to Washington, 1775, Nov. 7. 89, 77

1775
Nov. 6

Continental Army. General return. Cambridge. Statement of numbers. Transcript. Enclosed in Washington to the President of Congress 1775, Nov. 8. C. C. 169, 1, 401

1775
Nov. 7

Continental Congress, President. Philadelphia. To [George] Washington [Cambridge]. Enclosing resolves. A. L. S. of John Hancock. 1 p. Answered Nov. 19.* 89, 81

1775
Nov. 8

Washington, George. Cambridge. To [the President of Congress, Philadelphia]. Plan for destruction of British fleet at Boston; naval captures; reenlistments. A. L. S. 4 pp. Referred to Wythe, E. Rutledge, J. Adams, W. Livingston, Franklin, Wilson, and Johnson. Reported Nov. 23. Agreed to Nov. 25. For report as adopted see Journals of Congress that date. C. C. 152, 1, 275
Printed: Writings of Washington (Ford) N. Y. 1889. 3, 202.

1775
Nov. 8

Continental Congress, Resolve. Free postage of delegates mail. A. D. S. of Charles Thomson. Countersigned by John Hancock. Transmitted to Washington. 89, 100

1775
Nov. 8

Arnold, B[enedict]. Point Levi [Canada]. To Brig. Gen. [Richard] Montgomery [Camp near St. Johns]. Difficulties of march; condition of Quebec; crossing of St. Lawrence. Contemporary copy. In handwriting of Horatio Gates? Enclosed in Washington to the President of Congress, 1775, Dec. 4.   C. C. 152, 1, 317

1775
Nov. 8

Arnold, B[enedict]. Point Levi [Canada]. To [George] Washington [Cambridge]. Scarcity of provisions; Col. [Roger] Enos's retreat; Quebec. Contemporary copy. In handwriting of Horatio Gates? Enclosed in Washington to the President of Congress, 1775, Dec. 4.   C. C. 152, 1, 317

1775
Nov. 9

Enos, Roger. Brunswick, near Kennebec. To [George] Washington [Cambridge]. Reasons for his return; scarcity of provisions. Contemporary copy. In handwriting of Robert Hanson Harrison. Enclosed in Washington to the President of Congress, 1775, Nov. 19.   C. C. 152, 1, 287

1775
Nov. 10

Continental Congress, President. Philadelphia. To Gen. [George] Washington [Cambridge]. Forwarding resolves. A. L. S. of John Hancock. 1 p. Answered Nov. 19*.   89, 104

1775
Nov. 10

Continental Congress, Resolve. Free postage of Commander-in-chief's mail. A. D. S. of Charles Thomson. Countersigned by John Hancock. Transmitted to Washington.   89, 100

1775
Nov. 10

Continental Congress, Resolves. Spys to be sent to Nova Scotia; raising battalions of marines. A. D. S. of John Hancock. 2 pp. Enclosed in President of Congress to Washington, 1775, Nov. 10.
89, 101

1775
Nov. 11

Washington, George. Cambridge. To [the President of Congress, Philadelphia]. Captures by armed vessels; reenlistments; officers and men; movements of enemy. L. S. 3 pp. In handwriting of Stephen Moylan. Read in Congress Nov. 20.
C. C. 152, 1, 279
Printed: Writings of Washington (Ford) N. Y. 1889. 3, 213.

1775
Nov. 13

Lee, Richard Henry. Philadelphia. To [George Washington, Cambridge]. Intelligence from England; British army to remove to Long Island; goods sent into Canada to bribe the Indians; success at Chamblee; [John Murray, Earl] Dunmore in

Virginia; armed vessels; powder in Virginia; treaty with Ohio Indians. A. L. S. 3 pp. 7,185

1775
Nov. 13

Lynch, Thomas. Philadelphia. To [George Washington, Cambridge]. [Lt.] Col. [Joseph] Reed's delay in returning to camp; additional pay for officers; enlisting New Englanders; means of obtaining peace; powder; Canada; news from Virginia; articles of war and effect on officers. A. L. S. 4 pp.   7, 189

1775
Nov. 14

Arnold, Benedict. St. Marie, 2½ Leagues from Point Levi. To [George] Washington [Cambridge]. His situation. Contemporary copy. In handwriting of Horatio Gates? Enclosed in Washington to the President of Congress, 1775, Dec. 4.

C. C.   152, 1, 317

1775
Nov. 17

Montgomery, Richard. [Montreal.] To [Maj. Gen. Philip John Schuyler? Albany]. The situation; [Sir Guy] Carleton's strength. Contemporary copy. In handwriting of Horatio Gates? Enclosed in Washington to the President of Congress, 1775, Dec. 4.   C. C. 152, 1, 317

1775
Nov. 19

Washington, George. Cambridge. To the President of Congress [Philadelphia]. Raising of battalions of marines; accounts from Canada; reenlistments. L. S. 3 pp. In handwriting of Stephen Moylan. Read in Congress Nov. 27.   C. C. 152, 1, 283

Printed: Writings of Washington (Ford) N.Y. 1889. 3, 225.

1775
Nov. 19

Lovell, James. Boston. To [George] Washington [Cambridge]. His distressed condition. A. L. S. 2 pp. Enclosed in Washington to the President of Congress, 1775, Dec. 18.   C. C. 152, 1, 365

1775
Nov. 22

Carleton, [Sir] Guy. Quebec. Proclamation ordering all persons to quit the province who do not enroll in the militia. Broadside in English and French. 2 pp. Enclosed in Washington to the President of Congress, 1775, Dec. 31.   C. C. 152, 1,395

1775
Nov. 24

Bayley, Jacob. Newbury [New Hampshire]. To Col. [Moses] Little [Cambridge?]. Route to Canada via St. John; importance of the province. A. L. S. 4 pp. Enclosed in Washington to the President of Congress, 1775, Dec. 25.   C. C. 152, 1, 391

1775
Nov. 25

Continental Congress, Committee report. Nature of prizes of armed vessels; courts of admiralty; libel; shares of captors. Contemporary copy. In hand-

writing of Timothy Matlack. Signed by John
Hancock. Enclosed in President of Congress to
Washington, 1775, Dec. 22.   89, 106

> Committee of seven appointed Nov. 17: Wythe E. Rutledge, J. Ad-
> ams, W. Livingston, Franklin, Wilson and Johnson; 2d resolve of this
> report recommitted Dec. 14; and substitute resolution of Congress
> adopted Dec. 19. See: Journals of Congress (ed. 1904) of these dates.

1775
Nov. 26

Lee, Richard Henry. Philadelphia. To [George Washington, Cambridge]. Successes in Canada; British reenforcement of Boston; Canada committee.
A. L. S. 2 pp.   7, 233

1775
Nov. 28

Washington, George. Cambridge. To [the President of
Congress, Philadelphia]. Command of the artil-
lery; reenlistment of troops; fortifications. L.
S. 7 pp. In handwriting of Stephen Moylan.
"Considd. 7th" [December].   C. C.   152, 1, 291

> Printed: Writings of Washington (Ford) N. Y. 1889. 3, 241.

1775
Nov. 30

Washington, George. Cambridge. To [the President of
Congress, Philadelphia]. Capture [of the *Nancy*]
by Capt. [John] Manly. L. S. 1 p. In handwriting of Stephen Moylan. Read in Congress
Dec. 11.   C. C.   152, 1, 301

> Printed in part: Writings of Washington (Ford) N. Y. 1889. 3, 251.

1775
Nov. 30

Continental Congress. Resolves. Battalion of Marines;
pay, etc., for Army; prizes. A. D. S. of Charles
Thomson, countersigned by John Hancock. Enclosed in President of Congress to Washington,
1775, Dec. 2.   89, 108

1775
Dec. 1

Continental Army. General Court Martial. Cambridge.
Trial of Lt. Col. [Roger] Enos. Evidence and
decision of the court. Transcript. Enclosed in
Washington to the President of Congress, 1775,
Dec. 11.   C. C.   169, 1, 138

1775
Dec. 1

Putnam, Israel, Cambridge. To [George] Washington
[Cambridge]. Recommending Col. Henry Bab-
cock for brigadier general. L. S. 1 p. Enclosed in Washington to the President of Congress, 1775, Dec. 4.   C. C.   152, 1, 313

1775
Dec. 1

Massachusetts, House of Representatives. [Watertown.]
Order appointing committee to confer with Gen.
[George] Washington on defense of Cape Cod
harbour. Contemporary copy. 1 p. In handwriting of Stephen Moylan. Enclosed in Washington
to the President of Congress, 1775, Dec. 4.
                                    C. C.   152, 1, 325

1775
DEC. 2

Continental Congress, President. Philadelphia. To [George] Washington [Cambridge]. Money for army; Dr. [John] Connolly; [John Murray, Earl] Dunmore; prizes and miscellaneous matters. A. L. S. of John Hancock. 3 pp. **89, 113**

1775
DEC. 2

Continental Congress. Resolves. Artillery regiment; extract from resolves of Nov. 17; prisoners and goods taken in prizes; supplies for prisoners; payment of Army; exchanges; miscellaneous military matters; expresses; exchange of Ethan Allen. A. D. S. of Charles Thomson, countersigned by John Hancock. Enclosed in President of Congress to Washington, 1775, Dec. 2. **89, 108**

1775
DEC. 4

Washington, George. Cambridge. To [the President of Congress, Philadelphia]. Captures by armed vessels; troops returning home. Canadian affairs. L. S. 8 pp. In handwriting of Stephen Moylan. Read in Congress Dec. 13. Referred to the committee of Nov. 17. See: Committee report 1775, Nov. 25. **C. C. 152, 1, 305**
Printed: Writings of Washington (Ford), N.Y. 1889. 3, 256.

1775
DEC. 4

Continental Congress. Resolve. General and field officers' commands. A. D. S. of Charles Thomson. 1 p. Enclosed in President of Congress to Washington, 1775, Dec. 8. **89, 119**

1775
DEC. 5

Washington, George. Cambridge. To Jonathan Trumbull [Lebanon, Connecticut]. Enlistment of troops; new establishment: filling up of the army. Contemporary copy. 1 p. In handwriting of Robert Hanson Harrison. Enclosed in Washington to the President of Congress, 1775, Dec. 11. **C. C. 152, 1, 383**

1775
DEC. 6

Lee, Richard Henry. Philadelphia. To [George Washington, Cambridge]. Affairs in Virginia; armed vessels; matters on the Kanawha; news from Canada. A. L. S. 3 pp. **7, 265**

1775
DEC. 7

Washington, George. Cambridge. To the President of Congress, Philadelphia. Seizure of inhabitants of St. Johns by armed vessels; John Anderson's royalist sympathies. L. S. 2 pp. In handwriting of Stephen Moylan. **C. C. 152, 1, 329**
Printed: Writings of Washington (Ford), N.Y. 1889. 3, 257 and 261.

1775
DEC. 7

Continental Congress. Resolve. Authority to call out militia. A. D. S. of Charles Thomson, countersigned by John Hancock. 1 p. Enclosed in President of Congress to Washington, 1775, Dec. 8. **89, 120**

1775
Dec. 8

Continental Congress, President. Philadelphia. To [George]
Washington [Cambridge]. Forwarding money
for army. L. S. of John Hancock. 1 p. In handwriting of Charles Thomson.   89, 115

1775
Dec. 8

Continental Congress, President. Philadelphia. To [George]
Washington [Cambridge]. Cannon and lead;
backwardness of enlistments; Col. [Benedict] Ar-
nold in Canada. L. S. of John Hancock. 2 pp.
In handwriting of Charles Thomson. Answered
Dec. 18.*   89, 116

1775
Dec. 8

Lynch, Thomas. Philadelphia. To [George Washington,
Cambridge]. The situation; news from Canada;
a Member of Congress. [John Adams] going to
New England. A. L. S. 2 pp.   7, 272

1775
Dec. 11

Washington, George. Cambridge. To [the President of
Congress, Philadelphia]. Capt. [John] Manly's
captures; militia; enlistments; smallpox, etc.
L. S. 4 pp. In handwriting of Stephen Moylan.
C. C.   152, 1, 335
Printed: Writings of Washington (Ford), N. Y. 1889. 3. 270.

1775
Dec. 12

Morgan, John. General Hospital. [Cambridge]. To
[George] Washington, [Cambridge]. Hospital at
Roxbury; general hospital matters. A. L. S.
2 pp. Enclosed in Washington to the President
of Congress, 1775, Dec. 14.   C. C.   152, 1, 343

1775
Dec. 14

Washington, George. Cambridge. To [the President of
Congress, Philadelphia]. Marines; hospital; smallpox in Boston. L. S. 4 pp. In handwriting
of Stephen Moylan.   C. C.   152, 1, 339
Printed: Writings of Washington (Ford), N. Y. 1889. 3, 274.

1775
Dec. 14

Washington, George. Cambridge. To [the President of
Congress, Philadelphia]. Messrs. Penet & de
Pliarne's scheme to furnish arms and ammunition.
Letter-book copy. In handwriting of Robert
Hanson Harrison.   M. I, 155

1775
Dec. 16

Washington, George. Cambridge. To [the President of
Congress, Philadelphia]. Intelligence of troops
leaving Boston. L. S. 1 p. In handwriting of
Stephen Moylan.   C. C.   152, 1, 347

1775
Dec. 16

Wadsworth, Peleg. [Cambridge.] To [George] Washing-
ton [Cambridge]. Report on fortifying Cape
Cod. Contemporary copy. 1 p. In handwrit-
ing of Robert Hanson Harrison. Enclosed in
Washington to the President of Congress, 1775,
Dec. 25.   C. C.   152, 1, 379

1775
DEC. 18

Washington, George.   Cambridge.   To [the President of Congress, Philadelphia].   [John Murray,] Lord Dunmore in Virginia; works on Lechmere Hill; enlistments, etc.   L. S.   5 pp.   In handwriting of Stephen Moylan.   C. C.   152, 1, 351
Printed: Writings of Washington (Ford) N. Y. 1889. 3, 285.

1775
DEC. 18

Washington, George.   Cambridge.   To [Maj. Gen. Sir William Howe, Boston].   Retaliation for treatment of Col. [Ethan] Allen.   Contemporary attested copy.   2 pp.   In handwriting of Stephen Moylan.   Enclosed in Washington to the President of Congress, 1775, Dec. 18.   C. C.   152, 1, 361

1775
DEC. 19

Washington, George.   Cambridge.   To [the President of Congress, Philadelphia].   Transmitting letter. A. L. S.   1 p.   C. C.   152, 1, 369

1775
DEC. 20

Continental Congress, Resolve.   Trial of prizes of armed vessels.   Contemporary copy.   A. D. S. of Charles Thomson, countersigned by John Hancock.   Enclosed in President of Congress to Washington, 1775, Dec. 22.   89, 110

1775
DEC. 21

Howe, [Sir] William.   Boston.   To George Washington, Cambridge.   Treatment of [Col. Ethan] Allen. Contemporary copy.   1 p.   In handwriting of Robert Hanson Harrison.   Enclosed in Washington to the President of Congress, 1775, Dec. 25.
                                    C. C.   152, 1, 377
Printed, in part: Writings of Washington (Ford) N. Y. 1889. 3, 284, note.

1775
DEC. 22

Continental Congress, President.   Philadelphia.   To George Washington [Cambridge].   Reenlistments; prizes taken by armed vessels; attack on Boston and minor military matters.   A. L. S. of John Hancock.   3 pp.   Answered Jan. 4, 1776*.   7, 334

1775
DEC. 22

Continental Congress, Resolve.   Authorizing attack on Boston if expedient.   A. D. S. of Charles Thomson, countersigned by John Hancock.   1 p.   Enclosed in President of Congress to Washington, 1775, Dec. 22.   7, 333

1775
DEC. 25

Washington, George.   Cambridge.   To [the President of Congress, Philadelphia].   [Dr. John] Connolly; pay for the army; fortifications.   L. S.   4 pp. In handwriting of Stephen Moylan.
                                    C. C.   152, 1, 373
Printed: Writings of Washington (Ford) N. Y. 1889. 3, 294.

1775
DEC. 25

Bours, John.   Newport [Rhode Island].   Oath to refrain from assisting the British.   Contemporary copy. 1 p.   In handwriting of Robert Hanson Harrison.   Enclosed in Washington to the President of Congress, 1775, Dec. 31.   C. C.   152, 1, 389

1775
DEC. 26

Continental Congress, Committee report.   Imprisonment of soldiers for debt.   D. S. of John Hancock.   1 p. In handwriting of Timothy Matlack, attested by Charles Thomson.   Transmitted to Washington.
89, 121

Committee appointed Dec. 8: J. Wilson and W. Livingston.

1775
DEC. 26

Massachusetts, General Court.   Report of Committee respecting pay for militia at Braintree, Weymouth, and Hingham.   Resolve of Council thereon.   Contemporary copy.   3 pp.   In handwriting of Horatio Gates.   Enclosed in Washington to the President of Congress, 1775, Dec. 31.
C. C.   152, 1, 403

1775
DEC. 30

Continental Army.   General Return.   Cambridge.   Tabular statement of members by regiments.   1 p. A. D. S. of Horatio Gates.   Enclosed in Washington to the President of Congress, 1775, Dec. 31.   C. C.   152, 1, 399

1775
DEC. 31

Washington, George.   Cambridge.   To [the President of Congress, Philadelphia].   Pay for the army; employment of negroes.   L. S.   6 pp.   In handwriting of Stephen Moylan.   Received Jan. 15. Referred to Wythe, Adams, and Wilson..
C. C.   152, 1, 381

Printed: Writings of Washington (Ford) N. Y.   1889.   3, 305.

1776
JAN. 4

Washington, George.   Cambridge.   To the President of Congress, Philadelphia.   Situation of the army; British reinforcements; designs of enemy; the King's speech.   Unsigned.   3 pp.   In handwriting of Robert Hanson Harrison.   Read in Congress Jan. 13.   C. C.   152, 1, 407

Printed: Writings of Washington (Ford) N. Y.   1889.   3, 312.

1776
JAN. 5

Continental Congress, Resolves.   Patriotism of James Lovell.   A. D. S. of Charles Thomson, countersigned by John Hancock.   Enclosed in President of Congress to Washington, 1776, Jan. 6–18.
90, 53

1776
JAN. 6

Adams, John.   Watertown.   To [George Washington, Cambridge].   Opinion on Maj. Gen. [Charles] Lee's plan.   A. L. S.   3 pp.   8, 29

1776
JAN. 6–18

Continental Congress, President. Philadelphia. To [George] Washington [Cambridge]. Rank of aids; Allen Cameron, [Dr. John] Connolly, and [Dr. John F. D.] Smyth; formation of army in Canada; pay for troops; saltpetre; barbarity of British; militia; news from Canada. L. S. of John Hancock. 4 pp. In handwriting of Charles Thomson. **90, 56**

1776
JAN. 6–21

Continental Congress, President. Philadelphia. To [George] Washington, [Morristown, New Jersey]. [James] Lovell; rank of aids; [Allen] Cameron, [Dr. John] Connolly, and [Dr. John F. D.] Smyth; defense of Canada; paymaster's bills; saltpetre; [John Murray,] Lord Dunmore's barbarity; Massachusetts militia; powder; disaster at Quebec. L. S. of John Hancock. 4 pp. In handwriting of Charles Thomson. **90, 56**

1776
JAN. 8

Continental Congress, Resolves. Virginia troops; western frontiers. A. D. S. of Charles Thomson. 2 pp. Enclosed in President of Congress to Washington, 1776, Jan 10. **13, 53**

1776
JAN. 8

Continental Congress, Resolves. Troops to be raised for service in Canada; purchase of salt-petre. A. D. S. of Charles Thomson, countersigned by John Hancock. Enclosed in President of Congress to Washington, 1776, Jan. 6–18. **90, 53**

1776
JAN. 9

Continental Congress, Resolve. Free postage for soldiers. A. D. S. of Charles Thomson, countersigned by John Hancock. Transmitted to Washington. **89, 100**

1776
JAN. 9

Continental Congress, Resolves. Forwarding money; postage of soldiers' mail. A. D. S. of Charles Thomson, countersigned John Hancock. Enclosed in President of Congress to Washington, 1776, Jan. 6–18. **90, 53**
Postage resolve same as preceding entry.

1776
JAN. 11

Washington, George. Cambridge. To [the President of Congress, Philadelphia]. Defense of New York; Maj. [Thomas] Knowlton's exploit. L. S. 3 pp. In handwriting of Stephen Moylan. Read in Congress Jan. 22. **C. C. 152, 1, 411**
Printed: Writings of Washington (Ford) N. Y. 1889. 3, 332.

1776
JAN. 13

Schuyler, Ph[ilip John]. Albany [New York]. To [George] Washington [Cambridge]. Reenforcements for

Canada. Contemporary copy. 2 pp. In handwriting of George Lewis. Enclosed in Washington to the President of Congress, 1776, Jan. 19.

           C. C.   152, 1, 429

1776
JAN. 14

Washington, George. Cambridge. To [the President of Congress, Philadelphia]. Want of fire-arms; re-enforcements of the British. L. S. 3 pp. In handwriting of Robert Hanson Harrison. Read in Congress Jan. 25.   C. C.   152, 1, 415
Printed: Writings of Washington (Ford) N. Y. 1889. 3, 337.

1776
JAN. 14

Continental Congress, Resolve. Rank of officers. Contemporary copy. In handwriting of Joseph Reed. Transmitted to Washington.   15, 267

1776
JAN. 15

Rhode Island, General Assembly. Providence. To the Rhode Island delegates in Congress. Situation of the colony; its need of defense. Contemporary copy. 3 pp. Enclosed in Washington to the President of Congress, 1776, Apr. 30.

           C. C.   152, 1, 635

1776
JAN. 16

Continental Congress, Resolves. Drafts to pay army; enlistment of negroes; chaplains. A. D. S. of Charles Thomson, countersigned by John Hancock. Enclosed in President of Congress to Washington, 1776, Jan. 6–18.   90, 53

1776
JAN. 16

Massachusetts, House of Representatives [Watertown]. Report of Committee and resolve respecting recruits furnishing their own arms. Contemporary copy. 2 pp. In handwriting of George Lewis. Enclosed in Washington to the President of Congress, 1776, Jan. 19.   C. C.   152, 1, 433

1776
JAN. 16

Lynch, Thomas, Philadelphia. To [George] Washington [Cambridge]. Courts of Admiralty and military matters; delay in furnishing money; troops to be raised; expense; attitude of Britain; Lord Drummond and his information; powder. A. L. S. 3 pp.   8, 69

1776
JAN. 18

Continental Army. Council of War. Cambridge. Raising troops for Canada. Contemporary copy. 2 pp. In handwriting of Horatio Gates. Enclosed in Washington to the President of Congress 1776, Jan. 19.   C. C.   152, 1, 423

1776
JAN. 19

Washington, George. Cambridge. To [the President of Congress, Philadelphia]. Affairs in Canada; rais-

ing of troops for service there.   A. L. S.   4 pp.
Read in Congress Jan. 27.   Referred to Lynch,
Wythe, Sherman, Ward, and J. Adams.

C. C.   152, 1, 4

Printed: Writings of Washington (Ford) N. Y. 1889. 3, 359.

1776
JAN. 19

Washington, George. Cambridge. To the Colonies of
Massachusetts, Connecticut and New Hampshire.
Troops for Canada. L. S. 1 p. In handwriting
of George Baylor. Enclosed in Washington to
the President of Congress, 1775, Jan. 19.

C. C.   152, 1, 427

Printed: Writings of Washington (Ford) N. Y. 1889. 3, 362.

1776
JAN. 19

Continental Congress, Resolves. Enlistment of seamen for
South Carolina; reenforcements for Canada. A.
D. S. of Charles Thomson, countersigned by
John Hancock. 4 pp. Enclosed in President of
Congress to Washington, 1776, Jan. 20.   **90, 69**

1776
JAN. 20

Continental Congress, President. Philadelphia. To
[George] Washington [Cambridge]. Defeat in
Canada; reenforcements; raising of troops, etc.
L. S. of John Hancock. 3 pp. In handwriting
of Timothy Matlack.   **90, 57**

1776
JAN. 20

Continental Army. Commissary General's Department.
List of persons employed. A. D. of Joseph
Trumbull. 3 pp. Enclosed in Washington to
the President of Congress, 1776, Jan. 24.

C. C.   152, 1, 443

1776
JAN. 20

Continental Congress, President. Philadelphia. To
[George] Washington [Cambridge]. Canadian
situation; reenforcements; naming South Carolina armed vessels; capture of [Dr. John F. D.]
Smyth; raising of troops; minor matters. L. S.
of John Hancock. 3 pp. In handwriting of
Timothy Matlack.   **90, 58**

1776
JAN. 20

Continental Congress, Resolve. Officers and money for
Canada. A. D. S. of Charles Thomson, countersigned by John Hancock. Enclosed in President
of Congress to Washington, 1776, Jan 20.

90, 69

1776
JAN. 24

Washington, George. Cambridge. To [the President of
Congress, Philadelphia]. Commissary General's
department; accounts of the army; military situation; marines. L. S. 4 pp. In handwriting of
Robert Hanson Harrison.   C. C.   152, 1, 435

1776
JAN. 24

Continental Congress. Address to the Inhabitants of Canada. Exertions for their relief. Contemporary copy. 3 pp. In handwriting of Stephen Moylan. Transmitted to Washington.   **90, 72**

1776
JAN. 27

Washington, George. Cambridge. To [Maj.] Gen. [Philip John] Schuyler [Albany]. Canadian affairs; Coughnawaga Indians. Contemporary copy. 3 pp. In handwriting of George Lewis. Enclosed in Washington to the President of Congress, 1775, Jan. 30.   **C. C. 152, 1, 455**
Printed: Writings of Washington (Ford) N. Y. 1889. 3, 375.

1776
JAN. 29

Continental Congress, President. Philadelphia. To [George] Washington [Cambridge]. Raising of troops; prosecution of the war. L. S. of John Hancock. 2 pp. In handwriting of Timothy Matlack.   **8, 132**

1776
JAN. 29

Continental Congress, Resolves. Raising troops for Canada. A. D. S. of Charles Thomson, countersigned by John Hancock. 2 pp. Transmitted to Washington.   **90, 74**

1776
JAN. 29

Continental Congress, Resolves. Raising troops for Canada. A. D. S. of Charles Thomson, countersigned by John Hancock. Transmitted to Washington.   **90, 74**

1776
JAN. 30

Washington, George. Cambridge. To [the President of Congress, Philadelphia]. Affairs in Canada; pay of the army; powder; armed vessels. L. S. 3 pp. In handwriting of Robert Hanson Harrison. Read Feb. 9. Referred to Chase, J. Adams, Penn, Wythe and Edward Rutledge.   **C. C. 152, 1, 447**
Printed: Writings of Washington (Ford) N. Y. 1889. 3, 383.

1776
JAN. 30

W[ashingto]n, G[eorge]. Cambridge. To [Maj.] Gen. [Sir William] Howe [Boston.] Exchange of James Lovell. D. S. 1 p. In handwriting of George Lewis. Enclosed in Washington to the President of Congress, 1776, Feb. 9.   **C. C. 152, 1, 473**

1776
JAN. 30

Continental Congress, Resolves. Tent-cloth and arms. A. D. S. of Charles Thomson, countersigned by John Hancock. Transmitted to Washington.   **90, 74**

1776
JAN. 30

Coughnawaga Indians. [Cambridge.] Talk with Gen. [George] Washington. Offers of peace and alliance.

Pasmiquoddy Indians. Talk with Washington. Offers of peace; request for powder. 3 pp. In handwriting of Robert Hanson Harrison and George Lewis. Enclosed in Washington to the President of Congress, 1775, Jan. 30.

C. C.   152, 1, 459

Dated in error, Jan. 31.

1776
JAN.

Continental Army. Quartermaster General's Department. List of Clerks and Assistants. A. D. of Thomas Mifflin. 2 pp. Enclosed in Washington to the President of Congress, 1776, Jan. 24.

C. C.   152, 1, 439

1776
[JAN.]

Halifax, Proposed expedition against. General plan. Copied and attested by Stephen Moylan. 1 p. Enclosed in Washington to the President of Congress, 1775, Jan. 30.   C. C.   152, 1, 463

1776
FEB. 2

Howe, [Sir] W[illiam]. Boston. To George Washington [Cambridge]. Exchange of James Lovell. Contemporary copy. 1 p. In handwriting of George Lewis. Enclosed in Washington to the President of Congress, 1776, Feb. 9.   C. C.   152, 1, 475

1776
FEB. 5

Drummond, [Earl of Perth, James, Lord]. New York. To Brig. Gen. [James] Robertson, Boston. Suggested negotiation for peace. A. L. S.   3 pp. Enclosed in Washington to the President of Congress, 1776, Feb. 14.   C. C.   152, 1, 489

1776
FEB. 5

Lynch, Thomas. New York. To [George Washington, Cambridge]. Weak state of New York city; Lord Drummond's purposes. Recent copy. 2 pp.

8, 144

1776
FEB. 9

Washington, George. Cambridge. To [the President of Congress, Philadelphia]. Disadvantages arising from short enlistments. A. L. S.   4 pp. Read in Congress Feb. 22. Referred to Committee of the Whole.   C. C.   152, 1, 477

Printed: Writings of Washington (Ford) N. Y. 1889.   3, 406.

1776
FEB. 9

Washington, George. Cambridge. To the President of Congress, Philadelphia. Pay of the Connecticut troops. L. S.   1 p. In handwriting of Robert Hanson Harrison. Read in Congress Mar. 7.

C. C.   152, 1, 481

1776
FEB. 9

Washington, George. Cambridge. To [the President of Congress, Philadelphia]. Prize courts; recruit-

ing; prisoners; arms. L. S. 6 pp. In handwriting of Stephen Moylan. Read in Congress
Feb. 22.   C. C.   152, 1, 465

1776
FEB. 14

Washington, George. Cambridge. To [the President of
Congress, Philadelphia]. Lord Drummond's ad-
vances; reports from Nova Scotia; subsistence
of prisoners. L. S. 4 pp. In handwriting of
Robert Hanson Harrison. Read in Congress
Feb. 29. Referred to Chase, J. Adams, Penn,
Wythe, and Rutledge.   C. C.   152, 1, 485
Printed: Writings of Washington (Ford) N. Y. 3, 419.

1776
FEB. 16

Continental Army. Council of War. Cambridge. Advisa-
bility of attacking Boston. Contemporary copy.
3 pp. In handwriting of Robert Hanson Harrison. Enclosed in Washington to the President
of Congress, 1776, Feb. 18.   C. C.   152, 1, 501

1776
FEB. 18

Washington, George. Cambridge. To [the President of
Congress, Philadelphia]. Decision of Council of
War on attacking Boston; lack of powder. A.
L. S. 4 pp. Read in Congress Mar. 6.
                                  C. C.   152, 1, 497
Printed: Writings of Washington (Ford) N. Y. 1889. 3, 425.

1776
FEB. 26

Washington, George. Cambridge. To [the President of
Congress, Philadelphia]. Fortifying Dorchester
Heights; movements of enemy. Unsigned. 3
pp. In handwriting of Robert Hanson Harrison.
Read in Congress Mar. 6.   C. C.   152, 1, 505
Printed: Writings of Washington (Ford) N. Y. 1889. 3, 432.

[1776]
[FEB.]

Willard, Aaron and Moses **Child**. [Cambridge?] Report
[to George Washington, Cambridge]. Condi-
tions in Nova Scotia. A. D. S. of Willard, signed
also by Child. 1 p. Enclosed in Washington to
the President of Congress 1776, Feb. 14.
                                  C. C.   152, 1, 495

1776
MAR. 2

Continental Congress, Resolve. Settlement of seniority of
officers. Contemporary copy. In handwriting
of Joseph Reed, with explanatory note by Charles
Thomson.   15, 267

1776
MAR. 6

Continental Congress, President. Philadelphia. To George
Washington [Cambridge]. Accounts; establish-
ment of Middle and Southern Departments and
commanders for same; command in Canada; manufacture of powder and arms. L. S. of John
Hancock. 3 pp. In handwriting of Jacob Rush.
Answered Mar. 19*.   8, 210

1776
MAR. 7–9

Washington, George. Cambridge. To [the President of Congress, Philadelphia]. Fortifications at Dorchester Heights; plans for engagement; approaching evacuation of Boston by enemy. L. S. 8 pp. In handwriting of Robert Hanson Harrison. Read in Congress Mar. 15.   **C. C.   152,** 1, 509
Printed: Writings of Washington (Ford) N. Y. 1889. 3, 448.

1776
MAR. 8

Continental Congress. Minute of election of Henry B[eekman] Livingston to lieutenant-colonel. Contemporary copy. In handwriting of Joseph Reed.   **15, 267**

1776
MAR. 8

Boston, Selectmen. Statement looking toward preservation of the town on withdrawal of the British. [Unaddressed but sent to Washington.] Contemporary copy. In handwriting of William Palfrey. Enclosed in Washington to the President of Congress 1776, Mar. 7–9.   **C. C.   152,** 1 517
Printed: Writings of Washington (Ford) N. Y. 1889. 3, 457, note.

1776
MAR. 9

Learned, Ebenezer. Roxbury [Massachusetts]. To [Jonathan and Thomas] Amory and [Peter] Johannot [Roxbury]. [George] Washington's answer to statement of the Boston Selectmen. Contemporary copy. 1 p. In handwriting of William Palfrey. Enclosed in Washington to the President of Congress, 1776, Mar. 7.
C. C.   152, 1, 519
Printed: Writings of Washington (Ford) N. Y. 1889. 3, 458, note.

1776
MAR. 11

Continental Congress, President. Philadelphia. To [George] Washington [Cambridge]. Minor military matters. L. S. of John Hancock. 1 p. In handwriting of Charles Thomson. Answered Mar. 27*.   **8, 222**

1776
MAR. 13

Washington, George. Cambridge. To [the President of Congress, Philadelphia]. Approaching evacuation of Boston; preparations to defend New York. L. S. 5 pp. In handwriting of Robert Hanson Harrison. Read in Congress Mar. 22.
C. C.   152, 1, 521
Printed: Writings of Washington (Ford) N. Y. 1889. 3, 467.

1776
MAR. 13

Continental Army, Council of War. Roxbury [Massachusetts]. Marching troops to New York. Contemporary copy. 2 pp. In handwriting of William Palfrey. Enclosed in Washington to the President of Congress 1776, March 13.
C. C.   152, 1, 527

1776   **Lee**, Richard Henry. Philadelphia. To [George Wash-
Mar. 13   ington, Cambridge]. Forwarding letters; [Maj.]
             Gen. [Charles] Lee going south. A. L. S. 1 p.
                                                        8, 233

1776   **Washington**, George. Cambridge. To the officer com-
Mar. 14   manding the American forces at New York.
             [Maj. Gen. William Alexander, Lord Stirling].
             Defense of New York. L. S. 3 pp. In hand-
             writing of Stephen Moylan. Enclosed in Wash-
             ington to the President of Congress, 1776, Mar. 13.
                                         C. C. 152, 1, 531
                Printed: Writings of Washington (Ford) N. Y. 1889. 3, 471.

1776   **British Army**, Provision return. Contemporary copy. 1 p.
[Mar. 16?]   In handwriting of Thomas Mifflin? Enclosed in
             Washington to the President of Congress, 1776,
             Mar. 24.   C. C. 152, 1, 561

1776   **Continental Congress**, President. Philadelphia. To
Mar. 17   [George] Washington, [Cambridge]. Treatment
             of [Lt.] Col. [Archibald] Campbell in retalia-
             tion for that of [Maj.] Gen. [Charles] Lee; dis-
             couragement to foreigners proposing to come to
             America. L. S. of John Hancock. 3 pp. In
             handwriting of Jacob Rush. Answered Mar. 21.
                                                        90, 104

1776   **Cheever**, Ezekiel. [Boston.] Return of ordnance stores
Mar. 17   left in Boston by the British. Transcript. En-
             closed in Washington to the President of Congress,
             1776, Mar. 27.   C. C. 169, 1, 401

1776   **Frye**, Joseph. Cambridge. To [George] Washington
Mar. 18   [Cambridge]. Resigning his commission. A. L.
             S. 1 p. Enclosed in Washington to the Presi-
             dent of Congress, 1775, Mar. 14. C. C. 152, 1, 549

1776   **Washington**, George. Cambridge. To [Maj. Gen. Wil-
Mar. 19   liam Alexander, Lord Stirling, New York].
             Evacuation of Boston; troops ordered to New
             York. Contemporary copy. 2 pp. In hand-
             writing of William Grayson. Enclosed in Wash-
             ington to the President of Congress, 1776,
             Mar. 19.   C. C. 152, 1, 535
                Printed, in part: Writings of Washington (Ford) N. Y. 1889. 3, 479,
             note.

1776   **Washington**, George. Cambridge. To [the President of
Mar. 19   Congress, Philadelphia]. Occupation of Boston
             by the American Army. Unsigned. 2 pp. In

General Greenes Quarters
Nov. 16. 1776

Since I had the Honour of
addressing you last an important Event has taken
Place of which I wish to give you the earliest
Intelligence — The Preservation of the Passage of
the North River was an Object of so much Consequence that I thought no Pains or Expence too
great for that Purpose, & therefore after sending
off all the valuable Stores except such as were
necessary for its Defence I determined agreable
to the Advice of the most of the General Officers
to risque something to defend the Post on the East
Side called Mount Washington — When the Army
moved up in Consequence of Gen. Howe's landing at
Frog Point Col. Magaw was left in that Command
with about 1500 Men & Orders given to defend it
to the last. Afterwards reflecting upon the Smallness
of the Garrison & the Difficulty of their holding it
if Gen. Howe should fall down upon it with his
whole Force I wrote to Gen. Greene who had the Command
on the Jersey Shore directing him to govern himself

handwriting of William Palfrey. Read in Congress Mar. 25.   C. C.   152, 1, 537
Printed: Writings of Washington (Ford) N. Y. 1889. 3, 475.

1776
MAR. 20

Frazer, John G[izzard]. Boston. Inventory of King's stores left in Boston by the British. Contemporary copy. 4 pp. In handwriting of Robert Hanson Harrison. Enclosed in Washington to the President of Congress 1776, Mar. 24.
                                    C. C.   152, 1, 557

1776
MAR. 21

Washington, George. Cambridge. To the General Court [of Massachusetts, Watertown]. Departure of British; King's stores left in Boston; pay of Massachusetts army officers. Contemporary copy. 2 pp. In handwriting of George Lewis. Enclosed in Washington to the President of Congress, 1776, Mar. 24.   C. C.   152, 1, 553
Printed: Writings of Washington (Ford) N. Y. 1889. 3, 481.

1776
MAR. 22

Ward, Artemas. Roxbury. To [George] Washington, Cambridge. Resigning his commission. L. S. 1 p. Enclosed in Washington to Congress 1776, Mar. 24.   C. C.   152, 1, 545

1776
MAR. 23

Continental Congress, Resolves. Authorizing privateers; prizes. Broadside. 1 p. Printed by John Dunlap. Enclosed in President of Congress to Washington, 1776, Mar. 25.   **90, 78**

1776
MAR. 24

Washington, George. Cambridge. To [the President of Congress, Philadelphia]. Evacuation of Boston; military stores and other matters; Commissioners from England. L. S. 4 pp. In handwriting of Robert Hanson Harrison. Read in Congress, Apr. 2. Referred to Johnson, Jay and Wilson.
                                    C. C.   152, 1, 541
Printed: Writings of Washington (Ford) N. Y. 1889. 3, 487.

1776
MAR. 25

Continental Congress, President. Philadelphia. To [George] Washington [Cambridge]. Evacuation of Boston; lack of arms; troops for Canada. L. S. of John Hancock. 3 pp. In handwriting of Jacob Rush.   **8, 265**

1776
MAR. 27

Washington, George. Cambridge. To [the President of Congress, Philadelphia]. Sailing of enemy from Nantasket; troops sent to New York; petition from inhabitants of Nova Scotia. L. S. 3 pp. In handwriting of Robert Hanson Harrison. Received Apr. 6. Referred to Committee of the Whole.   C. C.   152, 1, 563
Printed: Writings of Washington (Ford) N. Y. 1889. 3, 494 and 496, notes.

1776
MAR. 31

Cooke, Nicholas. Providence [Rhode Island] To [George] Washington, Cambridge. Appearance of the British fleet off Rhode Island. Contemporary copy. 1 p. In handwriting of Robert Hanson Harrison. Enclosed in Washington to the President of Congress 1776, Apr. 1.

C. C. 152, 1, 575

[1776]
[MAR.?]

Nova Scotia, Inhabitants. Petition to George Washington [Cambridge] Calling for assistance. Contemporary copy. 2 pp. In handwriting of Caleb Gibbs. Enclosed in Washington to the President of Congress 1776, Mar. 27. C. C. 152, 1, 567

1776
APR. 1

Washington, George. Cambridge. To [the President of Congress, Philadelphia]. Alarm of enemy landing in Rhode Island. L. S. 2 pp. In handwriting of William Palfrey. C. C. 152, 1, 571

1776
APR. 1

Washington, George. Cambridge. To the President of Congress, Philadelphia. Introducing Jonathan Eddy and the Acadians. L. S. 1 p. In handwriting of William Palfrey. Read in Congress Apr. 10. Referred to Committee of the Whole.

C. C. 152, 1, 577

1776
APR. 1

Continental Congress, Resolves. Settlement of Treasury accounts. A. D. S. of Charles Thomson, countersigned by John Hancock. 2 pp. Transmitted to Washington. 89, 122

1776
APR. 1

Adams, John. Philadelphia. To [George] Washington [Cambridge] Introducing Francis Dana; thanks of Congress and medal commemorating evacuation of Boston. A. L. S. 1 p. 8, 280

1776
APR. 1

Cooke, Nicholas. Providence [Rhode Island]. To [George] Washington [Cambridge]. Foundation of report concerning the British fleet. Contemporary copy. 1 p. In handwriting of Caleb Gibbs. Enclosed in Washington to the President of Congress, 1776, Apr. 4. C. C. 152, 1, 585

1776
APR. 2

Continental Congress, President. Philadelphia. To [George] Washington [Cambridge]. Thanks of Congress on occasion of evacuation of Boston. L. S. of John Hancock. 2 pp. In handwriting of Jacob Rush. Answered Apr. 18.* 8, 283

1776
APR. 4

Washington, George. Cambridge. To [the President of Congress, Philadelphia]. Pay of militia; powder loaned by Massachusetts; Paymaster General.

L. S. 4 pp. In handwriting of Robert Hanson Harrison. Read in Congress Apr. 15.

C. C. 152, 1, 581

Printed: Writings of Washington (Ford) N. Y. 1889. 4, 9.

1776
APR. 12

Burbeck, William. Cambridge [Massachusetts]. To Col. Henry Knox [Cambridge]. Reasons for refusing to obey orders. Contemporary copy. 1 p. In handwriting of Caleb Gibbs. Enclosed in Washington to the President of Congress 1776, May 11. C. C. 152, 1, 679

1776
APR. 12

Knox, Henry. Cambridge. To Lt. Col. William Burbeck [Cambridge]. Ordering him to New York. Contemporary copy. 1 p. In handwriting of Caleb Gibbs. Enclosed in Washington to the President of Congress, 1776, May 11. C. C. 152, 1, 681

1776
APR. 15

Washington, George. New York. To [the President of Congress, Philadelphia]. The march to New York; miscellaneous matters. L. S. 3 pp. In handwriting of Robert Hanson Harrison. Recd. Apr. 18. Referred to Chase, Clinton, and Braxton. C. C. 152, 1, 587

Printed: Writings of Washington (Ford) N. Y. 1889. 4, 17.

1776
APR. 15

Continental Congress, Resolve.. Recruiting the rifle corps. A. D. S. of Charles Thomson, countersigned by John Hancock. 1 p. Transmitted to Washington. 89, 123

1776
APR. 16

Continental Congress, Resolves. Disposition of cannon and stores at New London with list of same. A. D. S. of Charles Thomson. 3 pp. Enclosed in President of Congress to Washington, 1776, Apr. 20. 89, 126

1776
APR. 17

Continental Congress, President. Philadelphia. To [George] Washington [New York] Troops for Cape May. A. L. S. of John Hancock. 1 p. 8, 335

1776
APR. 17

Continental Congress, Committee on fortifying coast. Philadelphia. To [George Washington, New York]. Fortifying of Cape Ann and New London. A. L. S. of John Adams, signed also by Benjamin Harrison and William Whipple. 2 pp. Answered Apr. 22.* 89, 124

Committee: Harrison, J. Adams and Whipple.

1776
APR. 17

New York, Committee of Safety, New York. To [George] Washington [New York]. Exchange of citizen prisoners. Contemporary copy. 1 p. Enclosed in Washington to the President of Congress, 1776, Apr. 22. In handwriting of William Palfrey.

C. C.   152, 1, 607

1776
APR. 18

Continental Army, Canadian Expedition. [New York.] Return of regiments going on command to Canada. Tabular statement. D. S. of Horatio Gates. 2 pp.   Enclosed in Washington to the President of Congress, 1776, Apr. 19.   C. C.   152, 1, 599

1776
APR. 18

Washington, George. New York. To [the President of Congress, Philadelphia]. Appreciation of Congress' approval. A. L. S.   2 pp.

C. C.   152, 1, 591

Printed: Writings of Washington (Ford) N. Y. 1889. 4, 26.

1776
APR. 19

Washington, George. New York. To [the President of Congress, Philadelphia]. Troops for Canada; aid of Indians; Canadian Committee. L. S.   3 pp.   In handwriting of William Palfrey.

C. C.   152, 1, 595

Printed in part: Writings of Washington (Ford) N. Y. 1889. 4, 30 and 31, notes.

1776
APR. 19

Continental Congress, Resolves.   Cannon; paymaster-general.   A. D. S. of Charles Thomson.   Enclosed in President of Congress to Washington, 1775, Apr. 20.   89, 126

1776
APR. 20

Continental Congress, President.   Philadelphia.   To [George] Washington [New York].   Troops for Canada.   L. S. of John Hancock.   2 pp.   In handwriting of Jacob Rush.

89, 128

1776
APR. 20

Hancock, John.   Philadelphia.   To [George] Washington, New York.   Desiring [Lt. Col. William] Palfrey's assistance.   A. L. S.   1 p.   8, 343

1776
APR. 22

Washington, George.   New York.   To [the President of Congress, Philadelphia].   Troops for Canada; lack of arms; exchange of prisoners; artillery; trouble with Commissary Department.   L. S. 4 pp.   In handwriting of William Palfrey.   Read in Congress Apr. 25.   Referred to R. H. Lee, J. Adams and Joseph Hewes.

C. C.   152, 1, 603

Printed: Writings of Washington (Ford) N. Y. 1889. 4, 34.

1776
APR. 22

Washington, George.   New York.   To [Committee of Congress, Philadelphia].   Fortifying Cape Ann and New London.   Letter-book copy.   In handwriting of Robert Hanson Harrison.   M. II, 44

Committee on fortifying forts: Harrison, J. Adams, and Whipple.

1776
APR. 23

Washington, George. New York. To [the President of Congress, Philadelphia]. Pay and rank of aid-de-camps. A. L. S. 3 pp. Read in Congress Apr. 25. Referred to R. H. Lee, J. Adams and Joseph Hewes.   **C. C. 152**, 1, 611
Printed: Writings of Washington (Ford) N. Y. 1889. 4, 39.

1776
APR. 23

Washington, George. New York. To the President of Congress, Philadelphia. Camp equipage for the Commander in chief. A. L. S. 1 p. Read in Congress May 4.   **C. C. 152**, 1, 614

1776
APR. 23

Continental Congress, President. Philadelphia. To [George] Washington [New York]. Reinforcements for Canada. L. S. of John Hancock. 3 pp. In handwriting of Jacob Rush. Answered Apr. 25.*   **8, 353**

1776
APR. 23

Continental Congress, Resolves. Respecting the Army in Canada; inquiries to inhabitants. A. D. S. of Charles Thomson, countersigned by John Hancock. 2 pp. Enclosed in President of Congress to Washington, 1776, Apr. 23.   **89, 130**

1776
APR. 23

Continental Army. General return. New York. Statement of numbers. Transcript. Enclosed in Washington to the President of Congress, 1776, Apr. 25.   **C. C. 169**, 1, 403

1776
APR. 25

Washington, George. New York. To [the President of Congress, Philadelphia]. Extract of prize agent's letter respecting Commodore [John] Manly's capture; pay of army; troops ordered to Canada. L. S. 12 pp. In handwriting of Stephen Moylan. Read in Congress Apr. 29. Referred to Harrison, Rutledge, Goldsborough, Paine and Rodney.   **C. C. 152**, 1, 627
Printed, in part: Writings of Washington (Ford) N. Y. 1889. 4, 44.

1776
APR. 25

Continental Congress, President. Philadelphia. To [George] Washington [New York]. Money for army in Canada. A. L. S. of John Hancock. 1 p.   **9, 6**

1776
APR. 26

Continental Congress, Resolves. Pay of aids to the Commander in chief; deficiency of arms; militia accounts, etc. A. D. S. of Charles Thomson, countersigned by John Hancock. 1 p. Enclosed in President of Congress to Washington, 1776, Apr. 27.   **89, 132**

1776
APR. 27

Continental Congress, President. Philadelphia. To [George] Washington [New York]. Transmit-

ting resolves of Congress. L. S. of John Hancock. 1 p.   **9, 8**

1776   **Continental Army**. Canadian Expedition. [New York.]
APR. 28   Return of regiments going on command to Can-
ada. Tabular statement. A. D. S. of Horatio
Gates. 2 pp. Enclosed in Washington to the
President of Congress, 1776, May 5.
C. C.   **152, 1, 653**

1776   **Continental Army**, General Court Martial. New York.
APR. 29   Trial of Lt. [Thomas] Grover for disobeying
orders and using insulting language to his superior officer. Contemporary copy. 4 pp. In
handwriting of Caleb Gibbs. Enclosed in Washington to the President of Congress 1776, May 5.
C. C.   **152, 1, 645**

1776   **Forts Montgomery and Constitution**. Returns of strength
APR. 29   of garrisons. Tabular statements. 1 p. A. D. S.
of Isaac Nicoll.   C. C.   **152, 1, 661**
Return for Fort Constitution is dated Apr. 23 and was enclosed in
Washington to the President of Congress, 1776, May 5.

1776   **Grover**, Thomas. [New York.] Defence before court
APR. 29   martial. Contemporary copy. 1 p. In handwriting of Caleb Gibbs. Enclosed in Washington to
the President of Congress, 1776, May 5.
C. C.   **152, 1, 647**

1776   **Washington**, George. New York. To [the President of
APR. 30   Congress Philadelphia]. Assistance for Rhode
Island. L. S. 2 pp. In handwriting of Robert
Hanson Harrison. Read in Congress May 2.
Referred to Committee on Eastern Department.
C. C.   **152, 1, 631**

Printed: Writings of Washington (Ford) N. Y. 1889, 4, 57.

1776   **Continental Congress**, President. Philadelphia. To
APR. 30   [George] Washington [New York]. The pay-
master-generalship. L. S. of John Hancock.
2 pp. In handwriting of Jacob Rush.   **89, 133**

1776   **Continental Congress**, Resolves. Miscellaneous military
MAY 3   matters. A. D. S. of Charles Thomson, counter-
signed by John Hancock. 1 p. Enclosed in
President of Congress to Washington, 1776,
May 4.   **89, 135**

1776   **Cushing**, Thomas. Watertown [Massachusetts]. To
MAY 3   [George] Washington [New York]. Rumor of
return of the British to Boston. Contemporary
copy. 1 p. In handwriting of Caleb Gibbs.

Enclosed in Washington to the President of Congress, 1776, May 7.   C. C. **152, 1, 667**

1776
MAY 4

Continental Congress, Resolve. Presenting cannon to Massachusetts. D. S. of John Hancock. 1 p. Transmitted to Washington.   **89, 136**

1776
MAY 4

Continental Congress, Resolve. Pay of militia. D. S. of John Hancock. Transmitted to Washington.
    89, 137

1776
MAY 4

Continental Congress, President. Philadelphia. To [George] Washington [New York]. Appointment [Matthias] Ogden to a lieutenant colonelcy. L. S. of John Hancock. 1 p. In handwriting of Charles Thomson, answered May 11*.   **9, 65**

1776
MAY 5

Washington, George. New York. To [the President of Congress, Philadelphia]. Pressing need of Arms. A. L. S. 4 pp. Read in Congress May 8. Referred to S. Adams, Wythe, Rodney, R. H. Lee, and Whipple.   C. C. **152, 1, 657**
Printed: Writings of Washington (Ford) N. Y. 1889. 4, 64.

1776
MAY 5

Washington, George. New York. To [the President of Congress, Philadelphia]. Settlement of accounts; new road to Canada; troops for Canada; other military matters. L. S. 5 pp. In handwriting of Robert Hanson Harrison. Read in Congress May 7. Referred to J. Adams, Braxton, and Duane.   C. C. **152, 1, 639**
Printed: Writings of Washington (Ford) N. Y. 1889. 4, 59.

1776
MAY 5

Continental Army, Artillery, New York. General return. Tabular statement. A. D. S. of Horatio Gates. 2 pp. Enclosed in Washington to the President of Congress, 1776, May 5.   C. C. **152, 1, 649**

1776
MAY 5

Grover, Thomas. New York. To George Washington [New York] acknowledging his offense and praying forgiveness. Additional acknowledgment dated May 8. A. L. S. 1 p. Enclosed in Washington to the President of Congress, 1776, May 11.   C. C. **152, 1, 677**

1776
MAY 6

Continental Congress, Resolve. Conduct toward Commissioners coming from England. A. D. S. of Charles Thomson, countersigned by John Hancock. 1 p. Enclosed in President of Congress to Washington, 1776, May 10.   **89, 138**

1776
MAY 7

Washington, George. New York. To [the President of Congress, Philadelphia]. Reports of enemy's

fleet; the [Peace] Commissioners. L. S.   2 pp.
In handwriting of Robert Hanson Harrison.
Read in Congress May 10.   Referred to Com-
mittee on State of the Eastern Colonies.

C. C.   152, 1, 663

Printed: Writings of Washington (Ford) N. Y. 1889. 4, 67, note.
Committee: Rutledge, Johnson, Wythe, Harrison, and Duane.

1776
MAY 7

Continental Congress, President.   Philadelphia.   To
[George] Washington.   Transmitting a resolve.
L. S. of John Hancock.   1 p.   Answered May
11*.   9, 92

1776
MAY 7

Continental Congress, Resolve.   Cannon for Boston.
D. S. of John Hancock.   Transmitted to Washington.   89, 137

1776
MAY 10

Continental Congress, President.   Philadelphia.   To
[George] Washington [New York].   Appoint-
ments; powder and arms; engagement in the
Delaware; money for army.   L. S. of John
Hancock.   2 pp.   9, 107

1776
MAY 10

Continental Congress, Resolve.   Accounts; recruiting expenses; Canada road; powder; money; returns;
promotions.   A. D. S. of Charles Thomson,
countersigned by John Hancock.   2 pp.   Enclosed in Washington, President of Congress
1776, May 10.   89, 138

1776
MAY 10

Schuyler, Philip John.   Fort George [New York].   To
[George] Washington [New York].   Affairs in
Canada; construction of gondolas; treatment re-
ceived by Schuyler.   Contemporary copy.   2 pp.
In handwriting of Caleb Gibbs.   Enclosed in
Washington to the President of Congress, 1776,
June 8.   C. C.   152, 2, 13

1776
MAY 10

Stringer, Samuel.   Albany [New York].   To [George]
Washington [New York].   Reenforcement and
supplies necessary for the hospital ordered to
Canada.   Contemporary copy.   1 p.   In handwriting of Caleb Gibbs.   Enclosed in Washington
to the President of Congress, 1776, May 15.

C. C.   152, 1, 689

[1776]
[MAY 10]

Stringer, Samuel.   [Albany.]   Estimate of hospital supplies necessary for Canada.   Contemporary copy.
1 p.   In handwriting of Caleb Gibbs.   Enclosed in
Washington to the President of Congress, 1776,
May 15.   C. C.   152, 1, 691

1776
MAY 11

Washington, George. New York. To [the President of Congress, Philadelphia]. Disciplinary measures; appointments; prisoners; coming of German troops. L. S. 4 pp. In handwriting of Robert Hanson Harrison. Read in Congress May 14. Referred to Livingston, Jefferson and J. Adams.
C. C. 152, 1, 669
Printed: Writings of Washington (Ford) N. Y. 1889. 4, 74.

[1776]
[MAY 11]

Washington, George. [New York] England's method of treatment of prisoners of war. A. D. of Horatio Gates. 2 pp. Enclosed in Washington to the President of Congress, 1776, May 11.
C. C. 152, 1, 683

1776
MAY 11

Continental Congress, Secret Committee. Philadelphia. To [George] Washington [New York]. Forwarding powder. A. L. S. of Robert Morris. 1 p. Answered May 20. 9, 133

1776
MAY 13

Continental Congress, President. Philadelphia. To [George] Washington, New York. Payment of troops; powder and arms. L. S. of John Hancock. 2 pp. In handwriting of Jacob Rush. Answered May 17*. 9, 139

1776
MAY 14

Continental Congress, Resolves. Command of the Eastern Department; troops to be raised in New Hampshire. D. S. of John Hancock. 1 p. Enclosed in President of Congress to Washington, 1776, May 16. 89, 140

1776
MAY 14

Continental Congress, Resolve. Raising of troops for the Eastern Department. D. S. of John Hancock. Enclosed in President of Congress to Washington, 1776, May 16. 89, 141

1776
MAY 15

Washington, George. New York. To [the President of Congress, Philadelphia] Intelligence of march of troops into Canada; hospital matters. L. S. 4 pp. In handwriting of Robert Hanson Harrison. Read in Congress May 16. Referred to Wm. Livingston, Jefferson and J. Adams.
C. C. 152, 1, 685
Printed: Writings of Washington (Ford) N. Y. 1889. 4, 80.

1776
MAY 16

Continental Congress, President. Philadelphia. To [George] Washington [New York]. Request to attend Congress; invitation to reside at his house; Mrs. Washington and the smallpox. L. S. of John Hancock. 3 pp. In handwriting of Jacob Rush. Answered May 20*. 89, 142

1776
MAY 16

Continental Congress, Secret Committee. Philadelphia. To [George] Washington [New York]. Muskets from Rhode Island. A. L. S. of Robert Morris. 1 p. Answered May 20*. **9, 172**

1776
MAY 16

Continental Congress, Resolve. Raising of troops in Massachusetts. D. S. of John Hancock. Enclosed in President of Congress to Washington, 1776, May 16. **89, 141**

1776
MAY 17

Washington, George. New York. To [the President of Congress, Philadelphia]. Reverses in Canada. L. S. 2 pp. In handwriting of Robert Hanson Harrison. Read in Congress May 18. Referred to Wm. Livingston, Jefferson, J. Adams, R. Morris, Duane, R. H. Lee, Rutledge, R. Livingston. **C. C. 152, 1, 693**

Printed, in part: Writings of Washington (Ford) N. Y. 1889. 4, 85, note.

1776
MAY 18

Washington, George. New York. To the President of Congress, Philadelphia. Transmitting important papers. L. S. 1 p. In handwriting of Robert Hanson Harrison. Read in Congress May 21. **C. C. 152, 1, 697**

Printed: Writings of Washington (Ford) N. Y. 1889. 4, 86, note.

1776
MAY 18

Continental Congress, Resolve. Increase of pay of assistant engineers. A. D. S. of Charles Thomson with autograph initialed note of John Hancock. Transmitted to Washington. **89, 167**

1776
MAY 19

Washington, George. New York. To [the President of Congress, Philadelphia]. Introducing [Maj.]Gen. Horatio Gates; his business. Unsigned. 2 pp. In handwriting of Robert Hanson Harrison. Read in Congress May 21. **C. C. 152, 1, 701**

Printed: Writings of Washington (Ford) N. Y. 1889. 4, 88, note.

1776
MAY 20

Washington, George. New York. To [the President of Congress, Philadelphia]. Approaching visit to Congress. A. L. S. 2 pp. Read in Congress May 21. **C. C. 152, 1, 704**

Printed: Writings of Washington (Ford) N. Y. 1889. 4, 88.

1776
MAY 20

Washington, George. New York. To [Chairman Secret Committee,] Robert Morris [Philadelphia]. Powder and invoices accompanying same. Letterbook copy. **M. II, 106**

1776
MAY 21

Washington, George. New York. To [the President of Congress, Philadelphia]. [John Dyer] Mercier's intelligence of attack on Quebec. Letter-book copy. In handwriting of Robert Hanson Harrison. **M.** II, 107

1776
MAY 21

Continental Congress, Resolves. Governing care and treatment of prisoners; form of parole. Broadside. 1 p. Transmitted to Washington. **89,** 144

1776
MAY 22

Continental Congress, Resolve. Cannon for vessels in Lake Champlain. A. D. S. of Charles Thomson. 1 p. Transmitted to Washington. **89,** 146

1776
MAY 22

Continental Congress, Resolve. Assistant clerk to Secretary to the Commander-in-chief. A. D. S. 1 p. Transmitted to Washington. **89,** 147

1776
MAY 24

Wilkinson, James. La Chine, near Montreal [Canada]. To ——— ? Defeat at the Cedars; weakness of troops; expectation of attack. Transcript. Enclosed in Washington to the President of Congress 1776, June 7. **C. C.** **169,** 1, 352

1776
MAY 25

Continental Congress, Resolve. Dismissal of Lt. Col. [William] Burbeck. A. D. S. of Charles Thomson, countersigned by John Hancock. 1 p. Transmitted to Washington. **89,** 148

1776
MAY 25

Continental Congress, Resolve. Disposal of arms and stores of armed schooners. A. D. S. of Charles Thomson. 1 p. Transmitted to Washington. **89,** 149

1776
MAY 27

Brown, Nicholas. Providence [Rhode Island]. To George Washington [Philadelphia]. Forwarding muskets to the army. Contemporary copy. 1 p. In handwriting of Caleb Gibbs. Enclosed in Washington to the President of Congress, 1776, June 9. **C. C.** **152,** 2, 21

1776
MAY 27–28

Chase, Samuel and Charles **Carroll** [of Carrollton]. Montreal To [the President of Congress, Philadelphia]. Report of the situation in Canada; miserable state of army; military movements; British barbarity. Contemporary copy. 8 pp. In handwriting of and attested by Jacob Rush. Enclosed in President of Congress to Washington, 1775, June 5–6. **89,** 150

1776
JUNE 1

Continental Congress, Resolve. Reenforcements for Canada. A. D. S. of Charles Thomson, countersigned by John Hancock. Enclosed in Washington to the President of Congress, 1776, June 3. **89,** 154

1776
JUNE 3

Washington, George. Philadelphia. To the President of Congress, Philadelphia. Application for arms

from Boston. L. S. 1 p. In handwriting of
Robert Hanson Harrison.   C. C. 152, 2, 1

1776
JUNE 3

Continental Congress, President. Philadelphia. To
[George] Washington [Philadelphia]. Thanks of
Congress. L. S. of John Hancock. 2 pp. In
handwriting of Jacob Rush.   9, 279

1776
JUNE 3

Continental Congress, Resolves. Reenforcement of army;
flying camp; militia; brigadier appointments; removal of stock, grain, etc.; lead mines; magazines of provisions. A. D. S. of Charles Thomson, countersigned by John Hancock. Enclosed
in Washington to the President of Congress, 1776,
June 3.   89, 154

1776
JUNE 3

Continental Congress, Resolves. General officer appointments. A. D. S. of Charles Thomson. 1 p.
Enclosed in President of Congress to Washington, 1776, June 3.   89, 156

1776
JUNE 4

Continental Congress, President. Philadelphia. Circular
letter to the Colonies. Designs of British; situation in Canada; calling forth of militia. Contemporary copy. 3 pp. In handwriting of Jacob
Rush. Enclosed in President of Congress to
Washington, 1776, June 11.   9, 322

1776
JUNE 4

Continental Congress, Resolve. Arms, etc. for militia.
A. D. S. of Charles Thomson. 1 p. Enclosed
in President of Congress to Washington, 1776,
June 5.   89, 157

1776
JUNE 5–6

Continental Congress, President. Philadelphia. To
[George] Washington [New York]. Promotions
and commissions; prizes captured. L. S. of John
Hancock. In handwriting of Jacob Rush. Answered June 7*.   9, 296

1776
JUNE 5

Continental Congress, Resolves. Returns; flying-camp,
militia; election of adjutant and quartermaster-
general and other military appointments. A. D.
S. of Charles Thomson, countersigned by John
Hancock. 2 pp. Enclosed in President of Congress to Washington, 1776, June 5–6.   89, 158

1776
JUNE 5

Arnold, B[enedict]. Montreal. To Brig. Gen. [John]
Sullivan [Sorel]. The military situation. Contemporary copy. 1 p. In handwriting of George
Lewis. Enclosed in Washington to the President
of Congress, 1776, June 16.   C. C. 152, 2, 55

1776
June 5

Dugan, J[eremiah]. St. Tours. [Canada]. To Brig. Gen. [John] Sullivan [Sorel]. Raising Canadian troops; Col. [Moses] Hazen's charges. Contemporary copy. 1 p. In handwriting of Caleb Gibbs. Enclosed in Washington to the President of Congress, 1776, June 16.   **C. C. 152**, 2, 57

1776
June 5

Sullivan, John. Sorel [Canada]. To [George] Washington [New York]. Military situation in Canada; disposition of the Canadians. Contemporary copy. 4 pp. In handwriting of Caleb Gibbs. Enclosed in Washington to the President of Congress, 1776, June 16.   **C. C. 152**, 2, 47

1776
June 6

Continental Congress, Resolves. Appointments and changes in officers of the northern army. A. D. S. part by Charles Thomson and part by John Hancock. 1 p. Enclosed in President of Congress to Washington, 1775, June 7.   **89**, 160

1776
June 6

Arnold, B[enedict]. Montreal [Canada]. To [Maj. Gen. Philip John Schuyler, Fort George? New York]. The military situation in Canada. Contemporary copy. 2 pp. In handwriting of George Baylor. Enclosed in Washington to the President of Congress 1776, June 16.   **C. C. 152**, 2, 41

1776
June 6

Sullivan, John. Sorel. To [Brig.] Gen. [William] Thompson [Sorel]. Instructions for his guidance; attack on enemy at Three Rivers. Contemporary copy. 1 p. In handwriting of George Lewis. Enclosed in Washington to the President of Congress, 1776, June 16.   **C. C. 152**, 2, 51

1776
June 6

Sullivan, John. Sorel. Commission to Francis Guillot as captain of a Canadian militia company. Contemporary copy. 1 p. In handwriting of George Lewis. Enclosed in Washington to the President of Congress, 1776, June 16.   **C. C. 152**, 2, 53

1776
June 7

Washington, George. New York. To [the President of Congress, Philadelphia]. Reverses in Canada; building gondolas. L. S. 4 pp. In handwriting of Robert Hanson Harrison. Read in Congress June 10.   **C. C. 152**, 2, 5

1776
June 7

Continental Congress, President. Philadelphia. To [George] Washington [New York]. Situation of army in Canada. L. S. 2 pp. In handwriting of Jacob Rush.   **9**, 303

1776
JUNE 7

Pellenger, Frederick. German Flats [New York]. To Col. Frederick Fisher, Mohawk River [New York]. Advance of British and Indians on the settlement. Contemporary copy. 1 p. In handwriting of Samuel Blatchley Webb. Enclosed in Washington to the President of Congress 1776, Aug. 7.

C. C.   152, 2, 351

1776
JUNE 7

Sullivan, John. Sorel. To [George] Washington, New York. Command in Canada. A. L. S. 1 p. Enclosed in Washington to the President of Congress 1776, June 16.   C. C.   152, 2, 71

1776
JUNE 8

Washington, George. New York. To [the President of Congress, Philadelphia]. Sir John Johnson; payment of troops; expresses. L. S. 4 pp. In handwriting of Robert Hanson Harrison. Read in Congress June 10. Referred to Sherman, Wythe, Sergent, F. Lee and Gwinnett.   C. C.   152, 2, 9
Printed: Writings of Washington (Ford) N. Y. 1889. 4, 115.

1776
JUNE 8

Washington, George. New York. To [Committee of Congress, Philadelphia]. Transmitting plans and reports on fortifying Cape Ann and New London. Letter-book copy. In handwriting of Alexander Contee Hanson.   M. II, 124
Committee on fortifying ports: Harrison, J. Adams and Whipple.

1776
JUNE 8

Albany, Committee. To. [Maj. Gen. Philip John Schuyler, Albany]. Asking assistance for expected Indian attack on Western frontier. Contemporary copy. 1 p. In handwriting of Samuel Blatchley Webb. Enclosed in Washington to the President of Congress 1776, Aug. 7.

C. C.   152, 2, 353

1776
JUNE 8–12

Sullivan, John. Sorel [Canada]. To [George Washington, New York]. Defeat at Three Rivers; weakness of army; the situation; Indians. Transcript. Enclosed in Washington to the President of Congress, 1776, June 23.   C. C.   169, 1, 371

1776
JUNE 9

Washington, George. New York. To [the President of Congress, Philadelphia]. Canadian affairs; payment of troops; supplies; [Maj.] Gen. [Philip John] Schuyler. L. S. 4 pp. In handwriting of Robert Hanson Harrison. Read in Congress June 11.   C. C.   152, 2, 17
Printed: Writings of Washington (Ford) N. Y. 1889. 4, 119.

1776
JUNE 9

Trumbull, Joseph. New York. To the President of Congress [Philadelphia] Pay for his services. Transcript.   C. C.   169, 1, 358

1776
JUNE 9

Ward, Artemas. Boston. To [George] Washington [New York]. Capture of British transport with troops. Extract of a letter. 1 p. In handwriting of George Lewis. Enclosed in Washington to the President of Congress, 1776, June 16.

C. C. **152,** 2, 45

1776
JUNE 10

Washington, George. New York. To [the President of Congress, Philadelphia]. Trouble in the Commissary Department; tories. A. L. S. 4 pp. Read in Congress June 11. C. C. **152,** 2, 25

Printed: Writings of Washington (Ford) N. Y. 1889. 4, 129.

1776
JUNE 10

Arnold, B[enedict]. Montreal [Canada]. To Maj. Gen. [Philip John] Schuyler [Albany]. Conferences with Indians; tories. Transcript. Enclosed in Washington to the President of Congress, 1776, June 16. C. C. **169,** 1, 363

1776
JUNE 10

Schuyler, Ph[ilip John]. Albany. To [George] Washington [New York]. Situation in the north. Contemporary copy. 2 pp. In handwriting of Samuel Blatchley Webb. Enclosed in Washington to the President of Congress, 1776, Aug. 7.

C. C. **152,** 2, 349

1776
JUNE 11

Continental Congress, President. Philadelphia. To [George] Washington [New York]. Proceedings in Congress; Indians; pay of troops; Mrs Washington. L. S. 2 pp. In handwriting of Jacob Rush. Answered June 13*. **9,** 317

1776
JUNE 11

Continental Congress, President. Philadelphia. To [George] Washington [New York]. March of militia; Canadian situation. L. S. of John Hancock. 2 pp. In handwriting of Jacob Rush. Answered June 14*. **9,** 319

1776
JUNE 11

Continental Congress, President. Philadelphia. Circular letter to the Colonies. Militia for defense of New York. Contemporary copy. 2 pp. In handwriting of Jacob Rush. Enclosed in President of Congress to Washington, 1776, June 11. **9,** 321

1776
JUNE 12

Continental Congress, Resolve. Establishing a Board of War. D. S. of Charles Thomson. 2 pp. In handwriting of Timothy Matlack. Enclosed in Board of War to Washington, 1776, June 21.

89, 161

1776
JUNE 12

Schuyler, Philip [John]. Albany [New York]. To [George] Washington [New York]. Canadian affairs.

Contemporary copy. 1 p. In handwriting of George Lewis. Enclosed in Washington to the President of Congress, 1776, June 16.

C. C. 152, 2, 59

1776
JUNE 12

Schuyler, Philip [John]. Albany. To [George] Washington [New York]. Reverses in Canada; batteaus and gondolas. Contemporary copy. 2 pp. In handwriting of George Lewis. Enclosed in Washington to Congress, 1776, June 16.

C. C. 152, 2, 61

1776
JUNE 12–13

Continental Congress, Resolves. The rifle regiment; establishment of Board of War and Ordnance, its duties etc.; members chosen for above board; complaints against [Esek] Hopkins, [Dudley] Saltonstall and [Abraham] Whipple. A. D. S. of Charles Thomson, countersigned by John Hancock. Enclosed in President of Congress to Washington, 1776, June 4. 89, 164

1776
JUNE 13

Washington, George. New York. To [the President of Congress, Philadelphia]. Intelligence from Canada; exportation of salt provisions. L. S. 3 pp. In handwriting of Alexander Contee Hanson.

C. C. 152, 2, 29

Printed: Writings of Washington (Ford) N. Y. 1889. 4, 139.

1776
JUNE 13

Washington, George. New York. To Samuel Chase [Philadelphia]. Character of Col. [Benjamin?] Nicholson; Court of Inquiry. Letter-book copy.

M. II, 148

1776
JUNE 13

Arnold, B[enedict]. St. Johns [Canada]. To Maj. Gen. Schuyler [Albany, New York]. Loss of goods; sick, etc.; general situation of affairs.

JUNE 13

Same to same. Chamblee. Measures for retreat from Canada. Contemporary copies. 4 pp. In handwriting of George Lewis. Enclosed in Washington to the President of Congress, 1776, June 23.

C. C. 152, 2, 93

1776
JUNE 13

Antill, E[dward]. Chamblee [Canada]. To [Maj.] Gen. [John] Sullivan [Sorrel]. Result of efforts to obtain complete return of American army in Canada. Transcript. Enclosed in Washington to the President of Congress, 1776, June 27.

C. C. 169, 1, 380

1776
JUNE 13

Arnold, B[enedict]. Chamblee [Canada]. To [Brig. Gen. John Sullivan, Sorel]. Retreat from Canada;

fortifying St. Johns; plundering of goods. Contemporary copy. 2 pp. In handwriting of Caleb Gibbs. Enclosed in Washington to the President of Congress, 1776, June 27.

C. C.   152, 2, 119

1776
JUNE 13

Hazen, M[oses]. Chamblee [Canada]. To [Maj.] Gen. [John] Sullivan [Sorel]. Charges against him; retreat from Canada; the situation. Transcript. Enclosed in Washington to the President of Congress, 1776, June 27.   C. C.   169, 1, 381

1776
JUNE 13

Lee, Richard Henry. Philadelphia. To [George] Washington [New York]. [John Murray,] Lord Dunmore's perusal of letters passing through the Virginia post-office; [Maj. Gen. Horatio] Gates to command in Canada. A. L. S. 2 pp.   10, 13

1776
JUNE 14

Washington, George. New York. To [the President of Congress, Philadelphia]. Clothing for troops in Canada; [Maj.] Gen. [Philip John] Schuyler. L. S. 3 pp. In handwriting of Robert Hanson Harrison. Read in Congress, June 15. Referred to Committee on War and Ordnance.

C. C.   152, 2, 33

Printed: Writings of Washington (Ford) N. Y. 1889. 4, 142.

1776
JUNE 14

Continental Congress, Resolves. Intercourse with enemy; exportation of salt meat; conference with Six Nations; post at Fort Stanwix. A. D. S. of Chas. Thomson, countersigned by John Hancock. Enclosed in President of Congress to Washington, 1776, June 14.   89, 164

1776
JUNE 14

Continental Congress, President. Philadelphia. To [George] Washington [New York]. Establishment of a Board of War; complaints against [Esek] Hopkins and others; salt-meat, money and other matters. L. S. of John Hancock. 3 pp. In handwriting of Timothy Matlack. Answered June 20.*   10, 15

1776
JUNE 16

Washington, George. New York. To [the President of Congress, Philadelphia]. [Maj.] Gen. [John] Sullivan's account of affairs in Canada. L. S. 3 pp. In handwriting of Robert Hanson Harrison. Read in Congress June 18.   C. C.   152, 2, 37

Printed in part: Writings of Washington (Ford) N. Y. 1889. 4, 150, note.

1776
JUNE 16

Palfrey, [William]. [New York.] To [George] Washington [New York]. Military chest exhausted. In

3d person. Transcript. Enclosed in Washington to the President of Congress, 1776, June 16.

                         C. C.   169, 1, 404

1776
JUNE 16

[Ward, Artemas.] Boston. To [George Washington, New York.] Forcing enemy's fleet from Nantasket Road; capture of British transports. [Extract of letter.] 2 pp. In handwriting of George Lewis. Enclosed in Washington to the President of Congress, 1776, June 23.   C. C.   152, 2, 99

1776
JUNE 17

Washington, George. New York. To the President of Congress [Philadelphia]. [Brig.] Gen. [David] Wooster. L. S. 1 p. In handwriting of Robert Hanson Harrison.   C. C.   152, 2, 63

1776
JUNE 17

Washington, George. New York. To [the President of Congress, New York]. Brig. Gen. [John] Sullivan's abilities; command in Canada. A. L. S. 3 pp. Read in Congress June 18.   C. C.   152, 2, 67

Printed: Writings of Washington (Ford) N. Y. 1889.   4, 156.

1776
JUNE 17

Continental Congress, Resolves. Commander for Canada and his powers; regulations for army in that province; roads, supplies; militia and Indians; prizes of armed vessels. A. D. S. of Charles Thomson, countersigned by John Hancock. 7 pp. Enclosed in President of Congress to Washington, 1776, June 18.   89, 171

1776
JUNE 17

Continental Congress, Resolve. Connecticut and New York troops for Canada; raising troops in Connecticut. A. D. S. of Charles Thomson, countersigned by John Hancock. 1 p. Enclosed in President of Congress to Washington, 1776, June 18.   89, 175

1776
JUNE 18

Continental Congress, President. Philadelphia. To [George] Washington [New York]. Affairs in Canada; [Maj.] Gen. [Horatio] Gates; Indians; militia. L. S. of John Hancock. 2 pp. In handwriting of Jacob Rush. Answered June 20*.

                                   10, 45

1776
[JUNE 18]

Continental Congress, Resolves. Mustermaster-general; settlement of accounts. A. D. S. of John Hancock. Enclosed in President of Congress to Washington, 1776, June 21.   89, 178

1776
JUNE 19

Continental Congress, President. Philadelphia. To [George] Washington [New York]. Minor military matters. L. S. of John Hancock. 2 pp. In handwriting of Jacob Rush. Answered June 21*.   10, 47

1776
JUNE 19

Continental Congress, Resolve. Colonies to furnish cloth-ing to troops. A. D. S. of Charles Thomson, countersigned by John Hancock. 1 p. Enclosed in President of Congress to Washington, 1776, June 21.   **89,** 176

1776
JUNE 19

Continental Congress, Resolves. Commissions granted by Brig. Gen. [John] Sullivan to officers in Canada; money for army. A. D. S. of John Hancock. Enclosed in President of Congress to Washington, 1776, June 21.   **89,** 178

1776
JUNE 20

Washington, George. New York. To [the President of Congress, Philadelphia]. Establishment of a war office; money for Canada; [Maj.] Gen. [Horatio] Gates; works at Kingsbridge. L. S. 4 pp. In handwriting of Robert Hanson Harrison. Read in Congress June 21. Referred to Board of War.   **C. C.** **152,** 2, 75
Printed: Writings of Washington (Ford) N. Y. 1889. 4, 164.

1776
JUNE 21

Washington, George. New York. To [the President of Congress, Philadelphia]. Proceedings of the In-dian commissioners; volunteer troop of horse. L. S. 3 pp. In handwriting of Robert Hanson Harrison. Read in Congress June 24. Referred to the Board of War.   **C.C.** **152,** 2, 79

1776
JUNE 21

Washington, George. New York. To the President of Congress, Philadelphia. Introducing Chevalier de Kermovan and Monsr. de Vermonet. L. S. 1 p. In handwriting of Alexander Contee Hanson. Read in Congress June 26. Read be-fore the Board of War 27th and referred for further consideration.   **C. C.** **152,** 2, 85

1776
JUNE 21

Continental Congress, President. Philadelphia. To [George] Washington [New York]. Inquiry into Canadian expedition; court martial of officers; clothes for army; minor matters. L. S. of John Hancock. 3 pp. In handwriting of Jacob Rush. Answered June 27*.   **10,** 80

1776
JUNE 21

Continental Congress, Resolves. New York regiment for Canada; inquiry into Canadian affairs; minor matters. A. D. S. of Charles Thomson, counter-signed by John Hancock. 2 pp. Enclosed in President of Congress to Washington, 1776, June 21.   **89,** 179

1776
JUNE 21

Board of War. Philadelphia. To [George] Washington, New York. Regular returns from army. L. S. John Adams, Roger Sherman, Benj. Harrison, James Wilson, Edward Rutledge. 1 p. In handwriting of Richard Peters.   89, 163

1776
JUNE 21

Goddard, William. New York. To Congress. Memorial of his services to the country; prays for commission in the army. Contemporary copy. 3 pp. Transmitted to Washington.   95, 95

1776
JUNE 21

[Hawley, Joseph]. Watertown. To [George] Washington [New York]. Slowness of Massachusetts in furnishing troops. Contemporary copy. 3 pp. In handwriting of Robert Hanson Harrison. Enclosed in Washington to the President of Congress 1776, June 30.   C. C. 152, 2, 145

Printed in part: Writings of Washington (Ford) N. Y. 1889. 4, 175, note.

1776
JUNE 21

Leary, John, jr. [New York.] To [George Washington, New York]. Conditions of service for a volunteer troop of horse. A. D. S. 1 p. Enclosed in Washington to the President of Congress, 1776, June 21.   C. C. 152, 2, 83

1776
JUNE 23

Washington, George. New York. To [the President of Congress, Philadelphia]. Sailing of British from Nantasket Road; misfortunes in Canada. L. S. 3 pp. In handwriting of Robert Hanson Harrison. Read in Congress June 25.   C. C. 152, 2, 89

Printed: Writings of Washington (Ford) N. Y. 1889. 4, 169.

1776
JUNE 23

Ward, Artemas. Boston. To [George Washington, New York]. Report of arrival of British fleet off Boston harbor. Extract of letter. 1 p. In handwriting of Caleb Gibbs. Enclosed in Washington to the President of Congress, 1776, June 30.   C. C. 152, 2, 143

1776
JUNE 24

Continental Congress, Resolves. Enlistment of Mohican and Stockbridge Indians; accounts of rifle companies; tents for Massachusetts; allegiance to the United Colonies and treason thereto; counterfeiting; ration. A. D. S. of Charles Thomson, countersigned by John Hancock. 3 pp. Enclosed in President of Congress to Washington, 1776, June 25.   89, 180

1776
JUNE 24

New York, Provincial Congress. Resolve authorizing [George] Washington to secure disaffected per-

Sir

I receiv'd yours of the 9th Instant, and could wish that it was in my power, consistent with the Duty I owe my Country to grant you the Relief you desire.— I have made repeated applications to General Howe to settle an Exchange of Prisoners, but he has not thought proper to return me any Answer.— It has been in his power to set you at liberty, and if you are still continued a Prisoner the blame must lay entirely upon him.—

The situation of your family is indeed distressing, but such is the fortune of War, that it is far from being singular— The brave Coll. Allen an Officer of Rank, has been torn from his dearest Connections, sent to England in Irons and is now confin'd to the most servile drudgery on board one of the King's Ships— Your treatment Sir, & that of the other Officers, taken in Arms against the Liberties of America, has been very different— for the truth of this I appeal to your own feelings—

Whenever it is in my power to release you by a mutual Exchange I shall do it with the greatest pleasure and am

Sir
Your most Obed. Serv.

New Haven 14 April 1776

Capt. Samuel Mackay

WRITING OF JOHN TRUMBULL.

sons. Contemporary copy. 1 p. In handwriting of Samuel Blatchley Webb. Enclosed in Washington to the President of Congress, 1776, June 28.
C. C.   **152**, 2, 133

1776
JUNE 24

Sullivan, John. Isle aux Noix [Richelieu River, Quebec]. To Maj. Gen. [Philip John] Schuyler [Albany]. Trouble with the army; sickness; military situation. Contemporary copy. 2 pp. In handwriting of George Lewis. Enclosed in Washington to the President of Congress, 1776, July 4.
C. C.   **152**, 2, 179

1776
JUNE 25

Continental Congress, President. Philadelphia. To [George] Washington [New York]. Enlistment of Indians; tents for Massachusetts; law and order in the colonies. L. S. of John Hancock. 2 pp. In handwriting of Jacob Rush. Answered June 27* and 28*.   **89**, 185

1776
JUNE 25

Continental Congress, Resolves. Reenforcement of Northern Army; Col. [Lewis] Dubois's commission; clothing; battalion accounts; bounties. A. D. S. of Charles Thomson, countersigned by John Hancock. 2 pp. Enclosed in President of Congress to Washington, 1776, June 26.   **89**, 182

1776
JUNE 25

Continental Congress, Resolve. Colonel's commission to [Lewis] Dubois. Contemporary copy. In handwriting of Jacob Rush. Enclosed in President of Congress to Washington, 1776, July 6.   **89**, 208

1776
JUNE 25

Arnold, B[enedict]. Albany. To [George] Washington [New York]. Retreat from Canada. Contemporary copy. 3 pp. In handwriting of George Lewis. Enclosed in Washington to the President of Congress, 1776, June 27. Read in Congress July 1.   C. C.   **152**, 2, 107

1776
JUNE 25

Schuyler, Philip [John]. Albany. To [George] Washington [New York]. The retreat from Canada. Contemporary copy. 2 pp. In handwriting of Samuel Blatchley Webb. Enclosed in Washington to the President of Congress, 1776, June 27.
C. C.   **152**, 2, 111

1776
JUNE 26

Continental Congress, President. Philadelphia. To [George] Washington [New York]. Reenforcements for the Northern Army. L. S. of John Hancock. 2 pp. In handwriting of Jacob Rush. Answered June 29*.   **10**, 91

1776
JUNE 26

Continental Congress, Resolves. Specifying officers for Col. Lewis Dubois regiment. A. D. S. of John Hancock. 2 pp. Enclosed in President of Congress to Washington, 1776, June 26. **89, 184**

1776
JUNE 26

Continental Army, Surgeons Mates of Spencer's brigade. New York. Memorial to Brig. Gen. [Joseph] Spencer [New York]. Increase of pay. A. D. S. of John R. Watrous, signed also by Gershom Beardsley, Silas Holmes, Zeckariah Keys and William Prentice. 1 p. Enclosed in Washington to the President of Congress. 1776, July 11. **C. C. 152, 2, 211**

1776
[JUNE 26?]

Continental Army, Surgeon's Mates of Stirling's brigade [New York]. Memorial to Brig. Gen. [William Alexander,] Lord Stirling [New York]. Increase of pay. A. D. S. of Daniel Menema, signed also by Isaac Ledyard, Asa Kingsberry and Preserve Wood. 1 p. Enclosed in Washington to the President of Congress, 1776, July 11. **C. C. 152, 2, 209**

1776
JUNE 27

Washington, George. New York. To [the President of Congress, Philadelphia]. Intelligence from Canada; Indians. L. S. 3 pp. In handwriting of Robert Hanson Harrison. Read in Congress July 1. **C. C. 152, 2, 103**
Printed: Writings of Washington (Ford) N. Y. 1889. 4, 181.

1776
JUNE 27

Washington, George. New York. To [the President of Congress, Philadelphia]. Maj. [Robert] Rogers. L. S. 1 p. In handwriting of Lewis Nicola. Read in Congress July 1. **C. C. 152, 2, 115**
Printed: Writings of Washington (Ford) N. Y. 1889. 4, 183, note.

1776
JUNE 27

Continental Congress, Resolves. Raising and officering of a rifle regiment. A. D. S. of. Charles Thomson, countersigned by John Hancock. 1 p. Enclosed in President of Congress to Washington, 1776, June 29. **89, 187**

1776
JUNE 27

Continental Congress, Resolves. Raising of a German regiment. A. D. S. of Charles Thomson, countersigned by John Hancock. 1 p. Enclosed in President of Congress to Washington, 1776, June 29. **89, 189**

1776
JUNE 27

Continental Congress, Resolve. Raising of German battalion. Contemporary copy. 1 p. In handwriting of Robert Hanson Harrison. Enclosed in President of Congress to Washington, 1776, June 29. **89, 191**

1776
JUNE 27

Davison, Joseph. Armed sloop *Schuyler*, off Fire Island. To [George] Washington [New York]. Prizes taken. Contemporary copy. 1 p. In handwriting of George Lewis. Enclosed in Washington to the President of Congress, 1776, June 28. **C. C. 152, 2, 131**

1776
JUNE 28

Washington, George. New York. To [the President of Congress, Philadelphia]. The Commissary General; chaplains; tories in New York city and on Long Island; Thomas Hickey; approach of Lord Howe. L. S. 7 pp. In handwriting of Robert Hanson Harrison. Read in Congress July 1. **C. C. 152, 2, 123**
Printed: Writings of Washington (Ford) N. Y. 1889. 4, 184.

1776
JUNE 28

Greene, Thomas. Providence [Rhode Island]. To Robert Morris, [Philadelphia]. Arrival of supplies from Europe. Contemporary copy. 1 p. In handwriting of Robert Morris. Enclosed in President of Congress to Washington, 1776, July 6. **89, 212**

1776
JUNE 29

Washington, George. New York. To [the President of Congress, Philadelphia]. Smallness of the army; arrival of the British at Sandy Hook. L. S. 3 pp. In handwriting of Robert Hanson Harrison. Read in Congress July 1. **C. C. 152, 2, 135**
Printed: Writings of Washington (Ford) N. Y. 1889. 4, 194.

1776
JUNE 29

Washington, George. New York. To the Board of War [Philadelphia]. Correspondence with the Board. Letter-book copy. In handwriting of Samuel Blatchley Webb. **M. II, 198**

1776
JUNE 29

Continental Congress, President. Philadelphia. To [George] Washington [New York]. The German battalion; loss of Canada; officering Rifle regiment. L. S. of John Hancock. 3 pp. In handwriting of Jacob Rush. Answered June 30.* **89, 192**

1776
JUNE 30

Washington, George. New York. To [the President of Congress Philadelphia]. Raising of troops; the retreat from Canada and other military matters. L. S. 4 pp. In handwriting of Robert Hanson Harrison. Read in Congress July 2. **C. C. 152, 2, 139**
Printed: Writings of Washington (Ford) N. Y. 1889. 4, 196.

1776
JUNE 30

[Schuyler, Philip John.] Albany. Substance of conversation with [Maj.] Gen. [Horatio] Gates respecting

command of the northern army. Contemporary
copy. 3 pp. In handwriting of Samuel Blatchley
Webb. Enclosed in Washington to the President
of Congress, 1776, July 4.   C. C.   152, 2, 181

1776
JULY 1
Continental Congress, President. Philadelphia. To
[George] Washington [New York]. Case of Maj.
[Robert] Rogers. A. L. S. of John Hancock.
1 p. Answered July 4.*   89, 194

1776
JULY 1
Continental Congress, President. Philadelphia. To
[George] Washington [New York]. Introducing
Antoine Felix Wybert. L. S. of John Hancock.
1 p. In handwriting of Jacob Rush. Answered
July 4.*   89, 195

1776
JULY 1
Schuyler, Philip John. Albany. To [George] Washing-
ton [New York]. Dispute over command of
the commissary department; dispute with [Maj.]
Gen. [Horatio] Gates; military situation, Indians.
Contemporary copy. 6 pp. Enclosed in Wash-
ington to the President of Congress, 1776, July 4.
In handwriting of Morgan Lewis.
                                         C. C.   152, 2, 175

1776
JULY 2
Lee, Charles. Charleston [South Carolina]. To the President of Congress [Philadelphia]. British repulse
at Charleston; cavalry for Georgia. Contemporary copy. 4 pp. In handwriting of John Hancock and Aaron D. Woodruff? Enclosed in
President of Congress to Washington, 1776,
July 19.   89, 195

1776
JULY 2
Charleston, (South Carolina). Accounts of various per-
sons of the attack on Fort Moultrie; damage to
British; strength. Contemporary copy, attested
by John Hancock. 4 pp. In handwriting of
Jacob Rush. Enclosed in President of Congress
to Washington, 1776, July 19.   89, 198

1776
JULY 3
Washington, George. New York. To [the President of
Congress, Philadelphia]. Arrival of enemy's
fleet; preparations for defense of New York. L.
S. 3 pp. In handwriting of Robert Hanson
Harrison. Read in Congress July 4.
                                         C. C.   152, 2, 149
Printed: Writings of Washington (Ford) N. Y. 1889. 4, 200.

1776
JULY 3
Continental Congress, Resolves. Troops to be raised in
Pennsylvania and New Jersey for the Flying

Camp. A. D. S. of John Hancock. 1 p. Enclosed in President of Congress to Washington, 1776, July 4.   **89**, 201

1776
JULY 4

Washington, George. New York. To [the President of Congress, Philadelphia]. Introducing Col. [Hugh] Stevenson; raising of the Maryland Rifle Battalion. L. S. 1 p. In handwriting of Robert Hanson Harrison. Read in Congress July 8. Referred to Board of War. Additional page: List of officers recommended to serve in the Rifle Battalion. In handwriting of John Fitzgerald?
                                           C. C.   152, 2, 153

1776
JULY 4

Washington, George. New York. To [the President of Congress, Philadelphia]. Slowness of New England in furnishing troops; militia; engaging Indians; preparations for defense; intelligence from Canada. L. S. 8 pp. In handwriting of Robert Hanson Harrison. Read in Congress July 6.   **C. C.   152**, 2, 159
Printed: Writings of Washington (Ford) N. Y. 1889. 4, 204.

1776
JULY 4

Continental Congress, President. Philadelphia. To [George] Washington [New York]. Troops for the Flying Camp; government in Pennsylvania. L. S. 2 pp. In handwriting of Jacob Rush. Answered July 10.*   **89**, 202

1776
JULY 4

Continental Congress, Resolves. Flints; Maryland and Delaware militia for the Flying Camp; seal for the United States. A. D. S. of John Hancock. Enclosed in President of Congress to Washington, 1776, July 6.   **89**, 205

1776
JULY 4

Continental Congress, Resolves. Conference on march of Pennsylvania militia to defense of New Jersey, and resolutions of same.

JULY 5

March of Pennsylvania troops to Trenton. Broadside. 1 p. Enclosed in President of Congress, to Washington, 1776, July 6.   **89**, 207

1776
JULY 4

Declaration of Independence. Broadside. 1 p. One of the first printed copies, by John Dunlap. Enclosed in President of Congress to Washington, 1776, July 6.   **89**, 204

1776
JULY 4

[Greene, Nathanael.] [Long Island.] To [George Washington, New York]. Intelligence of British. Extract of letter. 2 pp. In handwriting of George Lewis. Enclosed in Washington to the President of Congress, 1776, July 4.   **C. C.   152**, 2, 167

1776
JULY 4

Trumbull, Jonathan. Lebanon [Connecticut]. To [George] Washington [New York]. Smallpox and enlistments; exposure of northern frontier. Contemporary copy. 3 pp. In handwriting of Caleb Gibbs. Enclosed in Washington to the President of Congress, 1776, July 11.   C. C.   152, 2, 205
Printed, in part: Writings of Washington (Ford) N.Y. 1889. 4, 239, note.

1776
JULY 5

Continental Congress, Resolves. Vessels for defense of lakes [Champlain and George]; Delaware troops; force for Ticonderoga; chaplains; expresses; British prisoners. A. D. S. of John Hancock. Enclosed in President of Congress to Washington, 1776, July 6.   89, 205

1776
JULY 5

Continental Congress, Resolves. Regiment to be raised by officers who have served in Canada. Contemporary copy. In handwriting of Jacob Rush. Enclosed in President of Congress to Washington, 1776, July 6.   89, 208

1776
JULY 5

Continental Congress, Resolve. March of troops to Trenton. See: Continental Congress, Resolve 1776, July 4.

1776
JULY 6

Continental Congress, Resolves. Commissary for militia; arms and stores; Maj. [Robert] Rogers. A. D. S. of John Hancock. 1 p. Enclosed in President of Congress to Washington, 1776, July 6.
          89, 206

1776
JULY 6

Continental Congress, President. Philadelphia. To [George] Washington [New York]. Declaration of Independence; flints; militia; vessels for the lakes; arms and stores. L. S. of John Hancock. 3 pp. Answered July 10*.   89, 210

1776
JULY 6

Continental Congress, President. Philadelphia. To George Washington, New York. Carpenters for building vessels on the lakes [Champlain and George]. A. L. S. of John Hancock. 2 pp.   10, 162

1776
JULY 6

Board of War. Philadelphia. To [George] Washington, New York. Provision for sergeant majors drum and fife majors and quartermaster sergeants. A. L. S. of Richard Peters. 1 p. Answered July 9*.   95, 141

1776
JULY 6

Henshaw, William. Long Island. To [George] Washington, New York. Claim to higher rank. A. L. S. 2 pp. Enclosed in Washington to the President of Congress, 1776, Aug. 14.
          C. C.   152, 2, 405

1776
JULY 6

Rush, Jacob. Philadelphia. To George Washington, New York. Delay in preparing despatches. A. L. S. 1 p. **10, 164**

1776
JULY 7

Continental Army. Council of War. Crown Point [New York]. Retreat to and fortifying at Ticonderoga. Contemporary copy. 2 pp. In handwriting of Robert Hanson Harrison. Enclosed in Washington to the President of Congress, 1776, July 17. **C. C. 152, 2, 241**

1776
JULY 8

Washington, George. New York. To the President of Congress, Philadelphia. Recommending Lt. John David Woelpper for commission in the proposed German regiment. L. S. 1 p. In handwriting of Robert Hanson Harrison.
C. C. 152, 2, 185

1776
JULY 8

Continental Congress, Resolves. Command of the Northern Army; withdrawal of Continental troops from Massachusetts; Indians; Commissary General's power; quartermaster for Flying camp; rendezvous of recruits. A. D. S. of John Hancock. 3 pp. Enclosed in President of Congress to Washington, July 8. **89, 213**

1776
JULY 8

Continental Congress, President. Philadelphia. To [George] Washington [New York]. Dispute over command in Canada; rendezvous of troops. L. S. of John Hancock. 2 pp. In handwriting of Jacob Rush. Answered July 11*. **10, 174**

1776
JULY 9

Washington, George. New York. To the Board of War [Philadelphia]. Sergeant majors, quartermaster-sergeants and drum and fife majors. Letter-book copy. In handwriting of Robert Hanson Harrison. **M. II, 232**

1776
JULY 9

Continental Congress, Resolves. Raising and officering the Virginia rifle company; minor appointments. A. D. S. of John Hancock. Enclosed in the President of Congress to Washington, 1776, July 11. **89, 215**

1776
JULY 9

Knox, Henry. New York. To [George] Washington [New York]. Establishment of the artillery. Contemporary copy. 1 p. In handwriting of Morgan Lewis. Enclosed in Washington to the President of Congress, 1776, July 22.
C. C. 152, 2, 269

1776
JULY 10

Washington, George. New York. To [the President of Congress, Philadelphia]. Proclaiming the Declaration of Independence; militia and measures for defense of New York; bounties. L. S., 6 pp. In handwriting of Robert Hanson Harrison. Read in Congress July 11.   C. C.   **152, 2, 189**
Printed: Writings of Washington (Ford) N. Y. 1889. 4, 224.

1776
JULY 10

Continental Congress, Resolves. Flying camp; militia; medicines; powder. A. D. S. of John Hancock. Enclosed in the President of Congress to Washington, 1776, July 11.   **89, 215**

1776
JULY 10

Continental Congress, Committee report on capitulation at the Cedars; treatment of prisoners; resolutions of Congress thereon authorizing retaliation. D. S. of John Hancock. 8 pp. In handwriting of Jacob Rush. Enclosed in President of Congress to Washington, 1776, July 13.   **89, 217**
Committee: Jefferson, Braxton, Paine and Middleton.

1776
JULY 11

Washington, George. New York. To [the President of Congress, Philadelphia]. Indians; Connecticut horse; auditor for the army. Unsigned letter. 6 pp. In handwriting of Robert Hanson Harrison. Read in Congress July 14.
       C. C.   **152, 2, 197**
Printed: Writings of Washington (Ford) N. Y. 1889. 4, 237.

1776
JULY 11

Continental Congress, Resolve. Fortifying the lakes. A. D. S. of Charles Thomson, countersigned by John Hancock. 1 p. Enclosed in President of Congress to Washington, 1776, July 13.   **89, 222**

1776
JULY 11

Continental Congress, President. Philadelphia. To [George] Washington [New York]. Minor matters; establishment of double post; march of militia. L. S. of John Hancock. 2 pp. In handwriting of Jacob Rush. Answered July 14*.   **10, 184**

1776
JULY 12

Washington, George. New York. To [the President of Congress, Philadelphia]. Movement of enemy's ships; powder. L. S. 2 pp. In handwriting of Robert Hanson Harrison. Read in Congress July 14.   C. C.   **152, 2, 213**
Printed: Writings of Washington (Ford) N. Y. 1889. 4, 242.

1776
JULY 12

Schuyler, Ph[ilip John]. Albany. To [George Washington, New York]. Fortifying at Ticonderoga; supplies and intrenching tools; military miscellany. Contemporary copy. 4 pp. In handwriting of Morgan Lewis. Enclosed in Washington to the President of Congress, 1776, July 17. C. C. 152, 2, 237

1776
July 14

Washington, George. New York. To [the President of Congress, Philadelphia]. Enemy's ships in North River; refusal to receive Lord Howe's letter. L. S. 6 pp. In handwriting of Robert Hanson Harrison. Read in Congress July 16. Referred to the Board of War. C. C. 152, 2, 217
Printed: Writings of Washington (Ford) N. Y. 1889. 4, 247.

1776
July 14

Continental Congress, Resolves. Money for the Flying Camp; camp equipage; cartridges, powder, and lead; march of militia to Jersey; removal of British prisoners. D. S. of John Hancock. 3 pp. Enclosed in President of Congress to Washington, 1776, July 15. 89, 223

1776
July 15

Washington, George. New York. To [the President of Congress, Philadelphia]. Resolves of Congress to be sent to Generals Howe and Burgoyne; British treatment of prisoners. L. S. 2 pp. In handwriting of Robert Hanson Harrison.
C. C. 152, 2, 225
Printed: Writings of Washington (Ford) N. Y. 1889. 4, 258.

1776
July 15

Continental Congress, President. Philadelphia. To [George] Washington [New York]. Flying Camp; march of militia to Jersey. L. S. of John Hancock. 2 pp. In handwriting of Jacob Rush. Answered July 17.* 10, 231

1776
July 15

Continental Congress, Resolves. Flying camp; garrisoning of northern posts. A. D. S. of Charles Thomson. Enclosed in President of Congress to Washington, 1776, July 16. 89, 225

1776
July 15

Ward, Artemas. Boston. To [George] Washington [New York]. Forwarding troops; smallpox in Boston. Contemporary copy. 1 p. In handwriting of Samuel Blatchley Webb. Enclosed in Washington to the President of Congress, 1776, July 19.
C. C. 152, 2, 259

1776
July 16

Continental Congress, President. Philadelphia. To George Washington, New York. Transmitting resolves. A. L. S. of John Hancock. 89, 225

1776
July 16

Continental Congress, Resolves. Powder; noncommissioned officers; paymaster and auditing of accounts; bounties; military appointments; militia; Connecticut light horse. A. D. S. of Charles Thomson, countersigned by John Hancock. 4 pp. Enclosed in President of Congress to Washington, 1776, July 17.   **89, 229**

1776
JULY 16

Continental Congress, Resolves. Regimental paymasters; smallpox and the northern army; auditing of accounts. D. S. of John Hancock. 4 pp. Enclosed in President of Congress to Washington, 1776, July 24.   **89, 229**

1776
JULY 16

New York, Convention. White Plains. To George Washington [New York]. Requesting loan; powder and subsistence for levies. Contemporary copy. 2 pp. In handwriting of George Lewis. Enclosed in Washington to the President of Congress, 1776, July 19.   **C. C.   152, 2, 249**

1776
JULY 16

New York, Convention. White Plains. Resolve fixing death penalty for treason. Contemporary copy. 1 p. In handwriting of Morgan Lewis. Enclosed in Washington to the President of Congress, 1776, July 19.   **C. C.   152, 2, 253**

1776
JULY 16

New York, Convention. White Plains. Resolves calling out the militia. Contemporary copy. 3 pp. In handwriting of Caleb Gibbs. Enclosed in Washington to the President of Congress, 1776, July 19.
C. C.   152, 2, 255

1776
JULY 17

Washington, George. New York. To the President of Congress, Philadelphia. Regimentals for Col. [Edward] Hand's regiment. L. S. 1 p. In handwriting of Robert Hanson Harrison.
C. C.   152, 2, 229

1776
JULY 17

Washington, George. New York. To [the President of Congress, Philadelphia]. Militia; scarcity of food in northern army; British at Haverstraw. Bay. L. S. 3 pp. In handwriting of Robert Hanson Harrison. Read in Congress July 18. Referred to the Board of War. **C. C.   152, 2, 233**
Printed: Writings of Washington (Ford) N. Y. 1889. 4, 260.

1776
JULY 17

Continental Congress, President. Philadelphia. To [George] Washington [New York]. Powder; appointments; Maryland troops for Flying Camp; militia. L. S. of John Hancock. 2 pp. In handwriting of Jacob Rush. Answered July 19.*
89, 231

1776
[JULY] 17

Continental Congress, Resolves. Washington's refusal of Lord Howe's letter; officers, management, sup-

plies etc., of the hospital; German battalion, independent company, flying camp; removal of live stock from The Jersey coast. D. S. of John Hancock. 2 pp. In handwriting of Timothy Matlack. Enclosed in President of Congress to Washington, 1776, July 18. **89, 169**
Dated in error, June 17.

1776
JULY 17

Continental Congress, Resolve. [Richard,] Lord Howe's letter to Washington. D. S. of John Hancock. Enclosed in President of Congress to Washington, 1776, July 24. **89, 229**

1776
JULY 17

Trumbull, Jonathan. Lebanon. To [George Washington, New York]. Troops and cannon; supplies obtained by the enemy. July 19: Orders to row galleys. Contemporary copy. 3 pp. In handwriting of Samuel Blatchley Webb. Enclosed in Washington to the President of Congress, 1776, July 23. **C. C. 152, 2, 293**

1776
JULY 18

Continental Congress, President. Philadelphia. To [George] Washington [New York]. Transmitting resolves. L. S. of John Hancock. 1 p. In handwriting of Charles Thomson. Answered July 22*. **89, 233**

1776
JULY 19

Washington, George. New York. To [the President of Congress, Philadelphia]. The retreat from Crown Point; sundry matters. L. S. 5 pp. In handwriting of Robert Hanson Harrison. Read in Congress July 20. Referred to the Board of War. **C. C. 152, 2, 243**
Printed: Writings of Washington (Ford), N. Y. 1889. 4. 275.

1776
JULY 19

Continental Congress, President. Philadelphia. To [George] Washington [New York]. News from South Carolina [of attack on Fort Moultrie]. L. S. of John Hancock. 2 pp. In handwriting of Jacob Rush. Answered July 22.* **89, 236**

1776
JULY 19

Continental Congress, Resolves. Prices of goods sold to soldiers; harmony in Northern Army. D. S. of John Hancock. Enclosed in President of Congress to Washington, 1776, July 24. **89, 229**

1776
JULY 19

Continental Congress, Resolves. Engrossing the Declaration of Independence; affairs of the Northern Army; march of militia; publication of British terms of peace; auditing accounts; cannon. A. D. S. of Charles Thomson, countersigned by

John Hancock. 3 pp. Enclosed in President of
Congress to Washington, 1776, July 19. **89, 234**
The engrossing was done by Timothy Matlack.

1776
JULY 19

Goddard, William. Philadelphia. To the Board of War
[Philadelphia]. Appointment in the army.
A. L. S. 2 pp. Transmitted to Washington.

95, 145

[1776]
[JULY 19?]

Rutledge, Edward. [Philadelphia]. To [the President of
Congress, Philadelphia]. Extract of Hugh Rutledge's account of attack on Fort Moultrie.
A. L. S. 1 p. Enclosed in President of Con-
ress to Washington, 1776, July 19. **89, 200**

1776
JULY 20

Continental Congress, President. [Philadelphia.] To
[George] Washington [New York]. Transmit-
ting resolves. A. L. S. of John Hancock. 1 p.
Answered July 23.* **89, 238**

1776
JULY 20

Board of War. [Philadelphia.] To George Washington,
New York. William Goddard's appointment;
promotions. A. L. S. of Richard Peters. 1 p.
Answered July 29.* **95, 177**

1776
JULY 20

Glover, Jonathan. Marblehead [Massachusetts]. To
[George] Washington [New York]. Dispute with
John Bradford over authority. Contemporary
copy. 3 pp. In handwriting of Morgan Lewis.
Enclosed in Washington to the President of
Congress, 1776, Aug. 7. **C. C. 152, 2, 355**

1776
JULY 20

Mercer, Hugh. Elizabethtown [New Jersey]. To the
President of Congress, [Philadelphia]. Projected
expedition against Staten Island; need of boats;
officers for the Flying Camp. Contemporary
copy. 3 pp. In handwriting of Jacob Rush.
Enclosed in President of Congress to Washington, 1776, July 24. **89, 240**

1776
JULY 20

New York, Convention. [White Plains]. To [George]
Washington [New York]. Stock on Nassau
Island. Contemporary copy. 2 pp. In handwriting of Robert Hanson Harrison. Enclosed
in Washington to Congress, 1776, July 23.

C. C. 152, 2, 279

1776
JULY 20

New York, Convention. [White Plains]. Resolutions
respecting removal of stock from Nassau Island.
Contemporary copy. 4 pp. In handwriting of
George Lewis. Enclosed in Washington to the
President of Congress, 1776, July 23.

C. C. 152, 2, 283

1776
JULY 20

[Reed, Joseph] [New York.] Memorandum of interview of Col. [James] Patterson with Gen. George Washington. The address of [Sir William] Howe's letter; its contents; treatment of prisoners; question of pardons and exchanges. A. D. 5 pp. Enclosed in Washington to the President of Congress, 1776, July 22.   **96**, 10
Printed: Writings of Washington (Ford) N. Y. 1889, 4, 282, note.

1776
JULY 21

Washington, George. New York. To the President of Congress, Philadelphia. Acknowledging receipt of letters. L. S. 1 p. In handwriting of Robert Hanson Harrison. Read in Congress July 23. Referred to the Board of War.
                                  C. C. 152, 2, 261

1776
JULY 21

Gates, Horatio. Ticonderoga [New York]. To George Washington, New York. Court-martial of Col. [Donald] Campbell. A. L. S. 1 p. Enclosed in Washington to the President of Congress, 1776, Aug. 12.   **C. C. 152**, 2, 387

1776
JULY 22

Washington, George. New York. To [the President of Congress, Philadelphia]. Powers of the Peace Commissioners; interview with Lt. Col. [James] Patterson; artillery, tories. L. S. 3 pp. In handwriting of Robert Hanson Harrison. Read in Congress July 23.   **C. C. 152**, 2, 265
Printed: Writings of Washington (Ford), N. Y. 1889. 4, 282.

1776
JULY 22

Washington, George. New York. To the President of Congress, Philadelphia. Introducing [Capt. John David] Woelpper. L. S. 1 p. In handwriting of Robert Hanson Harrison. Read in Congress July 29. Referred to the Board of War.
                                  C. C. 152, 2, 271

1776
JULY 22

French, Christopher. Hartford [Connecticut]. To Gen. [George] Washington [New York]. Letters and his parole. A. L. S. 2 pp. Enclosed in Washington to the President of Congress, 1776, July 27.   **C. C. 152**, 2, 305

1776
JULY 22

New York, Convention. White Plains. Resolves respecting bounty for militia enlistments. Contemporary copy. 1 p. In handwriting of George Lewis. Enclosed in Washington to the President of Congress, 1776, July 23. **C. C. 152**, 2, 287

1776
JULY 22

Continental Congress. Resolve. Exchange of prisoners. D. S. of John Hancock. Enclosed in President of Congress to Washington, 1776, July 24.
                                        89, 229

1776   **Continental Congress**, Resolves. Mode of exchange of
JULY 22   prisoners. D. S. of John Hancock. 1 p. En-
                       closed in President of Congress to Washington,
                       1776, July 24.   **89, 242**

1776   **Washington**, George. New York. To [the President of
JULY 23   Congress, Philadelphia]. Resolves of the New
                       York Convention and minor military matters.
                       L. S. 1 p. In handwriting of Robert Hanson
                       Harrison. Read in Congress July 24. Referred
                       to the Board of War.   **C. C. 152, 2, 275**

1776   **Washington**, George. New York. To [the President of
JULY 23   Congress, Philadelphia]. Removal of stock;
                       enemies ships in North River; furnishing sup-
                       plies to enemy. L. S. 3 pp. In handwriting
                       of Robert Hanson Harrison. Read in Congress
                       July 25.   **C. C. 152, 2, 289**
                       Printed, in part: Writings of Washington (Ford) N. Y. 1889. 4,
                       294, note.

1776   **Continental Congress**, Resolves. Derangement of officers;
JULY 23   disposition of troops. D. S. of John Hancock.
                       Enclosed in President of Congress to Washington,
                       1776, July 24.   **89, 229**

1776   **Bigelow**, Timothy. Ticonderoga. Journal of his visit as
JULY 23   a flag to the Isle aux Noix. Contemporary copy.
                       4 pp. In handwriting of Tench Tilghman. En-
                       closed in Washington to the President of Con-
                       gress, 1776, Aug. 20.   **C. C. 152, 2, 451**

1776   **Continental Congress**, President. Philadelphia. To
JULY 24   [George] Washington [New York]. Flying
                       Camp; army accounts; exchange of prisoners.
                       L. S. of John Hancock. 2 pp. In handwriting
                       of Jacob Rush.   **89, 247**

1776   **Continental Congress**, Resolves. Lawful prizes; artillery
JULY 24   regiment; minor matters. A. D. S. of Charles
                       Thomson, countersigned by John Hancock. 2 pp.
                       Enclosed in President of Congress to Washington,
                       1776, July 24.   **89, 243**
                       Preamble, noting causes, etc., of war is crossed out and noted as
                       expunged.

[1776]   **Continental Congress**, Resolve. Virginia and Pennsylvania
[JULY 24]   troops for the Flying Camp. D. S. of John Han-
                       cock. 1 p. Enclosed in President of Congress
                       to Washington, 1776, July 24.   **89, 245**

1776   **Continental Congress**, Resolve. Prize ships. D. S. of John
JULY 24   Hancock. 1 p. Enclosed in President of Con-
                       gress to Washington, 1776, July 24.   **89, 246**

1776
JULY 24
Schuyler, Ph[ilip John].   German Flats [New York].   To [George] Washington [New York].   Relative advantages of Crown Point and Ticonderoga; waste of provisions; deputy quartermaster for St. Johns; lack of money.   Transcript.   Enclosed in Washington to the President of Congress, 1776, July 30.   C. C. **169**, 2, 445

1776
JULY 25
Washington, George.   New York.   To [the President of Congress, Philadelphia].   Necessity of additional aids-de-camp.   A. L. S.   2 pp.   Read in Congress July 29.   C. C. **152**, 2, 297
Printed: Writings of Washington (Ford) N. Y. 1889. 4, 297.

1776
JULY 27
Washington, George.   New York.   To [the President of Congress, Philadelphia].   Maj. [Christopher] French; enlistment bounty and other military matters.   L. S.   3 pp.   In handwriting of Robert Hanson Harrison.   Read in Congress July 29.
C. C. **152**, 2, 301
Printed: Writings of Washington (Ford) N. Y. 1889. 4, 301.

1776
JULY 29
Washington, George.   New York.   To [the President of Congress, Philadelphia].   Property of British subjects; need of musket powder; smallpox; prizes taken by armed vessels.   L. S.   2 pp. In handwriting of Robert Hanson Harrison. Read in Congress July 30.   Referred to the Board of War.   C. C. **152**, 2, 309
Printed, first paragraph only: Writings of Washington (Ford) N. Y. 1889. 4, 304, note.

1776
JULY 29
Washington, George.   New York.   To the Board of War [Philadelphia].   Vacancies and promotions in Army; case of [William] Goddard; mode of promotion.   Letter-book copy.   In handwriting of Robert Hanson Harrison.   **M**. III, 37

1776
JULY 29
Continental Congress, President.   Philadelphia.   To [George] Washington [New York].   Additional aid-de-camp.   A. L. S. of John Hancock.   1 p. Answered July 30.*   **11**, 18

1776
JULY 29
Continental Congress, Resolves.   Various military commissions granted.   A. D. S. of John Hancock. 2 pp.   Enclosed in President of Congress to Washington, 1776, July 30.   **89**, 248

1776
JULY 29
Bowdoin, James.   Boston.   To [George] Washington [New York].   Forwarding intelligence obtained through capture of a prize.   Contemporary copy. 1 p.   In handwriting of Samuel Blatchley Webb.

Enclosed in Washington to the President of Congress, 1776, Aug. 12.   C. C.   152, 2, 375

1776
JULY 29

Cooke, Nicholas. Providence [Rhode Island]. To Gen. [George] Washington [New York]. Account of prizes taken; news of British. Contemporary copy. 1 p. In handwriting of Morgan Lewis. Enclosed in Washington to the President of Congress, 1776, Aug. 5.   C. C.   152, 2, 339

1776
JULY 29

Kennedy, James. Boston. Statement of. Information of the Halifax fleet. Contemporary copy. 1 p. In handwriting of Samuel Blatchley Webb. Enclosed in Washington to the President of Congress, 1776, Aug. 12.   C. C.   152, 2, 377

1776
JULY 30

Washington, George. New York. To [the President of Congress, Philadelphia]. Evacuation of Crown Point; want of money; projected attempts on Staten Island; exchange of land and sea prisoners; Indians. L. S. 4 pp. In handwriting of Robert Hanson Harrison. Read in Congress Aug. 1.   C. C.   152, 2, 313

Printed, in part: Writings of Washington (Ford) N. Y. 1889. 4, 303, note.

1776
JULY 30

Washington, George. New York. To [Lt.] Gen. [Sir] William Howe [Staten Island]. Exchange of prisoners. Contemporary copy. In handwriting of Robert Hanson Harrison. Enclosed in Washington to the President of Congress, 1776, Aug. 5.   C. C.   152, 2, 333

Printed: Writings of Washington (Ford) N. Y. 1889. 4, 309.

1776
JULY 30

Continental Congress, President. Philadelphia. To [George] Washington [New York]. Miscellaneous military matters. L. S. of John Hancock. 2 pp. In handwriting of Jacob Rush. Answered Aug. 2*.   89, 260

1776
JULY 30

Continental Congress, Resolves. Investigation of failure of Canadian expedition; minor matters connected therewith; recruiting expenses; boats and cannon for [Brig.] Gen. [Hugh] Mercer; friendship of Cayashuta. D. S. of John Hancock. 6 pp. Enclosed in President of Congress to Washington, 1776, July 31.   89, 254

1776
JULY 30

Continental Congress, Resolve. War against Indians by the Southern colonies. A. D. S. of Charles Thomson, countersigned by John Hancock. 1 p. Enclosed in President of Congress to Washington, 1776, July 30.   89, 251

1776
JULY 30

Bowdoin, James.   Boston.   To [George Washington, New York].   Conference with Micmac and Penobscot Indians.   Contemporary copy.   3 pp.   In handwriting of Morgan Lewis.   Enclosed in Washington to the President of Congress, 1776, Aug. 12.   C. C.   152, 2, 379

1776
JULY 31

Washington, George.   New York.   To the President of Congress, Philadelphia.   Introducing Capt. Marquisie.   L. S.   1 p.   In handwriting of Robert Hanson Harrison.   Read in Congress, Aug. 5.
                                      C. C.   152, 2, 317

1776
JULY 31

Continental Congress, President.   Philadelphia.   To [George] Washington [New York].   Boats for the Flying Camp; Gates-Schuyler controversy.   L. S. of John Hancock.   2 pp.   In handwriting of Jacob Rush.   Endorsed by Robert Hanson Harrison with note of supplies received and captured on high seas.   Answered Aug. 4*.   89, 262

1776
JULY 31

Continental Congress, Resolves.   Powder; pay for Massachusetts militia; Canada investigation; powder, clothing and independent companies for North Carolina.   D. S. of John Hancock.   3 pp.   Enclosed in President of Congress to Washington, 1776, July 31.   89, 256

[1776]
[JULY]

Continental Army, Surgeons.   Memorial of Regimental Surgeons to Congress.   Supplies and instruments; regulations.   4 pp.   Transmitted to Washington.   96, 1

[1776]
[JULY?]

Elmore, Samuel.   Arrangement of field officers and captains of his regiment.
Wooster, David.   Arrangement of officers of regiment raised at Montreal.   Contemporary copy.   2 pp.   Enclosed in President of Congress to Washington, 1776, July 30.   89, 252

[1776]
[JULY]

Hazard, [Ebenezer]   [Marblehead? Massachusetts.]   To [George Washington, New York].   Account of arrival of Hessians.   Contemporary copy.   1 p.   In handwriting of Robert Hanson Harrison.   Enclosed in Washington to the President of Congress, 1776, Aug. 5.   C. C.   152, 2, 341

1776
AUG. 1

Howe, [Sir] William.   Staten Island.   To [George] Washington [New York].   Exchange of prisoners.

Contemporary copy. In handwriting of Robert Hanson Harrison. Enclosed in Washington to the President of Congress, 1776, Aug. 5.

C. C. 152, 2, 333

1776
Aug. 2
Washington, George. New York. To [the President of Congress, Philadelphia]. Troops from Massachusetts and Connecticut; enemy's reenforcement. L. S. 2 pp. In handwriting of Robert Hanson Harrison. Read in Congress, Aug. 5.

C. C. 152, 2, 325

Printed: Writings of Washington (Ford) N. Y. 1889. 4, 315.

1776
Aug. 2
Continental Congress, President. Philadelphia. To [George] Washington [New York]. Power of filling vacancies in the Army; paymaster and other departments; Stockbridge Indians; seamen. L. S. of John Hancock. 3 pp. Answered Aug. 8*.

89, 264

Printed in part: Writings of Washington (Ford) N. Y. 1889. 4, 306, note.

1776
Aug. 2
Continental Congress, Resolves. Money; Stockbridge Indians; paymaster, commissary and quartermaster monthly financial returns. D. S. of John Hancock. Transmitted to Washington. 89, 266

1776
Aug. 3
Penet, P[ierre]. Nantes [France]. To [George Washington, New York]. Requesting commission as aid-de-camp. Contemporary copy. 2 pp. In handwriting of Tench Tilghman. Enclosed in Washington to the President of Congress, 1776, Oct. 7. C. C. 152, 3, 135

1776
Aug. 5
Continental Congress, Resolves. Enlistment of seamen; commission to Rufus Putnam. D. S. of John Hancock. Transmitted to Washington. 89, 266

1776
Aug. 3
Tupper, Benjamin. Dobbs Ferry [New York]. To [George] Washington [New York]. Encounter of row galleys with enemy's ships. Contemporary copy. 1 p. In handwriting of George Lewis. Enclosed in Washington to the President of Congress, 1776. Aug. 5. C. C. 152, 2, 337

1776
Aug. 4
Carleton, Sir Guy. Quebec. Orders. Respecting flags-of-truce; prisoners. Contemporary copy. 3 pp. In handwriting of Francis Carr Clerke. Enclosed in Washington to the President of Congress, 1776, Aug. 20. C. C. 152, 2, 455

See note: Writings of Washington (Ford) N. Y. 1889. 4, 357.

1776
AUG. 4

D'Emory, Comte. San Domingo [West Indies]. To George Washington [New York]. Release of De Chambeau. Contemporary copy. 1 p. In handwriting of Tench Tilghman. Enclosed in Washington to the President of Congress, 1776, Oct. 7.   **C. C. 152, 3, 137**

1776
AUG. 5

Washington, George. New York. To [the President of Congress, Philadelphia]. Exchange of prisoners; engagement between enemy's ships and the row gallies; preparations for the coming battle. L. S. 3 pp. In handwriting of Robert Hanson Harrison. Read in Congress, Aug. 6.   **C. C. 152, 2, 329**
Printed: Writings of Washington (Ford) N. Y. 1889. 4, 317.

1776
AUG. 7

Washington, George. New York. To [the President of Congress, Philadelphia]. Appointment of Major Generals; disputes between agents for prizes; Indians. L. S. 4 pp. In handwriting of Robert Hanson Harrison. Read in Congress, Aug. 8.   **C. C. 152, 2, 343**
Printed: Writings of Washington (Ford) N. Y. 1889. 4, 321.

1776
AUG. 7

Washington, George. New York. To [the President of Congress, Philadelphia]. Reports of deserters; intended attack; news from Charleston, etc. L. S. 3 pp. In handwriting of Joseph Reed. Read in Congress, Aug. 8.   **C. C. 152, 2, 359**
Printed in part: Writings of Washington (Ford) N.Y. 1889. 4, 325, note.

1776
AUG. 7

Continental Congress, Resolves. British treatment of Lt. [James] Josiah. A. D. S. of Charles Thomson, countersigned by John Hancock. 1 p. Enclosed in President of Congress to Washington, 1776, Aug. 8.   **89, 268**

[1776]
[AUG. 7]

McMichael, Edward. Intelligence brought from Oswego. Intended attack on Fort Stanwix and the German Flats by British and Indians. Contemporary copy. 1 p. In handwriting of Caleb Gibbs. Enclosed in Washington to the President of Congress, 1776, Aug. 7.   **C. C. 152, 2, 347**

1776
AUG. 8

Washington, George. New York. To [the President of Congress, Philadelphia]. Stockbridge Indians; strength of army; preparations of enemy for an attack. L. S. 5 pp. In handwriting of Robert Hanson Harrison. Read in Congress, Aug. 12. Referred to the Board of War. **C. C. 152, 2, 363**
Printed: Writings of Washington (Ford) N.Y. 1889. 4, 331.

1776
AUG. 8

Continental **Congress**, President. Philadelphia. To [George] Washington [New York]. Case of Lt. [James] Josiah; [Maj.] Gen. [Charles] Lee. L. S. of John Hancock. 1 p. In handwriting of Charles Thomson.   **89, 269**

1776
AUG. 9

Continental **Congress**, Resolves. Election of Major and Brigadier Generals. D. S. of John Hancock. 1 p. Enclosed in President of Congress to Washington, 1776, Aug. 10.   **89, 270**

·1776
AUG. 10

Continental **Congress**, President. Philadelphia. To [George] Washington [New York]. Election of general officers; troops for Jersey. L. S. of John Hancock. 1 p. In handwriting of Jacob Rush. Answered Aug. 12.*   **89, 272**

1776
AUG. 10

Continental **Congress**, President. Philadelphia. To [George] Washington [New York]. Commissions. L. S. of John Hancock. 2 pp. In handwriting of Jacob Rush. Answered Aug. 12.*
    89, 274

1776
AUG. 10

Continental **Congress**, Resolve. Commissions to various officers. D. S. of John Hancock. 2 pp. Enclosed in President of Congress to Washington, 1776, Aug. 10.   **89, 276**

1776
AUG. 10

New York, Convention. Harlem. Resolve respecting securing of disaffected persons. Contemporary copy. 1 p. In handwriting of Samuel Blatchley Webb. Enclosed in Washington to the President of Congress, 1776, Aug. 12. **C. C.** **152, 2, 383**

1776
AUG. 12

Washington, George. New York. To [the President of Congress, Philadelphia]. Reenforcements; New York loyalists; cavalry for the South. L. S. 4 pp. In handwriting of Robert Hanson Harrison. Read in Congress, Aug. 14.
    C. C.   152, 2, 371
Printed in part: Writings of Washington (Ford) N. Y. 1889. **4, 337.**

1776
AUG. 12

Washington, George. New York. To the President of Congress, Philadelphia. Case of court-martial of Col. [Donald?] Campbell. L. S. 1 p. In handwriting of Robert Hanson Harrison.
    C. C.   152, 2, 385
Printed: Writings of Washington (Ford) N. Y. 1889. **4, 340, note.**

1776
AUG. 13

Washington, George. New York. To the President of Congress, Philadelphia. Sending his papers to

Camp above the Falls of Trenton
(15)
December 22d 1776

Sir,

When I wrote to you on the 14th Instant, I had little doubt of receiving considerable support from the Militia of this State, and was taught to believe that a large part of the old Troops (coming on with General Lee) had reinlisted—In the first, I have every reason in the world to fear a disappointment—In the latter, I find myself woefully deceiv'd—It is easier therefore to conceive, than describe the situation I am in—left or shall be, in a very few days, with only a very few Southern Regiments (reduced almost to nothing) to oppose Howes main Army, already posted in such a manner as to pour in his whole force upon us, so soon as the Frost affords him a passage over the Delaware, and our numbers such, as to give no effectual opposition.

Thus circumstanced, it is a matter of concern to me, that in my last, I directed you to take back any of the Militia designed for the support of the Army under my Command; and have to request that, instead of Ordering the return of any of those that were destined for this department (by order of their respective States) that you will hasten them on with all possible expedition, as I see no other chance of saving Philadelphia, and preventing a fatal blow to America in the loss of a City from whence so much of our Resources are drawn.

With respect to yourself, you will proceed agreeably to the directions in my former—It is not possible for me at this distance to lay down any particular Rule for your conduct

WRITING OF GEORGE BAYLOR.

Congress. L. S. 1 p. In handwriting of Robert Hanson Harrison.   C. C.   **152**, 2, 393

Printed: Writings of Washington (Ford) N. Y. 1889. 4, 342, note.

1776
Aug. 13

Continental Congress, Resolve. Massachusetts treaty with St. Johns and Micmac Indians. D. S. of John Hancock. In handwriting of Charles Thomson. Enclosed in President of Congress to Washington, 1776, Aug. 16.   **89**, 278

1776
Aug. 13

Continental Congress, President. [Philadelphia.] To [George] Washington [New York]. Nothing to communicate. A. L. S. of John Hancock. 1 p. Answered Aug. 15 *   **89**, 280

1776
Aug. 13

Givens, Thomas. Examination of. Information of strength, etc., of the British. Contemporary copy. 2 pp. In handwriting of George Lewis. Enclosed in Washington to the President of Congress, 1776, Aug. 14.   C. C.   **152**, 2, 409

1776
Aug. 13

Howe, Sir William. Staten Island. To [George] Washington [New York]. Requesting permission for Robert Temple to go into Massachusetts. Written by a secretary in the third person. 1 p. Enclosed in Washington to the President of Congress, 1776, Aug. 18.   C. C.   **152**, 2, 437

1776
Aug. 14

Washington, George. New York. To the President of Congress, Philadelphia. Introducing Capt. Moeballe. L. S. 1 p. In handwriting of Robert Hanson Harrison.   C. C.   **152**, 2, 397

1776
Aug. 14

Washington, George. New York. To [the President of Congress, Philadelphia]. Intelligence of the enemy; need of tents; miscellaneous matters. L. S. 2 pp. In handwriting of Robert Hanson Harrison. Read in Congress, Aug. 15.

C. C.   **152**, 2, 401

Printed, in part: Writings of Washington (Ford) N. Y. 1889. 4, 346, note.

1776
Aug. 14

Continental Congress, Secret Committee. Philadelphia. To [George] Washington [New York]. Powder in Rhode Island. A. L. S. of Robert Morris. 1 p.   **11**, 135

1776
Aug. 14

Continental Congress, Resolves. Land for Hessian deserters; [Antoine Felix] Wybert's appointment. D. S. of John Hancock. In handwriting of Charles Thomson. Enclosed in President of Congress to Washington, 1776, Aug. 16.   **89**, 278

1776
Aug. 14

Farrier, Isaac. [Amboy, New Jersey.] Examination of. Information of intentions of the British. Contemporary copy. 1 p. In handwriting of Tench Tilghman. Enclosed in Washington to the President of Congress, 1776, Aug. 17.

C. C.   152, 2, 431

1776
Aug. 14

Hand, Edward. West Chester [New York]. To [George Washington, New York]. Recommendations for officers' promotions. A. L. S. 2 pp. Enclosed in Washington to the President of Congress, 1776, Sep. 20.   C. C.   152, 2, 13

1776
Aug. 14

Hunter, Alexander. [Amboy.] Examination of. Information of strength etc. of British. Contemporary copy. 1 p. In handwriting of Tench Tilghman. Enclosed in Washington to the President of Congress, 1776, Aug. 17.   C. C.   152, 2, 429

1776
Aug. 15

Washington, George. New York. To [the President of Congress, Philadelphia]. The situation. L. S. 1 p. In handwriting of Robert Hanson Harrison. Read in Congress, Aug. 16.   C. C.   152, 2, 413
Printed: Writings of Washington (Ford) N. Y. 1889. 4, 346, note.

1776
Aug. 15

Continental Congress, Resolve. Col. James Livingston to raise companies of Canadians. D. S. of John Hancock. In handwriting of Charles Thomson. Enclosed in President of Congress to Washington, 1776, Aug. 16.   89, 278

1776
Aug. 15

Roberdeau, Daniel. Amboy [New Jersey]. To [George Washington, New York]. Forwarding prisoners. A. L. S. 1 p. Enclosed in Washington to the President of Congress, 1776, Aug. 17.

C. C.   152, 2, 425

1776
Aug. 16

Washington, George. New York. To [the President of Congress, Philadelphia]. Sickness in army; want of officers. L. S. 1 p. In handwriting of Robert Hanson Harrison.   C. C.   152, 2, 417
Printed: Writings of Washington (Ford) N. Y. 1889. 4, 346, note.

1776
Aug. 16

Continental Congress, President. Philadelphia. To [George] Washington [New York]. Transmitting resolves. A. L. S. of John Hancock. 1 p. Answered Aug. 18.*   89, 282

1776
Aug. 17

Washington, George. New York. To [Lt.] Gen. [Sir William] Howe [Staten Island]. Permission to Robert Temple to go to Massachusetts. Contem-

porary copy. 1 p. In handwriting of Tench
Tilghman. Enclosed in Washington to the President of Congress, 1776, Aug.18.   C. C.   152, 2, 441

1776
Aug. 17

Washington, George.   New York.   To [the President of
Congress, Philadelphia].   Intelligence of enemy;
attempt of fire ships.   L. S.   2 pp.   In handwriting of Robert Hanson Harrison.

C. C.   152, 2, 421

Printed, in part: Writings of Washington (Ford) N. Y. 1889. 4, 348,
note.

1776
Aug. 17

Washington, George.   New York.   To [Richard,] Viscount
Howe [off Staten Island].   Exchange of naval
prisoners.   Contemporary copy.   2 pp.   In handwriting of Tench Tilghman.   Enclosed in Washington to the President of Congress, 1776, Aug.
21.   C. C.   152, 2, 463

Printed: Writings of Washington (Ford) N. Y. 1889. 4, 348.

1776
Aug. 17

Continental Congress, President.   Philadelphia.   To
[George] Washington [New York].   Routine matters.   L. S. of John Hancock.   1 p.   In handwriting of Jacob Rush.   Answered Aug. 20.*

89, 284

1776
Aug. 17

Continental Congress, Resolves.   Conduct of Brig. Gen.
[David] Wooster; Quartermaster General's de-
partment; exchange of prisoners; Maryland
troops; articles [for the Flying Camp].   D. S. of
John Hancock.   5 pp.   Enclosed in President of
Congress to Washington, 1776, Aug. 17.

89, 286

1776
Aug. 18

Washington, George.   New York.   To [the President of
Congress, Philadelphia].   Resolutions respecting
foreign troops in British army; [James,] Lord
Drummond; delay of British in attacking; In-
dian treaties.   L. S.   2 pp.   In handwriting of
Robert Hanson Harrison.   Read in Congress,
Aug. 20.   C. C.   152, 2, 433

Printed, in part: Writings of Washington (Ford) N. Y. 1889. 4, 352,
note.

1776
Aug. 19

Washington, George.   New York.   To [the President of
Congress, Philadelphia].   The military situation;
militia.   L. S.   2 pp.   In handwriting of Robert
Hanson Harrison.   Read in Congress, Aug. 20.

C. C.   152, 2, 443

1776
Aug. 19

Drummond, [James, Lord]   *Polly* [Off Staten Island].   To
[George Washington, New York].   Question of

his parole. Contemporary copy. 2 pp. In handwriting of Tench Tilghman. Enclosed in Washington to the President of Congress, 1776, Aug. 26.   C. C.   152, 2, 497

1776
AUG. 19

Howe, [Richard, Viscount]. *Eagle*, off Staten Island. **To** George Washington [New York]. Exchange of Lt. [James] Josiah. Contemporary copy. 1 p. In handwriting of Tench Tilghman. Enclosed in Washington to the President of Congress, 1776, Aug. 21.   C. C.   152, 2, 467

1776
AUG. 20

Washington, George.   New York. To [the President of Congress, Philadelphia]. Exchange of prisoners; intentions of enemy. L. S. 3 pp. In handwriting of Robert Hanson Harrison. Read in Congress, Aug. 22.   C. C.   152, 2, 447
Printed: Writings of Washington (Ford) N. Y. 1889. 4, 355.

1776
AUG. 21

Washington, George.   New York. To [the President of Congress, Philadelphia]. Correspondence with British on subject of exchange of prisoners. L. S. 1 p. In handwriting of Robert Hanson Harrison. Read in Congress, Aug. 23.
                                   C. C.   152, 2, 459

1776
AUG. 21

Continental Congress, Resolves. Case of Bazil Bouderot; spies; money and cannon for army; Maj. Gen. [Artemas] Ward; copper. D. S. of John Hancock. 3 pp. Transmitted to Washington.
                                            89, 290

1776
AUG. 21

Hand, Edward.   The Narrows [Long Island]. To [Brig.] Gen. [John] Nixon [Long Island] Reports of enemy's movements. Contemporary copy. 1 p. In handwriting of Tench Tilghman. Enclosed in Washington to the President of Congress, 1776, Aug. 22.   C. C.   152, 2, 479

1776
AUG. 21

Livingston, William.   Elizabethtown [New Jersey]. To [George] Washington [New York]. Report of a spy of designs of the enemy. Contemporary copy. 2 pp. In handwriting of Tench Tilghman. Enclosed in Washington to the President of Congress, 1776, Aug. 22.   C. C.   152, 2, 475

1776
AUG. 22

Washington, George.   New York. To [the President of Congress, Philadelphia]. Expectations of attack. L. S. 2 pp. In handwriting of Robert Hanson Harrison. Read in Congress Aug. 26.
                                   C. C.   152, 2, 471

1776
AUG. 23

Washington, George. New York. To [the President of Congress, Philadelphia]. Approaching battle; prizes of armed vessels; treaty with Six Nations. L. S. 2 pp. In handwriting of Robert Hanson Harrison. Read in Congress, Aug. 26.

C. C. **152**, 2, 483

Printed, in part: Writings of Washington (Ford) N.Y. 1889. 4, 363, note.

1776
AUG. 23

Sullivan, John. Long Island. To [George] Washington [New York]. Account of skirmish on the Bedford Road. Contemporary copy. 1 p. In handwriting of Samuel Blatchley Webb. Enclosed in Washington to the President of Congress, 1776, Aug. 24.

C. C. **152**, 2, 491

1776
AUG. 24

Washington, George. New York. To [the President of Congress, Philadelphia]. Irregularity of the post; manœuvers of the enemy. A. L. S. 2 pp. Read in Congress, Aug. 26.

C. C. **152**, 2, 487

Printed, in part: Writings of Washington (Ford) N.Y. 1889. 4, 363, note.

1776
AUG. 24

Continental Congress, President. Philadelphia. To [George] Washington [New York]. [James,] Lord Drummond's officiousness. L. S. of John Hancock. 2 pp. In handwriting of Jacob Rush.

11, 200

1776
AUG. 26

Washington, George. New York. To [the President of Congress, Philadelphia]. Movements of the enemy; [James,] Lord Drummond. L. S. 3 pp. In handwriting of Robert Hanson Harrison. Read in Congress, Aug. 28.

C. C. **152**, 2, 493

1776
AUG. 26

Continental Congress, Resolve. Pensions for disabilities and death; Invalid corps. D. S. of John Hancock. 5 pp. Transmitted to Washington.

89, 292

1776
AUG. 27

Continental Congress, Resolve. Inducements to foreigners to desert from British. D. S. of John Hancock. 2 pp. Transmitted to Washington.

89, 296

1776
AUG. 27

Harrison, Rob[ert] H[anson]. New York. To [the President of Congress, Philadelphia]. Short account of the battle of Long Island. A. L. S. 2 pp.

C. C. **152**, 2, 499

1776
AUG. 29

Washington, George. Long Island. To the President of Congress, Philadelphia. The military situation. L. S. 2 pp. In handwriting of Robert Hanson Harrison. Read in Congress, Aug. 30.

C. C. **152**, 2, 503

Printed: Writings of Washington (Ford) N. Y. 1889. 4, 371.

1776
AUG. 29

Continental Army, Council of War. Long Island. Reasons for retreat. Contemporary copy. 3 pp. In handwriting of William Grayson. Enclosed in Washington to the President of Congress, 1776, Aug. 31. C. C. **152, 2, 511**

1776
AUG. 29

[Stirling, William Alexander, Lord.] Eagle [off Staten Island]. To [George Washington, New York]. Account of the battle of Long Island. Contemporary copy. 3 pp. In handwriting of William Grayson. Enclosed in Washington to the President of Congress, 1776, Aug. 31.

C. C. **152, 2, 515**

1776
AUG. 31

Washington, George. New York. To [the President of Congress, Philadelphia]. The retreat from Long Island; losses in the battle. L. S. 2 pp. In handwriting of Robert Hanson Harrison. Read in Congress, Sept. 2. C. C. **152, 2, 507**
Printed: Writings of Washington (Ford) N. Y. 1889. 4, 373.

1776
SEP. 1

De Lancey, Oliver. Jamaica [Long Island]. To Col. [Phinehas] Fanning [Long Island]. Submission of inhabitants of Suffolk county. Contemporary copy. 1 p. In handwriting of Henry Beekman Livingston. Enclosed in Washington to the President of Congress, 1776, Oct. 2.

C. C. **152, 3, 95**

1776
SEP. 2

Washington, George. New York. To [the President of Congress, Philadelphia]. Disorganized state of the army; militia. L. S. 4 pp. In handwriting of Robert Hanson Harrison. Read in Congress, Sept. 3. C. C. **152, 2, 519**
Printed: Writings of Washington, (Ford) N. Y. 1889. 4, 378.

1776
SEP. 2

De Lancey, Oliver. Huntington [Long Island]. To Col. Phinehas Fanning [Long Island]. Ordering taking oath of allegiance to King. Contemporary copy. 1 p. In handwriting of Henry Beekman Livingston. Enclosed in Washington to the President of Congress, 1776, Oct. 2. C. C. **152, 3, 97**

1776
SEP. 3

Continental Congress, Resolves. Preservation of New York city; reinforcements. D. S. of John Hancock. 2 pp. Enclosed in President of Congress to Washington, 1776, Sep. 3. **89, 298**

1776
SEP. 3

Continental Congress, President. Philadelphia. To [George] Washington [New York]. Preservation of New York; reinforcements. L. S. of John Hancock. 2 pp. In handwriting of Jacob Rush. **89, 300**

1776
SEP. 4

Washington, George. New York. To [the President of Congress, Philadelphia]. Movement of enemy's ships; intelligence from Canada; correspondence with Congress. Transcript. Read in Congress, Sep. 6. **C. C. 169, 2, 202**

Printed in part: Writings of Washington (Ford) N. Y. 1889. 4, 383, note.

1776
SEP. 5

'Continental Congress, Resolves. Exchange of prisoners. D. S. of John Hancock. Enclosed in President of Congress to Washington, 1776, Sep. 8.

89, 302

[1776]
[SEP. 4?]

Newell, Eliphalet. [New York.] To Col. Henry Knox [New York]. Report of damage being sustained from enemy's fire. L. S. 1 p. Enclosed in Washington to the President of Congress, 1776, Sep. 8. **C. C. 152, 2, 54**

1776
SEP. 5

Continental Congress, Resolves. Peace conference with [Richard,] Lord Howe. D. S. of John Hancock. Enclosed in President of Congress to Washington, 1776, Sep. 8. **89, 302**

1776
SEP. 5

De Lancey, Oliver. Jamaica [Long Island]. Proclamation offering commissions for raising companies of loyalists. Contemporary copy. 1 p. In handwriting of Henry Beekman Livingston. Enclosed in Washington to the President of Congress, 1776, Oct. 2. **C. C. 152, 3, 99**

1776
SEP. 6

Washington, George. New York. To [the President of Congress, Philadelphia]. Preservation of New York; intentions of enemy; pay for troops; exchanges. L. S. 3 pp. In handwriting of Robert Hanson Harrison. Read in Congress, Sep. 9. Referred to the Board of War. **C. C. 152, 2, 527**

Printed: Writings of Washington (Ford) N. Y. 1889. 4, 385.

1776
SEP. 6

Continental Congress, Resolves. Committee to wait on [Rear Adml. Richard,] Lord Howe; military appointments. D. S. of John Hancock. Enclosed in President of Congress to Washington, 1776, Sep. 8. **89, 302**

1776
SEP. 7

Washington, George. New York. To the President of Congress, Philadelphia. Claim of Capt. [Sion] Martindale and others for pay. L. S. 1 p. In handwriting of Robert Hanson Harrison. Read in Congress, Sep. 13. **C. C. 152, 2, 523**

1776
SEP. 8

Washington, George. New York. To [the President of Congress, Philadelphia]. Reasons for evacuation

of New York; militia. L. S. 7 pp. In hand-
writing of Robert Hanson Harrison. Read in
Congress, Sep. 10.   C. C. **152, 2, 531**
Printed: Writings of Washington (Ford) N. Y. 1889. 4, 390.

1776
SEP. 8

Continental Congress, President. Philadelphia. To [George]
Washington [New York]. Exchange of prisoners;
peace conference with [Rear Adml. Richard,]
Lord Howe; money; tents; intelligence to Congress. L. S. of John Hancock. 4 pp. In handwriting of Jacob Rush.   **89, 304**

1776
SEP. 8

Nicoll, Isaac. New Rochelle [New York]. To [George
Washington, New York]. Report of sources of
information; moves of enemy. A. L. S. 2 pp.
Enclosed in Washington to the President of Congress, 1776, Sep. 8.   C. C. **152, 2, 539**

1776
SEP. 10

Continental Congress, Resolve. Evacuation of New York.
A. D. S. of John Hancock. 1 p. Enclosed in
President of Congress to Washington, 1776, Sep.
16.   **89, 306**

1776
SEP. 11

Washington, George. New York. To [the President of
Congress, Philadelphia]. Exchange of prisoners;
moves of enemy; evacuation of city. L. S. 3 pp.
In handwriting of Robert Hanson Harrison.
Read in Congress Sep. 13.   C. C. **152, 2, 543**
Printed in part: Writings of Washington (Ford) N. Y. 1889. 4, 398.
402, and 404, notes.

1776
SEP. 11

[De Lancey, Oliver.] Jamaica. [Long Island]. To [Col.]
Phinehas Fanning [Long Island]. Ordering con-
fiscation of cattle. Contemporary copy. 1 p.
In handwriting of Henry Beekman Livingston.
Enclosed in Washington to the President of Con-
gress, 1776, Oct. 2.   C. C. **152, 3, 101**

1776
SEP. 12

W[ashington,] G[eorge]. New York. To Robert Morris
[Philadelphia]. Tents for the army. Letter-
book copy.   **M. III, 272**

1776
SEP. 12

Harrison, Rob[ert] H[anson]. New York. To the President of Congress, Philadelphia. Report of latest
military happenings. A. L. S. 1 p. Read in
Congress, Sep. 14.   C. C. **152, 2, 547**

1776
SEP. 12

Board of War. [Philadelphia.] To [George] Washington,
New York. Exchange of [Maj.] Gen. [Richard]
Prescott and [Brig. ?] Gen. [Allan ?] Macdonald
for [Maj.] Gen. [John] Sullivan and [Brig.] Gen.
[William Alexander,] Lord Stirling. A. L. S.
of Richard Peters. 1 p.   **95, 296**

1776
SEP. 12

Continental Congress, Resolves. Extent of command of the Commissary General; miscellaneous military matters. D. S. of John Hancock. 4 pp. Enclosed in President of Congress to Washington, 1776, Sep. 16.   **89,** 308

[1776]
[SEP. 12]

Rutledge, E[dward]. Brunswick [New Jersey]. To [George Washington, New York]. Conference with [Rear Adml. Richard,] Lord Howe. A. L. S. 1 p.   **12, 23**

1776
SEP. 14

Washington, George. New York. To [the President of Congress, Philadelphia]. Preparations for evacuation of New York; sick and pay of nurses. L. S. 4 pp. In handwriting of Robert Hanson Harrison. Read in Congress, Sep. 16.
                                        C. C. 152, 2, 551
Printed: Writings of Washington (Ford) N. Y. 1889. 4, 402.

1776
SEP. 14

Continental Congress, Resolves. Rations for militia officers; barracks; magazines; powder, flints; return of arms, etc., by discharged troops and militia. D. S. of John Hancock. Enclosed in President of Congress to Washington, 1776, Sep. 16.
                                                          89, 308

1776
SEP. 15–16

Continental Army, Prisoners. List of captures by the British on the island of New York. Contemporary copy. 1 p. In handwriting of Tench Tilghman. Enclosed in Washington to the President of Congress, 1776, Sep. 25.   **C. C. 152, 3, 55**

1776
SEP. 16

[**Washington,** George.] [Harlem Heights.] To [the President of Congress, Philadelphia]. Affair at Kips Bay. Unsigned letter. 3 pp. In handwriting of Robert Hanson Harrison. Read in Congress, Sep. 17.   **C. C. 152, 2, 555**
Printed: Writings of Washington (Ford) N. Y. 1889. 4, 406.

1776
SEP. 16

Continental Congress, President. Philadelphia. To [George] Washington [Harlem Heights, New York]. Transmitting resolves. L. S. of John Hancock. 2 pp. Answered Sep. 20.* **89,** 311

1776
SEP. 16

Continental Congress, Resolve. State quotas of troops; bounties of money and land. Broadside. Enclosed in Board of War to Washington, 1777, May 20.   **95,** 321

1776
SEP. 16

Continental Congress, Resolves. Brigadier appointments. D. S. of John Hancock. Enclosed in President of Congress to Washington, 1776, Sep. 24.
                                                          89, 314

1776
SEP. 16

Board of War. [Philadelphia.] To George Washington, New York. Memorial of 2d lieutenants of the Virginia regiments. A. L. S. of Richard Peters. 1 p. Answered Sep. 30.*   **95, 298**

1776
SEP. 16

Clark, John. Perth Amboy [New Jersey]. To George Washington [Harlem]. Resignation. A. L. S. 1 p. Enclosed in Washington to the President of Congress, 1776, Oct. 5.   **C. C. 152, 3, 117**

1776
SEP. 18

Washington, George. [Harlem Heights.] To [the President of Congress, Philadelphia]. The battle of Harlem Plains. L. S. 4 pp. In handwriting of Robert Hanson Harrison. Read in Congress, Sep. 20.   **C. C. 152, 2, 559**
Printed: Writings of Washington (Ford) N. Y. 1889. 4, 416.

1776
SEP. 18

Continental Congress, Resolves. Minor military appointments. D. S. of John Hancock. Enclosed in President of Congress to Washington, 1776, Sep. 24.   **89, 314**

1776
SEP. 18

Continental Congress, Resolves. Rations and bounties. Broadside. Enclosed in Board of War to Washington, 1777, May 20.   **95, 321.**

1776
SEP. 19

Washington, George. [Harlem Heights.] To [the President of Congress, Philadelphia]. Preparations for British to attack Harlem Heights. L. S. 1 p. In handwriting of Robert Hanson Harrison.
     C. C. 152, 3, 1
Printed, in part: Writings of Washington (Ford) N. Y. 1889. 4, 420, note.

1776
SEP. 19

Continental Congress, Resolves. Rank of adjutants and land assignments. Broadside. Enclosed in Board of War to Washington, 1777, May 20.   **95, 321**

1776
SEP. 19

Continental Congress, Resolves. Minor appointments of Frenchmen; drill of troops; accounts of Northern Army. D. S. of John Hancock. Enclosed in President of Congress to Washington, 1776, Sep. 24.   **89, 314**

1776
SEP. 19

Howe, [Richard, Viscount] and [Sir] W[illiam] **Howe.** New York. Declaration respecting disposition and intention of the King. 1 p. Broadside. Enclosed in Washington to the President of Congress, 1776, Sep. 27.   **C. C. 152, 3, 65**

1776
SEP. 19

McCumber, Matthew. Harlem Heights. Court-martial of. Contemporary copy. 3 pp. In handwriting of

Tench Tilghman. Auto. note by Washington. Enclosed in Washington to the President of Congress, 1776, Sep. 24.   C. C.   152, 3, 41

1776
SEP. 20
Washington, George. Harlem Heights. To [the President of Congress, Philadelphia]. Resolves respecting ammunition; commissions; short enlistments; clothing and tents. L. S. 3 pp. In handwriting of Robert Hanson Harrison. Read in Congress, Sep. 23.   C. C.   152, 3, 5
Printed, in part: Writings of Washington (Ford) N. Y. 1889. 4, 420.

1776
SEP. 20
Continental Congress, Resolves.- Raising of new army; supplies and wants of troops; physician for the Flying Camp. D. S. of John Hancock. Enclosed in President of Congress to Washington, 1776, Sep. 24.   89, 314

[1776]
[SEP. 20-27]
Continental Congress, Committee on State of the Army. Queries to be made at Headquarters. Supplies, the different military departments. 12 questions. First two answered in handwriting of Robert Hanson Harrison. 2 pp.   **W**
Committee: Sherman, Gerry and Lewis. Reported Oct. 3. See Journals of Congress Sep. 20, Oct. 8, 1776, and Writings of Washington (Ford) N. Y. 1889. 4, 451, note.

1776
SEP. 20
Board of War. [Philadelphia.] To George Washington, [Kingsbridge]. Introducing Marquis de Malmedy, Jean Louis Imbert, Christian de Colerus and [Jean] Louis de Vernejous. A. L. S. of Richard Peters. 1 p.   95, 299

[1776]
[SEP. 20 ?]
Ward, J[onathan] [Harlem.] To [George] Washington [Harlem]. Return of officers recommended for promotion in 21st Continental Infantry. A. D. S. 2 pp. Enclosed in Washington to the President of Congress 1776, Sep. 20.   C. C.   152, 3, 9

1776
SEP. 21
Howe, [Sir] W[illiam]. [New] York. To George Washington [Harlem]. Arrangements for exchange of prisoners. Contemporary copy. 2 pp. In handwriting of Robert Hanson Harrison. Enclosed in Washington to the President of Congress, 1776, Sep. 25.   C. C.   152, 3, 51

1776
SEP. 22
Washington, George. Kingsbridge [New York]. To the President of Congress [Philadelphia]. Plundering habits of the army. L. S. 3 pp. In handwriting of Joseph Reed. Read in Congress, Sep. 23.   C. C.   152, 3, 17
Printed: Writings of Washington (Ford) N. Y. 1889. 4, 424.

1776
SEP. 22
Washington, George. Harlem Heights. To [the Presi
dent of Congress, Philadelphia]. The fire in New
York. L. S. 1 p. In handwriting of Robert
Hanson Harrison. Read in Congress, Sep. 23.
C. C.   **152, 3, 21**
Printed: Writings of Washington (Ford) N. Y. 1889. 4, 430, note.

1776
SEP. 23
Washington, George. Harlem Heights. To [Lt.] Gen.
[Sir William] Howe [New York]. Exchange of
prisoners. Contemporary copy. 2 pp. In
handwriting of Robert Hanson Harrison. Enclosed in Washington to the President of Congress, 1776, Sep. 25.   C. C.   **152, 3, 53**
Printed, in part: Writings of Washington (Ford) N.Y. 1889. 4, 433–4,
notes.

1776
SEP. 23
Continental Congress, Resolve. Troops; clothing; powder
for Northern Army; Fort Montgomery and de-
fense of Highlands. D. S. of John Hancock.
2 pp.   **89, 318**

1776
SEP. 23
Greene, Nathanael. Fort Constitution [New York]. To
[George] Washington, Harlem Heights. Enemy
at Paulus Hook. A. L. S. 1 p. Enclosed in
Washington to the President of Congress, 1776,
Sep. 24.   C. C.   **152, 3, 27**

1776
SEP. 24
Washington, George. Harlem Heights. To [the President of Congress, Philadelphia]. Enemy's landing at Paulus Hook; discharge of militia. L. S.
1 p. In handwriting of Robert Hanson Harrison.
Read in Congress, 1776, Sep. 25.   C. C.   **152, 3, 23**
Printed, in part: Writings of Washington (Ford) N.Y. 1889. 4, 430,
note.

1776
SEP. 24
Washington, George. Harlem Heights. To [the Presi-
dent of Congress, Philadelphia]. Condition of
army; discipline; militia. A. L. S. 12 pp.
Read in Congress, Sep. 27.   C. C.   **152, 3, 29**
Printed: Writings of Washington (Ford) N. Y. 1889. 4, 438.

1776
SEP. 24
Continental Congress, President. Philadelphia. To
[George] Washington [Harlem Heights]. Aug-
menting the Army; enlistments for the war.
L. S. of John Hancock. 4 pp. In handwriting
of Jacob Rush. Answered Sep. 28*.

89, 320

1776
SEP. 24
Livingston, Henry B[eekman]. [Saybrook, New Jersey.]
To [George] Washington [Harlem]. Report of
his raid on Long Island. A. L. S. 3 pp. Enclosed in Washington to the President of Congress, 1776, Oct. 2.   C.C.   **152, 3, 91**

1776
SEP. 25

Washington, George. Harlem Heights. To [the President of Congress, Philadelphia]. Exchange of prisoners; commissaries; need of tents, clothing. L. S. 1 p. In handwriting of Robert Hanson Harrison.   C. C. 152, 3, 45
  <small>Printed, in part: Writings of Washington (Ford) N. Y. 1889. 4, 433, note.</small>

[1776]
[SEP. 25]

Washington, George. Harlem Heights. To [the President of Congress, Philadelphia]. Table of proposed increased pay for officers. 1 p. In handwriting of Tench Tilghman. Enclosed in Washington to the President of Congress, 1776, Sep. 25.
                               C. C. 152, 3, 49

1776
SEP. 25

SEP. 26

Continental Congress, Resolves: Payrolls of militia; clothing etc., for soldiers; blankets, shoes, provisions etc., for Northern Army; camp utensils; sundry military appointments; salt provision.
    Exchange of officers; desertion among Pennsylvania troops. D. S. of John Hancock. 8 pp. Enclosed in President of Congress to Washington, 1776, Oct. 2.   89, 324

1776
SEP. 26

Ballard, Robert. Fort Constitution [New York]. To [George]Washington [Harlem]. Requesting permission to resign. A. L. S. 2 pp. Enclosed in Washington to the President of Congress, 1776, Sep. 30.   C. C. 152, 3, 83

1776
SEP. 27

Washington, George. Harlem Heights. To [the President of Congress, Philadelphia]. The Congressional Committee; intelligence from Canada. L. S. 1 p. In handwriting of Robert Hanson Harrison. Read in Congress Sep. 30.
                               C. C. 152, 3, 59

[1776]
[SEP. 27]

Canada, British Army in. Estimate of troops, naval force. 1 p. Enclosed in Washington to the President of Congress, 1776, Sep. 27. In handwriting of Morgan Lewis.   C. C. 152, 3, 63

1776
SEP. 28

Washington, George. Harlem Heights. To [the President of Congress, Philadelphia]. Recommending Capt. Daniel Morgan for promotion. L. S. 2 pp. In handwriting of Robert Hanson Harrison. Read in Congress, Sep. 28.   C. C. 152, 3, 67
  <small>Printed: Writings of Washington (Ford) N. Y. 1889. 4, 454.</small>

1776
SEP. 28

Shepard, William. Bergen [New Jersey]. Petition to George Washington [Harlem Heights]. Praying for promotion. D. S. 2 pp. Enclosed in Washington to the President of Congress, 1776, Sep. 30.   C. C. 152, 3, 79

1776
SEP. 30

Washington, George. Harlem Heights. To [the President of Congress, Philadelphia]. Recommending Lt. Col. [William] Shepard for promotion. L. S. 1 p. In handwriting of Robert Hanson Harrison. Read in Congress, Oct. 2.   C. C. 152, 3, 75

1776
SEP. 30

Washington, George. New York. To the Board of War, Philadelphia. System of promotion. L. S. 1 p. In handwriting of Robert Hanson Harrison.
     C. C. 152, 3, 71
Printed: Writings of Washington (Ford) N. Y. 1889. 4, 460, note.

1776
SEP. 30

Continental Congress, Resolves. Trial of Ensign [Mathew] Macumber; exchange of officers; examination of surgeons for army; discharges. D. S. of John Hancock. Enclosed in President of Congress to Washington, 1776, Oct. 2.   89, 328

1776
[SEP.]

Continental Army, Prisoners. Return of prisoners sent from Canada by Sir Guy Carleton. 1 p. In handwriting of Tench Tilghman. Enclosed in Washington to the President of Congress, 1776, Sep. 25.   C. C. 152, 3, 57

[1776]
[SEP.]

Hand, Edward. [Harlem Heights]. To [George Washington, Harlem]. Recommending William Patten for third lieutenant. Transcript. Enclosed in Washington to the President of Congress, 1776, Oct. 5.   C. C. 169, 2, 202

1776
OCT. 1

Continental Congress, Resolves. The Quartermaster Generalship. D. S. of John Hancock. Enclosed in President of Congress to Washington, 1776, Oct. 2.   89, 328

1776
OCT. 2

Washington, George. Harlem Heights. To [the President of Congress, Philadelphia]. Enemy recruiting on Long Island; militia; movements of British. L. S. 4 pp. In handwriting of Robert Hanson Harrison. Read in Congress, Oct. 4.   C. C. 152, 3, 87
Printed with omission: Writings of Washington (Ford) N. Y. 1889. 4, 461.

1776
OCT. 2

Continental Congress, President. Philadelphia. To [George] Washington [Harlem Heights]. Transmitting resolves. L. S. of John Hancock. 1 p. Answered Oct. 5.*   89, 322

1776
OCT. 2

Continental Congress, Resolves. Report of Committee on supplies needed by army; resolves respecting

wagons; [Maj.] Gen. [Philip John] Schuyler's resignation. D. S. of John Hancock. 3 pp. In handwriting of Timothy Matlack. Enclosed in President of Congress to Washington, 1776, Oct. 4.   89, 333
Committee of Conference with Gen. Mifflin: R. H. Lee, Sherman, J. Adams and Gerry.

1776
Oct. 3
Continental Congress, Resolves. Minor military matters. D. S. of John Hancock. Enclosed in President of Congress to Washington, 1776, Oct. 14.
                                    89, 337

1776
Oct. 3
Continental Congress, Resolve. Loan of five million and establishment of loan offices. Broadside. Transmitted to Washington.   89, 330

1776
Oct. 3
Derby, Richard, jr. Salem [Massachusetts]. To [George Washington, Harlem Heights]. Intelligence of the British fleet. Contemporary copy. 2 pp. In handwriting of Tench Tilghman. Enclosed in Washington to the President of Congress, 1776, Oct. 8.   C. C. 152, 3, 143

1776
Oct. 3
Putnam, Rufus. [Harlem.] To G[eorge] Washington [Harlem]. Establishment for a corps of engineers. 2 pp. A. L. S. Enclosed in Washington to the President of Congress, 1776, Oct. 5.
                                    C. C. 152, 3, 127

1776
Oct. 4
Washington, George. Harlem. To [the President of Congress, Philadelphia]. Measures necessary to recruit the army. A. L. S. 7 pp. Read in Congress, Oct. 8.   C. C. 152, 3, 103
Printed: Writings of Washington (Ford) N. Y. 1889. 4, 466.

1776
Oct. 4
Continental Congress, President. Philadelphia. To [George] Washington [Harlem Heights]. Transmitting resolves; certain appointments. L. S. of John Hancock. 1 p.   89, 331

1776
Oct. 4
Howe, [Sir] W[illiam]. [New] York. To [George] Washington [Harlem]. Exchange of prisoners; Canadian prisoners. Contemporary copy. 2 pp. In handwriting of Tench Tilghman. Enclosed in Washington to the President of Congress, 1776, Oct. 5.   C. C. 152, 3, 123

1776
Oct. 5
Washington, George. Harlem Heights. To [the President of Congress, Philadelphia]. Exchange of prisoners; promotions; engineer corps; prizes; disputes of rank. L. S. 6 pp. In handwriting of Robert Hanson Harrison.   C. C. 152, 3, 111
Printed: Writings of Washington (Ford) N. Y. 1889. 4, 476.

1776
Oct. 7

Washington, George. Harlem Heights. To [the President of Congress, Philadelphia]. Dr. [Alexander] Skinner's errand; demands of regimental surgeons. Letter-book copy. In handwriting of George Lewis.   **M.** III, 83

1776
Oct. 7

Washington, George. Harlem Heights. To [the President of Congress, Philadelphia]. Release of Mons. De Chambeau; commission to P[ierre] Penet; Frenchmen in army. L. S. 2 pp. In handwriting of Robert Hanson Harrison. Read in Congress, Oct. 11.   **C. C.** 152, 3, 131
Printed: Writings of Washington (Ford) N. Y. 1889. 4, 482.

1776
Oct. 7

Continental Congress, Resolve. Counterfeiting. Broadside. Transmitted to Washington.   89, 330

1776
Oct. 7

Continental Congress, Resolves. Muster-master of the Flying Camp; commissary of prisoners; pay of officers. D. S. of John Hancock. Enclosed in President of Congress to Washington, 1776, Oct. 14.   89, 337

1776
Oct. 7

McCumber, Mathew. Harlem Heights. Court-martial. Report of members of court respecting the verdict. D. S.: Comfort Sage, Prest. Davd. Brearley. Ebr. Howell. Sam. Smith. Thoms. Bourk. Cornelius Higgins. Jacob Good. Leonard Bleeker. Jacob De Witt. 1 p. Enclosed in Washington to the President of Congress, 1776, Oct. 8.   **C. C.** 152, 3, 147

1776
Oct. 8

Washington, George. Harlem Heights. To [the President of Congress, Philadelphia]. Exchange of prisoners; bounty; Ensign McCumber's court-martial; enemy's movements. L. S. 4 pp. In handwriting of Robert Hanson Harrison.
    C. C. 152, 3, 139
Printed: Writings of Washington (Ford) N. Y. 1889. 4, 485.

1776
Oct. 8

Continental Congress, Resolves. Increase of army; officers. D. S. of John Hancock. Enclosed in President of Congress to Washington, 1776, Oct. 14.
    89, 337

1776
Oct. 9

Continental Congress, President. Philadelphia. To [George] Washington [Harlem Heights]. Pay, clothing and bounty for troops. L. S. of John Hancock. 2 pp. In handwriting of Jacob Rush.
    89, 335

1776
Oct. 9

Continental Congress, Resolves. Hospital matters; commissary department. D. S. of John Hancock. Enclosed in President of Congress to Washington, 1776, Oct. 14.   **89, 337**

1776
Oct. 10

Continental Congress, Resolves. Vessels for lakes [Champlain and George]; paymasters; exchange of officers; impressment of teams; miscellaneous military promotions; commissions; Canadians. D. S. of John Hancock. Enclosed in President of Congress to Washington, 1776, Oct. 14.

89, 337

1776
Oct. 10

New York, Committee of Safety. Fishkill. To Gen. [George] Washington [Harlem]. Activity of the New York loyalists. Contemporary copy. 1 p. In handwriting of Morgan Lewis. Enclosed in Washington to the President of Congress, 1776, Oct. 11.   **C. C.   152, 3, 153**

1776
Oct. 11

Washington, George. Harlem Heights. To [the President of Congress, Philadelphia]. Movements of enemy's ships; loyalists. L. S. 2 pp. In handwriting of Robert Hanson Harrison. Read in Congress, Oct. 15. "Nothing to be reported on this letter."   **C. C.   152, 3, 149**

Printed, in part: Writings of Washington (Ford) N. Y. 1889. 4, 497 and 498, notes.

1776
Oct. 12

Arnold, B[enedict]. Schuyler's Island [Lake Champlain, New York]. To [Maj. Gen. Horatio Gates, Albany]. Account of naval action off Valcour Island. Contemporary copy. 3 pp. In handwriting of William Grayson. Enclosed in Washington to the President of Congress, 1776, Oct. 18.   **C. C.   152, 3, 163**

1776
Oct. 12

Hoisington, Joab. Newbury [New Hampshire]. To Maj. Gen. [Horatio] Gates [Ticonderoga]. Reports of deserters. Contemporary copy. 1 p. In handwriting of William Grayson. Enclosed in Washington to the President of Congress, 1776, Nov. 9.   **C. C.   152, 3, 227**

1776
Oct. 14

Continental Congress, Resolves. Allowances and pay of officers. D. S. of John Hancock. Enclosed in President of Congress to Washington, 1776, Oct. 24.   **90, 3**

1776
Oct. 14

Harrison, Rob[ert] H[anson]. Harlem Heights. To [the President of Congress, Philadelphia]. Activity

of the New York loyalists; manœuvers of the two armies. A. L. S. 2 pp. Read in Congress, Oct. 21.   C. C. 152, 3, 155
<small>Printed, in part: Writings of Washington (Ford) N. Y. 1889. 4, 498, note.</small>

1776
Oct. 15

Continental Congress, Resolves. Clothing and blankets. D. S. of John Hancock. Enclosed in President of Congress to Washington, 1776, Oct. 24. **90, 3**

1776
Oct. 15

Board of War. [Philadelphia.] To George Washington, Harlem Heights. Monthly returns of military stores. L. S. of Richard Peters. 2 pp. In handwriting of Timothy Matlack. Answered Oct. 22* by Harrison.   **12, 87**

1776
Oct. 16

Continental Congress, Resolves. Commissaries of clothing in Northern and Main armies. D. S. of John Hancock. Enclosed in President of Congress to Washington, 1776, Oct. 24.   **90, 3**

1776
Oct. 16

Schuyler, Ph[ilip John]. Saratoga [New York]. To [George] Washington [Harlem]. Defeat on Lake Champlain. Contemporary copy. 1 p. In handwriting of Tench Tilghman. Enclosed in Harrison to the President of Congress, 1776, Oct. 20.   C. C. 152, 3, 171

1776
Oct. 17

Deane, S[ilas]. Paris. To [George] Washington [Harlem Heights, New York]. Introducing Mottin de la Balme. Contemporary copy. 1 p. In handwriting of Richard Kidder Meade. Enclosed in Washington to the President of Congress, 1777, May 9.   C. C. 152, 4, 169

1776
Oct. 18

Washington, George. Harlem Heights. To [the President of Congress, Philadelphia]. Intelligence from Canada; general situation. L. S. 1 p. In handwriting of Robert Hanson Harrison. Read in Congress, Oct. 21.   C. C. 152, 3, 159

1776
Oct. 18

Continental Congress, Resolves. [Thaddeus] Kosciusko's appointment; money for Northern Army; flints; Commissary deputies; rations; form of oath of allegiance. D. S. of John Hancock. Enclosed in President of Congress to Washington, 1776, Oct. 24.   **90, 5**

1776
Oct. 20

[**Harrison**, Robert Hanson]. Kingsbridge [New York]. To [the President of] Congress [Philadelphia]. Manoeuvers of the British and Continental armies. Auto. draft. 2 pp. Read in Congress, Oct. 21.   A. II, 1
<small>Printed: Writings of Washington, (Ford), N. Y. 1889. 4, 500, notes.</small>

1776
Oct. 21

Harrison, Rob[ert] H[anson]. Valentine's Hill [New York]. To the President of Congress, Philadelphia. Nothing of importance to communicate. A. L. S. 1 p. Read in Congress, Oct. 25.

C. C. 152, 3, 173

1776
Oct. 22

[**Harrison,** Robert Hanson]. Valentine's Hill. To the Board of War [Philadelphia]. French gentlemen; monthly returns of ordnance stores; Magazines; rations. Auto. draft. 2 pp. A. II, 3

1776
Oct. 23

Continental Congress, Resolves. Blankets and clothing in Rhode Island. D. S. of John Hancock. Enclosed in President of Congress to Washington. 1776, Oct. 24. 90, 5

1776
Oct. 23

Continental Congress, Resolve. Appointment of William Maxwell and William Smallwood as brigadiers. A. D. S. of John Hancock. 1 p. Enclosed in President of Congress to Washington, 1776, Oct. 24. 90, 9

1776
Oct. 24

Continental Congress, President. Philadelphia. To [George Washington, White Plains, New York]. Forwarding resolves. L. S. of John Hancock. 1 p. 90, 1

1776
Oct. 24

Board of War. [Philadelphia.] To [George] Washington [White Plains]. Ration returns and pay of discharged soldiers. A. L. S. of Richard Peters. 1 p. 95, 305

1776
Oct. 24

Board of War. [Philadelphia.] To [George] Washington [White Plains]. Situation of affairs in Pennsylvania. L. S. of Richard Peters. 2 pp. In handwriting of John Clark, jr. 95, 306

1776
Oct. 24

Board of War. Plan for returns of rations and pay of discharged soldiers. A. D., of Richard Peters. 2 pp. Enclosed in Board of War to Washington, 1776, Oct. 24. 95, 307

1776
Oct. 25

[**Harrison,** Robert Hanson.] White Plains. To [the President of] Congress [Philadelphia]. Movement of troops and stores; skirmishes [at Mamaroneck]; obstructing channel; advance of enemy; control of North River; formation of two armies to operate on both sides of river. Auto. draft. 3 pp. Read in Congress, Nov. 4. A. II, 5

1776
Oct. 26

Board of War. [Philadelphia.] To James Mease [Philadelphia]. Clothing issues; shoes, hats etc. Con-

temporary copy. 2 pp. Enclosed in Board of
War to Washington 1776, Oct. 27.   **95, 308**

1776
Oct. 27

Board of War. Philadelphia. To [George] Washington
[White Plains]. Returns of clothing issued.
A. L. S. of Richard Peters. 1 p. Answered
Nov. 11.   **95, 310**

1776
Oct. 27

Lee, Richard Henry. Philadelphia. To [George Washington, White Plains]. Military successes; intentions of Great Britain; military supplies; the
French court. A. L. S. 3 pp.   **12, 122**

1776
Oct. 28

Continental Congress, President. Philadelphia. To
[George] Washington, White Plains. Robbery
of the express. A. L. S. 2 pp. Answered Nov.
1* by Harrison.   **12, 124**

1776
Oct. 29

[Harrison, Robert Hanson.] White Plains. To [the
President of] Congress [Philadelphia]. Battle [of
White Plains]; difficulty of removing stores.
Auto. draft. 2 pp.   **A. II, 9**

1776
Oct. 31

Board of War. [Philadelphia.] To [George] Washington
[White Plains]. Introducing chevalier Lan-
tagniac. A. L. S. of Richard Peters. 1 p. Answered Nov. 8*.   **95, 312**

1776
Oct. 31

Gates, Horatio. Ticonderoga [New York]. To [Maj.] Gen.
[Philip John] Schuyler [Albany]. Enemy's feint
against Ticonderoga. Contemporary copy. 2 pp.
In handwriting of Tench Tilghman. Enclosed in
Washington to the President of Congress, 1776,
Nov. 9.   **C. C. 152, 3, 223**

1776
Oct. 31

Harrison, Rob[ert] H[anson]. White Plains. To [the
President of Congress, Philadelphia]. The mili-
tary situation; militia. A. L. S. 2 pp. Read in
Congress, Nov. 5.   **C. C. 152, 3, 189**

1776
Nov. 1

Harrison, Robert H[anson]. White Plains. To [the President of] Congress [Philadelphia]. Loss of letters;
situation of the army; difficulty in moving stores;
lack of flour. Auto. draft signed. 2 pp. Read
in Congress, Nov. 4.   **A. II, 11**
Printed in part: Writings of Washington (Ford) N.Y. 1890. 5, 25, note.

1776
Nov. 3

Washington, George. [White Plains.] To Dr. William
Shippen jr., Newark [New Jersey]. Establish-
ment of hospitals; Dr. [John] Morgan's authority.
L. S. 1 p. In handwriting of Tench Tilghman.
Read in Congress, Nov. 6.   **C. C. 152, 3, 197**

Sir   Head quarters Cambridge August 19: 1775.

I addressed you on the 11th Instant in Terms,
which gave the fairest Scope for the Exercise of that Humanity, & Politeness,
which were supposed to form a Part of your Character. I remonstrated with
you on the unworthy Treatment, shewn to the officers and Citizens of
America, whom the Fortune of War, chance, or a mistaken Confidence,
had thrown into your Hands.

Whether British or American Mercy,
Fortitude, and Patience are most pre-eminent. — whether our virtuous
Citizens whom the Hand of Tyranny has forced into arms to defend their
Wives, their Children, and their Property, or the mercenary Instruments
of lawless Domination, avarice and Revenge, best deserve the Appellation
of Rebels, and the Punishment of that Cord, which your affected Clemency
has forborne to inflict: whether the authority, under which I act, is
usurped, or founded upon the genuine Principles of Liberty, were altogether
foreign to the Subject. I purposely avoided all political Disquisition; nor
shall I now avail myself of those Advantages, which the sacred Cause of
my Country, of Liberty, and human Nature give me over you. Much less
shall I stoop to Retort and Invective. But the Intelligence you say you have
received from our Army requires a Reply — I have taken Time, Sir, to make
a strict Inquiry, and find it has not the least Foundation in Truth. Not
only your Officers and soldiers have been treated with a Tenderness
due to Fellow-Citizens, and Brethren, but even those execrable Parricides
whose Councels and Aid have deluged their Country with Blood, have been
protected from the Fury of a justly-enraged People. Far from compelling
or permitting their Assistance, I am embarrassed with the Numbers, who
crowd to our Camp, animated with the purest Principles of Virtue, and Love
of their Country — You advise me to give free operation to Truth, to punish
Misrepresentation and Falsehood. If Experience stamps Value upon Counsel,
yours must have a Weight, which few can claim. You best can tell, how far
the Convulsion, which has brought such Ruin on both Countries, and shaken
the mighty Empire of Britain to its Foundation, may be traced to these
malignant Causes.

You affect, Sir, to despise all Rank, not derived from
the same Source with your own. I cannot conceive one more honourable,
than that, which flows from the uncorrupted Choice of a brave and free People, the purest Source, and original Fountain of all Power. Far from
making it a Plea for Cruelty, a Mind of true Magnanimity, and
enlarged Ideas would comprehend, and respect it.

What may have been
the ministerial Views, which have precipitated the present Crisis, Lex-
ington, Concord, and Charles-Town can best declare. May that God to whom
you then appealed, judge between America and you. Under his

WRITING OF EDMUND RANDOLPH.

1776 Nov. 3	**Harrison,** Robert Hanson. White Plains. To [the President of] Congress [Philadelphia]. Desertion of troops. A. L. S. 1 p. Read in Congress, Nov. 6. C. C. **152,** 3, 201 Printed in part: Writings of Washington (Ford) N. Y. 1889. 5, 2, note.
1776 Nov. 4	**H[arrison,]** R[obert] H[anson]. White Plains. To the Board of War [Philadelphia]. Rations and payment of sick; defection in Pennsylvania. Auto. draft signed. 2 pp. **A.** II, 15 Printed: Writings of Washington (Ford) N. Y. 1890. 5, 2, note.
1776 Nov. 4	**Harrison,** Rob[ert] H[anson]. White Plains. To [the President of Congress, Philadelphia]. Introducing Monsieurs Robillard D'Antin and Bordes. A. L. S. 1 p. Read in Congress, Nov. 14. Referred to the Board of War. C. C. **152,** 3, 209
1776 Nov. 4	**Continental Congress,** Resolves. Appointment of officers to recruit the army. D. S. of John Hancock. 2 pp. Enclosed in President of Congress to Washington, 1776, Nov. 5. **90,** 10
1776 Nov. 5	**Continental Congress,** President. Philadelphia. To [George] Washington [White Plains]. Commissions for officers; power of appointment. L. S. of John Hancock. 2 pp. In handwriting of Jacob Rush. **90,** 7
1776 Nov. 6	**Washington,** George. White Plains. To [the President of] Congress [Philadelphia]. Movement of enemy; approaching dissolution of the army. Draft. 4 pp. In handwriting of Samuel Blatchley Webb. Read in Congress, Nov. 11. **A.** II, 19 Printed: Writings of Washington (Ford) N. Y. 1890. 5, 1.
1776 Nov. 6	**Continental Army,** Council of War. White Plains. Troops to be thrown into Jersey and on east side of the Hudson. Contemporary copy. 2 pp. In handwriting of Tench Tilghman. Enclosed in Washington to the President of Congress, 1776, Nov. 6. C. C. **152,** 3, 213
1776 Nov. 7	**Continental Congress,** Resolve. Allowance to officers for enlisting soldiers in camp. Contemporary copy. 1 p. Enclosed in Board of War to Washington, 1777, May 20. **95,** 319
1776 Nov. 7	**Continental Congress,** Resolves. Allowance for reenlistments; deserters; exchange of prisoners; military appointments. D. S. of John Hancock. 2 pp. Enclosed in President of Congress to Washington, 1776, Nov. 9. **90,** 14

1776
Nov. 7

Lovell, James. Fort Lee [New Jersey]. To [the President of Congress, Philadelphia]. Intelligence of enemy's designs. [Extract of letter.] Contemporary copy. 1 p. In handwriting of Charles Thomson.
         C. C. 152, 3, 233

1776
Nov. 8

Washington, George. White Plains. To [the Board of War, Philadelphia]. French gentlemen in the army. L. S. 2 pp. In the handwriting of Robert Hanson Harrison.   C. C. 152, 3, 229
Printed: Writings of Washington (Ford) N. Y. 1890. 5, 11.

1776
Nov. 8

Board of War. [Philadelphia.] To [George] Washington [White Plains]. Permission to certain ladies to enter New York. L. S.: Benj. Harrison, James Wilson, Edward Rutledge. 2 pp. Answered Nov. 15.*   95, 325

1776
Nov. 8

Howe, [Sir] W[illiam]. [New York.] To [George] Washington [White Plains]. Return of an officer's servant; exchange of prisoners. Contemporary copy. 1 p. In handwriting of Samuel Blatchley Webb. Enclosed in Washington to the President of Congress, 1776, Nov. 14.   C. C. 152, 3, 239

1776
Nov. 9

Washington, George. White Plains. To [the President of] Congress [Philadelphia]. Transmitting letters from the Northern Army; British expedition into the Jerseys. Draft. 1 p. In handwriting of Robert Hanson Harrison. Read in Congress, Nov. 12.   A. II, 21
Printed in part: Writings of Washington (Ford) N. Y. 1890. 5, 12, note.

1776
Nov. 9

Washington, George. [White Plains.] To [Lt.] Gen. [Sir William] Howe [New York]. Exchange of prisoners. Contemporary copy. 2 pp. Enclosed in Washington to the President of Congress, 1776, Nov. 14.   C. C. 152, 3, 235
Printed: Writings of Washington (Ford) N. Y. 1890. 5, 12.

1776
Nov. 9

Continental Congress, President. Philadelphia. To [George] Washington [White Plains]. Reenlistment allowance; deserters; exchange of prisoners; pay of Massachusetts troops. L. S. of John Hancock. 2 pp. In handwriting of Jacob Rush. Answered Nov. 19.*   90, 12

1776
Nov. 11

Washington, George. Peekskill. To [the President of] Congress [Philadelphia]. Recruiting service; designs of British; Massachusetts and Connecticut

pay to soldiers. Draft. 2 pp. In handwriting
of Robert Hanson Harrison. Read in Congress,
Nov. 15. **A. II, 23**
Printed: Writings of Washington (Ford) N. Y. 1890. 5, 20.

1776
Nov. 11
Howe, [Sir] W[illiam]. [New York.] To [George] Washington [Peekskill, New York]. Exchange of
prisoners. Contemporary copy. 2 pp. In handwriting of W...am Grayson. Enclosed in Washington to the President of Congress, 1776,
Nov. 14. **C. C. 152, 3, 241**
Printed: Writings of Washington (Sparks) Boston. 1834. 4, 529.

[1776]
[Nov. 13]
Searle, James. Long Branch [New Jersey]. To [John
Hancock? Philadelphia]. Conveyance of letters;
sailing of a British fleet. Contemporary copy.
2 pp. Enclosed in President of Congress to
Washington, 1776, Nov. 14. **90, 20**

1776
Nov. 14
Washington, George. "Genl. Greene's Qrs." [Fort Lee,
New Jersey.] To [the President of] Congress
[Philadelphia]. Movement of troops; increase of
field artillery; exchange of prisoners. Draft.
5 pp. In handwriting of Robert Hanson Harri-
son. Read in Congress, Nov. 18. **A. II, 29**

1776
Nov. 14
Continental Congress, President. Philadelphia. To
[George] Washington [White Plains]. Destina-
tion of a British fleet. L. S. of John Hancock.
1 p. In handwriting of Jacob Rush. **90, 18**

1776
Nov. 14
Board of War. [Philadelphia.] To [George] Washington
[Fort Lee, New Jersey]. British probable ad-
vance against Philadelphia; [Brig.] Gen. [Thomas]
Mifflin and defense of the city. A. L. S. of E.
Rutledge, signed also by Benj. Harrison, James
Wilson, and Francis Lightfoot Lee. 1 p.
95, 327

1776
Nov. 15
Washington, George. Hackensack [New Jersey]. To the
Board of War, Philadelphia. Permission to
ladies to go into New York. L. S. 1 p. In
handwriting of Robert Hanson Harrison.
C. C. 152, 3, 253

1776
Nov. 15
Continental Congress, Resolve. Cargo of the *Hancock &
Adams* appropriated for use of the Army. Con-
temporary copy, attested by Richard Peters. 1 p.
Enclosed in Board of War to Washington, 1776,
Nov. 18. **95, 329**

1776
Nov. 15

Washington, George. Hackensack. To the Board of War, Philadelphia. Exchange of prisoners. L. S. 1 p. In handwriting of Robert Hanson Harrison. C. C. 152, 3, 257

Printed, in part: Writings of Washington (Ford) N. Y. 1890. 5, 30; note.

1776
Nov. 16

Continental Congress, President. Philadelphia. To [George] Washington [Fort Lee, New Jersey]. Exchange of Hessians. L. S. of John Hancock. 1 p. In handwriting of Jacob Rush. Answered Nov. 19*. 90, 21

1776
Nov. 16

Washington, George. "Gen. Greene's Qrs." [Hackensack.] To [the President of] Congress. [Philadelphia]. The surrender of Fort Washington. Draft. 4 pp. In handwriting of Joseph Reed. Read in Congress, Nov. 19. A. II, 33

Printed: Writings of Washington (Ford) N. Y. 1890. 5, 33.

1776
Nov. 18

Board of War. [Philadelphia.] To [George] Washington [Hackensack]. Cargo of the *Hancock & Adams.* A. L. S. ? of Francis Lightfoot Lee, signed also by Benj. Harrison and James Wilson. 1 p. Answered Nov. 30*. 95, 331

1776
Nov. 19

Washington, George. Hackensack. To [the President of] Congress [Philadelphia]. Surrender of Fort Washington; capture of Fort Lee and loss of stores. Draft. 5 pp. In handwriting of Robert Hanson Harrison. Read in Congress, Nov. 23. A. II, 37–41

Printed: Writings of Washington (Ford) N. Y. 1890. 5, 41.

1776
Nov. 19

Continental Congress, Resolve. Monthly commissary returns; pay of sick; magazines of military stores; state quotas of troops. D. S. of John Hancock. Enclosed in President of Congress to Washington, 1776, Nov. 24. 90, 25

1776
Nov. 19

Continental Congress, Resolve. Pay of soldiers discharged from service through the hospitals. Contemporary copy, attested by Timothy Pickering jr. 2 pp. Enclosed in Board of War to Washington, 1778, May 12. 95, 333

1776
Nov. 19

Board of War. [Philadelphia.] To [George] Washington [Hackensack]. Prisoners ordered to Fort Lee; enlistment of prisoners in Continental Army. L. S. of Richard Peters. In handwriting of John Clark jr. 95, 339

1776
Nov. 21

Continental Congress, President. Philadelphia. To [George] Washington [Hackensack]. Troops for the new army; preparation for coming campaign. L. S. of John Hancock. 2 pp. In handwriting of Jacob Rush.   90, 23

1776
Nov. 22

Continental Congress, Resolve. Enlistments for the war. D. S. of John Hancock. Enclosed in President of Congress to Washington, 1776, Nov. 24.

90, 25

1776
Nov. 22

Continental Congress, Resolves. Power of appointment of army officers; committee to repair to head-quarters; hides and tallow. A. D. S. of John Hancock. Enclosed in President of Congress to Washington, 1776, Nov. 24.   90, 29

1776
Nov. 22

Continental Congress, Resolves. Reenforcements; troops from North; exchange of [Gov.] William Franklin. A. D. S. of John Hancock. Enclosed in President of Congress to Washington, 1776, Nov. 24.   90, 29

1776
Nov. 23

Washington, George. Newark [New Jersey]. To [the President of] Congress [Philadelphia]. Critical state of affairs; militia and payment of the Flying Camp. Draft. 2 pp. In handwriting of Robert Hanson Harrison. Read in Congress Nov. 25.
A. II, 43
Printed: Writings of Washington (Sparks) Boston. 1834. 4, 190.

1776
Nov. 23

Board of War. [Philadelphia.] To [George] Washington [Newark]. Prisoners sent to Brunswick. A. L. S. of Richard Peters. 1. p. Answered Nov. 30.*
95, 336

[1776]
[Nov. 23]

Continental Army. Abstract of returns of troops at Newark, fit for duty. 1 p. In handwriting of Joseph Reed. Enclosed in Washington to the President of Congress, 1776, Nov. 23.   C. C.   152, 3, 273

1776
Nov. 24

Continental Congress, President. Philadelphia. To [George] Washington [Newark]. Committee of Conference; troops from Pennsylvania and New Jersey; exchange of [Gov. William] Franklin; reenforcement measures. L. S. of John Hancock. 2 pp. In handwriting of Jacob Rush. Answered Nov 27.*   90, 27

1776
Nov. 25

Continental Congress, Resolves. Ordering Pennsylvania militia and Virginia light horse to join the Army;

[Brig.] Gen. [Thomas] Mifflin in Philadelphia. L. S. of John Hancock. 2 pp. Enclosed in President of Congress to Washington, 1776, Nov. 26. 90, 33

1776
Nov. 26

Continental Congress, President. Philadelphia. To [George] Washington [Newark]. Reenforcements for army. L. S. of John Hancock. 2 pp. In handwriting of Jacob Rush. Answered Nov. 30.* 90, 31

1776
Nov. 27

Washington, George. Newark. To [the President of] Congress [Philadelphia]. Northern troops; enemy in the Jerseys; exchange and enlistment of prisoners in the British army. Draft. 2 pp. In handwriting of Robert Hanson Harrison. Read in Congress, Nov. 30. A, II, 45
Printed in part: Writings of Washington (Ford) N. Y. 1890. 5, 53, note.

1776
Nov. 27

Anonymous. Boston. Extract of letter giving intelligence of British store ship. 1 p. In handwriting of George Lewis. Enclosed in Washington to the President of Congress, 1776, Nov. 27.
C. C. 152, 3, 347

1776
Nov. 28

Continental Congress, Resolves. Cannon casting; provisions at Albany; hospital for Northern Army; inquiry into hospital affairs; batteaux on the lakes. D. S. of John Hancock. Enclosed in President of Congress to Washington, 1777, Jan. 1. 20, 87

1776
Nov. 29

Clark, John jr. Tappan [New York]. To [George] Washington [New Brunswick, New Jersey]. Deserter's intelligence; removal of stores. Contemporary copy. 1 p. In handwriting of Morgan Lewis. Enclosed in Washington to the President of Congress, 1776, Dec. 4.
C. C. 152, 3, 315

1776
Nov. 30

Washington, George. Brunswick [New Jersey]. To [the President of] Congress [Philadelphia]. Reenforcement by militia; enemy's advance into Jersey; desertions. Draft. 2 pp. In handwriting of Robert Hanson Harrison. Read in Congress, Dec. 1. A. II, 47
Printed: Writings of Washington (Ford) N. Y. 1890. 5, 54.

1776
Nov. 30

Washington, George. Brunswick. To the Board of War [Philadelphia]. Stores captured from enemy;

enlistment of prisoners. Draft. 2 pp. In handwriting of Tench Tilghman.   A. II, 51
Printed: Writings of Washington (Ford) N. Y. 1890. 5, 58.

1776
Nov. 30

Deane, Silas. Paris. To [George] Washington [New
Brunswick]. Introducing Col. [Thomas] Conway. Contemporary copy. 1 p. In handwriting
of Richard Kidder Meade. Enclosed in Washington to the President of Congress 1777, May 9.
                                        C. C.   152, 4, 163

1776
[Nov.]

Miles, Samuel. [Long Island]. To William Wister, Philadelphia. His exchange. A. L. S. 1 p. En-
closed in President of Congress to Washington
1776, Nov. 7.   90, 16

1776
Dec. 1

Washington, George. Brunswick. To [the President of]
Congress [Philadelphia]. Designs of the enemy
on Philadelphia; exchange of Col. [Daniel] Mor-
gan and Maj. [William] Heath. Draft. 2 pp.
In handwriting of Robert Hanson Harrison.
Read in Congress, Dec. 2.   A. II, 53

1776
Dec. 1

Washington, George. Brunswick. To the President of
Congress, Philadelphia. Advance of the enemy
into Jersey. L. S. 1 p. In handwriting of
Robert Hanson Harrison. Read in Congress,
Dec. 2.   C. C. 152, 3, 291
Printed: Writings of Washington (Ford) N. Y. 1890. 5, 62, note.

1776
Dec. 1

Continental Congress, President. Philadelphia. To
[George] Washington [New Brunswick]. Troops
east of the Hudson; clothing. L. S. of John
Hancock. 2 pp. In handwriting of Jacob Rush.
Answered Dec. 2.*   90, 34

1776
Dec. 1

Continental Congress, Resolve. Clothing for Army; troops
on east side of the Hudson; relief of sick. D. S.
of John Hancock. 2 pp. Enclosed in President
of Congress to Washington, 1776, Dec. 1. 90, 36

1776
Dec. 2

Washington, George. Princeton [New Jersey]. To the
President of Congress, Philadelphia. Advance
of enemy into Jersey; removal of prisoners.
L. S. 1 p. In handwriting of Robert Hanson
Harrison. Read in Congress, Dec. 3.
                                        C. C. 152, 3, 295
Printed, in part: Writings of Washington (Ford) N. Y. 1890. 5, 63.

1776
Dec. 2

Washington, George. [Princeton.] To Capt. [Nicholas
Dietrich, Baron de] Ottendorff [Princeton]. Au-

thorizing raising of a German battalion. D. S.
1 p.   Enclosed in Washington to the President of
Congress, 1776, Dec. 2.   C. C.   152, 3, 299

1776
Dec. 3

Washington, George. Trenton [New Jersey]. To [the
President of] Congress [Philadelphia]. Transportation of stores; delay of [Maj.] Gen. [Charles]
Lee; Pennsylvania militia. Draft. 2 pp. In
handwriting of Tench Tilghman. Read in Congress, Dec. 4.   A. II, 55
Printed: Writings of Washington (Ford) N. Y. 1890. 5, 64.

1776
Dec. 3

Continental Congress, Resolves. Removal of prisoners into
the country; exchange of Gov. [William] Frank-
lin. Contemporary copy. In handwriting of
Jacob Rush. Transmitted to Washington with
President of Congress to Washington, 1776,
Dec. 4.   90, 38

1776
Dec. 4

Washington, George. Trenton. To [the President of]
Congress [Philadelphia]. [Maj.] Gen. [Charles]
Lee's delay; reports of enemy's movements.
Draft. 2 pp. In handwriting of Robert Hanson
Harrison. Read in Congress, Dec. 5. A. II, 57

1776
Dec. 4

Washington, George. Trenton. To the Board of War
[Philadelphia]. British prisoners not to be
allowed to come to the Continental army. Draft.
1 p. In handwriting of Tench Tilghman.
                                A. II, 59

1776
Dec. 4

Continental Congress, President. Philadelphia. To
[George] Washington, Trenton. Exchange of
Gov. [William] Franklin. L. S. of John Hancock. In handwriting of Jacob Rush. Answered Dec. 6.*   90, 38

1776
Dec. 5

Washington, George. Trenton. To [the President of]
Congress [Philadelphia]. Advance of the enemy;
disadvantages of depending on militia. A. L.
2 pp. and scrap.   A. II, 63
Printed: Writings of Washington (Ford) N. Y. 1890. 5, 66.

1776
Dec. 6

Washington, George. Trenton. To [the President of]
Congress [Philadelphia]. Movements of enemy;
Howe's proclamation of pardon. 1 p. In hand-
writing of Robert Hanson Harrison. Read in
Congress, Dec. 7.   A. II, 65
Printed: Writings of Washington (Ford) N. Y. 1890. 5, 69.

1776
Dec. 8

Washington, George. [Barclay's, Bucks County, Penn-
sylvania]. To [the President of] Congress [Phila-
delphia]. Retreat from Princeton; [Maj.] Gen.

[Charles] Lee's delay. A. D. 2 pp. Read in Congress, Dec. 9. **A. II, 67**
Printed: Writings of Washington (Ford) N. Y. 1890. 5, 71.

1776
Dec. 8
Cooke, Nicholas. Providence [Rhode Island]. To [George] Washington [Barclay's, Pennsylvania]. British descent on Newport. Contemporary copy. 1 p. In handwriting of Samuel Blatchley Webb. Enclosed in Washington to the President of Congress, 1776, Dec. 20. **C. C. 152, 3, 385**

1779
Dec. 9
Washington, George. Trenton Falls. To [the President of] Congress [Philadelphia]. Fortifications for defense of Philadelphia. Draft. 2 pp. In handwriting of Tench Tilghman. Read in Congress, Dec. 10. **A. II, 69**
Printed: Writings of Washington (Ford) N. Y. 1890. 5, 72.

1776
Dec. 10
Washington, George. Falls of Delaware. To [the President of] Congress [Philadelphia]. Movements of the enemy; Lee's delay. Draft. 1 p. In handwriting of Robert Hanson Harrison. Read in Congress, Dec. 11. **A. II, 73**
Printed: Writings of Washington (Note) N. Y. 1890. 5, 76, note.

1776
Dec. 11
Washington, George. Falls of Delaware. To [the President of] Congress [Philadelphia]. Crossing of the Delaware by the enemy; Lee's delay; valuable services of Major [Elisha] Sheldon's troop. Draft. 2 pp. In handwriting of Tench Tilghman. Read in Congress, Dec. 12. **A. II, 75**
Printed in part: Writings of Washington (Ford) N. Y. 1890. 5, 80.

1776
Dec. 11
Continental Congress, Secretary. [Philadelphia.] To Gen. [George] Washington [Barclay's]. Transmitting resolve. A. L. S. of Charles Thomson. 1 p. Answered Dec. 12.* **90, 40**

1776
Dec. 11
Continental Congress, Resolve. Dispersion of Congress. A. D. S. of Charles Thomson. Transmitted to Washington with Secretary of Congress to Washington, 1776, Dec. 11. **90, 40**

1776
Dec. 12
Washington, George. Trenton Falls. To [the President of Congress, Philadelphia]. Removal of Congress; military situation; payment of troops. Draft. 4 pp. In handwriting of Robert Hanson Harrison. Read in Congress, Dec. 20. **A. II, 77**
Printed: Writings of Washington (Ford). 1890. 5, 82.

1776
Dec. 12
Continental Congress, Secretary. Philadelphia. To [George] Washington [Barclay's]. Transmitting resolves. A. L. S. of Charles Thomson. **90, 44**

1776
DEC. 12

Continental Congress, Resolves. Frigates to defend Philadelphia; Sheldon's dragoons; adjournment of Congress; plenary power to Washington. A. D. S.
of Charles Thomson. Transmitted to Washington with Secretary of Congress to Washington,
1776, Dec. 12.   **90, 44**

1776
DEC. 13

Washington, George. Trenton Falls. To [the President
of Congress, Philadelphia]. Disposition of troops
for defense of the Delaware; recruiting. L. S.
2 pp. In handwriting of Tench Tilghman and
Robert Hanson Harrison.   **C. C.   152, 3, 351**
The draft, A II, 81, in handwriting of John Armstrong, Washington,
Tilghman and Harrison, is dated Dec. 12.
Printed: Writings of Washington (Ford) N. Y. 1890. 5, 89.

1776
DEC. 13

Sullivan, John. Germantown [Pennsylvania]. To [George]
Washington [Trenton Falls]. Capture of [Maj.]
Gen. [Charles] Lee. Contemporary copy. 1 p.
In handwriting of Morgan Lewis. Enclosed in
Washington to the President of Congress, 1776,
Dec. 15.   **C. C.   152, 3, 359**

1776
DEC. 13

[Trumbull, Joseph.] Morristown [New Jersey]. To
[George] Washington [Trenton Falls]. Salt provisions, supplies and commissary business. Contemporary copy. 2 pp. In handwriting of Morgan Lewis. Enclosed in Washington to the
President of Congress, 1776, Dec. 16.

C. C.   152, 3, 365

1776
DEC. 15

Washington, George. Keith's [Pennsylvania]. To [the
President of Congress, Philadelphia]. Capture
of Lee; movements of enemy. Draft. 2 pp.
In handwriting of Robert Hanson Harrison.
Read in Congress, Dec. 20.   **A. II, 85**
Printed: Writings of Washington (Ford) N. Ý. 1890. 5, 100.

1776
DEC. 16

Washington, George. Keith's. To [the President of Congress, Philadelphia]. Importance of increasing
the army; militia; Howe's designs; Commissary
General's need of money; clothing. Draft. 3
pp. In handwriting of Robert Hanson Harrison.
Read in Congress, Dec. 26.   **A. II, 87**
Printed, except paragraph relating to Commissary General: Writings
of Washington (Ford) N. Y. 1890. 5, 101.

[1776]
[DEC. 18]

[Knox, Henry.] Plan for establishing a corps of Continental Artillery, magazines, laboratories, etc.
Draft. 3 pp. In handwriting of John Fitzgerald. Enclosed in Washington to Congress 1776,
Dec. 20.   **A. II, 103**

1776
DEC. 20

W[ashingto]n, G[eorge]. Above Trenton Falls. To [the President of Congress, Baltimore]. Artillery; militia and short enlistments; system of army management; promotions. A. L. S. 9 pp. Read in Congress, Dec. 26. **A. II, 93**

Printed: Writings of Washington (Ford) N. Y. 1890. 5, 112.

1776
DEC. 20

Continental Congress, Resolve. British treatment of [Maj.] Gen. [Charles] Lee. D. S. of John Hancock. Enclosed in President of Congress to Washington, 1776, Dec. 23. **90, 46**

[1776]
[DEC. 20]

[Stephen, Adam.] Memorandum of plan of movements of Virginia troops. 2 pp. In handwriting of Samuel Blatchley Webb. Enclosed in Washington to the President of Congress, 1776, Dec. 20. **A. II, 91**

1776
DEC. 21

Continental Congress, Resolves. Suppression of publication of resolve by Washington; magazines of provisions; new levies; Robert Morris and George Clymer; money for militia; pay of troops. D. S. of John Hancock. Enclosed in President of Congress to Washington, 1776, Dec. 23. **90, 46**

1776
DEC. 21

Morris, Robert. Philadelphia. To George Washington [Trenton Falls]. Supply of blankets and muskets; supplies expected from France; safety in Philadelphia; captivity of [Maj. Gen. Charles] Lee. A. L. S. 3 pp. **12, 285**

1776
DEC. 21

Morris, Robert. Philadelphia. To George Washington [Trenton Falls]. Invoice of blankets and receipt of Hugh Peden for same. A. L. S. 1 p. **12, 289**

1776
DEC. 23

Continental Congress, President. Baltimore. To [George] Washington [above Trenton Falls]. British treatment of [Maj.] Gen. [Charles] Lee; approval of actions; committee left in Philadelphia; pay of militia. L. S. of John Hancock. 3 pp. In handwriting of Jacob Rush. Answered Dec. 29.* **90, 48**

1776
DEC. 23

Morris, Robert. Philadelphia. To [George Washington, Trenton Falls]. The situation and its causes; naval force; prisoners; cargo brought in; situation of [Maj.] Gen. [Charles] Lee. A. L. S. 3 pp. **12, 301**

1776
DEC. 24

Washington, George. Trenton Falls. To [the President of] Congress [Baltimore]. Condition of army;

militia; payment of troops. Draft. 4 pp. In
handwriting of Robert Hanson Harrison.

            A. II, 107

1776
DEC. 25

Washington, George. [McKonkey's Ferry, Pennsylvania.]
To Robert Morris [Philadelphia]. Blankets and
supplies; defection of people; continental ships
in the Delaware; exchange of prisoners. L. S.
3 pp. In handwriting of Tench Tilghman.

         C. C. 152, 3, 393

1776
DEC. 26

Morris, Robert. Philadelphia. To George Washington
[Trenton]. The Philadelphia Committee and cor-
respondence with Congress; success at Trenton.
A. L. S. 2 pp.   12, 310

1776
DEC. 26

Prisoners, British. Return of prisoners taken at Trenton.
Tabular statement. 1 p. In handwriting of Tench
Tilghman. Enclosed in Washington to the Presi-
dent of Congress, 1776, Dec. 27.

         C. C. 152, 3, 405

1776
DEC. 27

Washington, George. Newtown [Pennsylvania]. To the
President of Congress [Baltimore]. Account of
the battle of Trenton. Draft. 4 pp. In handwriting of Tench Tilghman. Read in Congress,
Dec. 31.   A. II, 111

  The first paragraph of draft describing the attacking maneuvers was
  altered to the form printed in Writings of Washington (Ford) N. Y.
  1890, 5, 132.

1776
DEC. 27

Washington, George. Newtown [Pennsylvania]. To
Robert Morris, Philadelphia. Transmitting account of battle of Trenton. L. S. 2 pp. In
handwriting of Robert Hanson Harrison.

         C. C. 152, 3, 397

1776
DEC. 27

Continental Congress, Resolves. Brig. Gen. of Artillery;
bounties; levies to join army; commissaries; system of promotion; magazine and elaboratory at
Carlisle; magazine at Brookfield; teams; small
arms from France; convalescents; North Carolina
troops; plenary power to Washington; Continental currency. D. S. of John Hancock. 6 pp.
Enclosed in President of Congress to Washington, 1776, Dec. 27.   91, 112

1776
DEC. 27

Continental Congress, President. Baltimore. To [George]
Washington [Newtown, Pennsylvania]. Trans-
mitting resolves. L. S. of John Hancock. 2 pp.
Answered Jan. 1, 1777.*   91, 116

1776
DEC. 28

Continental Congress, Resolves. Commissary General and the Northern Army; floating batteries and fortifications on Lake Champlain. D. S. of John Hancock. Enclosed in President of Congress to Washington, 1776, Jan. 1.   **20, 87**

1776
DEC. 28

Continental Congress, Committee at Philadelphia. To [George Washington, Newtown]. Success at Trenton; reenforcements of militia; expiration of enlistments; Hessian prisoners. A. L. S. of Robert Morris, signed also by Geo. Clymer and Geo. Walton. 3 pp.   **12, 317**
Committee: Morris, Clymer and Walton.

1776
DEC. 29

Washington, George. Newtown. To [the President of Congress, Baltimore]. Military movements; prisoners. Draft. 2 pp. In handwriting of Robert Hanson Harrison.   **A. II, 115**
Printed: Writings of Washington (Ford) N.Y. 1890. 5, 136.

1776
DEC. 29

Washington, George. Newtown. To Robert Morris, Philadelphia. Transmitting letters to be forwarded. L. S. 1 p. In handwriting of Robert Hanson Harrison.   **C. C.   152, 3, 409**

1776
DEC. 29

Continental Congress, Resolve. Foundry for cannon in New York State. D. S. of John Hancock. Enclosed in President of Congress to Washington, 1777, Jan. 1.   **20, 87**

1776
DEC. 30

Washington, George. Trenton. To Robert Morris, Philadelphia. Hard money for secret service; subsistence for troops. L. S. 1 p. In handwriting of Tench Tilghman.   **C. C.   152, 3, 417**
Printed: Writings of Washington (Ford) N.Y. 1900. 5, 138, note.

1776
DEC. 30

Continental Congress, Resolves, Elaboratory for Northern Army; batteaux men; wagons. D. S. of John Hancock. Enclosed in President of Congress to Washington, 1777, Jan. 1.   **20, 87**

1776
DEC. 30

Continental Congress, Committee at Philadelphia. To [George] Washington [Trenton]. Difficulty in obtaining hard money. A. L. S. of Robert Morris. 2 pp.   **12, 328**
List of hard money sent with above.   **12, 330**

1776
DEC. 30

Continental Congress, Committee at Philadelphia. To George Washington [Trenton]. Letters to go into New York. A. L. S. of Robert Morris. 1 p.   **12, 331**

1776 Washington, George. Trenton. To Robert Morris, Phila-
DEC. 31   delphia. Great need of money to retain the
             troops in service. L. S. 1 p. In handwriting
             of Joseph Reed.   C. C. 152, 3, 421
             Printed: Writings of Washington (Ford) N. Y. 1890. 5,145, note.

1776 Continental Congress, Resolve. Powder. D. S. of John
DEC. 31   Hancock. Enclosed in President of Congress to
             Washington, 1777, Jan. 1.   20, 87

1776 Continental Congress, Committee at Philadelphia. To
DEC. 31.   George Washington [Trenton]. Resolves of Con-
             gress vesting plenary powers in Washington.
             A. L. S. of Robert Morris; signed also by Geo.
             Clymer and Geo. Walton. 1 p.   12, 338

1776 Continental Congress, Resolves. Maryland levies; powder
DEC. 31.   for Northern Army; clothing. A. D. S. of John
             Hancock. Enclosed in President of Congress to
             Washington, 1777, Jan. 1.   20, 91

[1776] Continental Army. Route from Cambridge to New York.
             1 p. Endorsed by Washington: A route of the
             march to New York.   95, 31.

[1776] Chase, Samuel and Charles Carroll [of Carrollton]. Memo-
             randum of supplies needed in Canada. A. D. of
             Chase. 2 pp. Transmitted to Washington. 95, 32

1776 Enlistment form. Agreement (in blank) for enlistments
             from Massachusetts for service on the Canadian
             Expedition. Printed form. 1 p.   A. II, 61

1777 Washington, George. Trenton. To [the President of
JAN. 1.   Congress, Baltimore]. Powers vested in him by
             Congress; passage of the Delaware; military
             movements; militia; strength of army.   Draft.
             3 pp. In handwriting of Robert Hanson Harrison.
                                              A. II, 119
             Printed: Writings of Washington (Ford), N. Y. 1889. 5, 139.

1777 Washington, George. Trenton. To [the Committee of
JAN. 1.   Congress at Philadelphia]. Bounty to militia;
             Hessian prisoners; powers conferred by Congress.
             Draft. 3 pp. In handwriting of Tench Tilghman.
                                              A. II, 123
             Printed: Writings of Washington (Ford), N. Y. 1890. 5, 143.

1777 Continental Congress, President. Philadelphia. To
JAN. 1.   [George] Washington [Trenton]. The victory at
             Trenton. Horse for [Lt.] Col. [George] Baylor.
             L. S. of John Hancock. 4 pp. In handwriting
             of Jacob Rush.   13, 3

1777
JAN. 1.

Continental Congress, Resolve. Horse for [Lt.] Col. [George] Baylor. A. D. S. of John Hancock. Enclosed in President of Congress to Washington, 1777, Jan. 1.   **20**, 91

1777
JAN. 1.

Morris, Robert. Philadelphia. To George Washington [Trenton]. Forwarding money.. A. L. S. 1 p.
                                                            13, 2

1777
JAN. 2

Continental Congress, Resolves. Exchange of [Maj.] Gen. [Charles] Lee. D. S. of John Hancock. Enclosed in President of Congress to Washington, 1777, Jan. 6.   **13**, 22

1777
JAN. 3

Continental Congress, Resolves. Provisions for American prisoners; exchange of Col. Ethan Allen; treatment of Richard Stockton. D. S. of John Hancock. Enclosed in President of Congress to Washington, 1777, Jan. 6.   **13**, 22

1777
JAN. 4

Continental Congress, Resolves. March of troops; treatment of [Maj.] Gen. [Charles] Lee; pay to seamen. D. S. of John Hancock. Enclosed in President of Congress to Washington, 1777, Jan. 6.   **13**, 22

1777
JAN. 5

W[ashingto]n, G[eorge]. Pluckemin [New Jersey]. To [the President of Congress, Baltimore]. Account of the battle of Princeton. A. D. S. 4 pp.
                                                  A. II, 129
Printed: Writings of Washington (Ford) N. Y. 1890. 5, 146.

1777
JAN. 5

Washington, George. Pluckemin. To Robert Morris, Philadelphia. Transmitting letters to be forwarded; the situation. A. L. S. 1 p.
                                          C. C. 152, 3, 133

1777
JAN. 5

Continental Congress, Committee at Philadelphia. To [George] Washington [Pluckemin]. Awaiting news; naval captures. A. L. S. of Robert Morris, signed also by George Clymer and George Walton. 2 pp.   **13**, 18

1777
JAN. 5

Continental Congress, Resolves. Exchange of James Lovell. A. D. S. of Charles Thomson, countersigned by John Hancock. Enclosed in President of Congress to Washington, 1777, Jan. 6–21.
                                                        90, 54

1777
JAN. 6

Continental Congress, President. Baltimore. To [George] Washington [Morristown, New Jersey]. Case of

[Maj.] Gen. [Charles] Lee; military situation. L. S. of John Hancock. 3 pp. In handwriting of Jacob Rush. **13, 20**

1777
JAN. 7
Washington, George. Morristown [New Jersey]. To [the President of Congress, Baltimore]. Skirmishes and the post at Morristown. Draft. 1 p. In handwriting of Robert Hanson Harrison.

A. II, 133
Printed: Writings of Washington (Ford) N. Y. 1890. 5, 154.

1777
JAN. 7
Washington, George. Morristown. To [the Committee of Congress at Philadelphia.] Foundry work on cannon. L. S. 1 p. In handwriting of John Clark, jr. **C. C. 152, 3, 441**

1777
JAN. 7
Continental Congress, Committee at Philadelphia. To George Washington [Morristown]. The military situation; British treatment of prisoners; retaliation; exchange. A. L. S. of Robert Morris, Geo. Clymer, and Geo. Walton. 3 pp. **13, 28**
Dated in error: 1776.

1777
JAN. 7
[Schuyler, Philip John.] [Albany.] To [the President of Congress, Baltimore]. The situation in Canada. Extracts of letter. In handwriting of Joseph Nourse. Transmitted to Washington with Board of War to Washington, 1777, Jan. 23. **94, 166**

1777
JAN. 8
Continental Congress, Resolves. Exchange of prisoners; magazines of William Kennon in South Carolina and Georgia; attempt on Nova Scotia. A. D. S. of John Hancock. Enclosed in President of Congress to Washington, 1777, Jan. 10. **13, 51**

1777
JAN. 8
Continental Congress, Resolves. Canadian regiment and troops for Canada; salt-petre and powder. A. D. S. of Chas. Thomson, countersigned by John Hancock. Enclosed in President of Congress to Washington, 1777, Jan. 6–21. **90, 54**

1777
JAN. 9
Washington, George. Morristown. To [the President of Congress, Baltimore]. Honor conferred upon [Lt.] Col. [George] Baylor; movements of enemy. Draft. 1 p. In handwriting of Tench Tilghman.

A. II, 135
Printed, in part: Writings of Washington (Ford) N. Y. 1890. 5, 160, note.

1777
JAN. 9
Continental Congress, Resolves. Dismissal of Doctors John Morgan and Samuel Stringer, other hospital mat-

ters; progress of recruiting. A. D. S. of John Hancock. Enclosed in President of Congress to Washington, 1777, Jan. 10. **13, 51**

1777
JAN. 9

Continental Congress, Resolves. Pay for Massachusetts militia; postage of soldiers' letters. A. D. S. of Chas. Thomson, countersigned by John Hancock. Enclosed in President of Congress to Washington, 1777, Jan. 6–21. **90, 54**

1777
JAN. 9

Continental Congress, Resolves. Salting of meat in southern states; progress of recruiting. D. S. of John Hancock. 2 pp. Enclosed in President of Congress to Washington, 1777, Jan. 10. **13, 55**

1777
JAN. 9

Continental Congress, Committee at Philadelphia. To [George] Washington [Morristown]. Report of Joseph Traversie. L. S. of Robert Morris, Geo. Clymer and George Walton. 2 pp. **13, 32**

1777
JAN. 9

Continental Congress, Committee at Philadelphia. To [George Washington, Morristown]. Exchange of [Maj.] Gen. [Charles] Lee; agent for prisoners; British treatment; prisoners taken in merchant ships; exchange of certain sea-captains; military movements. A. L. S. of Robt. Morris. 2 pp. **13, 33**

1777
JAN. 9

Continental Congress, Committee at Philadelphia. To [George] Washington [Morristown]. Transmitting one hundred thousand dollars. Letter-book copy. **C. C. 133, 40**

1777
JAN. 9

Walton, George. Philadelphia. To George Washington [Philadelphia]. Exchange for officers and crew of an armed boat of Georgia. A. L. S. 2 pp. **13, 40**

[1777]
[JAN. 9]

Traversie, Joseph. [Philadelphia.] Intelligence of alleged plot amongst Canadian prisoners at Reading. Contemporary copy. 2 pp. Enclosed in Committee at Philadelphia to Washington, 1777, Jan. 9. **13, 30**

1777
JAN. 10

Continental Congress, President. Philadelphia. To [George] Washington [Morristown]. Attempt against Nova Scotia; dismissal of Drs. [John] Morgan and [Samuel] Stringer. L. S. of John Hancock. 2 pp. In handwriting of Jacob Rush. **13, 49**

1777
JAN. 10

Continental Congress, Resolves. Joseph Frye and Benedict Arnold to be brigadiers. A. D. S. of Chas.

Thomson, countersigned by John Hancock. Enclosed in President of Congress to Washington, 1777, Jan. 6–21.   **90, 54**

1777
JAN. 12

Washington, George. Morristown. To [the President of Congress, Baltimore]. Exchange of [Maj.] Gen. [Charles] Lee and Col. [Ethan] Allen; distressing the enemy. Draft. 2 pp. In handwriting of Tench Tilghman.   **A. II, 137**

Printed: Writings of Washington (Ford) N. Y. 1890. 5, 164, note.

1777
JAN. 12

Washington, George. Morristown. To [the Committee of Congress at Philadelphia]. British treatment of prisoners; exchange of certain officers; information from Canada; enemy at Brunswick. Draft. 2 pp. In handwriting of Tench Tilghman.

      A. II, 139

Printed, in part: Writings of Washington (Ford) N. Y. 1890. 5, 170, note.

1777
JAN. 13

Washington, George. Morristown. To [Lt.] Gen. [Sir William] Howe [New York]. Exchange of Maj. Gen. [Charles] Lee; British treatment of prisoners. Contemporary copy. 3 pp. In handwriting of Stephen Moylan. Enclosed in Washington to the President of Congress, 1777, Jan. 14.

      C. C. 152, 3, 465

Printed: Writings of Washington (Ford) N. Y. 1890. 5, 168.

1777
JAN. 13

Continental Congress, Resolve. British treatment of Walter Cruise and Richard Carpenter. Contemporary copy. In handwriting of Jacob Rush. Transmitted to Washington with President of Congress to Washington, 1777, Jan. 15.   **90, 79**

1777
JAN. 14

Washington, George. Morristown. To [the President of Congress, Baltimore]. Enemy's want of forage; exchange of Lee and treatment of prisoners. Draft. 1 p. In handwriting of Tench Tilghman.   **A. II, 141**

1777
JAN. 14

Continental Congress, Resolves. Supplies, etc., for the Northern Army; value of Continental bills, bills of credit; state debts; loan of two million. D. S. of John Hancock. 4 pp. Enclosed in President of Congress to Washington, 1777, Jan. 15.

      13, 66

1777
JAN. 15

Continental Congress, President. Baltimore. To [George] Washington [Morristown]. Continental currency; hospital and miscellaneous matters. L. S. of John Hancock. 2 pp. In handwriting of Jacob Rush.   **13, 86**

1777
JAN. 15

Bedford, Gunning. Philadelphia. To [George] Washington, Morristown. Quartermaster department business. A. L. S. 2 pp. Enclosed in Washington to the President of Congress, 1777, Jan. 19?
C. C.   152, 3, 477

1777
JAN. 15

Continental Congress, President. Baltimore. To George Washington [Morristown]. Employment of Walter Cruise and Richard Carpenter. L. S. of John Hancock. In handwriting of Jacob Rush. 90, 79

1777
JAN. 16

Continental Congress, Resolves. Bills to be drawn by the Paymaster-general; free negroes; engineers; chaplains. A. D. S. of Charles Thomson, countersigned by John Hancock. Enclosed in President of Congress to Washington, 1777, Jan. 6–21.
90, 54

1777
JAN. 16

Continental Congress, Resolves. Commissary of prisoners to reside within enemy's lines; clothing; New York Convention's address to people; Hessian treatment of prisoners. D. S. of John Hancock. Enclosed in President of Congress to Washington, 1777, Jan. 18.   13, 92

1777
JAN. 17

Washington, George. Morristown. To [the President of Congress, Baltimore]. Foraging of enemy; establishment of magazines of stores at Hartford and York. Draft. 2 pp. In handwriting of Tench Tilghman.   A. II, 143
Printed, in part: Writings of Washington (Ford) N. Y. 1890. 5, 175, note.

1777
JAN. 17

-Pelissier, Christopher. Philadelphia. Memorial to Congress. Appointment to chief command at Ticonderoga. D. S. 2 pp. Endorsed by Charles Thomson: " referred to the board of war." Transmitted to Washington.   90, 81

1777
JAN. 18

Continental Congress, President. Baltimore. To [George] Washington [Morristown]. Clothing for New York troops; prisoners. L. S. of John Hancock. 2 pp. In handwriting of Jacob Rush.
13, 90

1777
JAN. 18

Continental Congress, Resolves. Committee at Philadelphia; guard for prisoners at Lancaster; authority to use horses and oxen; case of [Major] Elisha Painter. D. S. of John Hancock. Enclosed in President of Congress to Washington, 1777, Jan. 18.   13, 92

1777
Jan. 19

Washington, George. Morristown. To [the President of Congress, Baltimore]. Fluctuating state of the army; militia. Draft. 3 pp. In handwriting of Tench Tilghman.   **A. II, 147**

Printed: Writings of Washington (Ford) N. Y. 1890. 5, 181.

1777
Jan. 19

Continental Congress, Resolves. Enlistments for South Carolina armed vessels; reenforcements for Canada. A. D. S. of Charles Thomson, countersigned by John Hancock. Enclosed in President of Congress to Washington, 1777, Jan 24.
90, 70

1777
Jan. 20

Washington, George. Morristown. To [the President of Congress, Baltimore]. Credits; recruiting service; proposal for raising a Canadian regiment; foreigners in army; surgeon for Northern Department; lost of storeship. Draft. 2 pp. In handwriting of Tench Tilghman.   **A. II, 151**

1777
Jan. 20

Continental Congress, Committee at Philadelphia. To [George] Washington [Morristown]. Papers from Pennsylvania Council of Safety respecting exchange of prisoners. Letter-book copy.
C. C.   133, 89

1777
Jan. 20

Continental Congress, Resolves. Commanding officer, specie, gunpowder, provisions, etc. for Canada; enlistment of Canadians. A. D. S. of Charles Thomson, countersigned by John Hancock. Enclosed in President of Congress to Washington, 1777, Jan. 24.   **90, 70**

1777
Jan. 21

Continental Congress, Resolves. Miscellaneous military matters; Maryland militia. D. S. of John Hancock. Enclosed in President of Congress to Washington, 1777, Jan. 24.   **13, 102**

1777
Jan. 22

Washington, George. Morristown. To [the President of Congress, Baltimore]. Report of capture of Fort Washington; appointment of general officers; raising of troops of horse, pay. Draft. 5 pp. In handwriting of Tench Tilghman and Washington.   **A. II, 153**

Printed: Writings of Washington (Ford) N. Y. 1890. 5, 190.

1777
Jan. 22

Continental Congress, Resolve. Subsistence allowance for recruits. D. S. of William. Churchill Houston. 1 p. Enclosed in Board of War to Washington, 1777, May 20.   **95, 324**

Head Qrs at Head Qrs Decr. 15th 1776

Sir

About one o'Clock to day I received a
Letter from Genl Sullivan a Copy of which you
have inclosed. I will not comment
upon the unpleasing intelligence it contains
but only add, that I sincerely regret the
unhappy fate of Genl Lee and feel much
for the loss of my Country in his Captivity.

Attached to the Enemy, they have been
industrious in their attempts
to get provided Boats, but as yet their efforts have
not succeeded. From the latest advice that
I have of their movements, they appear to be
leaving Trenton and to be falling off towards
Brunswick & Allen Town. What their designs
are, or whether they mean to retreat or only
a feint cannot be determined. I have parties
out to watch their motions, and to form
a possible an accurate Opinion of their Plans.
Our force since my last has received no
augmentation, but I am advised by a
Letter from the Council of Safety which just
came to hand, that Coll Hart & Gilbraith are
marching with their Battalions of
Militia and also that some small parties are
assembling in Cumberland County.

By Capt. Murray who is just returned
from his imprisonment, we are informed that

[Brig.] Gen. [Thomas] Mifflin. D. S. of John Hancock. Transmitted to Washington. **90, 80**

1777
JAN. 31

Washington, George. Morristown. To [the President of Congress, Baltimore]. Want of money; [Maj.] Gen. [William] Heath at Kingsbridge. Draft. 2 pp. In handwriting of Tench Tilghman.

A. II, 167

Printed, in part: Writings of Washington (Ford) N.Y. 1890. 5, 210, note.

1777
JAN. 31

Continental Congress, Committee at Philadelphia. To [George] Washington [Morristown]. Report from Rhode Island; case of Hugh Wallace; exchanges proposed; miscellaneous matters. A. L. S. of Robert Morris. 4 pp. **13, 156**

1777
JAN.

Bedford, Gunning. Philadelphia. To [George] Washington, Morristown. Quartermaster's department. A. L. S. 2 pp. Enclosed in Washington to the President of Congress, 1777, Jan. 19?

C. C. 152, 3, 481

1777
FEB. 1

Continental Congress, Resolve. Capt. Joseph Scott's Virginia company. D. S. of John Hancock. Transmitted to Washington. **90, 80**

1777
FEB. 4

Campbell, Archibald. Concord [Massachusetts]. To [George] Washington [Morristown]. Complaint of treatment received. A. L. S. 4 pp. Enclosed in Washington to the President of Congress, 1777, Mar. 6? **C. C. 152, 3, 585**

1777
FEB. 5

Washington, George. Morristown. To [the President of Congress, Baltimore]. Military matters; Maryland militia; smallpox; oath of allegiance. Draft. 5 pp. In handwriting of Tench Tilghman and John Clark, jr. **A. II, 171**
Printed in part: Writings of Washington (Ford) N. Y. 1890. 5, 218.

1777
FEB. 5

Washington, George. Morristown. To Robert Morris [Philadelphia]. Removal of stores; exchange of captains of merchant vessels; the King's speech in Parliament. Draft. 1 p. In handwriting of Tench Tilghman. **A. II, 175**

1777
FEB. 5

Washington, George. Morristown. To Samuel Chase [Philadelphia]. Barbarity of British toward prisoners. Draft. 2 pp. In handwriting of Tench Tilghman. **A. II, 177**
Printed: Writings of Washington (Sparks) Boston. 1834. 4, 309.

1777
FEB. 5

Continental Congress, Resolves. Brigadier F[rancis] Nash. A. D. S. of Charles Thomson. Enclosed in President of Congress to Washington, 1777, Feb. 23. **90, 85**

1777
FEB. 6

Washington, George. [Morristown.] To the Committee of Congress at Philadelphia. Requesting money for recruiting Col. [Stephen] Moylan's regiment. Contemporary copy. 1 p. In handwriting of John Fitzgerald. **A. II, 179**

1777
FEB. 6

Continental Congress, President. Baltimore. To [George] Washington [Morristown]. Introducing Mr. Burke, of Jamaica. L. S. of John Hancock. 1 p. **90, 86**

1777
FEB. 6

Board of War. Baltimore. To George Washington [Morristown]. Land grants to recruits for the war. L. S. of Richard Peters. 1 p. Answered Feb. 23.* **94, 167**

1777
FEB. 7

Continental Congress, Resolves. Pay for Connecticut light-horse; rank and pay of Maryland and Virginia regiments; howitzers for Ticonderoga. A. D. S. of John Hancock. 1 p. Transmitted to Washington. **90, 89**

1777
FEB. 11

[Lee, Arthur.] Nantes. To [Secret Committee of Congress]. British plan of campaign; exertions of Britain to raise troops; cutters for protection of the West India trade. Feb., 14: Letters of marque; transportation of prisoners to East Indies. Extract of letter. 3 pp. In handwriting of Richard Henry Lee. Enclosed in R. H. Lee, to Washington, 1777, Apr. 16? **20, 330**

1777
FEB. 12

Continental Congress, Committee at Philadelphia. To George Washington [Morristown]. Money for Lt. Col. [Moses] Rawlings and Lt. [Daniel] Cresap. L. S. of Robert Morris. 1 p. **13, 242**

1777
FEB. 13

Washington, George. Morristown. To [the Committee of Congress at Philadelphia]. Requesting money for recruiting in lower Jersey. Contemporary copy. 1 p. In handwriting of George Johnston. **A. II, 181**

1777
FEB. 13

Continental Congress, Medical Committee. Baltimore. To George Washington, Morristown. Inoculation of troops for smallpox. L. S. of Benjamin Rush. 2 pp. In handwriting of Thos. Burke. **13, 244**

1777
FEB. 13

Continental Congress, Resolves. Recommending Capt. [George] Gibson. D. S. of John Hancock. Enclosed in President of Congress to Washington, 1777, Feb. 23.   **90, 90**

1777
FEB. 14

Washington, George. Morristown. To [the President of Congress, Baltimore]. Military matters; establishment of cannon foundry; [Maj.] Gen. [Charles] Lee's letter to Congress. Draft. 4 pp. In handwriting of Robert Hanson Harrison.

A. II, 183

Printed: Writings of Washington (Ford) N. Y. 1890. 5, 236.

1777
FEB. 14

Washington, George. Morristown. To [the President of Congress, Baltimore]. Plan of establishment of hospital for the army; sickness last campaign; pay; Dr. [John] Morgan's vindication. Draft. 3 pp. In handwriting of Tench Tilghman.

A. II, 187

Printed in part: Writings of Washington (Ford) N. Y. 1890. 5, 240, note.

1777
FEB. 14

Morris, Robert. Philadelphia. To [George] Washington [Morristown]. Introducing Mr. Burke, of Jamaica. A. L. S. 1 p.   **13, 254**

1777
FEB. 14

Continental Congress, Resolves. Howitzers for Ticonderoga; French gentlemen in army. D. S. of John Hancock. Enclosed in President of Congress to Washington, 1777, Feb. 23.   **90, 90**

1777
FEB. 19

Continental Congress, Resolves. Promotions; Virginia troops to join army; election of major-generals. D. S. of John Hancock. Enclosed in President of Congress to Washington, 1777, Feb. 23. **90, 90**

1777
FEB. 19

Neil, Eliza. [East Jersey.] To [George] Washington [Morristown]. Pension for her support. A. L. S. 1 p. Enclosed in Washington to the President of Congress 1777, Feb. 28.   **C. C. 152, 3, 557**

1777
FEB. 20

Washington, George. Morristown. To [the President of Congress, Baltimore]. Military movements. Draft. 2 pp. In handwriting of Caleb Gibbs.

A. II, 191

Printed: Writings of Washington (Ford) N. Y. 1890. 5, 240.

1777
FEB. 20

Washington, George. Morristown. To [the President of Congress, Baltimore]. French officers in the army. Draft. 3 pp. In handwriting of Tench Tilghman.   **A. II, 193**

Printed: Writings of Washington (Ford) N. Y. 1890. 5, 244.

1777
FEB. 23

Washington, George. Morristown. To [the President of Congress, Baltimore]. Raising cavalry regiments and pay of their officers; forwarding of recruits; arms. Draft. 3 pp. In handwriting of Robert Hanson Harrison.   **A. II,** 199

Printed in part: Writings of Washington (Ford) N. Y. 1890. 5, 250, note.

1777
FEB. 23

Washington, George. Morristown. To [the Board of War, Baltimore]. Question of land bounty for enlistments. L. S. 2 pp. In handwriting of Robert Hanson Harrison. Endorsed: "This letter to be read in Congress & enquiry to be made whether any member remembir the Resolves of Congress respecting the Bounty of Land to be allowed Soldiers &c. The General is of opinion the 100 Acres Bounty is to be granted to those enlisting for three years. The Board of a diffr. opinion."   **C. C. 152, 3, 541**

1777
FEB. 23

Continental Congress, President. Baltimore. To [George] Washington [Morristown]. Minor matters; return of Congress to Philadelphia. L. S. of John Hancock. 2 pp. In handwriting of Jacob Rush. Answered Mar. 1.   **90, 92**

1777
FEB. 24

Continental Congress, Resolves. Troops to join the army; collection of arms. D. S. of John Hancock. Enclosed in President of Congress to Washington, 1777, Feb. 25.   **90, 95**

1777
FEB. 25

Continental Congress, President. Baltimore. To [George] Washington [Morristown]. Strengthening the army. L. S. of John Hancock. 2 pp. In handwriting of Jacob Rush. Answered Mar. 12.*   **90, 100**

1777
FEB. 25

Continental Congress, Resolves. Purchase of arms and woolens; punishment of deserters; appointment of Regnier de Rousie; profanity in army. D. S. of John Hancock. Enclosed in President of Congress to Washington, 1777, Feb. 25.   **90, 95**

1777
FEB. 26

Continental Congress, Committee at Philadelphia. To [George] Washington [Morristown]. [Maj.] Gen. [Charles] Lee's case; inconvenience of Baltimore as location of Congress. A. L. S. of Robert Morris, signed also by Geo. Clymer. 2 pp.   **14, 13**

1777
FEB. 26 .

Lee, Charles. New York. To [George] Washington [Morristown]. [Majors Jacob] Morris and [John Skey] Eustace. Contemporary copy. 1 p. Enclosed in Washington to the President of Congress, 1777, Mar. 6.   C. C. 152, 3, 579

1777
FEB. 27

Washington, George. Morristown. To [the Committee of Congress at Philadelphia]. Canadian prisoners; recruiting and militia reinforcements. Draft. 4 pp. In handwriting of Tench Tilghman.
A. II, 205

1777
FEB. 27

Continental Congress, Committee at Philadelphia. To [George] Washington [Morristown]. Condition of enemy; removal of stores; bright and gloomy side of affairs; loss of big men from Congress. A. L. S. of Robert Morris. 6 pp.   14, 27
Printed in part: Writings of Washington (Ford) N. Y. 1890. 5, 263, note.

1777
FEB. 27

Howe, [Sir] W[illiam]. Brunswick [New Jersey]. To [George] Washington [Morristown]. Arrangement of a cartel; treatment of Lt. Col. [Archibald] Campbell. Contemporary copy. 2 pp. Enclosed in Washington to the President of Congress, 1777, Mar. 6.   C. C. 152, 3, 581

1777
FEB. 27

Lee, Richard Henry. Baltimore. To [George Washington, Morristown]. Transmitting papers; glory of the recent campaign; news from London of British intent against eastern shore of Maryland; junction with Canada; aid from France and Spain. A. L. S. 2 pp.   14, 31

1777
FEB. 28

Washington, George. Morristown. To [the President of Congress, Baltimore]. Skirmishing; militia returning home; slow reinforcements; promotions of general officers; hospital. Draft. 3 pp. In handwriting of Tench Tilghman.   A. II, 209

1777
FEB. 29

Continental Congress, Committee at Philadelphia. To [George] Washington [Morristown]. Removal of stores; British ships in the Chesapeake; [Benjamin] Franklin in Europe. A. L. S. of Robert Morris. 2 pp. Answered Mar. 3.*   14, 39

1777
MAR. 1

Washington, George. Morristown. To [the President of Congress, Baltimore]. Resolve of Congress directing retaliatory measures on account of treatment [Maj.] Gen. [Charles] Lee. Draft. 3 pp. In handwriting of Caleb Gibbs.   A. II, 213
Printed: Writings of Washington (Ford) N. Y. 1890. 5, 257.

1777
MAR. 2

Washington, George. Morristown. To [Committee of Congress at Philadelphia]. Resolves of Congress respecting [Maj.] Gen. [Charles] Lee; removal of Congress to Lancaster; removal of public stores from Philadelphia. Draft. 1 p. In handwriting of Tench Tilghman.   **A. II, 217**

1777
MAR. 2

Washington, George. Morristown. To Robert Morris, Philadelphia. British designs; comparison of strength of British and American armies; removal of stores; hasty action of Congress as to retaliatory measures with prisoners; conference with [Maj.] Gen. [Charles] Lee. Transcript. **P. 1, 26**
Printed: Writings of Washington (Ford) N. Y. 1890. 5, 262.

1777
MAR. 3

Washington, George. Morristown. To [Committee of Congress at Philadelphia]. Enemy's design, by water, against Philadelphia; miscellaneous matters. L. S. 1 p. In handwriting of Robert Hanson Harrison.   **C. C. 152, 3, 571**

1777
MAR. 6

Washington, George. Morristown. To [the President of Congress, Philadelphia]. Resolves respecting Lt. Col. [Archibald] Campbell and [Maj.] Gen. [Charles] Lee. Draft. 2 pp. In handwriting of Robert Hanson Harrison.   **A. II, 219**
Printed: Writings of Washington (Ford) N. Y. 1890. 5, 274.

1777
MAR. 6

Morris, Robert. Philadelphia. To [George] Washington [Morristown]. Error of short enlistments; drink and bounties; [Maj.] Gen. [Charles] Lee's request and effect of compliance on France. A. L. S. 4 pp.   **14, 66**
Printed in part: Writings of Washington (Ford) N. Y. 1890. 5, 267.

1777
MAR. 1!

Washington, George. Morristown. To [Maj.] Gen. [Thomas] Mifflin [Reading, Pennsylvania]. Quartermaster business. L. S. 1 p. In handwriting of Tench Tilghman.   **C. C. 152, 3, 589**

1777
MAR. 12

Washington, George. Morristown. To [the President of Congress, Philadelphia]. State of the army; recruiting; hospitals and pay. Draft. 3 pp. In handwriting of Caleb Gibbs and Robert Hanson Harrison.   **A. II, 223**
Printed: Writings of Washington (Ford) N. Y. 1890. 5, 285.

1777
MAR. 12

Continental Congress, Resolves. Assessment and payment for blankets. D. S. of John Hancock. Enclosed in President of Congress to Washington, 1777, **Mar. 17.**   **90, 102**

1777
MAR. 13

Washington, George.   Morristown.   To Maj. Gen. [Thomas] Mifflin, Philadelphia.   Plan for Quartermaster's department; horses and wagons; cash for forage.   L. S.   2 pp.   In handwriting of George Johnston.   C. C.   152, 3, 591
Printed, in part: Writings of Washington (Ford) N. Y. 1890. 5, 285, note.

1777
MAR. 13

Continental Congress, Resolves.   Arms for Virginia troops; discouragement of foreign military men from coming to America.   D. S. of John Hancock. Enclosed in President of Congress to Washington, 1777, Mar. 17.   90, 102

1777
MAR. 14

Washington, George.   Morristown.   To [the President of Congress, Philadelphia].   Weak state of army; hospital; want of money.   L. S.   4 pp.   In handwriting of Robert Hanson Harrison.
C. C.   152, 3, 595
Printed: Writings of Washington (Ford) N. Y. 1890. 5, 285.

1777
MAR. 14

Continental Congress, Resolves.   Foreign corps from French [West Indies] islands; commissions for foreigners; pensions for widows; retaliation in treatment of prisoners; [Lt.] Col. [Archibald] Campbell's complaints.   D. S. of John Hancock.   Enclosed in President of Congress to Washington, 1777, Mar. 17.   90, 102

[1777]
[MAR. 15]

Washington, George.   [Morristown.]   To [the members of Congress, Philadelphia].   Introducing Maj. Gen. [Nathanael] Greene.   Draft.   1 p.   In handwriting of George Johnston.   A.   II, 227

1777
MAR. 15

Continental Army, Return of Continental troops and militia in New Jersey.   Tabular statement.   2 pp. In handwriting of Tench Tilghman.   Enclosed in Washington to the President of Congress, 1777, Mar. 18.   C. C.   152, 4, 15

1777
MAR. 18

Washington, George.   Morristown.   To [the President of Congress, Philadelphia].   Introducing Maj. Gen. [Nathanael] Greene; his errand to Congress.   L. S. 2 pp.   In handwriting of Robert Hanson Harrison.   Read in Congress, Mar. 20.   C. C.   152, 4, 1
Printed: Writings of Washington (Ford) N. Y. 1890. 5, 292, note.

1777
MAR. 19

Continental Congress, Resolves.   Minor matters and stores for Eastern and Northern departments.   D. S. of John Hancock.   Enclosed in President of Congress to Washington, 1777, Mar. 26.   90, 106

1777
MAR. 19

Continental Congress, Resolves. Certificate to foreigners; stockade for prisoners in Massachusetts. D. S. of John Hancock. Enclosed in President of Congress to Washington, 1777, Mar. 26.   **90, 106**

1777
MAR. 21

Washington, George. Morristown. To [the President of] Congress [Philadelphia]. [Maj.] Gen. [Nathanael] Greene's errand to Congress. Draft. 1 p. In handwriting of Robert Hanson Harrison.
                   A. II, 230

1777
MAR. 23

Washington, George. Morristown. To [the President of] Congress [Philadelphia]. Col. [William] Palfrey's accounts; estimates of expense. Draft. 1 p. In handwriting of Robert Hanson Harrison.
                   A. II, 231

1777
MAR. 23

Hays, A[nn] Hawkes. Haverstraw [New York]. **To** [George Washington, Morristown]. **Enemy's** burning of Peekskill; militia. Contemporary copy. 2 pp. Enclosed in Washington to the President of Congress, 1777, Mar. 26.
            C. C. 152, 4, 33

1777
MAR. 24

Continental Congress, Resolves. Judgment of Commander-in-chief and opinion of councils of war; exchange of prisoners and Maj. Gen. [Charles] Lee; purchase of arms. D. S. of John Hancok. Enclosed in President of Congress to Washington, 1777, Mar. 26.   **90, 106**

1777
MAR. 25

Continental Congress, Resolves. Western troops to join army; command at Ticonderoga. D. S. of John Hancock. Enclosed in President of Congress to Washington, 1777, Mar. 26.   **90, 106**

1777
MAR. 26

W[ashingto]n, G[eorge]. Morristown. To [the President of Congress, Philadelphia]. Affair at Peekskill; failure of the recruiting service; chaotic state of Army; militia. Auto. draft signed. 4 pp.
                  A. II, 235

1777
MAR. 26

Continental Congress, Resolves. [Maj.] Gen. [Philip John] Schuyler's general order; the Adjutant-Generalship; suspension of [Commodore] Esek Hopkins. D. S. of John Hancock. Enclosed in President of Congress to Washington, 1777, Mar. 26.
            90, 106

1777
MAR. 26

Continental Congress, President. Philadelphia. **To** [George] Washington [Morristown]. Exchange of prisoners; arms, etc. from France; appointment of [James] Clinton brigadier-general; conference with [Maj.] Gen. [Nathanael] Greene. L. S. of John Hancock. 2 pp. In handwriting of Jacob Rush. Answered Mar. 29.* 90, 108

1777
MAR. 26

Hazard, [Ebenezer]. Fishkill [New York.] To [George] Washington, Morristown. Arrival of storeship from France. A. L. S. in 3d person. 1 p. Enclosed in Washington to the President of Congress, 1777, Mar. 26. C. C. 152, 4, 43

1777
MAR. 26

Hoff, Christopher, jr. Hibernia Furnace [Morris County, New Jersey]. To [George] Washington [Morristown]. Inhabitants joining the enemy. Contemporary copy. 1 p. Enclosed in Washington to the President of Congress, 1777, Mar. 26.
C. C. 152, 4, 31

1777
MAR. 29

Washington, George. Morristown. To [the President of Congress, Philadelphia]. Attack on Peekskill; visit of Oneida Indians. Draft. 3 pp. In handwriting of Robert Hanson Harrison. A. II, 239
Printed: Writings of Washington (Ford) N. Y. 1890. 5, 296.

1777
MAR. 29

Washington, George. Morristown. To [the President of Congress, Philadelphia]. Arrival of storeship and French officers; affair at Peekskill. Draft. 2 pp. In handwriting of Robert Hanson Harrison. A. II, 243

1777
MAR. 29

Continental Congress, Resolve. [Maj.] Gen. [Charles] Lee's suggested conference with British; prisoners. D. S. of John Hancock. Enclosed in President of Congress to Washington, 1777, Apr. 4.
90, 113

1777
MAR. 29

McDougall, Alexander. Peekskill [New York]. To [George Washington, Morristown]. Report of enemy's expedition against Peekskill. Contemporary copy. 6 pp. Enclosed in Washington to the President of Congress, 1777, Apr. 2. C. C. 152, 4, 55

1777
MAR. 31

Washington, George. Morristown. To [the President of Congress, Philadelphia]. Reports of intentions of enemy. Draft. 1 p. In handwriting of Robert Hanson Harrison. A. II, 245

1777
MAR. 31

Continental Congress, Resolve. Execution of James Molesworth; officers of Northern department; reembursement of James Warren; appointment of Ephraim Blaine; appointment of brigadiers; lottery. D. S. of John Hancock. Enclosed in President of Congress to Washington, 1777, Apr. 4.
90, 113

[1777]   **Washington**, George. Morristown. Questions respecting
[MAR.]   organization, state, and establishment of the Con-
             tinental army to be decided by Congress. 2 pp.
             In handwriting of Alexander Hamilton. Enclosed
             in Washington to the President of Congress, 1777,
             Mar. 18.   C. C.   152, 4, 19

[1777]   **Prisoners**, American. Estimate of American prisoners in
[MAR.]   hands of British. 1 p. In handwriting of Robert
             Hanson Harrison. Enclosed in Washington to
             the President of Congress, 1777, Mar. 18.
                                                     C. C.   152, 4, 13
             This and the two following entries were not alluded to in the letter
             of Mar. 18.

[1777]   **Prisoners**, Cartel for exchange. Queries proposed respect-
[MAR.]   ing prisoners and arrangements for exchange. 4
             pp. In handwriting of Robert Hanson Harrison.
             Enclosed in Washington to the President of Con-
             gress, 1777, Mar. 18.   C. C.   152, 4, 5

[1777]   **Wolcott**, William and Robert Hanson Harrison. Objec-
[MAR.]   tions to British propositions respecting exchange
             of prisoners. Contemporary copy. 2 pp. In
             handwriting of Harrison. Enclosed in Washing-
             ton to the President of Congress, 1777, Mar. 18.
                                                     C. C.   152, 4, 9

[1777]   **Continental Congress**, Resolves. Regulations for payment
APR. 1   of army; rank of officers; Maj. Gen. [Arthur] St.
             Clair ordered to Ticonderoga. D. S. of John
             Hancock. Enclosed in President of Congress to
             Washington, 1777, Apr. 4.   90, 113

1777   **Continental Congress**, Resolves. Regulating pay of the
APR. 1   army. Broadside. Printed by Dunlap. En-
             closed in President of Congress to Washington,
             1777, Apr. 10.   90, 110

1777   **Washington**, George. Morristown. To [the President of
APR. 2   Congress, Philadelphia]. Affair at Peekskill; de-
             signs of enemy; establishment of expresses.
             Draft. 2 pp. In handwriting of George John-
             ston and Tench Tilghman.   A. II, 247

1777   **Continental Congress**, Resolve. Payrolls; removal of mili-
APR. 2   tary stores from Annapolis and Baltimore; hos-
             pital matters. D. S. of John Hancock. Enclosed
             in President of Congress to Washington, 1777,
             Apr. 4.   90, 113
             The payrolls resolution will also be found in the broadside form:
             90, 110.

1777
APR. 4

Continental Congress, President. Philadelphia. To [George] Washington [Morristown]. Pay of troops; execution of James Molesworth, [Joseph] Galloway's spy; officers to go to Ticonderoga. L. S. of John Hancock. 2 pp. In handwriting of Jacob Rush.   **90, 111**

1777
APR. 4

Continental Congress, Resolves. Military matters; muster and commissary departments; Henry Fisher and Independent Delaware Company; pay and miscellaneous matters. D. S. of John Hancock. Enclosed in President of Congress to Washington, 1777, Apr. 4.   **90, 113**
Above will be found in broadside form: 90, 184.

1777
APR. 4

Continental Congress, Resolves. Muster-master General's department. Broadside. Printed by Dunlap. Enclosed in President of Congress to Washington, 1777, May 3.   **91, 180**

1777
APR. 5

Washington, George. Morristown. To [the President of Congress, Philadelphia]. Appointment of Chevalier de Prudhomme de Borré to a brigadier-generalship. Draft. 1 p. In handwriting of Tench Tilghman.   **A. II, 249**

1777
APR. 7

Continental Congress, Resolves. Establishment, regulation etc. of the Continental Hospital. D. S. of John Hancock. Enclosed in President of Congress to Washington, 1777, Apr. 9.   **90, 127**

1777
APR. 8

Continental Congress, Resolves. Erection of monuments to Joseph Warren and Hugh Mercer; education of their sons. D. S. of John Hancock. 2 pp. Enclosed in President of Congress to Washington, 1777, Apr. 9.   **90, 121**

1777
APR. 8

Continental Congress, Resolves. Emergency provisions; schedule of pay. D. S. of John Hancock. Enclosed in President of Congress to Washington, 1777, Apr. 9.   **90, 127**

1777
APR. 9

Washington, George. Morristown. To [the President of Congress, Philadelphia]. Stores at Baltimore and Annapolis; regulation of Paymaster and Mustermaster General's Departments; hospital establishment; intentions of enemy. Draft. 2 pp. In handwriting of Tench Tilghman.   **A. II, 251**

1777
APR. 9

Continental Congress, President. Philadelphia. To [George] Washington [Morristown]. Establishment of hospital; monuments to Joseph Warren and Hugh Mercer. L. S. of John Hancock. 2 pp. In handwriting of Jacob Rush. Answered April 10.*   90, 129

1777
APR. 9

Continental Congress, Resolve. Deputy paymasters. Broadside. Printed by Dunlap. Enclosed in President of Congress to Washington, 1777, Apr. 10.   90, 110

1777
APR. 9

Continental Congress, Resolves. Opposition to enemy; commissary and hospital matters; command at Fort Pitt; minor matters; supplies from the people; paymasters; settlement of army accounts of New York and New Jersey; claims against the United States. D. S. of John Hancock. 6 pp. Enclosed in President of Congress to Washington, 1777, Apr. 9.   90, 136

1777
APR. 10

Washington, George. Morristown. To [the President of Congress, Philadelphia]. Hospital establishment; movements of enemy; lack of engineers; Lord Howe's letter relative to prisoners; money for recruiting service. Draft. 3 pp. In handwriting of Robert Hanson Harrison and Richard Kidder Meade.   A. II, 255

1777
APR. 10

Washington, George. Morristown. To [the President of Congress, Philadelphia]. Slowness in recruiting; hospital service. Draft. 4 pp. In handwriting of Tench Tilghman.   A. II, 259
Printed: Writings of Washington (Ford) N. Y. 1890. 5, 321.

1777
APR. 10

Continental Congress, President. Philadelphia. To [George] Washington [Morristown]. Transmitting resolves. A. L. S. of John Hancock. 1 p.   90, 132

1777
APR. 10

Continental Congress, Resolves. Rank of Commissary General of Musters and Deputy Mustermaster General. Broadside. Enclosed in President of Congress to Washington, 1777, Apr. 10.
     90, 184

1777
APR. 10

Continental Congress, Resolve. Rank of mustering officers. Broadside. Printed by Dunlap. Enclosed in President of Congress to Washington, 1777, May 3.   91, 180

1777
APR. 10

Continental Congress, Resolve. Payment of militia. Broadside. Printed by Dunlap. Enclosed in President of Congress to Washington, 1777, Apr. 10.   90, 110

1777
APR. 10

Continental Congress, Resolves. Formation of camp on west side of the Delaware; appointments of the commander-in-chief; pay of discharged troops; defense of the western frontier; appointments. D. S. of John Hancock. 4 pp. Enclosed in President of Congress to Washington, 1777, Apr. 10.   **90, 130**

1777
APR. 10

Continental Congress, Resolves. Election of minor military officers. D. S. of John Hancock. Enclosed in President of Congress to Washington, 1777, Apr. 16.   **90, 144**

1777
APR. 10

Lee, Richard Henry. Philadelphia. To [George] Washington [Morristown]. Ordering on of troops; British designs against Philadelphia; strengthening the army; inoculation of troops. A. L. S. 2 pp.   **14, 237**

1777
APR. 11

Continental Congress, Resolves. Election of hospital officers; provisions in Philadelphia; pay of certain officers. D. S. of John Hancock. Enclosed in President of Congress to Washington, 1777, Apr. 16.   **90, 144**

1777
APR. 12

Washington, George. Morristown. To the President of Congress, Philadelphia. Commission in army to Chev. [Mauduit] du Plessis. L. S. 1 p. In handwriting of Alexander Hamilton.
                                       C. C.   152, 4, 79

1777
APR. 12

Washington, George. Morristown. To [a Committee of Congress, Philadelphia]. Formation of army on west side of the Delaware; militia and Continentals; removal of stores from Philadelphia. Draft. 3 pp. In handwriting of Tench Tilghman.   **A. II, 263**
Committee for opposing progress of the enemy: Wilson, Clymer, R. H. Lee, Clark and J. Adams.

1777
APR. 12

Continental Congress, Resolves. Recruiting service; claims against the United States; hospital matters. D. S. of John Hancock. Enclosed in President of Congress to Washington, 1777, Apr. 16.   **90, 144**

1777
APR. 4

Continental Congress, Resolves. Magazine at Brookfield, Massachusetts. D. S. of John Hancock. Enclosed in Washington to the President of Congress, 1777, Apr. 16.   **90, 144**

1777
APR. 14

Continental Congress, Resolves. Investigation of recruiting service. Broadside. Printed by Dunlap. Transmitted to Washington.   **94, 289**

1777
APR. 14

Continental Congress, Resolves. Investigation of recruiting service; State returns of Continental troops; exemptions from service; drafts from militia; recruiting. Broadside. 1 p. Enclosed in President of Congress to Washington, 1777, Apr. 16.

90, 138

1777
APR. 14

Continental Congress, Resolves. Changes in regulations for government of troops; provisions; complaints of officers; courts-martial sentences. Broadside. 1 p. Enclosed in President of Congress to Washington, 1777, Apr. 16.

90, 143

1777
APR. 15

Continental Congress, Resolves. Various military appointments; designations of regiments. D. S. of John Hancock. Enclosed in President of Congress to Washington, 1777, Apr. 16.

90, 144

1777
APR. 16

Continental Congress, President. Philadelphia. To [George] Washington [Morristown]. Attempt on British in Rhode Island; augmenting army. L. S. of John Hancock. 2 pp. In handwriting of Jacob Rush. Answered Apr. 21*.

90, 140

1777
APR. 16

Continental Congress, Resolves. Recommending Rhode Island to expel enemy; Massachusetts and Connecticut's assistance. D. S. of John Hancock. 2 pp. Enclosed in President of Congress to Washington, 1777, Apr. 16.

90, 139

1777
APR. 16

Board of War. Invoice of military stores sent to French Creek from Mar. 25 to Apr. 16. Tabular statements. Enclosed in Board of War to Washington, 1777, Apr. 29.

94, 318

[1777]
[APR. 16?]

Lee, Richard Henry. [Philadelphia.] To [George] Washington [Morristown]. Troops ordered to Bristol; intelligence from Europe; British plan of campaign; scarcity of iron and remedy. A. L. S. 2 pp.

20, 328

1777
APR. 17

Washington, George. Morristown. To [the Board of War, Philadelphia]. Commissions to officers [of the 16 additional Continental regiments]. Draft. 2 pp. Endorsed: "To the Secy at War." In handwriting of Tench Tilghman.

A. II, 267

[1777]
[APR. 17]

Washington, George. List of officers appointed to the 16 additional Continental regiments. A. D. 1 p. Enclosed in Washington to the Board of War, 1777, Apr. 17.

A. II, 271

1777
APR. 17

Continental Congress, Resolves. Establishment of Committee of Foreign Affairs. D. S. of John Hancock. Enclosed in President of Congress to Washington, 1777, Apr. 20.   **90, 155**

1777
APR. 17

[Albany Committee.] Return of wheat and flour in Albany County that can be spared for the Continental service. Statement of quantities at various places. Contemporary copy. 1 p. In handwriting of John Lansing, jr. Enclosed in Schuyler to Washington, 1777, Apr. 30.   **15, 96**

1777
APR. 18

Washington, George. Morristown. To [the President of] Congress [Philadelphia]. Inhabitants supplying enemy with goods; relief of prisoners; designs of enemy. Draft. 5 pp. In handwriting of Robert Hanson Harrison.   **A. 11, 273**

Printed: Writings of Washington (Ford) N. Y. 1890. 5, 330.

1777
APR. 18

Continental Congress, Resolve. Inspection of magazines. D. S. of John Hancock. Enclosed in President of Congress to Washington, 1777, Apr. 20.

90, 155

1777
APR. 19

Continental Congress, Resolves. Deputy Adjutant General of the Northern Department; removal of provisions, cattle, etc. from reach of the enemy; minor matters. D. S. of John Hancock. Enclosed in President of Congress to Washington, 1777, Apr. 20.   **90, 155**

1777
APR. 19

Continental Congress, Resolves. Tory insurrection in Maryland. D. S. of John Hancock. 3 pp. Enclosed in President of Congress to Washington, 1777, Apr. 20.   **90, 153**

1777
APR. 20

Continental Congress, President. Philadelphia. To [George] Washington [Morristown]. Transmitting resolves. Unsigned letter. 1 p. In handwriting of Jacob Rush. Answered Apr. 21.*
90, 151

1777
APR. 20

[Caswell, Richard.] Newbern. [South Carolina]. To [Thomas Burke, Philadelphia]. Appointment of Col. Abraham Shepherd. Extract of letter. 2 pp. In handwriting of George Bond. Enclosed in President of Congress to Washington, 1777, June 13.   **90, 221**

1777
APR. 21

Washington, George. Morristown. To [the President of] Congress [Philadelphia]. Purchase of supplies

in Jersey; enemy in Rhode Island.   Draft.   2 pp.
In handwriting of Robert Hanson Harrison.
                                            A. II, 279

1777   Board of War. [Philadelphia.] To [George] Washington
APR. 21   [Morristown]. Recovery of cannon thrown in the
           Raritan by British; guns for city defenses;
           frigates. A. L. S. of Richard Peters. 1 p.
                                            17, 299

1777   [Heath, William.] Boston. To [George Washington, Mor-
APR. 21   ristown]. Shipment of arms from Massachusetts.
           [Extract of letter.] Contemporary copy. 1 p.
           In handwriting of George Johnston. Enclosed in
           Washington to the President of Congress, 1777,
           May 3.   C. C. 153, 4, 151

1777   Howe, [Sir] W[illiam]. New York. To George Washing-
APR. 21   ton [Morristown]. British treatment of prisoners.
           Contemporary copy. 3 pp. In handwriting of
           Richard Kidder Meade. Enclosed in Washing-
           ton to the President of Congress, 1777, Apr. 26.
                                   C. C. 152, 4, 113

1777   Continental Congress, Secretary. [Philadelphia.] To
APR. 22   [George] Washington, Morristown. Requesting
           originals resolves transmitted. A. L. S. of
           Charles Thomson. 1 p.   90, 157

1777   Continental Congress, Resolves. Forwarding troops; money
APR. 22   for American prisoners; hospital matters; case of
           Gov. William Franklin. D. S. of John Hancock.
           Enclosed in President of Congress to Washing-
           ton, 1777, Apr. 25.   90, 163

1777   Stephen, Adam. Newark [New Jersey]. To [George]
APR. 22   Washington [Morristown]. Intelligence of en-
           emy. A. L. S. 1 p. Enclosed in Washington
           to the President of Congress, 1777, Apr. 23.
                                   C. C. 152, 4, 99

1777   Washington, George. Morristown. To [the President of
APR. 23   Congress, Philadelphia]. Thomas Long, British
           spy. Draft. 1 p. In handwriting of Tench
           Tilghman.   A. II, 281

1777   Stephen, Adam. Chatham [New Jersey]. To [George]
APR. 23   Washington, Morristown]. Intelligence of en-
           emy's reenforcements, movements, etc. A. L. S.
           3 pp. Enclosed in Washington to the President
           of Congress, 1777, Apr. 23.   C. C. 152, 4, 103

1777
APR. 23

Stephen, Adam. Chatham. To [George] Washington, Morristown. Intelligence of enemy; state of their supplies, etc. A. L. S. 3 pp. Enclosed in Washington to the President of Congress, 1777, Apr. 23.   **C. C. 152, 4, 107**

1777
APR. 24

Continental Congress, Resolves. Calling out of Pennsylvania militia. D. S. of John Hancock. Enclosed in President of Congress to Washington, 1777, Apr. 25.   **90, 163**

1777
APR. 25

Continental Congress, President. Philadelphia. To [George] Washington [Morristown]. Calling out of the Pennsylvania militia; personal matters. L. S. of John Hancock. 3 pp. In handwriting of Jacob Rush. Answered Apr. 26.*   **90, 159**

1777
APR. 25

Continental Congress, Resolves. Case of Maj. Elisha Painter; calling out of Delaware and New Jersey militia; inspection of hospitals; forwarding troops. D. S. of John Hancock. 4 pp. Enclosed in President of Congress to Washington, 1777, Apr. 25.   **90, 167**

1777
APR. 25

Board of War. Return of provisions in Continental stores in Pennsylvania. Tabular statement. 1 p. Enclosed in Board of War to Washington, 1777, Apr. 29.   **94, 321**

1777
APR. 26

Washington, George. Morristown. To [the President of Congress, Philadelphia]. Relief of American prisoners; disaffection of inhabitants. Draft. 2 pp. In handwriting of Alexander Hamilton.   **A. II, 283**

1777
APR. 26

Continental Congress, President. Philadelphia. To [George] Washington [Morristown]. Forwarding troops; calling out militia of Philadelphia, Jersey and Delaware. L. S. of John Hancock. 2 pp. In handwriting of Jacob Rush. Answered Apr. 28.*   **90, 165**

1777
APR. 26

Board of War. Return of ammunition made up at Philadelphia. Tabular statement. Enclosed in Board of War to Washington, 1777, Apr. 29.   **94, 318**

1777
APR. 26

[Heath, William]. Boston. To [George Washington, Morristown]. Introducing Col. [Thomas] Conway. Extract of letter.ʼ 1 p. In handwriting of Richard Kidder Meade. Enclosed in Washington to the President of Congress, 1777, May 9.   **C. C. 152, 4, 161**

1777
APR. 26

Huntington, Jedediah. Danbury [Connecticut]. To B[rig]. G[en]. [Alexander] McDougall [Peekskill, New York]. Intelligence of enemy; manœuvers. [Three letters of same date.] Contemporary copies. 2 pp. In handwriting of Alexander Hamilton. Enclosed in Washington to the President of Congress, 1777, Apr. 30.
C. C. 152, 4, 129

1777
APR. 27

Arnold, B[enedict]. West Redding [Connecticut]. To Brig. Gen. [Alexander] McDougall [Peekskill]. The affair at Danbury. Contemporary copy. 2 pp. In handwriting of John Fitzgerald. Enclosed in Washington to the President of Congress, 1777, Apr. 30.   C. C. 152, 4, 139

1777
APR. 27

Campbell, John. Courtland's Manor [New York]. To Brig. Gen. [Alexander] McDougall [Peekskill]. Advance of enemy. Contemporary copy. 1 p. In handwriting of Tench Tilghman. Enclosed in Washington to the President of Congress, 1777, Apr. 30.   C. C. 152, 4, 131

1777
APR. 27

Campbell, John. Salem [Westchester county, New York]. To Brig. Gen. [Alexander] McDougall [Peekskill]. Movements of enemy. Contemporary copy. 1 p. In handwriting of Richard Kidder Meade. Enclosed in Washington to the President of Congress, 1777, Apr. 30.   C. C. 152, 4, 133

1777
APR. 27

Field, John. [Danbury? Connecticut.] To [Brig.] Gen. [Alexander] McDougall, Peekskill. March of enemy from Danbury. Contemporary copy. 1 p. In handwriting of Tench Tilghman. Enclosed in Washington to the President of Congress, 1777, Apr. 30.   C. C. 152, 4, 135

1777
APR. 27

Huntington, Jedediah. Danbury [Connecticut]. To [Brig.] Gen. [Alexander] McDougall [Peekskill]. The situation at Danbury. Contemporary copy. 1 p. In handwriting of Richard Kidder Meade. Enclosed in Washington to the President of Congress, 1777, Apr. 30.   C. C. 152, 4, 137

1777
APR. 27

McDougall, Alexander. Peekskill [New York]. To [George Washington, Morristown]. Affair at Danbury; the situation. Contemporary copy. 1 p. In handwriting of Tench Tilghman. Enclosed in Washington to the President of Congress, 1777, Apr. 28.   C. C. 152, 4, 125

WRITING OF STEPHEN MOYLAN.

1777
APR. 27

McDougall, Alexander. Peekskill. To [George Washington, Morristown]. Fruitless march against the enemy. Contemporary copy. 1 p. In handwriting of Richard Kidder Meade. Enclosed in Washington to the President of Congress, 1777, Apr. 30. C. C. **152, 4, 127**

1777
APR. 28

Washington, George. Morristown. To [the President of Congress, Philadelphia]. Recruiting service; destruction of stores at Danbury. Draft. 2 pp. In handwriting of Robert Hanson Harrison.

A. **II, 285**

Printed: Writings of Washington (Ford) N. Y. 1890. 5, 345.

1777
APR. 28

Arnold, B[enedict]. Saugatuck [Connecticut]. To [Brig. Gen. Alexander McDougall, Peekskill]. Skirmish at Ridgefield. Contemporary copy. 1 p. In handwriting of George Johnson. Enclosed in Washington to the President of Congress, 1777, Apr. 30. C. C. **152, 4, 145**

1777
APR. 28

Hughes, H[ugh]. "Sawgatouk Bridge" [Connecticut]. To [Brig. Gen. Alexander McDougall, Peekskill]. Account of enemy's foray into Connecticut. Contemporary copy. 2 pp. In handwriting of Alexander Hamilton. Enclosed in Washington to the President of Congress, 1777, Apr. 30.

C. C. **152, 4, 141**

1777
APR. 28

Huntington, Jedediah. Danbury. To [Brig. Gen. Alexander McDougall, Peekskill]. Loss of enemy; wounding of Brig. Gen. [David] Wooster; skirmishing. Contemporary copy. 1 p. In handwriting of George Johnston. Enclosed in Washington to the President of Congress, 1777, Apr. 30.

C. C. **152, 4, 143**

1777
APR. 29

Continental Congress, Resolves. Settlement of recruiting and paymaster's account. Broadside. Printed by Dunlap. Enclosed in President of Congress to Washington, 1777, Apr. 29–30. **94, 289**

1777
APR. 29

Continental Congress, Resolves. Calling out of Delaware militia; troops for Ticonderoga; measures for defense of the lakes. D. S. of John Hancock. 3 pp. Enclosed in President of Congress to Washington, 1777, Apr. 29–30. **90, 173**

1777
APR. 29

Gates, H[oratio]. [Albany.] To [the President of Congress, Philadelphia]. Reasons why British will make New York State main object of ensuing campaign; importance of posts in the Highlands; army in the Jerseys; horse for the Hudson. Contemporary copy. 4 pp. Enclosed in Board of War to Washington, 1777, May 7.   **15, 149**

1777
APR. 29

Lee, Richard Henry. Philadelphia. To [George] Washington [Morristown]. Ironworks in New Jersey; [Arthur] Lee's report of British plan of campaign. A. L. S. 1 p.   **15, 77**

1777
APR. 29–30

Continental Congress, President. Philadelphia. To [George] Washington [Morristown]. Defense of Ticonderoga; transmitting resolves. L. S. of John Hancock. 2 pp. In handwriting of Jacob Rush. Answered May 3*.   **90, 169**

1777
APR. 30

Washington, George. Morristown. To [the President of] Congress [Philadelphia]. Enclosing account of destruction of stores at Danbury. Draft. 1 p. In handwriting of Robert Hanson Harrison.

    A. II, 289

1777
APR. 30

Continental Congress, Resolves. Committees on the situation; removal of provisions; purchase of cattle; removal of grain from the Hudson; march of reenforcing troops. D. S. of John Hancock. 3 pp. Enclosed in President of Congress to Washington, 1777, Apr. 29–30.   **90, 175**

1777
APR. 30

Continental Congress, Resolves. Removal of salt beef and stores from Connecticut; supply of troops under [Brig.] Gen. [Alexander] McDougall; wheat in Albany county [New York]; flour magazines in Ulster county and supply of troops; purchase of cattle in Eastern States; removal of wheat from the Hudson; supply of cattle; salt. Contemporary copy. 4 pp. In handwriting of John Lansing, jr. In part, duplicate of preceding resolves. Enclosed in Schuyler to Washington, 1777, Apr. 30.   **15, 92**

1777
APR. 30

Continental Congress, Resolve. Report of committee of conference with the Commissary General on loss of provisions at Danbury to be sent to Gen. Washington, the Quartermaster and Commissary Generals. Contemporary copy. 1 p. In handwriting of John Lansing, jr. Enclosed in Schuyler to Washington, 1777, Apr. 30.   **15, 97**

The report on which above resolve was based is in C. C. 29, 55, and was made to Congress Apr. 30. The committee: Duer, Nelson, S. Adams and Gerry.

1777
APR. 30

Schuyler, Ph[ilip John]. Philadelphia. To [George] Washington [Morristown]. Transmitting resolves of Congress relating to Quartermaster and Commissary General's Departments; with explanations of reasons for their adoption; wheat and flour in Albany County [New York]; resignation. L. S. 3 pp. Answered May 3.   **15,** 90

1777
APR.

Board of War. Return of Continental stores at Baltimore and in New Hampshire, Rhode Island, North Carolina and Georgia. Tabular statement. 3 pp. Enclosed in Board of War to Washington, 1777, Apr. 29.   **94,** 319

[1777]
[APR.]

Anonymous, Intelligence of enemy's preparations. 1 p. In handwriting of John Fitzgerald. Enclosed in Washington to the President of Congress, 1777, Apr. 10.   **C. C.** 152, 4, 73

1777
MAY 1

Continental Congress, Resolves. Detention of Maryland troops. D. S. of John Hancock. Enclosed in President of Congress to Washington, 1777, May 3.   **90,** 181

1777
MAY 2

Continental Congress, Secret Committee. Philadelphia. To [George] Washington [Morristown]. Transmitting money for American prisoners. A. L. S. of Robert Morris, signed also by Richard Henry Lee, Wm. Whipple and Phil. Livingston. 1 p. Answered May 5*.   **90,** 177

1777
MAY 2

Continental Congress, Resolves. Mustering department matters. D. S. of John Hancock. Enclosed in President of Congress to Washington, 1777, May 3.   **90,** 181

1777
MAY 2

Continental Congress, Resolves. Duties of muster-masters. Broadside. Printed by Dunlap. Enclosed in President of Congress to Washington, 1777, May 3.   **91,** 180.

1777
MAY 3

Washington, George. Morristown. To [the President of Congress, Philadelphia]. Movements of troops and stores; arrival of *Amphitrite;* desertions. Draft. 5 pp. In handwriting of Robert Hanson Harrison. Read in Congress, May 6. **A.** II, 291
Printed in part: Writings of Washington (Ford) N. Y. 1890. 5, 343, note.

1777
MAY 3

Continental Congress, President. Philadelphia. To [George] Washington [Morristown]. Army baker; promotion of [Brig.] Gen. [Benedict] Arnold. L. S. of John Hancock]. 2 pp. In handwriting of Jacob Rush.   **90,** 179

1777
MAY 3

Continental Congress, Resolves. Baking for the Army; John Belton's improved musket; various appointments. D. S. of John Hancock. Enclosed in President of Congress to Washington, 1777, May 3.   **90, 181**

1777
MAY 5

Washington, George. Morristown. To [the President of Congress, Philadelphia]. Designs against Ticonderoga; Howe's bounty to deserters; loss at Danbury. Draft. 2 pp. In handwriting of Robert Hanson Harrison. Read in Congress, May 6.
                                                A. II, 297
                        Printed: Writings of Washington (Ford) N. Y. 1890. 5, 350.

1777
MAY 5

Washington, George. Morristown. To [the Secret Committee of Congress, Philadelphia]. Money for American prisoners of war. Draft. 1 p. In handwriting of Robert Hanson Harrison.
                                                A. II, 299

1777
MAY 6

Continental Congress, Resolves. Troops of horse for [Maj.] Gen. [Horatio] Gates. A. D. S. of Charles Thomson. 1 p. Transmitted to Washington.
                                                15, 148

1777
MAY 7

Board of War. [Philadelphia.] To George Washington, Morristown. Stores ordered to Springfield [Mass.]; case of Lt. Col. [George] Etherington. A. L. S. 1 p. Answered May 10*.   **15, 146**

1777
MAY 9

Washington, George. Morristown. To [the President of] Congress [Philadelphia]. Introducing Col. [Thomas] Conway. Draft. 2 pp. In handwriting of Robert Hanson Harrison. Read in Congress, May 12. A. II, 301.
                        Printed: Writings of Washington (Ford) N. Y. 1890. 5, 353, note.

1777
MAY 9

Washington, George. Morristown. To [the President of Congress, Philadelphia]. Introducing Mottin de la Balme; rank expected by Frenchmen. Draft. 2 pp. In handwriting of Tench Tilghman. Read in Congress, May 14. Referred to the Committee on Foreign Applications.   **A. II, 303**
                        Printed in part: Writings of Washington (Ford) N. Y. 1890. 5, 364, note.
                        Committee: Lovell, Heyward and Roberdeau.

1777
MAY 9

Continental Congress, Resolves. Investigation of pay matters. D. S. of John Hancock. 2 pp. Enclosed in President of Congress to Washington, 1777, May 10.   **90, 187**

1777
MAY 10

Washington, George. Morristown. To [the President of Congress, Philadelphia]. Movement of troops;

want of money; recruiting accounts. Draft. 2
pp. In handwriting of Richard Kidder Meade
and Robert Hanson Harrison. Read in Congress,
May 13. **A. II, 305**
Printed in part: Writings of Washington (Ford) N. Y. 1890. 5, 354,
note.

1777
MAY 10
Washington, George. Morristown. To [the Board of
War, Philadelphia]. Defense of passes of the
Hudson river. Draft. 1 p. In handwriting of
Tench Tilghman. **A. II, 307**

1777
MAY 10
Continental Congress, President. Philadelphia. To
[George] Washington [Morristown]. Investiga-
tion of withholding pay from soldiers; return of
army; Delaware and Pennsylvania militia. L. S.
of John Hancock. 3 pp. In handwriting of
Jacob Rush. Answered May 12*. **90, 185**

1777
MAY 10
Continental Congress, Resolves. Certain appointments.
D. S. of John Hancock. Enclosed in President
of Congress to Washington, 1777, May 15.
90, 191

1777
MAY 10
Morris, Robert. Philadelphia. To George Washington
[Morristown]. Introducing [Charles] Armand
[-Tufin], Marquis de la Rouerie. A. L. S. 2 pp.
15, 155

1777
MAY 11
Board of War. [Philadelphia.] To [George] Washington
[Morristown]. Letters to Gov. [William] Livingston and [Maj.] Gen. [Israel] Putnam; strength
of army in Jersey; disbanding militia. A. L. S.
of Richard Peters. Answered May 12*. **15, 154**

1777
MAY 12
Washington, George. Morristown. To [the President of]
Congress [Philadelphia]. Dishonesty of officers
in withholding pay of soldiers; state of army.
Draft. 3 pp. In handwriting of Robert Hanson
Harrison. Read in Congress, May 13.
A. II, 309
Printed: Writings of Washington (Ford) N. Y. 1890. 5, 359.

1777
MAY 12
Washington, George. Morristown. To [the President of
Congress, Philadelphia]. [Maj.] Gen. [Benedict]
Arnold's claim to rank. L. S. 2 pp. In hand-
writing of Robert Hanson Harrison.
C. C. 152, 4, 175
Printed: Writings of Washington (Ford) N. Y. 1890. 5, 362.

1777
MAY 12
Washington, George. Morristown. To [the President of]
Congress [Philadelphia]. [Maj.] Gen. [Benedict]

Arnold; charges against his character. **Draft.**
2 pp. In handwriting of Robert Hanson Harrison.　　　　　　　　　　　　　　　　**A. II, 313**

Printed: Writings of Washington (Ford) N. Y. 1890. 5, 362.

1777　　　**Washington,** George. Morristown. To [the Board of
MAY 12　　　War, Philadelphia]. Exchange of certain pris-
　　　　　　oners; militia. Draft. 1 p. In handwriting of
　　　　　　Tench Tilghman.　　　　　　　**A. II, 315**

1777　　　**Continental Congress,** Resolves. Brigadier appointments;
MAY 12　　　exemption of post-riders and others from military
　　　　　　duties. D. S. of John Hancock. Enclosed in
　　　　　　President of Congress to Washington, 1777, May
　　　　　　15.　　　　　　　　　　　　　　**90, 191**

1777　　　**Lovell,** James. Philadelphia. To [George] Washington
MAY 12　　　[Morristown]. [François, Marquis de] Malmedy's
　　　　　　rank. A. L. S. 2 pp.　　　　　　**15, 168**

1777　　　**Washington,** George. Morristown. To [the President
MAY 13　　　of Congress, Philadelphia]. Convict servants
　　　　　　recruited into the Virginia regiments. Draft.
　　　　　　2 pp. In handwriting of Robert Hanson Harri-
　　　　　　son.　　　　　　　　　　　　　　**A. II, 317**

1777　　　**Continental Congress,** Resolves. Relief of American sym-
MAY 13　　　pathizers in Nova Scotia; case of [Richard] Camp-
　　　　　　bell. D. S. of John Hancock. Enclosed in
　　　　　　President of Congress, 1777, May 15.　　**90, 191**

1777　　　**Rush,** B[enjamin]. Philadelphia. To [George] Washing-
MAY 13　　　ton [Morristown]. Danger to health of troops in
　　　　　　taking the field early. A. L. S. 2 pp. **15, 172**

1777　　　**Continental Congress,** Resolves. Forage-master's depart-
MAY 14　　　ment; intrenching tools; horses, wagons, etc.
　　　　　　Quartermaster's department; penalty for private
　　　　　　use of public stores. Broadside. 2 pp. Printed
　　　　　　by John Dunlap. Enclosed in President of Con-
　　　　　　gress to Washington, 1777, May 15.　　**90, 200**

1777　　　**Continental Congress,** Resolves. Clothing for Virginia
MAY 14　　　troops. D. S. of John Hancock. Enclosed in
　　　　　　President of Congress to Washington, 1777, May
　　　　　　27.　　　　　　　　　　　　　　　**90, 198**

1777　　　**Penet,** P[ierre]. Nantes [France]. To George Washington
MAY 14　　　[Morristown, New Jersey]. Introducing D'Avout,
　　　　　　A. L. S. 1 p. (In French). Enclosed in Wash-
　　　　　　ington to the President of Congress, 1777, July
　　　　　　25.　　　　　　　　**C. C. 152, 4, 421**

1777
MAY 15

Continental Congress, Resolves. Minor military matters.
D. S. of John Hancock. Enclosed in President
of Congress to Washington, 1777, May 27.
90, 198

1777
MAY 15

Continental Congress, President. Philadelphia. To
[George] Washington [Morristown]. Commis-
sions for brigadiers. L. S. of John Hancock.
In handwriting of Jacob Rush.   **90,** 189

1777
MAY 16

Washington, George. Morristown. To [the President
of Congress, Philadelphia]. Commission for
[Charles] Armand, [-Tufin, Marquis de la Rou-
erie]; expectations of French officers. Draft.
2 pp. In handwriting of Richard Kidder Meade.
Read in Congress, May 19.   **A.** II, 319
Printed: Writings of Washington (Ford) N. Y. 1890. 5, 367.

1777
MAY 18

Schuyler, Ph[ilip John]. Philadelphia. To [George]
Washington [Morristown]. Quakers and blankets; debate over Schuyler's supplanting Gates in
command in the North. L. S. 1 p. Answered
May 23.   **15,** 244

1777
MAY 20

Continental Congress, President. Philadelphia. To
[George] Washington [Morristown]. Introduc-
ing Mrs. Graydon of Philadelphia. L. S. of John
Hancock. 1 p.   **90,** 193

1777
MAY 20

Board of War. [Philadelphia.] To [George] Washington
[Morristown]. Inclosing resolves respecting the
recruiting service. A. L. S. of Richard Peters.
1 p.   **95,** 322

1777
MAY 21

Washington, George. Morristown. To [the President of]
Congress [Philadelphia]. Enclosing return of
forces in Jersey; need of secrecy as to state of
the army. 1 p. In handwriting of Robert Hanson
Harrison. Read in Congress, May 23. Referred
to the Board of War.   **A.** II, 321

1777
MAY 21

Continental Congress, Resolves. Northern Department
affairs. D. S. of John Hancock. Enclosed in
President of Congress, to Washington, 1777,
May 27.   **90,** 198

1777
MAY 22

Continental Congress, Resolves. [François] Louis [Teisse-
dre, Marquis de] Fleury. D. S. of John Hancock.
Enclosed in President of Congress to Washington, 1777, May 27.   **90,** 198

1777
MAY 22

Howe, [Sir] W[illiam]. New York. To [George Washington, Morristown]. Exchange of prisoners, ill

treatment of Lt. Col. [Archibald] Campbell.
Contemporary copy. 1 p. In handwriting of
Alexander Hamilton. Enclosed in Washington
to the President of Congress, 1777, May 28.

C. C.   152, 4, 199

Printed: Writings of Washington (Sparks) Boston. 1834. 4, 559.

1777
MAY 22

[Howe, Sir William.] New York. To [George] Washington [Morristown]. Complaints of Lt. Col. [Archi-
bald] Campbell's treatment. [Extract of letter.]
Contemporary copy. 1 p. In handwriting of
William Grayson? Enclosed in Washington to
the President of Congress, 1777, June 13–15.

C. C.   152, 4, 265

1777
MAY 22

Schuyler, Ph[ilip John]. Philadelphia. To [George]
Washington [Morristown]. James Fisher, a
tory. L. S. 1 p. Answered May 23.   15, 282

1777
MAY 24

Washington, George. Morristown. To [the President of
Congress, Philadelphia]. Col. [Timothy] Pickering as Adjutant-General; defense of Highlands;
artillery regiment. Draft. 3 pp. In handwriting of Robert Hanson Harrison and George
Lewis. Read in Congress, May 27. Referred to
Board of War.   A. II, 323

Printed: Writings of Washington (Ford) N. Y. 1890. 5, 386.

1777
MAY 24

Washington, George. Morristown. To [Charles Thomson, Philadelphia]. Papers respecting establishment of a cavalry corps. Draft. 1 p. In handwriting of Alexander Hamilton.   A. II, 327

1777
MAY 26

Continental Congress, Resolves. Command of the light
horse; pardoning power; chaplains; miscellaneous matters. D. S. of John Hancock. Enclosed
in President of Congress to Washington, 1777,
May 27.   90, 198

1777
MAY 26

Lovell, James. Philadelphia. To [George] Washington
[Morristown]. Introducing a German officer
[Maj. Henry Emanuel Lutterloh]; promotion of
[Charles] Armand [-Tufin, Marquis de la Rou-
erie]. A. L. S. 2 pp. Answered June 4.

15, 307

1777
MAY 26

Roberdeau, Daniel. Philadelphia. To [George] Washington [Morristown]. Personal matters; chaplains
and profanity in the army; recommending certain
clergymen. A. L. S. 4 pp.   15, 303

[1777]
[MAY 26]   [Schuyler, Philip John.] [Philadelphia] To [the President of Congress, Philadelphia.] Raising of horse in vicinity of Albany. Extract of letter. 1 p. In handwriting of William Churchill Houston. Transmitted to Washington.   90, 201

1777
MAY 27   Continental Congress, President. Philadelphia. To [George] Washington [Morristown]. Northern department; chaplains. L. S. of John Hancock. 2 pp. In handwriting of Jacob Rush. Answered May 29.*   90, 196

1777
MAY 27   Forman, David. Philadelphia. To the Board of War [Philadelphia]. Cutting off intercourse with enemy by way of Sandy Hook. Recent copy. 1 p. Original enclosed in Board of War to Washington, 1777, May 30.   15, 316

1777
MAY 27   Walton, George. Philadelphia. To [George] Washington [Morristown]. Col. [John] White's wish to recruit outside of Georgia. A. L. S. 2 pp.
   15, 312

1777
MAY 28   Washington, George. Morristown. To [the President of] Congress [Philadelphia]. Controversy with Howe over exchange of prisoners. Draft. 2 pp. In handwriting of Richard Kidder Meade. Read in Congress, May 29. Referred to the Board of War.   A. II, 329

Printed: Writings of Washington (Ford), N. Y. 1890. 5, 394.

1777
MAY 29   Washington, George. Middlebrook [New Jersey]. To [the President of Congress, Philadelphia]. Appointment of chaplains; raising troops of horse. Draft. 1 p. In handwriting of Richard Kidder Meade. Read in Congress, May 30.   A. II, 331

1777
MAY 29   Continental Congress, Resolves. Teams exempted from impressment; artillery from Virginia. D. S. of John Hancock. Enclosed in President of Congress to Washington, 1777, June 5.   90, 204

1777
MAY 29   Franklin, B[enjamin]. Paris. To [George] Washington [Middlebrook]. Introducing Comte [Casimir] Pulaski. Contemporary copy. 1 p. In handwriting of Caleb Gibbs. Enclosed in Washington to the President of Congress, 1777, Aug. 21.   C. C. 152, 4, 529

1777
MAY 29   [McDougall, Alexander.] Peekskill. To [George Washington, Middlebrook]. Arrival of reenforcements for enemy; desertions from Roger's Rangers.

[Extract of a letter.] Contemporary copy. 1 p. In handwriting of Richard Kidder Meade. Enclosed in Washington to the President of Congress 1777, May 31. C. C. 152, 4, 217

1777
MAY 29

Sullivan, John. Princeton [New Jersey]. To [George] Washington [Middlebrook]. Movements of enemy's ships. [Extract of letter.] Contemporary copy. 1 p. In handwriting of Tench Tilghman. Enclosed in Washington to the President of Congress, 1777, May 31. C. C. 152, 4, 219

1777
MAY 30

Continental Congress, Resolves. Commissions for Frenchmen. D. S. of John Hancock. Enclosed in President of Congress to Washington, 1777, June 5.
90, 204

1777
MAY 30

Continental Congress, Committee on Foreign Applications. To [George] Washington [Middlebrook]. Enclosing list of French officers arriving in the *Amphitrite;* [Charles Melchoir Garde de] Matigny's aptitude in English. A. L. S. of James Lovell, 2 pp. 16, 11

1777
MAY 30

Board of War. [Philadelphia.] To George Washington, Middlebrook. Relief of American prisoners; [Brig.] Gen. [David] Forman's letter; conduct of Capt. John Doyle. A. L. S. of Richard Peters, 2 pp. 15, 317

[1777]
[MAY 30]

French Officers. List of those who came over on the *Amphitrite.* 3 pp. (In French.) Enclosed in Committee on Foreign Applications to Washington, 1777, May 30. 16, 13

1777
MAY 31

Washington, George. Middlebrook. To [the President of Congress, Philadelphia]. Du Coudray and the command of the artillery. Draft. 2 pp. In handwriting of Robert Hanson Harrison. Read in Congress, June 2. Referred to the Board of War. A. II, 333
Printed: Writings of Washington (Ford), N. Y. 1890. 5, 401.

1777
MAY 31

Washington, George. Middlebrook. To [the President of Congress, Philadelphia]. Intentions of enemy; Pennsylvania militia as guard for Philadelphia; success at Sag Harbor. Draft. 3 pp. In handwriting of Tench Tilghman. A. II, 337

[1777]
[MAY]

Anonymous. Intelligence of enemy's designs. 2 pp. In handwriting of Tench Tilghman. Enclosed in Washington to the President of Congress, 1777, May 31. C. C. 152, 4, 215

1777
JUNE 2

Washington, George. Middlebrook. To [the President of Congress, Philadelphia]. News from the north; deficiencies in the armies; militia. Draft. 1 p. In handwriting of Alexander Hamilton. Read in Congress, June 5. Referred to the Board of War.   **A. II, 343**

1777
JUNE 2

Continental Congress, Resolves. Retaliation for treatment of [Maj.] Gen. [Charles] Lee; encouragement of desertion from British. D. S. of John Hancock. Enclosed in President of Congress to Washington, 1777, June 5.   **90, 204**

1777
JUNE 2

Washington, George. Middlebrook. To George Walton [Philadelphia]. Question of recruiting a regiment for Georgia. Draft. 1 p. In handwriting of Tench Tilghman.   **A. II, 345**

1777
JUNE 2

Washington, George. Middlebrook. To Lt. Gen. [Charles, Earl] Cornwallis, Brunswick [New Jersey]. Complaint of cruelty displayed in killing of Lt. [William] Martin. Contemporary copy. 1 p. In handwriting of William Grayson? Enclosed in Washington to the. President of Congress, 1777, June 13–15.   **C. C. 152, 4, 269**
Printed: Writings of Washington (Ford) N. Y. 1890. 5, 411, note.

1777
JUNE 2

Cornwallis, [Charles, Earl]. Brunswick [New Jersey]. To [George] Washington [Middlebrook]. Reply to charges of cruelty in case of Lt. [William] Martin. Contemporary copy. 1 p. In handwriting of William Grayson? Enclosed in Washington to the President of Congress, 1777, June 13–15.
    C. C. 152, 4, 271

1777
JUNE 3

Washington, George. Middlebrook. To [the President of Congress, Philadelphia]. Pardon for loyalists. L. S. 4 pp. In handwriting of Robert Hanson Harrison. Read in Congress, June 6. Referred to the Board of War.   **C. C. 152, 4, 225**
Printed: Writings of Washington (Ford) N. Y. 1890. 5, 407.

1777
JUNE 4

Washington, George. Middlebrook. To [James Lovell, Philadelphia]. Qualifications of Maj. [Henry Emanuel] Lutterloh. Draft. 1 p. In handwriting of Tench Tilghman.   **A. II, 351**

1777
JUNE 5

Washington, George. Middlebrook. To [the President of Congress, Philadelphia]. Requesting opinion of Congress on Howe's letter respecting prisoners. Draft. 1 p. In handwriting of Robert Hanson Harrison.   **A. II, 353**

1777
JUNE 5

Continental Congress, President. Philadelphia. To [George] Washington [Middlebrook]. [Brig.] Gen. [Thomas] Mifflin; encouragement of desertion from enemy. L. S. of John Hancock. 1 p. In handwriting of Jacob Rush. Answered June 6*.   90, 202

1777
JUNE 5

Howe, [Sir] W[illiam]. New York. To [George] Washington [Middlebrook]. Answer to his letter of May 22. Contemporary copy. 1 p. In handwriting of Alexander Hamilton. Enclosed in Washington to the President of Congress, 1777, June 5.   C. C. 152, 4, 231

1777
JUNE 5

Knox, Henry. Middlebrook. To [George] Washington [Middlebrook]. Resolution of Congress as to ranking of French officers in the artillery. Contemporary copy. 3 pp. In handwriting of William Grayson? Enclosed in Washington to the President of Congress, 1777, June 5.
C. C. 152, 4, 241

1777
JUNE 5

Willis, Enoch. [Middlebrook.] Examination of. Preparations of enemy for embarkation. 1 p. In handwriting of Richard Kidder Meade. Enclosed in Washington to the President of Congress, 1777, June 8.   C. C. 152, 4, 251

1777
JUNE 6

Washington, George. Middlebrook. To [the President of] Congress [Philadelphia]. Rank of French officers in the artillery: intentions of enemy. Draft. 4 pp. In handwriting of Richard Kidder Meade and Robert Hanson Harrison. Read in Congress, June 9. Referred to Board of War.
A. II, 355

Printed, in part: Writings of Washington (Ford) N. Y. 1890. 5, 411.

1777
JUNE 6

Washington, George. Middlebrook. To [the Board of War, Philadelphia]. Prisoners and minor military matters. Draft. 2 pp. In handwriting of Tench Tilghman.   A. II, 359

1777
JUNE 6

Washington, George. Middlebrook. To James Lovell [Philadelphia]. Question of seniority of French officers. Draft. 1 p. In handwriting of Tench Tilghman.   A. II, 351

1777
JUNE 6

Washington, George. Middlebrook. To [Robert Morris, Philadelphia]. Major Apollos Morris. Draft. 2 pp. In handwriting of Tench Tilghman.
A. II, 361

1777
JUNE 6

Continental Congress, President.   Philadelphia.   To [George] Washington [Middlebrook].   Exchange negotiations and miscellaneous matters.   L. S. of John Hancock.   2 pp.   In handwriting of Jacob Rush.   Answered June 8.*   **90, 208**

1777
JUNE 6

Continental Congress, Resolves.   Negotiations for exchange of prisoners; Deputy-judge advocates general; Commissary general of prisoners.   D. S. of John Hancock.   2 pp.   Enclosed in President of Congress to Washington, 1777, June 6.   **90, 206**

1777
JUNE 7

Continental Congress, President.   Philadelphia.   To [George] Washington [Smith's Clove, New York].   Transmitting resolves; Maj. Gen. [Horatio] Gates's letter referred to the Treasury.   L. S. of John Jay.   1 p.   Answered June 14.*   **93, 201**

1777
JUNE 7

Continental Congress, Resolves.   Regimental paymasters. D. S. of John Hancock.   Enclosed in President of Congress to Washington, 1777, June 13.
                                                            90, 215

1777
JUNE 7

Mitchell, William.   Middlebrook.   Examination of.   Information of enemy's designs.   1 p.   In handwriting of Tench Tilghman.   Enclosed in Washington to the President of Congress, 1777, June 8.
                                        C. C.   152, 4, 249

1777
JUNE 8

Washington, George.   Middlebrook.   To [the President of Congress, Philadelphia].   Exchange of prisoners; chaplains; enemy's movements.   Draft.   3 pp.   In handwriting of Robert Hanson Harrison.   Read in Congress, June 9.   Referred to Board of War.   **A.   II, 363**
Printed: Writings of Washington (Ford) N.Y. 1890. 5, 418.

1777
JUNE 8

[Jackson, Henry].   Boston.   To [Brig.] Gen. [Henry] Knox [Middlebrook].   Captures of transports by Continental armed vessels.   [Extract of letter.]   Contemporary copy.   1 p.   In handwriting of Alexander Hamilton.   Enclosed in Washington to the President of Congress, 1777, June 20.
                                        C. C.   152, 4, 283

1777
JUNE 9

Continental Congress, Resolve.   Arrest of Maj. Apollos Morris.   D. S. of John Hancock.   Enclosed in President of Congress to Washington, 1777, June 13.   **90, 215**

1777
JUNE 10

Continental Congress, Resolve.   [Maj.] Gen. [Benedict] Arnold ordered to Trenton.   D. S. of John Han-

cock.   Enclosed in President of Congress to
Washington, 1777, June 13.   90, 215

1777
JUNE 10

Continental Congress, Resolves.   Retaliation in treatment
of prisoners; Col. Abraham Sheppard; rank of
officers.   A. D. S. of John Hancock.   2 pp.   Enclosed in President of Congress to Washington,
1777, June 13.   90, 213

1777
JUNE 10–11

Continental Congress, Resolves.   Commissaries General of
Purchases, Issues, etc.; duties.   **Broadside.**
Printed by Dunlap.   Enclosed in President of
Congress to Washington, 1777, June 24.   90, 209

1777
JUNE 11

Continental Congress, Resolve.   New Jersey militia.   D. S.
of John Hancock.   Enclosed in President of Congress to Washington, 1777, June 13.   90, 215

1777
JUNE 13

Washington, George.   Middlebrook.   To Charles Thomson [Philadelphia].   Plan for establishment of
cavalry.   Draft.   2 pp.   In handwriting of Alexander Hamilton.   A. II, 365

1777
JUNE 13–15

Washington, George.   Middlebrook.   To [the President
of] Congress [Philadelphia].   British outrages;
treatment of prisoners; difficulty with Howe over
an exchange; ownership of horses for cavalry;
designs of enemy against Philadelphia; execution
of Abraham Patton; advance of the enemy;
[Brig.] Gen. [John Philip] De Haas.   Draft.   4
pp.   In handwriting of Richard Kidder Meade,
Robert Hanson Harrison and Caleb Gibbs.   Read
in Congress, June 16.   Referred to Board of
War.   A. II, 367

1777
JUNE 13

Continental Congress, President.   Philadelphia.   To
[George] Washington [Middlebrook].   Retalia-
tion in treatment of prisoners; Col. Abraham
Sheppard; fortifications on the Delaware.   L. S.
of John Hancock.   2 pp.   In handwriting of
Jacob Rush.   90, 211

1777
JUNE 14

Washington, George.   Middlebrook.   To [the President
of Congress, Philadelphia].   Advance of enemy.
L. S.   1 p.   In handwriting of Robert Hanson
Harrison.   Referred to the Board of War.
                                        C. C.   152, 4, 273

1777
JUNE 14

Washington, George.   Middlebrook.   To [the Board of
War, Philadelphia].   Enclosing establishment and
pay of light dragoons.   Draft.   1 p.   In handwriting of Tench Tilghman.   A. II, 371

1777
JUNE 15

[Schuyler, Philip John.] Saratoga [New York]. To [George Washington, Middlebrook]. Intelligence of a prisoner as to British in Canada. Contemporary copy of all but last paragraph of original letter. 2 pp. In handwriting of John Fitzgerald. Enclosed in Washington to the President of Congress, 1777, June 20. C. C. 152, 4, 281

1777
JUNE 16

Continental Congress, Resolve. Pay of Commissary Generals. Broadside. Printed by Dunlap. Enclosed in President of Congress to Washington, 1777, June 24. 90, 209

1777
JUNE 16

Continental Congress, Resolves. [Brig.] Gen. [John Philip] De Haas. D. S. of John Hancock. Enclosed in President of Congress to Washington, 1777, June 20. 90, 224

1777
JUNE 16

Board of War. [Philadelphia.] To George Washington, Middlebrook. Spears, cartridge-boxes, etc.; quartermaster of militia horse. A. L. S. of Richard Peters. 1 p. 95, 91

1777
JUNE 16

Schuyler, Ph[ilip John]. Fort Edward [New York]. To [George Washington, Middlebrook]. Expected attack on Ticonderoga; supplies and reenforcements. Contemporary copy. 2 pp. In handwriting of John Fitzgerald. Enclosed in Washington to the President of Congress, 1777, June 20. C. C. 152, 4, 282

1777
JUNE 17

Continental Congress, Resolves. Monument to [David] Wooster; Col. Abraham Sheppard's command. D. S. of John Hancock. Enclosed in President of Congress to Washington, 1777, June 20.

90, 224

1777
JUNE 18

Washington, George. Middlebrook. To [Lt.] Gen. [Sir William] Howe [New York]. British treatment of prisoners. Contemporary copy. 4 pp. In handwriting of Richard Kidder Meade. Enclosed in Washington to the President of Congress, 1777, June 13–15. C. C. 152, 4, 261
Printed: Writings of Washington (Ford) N. Y. 1890. 5, 423.

1777
JUNE 18

Continental Congress, Resolves. Appointments of Commissaries and others. D. S. of John Hancock. Enclosed in President of Congress to Washington, 1777, June 24. 90, 230

1777
JUNE 18

Continental Congress, Resolve. Power of general officer on separate command. D. S. of John Hancock.

Enclosed in President of Congress to Washington,
1777, June 20.   90, 224

1777
JUNE 18–
AUG. 6

[**Houston**, William Churchill] Memorandum of appointments of commissaries and deputies. A. D. 1 p.
Transmitted to Washington.   90, 266

1777
JUNE 19

Board of War. [Philadelphia.] To [George] Washington [Middlebrook]. Returns of arms and military stores from Continental agents. A. L. S. of Richard Peters. 2 pp.   16, 152

1777
JUNE 20

Washington, George. Middlebrook. To [the President of] Congress [Philadelphia]. Puzzling movements of the British. Draft. 4 pp. In handwriting of Robert Hanson Harrison and Caleb Gibbs. Read in Congress, June 23. A. II, 373
Printed in part: Writings of Washington (Ford) N. Y. 1890. 5, 444.

1777
JUNE 20

Washington, George. Middlebrook. To [the Board of War Philadelphia]. Spears and tin cartridge cases; quartermasters of troops of horse. Draft. 2 pp. In handwriting of Tench Tilghman.
                                        A. II, 377

1777
JUNE 20

Continental Congress, President. Philadelphia. To [George] Washington [Middlebrook]. Transmitting resolves. L. S. of John Hancock. 2 pp. In handwriting of Jacob Rush. Answered June 21. *   90, 222

1777
JUNE 20

Continental Congress, Resolve. Formation of an invalid corps. D. S. of John Hancock. Enclosed in President of Congress to Washington, 1777, June 24.   90, 230

1777
JUNE 21

Washington, George. Middlebrook. To [the President of Congress, Philadelphia]. Business of the Commissary Department. Draft. 1 p. In handwriting of Robert Hanson Harrison.
                                        A. II, 379

1777
JUNE 22

Washington, George. Middlebrook. To [the President of Congress, Philadelphia]. Retirement of the British from Brunswick. Draft. 3 pp. In handwriting of Tench Tilghman. Read in Congress, June 24.   A. II, 381
Printed: Writings of Washington (Ford) N. Y. 1890. 5, 447.

1777
JUNE 23

Flower, Benjamin. Philadelphia. To [the Board of War, Philadelphia]. Design of pike for riflemen; cartridges cannisters, etc. L. S. 1 p. Transmitted to Washington.   16, 154

1777
June 23

Continental Congress, Resolves. Provision supplies; commissary of prisoners. D. S. of John Hancock. Enclosed in President of Congress to Washington, 1777, June 24.   **90, 230**

1777
June 24

Continental Congress, President. Philadelphia. To [George] Washington [Middlebrook]. British retreat from Brunswick; commissary department. L. S. of John Hancock. 2 pp. In handwriting of Jacob Rush.   **90, 228**

1777
June 24

Continental Congress, Resolves. Reciprocal provision, arrangement with enemy for prisoners; contracts. D. S. of John Hancock. Enclosed in President of Congress to Washington, 1777, June 24.

    90, 230

1777
June 24

Williamson, Matthew jr. Elizabethtown [New Jersey]. To [George Washington, Middlebrook]. Intelligence of enemy. Contemporary copy. 1 p. In handwriting of John Fitzgerald. Enclosed in Washington to the President of Congress, 1777, June 25.   **C. C. 152, 4, 299**

1777
June 25

Washington, George. Quibbletown [New Jersey]. To [the President of Congress, Philadelphia]. Retreat and pursuit of the enemy to Amboy. Draft. 3 pp. In handwriting of Robert Hanson Harrison. Read in Congress, June 26.   **A. II, 385**
Printed: Writings of Washington (Ford) N. Y. 1890. 5, 450.

1777
June 25

Washington, George. Quibbletown. To Col. [Baron] D'Arendt [Quibbletown?]. Permission to go to Philadelphia; treaty with Prussia. L. S. 1 p. In handwriting of Alexander Hamilton.

    C. C. 152, 4, 301

1777
June 25

St Clair, Arthur. Ticonderoga. [New York]. To Maj. Gen. [Philip John] Schuyler [Saratoga, New York]. Enemy at Crown Point; militia; inability to defend Ticonderoga. Contemporary copy. 1 p. In handwriting of Caleb Gibbs. Enclosed in Washington to the President of Congress, 1777, July 2.   **C. C. 152, 4, 325**

1777
June 28

Washington, George. Middlebrook. To [the President of Congress, Philadelphia]. Advance of enemy and consequent manoevers [skirmish of Short Hills, New Jersey]. Draft. 2 pp. In handwriting of Robert Hanson Harrison. Read in Congress, June 30.   **A. II, 389**
Printed: Writings of Washington (Ford) N. Y. 1890. 5, 452.

1777   **Board of War**. Philadelphia. To [George] Washington,
JUNE 28   Quibbletown [Middlebrook]. Disposition of cannon from France. Note of this letter being found in papers of Lt. [Charles?] Cameron. A. L. of Richard Peters. 1 p.   **17, 137**

1777   **Washington**, George. Middlebrook. To [the President
JUNE 29   of Congress, Philadelphia]. Loss of British in retreat to Amboy; object of their movements. Draft. 3 pp. In handwriting of Robert Hanson Harrison.   **A. II, 393**

1777   **Hicks**, William. New York. To [Gov.] William Franklin,
JUNE 29   Litchfield [Connecticut]. Mrs. Franklin's poor health. A. L. S. 1 p. Enclosed in Washington to the President of Congress, 1777, July 25.
       C. C. 152, 4, 389

1777   **Washington**, George. Middlebrook. To [the Board of
JUNE 30   War, Philadelphia]. Arrival of artillery in the *Amphitrite;* distribution of the guns; irregularity of system of obtaining supplies. Draft. 4 pp. In handwriting of Alexander Hamilton.
       A. II, 397

[1777]   **Du Coudray**, Philip Charles Jean Baptiste Tronson.
[JUNE]   [Philadelphia.] Observations on the fortifications of the Delaware: Billingsport, and Red Bank. Contemporary copy. 7 pp. In handwriting of William Churchill Houston. Enclosed in President of Congress to Washington, 1777, June 13.
       90, 217

1777   **Washington**, George. Middlebrook. To [the President
JULY 1   of Congress, Philadelphia]. Retreat of British from Amboy. Draft. 1 p. In handwriting of Robert Hanson Harrison. Read in Congress, July 3.   **A. II, 401**

1777   **Continental Congress**, Resolves. Harrison's artillery; elec-
JULY 1   tion of Deputy Commissary of Issues, Robert Hoops and Physician General of Hospital, Middle Department, Dr. Benjamin Rush; arms for Connecticut. D. S. of John Hancock. Enclosed in President of Congress to Washington, 1777, July 5.   **16, 244**

1777   **Sullivan**, John. Middlebrook. To [the President of Con-
JULY 1   gress, Philadelphia]. Conditional resignation.
       Greene, Nathanael. To Congress. Conditional resignation.

JULY 1   **Knox**, Henry. To Congress. Conditional resignation. A. D. S. of Charles Thomson. 2 pp. Enclosed in President of Congress to Washington, 1777, July 8   **90, 238**

1777   **Washington**, George. Middlebrook. To [the President
JULY 2   of Congress, Philadelphia]. Uncertainty of British intentions; Howe's junction with Burgoyne; designs against Philadelphia. Draft. 4 pp. In handwriting of Robert Hanson Harrison and Richard Kidder Meade. Read in Congress, July 3.   **A. II, 403**

Printed: Writings of Washington (Ford) N. Y. 1890. 5, 461.

1777   **Continental Congress**, Resolves. Travelling expenses of
JULY 2   Deputy Commissary Generals of Purchases; election of Dr. William Brown in room of Dr. [Benjamin] Rush. D. S. of John Hancock. Enclosed in President of Congress to Washington, 1777, July 5.   **16, 244**

1777   **Washington**, George. Morristown [New Jersey]. To
JULY 5   [the President of Congress, Philadelphia]. Disposition of troops; enemy's intentions; questions of pay to certain officers; low state of funds. Draft. 3 pp. In handwriting of Tench Tilghman.   **A. II, 407**

1777   **Continental Congress**, President. Philadelphia. To
JULY 5   [George] Washington [Morristown]. Transmitting resolves. L. S. of John Hancock. 1 p.   **16, 241**

1777   **Washington**, George. Morristown. To [the President of
JULY 7   Congress, Philadelphia]. Preparations for embarkation of enemy; scarcity of arms; pay of troops. Draft. 2 pp. In handwriting of Tench Tilghman. Read in Congress, July 8.   **A. II, 411**

1777   **Washington**, George. Morristown. To [the Board of
JULY 7   War, Philadelphia]. Spears and cartridge canisters. Draft. 1 p. In handwriting of Tench Tilghman.   **A. II, 413**

1777   **Continental Congress**, Resolves. Impropriety of letters of
JULY 7   Sullivan, Greene and Knox. A. D. S. of William Churchill Houston, countersigned by John Hancock. 1 p. Enclosed in President of Congress to Washington, 1777, July 8.   **90, 237**

1777
JULY 7

Continental Congress, Resolves. Thanks of Congress for march of army and battle of Monmouth. Contemporary copy, attested by Charles Thomson. 1 p. Enclosed in President of Congress to Washington, 1778, July 8.   **91, 227**

1777
JULY 8

Continental Congress, President. Philadelphia. To [George] Washington [Morristown]. Letters of Sullivan, Greene and Knox to Congress. L. S. of John Hancock. 2 pp. In handwriting of Jacob Rush. Answered July 12.*   **90, 235**

1777
JULY 8

Continental Congress, Resolves. Defense of the Delaware; appointments of Frenchmen; [Maj.] Gen. [Horatio] Gates. Contemporary copy, attested by Charles Thomson, countersigned by John Hancock. 2 pp. Enclosed in President of Congress to Washington, 1777, July 8.   **90, 234**

1777
JULY 8

Board of War. [Philadelphia.] To George Washington, Morristown. Want of arms and clothing in Northern Department; returns and responsibility of noncommissioned officers; arms at Springfield; spears and cartridge cannisters; Du Coudray's letter. A. L. S. of Richard Peters. 2 pp. Answered July 12.*   **16, 266**

1777
JULY 9

Washington, George. Morristown. To [the President of Congress, Philadelphia]. Confusion in the Commissary of Provisions department. Draft. 1 p. In handwriting of Robert Hanson Harrison.
                    A. II, 415

1777
JULY 9

Schuyler, Ph[ilip John]. Fort Edward [New York]. To [George] Washington [Morristown]. Retreat of army; consternation of country; lack of men, ammunition and supplies; Ticonderoga. Contemporary copy. 2 pp. In handwriting of Alexander Hamilton. Enclosed in Washington to the President of Congress, 1777, July 12.
                    C. C. 152, 4, 345

1777
JULY 9

Trumbull, Joseph. Morristown. To [George] Washington [Morristown]. Difficulties of the Commissary under Congress' new regulations. Contemporary copy. 1 p. In handwriting of John Fitzgerald. Enclosed in Washington to the President of Congress, 1777, July 9.   **C. C. 152, 4, 335**

1777
JULY 10

Washington, George. Morristown. To [the President of] Congress [Philadelphia]. Evacuation of Ticon-

New York 10 April 1776

Sir,

I have the honour to inclose a Letter from General Schuyler containing intelligence of a very important nature. Copies of which I imagine are contained in the enclosed Letters to you which I thought it my duty immediately to forward by Express, that they may be laid before the Honorable Congress and proper measures pursued to prevent the fatal effects which are therein apprehended. For my own part I have done my utmost to forward the four Regiments ordered by Congress, but a variety of incidents have hitherto conspired to prevent their embarkation. The men had scarcely recovered themselves from the fatigues of their march from Boston, and are quite unprovided with necessaries— The Colonels of the Regiments, though repeatedly called upon for that purpose, had neglected making out the abstracts for their pay. All Obstacles however are now removed, and I hope to begin the embarkation this day,— Indeed it would have been best in my opinion, to have sent the Regiments rais'd in this Province and New Jersey upon that Service, had not the peculiar circumstances under which they were rais'd prevented it, by the terms of their inlistment they are to serve during the War, and at five dollars pMonth, on Condition (as I am inform'd) that they should not be sent out of those Provinces— Besides, they are very ill provided with Arms, some Companies not having any— It must be a great Burthen upon the Continent to keep such a number of useless men in pay, and yet if they should be dismissed, and an unexpected Supply of Arms should arrive it may be found very difficult to replace them—

The Officers of the several Corps that have arrived here have

deroga; [Maj.] Gen. [Benedict] Arnold to be sent
to the north. Draft. 3 pp. In handwriting
of Robert Hanson Harrison. Read in Congress,
July 11. **A. II, 417**

Printed: Writings of Washington (Ford) N. Y. 1890. 5, 472.

1777
JULY 10

Board of War. [Philadelphia.] To George Washington,
Morristown. Lack of arms in Armand's corps;
inquiry as to cause. A. L. S. of Richard Peters.
1 p. Answered July 16.* **16, 280**

1777
JULY 11

Continental Congress, Resolve. Committee to repair to
headquarters to enquire into state of army, in-
vestigate the commissaries and other departments:
Livingston, Gerry and Clymer. A. D. of Gerry.
Transmitted to Washington with Committee to
Washington, 1777, July 16? **90, 239**

1777
JULY 11

[Spencer, Joseph.] Providence [Rhode Island]. To [George
Washington, Morristown]. Capture of Maj. Gen.
[Robert] Prescott. [Extract of letter.] Contem-
porary copy. 2 pp. In handwriting of Caleb
Gibbs. Enclosed in Washington to the President
of Congress, 1777, July 16. **C. C. 152, 4, 359**

1777
JULY 12

Washington, George. Pompton Plains [New Jersey]. To
[the President of] Congress [Philadelphia].
Evacuation of Ticonderoga; reenforcements and
supplies for [Maj.] Gen. [Philip John] Schuyler;
[Maj.] Gen. [Benedict] Arnold to go to the north;
movement of Continental Army and intentions of
British. Draft. 4 pp. In handwriting of
Robert Hanson Harrison. **A. II, 421**

Printed in part: Writings of Washington (Ford) N. Y. 1890. 5, 475, note.

1777
JULY 12

Washington, George. Pompton Plains. To [the Board of
War, Philadelphia]. Lack of arms in the northern army; want of clothes; distribution of supplies under control of one person. Draft. 3 pp.
In handwriting of Tench Tilghman. **A. II, 425**

1777
JULY 12

Continental Congress, Resolves. Reenforcements for the
army. Contemporary copy, attested by Charles
Thomson, countersigned by John Hancock.
1 p. Enclosed in President of Congress to Washington, 1777, July 14. **90, 242**

1777
JULY 14

Washington, George. "Vanaulen 8 miles from Pumpton
Plains." To [the President of] Congress [Phila-
delphia]. Movement of army toward the North

river. Draft. 1 p. In handwriting of Robert Hanson Harrison. Read in Congress, July 16.
A. II, 429

1777
JULY 14

Continental Congress, President. Philadelphia. To [George]Washington[en route to Suffern'sTavern, New York]. Troops to join the army. L. S. of John Hancock. 2 pp. In handwriting of Jacob Rush.
90, 240

1777
JULY 14

Board of War. Return of tents sent from Philadelphia since commencement of this campaign. Tabular statement, contemporary copy. 1 p. Enclosed in Board of War to Washington, 1780, July 15.
95, 163

1777
JULY 14

Schuyler, Ph[ilip John]. Fort Edward [New York]. To [George] Washington [en route to Suffern's]. Situation; confusion and weakness of the army; want of supplies; removal of stores from Fort George and retreat of army. Contemporary copy. 4 pp. In handwriting of Caleb Gibbs. Enclosed in Washington to the President of Congress, 1777, July 18.   C. C. 153, 4, 365

1777
JULY 15

Board of War. [Philadelphia.] To [George] Washington [Suffern's]. Case of Hudson Burr; tents. A. L. S. of Richard Peters. 2 pp. Answered July 28.*
95, 161

1777
JULY 15

Heath, W[illiam]. Boston. To [George] Washington [Suffern's]. Introducing Mons. D'Avout; loss of Northern army in the retreat. L. S. 1 p. Transmitted to Congress.   C. C. 152, 4, 425

1777
JULY 16

Washington, George. Near [Smith's] Clove [New York]. To [the President of Congress, Philadelphia]. Intentions of British; artillery; militia; commissary's department. Draft. 1 p. In handwriting of Tench Tilghman. Read in Congress, July 17.
A. II, 431

1777
JULY 16

Washington, George. At [Smith's] Clove. To [the President of Congress, Philadelphia]. Capture of [Brig.] Gen. [Robert] Prescott; movement of troops. Draft. 1 p. In handwriting of Robert Hanson Harrison. Read in Congress, July 19.
A. II, 433

1777
JULY 16

Washington, George. "New Jersey" [Smith's Clove]. To [Lt. Gen. Sir] William Howe [New York]. Exchange of Maj. Gen. [Robert] Prescott for

Maj. Gen. [Charles] Lee. Contemporary copy.
1 p. In handwriting of Richard Kidder Meade.
Enclosed in Washington to the President of Congress, 1777, July 25.   C. C.   152, 4, 391
Printed: Writings of Washington (Ford) N. Y. 1890. 5, 487.

1777 **Washington**, George. [Smith's] Clove. To [the Board
July 16 of War, Philadelphia]. ·Lack of arms. Draft.
1 p. In handwriting of John Fitzgerald.
                                                    A. II, 435

1777 **Board of War.** [Philadelphia.] To [George] Washington
July 16 [Smith's Clove]. Employment of Dupré as
armourer. L. S. of Richard Peters. 1 p. 16, 330

1777 **Continental Congress,** Committee. [Suffern's Tavern, New
[July 16?] York]. To George Washington·[Morristown].
Committee to enquire into state of army. A.
D. S. of Elbridge Gerry in 3d person.   90, 239
Committee: Livingston, Gerry and Clymer.

1777 **Washington**, George. At [Smith's] Clove. To [the Presi-
July 18 dent of] Congress [Philadelphia]. Condition of
affairs at the North. Draft. 2 pp. In handwriting of Robert Hanson Harrison.   A. II, 437

1777 **Washington**, G[eorge]. At [Smith's] Clove. To [the Com-
July 19 mittee of Congress at camp]. Food for the army;
clothes; printing-press at headquarters; geographer. Auto. draft signed. 6 pp. Read in
Congress, July 24. Referred to Board of War.
                                                    A. II, 439

Printed: Writings of Washington (Ford) N. Y. 1890. 5, 493.
Committee to repair to camp: Livingston, Gerry and Clymer.

1777 **Nixon**, John. Kingsborough [New York]. To Maj. Gen.
July 21 [Philip John] Schuyler [Fort Edward, New York].
Reports of arrival of British and Indians; fate of
scouting parties. Contemporary copy. 1 p.
In handwriting of Robert Hanson Harrison. Enclosed in Washington to the President of Congress, 1777, July 25.   C. C.   152, 4, 395

1777 **Washington**, George. [Smith's] Clove. To [the President
July 22 of Congress, Philadelphia]. Uncertainty as to
movements of the enemy. Draft. 2 pp. In
handwriting of Robert Hanson,Harrison. Read
in Congress July 24. Referred to Board of War
"who are directed to confer with the executive
powers of Pennsylvania and take immediate and

effectual measures to carry into execution the
views and wishes of the general." **A. II, 445**

Printed: Writings of Washington (Ford) N. Y. 1890. 5, 502.

1777
JULY 22
Franklin, W[illiam]. Litchfield [Connecticut]. To
[George] Washington [Smith's Clove]. Mrs.
Franklin's ill health; requests permission to go
to her. A. L. S. 4 pp. Enclosed in Washing-
ton to the President of Congress, 1777, July 25.

C. C. 152, 4, 385

1777
JULY 22
Schuyler, Ph[ilip John]. Fort Edward [New York]. To
[George] Washington [Smith's Clove]. Evacua-
tion of Ticonderoga; weak state of army; lack of
everything; Maj. Gen. [Benedict] Arnold and re-
inforcements. Contemporary copy. 2 pp. In
handwriting of John Fitzgerald. Enclosed in
Washington to the President of Congress, 1777,
July 25. **C. C. 152, 4, 393**

1777
JULY 23
Board of War. [Philadelphia.] To George Washington,
Ramapaugh [New Jersey]. Returns from Maj.
Gen. [Israel] Putnam; resolves respecting invalid
corps. A. L. S. of Richard Peters. 1 p.
Answered July 28*. **95, 192**

1777
JULY 24
Lovell, James. Philadelphia. To [George] Washington
[Ramapaugh]. Case of Du Portail, La Radière
and Gouvion; engagements of Congress; Du
Coudray's pretensions; foreigners in the service.
A. L. S. 8 pp. **17, 105**

1777
JULY 25
Washington, George. Ramapaugh [New Jersey]. To
[the President of Congress, Philadelphia]. Gov.
[William] Franklin's enlargement. Draft. 1 p.
In handwriting of Robert Hanson Harrison.
Read in Congress July 28. **A. II, 451**

Printed: Writings of Washington (Sparks) Boston. 1834. 5, 6.

1777
JULY 25
Washington, George. Ramapaugh. To the President of
Congress, Philadelphia. Introducing Mons.
D'Avout. L. S. 1 p. In handwriting of Alex-
ander Hamilton. Read in Congress July 31.
Referred to Committee on Foreign Applications.

C. C. 152, 4, 413

1777
JULY 25
Washington, George. Ramapaugh. To [the President of
Congress, Philadelphia]. Uncertainty as to des-
tination of the enemy; disposition of troops.
Draft. 2 pp. In handwriting of Robert Hanson
Harrison. Read in Congress July 26.

A. II, 447

Printed: Writings of Washington (Ford) N. Y. 1890. 5, 515.

1777
July 25

Continental Congress, Resolves. Approbation of Lt. Cols. [Return Jonathan] Meigs and [William] Barton; beer, vegetables, etc., for army; settlement of accounts; appointment of Robert Erskine. Contemporary copy, attested by Charles Thomson, countersigned by John Hancock. 2 pp. Enclosed in President of Congress to Washington, 1777, July 26.   **90, 245**

[1777]
[July 25?]

D'Avout, ———. [Ramapaugh?] Memorial to Congress applying for a commission in the Continental Army. A. D. S. in 3ᵈ person. 1 p. (In French.) Enclosed? in Washington to the President of Congress, 1777, July 25.   **C. C. 152, 4, 423**

1777
July 26

Continental Congress, President. Philadelphia. To [George] Washington [Ramapaugh]. Swords for Lt. Cols. [Return Jonathan] Meigs and [William] Barton. L. S. of John Hancock. 2 pp. In handwriting of Jacob Rush.   **90, 243**

1777
July 26

Board of War. Philadelphia. To [George] Washington [Ramapaugh]. Money for use of Northern Department. A. L. S. of Richard Peters. 1 p.   **17, 126**

1777
July 27

Washington, George. Morristown. To [the President of] Congress [Philadelphia]. Proposed expedition against St. Johns; question of rank; troops marching toward Philadelphia. Draft. 2 pp. In handwriting of Robert Hanson Harrison. Read in Congress July 28.   **A. II, 453**

1777
July 27

Brown, John. Kinderhook [New York]. To [Maj. Gen. Philip John Schuyler, Saratoga]. Escape of [the British] express. Contemporary copy. 1 p. In handwriting of Richard Kidder Meade. Enclosed in Washington to the President of Congress, 1777, Aug. 7.   **C. C. 152, 4, 451**

1777
July 28

Washington, George. Flemingtown [New Jersey]. To [Board of War, Philadelphia]. Accusations against Hudson Burr; tents for [Maj.] Gen. [Philip John] Schuyler; returns of [Maj.] Gen. [Israel] Putnam's force. Draft. 2 pp. In handwriting of Robert Hanson Harrison.   **A. II, 455**

1777
July 28

Washington, George. Flemingtown [New Jersey]. To [James Lovell? Philadelphia]. Ordinance respecting Royal Corps of French Engineers;

Exchange of prisoners. L. S. 2 pp. In handwriting of Robert Hanson Harrison.

C. C. 152, 4, 405

1777
JULY 29

Continental Congress, Resolves. Inquiry into evacuation of Ticonderoga. D. S. of John Hancock. 1 p. Enclosed in President of Congress to Washington, 1777, Aug. 2. 90, 255

1777
JULY 29

Spencer, Joseph. Oneida [New York]. To [Maj.] Gen. [Philip John] Schuyler [Saratoga]. Meeting of Oneida chiefs; need of troops; defense of Fort Schuyler. Contemporary copy. 2 pp. In handwriting of Richard Kidder Meade. Enclosed in Washington to the President of Congress, 1777, Aug. 7. C. C. 152, 4, 449

Signed by copyist: "Thomas Spencer."

1777
JULY 30

Washington, George. Coryells Ferry [New] Jersey. To [the President of Congress, Philadelphia]. Moving to defense of Philadelphia. Draft. 1 p. In handwriting of Robert Hanson Harrison. Read in Congress July 31. A. II, 459

1777
JULY 30

Continental Congress, Resolve. Maj. Gen. [Arthur] St. Clair. D. S. of John Hancock. Enclosed in President of Congress to Washington, 1777, Aug. 2. 90, 255

1777
JULY 31

Washington, George. Coryells Ferry. To the President of Congress, Philadelphia. March of army to defense of Philadelphia. L. S. 1 p. In handwriting of John Fitzgerald. C. C. 152, 4, 429

1777
JULY 31

Continental Congress, Resolves. Seizure of disaffected in Pennsylvania; guards for prisoners; militia; naval matters; commission to Marquis de Lafeyette; recruiting measures, etc. Contemporary copy, attested by Charles Thomson. 3 pp. Enclosed in President of Congress to Washington, 1777, Aug. 2. 90, 249

1777
AUG. 1

Continental Congress, President. Philadelphia. To [George] Washington, Chester [Pennsylvania]. News of British fleet. A. L. S. of John Hancock. 1 p. 90, 251

1777
AUG. 1

Continental Congress, Resolve. Maj. Gen. [Philip John] Schuyler and other officers ordered to head-quarters. D. S. of John Hancock. Enclosed in President of Congress to Washington, 1777, Aug. 2. 90, 255

1777
Aug. 1

Continental Congress, Resolves. Establishment of post in Georgia. A. D. S. of William Churchill Houston. Enclosed in President of Congress to Washington, 1777, Aug. 8. **90, 265**

1777
Aug. 1

Heath, William. Boston. To [George] Washington [Chester]. Destination of enemy's fleet. Transcript. Enclosed in Washington to the President of Congress, 1777, Aug. 9. **C. C. 169, 3, 316**

1777
Aug. 1

Massachusetts, Council. Boston. To [George] Washington [Chester]. Appearance of a fleet off the coast. Contemporary copy. 1 p. In handwriting of Richard Kidder Meade. Enclosed in Washington to the President of Congress, 1777, Aug. 9.
C. C. 152, 4, 463

1777
Aug. 1

Schuyler, Ph[ilip John]. Saratoga. To [George] Washington [Chester]. Panicky state of troops; Howe's junction with Burgoyne; departure of Massachusetts militia; [Maj.] Gen. [Benedict] Arnold's wish to retire. Contemporary copy. 1 p. In handwriting of Alexander Hamilton. Enclosed in Washington to the President of Congress, 1777, Aug. 6. **C. C. 152, 4, 447**

1777
Aug. 2

Continental Congress, President. Philadelphia. To [George] Washington, Philadelphia. Transmitting resolves. A. L. S. of John Hancock. 1 p. Answered Aug 6.* **90, 253**

1777
Aug. 2

Adams, John and Others. Philadelphia. To [George] Washington [Philadelphia]. Recommending Maj. Gen. [Horatio] Gates to command the Northern Army. L. S., signed also: Nathl. Folsom, Saml. Adams, Hy. Marchant, Elbridge Gerry, Elipht. Dyer and Wm. Williams. 1 p. In handwriting of Williams. **17, 169**

1777
Aug. 2

Heath, William. Boston. To [George] Washington [Philadelphia]. British fleet. Transcript. Enclosed in Washington to the President of Congress, 1777, Aug. 9. **C. C. 169, 3, 315**

1777
Aug. 2

Schuyler, Ph[ilip John]. Albany. To [George] Washington [Philadelphia]. Gates in command; Bennington; Indians. A. L. S. 2 pp. **90, 287**

1777
Aug. 2

Walton, George. Philadelphia. To [George] Washington [Philadelphia]. Employment of enlisted deserters in the South. A. L. S. 2 pp. **17, 165**

1777
AUG. 3

Washington, George. Philadelphia. To [the President of Congress, Philadelphia]. Choice of commander for the Northern Department; reenforcements of militia. Draft. 2 pp. In handwriting of Tench Tilghman. Read in Congress, Aug. 4. "Ordered to be taken into consideration at 1 o'clock." A. II, 461

Printed: Writings of Washington (Ford) N. Y. 1890. 6, 3.

1777
AUG. 3

Continental Congress, President. Philadelphia. To [George] Washington [Philadelphia]. Transmitting resolves. A. L. S. of John Hancock. 1 p. Answered Aug. 3*. 17, 174

1777
AUG. 3

Continental Congress, Resolves. Command of and militia reenforcements for the Northern Army; recall of brigadiers. A. D. S. of William Churchill Houston, countersigned by John Hancock. 2 pp.
17, 176

1777
AUG. 3

Board of War. Philadelphia. To [George] Washington [Philadelphia]. Supply of deficiency of arms. A. L. S. of Richard Peters. 2 pp. 17, 170

1777
AUG. 4

Continental Congress, Resolves. Command of the Northern Army. A. D. S. of William Churchill Houston, countersigned by John Hancock. 1 p. Enclosed in President of Congress to Washington, 1777, Aug. 4. 90, 257

1777
AUG. 4

Continental Congress, President. Philadelphia. To [George] Washington, Philadelphia. Maj. Gen. [Horatio] Gates to command Northern Army. L. S. of John Hancock. 1 p. In handwriting of Jacob Rush. 90, 258

1777
AUG. 4

Board of War. [Philadelphia.] To Benjamin Flower [Philadelphia]. Arms placed at Washington's disposal. Copy by Flower.

Flower, Benjamin. To [Washington, Philadelphia]. Commissaries to issue arms. A. L. S. 1 p. 95, 223

1777
AUG. 5

Washington, George. Philadelphia. To [the Board of War, Philadelphia]. Scarcity of arms; need of an armourer; beer, cider and vinegar for troops. Draft. 3 pp. In handwriting of Tench Tilghman. A. II, 463

1777
AUG. 5

Board of War. [Philadelphia.] To [George] Washington [Philadelphia]. Returns of Commissary General of arms and stores; repairs. A. L. S. of Richard Peters. 1 p. 17, 172

1777
Aug. 5

Walton, George. Philadelphia. To [George] Washington [Philadelphia]. Recall of Brig. Gen. [Lachlan] McIntosh from Georgia. A. L. S. 2 pp.

17, 182

1777
Aug. 6

Washington, George. Near Germantown [Schuylkill Falls, Pennsylvania]. To [the President of] Congress [Philadelphia]. Recall of [Maj.] Genls. [Philip John] Schuyler and [Arthur] St. Clair to headquarters. Draft. 1 p. In handwriting of Robert Hanson Harrison. A. II, 467

1777
Aug. 6

Washington, George. [Schuylkill Falls.] To George Walton, Philadelphia. Appointment of [Brig.] Gen. [Lachlan] McIntosh to a brigade. In handwriting of John Fitzgerald. Draft. 1 p.

A. II, 469

1777
Aug. 6

Continental Congress, Resolves. Troops for Northern Department; Commissaries of Issues and Musters. Contemporary copy, attested by William Churchill Houston, countersigned by John Hancock. 1 p. Enclosed in President of Congress to Washington, 1777, Aug. 8. 90, 264

1777
Aug. 6

Continental Congress, Resolve. Brig. [Gen. Lachlan] McIntosh ordered to headquarters. A. D. S. of William Churchill Houston. Enclosed in President of Congress to Washington, 1777, Aug. 8.

90, 265

1777
Aug. 6

Continental Congress, Resolves. Resignation of Joseph Trumbull. Contemporary copy, attested by William Churchill Houston, countersigned by John Hancock. 1 p. Enclosed in President of Congress to Washington, 1777, Aug. 8. 90, 263

1777
Aug. 7

Washington, George. [Schuylkill Falls.] To [the President of Congress, Philadelphia]. Unpromising state of affairs in the North. Draft. 1 p. In handwriting of Robert Hanson Harrison.

A. II, 471

1777
Aug. 7

Continental Congress, Resolves. Maj. Gen. [Robert] Prescott's treatment; exchange of prisoners. Contemporary copy, attested by Charles Thomson, countersigned by John Hancock. 1 p. Enclosed in President of Congress to Washington, 1777, Aug. 7. 90, 262

1777
Aug. 7

Continental Army, Board of General Officers. [Near Germantown, Pennsylvania.] To [George] Washington [near Germantown]. Resolve of Congress obliging officers to draw rations with the men; disadvantages. A. D. S. of Nath. Greene, Prest. 1 p. Enclosed in Washington to Congress, 1777, Aug. 9.   **Miscel.**

1777
Aug. 7

Purnell, Zadoc. [Worcester County? Maryland] To [the President of Congress, Philadelphia]. British fleet off Sinepuxent [Bay, Maryland]. Contemporary copy. 1 p. Enclosed in President of Congress to Washington, 1777, Aug. 10.   **90, 269**

1777
Aug. 8

Continental Congress, President. Philadelphia. To [George] Washington [Schuylkill Falls]. Transmitting resolves. A. L. S. of John Hancock. 1 p. Answered Aug. 9.*   **90, 260**

1777
Aug. 9

Washington, George. [Schuylkill Falls.] To [the President of] Congress [Philadelphia]. Exchange of officers; military matters; [Maj.] Genls. [Philip John] Schuyler and [Arthur] St. Clair. Draft. 2 pp. In handwriting of Robert Hanson Harrison. Read in Congress, Aug. 11. Referred to Wilson, J. B. Smith and William Smith.
A. II, 473

Printed: Writings of Washington (Ford) N. Y. 1890. 6, 16.

1777
Aug. 9

Washington, George. [Schuylkill Falls.] To the President of Congress, Philadelphia. Enclosing intelligence. L. S. 1 p. In handwriting of Robert Hanson Harrison.   **C. C.   152, 4, 445**

1777
Aug. 9

Burgoyne, J[ohn]. [Battenkill, New York.] Instructions for Lt. Col. [Friedrich] Baum. Purposes to be effected; seizure of horses and cattle. In handwriting of Caleb Gibbs. Endorsed by Charles Thomson: "Published by Order of Congress." Referred to the Comtt. of Intelligence. Contemporary copy. 4 pp.   **C. C.   152, 4, 533**
Committee: Rush, R. H. Lee and Hopkinson.

1777
Aug. 9

Meade, R[ichard] K[idder]. [Schuylkill Falls.] To [the Board of War, Philadelphia]. Difficulties connected with obtaining horses. Auto. draft signed. 1 p.   **A. II, 475**

[1777]
[Aug. 10]

Washington, George. Near Germantown [Neshaminy Camp, Bucks County, Pennsylvania]. To the President of Congress, Philadelphia. Acknowledging receipt of intelligence. L. S. 1 p. In

handwriting of Robert Hanson Harrison.   Read
in Congress, Aug. 11.   C. C.   152, 4, 459

Washington's headquarters from Aug. 10 to 23, while the Army was
at Neshaminy Camp, were about half a mile from Cross Roads, later
called Hartsville, on Little Neshaminy Creek, Bucks County. His
letters during this period are indifferently dated: Near Germantown,
Bucks County, Neshaminy and Cross Roads.

1777
AUG. 10

Washington, George.   [Neshaminy Camp.]   To [the President of Congress, Philadelphia].   Comparative
advantages of Billingsport and Fort Island as
defenses of the Delaware river.   Draft.   5 pp.
In handwriting of Richard Kidder Meade.   Read
in Congress, Aug. 11.   "Referred to the board
of war who are directed to carry the general's
plan into execution with all possible despatch."
                                   A. II, 477

Printed: Writings of Washington (Ford) N. Y.   1890.   6, 17.

1777
AUG. 10

Continental Congress, President.   Philadelphia.   To
[George] Washington [Neshaminy Camp].   Brit-
ish fleet off Sinepuxent [Bay, Maryland].   L. S. of
John Hancock. 1 p.   Answered Aug. 10.* **90, 267**

1777
AUG. 11

Jones, Joseph.   Philadelphia.   To [George] Washington
[Neshaminy Camp].   Capt. [James] Monroe's
efforts to recruit in Virginia.   A. L. S.   2 pp.
                                   17, 206

1777
AUG. 12

Washington, George.   [Neshaminy Camp.]   To [the President of Congress, Philadelphia].   The Jersey
militia.   Draft.   1 p.   In handwriting of Alexander Hamilton.   Read in Congress, Aug. 13.
Referred to the Board of War.   **A.** II, 483

1777
AUG. 13

Clinton, George.   New Windsor [New York].   To [George]
Washington [Neshaminy Camp].   Situation in the
north; New York militia; promises but no troops
from New England.   Contemporary copy.   2 pp.
In handwriting of John Fitzgerald.   Enclosed in
Washington to the President of Congress, 1777,
Aug. 16.   **C. C.**   152, 4, 497

1777
AUG. 13

Washington, George.   Neshaminy Camp.   To [Silas] Deane
[Paris].   French officers coming to America.
Draft.   2 pp.   In handwriting of Tench Tilgh-
man.   **A.** II, 485

1777
AUG. 15

Washington, George.   [Neshaminy Camp.]   To [the President of Congress, Philadelphia].   Construction
of chevaux-de-frize to protect Fort Island.
Draft.   1 p.   In handwriting of Alexander Hamilton.   Read in Congress, Aug. 16.   **A.** II, 487

1777
Aug. 15
Nelson, Thomas. York [Virginia]. To [Col. Benjamin Harrison, Philadelphia]. Appearance of British fleet at the Capes. Contemporary copy. 2 pp. In handwriting of Jacob Rush. Enclosed in President of Congress to Washington, 1777, Aug. 21. **17, 257**

1777
Aug. 16
Washington, George. Neshaminy Camp. To [the President of] Congress [Philadelphia]. Exorbitant price of supplies; establishment of tanneries and distilleries for the army; guards for stores at Carlisle; horses and pay of cavalry officers. Draft. 3 pp. In handwriting of Robert Hanson Harrison and Caleb Gibbs. Read in Congress, Aug. 18. **A. II, 489**

1777
Aug. 16
Continental Congress, Resolve. Riflemen to be sent to Northward. Contemporary copy, attested by Charles Thomson, countersigned by John Hancock. 1 p. Enclosed in President of Congress to Washington, 1777, Aug. 17. **90, 272**

1777
Aug. 16
D'Avout, ——. Derby [Connecticut]. To James Lovell, Philadelphia. His application for commission in the Continental Army. A. L. S. 2 pp. (In French.) **C. C. 152, 4, 417**

1777
Aug. 17
Washington, George. Neshaminy Camp. To [the President of Congress, Philadelphia]. Van Cortlandt's, Livingston's and Morgan's corps ordered to Schuyler's relief. Draft. 1 p. In handwriting of Robert Hanson Harrison. Read in Congress, Aug. 18. Referred to Committee on Western Frontier and Northern Department. **A. II, 493**

Committee: Duer, Lee, Wilson, J. Adams and Chase.

[1777]
[Aug. 17]
Washington, George. Neshaminy Camp. To [the President of Congress, Philadelphia]. Horses and servants for Col. [Louis Le Bègue] Duportail. Draft. 1 p. In handwriting of Alexander Hamilton. Read in Congress, Aug. 18. **A. II, 495**

1777
Aug. 17
Washington, George. Neshaminy Camp. To the Maryland delegates in Congress, Philadelphia. Arrest of Lt. [James] McNair by State authorities for enlisting men. Draft. 2 pp. In handwriting of Robert Hanson Harrison. **A. II, 499**

1777
Aug. 17
Washington, George. [Neshaminy Camp.] To [Benjamin Franklin, Passy]. Mons. de Cenis and expecta-

tions of French officers. Draft. 2 pp. In handwriting of Alexander Hamilton.   A. II, 501
Printed: Writings of Washington (Ford) N. Y. 1890. 6, 36.

1777
AUG. 17   **Continental Congress,** President. Philadelphia. To
[George] Washington [Neshaminy Camp]. Rifle-
men for the northward; defense of the Delaware.
L. S. of John Hancock. 2 pp. In handwriting
of Jacob Rush. Answered Aug. 18.*   **90, 270**

1777
AUG. 17   **Wilkinson,** James. [Albany.] General return of troops
under command of Maj. Gen. [Philip John]
Schuyler at Forts near Half Moon. Tabular
statement. Contemporary copy. 1 p. In handwriting of Richard Varick. Enclosed in President of Congress to Washington, 1777, Aug. 24.
90, 290

1777
AUG. 18   **Washington,** George. Neshaminy Camp. To [the Presi-
dent of] Congress [Philadelphia]. Col. [Daniel]
Morgan ordered to reenforce the northern army.
Draft. 1 p. In handwriting of Robert Hanson
Harrison.   **A. II, 503**

1777
AUG. 19   **Washington,** George. "Neshamony Bridge." To [Benja-
min Harrison, Philadelphia]. Marquis de La-
fayette's commission. Draft. 2 pp. In handwriting of Richard Kidder Meade.   **A. II, 505**
Printed: Writings of Washington (Ford) N. Y. 1890. 6, 39.

1777
AUG. 19   **Board of War.** [Philadelphia.] To [George] Washington,
Neshaminy. Unmounted men from North Caro-
lina. A. L. S. of Richard Peters. 1 p.   **17, 287**

1777
AUG. 19   **Greene,** Nathanael. [Neshaminy Camp.] To Gen. [George]
Washington. [Neshaminy Camp.] Proceedings
of a board of General Officers, on settlement of
rank of Pennsylvania field officers. D. S. 2 pp.
In handwriting of John Fitzgerald. Enclosed in
Washington to the President of Congress, 1777,
Nov. 10.   **C. C. 152, 5, 177**

1777
APR. 19.   **Lincoln,** B[enjamin]. Bennington [Vermont]. To Maj.
Gen. [Philip John] Schuyler [Albany] The situ-
ation. Contemporary copy. 1 p. In handwriting of John Lansing, jr. Enclosed in President
of Congress to Washington, 1777, Aug. 24.
90, 289

1777
AUG. 19   **Maryland,** Delegates to Continental Congress. Philadel-
phia. To [George Washington, Neshaminy].
Arrest of Lt. [James] McNair in Maryland.

A. L. S. of William Paca, signed also by Samuel
Chase. 1 p. 17, 289

1777
Aug. 20
Washington, George. [Neshaminy camp.] To the President of Congress, Philadelphia. Forwarding packet from [Maj.] Gen. [Philip John] Schuyler. L. S. 1 p. In handwriting of Tench Tilghman. Read in Congress, Aug. 20. C. C. 152, 4, 505

1777
Aug. 20
Continental Congress, Resolve. New Jersey militia to garrison forts on the Hudson. A. L. S. of Charles Thomson. 1 p. Enclosed in President of Congress to Washington, 1777, Aug. 21. 17, 259

1777
Aug. 20
Continental Congress, Resolve. Call for New Jersey militia. A. D. S. of Charles Thomson. 1 p. Enclosed in President of Congress to Washington, 1777, Aug. 21. 17, 259

1777
Aug. 20
Continental Congress, Resolve. New Jersey militia to garrison the Highlands. A. D. S. of Charles Thomson. 1 p. Enclosed in President of Congress to Washington, 1777, Aug. 21. 17, 259

1777
Aug. 20
Gates, Horatio. Van Schaaks Island [New York]. To [the President of Congress, Philadelphia]. The situation; Bennington. Contemporary copy. 1 p. In handwriting of John Lansing, jr. Enclosed in President of Congress to Washington, 1777, Aug. 24. 90, 291

1777
Aug. 20
Harrison, Benjamin. Philadelphia. To [George Washington, Neshaminy]. Lafayette's commission and the general understanding of Congress regarding same; Howe, Burgoyne and Gates. A. L. S. 2 pp. 17, 295

1777
Aug. 20
Newcomb, Silas. Woodbury [New Jersey]. To [George] Washington [Neshaminy Camp]. Requesting permission to march his detachment home. A. L. S. 1 p. Enclosed in Washington to the President of Congress, 1777, Aug. 21. C. C. 152, 4, 513

1777
Aug. 20
Schuyler, Ph[ilip John]. Albany. To [George] Washington [Neshaminy Camp]. [Maj.] Gen. [Horatio] Gates in command; the situation. Contemporary copy. 1 p. In handwriting of John Fitzgerald. Enclosed in Washington to the President of Congress, 1777, Aug. 25. C. C. 152, 4, 551

1777
AUG. 21
Washington, George. [Neshaminy Camp.] To the President of Congress, Philadelphia. Introducing Comte [Casimir] Pulaski. L. S. 1 p. In handwriting of John Fitzgerald. Read in Congress, Aug. 28. Referred to Committee on Foreign Applications. **C. C. 152**, 4, 531

1777
AUG. 21
Washington, George. Neshaminy. To [the President of Congress, Philadelphia]. Discharge of the Jersey militia. Draft. 1 p. In handwriting of Tench Tilghman. Read in Congress Aug. 22. Referred to Board of War. **A. II, 511**

1777
AUG. 21
Washington, George. Neshaminy. To [the President of Congress, Philadelphia.] Intentions of British; danger to Charleston. Draft. 1 p. In handwriting of Caleb Gibbs. Read in Congress, Aug. 22. **A. II, 513**

1777
AUG. 21
Washington, George. Neshaminy Camp. To [the President of Congress, Philadelphia]. Intentions of enemy; deliberations of a council of war. Draft. 3 pp. In handwriting of Richard Kidder Meade and Robert Hanson Harrison. **A. II, 50.**

Printed: Writings of Washington (Ford), N. Y. 1890. 6, 45.

1777
AUG. 21
Washington, George. Neshaminy. To John Page [Virginia]. Militia; intentions of the enemy. Draft, 1 p. In handwriting of Robert Hanson Harrison. **A. II, 515**

1777
AUG. 21
Continental Congress, President. Philadelphia. To [George] Washington [Neshaminy]. Appointment of George Ewing, commissary of hides; garrisoning forts on the Hudson with Jersey militia; intelligence from Virginia. L. S. of John Hancock. 2 pp. In handwriting of Jacob Rush.
17, 260

1777
Aug. 21
Continental Congress, President. Philadelphia. To [George] Washington [Neshaminy Camp]. Commissary of hides; letters from the north; New York militia. L. S. of John Hancock. 2 pp. In handwriting of Jacob Rush.
17, 260

1777
AUG. 21
Continental Congress. Resolve. March of army toward the Hudson. D. S. of John Hancock. 1. p. Enclosed in President of Congress, 1777, Aug. 22.
90, 275

1777
AUG. 21

Board of War. Philadelphia. To [George] Washington [Neshaminy]. Recovery of British cannon thrown into the Raritan; guns for defenses at Red Bank and Billingsport; frigates. A. L. S. of Richard Peters. 1 p.   **17, 299**

1777
AUG. 21

Continental Army. Council of War. Neshaminy Camp. Destination of enemy; movement of Continental army. Contemporary copy. 2 pp. In handwriting of Tench Tilghman. Enclosed in Washington to the President of Congress, 1777, Aug. 21.   **C. C. 152, 4, 525**

1777
AUG. 21

Bordley, W[illiam]. [Maryland.] To [William Paca, Philadelphia]. British fleet in the Chesapeake. Contemporary copy. 2 pp. In handwriting of, and attested by Charles Thomson. Enclosed in President of Congress to Washington, 1777, Aug. 22.   **90, 279**

1777
AUG. 22

Washington, George. [Neshaminy Camp.] To [the President of Congress, Philadelphia]. Enemy in the Chesapeake; movement of troops. Draft. 1 p. In handwriting of Alexander Hamilton. Read in Congress, Aug. 23.   **A. II, 517**
Printed: Writings of Washington (Ford) N. Y. 1890. 6, 49.

1777
AUG. 22

Washington, George. [Neshaminy Camp.] To [the Board of War, Philadelphia]. Disposition of cannon; difficulty with the Carolinians and Col. [George] Baylor's regiment. Draft. 2 pp. In handwriting of Tench Tilghman.   **A. II, 519**

1777
AUG. 22

Continental Congress, President. Philadelphia. To [George] Washington [Neshaminy Camp]. Military matters; British fleet; victory [at Bennington]. L. S. of John Hancock. 2 pp. In handwriting of Jacob Rush.   **90, 273**

1777
AUG. 22

Continental Congress, President. Philadelphia. To [George] Washington [Neshaminy Camp]. British in the Chesapeake; removal of stores and prisoners. A. L. S. of John Hancock. 1 p. Answered Aug. 22.*   **90, 277**

1777
AUG. 22

Continental Congress, Resolve. British in the Chesapeake; movement of army. A. D. S. of Charles Thomson. 1 p. Enclosed in President of Congress to Washington 1777, Aug. 22.   **90, 276**

1777
AUG. 22

Continental Congress, Resolves. Calling out militia from Maryland, Delaware, Virginia and Pennsylvania;

removal of boats, stock, etc. A. D. S. of John Hancock. 2 pp. Enclosed in President of Congress to Washington, 1777, Aug. 23. **90, 283**

1777
Aug. 23

Washington, George. Neshaminy. To [the President of Congress, Philadelphia]. March of the army to oppose the British. Draft. 1 p. In handwriting of Robert Hanson Harrison. Read in Congress, Aug. 23. Referred to the Board of War.
A. II, 521
Printed: Writings of Washington (Ford) N. Y. 1890. 6, 50.

1777
Aug. 23

Continental Congress, President. Philadelphia. To George Washington, Neshaminy Camp. Strengthening the army. L. S. of John Hancock. 1 p. In handwriting of Jacob Rush. **90, 281.**

1777
Aug. 23

Continental Congress, Resolve. Repudiating intention of limiting Gen. Washington's power as Commander-in-Chief of all land forces. A. D. S. of John Hancock. 1 p. Enclosed in President of Congress to Washington, 1777, Aug. 23. **17, 312**

1777
Aug. 24

Continental Congress, President. Philadelphia. To [George] Washington [Philadelphia]. Letters from the north; report of success at Staten Island. A. L. S. of John Hancock. 1 p. **90, 286**

1777
Aug. 24

Hollingsworth, H[enry]. Head of Elk [Maryland]. To [the President of Congress, Philadelphia]. Force of enemy in the Chesapeake. Contemporary copy. 1 p. In handwriting of John Hancock. Enclosed in President of Congress to Washington, 1777, Aug. 24. **90, 292**

1777
Aug. 25

Washington, George. Wilmington [Delaware]. To [the President of Congress, Philadelphia]. Preparations to oppose the enemy. Draft. 2 pp. In handwriting of Tench Tilghman. **A. II, 523**
Printed: Writings of Washington (Ford) N. Y. 1890. 6, 51.

1777
Aug. 25

Washington, George. Chester [Pennsylvania]. To [the President of Congress, Philadelphia]. News from the north; preparations to oppose British; Burgoyne's instructions. Draft. 1 p. In handwriting of Robert Hanson Harrison. Read in Congress, Aug. 25. **A. II, 525**

1777
Aug. 25

Chase, Samuel. Philadelphia. To [George Washington, Wilmington]. Information respecting probable seat of next campaign [Maryland]; names of persons who can furnish data. A. L. S. 4 pp. **17, 319**

1777
[AUG. 25]

Hollingsworth, H[enry]. Head of Elk [Maryland]. To Brig. Gen. [John] McKinley. Landing of the British at Head of Elk. Contemporary copy. 1 p. In handwriting of John Fitzgerald. Enclosed in Washington to the President of Congress, 1777, Aug. 25.   C. C.   152, 4, 541

1777
AUG. 26

Continental Congress, Resolves. Cannon; lead from houses; seizure of disaffected; seizure of arms. Contemporary copy, attested by Charles Thomson. 2 pp. Enclosed in President of Congress to Washington, 1777, Aug. 27.   90, 298

1777
AUG. 27

Washington, George. Wilmington. To [the President of] Congress [Philadelphia]. Reconnoissance of enemy. Draft. 1 p. In handwriting of Robert Hanson Harrison. Read in Congress, Aug. 29.
          A. II, 527

Printed: Writings of Washington (Ford) N. Y. 1890. 6, 53.

1777
AUG. 27

Washington, George. Wilmington. To Samuel Chase [Philadelphia]. Militia and disaffected in Maryland; engineer for Baltimore. Draft. 1 p. In handwriting of Tench Tilghman and Timothy Pickering, jr. ?   A. II, 529

1777
AUG. 27

Continental Congress, President. Philadelphia. To [George] Washington [Wilmington]. Seizure of disaffected. L. S. of John Hancock. 1 p. In handwriting of Jacob Rush.   90, 297

1777
AUG. 27

Continental Congress, Resolves. Enquiry into the evacuation of Ticonderoga. A. D. S. of William Churchill Houston, countersigned by John Hancock. Enclosed in President of Congress to Washington, 1777, Sep. 1.   90, 302

1777
AUG. 27

Morris, Robert. Philadelphia. To George Washington [Wilmington]. Introducing Capt. des Epinières. A. L. S. 1 p.   17, 325

1777
AUG. 28

Washington, George. Wilmington. To [the President of Congress, Philadelphia]. Employment of Comte [Casimir] Pulaski. Draft. 2 pp. In handwriting of Alexander Hamilton. Referred to Board of War.   A. II, 531

Printed: Writings of Washington (Ford) N. Y. 1890. 6, 56, note.

1777
AUG. 28

Continental Congress, Resolve. Committee to conduct enquiry into evacuation of Ticonderoga: Laurens, R. H. Lee and J. Adams. A. D. S. of William Churchill Houston, countersigned by

John Hancock. Enclosed in President of Congress to Washington, 1777, Sep. 1.   **90, 302**

1777   **White**, Robert. Wilmington. To [the President of Con-
AUG. 28   gress, Philadelphia]. Difference between established ration and the one drawn. A. L. S. 2 pp.
Enclosed in Board of War to Washington, 1777,
Sep. 6.   **17, 334**

1777   **Washington**, George. Wilmington. To [the President
AUG. 29   of] Congress [Philadelphia]. Movements of
enemy; request for commissions from [Maj.]
Gen. [Horatio] Gates. Draft. 2 pp. In handwriting of Tench Tilghman and Robert Hanson
Harrison. Read in Congress Aug. 30.
A. II, 533
Printed in part: Writings of Washington (Ford) N. Y. 1890. 6, 58, note.

1777   **Washington**, George. Wilmington. To [the President
AUG. 30   of] Congress [Philadelphia]. The military situation. Draft. 1 p. In handwriting of Robert
Hanson Harrison. Read in Congress Sep. 1.
A. II, 537
Printed: Writings of Washington (Ford) N. Y. 1890. 6, 56.

1777   **Continental Congress**, Resolve. Repair of arms. A. D. S.
AUG. 30   of William Churchill Houston, countersigned by
John Hancock. 1 p. Enclosed in President of
Congress to Washington, 1777, Sep. 1.   **91, 1**

1777   **Anonymous.** Camp near Wilmington. To ——? [Phila-
AUG. 30   delphia]. Complaint of manner of serving rations
to the Virginia Line; officers' difficulties; effect
on reenlistments. Contemporary copy. 4 pp.
Enclosed in Board of War to Washington, 1777,
Sep. 5.   **18, 16**
Above letter was written by a Colonel of the Virginia Line to a
Virginia delegate in Congress. Both writer's and recipient's name
are carefully omitted from this copy, which is in the handwriting of
Jos. Nourse.

1777   **Rush**, Benjamin. Philadelphia. To [George] Washing-
AUG. 30   ton [Wilmington]. Requesting permission for
Capt. [John] Macpherson to go to New York on
parole. A. L. S. 2 pp.   **18, 7**

1777   **Alexander**, Francis. New Castle County [Delaware].
AUG. 31   Deposition respecting outrages of British. Contemporary copy. 1 p. In handwriting of
Richard Kidder Meade. Enclosed in Washington to the President of Congress, 1777, Sep. 1.
C. C. 152, 5, 21

1777   **Hopkins,** David [Head of Elk].   To [George Washington,
[AUG. 31]   Wilmington, Delaware].   Movements of enemy.
               Contemporary copy.   1 p.   In handwriting of
               John Fitzgerald.   Enclosed in Washington to the
               President of Congress 1777, Sep. 1.

                                              C. C.   152, 4, 23

[1777]   **Board of War,** Report.   Settlement of rank in army.   D. S.
[AUG.]   of John Hancock.   6 pp.   Transmitted to Wash-
               ington.   90, 293

1777   **Washington,** George.   Wilmington.   To [the President of
SEP. 1   Congress, Philadelphia].   Movements of the
               enemy; militia.   Draft.   2 pp.   In handwriting
               of Robert Hanson Harrison.   Read in Congress,
               Sep. 2.   A. III, 1

               Printed: Writings of Washington (Ford) N. Y. 1890. 6, 58.

1777   **Washington,** George.   Wilmington.   To [the President of]
SEP. 1   Congress [Philadelphia].   News from the north
               [of the battle of Bennington].   Draft.   1 p.   In
               handwriting of Robert Hanson Harrison.   Read
               in Congress Sep. 2.   A. III, 3

1777   **Continental Congress,** President.   Philadelphia.   To
SEP. 1   [George] Washington [Wilmington].   Evacuation
               of Ticonderoga; repair of firearms; relief of Fort
               Schuyler.   L. S. of John Hancock.   2 pp.   In
               handwriting of Jacob Rush.   Answered Sep. 1.*
                                                            90, 300

1777   **Continental Congress,** Resolve.   Court of inquiry on failure
SEP. 1   of Sullivan's expedition against Staten Island.
               A. D. S. of Charles Thomson, countersigned by
               John Hancock.   1 p.   Enclosed in President of
               Congress to Washington, 1777, Sep. 3.   90, 309

1777   **Continental Congress,** Committee of Intelligence.   Phila-
SEP. 2   delphia.   To [George] Washington [Wilmington].
               Transmitting printed handbills for distribution
               through the army.   A. L. S. of Richard Henry
               Lee, signed also by William Heyward, Jonathan
               D. Sergeant, and William Duer.   1 p.   Answered
               Sep. 3.*   90, 304

1777   **Continental Congress,** Resolve.   Col. [William] Richard-
SEP. 2   son's battalion.   A. D. S. of Charles Thomson,
               countersigned by John Hancock.   1 p.   Enclosed
               in President of Congress to Washington, 1777,
               Sep. 3.   90, 308

Head Quarters West-point
20th Novr 1779

Sir

On monday evening I had the honor to receive your Excellency's Letter of the 16th with the Inclosure to which it refers, by Major Clarkson. I also had the honor since, on the night of the 17th to receive your favor of the 18th.

I regret much the failure of the expedition against Savannah, and the causes which seem to have produced it. The North Carolina Troops proceeded yesterday to New Windsor, from whence they would begin their march for the Southward to day — They could not commence it sooner. From the state of matters in the Southern quarter as communicated by General Lincoln in his Letter to the Honble the Committee of Correspondence, I most sincerely wish it were in my power to afford him further succor from this Army, than the North Carolina Troops; but from the fullest consideration of the point, it does not appear to me practicable. I had determined to send that part of Baylor's Regiment, which is under the Command of Lt Col. Washington, and accordingly wrote him yesterday to march, but unfortunately I found by the report of an Officer belonging to the Regiment whom I saw to day, that it would answer but little if any purpose, as the Inlistments of many, if not all the men would expire, before, or not long after they could arrive. From this circumstance I have been obliged to send a Countermanding Order. I have however called for an exact return of the mens engagements, and when I receive it shall act with respect to them as circumstances may authorise. The Letter which I had the honor of addressing to your

WRITING OF CALEB GIBBS.

1777
SEP. 3

Washington, George. Wilmington. To [the President of Congress, Philadelphia]. Skirmish with the enemy [Iron Hill, Delaware]. Draft. 2 pp. In handwriting of Robert Hanson Harrison. Read in Congress Sep. 4. **A. III, 5**

Printed: Writings of Washington (Ford) N. Y. 1890. 6, 64.

1777
SEP. 3

Washington, George. Wilmington. To [Committee of Intelligence of Congress, Philadelphia]. Hand-bills of success in the north [Bennington]. Draft. 1 p. In handwriting of Tench Tilghman.
A. III, 7

Printed in part: Writings of Washington (Ford) N.Y. 1890. 6, 65, note.
Committee: Rush, R. H. Lee, and Hopkinson.

1777
SEP. 3

Continental Congress, President. Philadelphia. To [George] Washington [Wilmington]. Transmitting resolves; Sullivan's failure against Staten Island. L. S. of John Hancock. 2 pp. In handwriting of Jacob Rush. **90, 306**

1777
SEP. 4

Continental Congress, Resolves. Resignation of certain officers; Pennsylvania and New Jersey militia. A. D. S. of William Churchill Houston. Countersigned by John Hancock. 2 pp. Enclosed in President of Congress to Washington, 1777, Sep. 6. **90, 313**

1777
SEP. 5

Washington, George. Wilmington. To [the President of Congress, Philadelphia]. Movements of enemy and their loss [at Iron Hill]. Draft. 1 p. In handwriting of Tench Tilghman. Read in Congress, Sep. 6. **A. III, 9**

1777
SEP. 5

Board of War. [Philadelphia.] To [George] Washington, Wilmington. Peculations of bacon and meat by commissaries and sutlers. A. L. S. of Richard Peters. 1 p. **18, 18**

1777
SEP. 6

Continental Congress, President. Philadelphia. To [George] Washington [Wilmington]. Pennsylvania and Maryland militia; [Maj.] Gen. [Philemon] Dickinson. L. S. of John Hancock. 2 pp. In handwriting of Jacob Rush. Answered Sep. 7* by Harrison. **90, 311**

1777
SEP. 6

Continental Congress, Resolves. Clothing for army. Broadside, 1 p. Printed by Dunlap. Enclosed in President of Congress to Washington, 1777, Sep. 6. **90, 310**

1777
SEP. 6

Board of War. [Philadelphia.] To [George] Washington, Wilmington. Size of ration. A. L. S. of Richard Peters. 1 p.   **17, 335**

1777
SEP. 6

Continental Congress, Committee. To [George] Washington [Wilmington]. Representation of regimental officers on inconvenience of method of drawing rations; proposed resolve. A. L. S. of E[lbridge] Gerry, signed also, Richard Henry Lee and Nathl. Folsom. 1 p. Answered Sep. 10. **18, 48**

Above committee to consider regulations for issuing rations to regimental officers appointed Sep. 4.

[1777]
[SEP. 6]

Continental Congress, Committee. Regulation of Commissary Department respecting provision issues; proposed resolve of Congress on issues to officers. A. D. of Elbridge Gerry. Enclosed in Committee to Washington, 1777, Sep. 6.   **18, 47**

Above preamble and resolve adopted verbatim, Sep. 11.

1777
SEP. 7

Harrison, Robert H[anson]. Newport [Delaware]. To [the President of Congress, Philadelphia]. The Jersey militia; intelligence of the enemy. Auto. draft signed. 1 p. Read in Congress, Sep. 8.

    A. III, 11

1777
SEP. 7

Livingston, William. Philadelphia. To [the President of Congress, Philadelphia]. Call for Continental troops to protect the eastern shore of New Jersey. Contemporary copy, attested by Charles Thomson. Enclosed in President of Congress to Washington, 1777, Sep. 9.   **91, 2**

1777
SEP. 7

Du Coudray, [Philip Charles etc.] Philadelphia. To the President of Congress [Philadelphia]. Disputing march of British on Philadelphia; fortified camp and other military advice. L. S. 8 pp. Enclosed in President of Congress to Washington, 1777, Sep. 9.   **91, 3**

1777
SEP. 8

Continental Congress, Resolve. Employment of French officers; Baron de Kalb and others. A. D. S. of Charles Thomson. 2 pp. Enclosed in President of Congress to Washington, 1777, Sep. 9.

    91, 7

1777
SEP. 8

Continental Congress, Resolve. Movement of troops at North River; du Coudray's letter. A. D. S. of Charles Thomson, countersigned by John Hancock. 1 p. Enclosed in President of Congress to Washington, 1777, Sep. 9.   **91, 8**

1777
SEP. 9

Washington, George. Six miles from Wilmington. To [the President of] Congress [Philadelphia]. Advance of the enemy. Draft. 1 p. In handwriting of Robert Hanson Harrison. Read in Congress, Sep. 10. **A.** III, 13
Printed: Writings of Washington (Ford) N. Y. 1890. 6, 67.

1777
SEP. 9

Continental Congress, President. Philadelphia. To [George] Washington [near Wilmington]. British on Staten Island; establishment of camp between Wilmington and Philadelphia. L. S. of John Hancock. 2 pp. In handwriting of Jacob Rush. **90, 314**

1777
SEP. 9

Continental Congress, Resolve. Correspondence with headquarters and establishment of expresses. Contemporary copy, attested by Charles Thomson. 1 p. Enclosed in President of Congress to Washington, 1777, Sep. 9. **91, 10**

1777
SEP. 9

Continental Congress, Resolve. Correspondence with Congress. Contemporary copy, attested by Charles Thomson. 1 p. Enclosed in Board of War to Washington, 1777, Sep. 9. **18, 70**

1777
SEP. 9

Board of War. [Philadelphia]. To [George] Washington [near Wilmington]. Correspondence between the Commander in chief and Congress. A. L. S. of Richard Peters. 1 p. **18, 69**

1777
SEP. 9

Board of War. [Philadelphia.] To [George] Washington [near Wilmington]. Providing for expresses. A. L. S. of Richard Peters. 1 p. **18, 69**

1777
SEP. 10

[Washington, George.] Chadd's Ford [Pennsylvania]. To [the President of Congress Philadelphia]. Detachment from [Maj.] Gen. [Israel] Putnam; uselessness of constructing works; manœvering of enemy. Draft. 1 p. In handwriting of, and signed "R. H. H." by Robert Hanson Harrison. Read in Congress, Sep. 11. **A.** III, 15

1777
SEP. 10

Washington, George. Chadd's Ford. To [the Board of War, Philadelphia]. Complaint of partiality shown by Commissary of Provisions; question as to ration. Draft. 1 p. In handwriting of Tench Tilghman. **A.** II, 17

1777
SEP. 10

Continental Congress, President. Philadelphia. To [George] Washington [Chadd's Ford]. Transmitting resolves. L. S. of John Hancock. 1 p. **91, 9**

1777
SEP. 10

Harrison, Rob[ert] H[anson]. Chadd's Ford. To the President of Congress, Philadelphia. Position of the enemy. A. L. S. 1 p. Read in Congress, Sep. 11. C. C. 152, 4, 41

1777
SEP. 11

Washington, George. Chester [Pennsylvania]. To [the President of Congress, Philadelphia]. Account of the battle [of Brandywine]. Draft. 1 p. In handwriting of Timothy Pickering, jr. Read in Congress, Sep. 12. "Published by order of Congress. Chas Thomson Secy." A. III, 23
Printed: Writings of Washington (Ford). N. Y. 1890. 6, 69.

1777
SEP. 11

Harrison, Robert H[anson]. Chadd's Ford. To [the President of Congress, Philadelphia]. Advance of the enemy. Auto. draft signed. 1 p. A. III, 19
Printed: Writings of Washington (Ford). N. Y. 1890. 6, 67, note.

1777
SEP. 11

Harrison, R[obert] H[anson]. Chadd's Ford. To [the President of Congress, Philadelphia]. Account of the battle [of Brandywine]. Auto. draft signed. 2 pp. Read in Congress Sep. 12. "Published by order of Congress Chas Thomson Secy." A. III, 21
Printed: Writings of Washington (Ford) N. Y. 1890. 6, 68, note.

1777
SEP. 11

British Army. State of and return of killed and wounded at Brandywine. Contemporary copy. 1 p. Enclosed in Washington to the President of Congress, 1777, Oct. 5. C. C. 152, 4, 87

1777
SEP. 12

Continental Congress, President. Philadelphia. To George Washington [Germantown]. Result of battle of Brandywine. L. S. of John Hancock. 1 p. 18, 90

1777
SEP. 12

Continental Congress, President. Philadelphia. To [George] Washington [En route to Philadelphia]. Spirits of Army. L. S. of John Hancock. 1 p. In handwriting of Jacob Rush. 18, 90

1777
SEP. 13

Washington, George. [Schuylkill Falls.] To [the President of Congress, Philadelphia]. Construction of redoubts; conduct of [Brig.] Gen. [Prudhomme] de Borré. Draft. 1 p. In handwriting of John Fitzgerald? Read in Congress Sep. 14. A. III, 25
Printed: Writings of Washington (Ford) N. Y. 1890. 6, 71.

1777
SEP. 13

Continental Congress, President. Philadelphia. To [George] Washington [Schuylkill Falls]. Conduct of Brig. Gen. [Prudhomme de] Borré. L. S. of John Hancock. 1 p. Answered Sep. 13.* 91, 12

1777
SEP. 14

Lincoln, B[enjamin]. Pawlet [Vermont]. To Maj. Gen. [Horatio] Gates [Bemus Heights, New York]. Plans against British on Lake George, Mt. Independence, Ticonderoga and elsewhere. Contemporary copy. 2 pp. Enclosed in President of Congress to Washington, 1777, Sep. 30.   **91, 56**

1777
SEP. 15

Washington, George. [Bucks Tavern, Pennsylvania.] To [the President of Congress, Philadelphia]. Recall of [Maj.] Gen. [John] Sullivan; withdrawal of general officers from the army; supplies. Draft. 2 pp. In handwriting of Robert Hanson Harrison. Read in Congress, Sep. 16.   **A. III, 29**

Printed: Writings of Washington (Ford) N. Y. 1890. 6, 72.

1777
SEP. 15

Continental Congress, Resolves. Commissions for Du Coudray and companions; Pulaski's appointment; and those of Frederick de Bedaulx and Baron de Kalb. A. D. S. of Charles Thomson, countersigned by John Hancock. 2 pp.   **91, 29**

1777
SEP. 15

Chase, Samuel. Philadelphia. To [George] Washington [Buck's Tavern]. Col. [Mordecai] Gist and the Maryland militia at Christiana Bridge; reenforcements; British at Wilmington. A. L. S. 3 pp.
18, 123

1777
SEP. 15

Gates, Horatio. Bemus Heights [New York]. To [Maj.] Gen. [Benjamin] Lincoln [Pawlet, Vermont]. Movements of enemy. Contemporary copy. Enclosed in ,President of Congress to Washington, 1777, Sep. 30.   **91, 53**

1777
SEP. 16

Washington, George. Camp between Warren and White Horse taverns. To the President of Congress, Philadelphia. Preparations to meet the enemy; lack of arms and ammunition. L. S. 1 p. In handwriting of Robert Hanson Harrison. Read in Congress, Sep. 16.   **C. C. 152, 4, 65**

1777
SEP. 16

Continental Congress, President. Philadelphia. To [George] Washington [Near Whitehorse Tavern]. [Maj.] Gen. [Philemon] Dickinson's letter; transmitting resolves. A. L. S. of John Hancock. 1 p. Answered Sep. 17.*   **91, 31**

1777
SEP. 16

Continental Congress, President. Philadelphia. To [George] Washington [Near Whitehorse Tavern]. Transmitting resolves; Pulaski's commission. L. S. of John Hancock. 1 p. In handwriting of Jacob Rush. Answered Sep. 17.*   **91, 27**

1777   **Lincoln,** Benjamin. Pawlet [Vermont]. To Maj. Gen.
SEP. 17   [Horatio] Gates [Bemus Heights]. March of his
            army.

SEP. 17   **Gates,** Horatio. To Lincoln. Cooperation of forces.
            Contemporary copies. Enclosed in President of
            Congress to Washington, 1777, Sep. 30.   **91,** 53

1777   **Livingston,** William. Haddonfield [New Jersey]. To
SEP. 17   the President of Congress, Philadelphia. Militia;
            advance of British. A. L. S. 1 p. Enclosed
            in President of Congress to Washington, 1777,
            Sep. 17.   **91,** 23

1777   **Pennsylvania,** Supreme Executive Council. Philadelphia.
SEP. 17   To the President of Congress [Philadelphia]. Re-
            solves of Congress respecting provisions and seiz-
            ure of blankets. Contemporary copy. 4 pp.
            Enclosed in President of Congress to Washing-
            ton, 1777, Sep. 17.   **91,** 39

1777   **Washington,** George. Reading Furnace [Pennsylvania].
SEP. 18   To [the President of] Congress [Philadelphia].
            Manœvers of troops and enemy; removal of sup-
            plies from Trenton. Draft. 2 pp. In hand-
            writing of Robert Hanson Harrison. **A. III,** 35
            Printed in part: Writings of Washington (Ford) N. Y. 1890. 6, 77,
            note.

1777   **Continental Congress,** President. Philadelphia. To
SEP. 18   [George] Washington [Warwick Furnace]. For-
            warding letters; intelligence of enemy. L. S. of
            John Hancock. 2 pp. In handwriting of Jacob
            Rush.   **91,** 41

1777   **Brown,** John. North end of Lake George [New York].
SEP. 18   To [Maj.] Gen. [Benjamin] Lincoln [Castletown,
            Vermont ?]. Defeat of British; capture of Mt.
            Defiance; the situation. Contemporary copy.
            Enclosed in President of Congress to Washing-
            ton, 1777, Sep. 30.   **91,** 51

1777   **Dickinson,** Philemon. Near Brunswick [New Jersey]. To
SEP. 18   [the President of Congress, Philadelphia]. Incur-
            sion of British from New York; militia. Con-
            temporary copy. Initialed by Hancock. 2 pp.
            Enclosed in President of Congress to Washing-
            ton, 1777, Sep. 18.   **91,** 43

1777   **Washington,** George. Parker's Ford [Pennsylvania]. To
SEP. 19   [Henry Laurens, Lancaster? Pennsylvania]. Ma-
            nœvers; damage to ammunition from rain. Draft.

2 pp. In handwriting of Robert Hanson Harrison. Endorsed "To Congress." **A. III, 37**
Printed: Writings of Washington (Ford) N.Y. 1890. 6, 75.

1777
SEP. 19
Gates, Horatio. Bemus Heights [New York]. To [Maj.] Gen. [Benjamin] Lincoln [Castletown, Vermont?]. Ordering him to Stillwater. Contemporary copy. Enclosed in President of Congress to Washington, 1777, Sep. 30. **91, 51**

1777
SEP. 20
Lincoln, B[enjamin]. Castletown [Vermont?]. [Maj.] Gen. [Horatio] Gates [Bemus Heights, New York]. The military situation in the North. Contemporary copy. 2 pp. Enclosed in President of Congress to Washington, 1777, Sep. 30. **91, 50**

1777
SEP. 22
Carroll, Charles "of Carrollton." Potts Grove, [Pennsylvania]. To [George] Washington [Potts Grove]. Impress of teams for removal of stores. A. L. S. 1 p. **18, 160**

1777
SEP. 22
Chase, Samuel. Potts Grove. To [George] Washington [Potts Grove]. Tory concealment of stores. A. L. S. 1 p. **18, 161**

1777
SEP 22
Gates, Horatio. Bemus Heights [New York]. To [the President of Congress, Philadelphia.] Account of battle of Bemus Heights. Contemporary copy. 2 pp. In handwriting of John Hancock. Enclosed in President of Congress to Washington, 1777, Sep. 30. **91, 48**

1777
SEP. 23
Washington, George. Near Potts Grove [Pennsylvania]. To [the President] "or any member of Congress, Lancaster" [Pennsylvania]. Manœvers of the armies; want of shoes and arms; Virginia militia. Draft. 4 pp. In handwriting of Tench Tilghman. Read in Congress Sep. 27.
A. III, 41
Printed in part: Writings of Washington (Ford) N.Y. 1890. 6, 80.

1777
SEP. 24
Nicholas, Samuel. Lebanon, Connecticut. To [the Board of War, Philadelphia]. Forwarding of arms from Boston; supplies at Springfield. Contemporary copy. 1 p. In handwriting of Richard Peters. Enclosed in Board of War to Washington, 1777, Oct. 1. **18, 192**

1777
SEP. 25
Gerry, E[lbridge]. Lancaster. To [George Washington, Potts Grove]. Collection of fire-arms, blankets and shoes. A. L. S. 1 p. Answered Sep. 27*.
18, 163

[1777]
[SEP. 26]

Washington, George. [Pottsgrove, Pennsylvania.] To Elbridge Gerry [Lancaster]. Want of arms for the Virginia militia; need of shoes and blankets. Movements of enemy. Draft. 2 pp. In handwriting of Robert Hanson Harrison.   A. III, 45

Printed in part: Writings of Washington (Ford) N. Y. 1890. 6, 88, note.

1777
SEP. 26

Continental Congress, President. Lancaster. To [George] Washington [Pennybacker's mills, Pennsylvania]. Commodore [John] Hazelwood and Capt. [Charles] Alexander. A. L. S. of John Hancock. 1 p.

18, 169

1777
SEP. 27

Washington, George. Pennybacker's mills [Pennsylvania]. To E[lbridge] Gerry [Lancaster]. Collection of arms for militia; shoes and blankets for the army. Draft. 2 pp. In handwriting of Tench Tilghman.   A. III, 47

Printed in part: Writings of Washington (Ford) N. Y. 1890. 6, 79, note.

1777
SEP. 27

Carroll, Charles, "of Carrollton." Lancaster. To [George] Washington [Pennybacker's mills]. Tin cartridge boxes; certain officers addicted to liquor; punishment of quartermaster and commissaries. A. L. S. 1 p.   **18, 170**

1777
SEP. 27

Continental Congress, Resolve. Seizure of supplies for the Army. A. D. S. of John Hancock. 1 p. Enclosed in President of Congress to Washington, 1777, Sep. 30.   **91, 47**

1777
SEP. 28

Washington, George. Pennybacker's mills. To [the Board of War, Lancaster]. The need of militia reenforcements. Draft. 1 p. In handwriting of Alexander Hamilton.   A. III, 51

1777
SEP. 29

Washington, George. Pennybacker's mills. To [the President of Congress, Lancaster]. Minor military movements. Draft. 1 p. In handwriting of Caleb Gibbs.   A. III, 49

1777
SEP. 29

Peters, Richard. Lancaster. To [Lt.] Col. Tench Tilghman [Pennybacker's mills]. Scarcity of arms at Springfield; confusion of accounts of stores. A. L. S. 1 p.   **18, 172**

1777
SEP. 29

Putnam, Israel. Peekskill. To the President [of Congress, York, Pennsylvania]. Cannon; movement of British at New York; weak state of Peekskill garrison. Contemporary copy. 3 pp. Partly in handwriting of Jacob Rush. Enclosed in President of Congress to Washington 1777, Oct. 7.

91, 59

1777
SEP. 30

Continental Congress, President. York, Pennsylvania. To [George] Washington [Skippack, Pennsylvania]. Convening of Congress; news from the north L. S. of John Hancock. 2 pp.   **91, 45**

1777
SEP. 30

Jones, Joseph. York. To [George Washington, Skippack]. Condition of phaeton; clothing for militia; seizure of necessaries from disaffected, subsisting army. A. L. S. 3 pp.   **18, 178**

[1777]
[SEP.]

Anonymous. [New York.] Memorandum of British force in New York; British, Hessians, number of ships; general officers names. Contemporary copy. 1 p. In handwriting of Jacob Rush. Enclosed in President of Congress to Washington, 1777, Sep. 16.   **91, 34**

1777
OCT. 1

Board of War. York [Pennsylvania]. To [George] Washington [Skippack]. Reenforcements; march of militia; blankets and shoes; scarcity of arms; fitting out of recruits, militia. A. L. S. of Richard Peters. 3 pp. Answered Oct. 7.*   **18, 181**

1777
OCT. 2

Board of War. York. To [George] Washington [near Skippack]. Recruits of Virginia and Maryland need of clothing. A. L. S. of Richard Peters. 1 p. Answered Oct. 7.*   **18, 190**

1777
OCT. 3

Washington, George. Camp. 20 miles from Philadelphia [Worcester]. To [the President of Congress, York, Pennsylvania]. News from the north; shoes, blankets etc. for the army; capture of the *Delaware.* Draft. 2 pp. In handwriting of Robert Hanson Harrison. Read in Congress, Oct. 6.   **A. III, 53**

Printed: Writings of Washington (Ford) N. Y. 1890. 6, 91.

1777
OCT. 4

Washington, George. [Near Pennybacker's mills.] General Orders for the attack at Germantown. Contemporary copy. 2 pp. In handwriting of Timothy Pickering, jr. ? Enclosed in Washington to the President of Congress, 1777, Oct. 5.

C. C. 152, 5, 85

1777
OCT. 4

Continental Congress, Resolve. Commission of Chevalier Du Buysson. A. D. S. 1 p. Enclosed in President of Congress to Washington, 1777, Oct. 7.

91, 83

1777
OCT. 4

Continental Congress, Resolves. Deputy commissaries general of purchases and issues, assistants, purchases etc; Baron de Kalb's commission; various military appointments; resolutions of thanks for Bennington and other enterprises; barracks for prisoners. D. S. of John Hancock. 7 pp. Enclosed in President of Congress to Washington, 1777, Oct. 7.   **91, 61**

1777
OCT. 5

Washington, George. Near Pennybackers mills. To [the President of Congress, York]. Account of the battle of Germantown. Draft. 3 pp. In handwriting of Robert Hanson Harrison and Alexander Hamilton. Read in Congress, Oct 8.
        A. III, 55
Printed: Writings of Washington (Ford) N. Y. 1890. 6, 93.

1777
OCT. 6

Continental Congress, Resolves. [Maj.] Gen. [Israel] Putnam's letter; reenforcements; commissaries' power of seizure. D. S. of John Hancock. 2 pp. Enclosed in President of Congress to Washington 1777, Oct. 7.   **91, 65**

1777
OCT. 6

Mifflin, Jonathan. Trenton [New Jersey] To Col. [Clement] Biddle. [Near Pauling's mills, Pennsylvania]. British feeling regarding the battle of Germantown; conditions in Philadelphia. Contemporary copy. 3 pp. In handwriting of Caleb Gibbs. Enclosed in Washington to the President of Congress, 1777, Oct. 7.   **C. C. 152, 5, 93**

1777
OCT. 7

Washington, George. Near Pennybacker's mills. To [the President of Congress, York]. Loss of the enemy at Germantown; water defense of Philadelphia; want of brigadiers. Draft. 3 pp. In handwriting of Robert Hanson Harrison and Alexander Hamilton. Read in Congress, Oct. 13. Referred to the Board of War.   **A. III, 59**
Printed: Writings of Washington (Ford) N. Y. 1890. 6, 98.

1777
OCT. 7

Washington, George. Near Pauling's mills [Pennsylvania]. To [the Board of War, York]. Want of blankets, clothing and shoes for the army; arms in use in Connecticut. Draft. 2 pp. In handwriting of of Tench Tilghman.   **A. III, 63**
Paulings Mill was the former name of Pennybacker's mills.

1777
OCT. 7

Continental Congress, President. York. To [George] Washington [Pennybacker's mills]. Transmitting resolves; the Highlands; rumors of battle of

Germantown. L. S. of John Hancock. 2 pp. In handwriting of Jacob Rush. Answered Oct. 10.* **91, 57**

1777
OCT. 7

Board of War. York. To [George] Washington [near Pennybacker's mills]. Capt. Thomas Rowland's invention; pay of certain French officers. A. L. S. of Richard Peters. 1 p. Answered Oct. 15. Endorsed by Tilghman: "Capt. Rowland's invention not useful." **18, 233**

1777
OCT. 8

Washington, George. Pennybacker's mills. To [the President of] Congress [York]. Need of artillerymen; Col. [Charles] Harrison's regiment. Draft. 1 p. In handwriting of Robert Hanson Harrison. Referred to the Board of War. **A. III, 65**

1777
OCT. 8

Continental Army, General Court Martial. Williamsburg [Virginia]. Trial of Godfrey Roberts, John More, and George Isden. D. S.: Ed. Carrington Prest. Auto.-signed note on findings as above by Col. David Mason. 3 pp. Transmitted to Washington. **91, 75**

1777
OCT. 8

Continental Congress, Resolve. Thanks to Washington and army for actions at Germantown. D. S. of John Hancock. 1 p. Enclosed in President of Congress to Washington, 1777, Oct. 9. **91, 68**

1777
OCT. 8

Burgoyne, J[ohn]. [Freeman's Farm, New York]. To M[aj]. Gen. [Horatio] Gates [Freeman's]. Commending the British sick and wounded to his care. Contemporary copy. 1 p. Enclosed in President of Congress to Washington, 1777, Oct. 17. **91, 87**

1777
OCT. 8

Duché, Jacob. Philadelphia. To [George] Washington [Pennybacker's mills, Pennsylvania]. Hopelessness of the present; rescinding Declaration of Independence; Washington's influence for peace. A. L. S. 13 pp. Enclosed in Washington to the President of Congress, 1777, Oct. 16.
C. C. 152, 5, 127
See: Writings of Washington (Ford) N. Y. 1890. 6, 116, note.
This letter was enclosed in Duché's Washington, Oct. 13.

1777
OCT. 9

Continental Congress, President. York. To [George] Washington [Towamencin, Pennsylvania]. Punishment of persons assisting enemy. L. S. of John Hancock. 2 pp. In handwriting of Jacob Rush. **91, 66**

1777
Oct. 9

Continental Congress, President. York. To [George] Washington [Towamencin]. Thanks of Congress for behavior at Germantown. L. S. of John Hancock. 2 pp. In handwriting of Jacob Rush.
91, 67

1777
Oct. 9

Burgoyne, J[ohn]. [Saratoga, New York]. To M[aj]. Gen. [Horatio] Gates [Wilbur's Basin]. Introducing Lady Harriet Ackland. Contemporary copy. 1 p. Enclosed in President of Congress to Washington, 1777, Oct. 17. 91, 89

1777
Oct. 10

Washington, George. 26 miles from Philadelphia [Towamencin]. To [the President of Congress, York]. Quarters for the troops; enemy's feint against the Highlands; militia; cannonade by enemy; want of shoes, blankets; scarcity of money. Draft. 3 pp. In handwriting of Robert Hanson Harrison. Referred to Board of War. "Acted upon." A. III, 67

1777
Oct. 10

Continental Congress, Resolve. Promotion of Capt. Silas Talbot. D. S. of Charles Thomson, countersigned by John Hancock. 1 p. Enclosed in President of Congress to Washington, 1777, Oct. 12. 91, 80

1777
Oct., 10

Hazelwood, John. Fort Island [Schuylkill River]. To [George Washington, Towamencin]. Assistance to officer sent from camp; demand of enemy; defense of the post. Contemporary copy. 2 pp. In handwriting of Tench Tilghman. Enclosed in Washington to the President of Congress, 1777, Oct. 13. C. C. 152, 5, 109

1777
Oct. 11

Continental Congress, Resolves. British treatment of prisoners; resignation of La Balmé. A. D. S. of John Hancock. 1 p. Enclosed in President of Congress to Washington, 1777, Oct. 12. 91, 81

1777
Oct. 11

Continental Congress, Resolves. Hides; impress of teams for commissary of hides; returns of work, business of the department. D. S. of Charles Thomson, countersigned by John Hancock. 3 pp. Enclosed in President of Congress to Washington, 1777, Oct. 12. 91, 78

1777
Oct. 11

Bradford, William and John Hazelwood. Fort Mifflin [Pennsylvania]. To [George Washington, Towamencin]. Capture of a British redoubt; defense of Fort Mifflin. Contemporary copy. 2 pp. In

handwriting of Caleb Gibbs. Enclosed in Washington to the President of Congress, 1777, Oct. 13.
C. C. 152, 5, 111

1777
Oct. 11

[**Mason,** David. Williamsburgh, Virginia.] To [the President of Congress, York]. Case of John More. [Extract of letter.] Contemporary copy. 1 p. Transmitted to Washington. 91, 69

1777
Oct. 12

Continental Congress, President. York. To [George] Washington [Towamencin]. British treatment of prisoners. L. S. of John Hancock. 2 pp. In handwriting of Jacob Rush. 91, 77

1777
Oct. 12

Gates, Horatio. [Saratoga, New York]. To Lt. Gen. [John] Burgoyne [Saratoga]. Lady [Harriet] Ackland; treatment of British wounded; burning of houses by British. Contemporary copy. 2 pp. Enclosed in President of Congress to Washington, 1777, Oct. 17. 91, 92

1777
Oct. 12

Gates, Horatio. Saratoga [New York]. To [the President of Congress, Philadelphia]. Account of battle of Freeman's Farm and retreat of Burgoyne. Contemporary copy. 1 p. Enclosed in President of Congress to Washington, 1777, Oct. 17. 91, 90

1777
Oct. 12

Sullivan, John. Towamencin. Court of Inquiry on conduct in expedition against Staten Island in August. D. S.: Stirling. Henry Knox. Alex: McDougall. Oliver Spencer. T. Clark. 2 pp. Enclosed in Washington to the President of Congress, 1777, Oct. 13. C. C. 152, 5, 113

1777
Oct. 13

Washington, George. [Towamencin.] To [the President of Congress, York]. Attack on Fort Mifflin; capture of Fort Montgomery and evacuation of Peekskill; wants of the army; cartouche boxes; enlistments and drafts; court of inquiry on [Maj.] Gen. [John] Sullivan. Draft. 4 pp. In handwriting of Robert Hanson Harrison. Read in Congress, Oct. 16. Referred to the Board of War. A. III, 71

1777
Oct. 13

Continental Congress, Resolves. Money for army; French officers; shoes, stockings, etc. for army. D. S. of John Hancock. 1 p. Enclosed in President of Congress to Washington, 1777, Oct. 14. 91, 84

1777
Oct. 13

Continental Army, Towamencin. Return of clothing wanting in the several brigades. Tabular statement. A. D. S. of T[imothy] Pickering, jr. 2 pp. Enclosed in Washington to the President of Congress, 1777, Oct. 15.   C. C.   152, 5, 117

1777
Oct. 13
Duché, Jacob. Philadelphia. To [George] Washington [Towamencin]. Forwarding his thoughts on present conditions. A. L. S. 1 p. Enclosed in Washington to the President of Congress, 1777, Oct. 16.   C. C.   152, 5, 123

1777
Oct. 14
Continental Congress, President. York. To [George] Washington [Towamencin]. Intercourse with enemy; transmitting resolves. L. S. of John Hancock. 1 p. In handwriting of Jacob Rush.
91, 82

1777
Oct. 16
Washington, George. Peter Wentz's [Worcester, Pennsylvania]. To [the President of Congress, York]. British treatment of prisoners; successes of the northern army; [Jacob] Duché's letter. Draft. 2 pp. In handwriting of Robert Hanson Harrison. Read in Congress, Oct. 20.   A. III, 75
Printed: Writings of Washington (Ford) N. Y. 1890. 6, 114.

1777
Oct. 16
Washington, George. [Worcester.] To [the Board of War, York]. Requesting blank commissions. Draft. 1 p. In handwriting of Tench Tilghman.
A. III, 77

1777
Oct. 17
Washington, George. "Metuchen Hill, Philadelphia." [Worcester.] To Richard Henry Lee [York]. Promotion of Brig. Gen. [Thomas] Conway; his ability; difficulties; clothing. Transcript.
P. I, 41
Printed· Writings of Washington (Ford) N. Y. 1890. 6, 120.

1777
Oct. 17
Continental Congress, President. York. To [George] Washington [Worcester]. Retirement from Congress; escort for protection on journey to Boston. A. L. S. of John Hancock. 2 pp. Answered Oct. 22.*   19, 11

1777
Oct. 17
Continental Congress, President. York. To [George] Washington [Worcester, Pennsylvania]. Transmitting resolves; victory in the north [Saratoga]. L. S. of John Hancock. 2 pp. In handwriting of Jacob Rush. Answered Oct. 21.*   91, 85

1777
Oct. 17
Continental Congress, Resolve. Management of the Post-office. Contemporary copy, attested by Charles Thomson. 2 pp. Enclosed in President of Congress to Washington, 1777, Oct. 17.   91, 72

1777
Oct. 17

Continental Congress, Resolve. Approval of Commodore [John] Hazelwood's defense of Philadelphia. A. D. S. of Charles Thomson. 1 p. Enclosed in President of Congress to Washington, 1777, Oct. 17. **91, 94**

1777
Oct. 17

Continental Congress, Resolves. Completion of state battalions; reward for deserters; recruiting service. Contemporary copy, attested by Charles Thomson, countersigned by John Hancock. 3 pp. Enclosed in Washington to the President of Congress, 1777, Oct. 17. **91, 96**

1777
Oct. 18

Washington, George. [Worcester.] To [the President of Congress, York]. Sending intelligence [of the surrender of Burgoyne]. Draft. 1 p. In handwriting of Tench Tilghman. A. **III, 80**

1777
Oct. 18

Board of War. [York]. To George Washington [Worcester]. Scarcity of lead; sources of supply; seizure of blankets, etc. from the disaffected; cartouche boxes. A. L. S. of Richard Peters. 2 pp. **19, 13**

[1777]
[Oct. 18]

Board of War. Abstract of arms and accoutrements issued from Apr. 1 to Aug. 1; estimate of lead on hand, Aug. 11; estimate of powder on hand, Aug. 11. Tabular statement. D. S. of Richard Peters. 3 pp. Enclosed in Board of War to Washington, 1777, Oct. 18. **91, 15**

1777
Oct. 18

Gates, Horatio. Saratoga. To [the President of Congress [York]. Transmitting articles of Saratoga Convention; recommending [Lt.] Col. [James] Wilkinson. Contemporary copy. 1 p. Enclosed in Charles Thomson to Washington, 1777, Oct. 31. **19, 99**

1777
Oct. 19

[**Gates**, Horatio.] Albany. To Maj. Gen. John Vaughan [near Kingston]. Ravages of his army. Contemporary copy. 1 p. In handwriting of Charles Thomson. Enclosed in Thomson to Washington, 1777, Oct. 31. **19, 100**

1777
Oct. 19

Saratoga Convention. Articles agreed upon between Gates and Burgoyne. Contemporary copy. 4 pp. In handwriting of Charles Thomson. Enclosed in Thomson to Washington, 1777, Oct. 31. **19, 96**

1777
Oct. 20

Continental Congress, Resolves. Artillerymen from Maryland; court of inquiry on [Maj.] Gen. [John]

Sullivan; promotions and appointments. A. D. S. of Charles Thomson. 1 p. Enclosed in President of Congress to Washington, 1777, Oct. 25.   **91, 73**

1777
Oct. 20

[**Gates**, Horatio.] Albany. To [the President of Congress, York]. Letter to Maj. Gen. [John] Vaughan; recommending Dr. John Potts. Contemporary copy. 1 p. Enclosed in Charles Thomson to Washington, 1777, Oct. 31.   **91, 101**

1777
Oct. 20

Lee, Richard Henry. York. To [George Washington, Worcester]. [Thomas] Conway and a Maj. Generalship; new Board of War and proposed membership; Conway for Adjutant-general; his retirement. A. L. S. 3 pp.   **18, 21**

1777
Oct. 21

Washington, George. Near White Marsh [Pennsylvania]. To [the President of Congress, York]. Filling the battalions; deserters; movements of enemy; cannonade of Fort Mifflin. Draft. 2 pp. In handwriting of Robert Hanson Harrison. Read in Congress, Oct. 24.   **A. III, 81**

1777
Oct. 22

Washington, George. Whitpain [Pennsylvania]. To [the President of Congress, York]. His retirement from Congress. Draft. 1 p. In handwriting of Alexander Hamilton.   **A. III, 83**
Printed: Writings of Washington (Ford) N. Y. 1890. 6, 132.

1777
Oct. 22

Washington, George. [Whitpain.] To [the Board of War, York]. Supplies for the army; lead at Boston; cartouche boxes; general returns of the army. Draft. 2 pp. In handwriting of Tench Tilghman.   **A. III, 85**
Printed in part: Writings of Washington (Ford) N. Y. 1890. 6, 134, note.

1777
Oct. 22

Continental Congress, Resolves. Case of John More; commissary of issues; army ration. A. D. S. of Charles Thomson. 1 p. Enclosed in President of Congress to Washington, 1777, Oct. 25.   **91, 74**

1777
Oct. 23

Ballard, Robert. Red Bank [Fort Mercer, New Jersey]. To [George] Washington [Whitpain]. Enemy's attack on Fort Mifflin. Contemporary copy. 2 pp. In handwriting of Caleb Gibbs. Enclosed in Washington to the President of Congress, 1777, Oct. 21.   **C. C. 152, 5, 155**

1777
Oct. 23

Hazelwood, John. Red Bank [New Jersey]. To George Washington [Whitpain]. Naval action off Fort Mifflin. Contemporary copy. 2 pp. In handwriting of George Lewis. Enclosed in Washington to the President of Congress, 1777, Oct. 24.

C. C. 152, 5, 151

1777
Oct. 23

Ward, Samuel. Red Bank [New Jersey]. To [George] Washington [Whitpain]. Repulse of British at Red Bank; losses; bravery of Mauduit Du Plessis. Contemporary copy. 2 pp. In handwriting of Caleb Gibbs. Enclosed in Washington to the President of Congress, 1777, Oct. 23.

C. C. 152, 5, 153

1777
Oct. 24

Washington, George. [Whitpain.] To [the President of Congress, York]. British repulse at Red Bank [Fort Mercer]; want of shoes and blankets. Draft. 2 pp. In handwriting of Robert Hanson Harrison. Read in Congress, Oct. 27.

A. III, 87
Printed: Writings of Washington (Ford) N. Y. 1890. 6, 136.

1777
Oct. 24

Board of War. [York.] To George Washington [Whitpain]. Lead, salt petre, etc. at Boston; cartouche boxes; minor matters. A. L. S. of Richard Peters. 1 p. Answered Nov. 3.*   19, 38

1777
Oct. 25

Continental Congress, President. York. To [George] Washington [Whitpain]. Transmitting resolves; commissions; news from north. L. S. of John Hancock. 2 pp. In handwriting of Jacob Rush.

91, 70

1777
Oct. 25

Navy Board, Bordentown [New Jersey]. To [George] Washington [Whitpain]. Action at Red Bank; want of ammunition. A. L. S. of Francis Hopkinson, signed also by John Wharton. 2 pp.

19, 61

1777
Oct. 25

Hancock, John. York. To [George] Washington [Whitpain]. Journey to Boston; escort of horse. L. S. 1 p. In handwriting of Jacob Rush.   19, 54

1777
Oct. 31

Continental Congress, Secretary. York. To [George] Washington [Whitpain]. Transmitting letters from [Maj.] Gen. [Horatio] Gates. A. L. S. of Charles Thomson. 1 p.   19, 95

[1777]
[Oct. ?]

[Shippen, William, jr.] [Whitpain.] To [George Washington, Whitpain]. Plan for establishment of the hospital department. Contemporary copy. 3 pp. In handwriting of Tench Tilghman. Enclosed in Washington to the President of Congress, 1777, Oct. 24?   C. C. 152, 5, 157

1777
Nov. 1

Washington, George. Whitemarsh. To the President of Congress [York]. The military situation; Lafayette; militia. Draft. 8 pp. In handwriting of Robert Hanson Harrison. Read in Congress, Nov. 6. Referred to Board of War.

A.   III, 89

Printed: Writings of Washington (Ford) N. Y. 1890.   6, 156.

1777
Nov. 2

Washington, George. Whitemarsh. To [the President of Congress, York]. His retirement from Congress. Draft. 1 p. In handwriting of Robert Hanson Harrison.   A.   III, 97

1777
Nov. 3

Washington, George. Whitemarsh. To [the Board of War, York]. Cartouche boxes; Col. [Louis Le Bègue] Duportail's rank. Draft. 2 pp. In handwriting of Tench Tilghman.   A.   III, 99

1777
Nov. 4

Washington, George. [Whitemarsh.] To [Lt. Gen. Sir] William Howe [Philadelphia]. Exchange of prisoners. Contemporary copy. 1 p. In handwriting of John Laurens. Enclosed in Washington to the President of Congress, 1777, Nov. 4.

C. C.   152, 5, 207

Printed: Writings of Washington (Ford) N. Y. 1890.   6, 172.

1777
Nov. 4

Continental Congress, President. York. To [George] Washington [Whitemarsh]. Transmitting resolves. Letterbook copy.   C. C.   13, I, 2

1777
Nov. 4

Continental Congress, Report of Marine Committee on frigates in the Delaware and order of Congress thereon. A. D. S. of Charles Thomson. 2 pp. Enclosed in President of Congress to Washington, 1777, Nov. 5.   91, 100

1777
Nov. 4

Continental Congress, Resolves. Monument to Brig. Gen. Francis Nash; resolutions of thanks to commanding officers at Saratoga, Red Bank, Fort Mifflin and of the naval force in the Delaware. A. D. S. of Charles Thomson. 2 pp. Enclosed in President of Congress to Washington 1777, Nov. 5.   91, 102

1777
Nov. 4

Board of War. [York.] To George Washington, Whitemarsh. Question of passport for Joseph Simons and Bernard Gratz. A. L. S. of Richard Peters. 1 p.   95, 317

1777
Nov. 5

Continental Congress, President. York. To [George] Washington [Whitemarsh]. Transmitting sun-

WRITING OF GEORGE LEWIS.

dry resolves, letters, and documents.   A. L. S. of
Henry Laurens.   2 pp.   Answered Nov. 10.*

91, 98

1777
Nov. 5

Continental Congress, Resolves.   Recapture of forts in the
Highlands; directions to [Maj]. Gen. [Horatio]
Gates, militia; aid from New York state.
A. S. D. of Charles Thomson.   3 pp.   Enclosed
in President of Congress to Washington, 1777,
Nov. 5.   **91, 103**

1777
Nov. 5

Howe, [Sir.] W[illiam].   Philadelphia.   To George Washington [Whitemarsh].   Exchange of prisoners;
complaints.   Contemporary copy.   3 pp.   In handwriting of Richard Kidder Meade.   Enclosed in
Washington to the President of Congress, 1777,
Nov. 10.   **C. C.   152,** 5, 209

1777
Nov. 7

Continental Congress, President.   York.   To [George]
Washington [Whitemarsh].   Forwarding resolves.
A. L. S. of Henry Laurens.   1 p.   Answered
Nov. 10.*   **91, 106**

1777
Nov. 7

Continental Congress, Resolve.   Resignation of Maj. Gen.
[Thomas] Mifflin; election of board of war.   A. D.
S. of Charles Thomson.   1 p.   Enclosed in Presi-
dent of Congress to Washington, 1777, Nov. 7.

91, 105

1777
Nov. 7

Board of War.   [York.]   To [George] Washington, Whitemarsh.   Seizure of blankets and shoes from disaffected.   A. L. S. of Richard Peters.   1 p.   **19, 166**

1777
Nov. 8

Washington, George.   Whitemarsh.   To [the President of
Congress, York].   Movements of enemy; sup-
port of Fort Mifflin; lack of money; salt provisions.   Draft.   2 pp.   In handwriting of Tench
Tilghman.   Read in Congress, Nov. 12.   Referred
to Board of Treasury.   **A. III, 101**

1777
Nov. 8

Dickinson, Philemon.   Whitemarsh.   [Pennsylvania].
To [George] Washington [Whitemarsh].   Sailing
of fleet from New York; militia.   Contemporary
copy.   1 p.   In handwriting of Richard Kidder
Meade.   Enclosed in Washington to the President of Congress, 1777, Nov. 8.
C. C.   152, 5, 185

1777
Nov. 10.

Washington, George.   Whitemarsh.   To the President of
Congress [York].   Sinking of the frigates; military matters, rank etc.; foreign engineer officers;

money. Draft. 2 pp. In handwriting of Robert
Hanson Harrison. Read in Congress, Nov. 12.

A. III, 103

Printed: Writings of Washington (Ford) N. Y. 1890. 6, 180.

1777
Nov. 11

Washington, George. Whitemarsh. To [the President of
Congress, York]. Want of clothes and blankets;
movements of the enemy; militia. Draft. 3 pp.
In handwriting of Robert Hanson Harrison.
Read in Congress, Nov. 14.   A. III, 107

Printed: Writings of Washington (Ford) N. Y. 1890. 6, 184.

1777
Nov. 11

Washington, George. Whitemarsh. To the Board of War
[York]. Practice of substitutes; arms for militia;
clothing for the army. Draft. 1 p. In handwriting of Robert Hanson Harrison. A. III, 111

1777
Nov. 12

Board of War. [York.] To [George Washington, White-
marsh]. Col. Benjamin Flower's claim to a commission. A. L. S. of Richard Peters.   1 p.

32, 144

1777
Nov. 13

Continental Congress, President. York. To [George]
Washington [Whitemarsh]. Difficulty of Treasury as to money; appointment to chair of Congress; approval of Washington's course respecting
the frigates; commissions for Pennsylvania offices;
methods of transacting business in Congress;
resolves enclosed; comment; clothing; French
officers. Letter-book copy.   C. C. 13, I, 15

1777
Nov. 14

Washington, George. [Whitemarsh.] To [Lt. Gen. Sir]
William Howe [Philadelphia]. Exchange of officers; charges of cruelty. Contemporary copy.
3 pp. In handwriting of John Laurens. Enclosed
in Washington to the President of Congress, 1777,
Nov. 23.   C. C. 152, 5, 213

Printed: Writings of Washington (Ford) N. Y. 1890. 6, 193.

1777
Nov. 15

Cloyd, Joseph, and William **Dewees**, jr. Philadelphia
county. Depositions of their treatment while
prisoners of the British. Contemporary copy.
2 pp. Enclosed in Washington to the President
of Congress, 1777, Nov. 23.   C. C. 152, 5, 217

1777
Nov. 17

Washington, George. Whitemarsh. To [the President of
Congress, York]. Evacuation of Fort Mifflin;
want of clothing; delay of troops from the north.
Draft. 6 pp. In handwriting of Tench Tilghman. Read in Congress, Nov. 21. Referred to
the Board of War.   A. III, 113

Printed: Writings of Washington (Ford) N. Y. 1890. 6, 200.

1777
Nov. 18

Washington, George. Whitemarsh. [York.] To Richard Henry Lee. The Adjutant Generalship; can-
didates and their qualifications; the Quartermaster General vacancy; salt provision. Transcript.
P. 1, 49
Printed: Writings of Washington (Ford) N. Y. 1890. 6, 207.

1777
Nov. 19

Continental Congress, President. York. To [George]
Washington, Whitemarsh. Transmitting resolves; John Brown's claim as messenger from
Sir William and Lord [Richard] Howe. Letter-
book copy. C. C. 13, I, 33

1777
Nov. 20

Lee, Richard Henry. York. To [George] Washington
[Whitemarsh]. [Brig.] Gen. [Thomas] Mifflin
and the Board of War; the Adjutant Generalship;
Mifflin's plan for the Quartermaster's Department; British faith and the Saratoga Convention;
feeling in Pennsylvania and Delaware; taxation;
change in Commissary Department; news from
Europe. A. L. S. 6 pp. 20, 6

1777
Nov. 23

Washington, George. Whitemarsh. To [the President
of Congress, York]. Devices of enemy to deceive
the people; loss of Red Bank; movements of
enemy; militia. Draft. 4 pp. In handwriting
of Robert Hanson Harrison. Read in Congress,
Nov. 27. A. III, 121
Printed: Writings of Washington (Ford) N. Y. 1890. 6, 214.

1777
Nov. 23

Washington, George. [Whitemarsh.] To [Lt.] Gen. [Sir
William] Howe [Philadelphia]. Retaliation for
treatment of American prisoners. Contemporary copy. 1 p. In handwriting of Robert
Hanson Harrison. Enclosed in Washington to
the President of Congress, 1777, Nov. 23.
C. C. 152, 5, 221

1777
Nov. 26

Washington, George. [Whitemarsh.] To [the President
of Congress, York]. Foreign intelligence; Lafayette's command; Convention troops; exchange
of prisoners. Draft. 4 pp. In handwriting of
Robert Hanson Harrison. Read in Congress,
Dec. 1. A. III, 125
Printed: Writings of Washington (Ford) N. Y. 1890. 6, 222.

1777
Nov. 26

Continental Congress, President. York. To [George]
Washington, Whitemarsh. Transmitting resolves; Lt. Col. [François Louis Teisseidre, Marquis de] Fleury's brevet. Letter-book copy.
C. C. 13, I, 40

1777
Nov. 27

Washington, George. Whitemarsh. To [the Board of War, York]. Lack of clothing; inattention to general orders; reforms in the army. Draft. 2 pp. In handwriting of Tench Tilghman.

           A. III, 129

1777
Nov. 28

Continental Congress, President. York. To [George] Washington, Whitemarsh. Delay in reports from Boards of War and Treasury; transmitting resolves. Letter-book copy. **C. C. 13, I, 36**

1777
Nov. 28

Navy Board. Bordentown [New Jersey]. To [George] Washington [Whitemarsh]. Disposition of the sunken frigates. A. L. S. of Francis Hopkinson, signed also by John Wharton. 2 pp. **20, 85.**

1777
Nov. 30

Continental Congress, President. York. To [George] Washington, Whitemarsh. Transmitting resolves and other papers. Letter-book copy.

           C. C. 13, I, 49

1777
Dec. 1

Washington, George. Whitemarsh. To [the President of Congress, York]. Want of cloathing; uneasiness caused by promotions. Draft.. 2 pp. In handwriting of Robert Hanson Harrison. Read in Congress, Dec. 4. Referred to R. H. Lee, Duer, Dana, Duane and Harvie. **A. III, 131**
Printed: Writings of Washington (Ford) N. Y. 1890. 6, 229.

1777
Dec. 1

Continental Congress, President. York. To [George] Washington, Whitemarsh. Port of embarkation of the Convention troops; Lafayette's command of a division; report of arrival of stores from France. Letter-book copy. **C. C. 13, I, 52**

1777
Dec. 2

Washington, George. Whitemarsh. To Maj. Gen. [Israel] Putnam [Fishkill, New York]. Fortifying the Hudson. Contemporary copy. 2 pp. In handwriting of Caleb Gibbs. Enclosed in Washington to the President of Congress, 1778, Mar. 17. **C. C. 152, 5, 397**
Printed: Writings of Washington (Ford) N. Y. 1890. 6, 231.

1777
Dec. 3

Continental Congress, Resolves. 'Secret enterprise against British at St Johns and elsewhere on Lake Champlain. Contemporary copy. 3 pp. In handwriting of John Lansing, jr. Enclosed in John Stark to Washington 1778, July 31, which letter is not included in this calendar. **25, 114**

1777
Dec. 8

Continental Congress, President. York. To [George] Washington, Whitemarsh. Transmitting resolve; [Lt.] Gen. [Sir William] Howe's answer to Washington's letter. Letter-book copy.

               C. C. 13, I, 58

1777
DEC. 10

Washington, George. Whitemarsh. To [the President of Congress, York]. Skirmishes with enemy at Whitemarsh, Chestnut Hill and other places. Draft. 3 pp. In handwriting of Robert Hanson Harrison. Read in Congress, Dec. 13. . **A. III, 133**

Printed: Writings of Washington (Ford) N. Y. 1890. 6, 237.

1777
DEC. 10

Continental Congress, Committee of conference with Gen. Washington. Whitemarsh. To George Washington [Whitemarsh]. Measures to be recommended to Congress for increasing efficiency of the army. A. L. S. of Robert Morris, signed also by Elbridge Gerry and Joseph Jones. 2 pp.

               91, 110

1777
DEC. 12

Continental Congress, President. York. To [George] Washington, Whitemarsh. Transmitting resolve. Letter-book copy.   **C. C. 13, I, 59**

1777
DEC. 14

Washington, George. Gulf Creek [Pennsylvania]. To [the Board of War, York]. Seizure of clothing; minor military matters; loss of arms by deserters. Draft. 4 pp. In handwriting of Tench Tilghman.   **A. III, 137**

1777
DEC. 14

Washington, George. "Near the Gulph." To [the President of Congress, York]. Movement of the army; Burgoyne and the Convention; supplies and exercise of military authority. Draft. 4 pp. In handwriting of Robert Hanson Harrison.

               A. III, 141

Printed: Writings of Washington (Ford) N. Y. 1890. 6, 242.

1777
DEC. 16

Continental Congress, Committee of Conference with Gen. Washington. Report to Congress; attempt on Philadelphia; militia and reenforcements for army. Contemporary copy. 1 p. In handwriting of Joseph Jones. Enclosed in Committee to Washington, 1777, Dec. 10. Report considered in Congress, Dec. 18 and 19.   **91, 108**

Committee consisted of R. Morris, Gerry and Jones.

1777
DEC. 17

Continental Congress, President. York. To [George] Washington, Gulf [mill, Pennsylvania]. [Lt.] Gen. [John] Burgoyne's letter. Letter-book copy.

               C. C. 13, I, 61

1777
Dec. 17
     Navy Board. Bordentown [New Jersey]. To [George] Washington [Gulf mill]. Progress of an experiment. A. L. S. of Francis Hopkinson, signed also by John Wharton. 1 p.   **20, 171**

1777
Dec. 19
     Continental Congress, Resolve. Supply of provisions for British prisoners. Broadside. With auto. note of Robert Hanson Harrison of names of American officers confined in goal. Enclosed in Washington to the President of Congress, 1778, Apr. 18.   **C. C. 152, 5, 471**

1777
Dec. 20
     Continental Congress, President. York. To [George] Washington, Gulf [mill]. Transmitting resolves and other papers; [Gov.] William Tryon's cruelties.   **C. C. 13, I, 63**

1777
Dec. 22
     Washington, George. Valley Forge [Pennsylvania]. To [the President of Congress, York]. Lack of provisions; sufferings of the army. Draft. 4 pp. In handwriting of Robert Hanson Harrison.
                                               A. III, 145
                Printed: Writings of Washington (Ford) N. Y. 1890. 6, 252.

1777
Dec. 23
     W[ashingto]n, G[eorge]. Valley Forge. To [the President of Congress, York]. Starvation; impossibility of collecting supplies; critics of the service. Auto. draft signed. 7 pp.   **A. III, 151**
                Printed: Writings of Washington (Ford) N. Y. 1890. 6, 257.

1777
Dec. 23
     Continental Congress, President. York. To [George] Washington [Valley Forge]. Transmitting papers; mutiny of crew of British merchant-ship and carrying of vessel into Charleston. Letter-book copy.   **C. C. 13, I, 65**

1777
Dec. 24
     Washington, George. Valley Forge. To the Board of War [York]. Exchange of [Brig] Gen. [William] Thompson. Draft. 1 p. In handwriting of Robert Hanson Harrison.   **A. III, 149**

1777
Dec. 24
     Continental Congress, President. York. To [George] Washington [Valley Forge]. Transmitting resolve; opinion of France's attitude toward the United States.   **C. C. 13, I, 77**

1777
Dec. 25
     Continental Congress, President. York. To [George] Washington [Valley Forge]. Commission to Col. [William] Barton. Letter-book copy.
                                          C. C. 13, I, 78

1777
Dec. 26

Washington, George. Valley Forge. To the President of Congress [York]. Claim of rank of [Brig.] Gen. [William] Woodford. Draft. 1 p. In handwriting of Robert Hanson Harrison.

A. III, 161

1777
Dec. 27

Washington, George. Valley Forge. To Maj. Gen. [Israel] Putnam [Fishkill, New York]. Fortifications in Highlands; return of troops at Fishkill. Contemporary copy. 2 pp. In handwriting of Caleb Gibbs. Enclosed in Washington to the President of Congress, 1778, Mar. 17. C. C. **152**, 5, 397

1777
Dec. 29

Washington, George. Valley Forge. To the Board of War [York]. Suffering of garrison of Fort Pitt for want of clothing. Draft. 1 p. In handwriting of John Laurens. A. III, 159

1777
Dec. 30

Washington, George. Valley Forge. To the Board of War [York]. Horses for Capt. [Cadwallader] Jones's troop. Draft. 1 p. In handwriting of Tench Tilghman. A. III, 163

1777
Dec. 30

Washington, George. [Valley Forge.] To Maj. Gen. [Thomas] Conway [Camp]. Commencement of duties as Inspector General; promotions. Contemporary copy. 2 pp. In handwriting of John Fitzgerald. Enclosed in Washington to the President of Congress, 1778, Jan. 2.

C. C. **152**, 5, 241

1777
Dec. 30

Navy Board, Middle District. Bordentown [New Jersey]. Present of fish; an experiment; advance to Col. [Asa?] Worthington. A. L. S. of Francis Hopkinson, signed also by John Wharton. **W**

1777
Dec. 31

Lovell, James. [York.] To [George] Washington [Valley Forge]. Printing and hiding of the Journals of Congress from the British. A. L. S. 3 pp.

20, 320

1778
Jan. 1

Washington, George. Valley Forge. To [the President of Congress, York]. Appointments of Quartermaster and Adjutant General; [Brig] Gen. [George] Weedon's complaint as to rank. Draft. **4 pp.** In handwriting of Tench Tilghman.

A. III, 165

Printed: Writings of Washington (Ford) N. Y. 1890. 6, 273.

1778
Jan. 1

Continental Congress, President. York. To [George] Washington [Valley Forge]. Committee of Con-

ference; transmitting resolves. Letter-book
copy.   C. C.   13, I, 94

1778   Forman, David. [Valley Forge.] Memorial [to George
JAN. 1   Washington, Valley Forge,] praying for guard
             for salt works at Barnegat.

         Same to same. Letter transmitting above. Contempo-
             rary copies. 3 pp. In handwriting of Tench
             Tilghman. Enclosed in Washington to the Presi-
             dent of Congress, 1778, Jan. 31.

                                      C. C.   152, 5, 279

1778   Washington, George. Valley Forge. To [the President
JAN. 2   of Congress, York]. [Maj] Gen. [Thomas] Con-
             way and the office of Inspector-General. Draft.
             2 pp. In handwriting of Robert Hanson Harri-
             son. Read in Congress, Jan. 7. Referred to
             Board of War.   A. III, 169
             Printed: Writings of Washington (Ford) N.Y. 1890. 6, 276.

1778   Washington, George. Valley Forge. To [the President
JAN. 2   of Congress, York]. Introducing Maj. John
             Clark [jr]. Draft. 1 p. In handwriting of Tench
             Tilghman. Read in Congress, Jan. 10. Referred
             to Board of War.   A. III, 171

1778   Washington, George. Valley Forge. To [the Board of
JAN. 2   War, York]. Virginia clothing for Virginia
             troops; want of blankets; cattle in Delaware;
             Adjutant-generalship: clothing and tailors; [Maj.]
             Gen. [Thomas] Conway's machinations; weakness
             of army; seizure of clothes. Draft. 5 pp. In
             handwriting of Robert Hanson Harrison.

                                                  A. III, 173
             Conway paragraph printed: Writings of Washington (Ford) N.Y.
             1890. 6, 277, note.

1778   Eyre, Thomas. Philadelphia. To [Lt. Gen.] Sir William
JAN. 2   Howe [Philadelphia]. Account of his treatment
             while a prisoner of war. Contemporary copy.
             2 pp. In handwriting of Alexander Hamilton.
             Enclosed in Washington to the President of Con-
             gress, 1778, Apr. 18.   C. C.   152, 5, 453

1778   Wiggins, Thomas. Philadelphia. Deposition of having
JAN. 3   been fired upon while acting as a flag. Contempo-
             rary copy. 1 p. In handwriting of John Lau-
             rens. Enclosed in Washington to the President
             of Congress, 1778, Apr. 18.   C. C.   152, 5, 455
             Dated in error 1777.

1778
JAN. 4

Washington, George. Valley Forge. To [the President of Congress, York]. Enclosing his answer to [Maj.] Gen. [Horatio] Gates. Auto. draft signed. 1 p. Read in Congress, Jan. 13. Referred to the Board of War. **A. III, 179**
Printed: Writings of Washington (Ford) N. Y. 1890. 6, 278, note.

1778
JAN. 5

Washington, George. Valley Forge. To [the President of Congress, York]. Distress of the army. Draft. 2 pp. In handwriting of Robert Hanson Harrison. Read in Congress, Jan. 13. Referred to Board of War. **A. III, 182**
Printed: Writings of Washington (Ford) N. Y. 1890. 6, 280.

1778
JAN. 5

Continental Congress, President. York. To [George] Washington, Valley Forge. Election of Col. [Alexander] Scammel, Adjutant General; detention of Convention troops; heavy burdens upon Members of Congress. Letter-book copy.
C. C. 13, I, 112

1778
JAN. 8

Washington, George. [Valley Forge.] To [Lt.] Gen. [Sir William] Howe [Philadelphia]. Retaliation for treatment received by American prisoners in England; firing upon a flag. Contemporary copy. 1 p. In handwriting of Tench Tilghman. Enclosed in Washington to the President of Congress, 1778, Apr. 18. **C. C. 152, 5, 451**

1778
JAN. 8

Howe, [Sir] W[illiam]. Philadelphia. To [George Washington, Valley Forge]. Lt. [Thomas] Eyre's case; firing on a flag. Contemporary copy. 1 p. In handwriting of Richard Kidder Meade. Enclosed in Washington to the President of Congress, 1778, Apr. 18. **C. C. 152, 5, 457**

1778
JAN. 9

Washington, George. Valley Forge. To [the President of Congress, York]. Appointment of aides; detention of Convention troops; resolves granting extra month's pay to soldiers. Draft. 3 pp. In handwriting of Robert Hanson Harrison. Read in Congress, Jan. 13. Referred to the Board of War. **A. III, 183**
Printed: Writings of Washington (Ford) N. Y. 1890. 6, 282.

1778
JAN. 9

Washington, George. [Valley Forge.] To James Lovell [York]. Recovery of the Journals of Congress. Draft. 1 p. In handwriting of John Laurens.
A. III, 187

1778
JAN. 10

[Boudinot, Elias.] [Valley Forge?] To [Hugh Ferguson, Philadelphia.] Subsistence for British prisoners. Extract of letter. 2 pp. Enclosed in Howe to Washington, 1778, Jan. 19.   **92, 95**

1778
JAN. 12

Washington, George. Valley Forge. To [the President of Congress, York]. Questions respecting disposition of captured articles. Draft. 3 pp. In handwriting of Robert Hanson Harrison. Read in Congress, Jan. 20. Referred to Marine Committee.   **A. III, 189**

1778
JAN. 13

Washington, George. [Valley Forge.] To the President of Congress [York]. Recommending Chevalier de Mauduit du Plessis for a commission. Draft. 2 pp. In handwriting of John Laurens. Read in Congress, Jan. 19. Request granted.   **A. III, 193**

1778
JAN. 13

Gerry, E[lbridge]. York. To [George] Washington [Valley Forge]. Committee of Conference, its purpose and powers; members chosen; various resolves on military matters; pensions; Col. [James] Wilkinson appointed Secretary to Board of War; bell tents for army. A. L. S. 3 pp.   **21, 88**

1778
JAN. 14

Continental Congress, President. York. To [George] Washington, Valley Forge. Transmitting resolves; proceedings of Congress relative to the Convention troops; appointment of Maj. [John] Clark [jr.] Auditor of Public Accounts in Camp. Letter-book copy.   **C. C. 13, I, 124**

1778
JAN. 17

Anonymous. To Congress. "Thoughts of a Freeman" Criticisms of the Commander in Chief and the Army. Contemporary copy. 4 pp. In handwriting of Robert Hanson Harrison. Transmitted to Washington by Patrick Henry? **21, 204**
Printed: Writings of Washington (Sparks) Boston. 1834. **5, 497**.

1778
JAN. 18

Howe, [Sir] W[illiam]. Philadelphia. To [George] Washington [Valley Forge]. American prisoners in England. Contemporary copy. 1 p. In handwriting of Robert Hanson Harrison. Enclosed in Washington to Congress, 1778, Apr. 18.   **C. C. 152, 5, 459**

1778
JAN. 19

Continental Congress, President. [York.] To [George] Washington, Valley Forge. Suspension of [Lt.] Gen. [John] Burgoyne's embarkation. Letter-book copy.   **C. C. 13, I, 143**

1778
JAN. 19

Howe, [Sir] W[illiam]. Philadelphia. To [George] Washington [Valley Forge]. Subsistence of British
prisoners; clothing; agents. L. S. 3 pp. Copy
of this letter enclosed in Washington to the
President of Congress, 1778, Apr. 18.   **92, 93**

1778
JAN. 19

Prisoners. Quantity of weekly provisions issued by British to American prisoners. 1 p. Enclosed in
Howe to Washington, 1778, Jan. 19.   **92, 97**

1778
JAN. 19

Prisoners, American. Philadelphia. Allowance of provision. Contemporary copy. 1 p. In handwriting of John Laurens. Enclosed in Washington to the President of Congress, 1778, Apr.
18.   **C. C. 152, 5, 465**

1778
JAN. 20

Washington, George. Valley Forge. To [Lt.] Gen. [Sir]
William Howe [Philadelphia]. Lt. [Thomas]
Eyre's case. Contemporary copy. 2 pp. In
handwriting of Richard Kidder Meade. Enclosed in Washington to the President of Congress, 1778, Apr. 18.   **C. C. 152, 5, 467**

1778
JAN. 21

Continental Congress, Resolves. Report of Board of War
on state of prisoners, correspondence with [Sir
William] Howe and consequent resolutions.
Broadside. With auto. note of Robert Hanson
Harrison of names of American officers confined
in goal. Enclosed in Washington to the President of Congress, 1778, Apr. 18.

C. C. 152, 5, 471

1778
JAN. 22

Continental Congress, President. [York.] To [George]
Washington, Valley Forge. Brevet of Lt. Col.
of Artillery to [Chevalier Mauduit] du Plessis;
transmitting resolves. Letter-book copy.

C. C. 13, I, 146

1778
JAN. 22

Navy Board. Bordentown. [New Jersey]. To [George
Washington, Valley Forge]. Capt. [Charles]
Alexander's desire to annoy enemy. Recent copy.
1 p.   **21, 175**

1778
JAN. 23

Washington, George. [Valley Forge.] To [the President of Congress, York]. Introducing French
officers to Congress. Draft. 1 p. In handwriting of John Laurens.   **A. III, 195**

1778
JAN. 24

Washington, George. Valley Forge. To [the Board of
War, York]. Securing of leather at German-

town and exchange of certain prisoners. Draft.
3 pp. In handwriting of Tench Tilghman.

> A. III, 197

1778
JAN. 25

Continental Congress, President. [York.] To [George]
Washington, Valley Forge. Transmitting resolves. Letter-book copy.   **C. C. 13, I 154**

1778
JAN. 26

Washington, George. Valley Forge. To the Board of
War, York. Seizure of British officers who have
permission to visit prisoners. Draft. 2 pp.
In handwriting of Robert Hanson Harrison.

> A. III, 201

Extract printed. Writings of Washington (Ford) N. Y. 1890. 6, 353,
note.

1778
JAN. 27

Washington, George. Valley Forge. To the Board of
War, York. Seizure of the British officers and
supplies intended for British prisoners; the Canadian expedition. Draft. 2 pp. In handwriting
of Robert Hanson Harrison.   A. III, 203

1778
JAN. 28

Continental Congress, President. [York.] To [George]
Washington, Valley Forge. Transmitting resolves. Letter-book copy.   **C. C. 13, I, 156**

[1778]
[JAN. 29]

Washington, George. [Valley Forge.] To [a Committee
of Congress, Valley Forge]. State of the army
considered by departments. D. S. 38 pp. In
handwriting of Alexander Hamilton. Endorsed:
"Jany. 10. Members chosen. Messrs. Dana,
Reed, Folsom & Harvie. Jany. 20.—Messrs.
[Charles] Carroll, [Gouverneur] Morris."

> A. III, 205.

Printed. Writings of Washington (Ford) N. Y. 1890. 6, 300.
This was the committee appointed to repair to camp and is generally
known as the Committee of Conference. Extract from above, made
on occasion of the Newburgh Addresses, in handwriting of Benjamin
Walker, 6 pp., was enclosed in Washington to the President of Congress, 1783, Mar. 18. C. C. 152, 11, 159

1778
JAN. 30

Washington, George. Valley Forge. To [Lt.] Gen. [Sir
William] Howe [Philadelphia]. Provisions and
clothing for British prisoners. Contemporary
copy. 2 pp. Enclosed in Washington to the
President of Congress, 1778, Apr. 18.

> C. C. 152, 5, 469

1778
JAN. 31

Washington, George. Valley Forge. To [the President
of Congress, York]. Minor matters; salt for the
army. Draft. 1 p. In handwriting of Robert
Hanson Harrison.   A. III, 245

1778
JAN. 31

Washington, George. Valley Forge. To Henry Laurens, York. Enemies in Congress; his conduct. Draft. 2 pp. In handwriting of Robert Hanson Harrison. **P.** I, pt. II, 5

Printed: Writings of Washington (Ford) N. Y. 1890. 6, 353.

[1778]
[JAN.]

[Sandford, Thomas.] [Philadelphia.] Report of treatment received in attempted performance of duty to relieve distresses of British prisoners. [Extract.] Contemporary copy. 12 pp. Transmitted to Washington. **91,** 218

1778
FEB. 3

Washington, George. Valley Forge. To [the President of Congress, York]. Food supplies for American prisoners; pressing need of money. Draft. 1 p. In handwriting of Robert Hanson Harrison. Read in Congress, Feb. 5. Referred to Board of Treasury. **A.** III, 247

Printed in part: Writings of Washington (Ford) N. Y. 1890. 6, 387, note.

1778
FEB. 3

Continental Congress, President. [York.] To [George] Washington, Valley Forge. [Brig.] Gen. [David] Forman's petition; transmitting resolves. Letter-book copy. **C. C.** 13, I, 160

1778
FEB. 5

Howe, [Sir] W[illiam]. Philadelphia. To [George] Washington [Valley Forge]. Liquidation of accounts of the Convention prisoners; supplies for American prisoners; commissioners for a cartel. Contemporary copy. 4 pp. In handwriting of John Laurens. Enclosed in Washington to the President of Congress, 1778, Apr. 18. **C. C.** 152, 5, 473

Printed: Writings of Washington (Ford) N. Y. 1890. 6, 369, note.

1778
FEB. 7

Continental Congress, President. York. To George Washington [Valley Forge]. Transmitting papers relating to investigation of evacuation of Ticonderoga. L. S. of Henry Laurens. 1 p. Answered Feb. 14. **92,** 67

1778
FEB. 8

Washington, George. Valley Forge. To [the President of Congress, York]. The Canadian expedition; prisoners; inquiries into losses of Forts Montgomery, Clinton and Mifflin. Draft. 3 pp. In handwriting of Robert Hanson Harrison. Read in Congress, Feb. 17. "Accompanied with the following letters. 1 from Genl. Howe Jany 8. 1778 Answer from G Wash: 20. 1 from Gen

Howe 19. G. W's answer 30. G W to Gen
Howe 8   Gen Howe to Gen W 18   Gen H to G
Wash 5 Feby   G W's answer 10 Feby "

A. III, 249

1778
FEB. 8

Continental Congress, President. [York.] To [George]
Washington, Valley Forge. Transmitting resolves; oaths of allegiance. Letter-book copy.

C. C. 13, I, 165

1778
FEB. 10

Washington, George. Valley Forge. To [the Board of
War, York]. Minor military matters; British
officers sent to relieve prisoners; collection of
clothing in Pennsylvania. Draft. 2 pp. In
handwriting of Tench Tilghman.   A. III, 253

1778
FEB. 10

Washington, George. Valley Forge. To Maj. Gen.
[Horatio] Gates [York]. British officers with
clothing for their prisoners; clothing for Pennsylvania troops. L. S. 2 pp. In handwriting
of Tench Tilghman.   C. C. 152, 5, 253

1778
FEB. 10

Washington, George. [Valley Forge.] To [Lt.] Gen. [Sir
William] Howe [Philadelphia]. Exchange of
prisoners. Contemporary copy. 2 pp. In handwriting of Robert Hanson Harrison. Enclosed
in Washington to the President of Congress 1778,
Apr. 18.   C. C. 152, 5, 477

Printed: Writings of Washington (Ford) N. Y. 1890. 6, 369.

1778
FEB. 11

Washington, George. [Valley Forge.] To the President of
Congress, Philadelphia. Claims of Mons. Romand de Lisle and Robillard D'Antin; trouble
with foreigners. L. S. 1 p. In handwriting
of Tench Tilghman. Read in Congress Feb. 18.

.C. C. 152, 5, 291

Dated in error, Morristown, 1777.

1778
FEB. 11

Continental Congress, Resolves. Commissaries General
departments; duties, management; table of pay.
Broadside. 1 p. Printed by Dunlap.

24, 29

1778
FEB. 11

Continental Congress, Committee of Conference. Moore
Hall [near Valley Forge]. To [George] Washington [Valley Forge]. Exchange of prisoners;
status of citizens. A. L. S. of Francis Dana.
2 pp.   92, 71

1778
FEB. 13

Continental Congress, President. [York.] To [George]
Washington, Valley Forge. Transmitting resolves. Letter-book copy.   C. C. 13, I, 188

1778
FEB. 13

Putnam, Israel. West Point. To [George Washington, Valley Forge]. Great need of money. [Extract of letter.] 1 p. In handwriting of Richard Kidder Meade. Enclosed in Washington to the President of Congress 1778, Feb. 27.

C. C. 152, 5, 315

1778
FEB. 14

Howe, [Sir] W[illiam]. Philadelphia. To [George] Washington [Valley Forge]. Exchange of prisoners. Contemporary copy. 2 pp. In handwriting of Richard Kidder Meade. Enclosed in Washington to the President of Congress, 1778, Mar. 7. C. C. 152, 5, 325

Printed: Writings of Washington (Sparks) Boston. 1834. 5, 537.

1778
FEB. 15

Washington, George. Valley Forge. To Robert Hooper, Nathaniel Falconer and Jonathan Mifflin jr., Reading [Pennsylvania]. Distress of army for meat and forage. Attested contemporary copy by Jonathan Mifflin jr. 2 pp. Transmitted to Congress. C. C. 152, 5, 303

1778
FEB. 16

Franklin, Thomas. Philadelphia. Deposition respecting British treatment of prisoners. Contemporary copy. 1 p. In handwriting of Richard Kidder Meade. Enclosed in Washington to the President of Congress, 1778, Mar. 7.

C. C. 152, 5, 341

1778
FEB. 19

Washington, George. Valley Forge. To [the President of Congress, York]. Resolve respecting abuses in the several states. Draft. 1 p. In handwriting of Robert Hanson Harrison. Read in Congress Feb. 23. A. III, 255

1778
FEB. 19

Continental Congress, President. [York.] To [George] Washington, Valley Forge. Transmitting resolves; John Clark [jr] and Mathew Clarkson, Auditors of army accounts; Baron Steuben. Letter-book copy. C. C. 13, I, 191

1778
FEB. 19

North, [Frederick,] Lord. Speech on his conciliatory motion with drafts of bills on taxation of the colonies and peace commissioners.

See: Pennsylvania Gazette, 1778, Apr. 24.

1778
FEB. 21

Washington, George. [Valley Forge.] To [the Board of War, York]. Removal of artillery at Albany. Draft. 1 p. In handwriting of Alexander Hamilton. A. III, 257

1778
FEB. 21

Continental Congress, President. [York.] To [George] Washington, Valley Forge. Transmitting sundry resolves. Letter-book copy.

C. C. 13, I, 197.

1778
FEB. 21

Howe, [Sir] W[illiam]. Philadelphia. To [George Washington, Valley Forge]. British treatment of prisoners; accusations against Americans. Contemporary copy. 14 pp. In handwriting of John Fitzgerald. Enclosed in Washington to the President of Congress, 1778, Mar. 7.

C. C. 152, 5, 337

[1778]
FEB. 23

Meyers, Anne. [of Philadelphia.] Report respecting loyalist refugees. Contemporary copy by Richard Kidder Meade. 1 p. Enclosed in Washington to Board of War, 1778, Feb. 23.   A. III, 259

1778
FEB. 23

Washington, George. Valley Forge. To [the Board of War, New York]. Minor military matters; ordnance supplies for next campaign. Draft. 1 p. In handwriting of Alexander Hamilton.

A. III, 261

1778
FEB. 27

Washington, George. Valley Forge. To [the President of Congress, York]. Court-martial of various officers; disturbed condition of western troops. Draft. 3 pp. In handwriting of Caleb Gibbs and Robert Hanson Harrison. Read in Congress, Mar. 5.   A. III, 263

Printed: Writings of Washington (Ford) N. Y. 1890. 6, 385.

1778
FEB. 27

Washington, George. Valley Forge. To [the Board of War, York]. Need of writing paper. Draft. 1 p. In handwriting of Tench Tilghman.

A. III, 267

1778
FEB. 28

Champion, Henry. Hartford, Connecticut. To [George] Washington [Valley Forge]. Trouble caused by Connecticut's Regulating Act for price of beef. [Extract of letter.] Contemporary copy. In handwriting of Tench Tilghman. Enclosed in Washington to the President of Congress, 1778, Mar. 12.   C. C. 152, 5, 363

1778
FEB. 29

Washington, George. Valley Forge. To the Committee [of Conference], Moore Hall. Disorder in the Armourer's department. L. S. 1 p. In handwriting of Alexander Hamilton.   C. C. 33, 225

[1778]
[FEB.]

[Knox? Henry.] Memoranda of alterations proposed in resolves of Congress of Feb. 11 respecting the Commissaries' departments as regards the artillery. Contemporary copy. In handwriting of Samuel Shaw. A. D. 1 p. **24, 30**

[1778]
[FEB.]

Lisle, [Charles Noel François] Romand de. [Valley Forge?] To [George] Washington, Morristown [Valley Forge]. Claim to chief command of the artillery. A. L. S. 2 pp. Enclosed in Washington to the President of Congress, 1778, Feb. 11.
C. C. 152, 5, 295

[1778]
[FEB.]

Robillard D'Antin, Lewis Joseph Henry [Valley Forge]. To [George] Washington, Morristown [Valley Forge]. Claim to a captaincy in the artillery. A. L. S. 2 pp. Enclosed in Washington to the President of Congress, 1778, Feb. 11.
C. C. 152, 5, 299

1778
MAR. 1

Washington, George. Valley Forge. To the Committee [of Conference], Moore Hall. Controversy over rank between Brig. Gens. [William] Woodford, [George] Weedon, and [Charles] Scott; cavalry; exchange negotiations; command in Rhode Island; delay in appointing General Officers; [Maj.] Gen. [Nathanael] Greene and the Quartermasters' department; Du Portail and the Engineers. A. L. S. 2 pp. **C. C. 33, 209**

1778
MAR. 1

Continental Congress, President. [York.] To [George] Washington, Valley Forge. Transmitting resolves; approbation of Washington's letter to Howe; exchange of prisoners. Letter-book copy.
C. C. 13, 1, 201

1778
MAR. 1

Navy Board. [Bordentown, New Jersey.] To [George] Washington [Valley Forge]. Removal of flatboats, galleys and naval stores from Bordentown. A. L. S. of Francis Hopkinson, signed also by John Wharton. 1 p. **22, 77**

1778
MAR. 2

Howe, [Sir] W[illiam]. Philadelphia. To [George] Washington [Valley Forge]. Commission for exchange of prisoners. Contemporary copy. 1 p. In handwriting of Richard Kidder Meade. Enclosed in Washington to the President of Congress, 1778, Mar. 7. **C. C. 152, 5, 343**

1778
MAR. 3

Continental Congress, Resolve. Passports for British officers seeking exchange. Contemporary copy,

attested by Charles Thomson. 1 p. Enclosed in
President of Congress to Washington, 1778,
May 6.   92, 34

1778 **Reed**, James. To Gov. George Clinton [Poughkeepsie?
MAR. 4   New York].   Regulating Act [of price of beef,
in Connecticut]. [Extract of letter.] 1 p. In
handwriting of Tench Tilghman. Enclosed in
Washington to the President of Congress, 1778,
Mar. 12.   C. C. 152, 5, 365

1778 **Sullivan**, John and Others. [Valley Forge.] To [George]
MAR. 4   Washington [Valley Forge.] Decision of board
of general officers on settlement of rank of brigadiers Woodford, Muhlenberg, Scott, and Weedon. A. L. S. of Sullivan, signed also: Nath
Greene, Stirling, Lachn. McIntosh, Wm. Maxwell, J. M. Varnum, J. Huntington. 1 p. Enclosed in Washington to the President of Congress, 1778, Mar. 12.   C. C. 152, 5, 369

1778 **Continental Congress**, President. [York.] To [George]
MAR. 5   Washington, Valley Forge. Transmitting resolves. Letter-book copy.   C. C. 13, I, 207

1778 **Howe**, [Sir] William. Philadelphia. Commission to Cols.
MAR. 5   Charles O'Hara and Humphrey Stephens and
Capt. Richard Fitzpatrick to arrange for an exchange of prisoners. Contemporary copy. 2 pp.
In handwriting of Richard Kidder Meade. Enclosed in Washington to the President of Congress, 1778, Apr. 18.   C. C. 152, 5, 481

1778 **Wadsworth**, Jeremiah. Hartford. To [George] Wash-
MAR. 5   ington [Valley Forge]. Endorsement of Henry
Champion's complaint of trouble caused by Connecticut's Regulating Act of price of beef. Contemporary copy. In handwriting of Tench Tilghman. Enclosed in Washington to the President
of Congress, 1778, Mar. 12.   C. C. 152, 5, 363

1778 **W[ashingto]n**, G[eorge]. Valley Forge. To the Commit-
MAR. 6   tee [of Conference], Moore Hall. Transfer of
[Maj.] Gen. [Israel] Putnam to Rhode Island.
Auto. draft signed. 1 p.   A. III, 269
Printed, in part: Writings of Washington (Ford) N. Y. 1890. 6, 388,
note.
The personnel of the Committee at this date was: Duane, Root,
M. Smith, G. Morris and Laurens.

1778 **Washington**, George. Valley Forge. To the Board of
MAR. 6   War [York]. Need of arms and accoutrements

for the coming campaign; leather for cartouche boxes and shoes. Draft. 3 pp. In handwriting of Tench Tilghman. **A.** III, 271

1778
MAR. 6

Continental Congress, Committee of Conference [Moore Hall]. To [George Washington, Valley Forge]. Considerations respecting settlement of a cartel; money and supplies for prisoners; convention troops; exchange of citizens; State and Continental prisoners; loyalists; tariff of exchange; Fort Washington prisoners; distresses. Draft. 13 pp. In handwriting of Gouverneur Morris. Endorsed: " . . . . superseded by a Conference."
C. C. 33, 241

1778
MAR. 6

Continental Congress, Committee of Conference. Moore Hall [near Valley Forge]. To [George] Washington [Valley Forge]. Selection of commander for posts on the Hudson. L. S. of Francis Dana. 1 p. 92, 116

1778
MAR. 6

Clinton, George. Poughkeepsie. To Jonathan Trumbull [Lebanon, Connecticut]. Raising of troops for defense of the Highlands. Contemporary copy. 2 pp. In handwriting of Richard Kidder Meade. Enclosed in Washington to the President of Congress, 1778, Mar. 16. **C. C.** 152, 5, 383

1778
MAR. 7

Washington, George. Valley Forge. To [the President of Congress, York]. Resolves of Congress respecting exchange of prisoners. Draft. 8 pp. In handwriting of Robert Hanson Harrison. Referred to Board of War. **A.** III, 279
Printed: Writings of Washington (Ford) N.Y. 1890. 6, 397.

1778
MAR. 7

Parsons, Sam[uel] H[olden]. West Point. To [George] Washington [Valley Forge]. Confusion as to command in the Highlands; fortification work. Contemporary copy. 3 pp. In handwriting of Richard Kidder Meade. Enclosed in Washington to the President of Congress, 1778, Mar. 17. **C. C.** 152, 5, 401

1778
MAR. 9

Washington, George. Valley Forge. To [the Board of War, York]. Artillery from Albany; exchange of convention officers and general exchange of prisoners; western regiments; deserters; clothing. Draft. 3 pp. In handwriting of Tench Tilghman. **A.** III, 283

1778
MAR. 9

Washington, George. [Valley Forge.] To [Lt.] Gen. [Sir] W[illiam] Howe [Philadelphia]. Postponement of meeting of exchange commissioners; exchange of [Maj.] Gen. [Charles] Lee. Contemporary copy. 1 p. In handwriting of Richard Kidder Meade. Enclosed in Washington to the President of Congress, 1778, Mar. 12.

C. C.   **152**, 5, 353

Printed: Writings of Washington (Ford) N. Y. 1890. 6, 406, 415, notes.

1778
MAR. 9

Barry, John.   Port Penn [Delaware].   To [George Washington, Valley Forge].   Account of capture of prizes. [Extract of letter.] 2 pp. In handwriting of Richard Kidder Meade. Enclosed in Washington to the President of Congress, 1778, Mar. 12.   C. C.   **152**, 5, 367

1778
MAR. 10

Continental Congress, President. [York.] To [George] Washington, Valley Forge. Transmitting resolves.   Letter-book copy.   C. C.   **13**, I, 218

1778
MAR. 10

Howe, [Sir] W[illiam].   Philadelphia.   To [George] Washington [Valley Forge].   Postponed meeting of exchange commissioners; exchange of [Maj.] Gen. [Charles] Lee and British officers. Contemporary copy. 2 pp. In handwriting of Richard Kidder Meade. Enclosed in Washington to the President of Congress, 1778, Mar. 12.

C. C.   **152**, 5, 355.

Printed: Writings of Washington (Sparks) Boston. 1834. 5, 538.

1778
MAR. 12

Washington, George.   Valley Forge.   To [the President of Congress, York].   Exchange of prisoners; enlistment of prisoners; minor military matters; supplies.   Draft. 3 pp.   In handwriting of Timothy Pickering, jr?.   Referred to Board of War.   **A**.   III, 287

Printed: Writings of Washington (Ford) N. Y. 6, 414.

1778
MAR. 12

Washington, George.   Valley Forge.   To [Lt. Gen. Sir William Howe, Philadelphia].   Exchange of Lt. Col. [Archibald] Campbell and [Maj.] Gen. [Charles] Lee.   Contemporary copy. 2 pp.   In handwriting of Richard Kidder Meade.   Enclosed in Washington to the President of Congress, 1778, Mar. 12.   C. C.   **152**, 5, 359

Printed, in part: Writings of Washington (Ford) N. Y. 1890. 6, 416, note.

1778
MAR. 13

Huntington, Jedediah.   Valley Forge.   To George Washington [Valley Forge].   Resignation of Col.

Charlestown Octo.^r 27 1789

Honoured and much Esteemed

Sir,

I am prevented by the Weather, (being Unwell) of Personally waiting on You, a Duty, I should have performed with great Pleasure,

Its to be Regreted, Your Continuance among us, is so short,

I look back with Gratitude, on Your Goodness, and Condescension, to me, when Your Family, was at Cambridge, and my Friend, the late Mr Reed, was Your Secretary,

WRITING OF RICHARD CARY.

[Charles] Webb. A. L. S. 1 p. Enclosed in Washington to the President of Congress, 1778, Mar. 16. **C. C. 152, 5, 389**

1778
MAR. 13

Webb, Charles. Valley Forge. To the President of Congress [York]. Resignation. L. S. 1 p. In handwriting of Jedediah Huntington with auto. signed approval. Enclosed in Washington to the President of Congress, 1778, Mar. 16.
C. C. 152, 5, 391

1778
MAR. 14

Washington, George. [Valley Forge.] To the President of Congress [York]. Comte [Casimir] Pulaski and his proposed regiment of dragoons. Draft. 2 pp. In handwriting of John Laurens. Referred to Board of War. **A. III, 291**
Printed: Writings of Washington (Ford) N. Y. 1890. 6, 422.

1778
MAR. 14

Continental Congress, President. [York.] To [George] Washington, Valley Forge. Transmitting resolves. Letter-book copy. **C. C. 13, I, 224**

1778
MAR. 15

Continental Congress, President. [York.] To [George] Washington, Valley Forge. Marquis de Lafayette and Baron de Kalb to rejoin army. Letter book copy. **C. C. 13, I, 229**

1778
MAR. 16

Washington, George. Valley Forge. To [the President of Congress, York]. Command and garrison in the Highlands. Draft. 2 pp. In handwriting of Alexander Hamilton. Referred to Board of War. **A. III, 293**
Printed: Writings of Washington (Ford) N. Y. 1890. 6, 430.

1778
MAR. 16

Washington, George. Valley Forge. To the President of Congress [York]. Capt. [Ebenezer] Sullivan's claim; minor military matters. Draft. 2 pp. In handwriting of Robert Hanson Harrison and Caleb Gibbs. Referred to Board of War as far as respects Capt. Sullivan. **A. III, 295**

1778
MAR. 16

Navy Board. Bordentown [New Jersey]. To [George] Washington [Valley Forge]. Seizure of Capts. [Isaiah] Robinson and [Nathaniel] Galt while under protection of a flag. A. L. S. of Francis Hopkinson. 2 pp. **22, 185**

1778
MAR. 17

Washington, George. Valley Forge. To [the President of Congress, York]. Confusion of command and state of the works in the Highlands. Draft. 1 p. In handwriting of Robert Hanson Harrison.
A. III, 297

1778
MAR. 17

Smallwood, William. Wilmington [Delaware]. To [George] Washington [Valley Forge]. Sailing of fleet toward Philadelphia. Contemporary copy. 1 p. In handwriting of Caleb Gibbs. Enclosed in Washington to the President of Congress, 1778, Mar. 18.   **C. C. 152, 5, 409**

1778
MAR. 18

Washington, George. [Valley Forge.] To the President of Congress [York]. Preparations of the enemy. Draft. 1 p. In handwriting of John Laurens. Read in Congress, Mar. 23.   **A. III, 299**

1778
MAR. 19

Washington, George. [Valley Forge.] To [the Committee of Conference, Moore Hall]. Col. [Rufus] Putnam's rank. Draft. 1 p. In handwriting of Richard Kidder Meade.   **A. III, 301**

1778
MAR. 20

Washington, George. Valley Forge. To [the Board of War, York]. Intelligence respecting enemy; artillery magazine at Carlisle [Pennsylvania]; recruits. Draft. 3 pp. In handwriting of Tench Tilghman.   **A. III, 303**

1778
MAR. 20

Seely, Silvanus. Elizabethtown [New Jersey]. To [George] Washington [Valley Forge]. Embarkation of British from New York. Contemporary copy. 1 p. In handwriting of Richard Kidder Meade. Enclosed in Washington to the President of Congress, 1778, Mar. 24.   **C. C. 152, 5, 377**

1778
MAR. 21

Washington, George. Valley Forge. To [the President of Congress, York]. Troops from Albany; charges against Dr. [William] Shippen [jr.]. Draft. 2 pp. In handwriting of Tench Tilghman. Read in Congress, Apr. 3. Referred to Drayton, Huntington and Bannister.

     A. III, 307

Printed: Writings of Washington (Ford) N.Y. 1890. 6,437.

1778
MAR. 21

Continental Congress, President. York. To [George] Washington, Valley Forge. Feeling of Congress about expressions in letters of Sir William Howe; transmitting resolves. Letter-book copy.

     C. C. 13, I, 237

1778
MAR. 24

W[ashington,] G[eorge]. Valley Forge. To [the President of Congress, York]. Establishment of the army; resignations; recruits. Auto draft signed. 3 pp. Read in Congress. Mar. 27. Referred to Board of War.   **A. III, 309**

Printed: Writings of Washington (Ford) N. Y. 1890. 6, 443.

1778
MAR. 24

Washington, George. Valley Forge. To [the President of Congress, York]. Resignation of Col. Charles Lewis. Draft. 1 p. In handwriting of Robert Hanson Harrison. Read in Congress, Mar. 28.

A. III, 313

1778
MAR. 24

Navy Board. Bordentown [New Jersey]. To [George] Washington [Valley Forge]. Case of Capts. [Isaiah] Robinson and [Nathaniel] Galt; removal of cannon and stores. A. L. S. of Francis Hopkinson. 2 pp. Answered Mar. 27.   **22**, 255

1778
MAR. 24

Lovell, James. [York.] To [George] Washington [Valley Forge]. Extract of letter of Thomas Cushing: Embarkation preparations of British; exchange of marine prisoners; case of John Gray; news from Martinique. A. L. S. 5 pp. Answered Mar. 29.*   **22**, 251

1778
MAR. 25

Washington, George. Valley Forge. To [the Board of War, York]. Virginia regiments; troops for and on the western frontier. Draft. 2 pp. In handwriting of Tench Tilghman.   A. III, 315

1778
MAR. 25

Continental Congress, President. York. To [George] Washington, Valley Forge. Transmitting resolves. Letter-book copy.   **C. C.** 13, I, 242

1778
MAR. 26

Lovell, James. York. To [George] Washington [Valley Forge]. Delivery of articles shipped to Washington from France. A. L. S. 2 pp. Answered Mar. 29.*   **22**, 253

1778
MAR. 27

Howe, [Sir] W[illiam]. Philadelphia. To [George] Washington [Valley Forge]. Meeting of Commissioners for exchange at Germantown. Contemporary copy. 1 p. In handwriting of Richard Kidder Meade. Enclosed in Washington to the President of Congress, 1778, Apr. 18.   **C. C.** 152, 5, 485

1778
MAR. 28

Washington, George. Valley Forge. Commission to Col. William Grayson, Lt. Cols. Robert Hanson Harrison and Alexander Hamilton and Commissary Elias Boudinot to arrange for an exchange of prisoners. Contemporary copy. 2 pp. In handwriting of Tench Tilghman. Enclosed in Washington to the President of Congress, 1778, Apr. 18.   **C. C.** 152, 5, 489

Printed: Writings of Washington (Ford) N. Y. 1890. 6,442, note.

1778
MAR. 28
New Jersey, Officers, civil and military. Roadstown. Petition to Gov. William Livingston [Trenton]. Devastations of the British; praying for relief. Contemporary copy of D. S. of 23 names. 2 pp. In handwriting of Charles Thomson. Enclosed in President of Congress, 1778, Apr. 18. **92, 91**

1778
MAR. 29
Washington, George. Valley Forge. To [the President of Congress, York]. Intelligence of reinforcements from New York to Howe. . Draft. 1 p. In handwriting of Tench Tilghman. Read in Congress, Apr. 1. Referred to Board of War.
A. III, 317

1778
MAR. 29
Continental Congress, President. [York.] To [George] Washington, Valley Forge. Transmitting resolves. Letter-book copy. **C. C. 13, I, 245**

1778
MAR. 29
Washington, George. Valley Forge. To [Lt.] Gen. [Sir William] Howe [Philadelphia]. Arrangements for meeting of Commissioners for exchange of prisoners at Germantown. Contemporary copy. 1 p. In handwriting of Richard Kidder Meade. Enclosed in Washington to the President of Congress, 1778, Apr. 18. **C. C. 152, 5, 487**
Printed, in part: Writings of Washington (Ford) N. Y. 1890. **6, 442,** note.

1778
MAR. 29
Washington, George. Valley Forge. To James Lovell [York]. Intelligence of enemy; French protection of American trade. Draft. 1 p. In handwriting of Tench Tilghman. **A. III, 319**

1778
MAR. 30
Continental Congress, President. York. To [George] Washington, Valley Forge. Transmitting resolves. Letter-book copy. **C. C. 13, I, 247**

1778
MAR. 31
Navy Board, Bordentown [New Jersey]. To. [George] Washington [Valley Forge]. Forwarding stores to camp. A. L. S. of Francis Hopkinson, signed also by John Wharton. 1 p. Answered Apr. 11.
22, 293

1778
MAR. 31
Clymer, George and Samuel Mathews, Pittsburgh. To [the President of Congress, York]. Investigation of conditions and recommendations for defense of the Western frontier. Contemporary copy. 3 pp. Enclosed in President of Congress to Washington, 1778, May 3. **92, 28**

1778
APR. 1
Washington, George. Valley Forge. To [the President of Congress, York]. Charges against [Maj.] Gen.

[Arthur] St. Clair. Draft. 2 pp. In handwriting of Tench Tilghman. Read in Congress, Apr. 6.   **A. III, 321**

1778
APR. 3

Washington, George. [Valley Forge.] To [the President of Congress, York]. Promotion of Capt. [Henry] Lee. Draft. 1 p. In handwriting of Alexander Hamilton. Read in Congress, Apr. 7.

A. III, 323

1778
APR. 3

New Jersey, Legislature. Trenton. Memorial to Congress. Raising the State quota of Continental troops. Contemporary copy. 3 pp. Enclosed in President of Congress to Washington, 1778, Apr. 18.

92, 89

1778
APR. 4

Washington, George. [Valley Forge.] To [the President of Congress, York]. Exchange of prisoners and resolves of Congress respecting same. Draft. 4 pp. In handwriting of Robert Hanson Harrison.   **A. III, 325**

Printed: Writings of Washington (Ford) N. Y. 1890. 6, 459.

1778
APR. 4

Continental Congress, President. York. To [George] Washington [Valley Forge]. Transmitting resolves; delay in Ticonderoga inquiry. A. L. S. of Henry Laurens. 1 p.   **92, 74**

1778
APR. 4

Continental Congress, Resolve. Maryland, Pennsylvania and New Jersey militia. Contemporary copy, attested by Charles Thomson. 1 p. Enclosed in President of Congress to Washington, 1778, Apr. 4.   **92, 73**

1778
APR. 4

Grayson, William; Robert Hanson **Harrison**; Alexander **Hamilton** and Elias **Boudinot.** Valley Forge. To George Washington [Valley Forge]. Report of conference of Commissioners at Germantown, for exchange of prisoners. Contemporary copy. 3 pp. In handwriting of Robert Hanson Harrison. Enclosed in Washington to the President of Congress, 1778, Apr. 18.   **C. C. 152, 5, 493**

1778
APR. 7

Continental Congress, Resolve. Promotion of Henry Lee and others of the Light Horse. Contemporary copy, attested by Charles Thomson. 1 p. Enclosed in President of Congress to Washington, 1778, Apr. 8.   **92, 78**

1778
APR. 8

Continental Congress, President. York. To [George] Washington [Valley Forge]. Inquiry into evacuation of Ticonderoga; Maj. [Henry] Lee; miscellaneous military matters. A. L. S. of Henry Laurens. 2 pp. Answered Apr. 10.*   **92, 76**

1778
APR. 9

Washington, George. [Valley Forge.] To [the Committee of Conference, Moore Hall]. Officers for Count [Casimir] Pulaski's corps. Draft. 1 p. In handwriting of John Laurens. Read in Congress, Apr. 18.   **A. III, 329**

1778
APR. 10

Washington, George. Valley Forge. To the President of Congress [York]. The militia; confused state of the army; resignations; delays; clothing, etc. Draft. 10 pp. In handwriting of John Laurens and Washington. Read in Congress, Apr. 13. Referred to Duer, Chase and Dana. **A. III, 331**
Printed: Writings of Washington (Ford) N. Y. 1890. 6, 461.

1778
APR. 10

Grayson, Harrison, Hamilton and Boudinot to O'Hara, Stephens and Fitzpatrick. See: Grayson, Harrison, etc., to Washington, 1778, Apr. 15.

1778
APR. 11

Grayson, Harrison, Hamilton and Boudinot to O'Hara, Stephens and Fitzpatrick. See: Grayson, Harrison, etc., to Washington, 1778, Apr. 15.

1778
APR. 11

O'Hara, Stephens and Fitzpatrick to Grayson, Harrison, Hamilton and Boudinot. See: Grayson, Harrison, etc., to Washington, 1778, Apr. 15.

1778
APR. 13

Continental Congress. Resolves. Survey of the Susquehannah River. Contemporary copy. 1 p. Enclosed in Board of War to Washington, 1778, May 6.   **94, 341**

[1778]
[APR. 13]

George III. Westminster. Commission to Frederick, Earl of Carlisle, Richard, Viscount Howe, Sir William Howe, William Eden and George Johnstone to treat for peace with the United States. Contemporary copy. 7 pp. In handwriting of Moses Young. Enclosed in Laurens, Henry to Washington, 1778, June 18.   **24, 54**

[1778]
APR. 14

Continental Congress, President. York. To George Washington [Valley Forge]. Resolutions respecting cartel for exchange; disclaimer by Congress of intention to offend; instructions, intentions etc.

L. S. of Henry Laurens. 3 pp. In handwriting of Charles Thomson. Answered Apr. 18.*

92, 45

In letter book, C. C. 13, I, 258, the copy of above is annotated as follows by Laurens: " . . . Copy of a letter, produced by amendments in Congress on a draft prepared by a comm⁻ in answer to Gen. Washington's Letter of the 4th. April—the draught presented the 9th, debated at divers meetings & Resolved the 13 April ½ p 9 0C to P. M.—"

1778
APR. 14

Continental Congress, President. York. To [George] Washington [Valley Forge]. Transmitting papers. A. L. S. of Henry Laurens. 1 p. Answered Apr. 18.* 93, 94

1778
APR. 14

Continental Congress, Resolves. Commissary General's department; management etc. Contemporary copy, attested by Charles Thomson. 3 pp. Enclosed in President of Congress to Washington, 1778, Apr. 17. 92, 83

1778
APR. 15

Continental Congress, Resolves. Command at Fishkill; militia for defense of the Hudson. Contemporary copy, attested by Charles Thomson. 1 p. Enclosed in President of Congress to Washington, 1778, Apr. 17. 92, 82

1778
APR. 15

Grayson, William; Robert Hanson Harrison, Alexander Hamilton and Elias Boudinot. Valley Forge. To George Washington [Valley Forge]. Report of conference of Commissioners at Newtown, for exchange of prisoners, containing copies of letters of Apr. 10 and 11 between O'Hara, Stephens and Fitzpatrick and Grayson, Harrison etc. respecting their powers. Contemporary copy. 7 pp. In handwriting of Robert Hanson Harrison. Enclosed in Washington to the President of Congress, 1778, Apr. 18. C. C. 152, 5, 497

1778
APR. 16

Bannister, John. York. To [George Washington, Valley Forge]. Additional state bounty to Virginia soldiers; present state of army and the new establishment; troops from Virginia; volunteers. A. L. S. 3 pp. 22, 35

1778
APR. 17

Washington, George. Valley Forge. To [the President of Congress, Yorktown]. Introducing a Mr. Earnest. Draft. 1 p. In handwriting of Robert Hanson Harrison. A. III, 343

1778
APR. 17

Continental Congress, President. York. To [George] Washington [Valley Forge]. Transmitting resolves. A. L. S. of Henry Laurens. 1 p. Answered Apr. 20.*   **92,** 80

1778
APR. 17

Continental Congress, Resolve. Empowering Board of War to order courts martial. Copy made in 1780. 1 p. In handwriting and attested by Benjamin Stoddert.   **94,** 296

1778
APR. 17

Continental Congress, Resolve. Troops from New Jersey. Contemporary copy, attested by Charles Thomson. 1 p. Enclosed in President of Congress to Washington, 1778, Apr. 18.   **92,** 88

1778
APR. 17

Continental Congress, Resolve. General courts martial. Contemporary copy, attested by Charles Thomson. 1 p. Enclosed in President of Congress to Washington, 1778, Apr. 17.   **92,** 79

1778
APR. 17

Board of War. [Philadelphia.] To [George] Washington, Valley Forge. Introducing Mons. de Wolffen. L. S. of Horatio Gates. 1 p. In handwriting of Timothy Pickering jr.   **94,** 294

1778
APR. 17

Tryon, William. New York. To [George] Washington [Valley Forge]. Transmitting papers for circulation. L. S. 1 p. Enclosed in Washington to the President of Congress, 1778, Apr. 23.
     C. C. 152, 5, 519
Printed: Writings of Washington (Ford) N. Y. 1890. 6, 492, note.

1778
APR. 18

Washington, George. Valley Forge. To [the President of Congress, York]. Cartel for exchange of prisoners; spurious letters of Washington and forged resolves of Congress. Draft. 2 pp. In handwriting of Robert Hanson Harrison. Read in Congress, Apr. 20. Referred to Morris, Drayton and Dana.   **A.** III, 345
Printed: Writings of Washington (Ford) N. Y. 1890. 6, 472.

1778
APR. 18

Continental Congress, President. York. To [George] Washington [Valley Forge]. Petition of civil and military officers of New Jersey and resolves of Congress thereon; transmitting also other resolves. A. L. S. of Henry Laurens. 1 p. Answered Apr. 23.*   **92,** 85

1778
APR. 18

Continental Congress, Resolve. Council of War to settle a plan of campaign. Contemporary copy, attested by Charles Thomson. 1 p. Enclosed in President of Congress to Washington, 1778, Apr. 18.
     92, 87

1778
APR. 18

Morris, Gouverneur. York. To [George] Washington, Valley Forge. Dilatoriness of Congress; [Maj.] Gen. [Horatio] Gates's command; the Board of War; Congress and secrecy. A. L. S. 2 pp.

23, 38.

1778
APR. 20

Washington, George. Valley Forge. To [the President of Congress, York]. Authenticity of a Parliamentary bill; Lord North's speech. Draft. 1 p. In handwriting of Robert Hanson Harrison. Read in Congress, Apr. 23. **A.** III, 347

Printed, in part: Writings of Washington (Ford) N. Y. 1890. 6, 474, note.

1778
APR. 20

Continental Congress. Instructions to Maj. Gen. [Horatio] Gates for his guidance in command of posts on the Hudson. D. S. of H[enry] L[aurens]. 2 pp. Enclosed in President of Congress to Washington, 1778, Apr. 24. **92**, 106

1778
APR. 21

[Washington, George.] Valley Forge. To John Bannister [York]. Resignations; contrast between position of British and American officers; patriotism; exertions necessary; European aid; character of Congress; Independence; jealousy of the army on part of Congress; sufferings of former; remonstrances; volunteers; tories. Draft. 8 pp. In handwriting of Robert Hanson Harrison and Washington. **P.** I, pt. II, 49

Printed: Writings of Washington (Ford) N. Y. 1890. 6, 477.

1778
APR. 21

Continental Congress, Resolves. Approval of conduct of American commissioners for exchange of prisoners. Contemporary copy, attested by Charles Thomson. 1 p. Enclosed in President of Congress to Washington 1778, Apr. 24. **92**, 105

1778
APR. 22

Continental Congress, Resolves. On conciliation. See: Pennsylvania Gazette, 1778, Apr. 24.

1778
APR. 22

Boudinot, Elias. [Valley Forge.] To [George] Washington [Valley Forge]. Exchange of prisoners; list of officers names. A. L. S. 1 p. Enclosed in Washington to the President of Congress, 1778, Apr. 23. **C. C.** 152, 5, 523

1778
APR. 23

Washington, George. [Valley Forge]. To [the President of Congress, York]. Lord North's bill; British forgeries; plan of campaign. Draft. 2 pp. In handwriting of Richard Kidder Meade. Read in

Congress, Apr. 25.   Referred to Drayton, Morris and Dana.   **A. III, 349**
Printed: Writings of Washington (Ford) N. Y. 1890. 6, 492.

1778
APR. 23

Washington, George. Valley Forge. To Francis L[ight-
foot] Lee and John Bannister [York]. Payment
of bounty to the Virginia troops. Draft. 1 p.
In handwriting of Tench Tilghman. **A. III, 351**

1778
APR. 23

Continental Congress, Resolves. Pardon to disaffected.
Contemporary copy, attested by Charles Thom-
son. 1 p. Enclosed in President of Congress to
Washington, 1778, Apr. 24.   **92, 103**

1778
APR. 23

Continental Congress, Resolve. Renewal and extension to
Aug. 10 of powers granted Washington. Contemporary copy, attested by Charles Thomson.
1 p. Enclosed in President of Congress to Washington, 1778, Apr. 24.   **92, 104**

1778
APR. 24

Continental Congress, President. York. To [George]
Washington [Valley Forge]. Transmitting re-
solves, printed matter etc.; pardon acts of states.
A. L. S. of Henry Laurens. 2 pp. Answered
Apr. 27 *   **92, 101**

1778
APR. 24

Duane, James. Albany. To the President [of Congress,
York]. Oneidas and Tuscarora Indians for the
army; conditions at the north; troops, stores,
artillery; need of money. Contemporary copy.
3 pp. Transmitted to Washington.   **92, 36**

1778
APR. 24

Pennsylvania Gazette (The) containing:
     Lord North's speech on his conciliatory motion.
Feb. 19.
     Draft of bill declaring intentions of Parliament
regarding taxation of colonies. [Feb. 19.]
     Draft of bill to appoint Peace Commissioners
[Feb. 19].
     Resolutions of Congress, of Apr. 22 on above.
     Lord North's conciliatory propositions of Feb.
20 and various news items of the war.
     4 pp. Yorktown. Printed by Hall & Sellers.
Enclosed in President of Congress to Washington, 1778, Apr. 24.   **92, 99**

1778
APR. 25

Washington, George. Valley Forge. To [the President
of Congress, York]. British peace commissioners. Draft. 1 p. In handwriting of Robert
Hanson Harrison. Read in Congress, Apr. 26.
                                      A. III, 353
Printed: Writings of Washington (Ford) N. Y. 1890. 6, 497.

1778
APR. 25

Washington, George. Valley Forge. To Gouverneur Morris [York]. Formation of military council [Committee of Conference at Headquarters]; chief of artillery; resignations. Draft. 2 pp. In handwriting of Robert Hanson Harrison and Washington. **P. I, pt. II, 57**

Printed: Writings of Washington (Ford) N. Y. 1890. 6, 495.

1778
APR. 25

Board of War. [York.] To [George] Washington [Valley Forge]. Exchange of [Brig.] Gen. [William] Thompson. L. S. of Horatio Gates. 1 p. In handwriting of Richard Peters. Answered May 1* **23, 44**

1778
APR. 25

Chase, Samuel. York. To George Washington [Valley Forge]. British seizure of civilians; case of Gunning Bedford. A. L. S. 2 pp. **23, 40**

1778
APR. 26

Washington, George. Valley Forge. To Maj. Gen. [William] Tryon, New York. Conciliatory bills; resolutions of Congress. Contemporary copy. 1 p. In handwriting of Robert Hanson Harrison. Enclosed in Washington to the President of Congress, 1778, Apr. 27. **C. C. 152, 5, 533**

1778
APR. 27

Washington, George. Valley Forge. To [the President of Congress, York]. Resolve of Congress respecting Lord North's bills; plans for the campaign. Draft. 3 pp. Read in Congress, Apr. 29. **A. III, 357**

Printed: Writings of Washington (Ford) N. Y. 1890. 6, 500.

1778
APR. 27

Washington, George. Valley Forge. To [the Board of War, York]. Manufacture of musket cartridges. Draft. 1 p. In handwriting of Tench Tilghman. **A. III, 361**

1778
APR. 27

Washington, George. Valley Forge. To Robert Morris [York]. Manufacture of musket cartridges. Draft. 1 p. In handwriting of Tench Tilghman. **A. III, 367**

[1778]
[APR. 27]

Washington, George. [Valley Forge.] To [Samuel Chase, York]. British imprisonment of civilians; exchange of [Gunning] Bedford. Draft. 2 pp. In handwriting of Alexander Hamilton. **A. III, 369**

Printed in part: Writings of Washington (Ford) N. Y. 6, 499, note.

1778
APR. 27

Continental Congress, President. York. To [George] Washington [Valley Forge]. Delay of express; oath of allegiance; pensions for officers. A. L. S. 1 p. Answered Apr. 31. **92, 108**

1778
APR. 27

Laurens, Henry. York. To [George] Washington [Valley Forge]. British forgeries; Commissioners to treat for peace. A. L. S. 1 p.   **23, 48**

1778
APR. 27

Continental Congress, Resolve. Commander of the Artillery to be of the council for planning the campaign. A. D. S. of Charles Thomson. 1 p. Enclosed in President of Congress to Washington, 1778, Apr. 28.   **92, 112**

1778
APR. 28

Washington, George. [Valley Forge.] To [the President of Congress, York]. The Inspector-General's office and work performed by Baron Steuben. Draft. 4 pp. In handwriting of John Laurens.
     A. III, 363
Printed, under date of Apr. 30: Writings of Washington (Ford) N. Y. 1890. 6, 504.

1778
APR. 28

Continental Congress, President. York. To George Washington [Valley Forge]. Miscellaneous military matters; oaths of allegiance; resignation of Maj. Gen. [Thomas] Conway. A. L. S. of Henry Laurens. 1 p. Answered May 1.*   **92, 110**

1778
APR. 28

Continental Congress, President. Philadelphia. To [George] Washington [Middlebrook]. Transmitting resolve. L. S. of John Jay.   **93, 119**

1778
APR. 29

Bannister, J[ohn]. York. To [George] Washington [Valley Forge]. Bounty to reenlisting Virginia soldiers. A. L. S. 1 p.   **22, 61**

1778
APR. 30

Washington, George. [Valley Forge.] To [the President of Congress, York]. Baron Steuben and the Inspectorship. L. S. 4 pp. In handwriting of John Laurens. Read in Congress, May 4. Referred to R. H. Lee, Drayton and Chase.
     C. C. 152, 5, 535
Printed: Writings of Washington (Ford) N. Y. 1890. 6, 504.

1778
APR. 30

W[ashingto]n, G[eorge]. Valley Forge. To Henry Laurens [York]. British Peace Commissioners; Independence; half-pay; lack of information. Draft. 3 pp. In handwriting of Robert Hanson Harrison and Washington.   **P. I, pt. II, 67**
Printed: Writings of Washington (Ford) N. Y. 1890. 6, 508.

1778
APR. 30

Continental Congress, President. York. To [George] Washington [Valley Forge]. Papers relating to the Ticonderoga investigation. A. L. S. of Henry Laurens. 1 p. Answered May 1.*
     92, 69

1778
APR. 30

Continental Congress, Resolve. Brevet commissions. Contemporary copy, attested by Charles Thomson. 1 p. Enclosed in President of Congress to Washington, 1778, May 3.   **92, 113**

1778
APR. 30

Stirling, [William Alexander, Lord.] Valley Forge. Account against the United States for losses sustained in the service. A. D. S. 1 p. Enclosed in Washington to the President of Congress, 1778, May 1.   C. C. **152, 6, 17**

[1778]
[APRIL.]

[Phillips, William.] Cambridge [Massachusetts]. To [Sir Guy Carleton, Quebec?]. American prisoners to be sent to Boston. [Extract of letter.] 1 p. Enclosed in President of Congress to Washington, 1779, Aug. 26.   **93, 324**

1778
MAY 1

Washington, George. Valley Forge. To [the President of Congress, York]. Returning papers respecting loss of Ticonderoga. Draft. 1 p. In handwriting of Robert Hanson Harrison. Read in Congress, May 4.   **A. III, 375**

1778
MAY 1

Washington, George. Valley Forge. To [the President of Congress, York]. Oaths of allegiance; news from France. Draft. 3 pp. In handwriting of Robert Hanson Harrison. Read in Congress, May 4.   **A. III, 371**
Printed: Writings of Washington (Ford) N. Y. 1890. 7, 1.

1778
MAY 1

Washington, George. Valley Forge. To [the Board of War, York]. Exchange of [Brig.] Gen. [William] Thompson; state of the military laboratories; cartridges and lead. Draft. 3 pp. In handwriting of Tench Tilghman.   **A. III, 377**

1778
MAY 1

Morris, Gouverneur. York. To [George] Washington [Valley Forge]. Half-pay and how the states stand on the question. A. L. S. 1 p.   **23, 63**
Printed: Writings of Washington (Ford) N. Y. 1890. 6, 496, note.

1778
MAY 1

Stirling, [William Alexander, Lord.] Valley Forge. To [George] Washington [Valley Forge]. Schedule of losses of property sustained in the service. A. L. S. 1 p. Enclosed in Washington to the President of Congress, 1778, May 1.
            C. C. **152, 6, 13**

1778
MAY 2

Continental Congress, Resolves. Protection of Western frontier; command at Fort Pitt; quartermaster etc. for southwestern Virginia counties. A. D.

of Charles Thomson.   Enclosed in President of
Congress to Washington 1778, May 6.   **92, 35**
<sub>Second copy of resolves attested by Thomson and enclosed in letter
of May 3. 92, 27.</sub>

1778

MAY 3   **Washington, George.** Valley Forge. To [the President
of Congress, York].   Negotiations with the northern Indians.   Draft.   2 pp.   In handwriting of
Alexander Hamilton.   Read in Congress, May 5.

A. III, 381

1778   **Continental Congress,** President. York. To [George]

MAY 3   Washington [Valley Forge].   Transmitting resolves; treaty with France. A. L. S. of John
Laurens.   2 pp.   **92, 114**

1778   **Continental Congress,** President. York. To [George]

MAY 3   Washington [Valley Forge].   Transmitting resolves, broadsides of intelligence and address to
foreigners in the British army. A. L. S. of
Henry Laurens.   1 p.   Answered May 12.*

92, 25

1778   **[Sullivan, John.]** [Providence, Rhode Island]. To [the

MAY 3   President of Congress, York].   Applying for
[Brig.] Gen. John Stark's services. A. D. S. of
Charles Thomson.   Enclosed in President of
Congress to Washington, 1778, May 20.   '**92, 53**

1778   **Washington, George.** Valley Forge. To [the President

MAY 4   of Congress, York].   Alliance with France; Lord
Stirling's letter.   Draft.   1 p.   In handwriting
of Tench Tilghman.   Read in Congress, May 5.

A. III, 383

<sub>Printed, in part: Writings of Washington (Ford) N. Y. 1890. 7, 3,
note.</sub>

1778   **Continental Congress,** Resolves. Inspector-General's de-

MAY 5   partment. A. L. S. of Charles Thomson with
auto. note of Henry Laurens respecting pay of
Baron Steuben.   1 p.   Enclosed in President of
Congress to Washington, 1778, May 6.   **92, 33**

1778   **Continental Congress,** Resolve. Pay of Virginia militia

MAY 5   officers. A. D. of Charles Thomson.   Enclosed
in President of Congress to Washington, 1778,
May 6.   **92, 35**

1778   **Laurens,** Henry.   York. To [George] Washington [Valley

MAY 5   Forge].   Intelligence from Europe; trouble
among the U. S. Commissioners; British Peace
Commissioners and feeling of British mer-

cantile classes; arrangement of army; pensions
and feeling against them. A. L. S. 4 pp.   **23**, 90

1778
MAY 5
Smallwood, [William].   Wilmington [Delaware].   To
[George Washington, Valley Forge].   Repre-
sentation of privates, prisoners in Philadelphia.
[Extract of letter.]   1 p.   In handwriting of
Richard Kidder Meade.   Enclosed in Washington
to the President of Congress, 1778, May 11.
C. C.   **152**, 6, 29

1778
MAY 6
Continental Congress, President.   York.   To [George]
Washington [Valley Forge].   Transmitting
papers; exchange of officers.   A. L. S. of Henry
Laurens.   1 p.   Answered May 12.*   **92**, 31

1778
MAY 6
Board of War.   [York, Pennsylvania.]   To [George]
Washington [Valley Forge].   Survey of the
Susquehannah and creeks; inducement to Ger-
mans to desert from the British.   A. L. S. of
Richard Peters.   2 pp.   Answered May 9.*
94, 339

1778
MAY 6
Board of War.   [York, Pennsylvania.]   To Capt. William
Scull, Lancaster.   Survey of the Susquehannah
river for military purposes.   Contemporary copy.
1 p.   Enclosed in Board of War to Washington,
1778, May 6.   **94**, 338

1778
MAY 6
Lee, Richard Henry.   York.   To [George] Washington
[Valley Forge].   The forged letters; treaty with
France; Great Britain and commerce; Britain's
difficulty in raising men; European situation;
slowness of draft troops in coming in; intention
to bribe Congress.   A. L. S.   3 pp.   **22**, 108

1778
MAY 7
Washington, George.   [Valley Forge.]   To [the President
of Congress, York].   Transmitting letters relating
to Chevalier de la Neufville.   Draft.   1 p.   In
handwriting of John Laurens.   **A.** III, 385

[1778]
[MAY 8]
Dircks, Jacob Gerhard.   Petition to Congress for service
in the field; raising partisan companies.   A. D. S.
2 pp.   Enclosed in President of Congress to
Washington, 1778, May 9.   **92**, 40

1778
MAY 9
Continental Congress, President.   York.   To [George]
Washington [Valley Forge].   Petition of Lt. Col.
[Jacob Gerhard] Dircks; treaty of Paris.   A.L.S.
of Henry Laurens.   1 p.   Answered May 12.*
92, 38

1778
MAY 9

Washington, George. [Valley Forge.] To [the Board of War, York]. Survey work and lack of engineers. Draft. 2 pp. In handwriting of John Laurens.
A. III, 387

1778
MAY 9

Morris, Robert. Manheim, Pennsylvania. To George Washington [Valley Forge]. Wine and news from Europe. A. L. S. 2 pp.   **23, 123**

1778
MAY 9

Allen, Ethan. Valley Forge. To the President of Congress [York]. Thanks for his exchange. A. L. S. 2 pp. Read in Congress, May 14. Referred to the Board of War. Enclosed in Washington to the President of Congress, 1778, May 12.
C. C. 152, 6, 35

1778
MAY 10

Howe, [Sir] W[illiam]. Philadelphia. To [George Washington, Valley Forge]. Proposal for exchange of prisoners. Contemporary copy. 2 pp. In handwriting of Tench Tilghman. Enclosed in Washington to the President of Congress, 1778, May 11.   C. C. 152, 6, 25

1778
MAY 11

Washington, George. Valley Forge. To [the President of Congress, York]. Howe's letter respecting prisoners; exchange. Draft. 1 p. In handwriting of Robert Hanson Harrison. Read in Congress, May 13. Referred to Duer, R. H. Lee and Carroll.   A. III, 389

1778
MAY 11

Continental Congress, President. York. To [George] Washington [Valley Forge]. Forwarding address of Congress to the inhabitants of America. A. L. S. of Henry Laurens. 1 p.   **92, 43**

1778
MAY 11

Continental Congress, Resolve. Col. Francis Johnson elected commissary of prisoners. A. D. S. of Charles Thomson. 1 p. Enclosed in President of Congress to Washington, 1778, May 11.
92, 42

1778
MAY 11

Smith, Thomas. Bedford [Pennsylvania]. To James Smith [Philadelphia]. Indian ravages on Western frontier; Col. William Butler and the Rifle battalion. Contemporary copy. 3 pp. Enclosed in Board of War to Washington, 1778, May 19.
95, 8

1778
MAY 12

Washington, George. Valley Forge. To [the President of Congress, York]. The command at Fort Pitt; exchange of officers; Col. [Jacob Gerhard] Dircks's petition; fate of continental frigates in

the Delaware; Lt. Col. [Ethan] Allen; French King's message to the Court at London. Draft. 3 pp. In handwriting of Robert Hanson Harrison. Read in Congress, May 14. Referred to the Board of War.   **A. III, 391**
Printed in part: Writings of Washington (Ford) N. Y. 1890. 7: 7 12 & 20, notes.

1778
MAY 12
Board of War. [Yorktown, Penna.] To [George] Washington [Valley Forge]. Pay of discharged soldiers; officers and soldiers. A. L. S. of Timothy Pickering, jr. Answered May 16.*   **95, 335**

1778
MAY 13
Board of War. York. To George Washington, Valley Forge. Discharge of militia at Reading, Bethlehem and Easton; expense. A. L. S. of Richard Peters. 1 p.   **94, 348**

1778
MAY 15
Continental Congress, President. York. To [George] Washington [Valley Forge]. Half-pay and gratuity; transmitting papers. A. L. S. of Henry Laurens. 2 pp. Answered May 18.*   **92, 47**

1778
MAY 15
Continental Congress, Resolve. Half-pay for officers at close of war and gratuity to non-commissioned officers and privates. A. D. S. of Charles Thomson. 1 p. Enclosed in President of Congress to Washington, 1778, May 15.   **92, 49**

1778
MAY 16
Washington, George. Valley Forge. To the Board of War [York]. Forwarding supplies from the south; case of Capt. [Nathaniel] Galt; establishment of stages; duplication of soldiers pay. Draft. 3 pp. In handwriting of Richard Kidder Meade and John Fitzgerald.   **A. III, 395**

1778
MAY 18
Washington, George. Valley Forge. To [the President of Congress, York]. Resolves [respecting half-pay for officers]; evacuation of Philadelphia; prisoners. Draft. 3 pp. In handwriting of Robert Hanson Harrison. Read in Congress May 20. Referred to the Committee of Conference, "lately from camp."   **A. III, 399**
Printed: Writings of Washington (Ford) N. Y. 1890. 7, 19.

1778
MAY 18
Washington, George. Valley Forge. To [the Board of War, York]. Unnecessary force of militia at Easton, Bethlehem and Reading. Draft. 2 pp. In handwriting of Tench Tilghman.   **A. III, 403**

1778
MAY 18
W[ashingto]n, G[eorge]. Valley Forge. To Gouverneur Morris [York]. Half-pay; council [Committee of

Conference]; [Maj. Gen. Thomas Mifflin's] conduct; [Maj. Gen. Thomas] Conway's imperti-
nence. A. D. S. 3 pp.   P. I, pt. II, 81
Printed: Writings of Washington (Ford) N. Y. 1890. 7, 16.

1778
MAY 18

Continental Congress, Resolve. Relief for Western frontiers. Contemporary copy, attested by Charles
Thomson. 1 p. Transmitted to Washington.
95, 7

1778
MAY 19

Continental Congress, Resolve. Pay and rations of officers
while prisoners of the enemy. Contemporary
copy, attested by Charles Thomson. 1 p. Enclosed in President of Congress to Washington,
1778, May 20.   92, 50

1778
MAY 19

Board of War. [Philadelphia]. To [George] Washington
[Valley Forge]. Atrocities on the Western frontier; Col. William Butler; relief of frontier; proposed expedition against Detroit. A. L. S. of
Timothy Pickering, jr. 3 pp.   95, 5

1778
MAY 20

Continental Congress, President. York To [George]
Washington [Valley Forge]. Transmitting pa-
pers relating to Army matters; title of "The
United States of North America" adopted. A.
L. S. of Henry Laurens. 1 p. Answered May
24*   92, 51

1778
MAY 20

Continental Congress, Resolve. [Maj.] Gen. [John] Sullivan's request for [Brig.] Gen. [John] Stark's
services. A. D. S. of Charles Thomson. Enclosed in President of Congress to Washington,
1778, May 20.   92, 52

1778
MAY 20

Continental Army, Provost. Establishment of. A. D. S.
of Charles Thomson. 1 p. Enclosed in President of Congress to Washington 1778, May 20.
92, 54

1778
MAY 21

Washington, George. Valley Forge. To [the President
of Congress, York]. [Brig.] Gen. [Lachlan]
McIntosh to command at Fort Pitt; his travel-
ling expenses. ,Draft. 1 p. In handwriting of
Robert Hanson Harrison. Read in Congress
June 1. Referred to the Board of War.
A. III, 405

1778
MAY 21

Continental Congress, President. York. To George Wash-
ington [Valley Forge]. Transmitting resolve.
A. L. S. of Henry Laurens. 1 p. Answered
May 24*   92, 56

1778
MAY 21

Continental Congress, Resolve. Exchange and treatment of prisoners. Contemporary copy, attested by Charles Thomson. 1 p. Enclosed in President of Congress to Washington, 1778, May 21.   92, 55

1778
MAY 21

Morris, Gouverneur. York. To [George] Washington [Valley Forge]. Excessive wisdom of Congress; probable moves of British; man's self-interest; resignation [of Maj. Gen. Thomas Conway]. A. L. S. 3 pp.   22, 178

1778
MAY 22

Continental Congress, Resolve. Exempting deserters from British from military service. Broadside. 1 p. Printed by Hall & Sellers. Enclosed in President of Congress to Washington 1778, May 25.
92, 60

1778
MAY 23

Washington, George. Valley Forge. To [the Board of War, York]. Troops sent to Fort Pitt; difficulty with officers. Draft. 2 pp. In handwriting of Tench Tilghman.   A. III, 407

1778
MAY 23

Morris, Gouverneur. York. To [George] Washington [Valley Forge]. Commander for Rhode Island; exchange of prisoners and retaliations. A. L. S. 1 p.   22, 195

1778
MAY 24

Washington, George. Valley Forge. To [the President of Congress, York]. Exchange of prisoners; affair of Lafayette [at Barren Hill]; evacuation of Philadelphia; case of Capt. John Vance's commission. Draft. 2 pp. In handwriting of Robert Hanson Harrison.   A. III, 409

1778
MAY 25

Continental Congress, President. York. To [George] Washington [Valley Forge]. Transmitting resolves to be distributed among enemy. A. L. S. of Henry Laurens. 1 p. Answered May 31.*
92, 58

1778
MAY 27

Continental Congress, Resolves. Establishment of the Army; pay, rations, quartermasters and others. Broadside. Printed by Dunlap. Enclosed in President of Congress to Washington, 1778, June 4.   91, 132

1778
MAY 27

Howe, [Sir William]. Philadelphia. To [George] Washington [Valley Forge]. Transmitting copies of conciliatory Acts of Parliament. Contemporary copy. 1 p. In handwriting of Tench Tilghman. Enclosed in Washington to the President of Congress, 1778, June 4.   C. C. 152, 6, 71

1778 MAY 27	**Morris,** Gouverneur. York. To [George] Washington [Valley Forge]. Discussion of the rule of promotion; action of Congress; measures to be adopted on evacuation of Philadelphia by the British. A. L. S. 2 pp. **23, 239**
1778 MAY 28	**Washington,** George. Valley Forge. To [the President of Congress, York]. Enemy's preparations to evacuate Philadelphia. Draft. 1 p. In handwriting of Robert Hanson Harrison. Read in Congress, June 1. **A. III, 411**
1778 MAY 28	**Washington,** George. Valley Forge. To [the President of Congress, York]. Commission for Lt. Col. John Gibson. Draft. 1 p. Read in Congress, June 3. Referred to Board of War. **A. III, 413**
1778 MAY 28	**Continental Congress,** Resolve. Appointment of Commissary of prisoners. A. D. S. of Charles Thomson. 1 p. Enclosed in President of Congress to Washington 1778, May 29. **92, 63**
1778 MAY 28	**Continental Congress,** Resolve. Strength of Maj. Henry Lee's Corps of light dragoons. A. D. S. of Charles Thomson. 1 p. Enclosed in President of Congress to Washington, 1778, May 29. **92, 64**
1778 MAY 29	**W[ashingto]n,** G[eorge]. Valley Forge. To [Henry Laurens]. Disagreement between the U. S. Commissioners in France; British Peace Commissioners; military arrangement. Draft. 2 pp. In handwriting of Robert Hanson Harrison and Washington. **P. I, pt. II, 89** Printed: Writings of Washington (Ford) N. Y. 1890. 7,33.
1778 MAY 29	**Continental Congress,** President. York. To George Washington [Valley Forge]. Transmitting resolves making minor appointments. A. L. S. of Henry Laurens. 1 p. Answered May 31.* **92, 61**
1778 MAY 29	**Continental Congress,** Resolve. Rank of civil staff appointees. Broadside. Printed by Dunlap. Enclosed in President of Congress to Washington, 1778, June 4. **91, 132**
1778 MAY 30	**Clinton,** [Sir] H[enry]. [Philadelphia.] To [George] Washington [Valley Forge]. Transmission of Acts of Parliament. Contemporary copy. 1 p.

White Plains Novr 6th 1776.

Sir

I have the honor to inform you that on Yesterday morning the Enemy made a sudden and unexpected removal from the several Posts they had taken in our front, they broke up their whole encampment the preceding night, and have advanced towards Kings-bridge and the North River. The design of this manoeuvre is a matter of much conjecture and speculation, and cannot be accounted for with any degree of certainty, the grounds we had taken possession off were strong and advantageous, and such as they could not have gained without much loss of Blood in case an attempt had been made, I had taken every possible precaution to prevent their outflanking us, which may have led to the present measure. they may still have in view their Original plan, and by a sudden wheel try to accomplish it. Detachments are constantly out to observe their motions, and to harrass them as much as possible.

In Consequence of this movement it call'd a council of General Officers to day to consult of such measures as should be adopted in case they pursued their retreat to NewYork. the result of which is herewith transmitted. In respect to myself I can indulge an Idea that General Howe, supposing ___ going to NewYork ___ to close the Cam...

WRITING OF SAMUEL BLATCHLEY WEBB.

In handwriting of James McHenry. Enclosed
in Washington to the President of Congress, 1778,
June 4.   C. C. 152, 6, 75

1778   Washington, George. Valley Forge. To [the President
May 31   of Congress, York]. Evacuation of Philadelphia;
            disposition of public and private stores left therein.
            Draft. 2 pp. In handwriting of Robert Hanson
            Harrison. Read in Congress, June 2. Referred
            to McKean, Witherspoon and James Smith.
                                           A. III, 415

1778   Washington, George. [Valley Forge.] To [Lt. Gen.] Sir
May 31   Henry Clinton [Philadelphia]. Letters or de-
            spatches for Congress. Contemporary copy. 1 p.
            In handwriting of Tench Tilghman. Enclosed in
            Washington to the President of Congress, 1778,
            June 4.   C. C. 152, 6, 79
            Printed: Writings of Washington (Ford) N. Y. 1890. 6, 43.

1778   Continental Congress, President. York. To George
May 31   Washington [Valley Forge]. Transmitting re-
            solves. A. L. S. of Henry Laurens. 1 p. An-
            swered June 2.*   92, 65

1778   Washington, George. Valley Forge. To the President
June 2   of Congress [York]. Proscription of Philadel-
            phia loyalists. Draft. 2 pp. In handwriting of
            Robert Hanson Harrison. Read in Congress,
            June 4.   A. III, 419
            Printed: Writings of Washington (Ford) N. Y. 1890. 7, 51.

1778   Continental Congress, Resolve. Ration allowances. Broad-
June 2   side. Printed by Dunlap. Enclosed in President
            of Congress to Washington, 1778, June 4.   91, 132

1778   Clinton, [Sir] H[enry]. Philadelphia. To [George]
June 3   Washington. Transmitting conciliatory Acts of
            Parliament. Contemporary copy. 1 p. In
            handwriting of James McHenry. Enclosed in
            Washington to the President of Congress 1778,
            June 4.   C. C. 152, 6, 67

1778   Washington, George. Valley Forge. To [the President
June 4   of Congress, York]. Transmitting letters from
            Clinton and Howe. Draft. 1 p. In handwriting
            of Robert Hanson Harrison. Read in Congress,
            June 6.   A. III, 423

1778   Continental Congress, President. York. To [George]
June 4   Washington [Valley Forge]. Forwarding printed

copies of establishment of the army and blank oaths of "Abjuration." A. L. S. of Henry Laurens. 2 pp. Answered June 7.* 91, 130

1778
JUNE 4

Continental Congress, Resolve. Duties of committee of arrangement of the Army. A. D. S. of Charles Thomson. 1 p. Enclosed in President of Congress to Washington, 1778, June 4. 92, 1

1778
JUNE 4

Continental Congress, Resolve. Protection of Philadelphia and property on evacuation by British. A. D. S. of Charles Thomson. 1 p. Enclosed in President of Congress to Washington, 1778, June 5. 92, 4

1778
JUNE 4

Roberdeau, Daniel. York. To [George] Washington [Valley Forge]. Application for lead smelters from the army. A. L. S. 3 pp. 23, 288

1778
JUNE 5

Continental Congress, President. York. To George Washington [Valley Forge]. Measures respecting evacuation of Philadelphia by the British. A. L. S. of Henry Laurens. 1 p. Answered June 7.* 91, 2

1778
JUNE 6

Washington, George. Valley Forge. To [the Board of War, York]. Want of cartouche boxes. Draft. 2 pp. In handwriting of Tench Tilghman. A. III, 427

1778
[JUNE] 6

Continental Congress, President. York. To [George] Washington [Valley Forge]. Replies of Congress to Howe and Clinton. A. L. S. of Henry Laurens. 1 p. Answered June 9.* 92, 5
Dated in error May 6.

1778
[JUNE] 6

Continental Congress, President. York. To [Richard,] Lord Howe [Philadelphia]. Acts of Parliament; peace. Auto. draft signed of Henry Laurens. 1 p. Enclosed in President of Congress to Washington, 1778, June 6. The same letter to Sir Henry Clinton. 92, 7
Dated in error May 6.

1778
JUNE 7

Washington, George. Valley Forge. To [the President of Congress, York]. Arrival of the British peace commissioners. Draft. 1 p. In handwriting of Robert Hanson Harrison. Read in Congress, June 9. Referred to R. H. Lee, S. Adams, and Marchant. A. III, 429

1778
JUNE 8

Laurens, Henry. York. To [George] Washington [Valley Forge]. Delay in the Ticonderoga investigation; trouble among the commissioners in France. A. L. S. 2 pp.   **23,** 330

1778
JUNE 9

Washington, George. Valley Forge. To [the President of Congress, York]. Letters of Lord Howe and Sir Henry Clinton; passport for Dr [Adam] Ferguson. Draft. 2 pp. In handwriting of James McHenry. Read in Congress June 11. Referred to R. H. Lee, S. Adams and Marchant.

A. III, 431

1778
JUNE 9

Washington, George. [Valley Forge.] To [Lt. Gen.] Sir Henry Clinton [Philadelphia]. Passport for [Dr. Adam] Ferguson. Contemporary copy. 1 p. In handwriting of James McHenry. Enclosed in Washington to the President of Congress, 1778, June 9.   **C. C.** 152, 6, 93

1778
JUNE 9

Washington, George. Valley Forge. To [Francis] Dana [York]. Requesting his presence in camp. Draft. 1 p. In handwriting of James McHenry.

A. III, 433

1778
JUNE 9

Continental Congress, Resolves. Payment for officers rations. Contemporary copy, attested by Charles Thomson. 1 p. Enclosed in President of Congress to Washington, 1777, June 14.   **92,** 16

1778
JUNE 9

Board of War. York. To [George] Washington [Valley Forge]. Blankets from North Carolina; cartridge-boxes; shoes. A. L. S. of Timothy Pickering, jr. 2 pp. Answered June 15.*   **27,** 344

1778
JUNE 9

British Peace Commissioners. Philadelphia. To the President and members of Congress [York]. Proposition for cessation of hostilities; designs of France, etc. Contemporary copy. 5 pp. In handwriting of Henry Laurens. Enclosed in Laurens to Washington, 1778, June 18.   **24,** 58

1778
JUNE 9

Clinton, [Sir] H[enry]. Philadelphia. To [George] Washington [Valley Forge]. Arrival of British Peace Commissioners. Contemporary copy. 1 p. In handwriting of Tench Tilghman. Enclosed in Washington to the President of Congress, 1778, June 9.   **C. C.** 152, 6, 91

1778
JUNE 9

Duane, James; Volkert P. **Douw.** Albany [New York]. To [George Washington, Valley Forge]. Errand of the Seneca chiefs; depredations and conditions on the northern frontier. Contemporary copy. 4 pp. In handwriting of James McHenry. Enclosed in Washington to the President of Congress, 1778, June 21. C. C. 152, 6, 131

1778
JUNE 9

Morris, Gouverneur. York. To [George] Washington [Valley Forge]. Arrangement of army; measures on evacuation of Philadelphia; minor military matters. A. L. S. 2 pp. 23, 342

1778
JUNE 10

Washington, George. Valley Forge. To [the President of Congress, York]. Maj. [Richard] Campbell's commission. Draft. 1 p. In handwriting of Robert Hanson Harrison. Read in Congress June 15. Referred to Board of War. "(Acted upon)" A. III, 435

1778
JUNE 11

Washington, George. [Valley Forge.] To [the President of Congress, York]. Transmitting letters. Draft. 1 p. In handwriting of Robert Hanson Harrison. Read in Congress June 13. A. III, 437

[1778]
[JUNE 11]

Washington, George. Valley Forge. To Henry Laurens [York]. Opening of letters; caution in delivery [of epistles from the British Peace Commissioners]. Draft. 1 p. In handwriting of Robert Hanson Harrison. P. I, pt. II, 93
Printed: Writings of Washington (Ford) N. Y. 1890. 7, 57.

1778
JUNE 11

Continental Congress, President. York. To [George] Washington [Valley Forge]. Passport for [Dr.] Adam Ferguson; inquiry into the late Quartermaster-General [Thomas Mifflin]'s conduct. A. L. S. of Henry Laurens. 1 p. Answered June 15.* 92, 9

1778
JUNE 11

Continental Congress, Resolve. Inquiry into conduct of Maj. Gen. [Thomas] Mifflin, late Quartermaster General. Contemporary copy, attested by Charles Thomson. 1 p. Enclosed in President of Congress to Washington, 1778, June 11. 92, 11

1778
JUNE 11

Continental Congress, Report of Board of War on Expedition into the Indian country; recommendations etc. Contemporary copy, attested by Charles Thomson. 4 pp. Enclosed in President of Congress to Washington, 1778, June 14. 92, 14

1778
JUNE 11

Continental Congress, Resolves. Report of Board of War on the Indian situation; causes of the raids; hostile and friendly tribes; reduction of Detroit;

expedition against the Senecas. Contemporary copy. 4 pp. Enclosed in Board of War to Washington, 1778, July 27.   **25, 86**

1778
JUNE 11

Dana, Francis. York. To [George] Washington [Valley Forge]. Work of arranging the army. A. L. S. 2 pp.   **24, 5**

1778
JUNE 14

Continental Congress, President. York. To [George] Washington [Valley Forge]. Address of British Peace Commissioners; rations to officers; certain appointments. A. L. S. of Henry Laurens. 1 p. Answered June 15.*   **92, 12**

1778
JUNE 14

Laurens, Henry. York. To [Gov.] George Johnstone, Philadelphia. The Peace Commissioners; attitude of Congress. Contemporary copy. 2 pp. In handwriting of Laurens. Enclosed in Laurens to Washington, 1778, June 18.   **24, 61**

1778
JUNE 15

Washington, George. [Valley Forge.] To [the President of Congress, York]. Value of rations; case of [Maj.] Gen. [Thomas] Mifflin; evacuation of Philadelphia; exchange of prisoners. Draft. 2 pp. In handwriting of Robert Hanson Harrison. Read in Congress June 18. Referred to the Board of War "who are directed to report to Congress the grounds & terms upon which the exchange of prisoners between Genl. Washington & Genl. Clinton has taken place."   **A. III, 439**

1778
JUNE 15

Washington, George. Valley Forge. To Joseph Reed [York]. His letter to Gov. [George] Johnstone. Auto. draft signed. 1 p.   **P. I, pt. II, 105**

1778
JUNE 15

Washington, George. [Valley Forge.] Orders establishing the office of Inspector-General; plan of duties etc. "Extract from the Orders. Rob. H. Harrison." 2 pp. In handwriting of Robert Hanson Harrison. Enclosed in Washington to the President of Congress, 1778, June 18? **C. C. 152, 6, 111**

1778
JUNE 15

Washington, George. Valley Forge. To [the Board of War, York]. Blankets; draft of mechanics and workmen from the ranks; cannisters to supply the place of cartouche boxes. Draft. 1 p. In handwriting of Tench Tilghman.   **A. III, 443**

1778
JUNE 15

Washington, George. [Valley Forge.] To [Daniel Roberdeau, York]. Men from the ranks to work at the lead mines. Draft. 2 pp. In handwriting of James McHenry.   **A. III, 447**

1778
JUNE 15

Knox, H[enry]. [White Plains.] To [George] Washington [White Plains]. Embarrassment caused by regulations of Congress of Feb. 12. Contemporary copy. 2 pp. In handwriting of Richard Kidder Meade. Enclosed in Washington to the President of Congress, 1778, Aug. 3.

C. C. 152, 6, 205

1778
JUNE 16

Board of War, [York, Pennsylvania.] To [George] Washington [Valley Forge]. Need of arms in the Northern army. A. L. S. of Timothy Pickering, jr. 2 pp. **95, 89**

1778
JUNE 17

Continental Congress, President. York. To [George] Washington [Valley Forge]. Enclosing certain commissions, resolves, letters, etc. A. L. S. of Henry Laurens. 1 p. **92, 17**

1778
JUNE 17

Continental Congress, President. York. To the Earl of Carlisle, William Eden and [Gov.] George Johnstone [Philadelphia]. British disposition for peace. Contemporary copy. 1 p. Enclosed in President of Congress to Washington, 1778, June 17. **92, 21**

1778
JUNE 17

Continental Congress, Resolves. Correspondence with the enemy. A. D. S. of Charles Thomson. 1 p. Enclosed in President of Congress to Washington, 1777, June 17. **92, 19**

1778
JUNE 18

Washington, George. [Valley Forge.] To [the President of Congress, York]. Evacuation of Philadelphia has taken place; army is in pursuit. Draft. 2 pp. In handwriting of Robert Hanson Harrison. Read in Congress June 20. Referred to the Committee of Intelligence. A. III, 449

Printed: Writings of Washington (Ford) N. Y. 1890. 7, 66.

1778
JUNE 18

Washington, George. [Valley Forge.] To [the President of Congress, York]. Correspondence with the British Peace Commissioners; [Maj.] Gen. [Benedict] Arnold to command in Philadelphia. Draft. 2 pp. In handwriting of Robert Hanson Harrison. Read in Congress June 20. A. III, 451

Printed. Writings of Washington (Ford) N. Y. 1890. 7, 68.

1778
JUNE 18

Washington, George. [Valley Forge.] To [the President of Congress, York]. Baron Steuben's visit to Congress; promotion of Capt. [Caleb] Gibbs; the commander in chief's guard. Draft. 2 pp. In handwriting of Robert Hanson Harrison.

A. III, 445

Printed, in part: Writings of Washington (Ford) N. Y. 1890. 7, 66, note.

1778
JUNE 18

Laurens, Henry. York. To George Washington [Valley Forge]. British Peace Commissioners; correspondence with members of Congress; power of Congress over private letters. A. L. S. 3 pp.

24, 52

1778
JUNE 19

Board of War. [York.] To [George] Washington [Valley Forge]. Detaching troops for defense of the western frontier. A. L. S. of Timothy Pickering, jr. 2 pp. Answered June 22.* 95, 102

1778
JUNE 20

Washington, George. [Doylestown, Pennsylvania.] To [the President of Congress, York]. Pursuit of the enemy. Draft. 1 p. In handwriting of Robert Hanson Harrison. Read in Congress June 23. A. III, 455

1778
JUNE 20

Continental Congress, President. York. To [George] Washington [Doylestown]. Ticonderoga investigation; British Peace Commission. A. L. S. of Henry Laurens. 1 p. Answered June 28.*

92, 22

1778
JUNE 21

Washington, George. "10 miles from Coryell's" [Ferry, New Jersey]. To [the President of] Congress [York]. Visit of Seneca chiefs to camp. Draft. 2 pp. In handwriting of Robert Hanson Harrison. A. III, 457

1778
JUNE 22

Washington, George. Near Coryell's. To [the President of Congress, York]. Route of the enemy. Draft. 1 p. In handwriting of Robert Hanson Harrison. A. III, 461

Printed: Writings of Washington (Ford) N. Y. 1890. 7, 73.

1778
JUNE 22

Washington, George. Near Coryell's. To the Board of War [York]. Indian war in the Western Department; companies ordered thither; question of commander. Draft. 1 p. In handwriting of Robert Hanson Harrison. A. III, 463

1778
JUNE 25

Continental Congress, President. [York] To [George] Washington [Kingston, New Jersey]. Adjournment of Congress to Philadelphia. Letter-book copy. C. C. 13, 11, 11

1778
JUNE 25

Continental Congress, Resolves. Troops to be raised by Massachusetts; Rhode Island battalion; arms for [Maj.] Gen. [John] Sullivan; building of armed galleys. Contemporary copy, attested by Charles Thomson. 2 pp. Transmitted to Washington. **92, 24**

1778
JUNE 27

Continental Congress, President. [York.] To [George] Washington [near Englishtown, New Jersey]. Note of resolves transmitted. Letter-book copy. **C. C. 13, II, 15**

1778
JUNE 28

Washington, George. Englishtown [New Jersey]. To [the President of Congress, York]. The military situation. Draft. 2 pp. In handwriting of Robert Hanson Harrison. **A. III, 465**
Printed: Writings of Washington (Ford) N. Y. 1890. 7, 76.

1778
JUNE 28

Monmouth, (Battle of). Return of killed, wounded and missing of the Continental Army. A. D. of Tench Tilghman. Enclosed in Washington to the President of Congress, 1778, July 1. **C. C. 152, 6, 159**

1778
JUNE 29

Washington, George. "Fields near Monmouth Court House." To [the President of Congress, York]. Brief announcement of the engagement at Monmouth. Draft. 1 p. In handwriting of Robert Hanson Harrison. **A. III, 467**

1778
JULY 1

Washington, George. Englishtown. To [the President of Congress, York]. Account of preliminary manœvers and the battle of Monmouth. Draft. 9 pp. In handwriting of Robert Hanson Harrison. **A. III, 469**
Printed: Writings of Washington (Ford) N. Y. 1890. 7, 78.

[1778]
[JULY 7]

Washington, George. [New Brunswick, New Jersey.] To [the President of Congress, Philadelphia.] Movements of enemy; unsettled state of rank. Draft. 2 pp. In handwriting of Robert Hanson Harrison and Alexander Hamilton. Read in Congress, July 9. **A. III, 481**
Printed: Writings of Washington (Ford) N. Y. 1890. 7, 93.

1778
JULY 7

Laurens, Henry. Philadelphia. To [George] Washington [New Brunswick]. Publication of Washington's letters to Congress; the victory at Monmouth. A. L. S. 2 pp. **24, 277**

1778
JULY 8

Continental Congress, President. Philadelphia. To [George] Washington [near New Brunswick, New Jersey]. Thanks of Congress for movements preceding and during battle of Monmouth. A. L. S. of Henry Laurens. 1 p. Answered July 12*.   91, 225

1778
JULY 9
Continental Congress, Resolve. Committee to arrange the army. Contemporary copy, attested by Henry Laurens. 1 p. Enclosed in President of Congress to Washington, 1777, July 11.   91, 124

1778
JULY 10
Continental Congress, President. Philadelphia. To [George] Washington [near Paramus, New Jersey]. Accounts of D'Estaing's fleet; British naval strength at New York. A. L. S. of Henry Laurens. 2 pp. Answered July 14.*   91, 118

1778
JULY 11
Washington, George. Paramus. To Henry Laurens [Philadelphia]. Thanks of Congress on occasion of the battle of Monmouth. Draft. 1 p. In handwriting of Alexander Hamilton.
P. I, pt. II, 109

1778
JULY 11
Continental Congress, President. Philadelphia. To [George] Washington [Paramus]. Transmitting resolves; suggested attack on British at Rhode Island; adoption of word "America." A. L. S. of Henry Laurens. 2 pp. Answered July 22.*   91, 122

1778
JULY 11
Continental Congress, Resolve. Washington's cooperation with D'Estaing. A. D. S. of Charles Thomson. 1 p. Enclosed in President of Congress to Washington, 1778, July 11.   91, 120

1778
JULY 11
Continental Congress, Resolve. Militia for cooperation with the French. Contemporary copy, attested by Henry Laurens. 1 p. Enclosed in President of Congress to Washington, 1778, July 11.
91, 121

1778
JULY 12
Washington, George. Paramus. To [the President of Congress, Philadelphia]. March of the army; French fleet's arrival. Draft. 2 pp. In handwriting of Robert Hanson Harrison. Read in Congress, July 15.   A. III, 483
Printed: Writings of Washington (Ford) N. Y. 1890. 7, 96.

1778
JULY 12
[Washington, George.] Paramus. To William Henry Drayton [Philadelphia]. Approbation of his countrymen; friendship. Draft. 1 p. In handwriting of Alexander Hamilton. P. I, pt. II, 111
Printed: Writings of Washington (Sparks) Boston. 1834. 5, 439.

1778
JULY 14
Washington, George. Paramus. To [the President of Congress, Philadelphia]. Communication with the French fleet and movement of army. Draft. 2 pp. In handwriting of James McHenry. Read in Congress, July 17.   A. III, 487

1778
JULY 14
Washington, George. Paramus. To Comte D'Estaing [off Sandy Hook?] Strength of British fleet; facilities for correspondence, etc. Contemporary copy. 2 pp. In handwriting of James McHenry. Enclosed in Washington to the President of Congress, 1778, July 22.   C. C.   152, 6, 191
Printed: Writings of Washington (Ford) N. Y. 1890. 6, 99.

1778
JULY 15
Washington, George. Paramus. To Comte D'Estaing [off Sandy Hook?] Present of live stock. Contemporary copy. 1 p. In handwriting of James McHenry. Enclosed in Washington to the President of Congress, 1778, July 28.

C. C.   152, 6, 197

1778
JULY 15
Continental Congress, Resolves. Prisoners taken by the French. Contemporary copy, attested by Charles Thomson. 1 p. Enclosed in President of Congress to Washington, 1778, July 17.   91, 125

1778
JULY 17
Washington, George. Haverstraw Bay [New York]. To Comte D'Estaing [off Sandy Hook?]. Co-operation. Contemporary copy. 3 pp. In handwriting of James McHenry. Enclosed in Washington to the President of Congress, 1778, July 22.   C. C.   152, 6, 193
Printed: Writings of Washington (Ford) N. Y. 1890. 6, 101.

1778
JULY 17
Continental Congress, President. Philadelphia. To [George] Washington [Haverstraw, New York]. Transmitting resolves. A. L. S. of Henry Laurens. 1 p.   Answered July 22.*   91, 126

1778
JULY 18
Laurens, Henry. Philadelphia. To [George] Washington [Haverstraw]. Letters for Comte D'Estaing; letter from the British Peace Commissioners. A. L. S.   2 pp.   24, 347

1778
JULY 19
Schuyler, Ph[ilip John]. Albany. To [the President of Congress, Philadelphia]. Expedition against Indian country; Oneida and Tuscarora chiefs. Contemporary copy. 2 pp. Enclosed in Board of War to Washington, 1778, July 27.   25, 91

1778
JULY 22

Washington, George. Near White Plains [New York]. To [the President of Congress, Philadelphia]. D'Estaing's project against New York; expedition to Rhode Island; Indians on the Western frontier. Draft. 5 pp. In handwriting of Robert Hanson Harrison and James McHenry?. Read in Congress, July 27. Referred to Board of War in what respects Capt. Gibbs.   A. III, 491
Printed: Writings of Washington (Ford) N. Y. 1890. 7, 108.

1778
JULY 22

Washington, George. Near White Plains. To the President of Congress [Philadelphia]. Baron D'Arendt's resignation. Draft signed. 1 p. In handwriting of John Laurens.   A. III, 495

1778
JULY 24

W[ashington,] G[eorge]. White Plains. To Henry Laurens [Philadelphia]. Captures by American vessels; British Peace Commissioners' letter; Chevalier de la Neufville and foreign officers in the army; Baron Steuben's desires. Draft. 4 pp. In handwriting of Robert Hanson Harrison.
          P. I, pt. II, 113
Printed: Writings of Washington (Ford) N. Y. 1890. 7, 119.

1778
JULY 25

Continental Congress, Resolves. Deferring expedition against Detroit; Brig. Gen. [Lachlan] McIntosh's expedition against Indian towns; Virginia troops. Contemporary copy. 3 pp. Enclosed in Board of War to Washington, 1778, July 27.   25, 88

1778
JULY 26

Washington, George. White Plains. To [the President of Congress, Philadelphia]. The question of Baron Steuben's command. Draft. 2 pp. In handwriting of Alexander Hamilton. Read in Congress, Aug. 1. Referred to Reed, Boudinot and Chase.   A. III, 497
Printed: Writings of Washington (Ford) N. Y. 1890. 7, 124.

1778
JULY 27

Board of War. [Philadelphia.] To George Washington [White Plains]. Expeditions into the Indian country; the Six Nations; news from the frontier. A. L. S. of Richard Peters. 3 pp.   25, 84

1778
JULY 28

Washington, George. White Plains. To [the President of Congress, Philadelphia]. Decision respecting the court of inquiry on [Maj.] Gen. [Israel] Putnam. Draft. 1 p. In handwriting of Robert Hanson Harrison. Read in Congress, Aug. 4. Referred to Hosmer, R. H. Lee and Scudder.
          A. III, 499

252 LIBRARY OF CONGRESS

1778
July 28
Board of War. [Philadelphia.] To [George] Washington [White Plains]. The Invalid Corps. A. L. S. of Richard Peters. 1 p.   **95, 211**

1778
July 29
Phillips, W[illiam]. Cambridge [Massachusetts]. To Maj. Gen. [William] Heath [Boston]. Clothing for Convention troops; officer to go to Canada. Contemporary copy. 1 p. In handwriting of James McHenry. Enclosed in Washington to the President of Congress, 1778, Aug. 16.   **C. C. 152, 6, 261**

1778
July 30
Continental Congress, President. Philadelphia. To [George] Washington [White Plains]. Military appointments; brevets for foreigners. A. L. S. of Henry Laurens. 1 p. Answered Aug. 7.*
   91, 128

1778
July 30
Keppel, A[ugustus, Viscount]. [H. M. S.] *Victory*, at Sea. To Philip Stephens [Whitehall]. Account of engagement between French and British fleets with list of British losses. Contemporary copy. 4 pp. In handwriting of Tench Tilghman. Enclosed in Washington to the President of Congress, 1778, Oct. 14.   **C. C. 152, 6, 403**

1778
Aug. 1
Sullivan, John. Providence [Rhode Island]. To [George Washington, White Plains]. The military situation in Rhode Island. Contemporary copy. 2 pp. In handwriting of John Fitzgerald. Enclosed in Washington to the President of Congress, 1778, Aug. 3.   **C. C. 152, 6, 209**

1778
Aug. 2
Morris, Gouverneur. Philadelphia. To [George] Washington [White Plains]. Baron de la Neufville's brevet; victory at Monmouth and the aftermath. A. L. S. 2 pp.   **25, 116**

1778
Aug. 3
Washington, George. White Plains. To [the President of Congress, Philadelphia]. Disputes of rank; confusion in the cavalry service; Rhode Island expedition; D'Estaing; Clothier general. Draft. 8 pp. In handwriting of Robert Hanson Harrison. Read in Congress, Aug. 10.   **A. III, 503**
Printed: Writings of Washington (Ford) N. Y. 1890. 7, 137.

1778
Aug. 3
Washington, George. White Plains. To [the Board of War, Philadelphia]. Arguments against the proposed expedition into the Indian country. Draft. 6 pp. In handwriting of Alexander Hamilton.
   A. III, 511
Printed: Writings of Washington (Ford) N. Y. 1890. 7, 131.

1778
AUG. 3

D'Estaing, [Charles Henri Theodar, Comte]. At sea. To [George] Washington [White Plains]. Disappointments at Sandy Hook; [Maj.] Gen. [John] Sullivan; health of the fleet; Lt. Col. [John] Laurens; general arrangements. Contemporary copy. 3 pp. In handwriting of Alexander Hamilton. (In French.) Enclosed in Washington to the President of Congress, 1778, Aug. 7.
C. C. **152**, 6, 219

1778
AUG. 4

Laurens, John. Providence [Rhode Island]. To [George] Washington [White Plains]. Journal of operations of French fleet at Rhode Island from July 25 to Aug. 4. Contemporary copy. 16 pp. In handwriting of James McHenry, Tench Tilghman and Robert Hanson Harrison. Enclosed in Washington to the President of Congress, 1778, Aug. 7.
C. C. **152**, 6, 223

1778
AUG. 6

[Heath, William.] Boston. To [George Washington, White Plains]. Convention officer to go to Canada by way of the lakes. [Extract of letter.] Contemporary copy. 1 p. Enclosed in Washington to the President of Congress, 1778, Aug. 16.
C. C. **152**, 6, 259

1778
AUG. 6

Sullivan, John. Providence [Rhode Island]. To [George] Washington [White Plains]. Destruction of British frigates; tardiness of militia. Contemporary copy. 2 pp. In handwriting of James McHenry. Enclosed in Washington to the President of Congress, 1778, Aug. 13.
C. C. **152**, 6, 251

1778
AUG.

Washington, George. White Plains. To [the President of Congress, Philadelphia]. Major [Caleb] Gibbs's commission; advices from Rhode Island; fire in New York City. Draft. 2 pp. In handwriting of Robert Hanson Harrison. Read in Congress, Aug. 10.
A. III, 517

1778
AUG. 7

Washington, George. [White Plains.] To [the President of Congress, Philadelphia]. Transmitting copies of Comte D'Estaing's letters. Draft. 1 p. In handwriting of Robert Hanson Harrison. Read in Congress, Aug. 10.
A. III, 519

1778
AUG. 7

Washington, George. White Plains. Extract of General Orders. Establishment of rank of dragoon

officers. D. S.: "S. Moylan. Col. C. L. D."
1 p. Enclosed in Washington to the President
of Congress, 1778, Sept. 23. **C. C. 152, 6, 379**

1778
Aug. 9

Washington, George. White Plains. To [the President
of Congress, Philadelphia]. British fleet sailing
from New York. Draft. 1 p. In handwriting
of Robert Hanson Harrison. **A. III, 521**

1778
Aug. 9

Washington, George. White Plains. To [the President
of Congress, Philadelphia]. Employment of
Hessian officers who wish to join the Continental
Army. Draft. 2 pp. In handwriting of
Alexander Hamilton. Read in Congress, Aug.
18. Referred to the Board of War. **A. III, 523**

1778
Aug. 9

Washington, George. White Plains. To Richard H[enry]
Lee [Philadelphia]. Resignation of Col. [Alex-
ander] Spotswood. Draft. 3 pp. In handwriting of Robert Hanson Harrison and Washington.
A. III, 525

1778
Aug. 11

Washington, George. White Plains. To the President of
Congress [Philadelphia]. Military chest ex-
hausted. Draft. 1 p. In handwriting of Robert
Hanson Harrison. **A. III, 529**

1778
Aug. 13

Washington, George. White Plains. To [the President
of Congress, Philadelphia]. News from Rhode
Island; minor military matters. Draft. 1 p.
In handwriting of Alexander Hamilton. Read
in Congress, Aug. 15. **A. III, 531**

1778
Aug. 13

Continental Congress, President. Philadelphia. To
[George] Washington [White Plains]. Transmitting resolves and sundry papers relating to
British Peace Commissioners. Letter-book
copy. **C. C. 13, II, 44**

1778
Aug. 16

Washington, George. White Plains. To [the President
of Congress, Philadelphia]. Clothing for the
Convention troops. Draft. 1 p. In handwriting of Robert Hanson Harrison. Referred to
Chase, Duer and R. H. Lee. **A. III, 533**

1778
Aug. 16

Washington, George. White Plains. To [the President
of Congress, Philadelphia]. Advices from Rhode
Island. Draft. 1 p. In handwriting of Robert
Hanson Harrison. Read in Congress Aug. 21.
A. III, 535

Printed: Writings of Washington (Ford) N. Y. 1890. 7, 153.

1778
Aug. 16

Continental Congress, President. Philadelphia. To [George] Washington, White Plains. Correspondence; papers relative to charges against [Maj.] Gen. [Arthur] St. Clair; various resolves. Letter-book copy.   **C. C.** **13,** II, 46

1778
Aug. 19

Washington, George. White Plains. To [the President of Congress, Philadelphia]. Situation in Rhode Island; reenlistments. Draft. 1 p. In handwriting of Robert Hanson Harrison. **A.** III, 537

1778
Aug. 20

Washington, G[eorge]. White Plains. To Henry Laurens [Philadelphia]. Conduct of Gov. [George] Johnstone; trouble caused by French officers. Draft. 2 pp. In handwriting of Robert Hanson Harrison.   **P.** I, pt. II, 129
Printed: Writings of Washington (Ford) N. Y. 1890. 7, 155.

1778
Aug. 20

Continental Congress, President. Philadelphia. To [George] Washington, White Plains. Transmitting resolve. Letter-book copy.
C. C. **13,** II, 49

1778
Aug. 20

Continental Congress, President. Philadelphia. To [George] Washington. White Plains. Enclosing Committee report on letter relating to Baron Steuben. Letter-book copy. **C. C.** **13,** II, 51

1778
Aug. 20

Continental Army, Council of War. White Plains. Degrees of punishment in the army. Contemporary copy. 4 pp. In handwriting of Tench Tilghman. Enclosed in Washington to the President of Congress, 1778, Aug. 31.   **C. C.** **152,** 6, 317

1778
Aug. 21

Washington, George. White Plains. To [the President of Congress, Philadelphia]. Advices from Rhode Island; ships returning to Sandy Hook. Draft. 1 p. In handwriting of Robert Hanson Harrison. Read in Congress, Aug. 25.   **A.** III, 539

1778
Aug. 21

Washington, George. White Plains. To [the President of Congress, Philadelphia]. Memorial of Col. [Moses] Rawlings and the Maryland officers. Draft. 1 p. In handwriting of Robert Hanson Harrison. Read in Congress, Aug. 25. Referred to the Board of War.   **A.** ,III, 541

1778
Aug. 21

D'Estaing, [Charles Henri Theodat, Comte]. [Rhode Island] To Maj. Gen. [John] Sullivan [Before Newport]. Sailing for Boston; condition of fleet; orders from the king. Contemporary copy.

3 pp. In handwriting of Alexander Hamilton. (In French.) Enclosed in Washington to the President of Congress, 1778, Aug. 25.

C. C. 152, 6, 297

English translation of same in handwriting of Charles Thomson. 3 pp.   C. C. 152, 6, 301

1778
Aug. 21

Greene, N[athanael]. On board the *Languedoc*. To Comte D'Estaing. Remonstrance against French fleet leaving for Boston; urging attack. Contemporary copy. 4 pp. In handwriting of Tench Tilghman. Enclosed in Washington to the President of Congress, 1778, Aug. 25.   C. C. 152, 6, 293

1778
Aug. 22

Continental Army, General Officers. Before Newport. To [Comte D'Estaing, Rhode Island]. Protest against French fleet going to Boston. Contemporary copy. 1 p. In handwriting of Richard Kidder Meade. Enclosed in Washington to the President of Congress 1778, Aug. 25.

C. C. 152, 6, 305

1778
Aug. 23

Continental Congress, President. Philadelphia. To [George] Washington, White Plains. Proceedings of Maj. Gen. [Charles] Lee's court-martial before Congress. Letter-book copy, marked "not sent"

C. C. 13, II, 51

1778
Aug. 23

Sullivan, John. Before Newport · [Rhode Island]. To [George] Washington [White Plains]. Sailing of French fleet for Boston; delicate situation. Contemporary copy. 2 pp. In handwriting of Robert Hanson Harrison. Enclosed in Washington to the President of Congress 1778, Aug. 25.

C. C. 152, 6, 289

1778
Aug. 23

Sullivan, John. Before Newport. To the General Officers in camp. Questions as to operations of the army. Contemporary copy. 2 pp. In handwriting of James McHenry. Enclosed in Washington to the President of Congress, 1778, Aug. 25.

C. C. 152, 6, 309

1778
Aug. 24

Washington, George. White Plains. To [the President of Congress, Philadelphia]. Transmitting letter from [Maj.] Gen. [John] Sullivan. Draft. 1 p. In handwriting of Robert Hanson Harrison.

A. III, 545

1778
Aug. 25

Washington, George. White Plains. To [the President of Congress, Philadelphia]. Situation in Rhode Island. Draft. 1 p. In handwriting of Robert Hanson Harrison. Read in Congress, Aug. 28.
A. III, 547

1778
Aug. 25

Washington, George. White Plains. To Henry Laurens [Philadelphia]. Need of gold for secret service. Auto. draft signed. 1 p. P. I, pt. II, 141
Printed in part: Writings of Washington (Ford) N. Y. 1890. 7, 163, note.

1778
Aug. 28

Washington, George. White Plains. To the Board of War [Philadelphia]. Returns of officers; rank, etc. Draft. 1 p. In handwriting of Robert Hanson Harrison. A. III, 549

1778
Aug. 28

Continental Congress, President. Philadelphia. To [George] Washington, White Plains. Printing of proceedings of court-martial of Maj. Gen. [Charles] Lee; transmitting resolve. Letterbook copy. C. C. 13, II, 55

1778
Aug. 29

Laurens, Henry. Philadelphia. To [George] Washington [White Plains]. Hard money for special uses; attitude of British Peace Commissioners; minor matters and the present situation. A. L. S. 2 pp. 25, 276

1778
Aug. 30

Continental Congress, President. Philadelphia. To [George] Washington, [White Plains]. Money for secret service; Capt. Josiah Stoddard's memorial. Letter-book copy. C. C. 13, II, 57

1778
Aug. 30

Continental Army, Artillery. Captain-Lieutenants [White Plains]. To [George Washington, White Plains]. Pay question. Contemporary copy. 3 pp. In handwriting of Peter Presley Thornton? Enclosed in Washington to the President of Congress, 1779, Apr. 24. C. C. 152, 7, 271

1778
Aug. 30

[Heath, William.] Boston. To [George Washington, White Plains]. Supplies wanted by the French fleet. [Extract of letter.] 1 p. In handwriting of Robert Hanson Harrison. Enclosed in Washington to the President of Congress, 1778, Sep. 7. C. C. 152, 6, 349

1778
Aug. 31

Washington, George. White Plains. To [the President of Congress, Philadelphia]. Commissions in Armand's corps; contentions of Du Portail; capital punishment in the Army; situation in Rhode Island. Draft. 4 pp. In handwriting of Robert Hanson Harrison. Read in Congress, Sep. 3. Referred to the Board of War.   A. III, 551

1778
Aug. 31

Continental Congress, President. Philadelphia. To [George] Washington, White Plains. Enlistment of militia for the war; bounty. Letter-book copy.   C. C. 13, II, 60

1778
Aug. 31

Morris, Gouverneur. [Philadelphia.] To [George] Washington [White Plains]. Recruiting the army; hard money bounty. A. L. S. 1 p.   **25, 311**

[1778]
[Aug. ?]

Collier, William. [Quebec?] Report respecting American prisoners started toward Boston. Contemporary copy. 2 pp. Enclosed in President of Congress to Washington, 1779, Aug. 26.   **93, 325**

1778
Sep. 1

Washington, George. White Plains. To [the President of Congress, Philadelphia]. Retreat from Rhode Island. Draft. 1 p. In handwriting of Robert Hanson Harrison. Referred to the Committee of Intelligence.   A. IV, pt. I. 1

1778
Sep. 2

Washington, George. White Plains. To Silas Deane, Philadelphia. Exchange of Col. [Samuel Blatchley] Webb; news from Rhode Island. Draft. 2 pp. In handwriting of Robert Hanson Harrison.   A. IV, pt. I, 3

1778
Sep. 3

Sullivan, John. Providence. To [George Washington, White Plains]. Protest of officers against French fleet going to Boston. Contemporary copy. 3 pp. In handwriting of Tench Tilghman. Enclosed in Washington to the President of Congress, 1778, Sep. 4.   C. C. 152, 6, 333

1778
Sep. 4

Washington, George. White Plains. To [the President of Congress, Philadelphia]. Retreat from Rhode Island; arrival of [Sir Peter] Parker off New York. Draft. 1 p. In handwriting of Robert Hanson Harrison. Read in Congress, Sep. 7.
          A. IV, pt. I, 5

1778
Sep. 4

Washington, George. White Plains. To [the President of Congress, Philadelphia]. Protest of Continental officers to Comte D'Estaing; designs of enemy; bounty for enlistments. Draft. 5 pp. In handwriting of Robert Hanson Harrison.
          A. IV, pt. I, 7

1778
SEP. 4

Washington, George. White Plains. To Henry Laurens [Philadelphia]. Report of Lt. Col. [John] Laurens's bravery at Rhode Island; return of gold. Auto. draft signed. 2 pp.   P. I, pt. II, 147

1778
SEP. 5

W[ashington,] G[eorge]. White Plains. To Gouverneur Morris [Philadelphia]. Danger in bounties of coin. Draft. 2 pp. In handwriting of Robert Hanson Harrison.   P. I, pt. II, 149
Printed: Writings of Washington (Ford) N. Y. 1890. 7, 179.

1778
SEP. 5

Continental Congress, President. Philadelphia. To [George] Washington, White Plains. Transmitting resolves. Letter-book copy.
C. C. 13, II, 63

1778
SEP. 6

Continental Army, Blankets. White Plains. Return of blankets wanting in the several brigades. Tabular statement. D. S. of Alexander Scammell. 1 p. Enclosed in Washington to the President of Congress, 1778, Sep. 7.   C. C. 152, 6, 345

1778
SEP. 7

Washington, George. White Plains. To [the President of Congress, Philadelphia]. Provisions and wood for French fleet; want of blankets. Draft. 1 p. In handwriting of Robert Hanson Harrison. Read in Congress, Sep. 10. Referred to Board of War.   A. IV, pt. I, 13

1778
SEP. 10

Continental Congress, President. Philadelphia. To [George] Washington, White Plains. Acknowledging letters and transmitting resolves. Letter-book copy.   C. C. 13, II, 72

1778
SEP. 10

Gates, Horatio, Jacob **Bayley** and Moses **Hazen**. White Plains. To [George Washington, White Plains]. Report on proposed expedition to Canada; routes, supplies, etc. Contemporary copy. 5 pp. In handwriting of John Laurens. Enclosed in Washington to the President of Congress, 1778, Sep. 12.   C. C. 152, 6, 359

1778
SEP. 12

W[ashington,] G[eorge]. White Plains. To [the President of Congress, Philadelphia]. Inspector-General-ship and Baron Steuben's appointment; outrages of British; position of Continental Army. Draft. 3 pp. In handwriting of Robert Hanson Harrison. Read in Congress, Sep. 14.   A. IV, pt. I, 19
Printed, in part: Writings of Washington (Ford) N.Y. 1890. 7, 189, note.

1778
SEP. 12

Washington, George. White Plains. To [the President of Congress, Philadelphia]. Proposed expedition to Canada and preparations necessary. Draft. 3 pp. In handwriting of Alexander Hamilton. Read in Congress, Sep. 15. Referred to Lee and Drayton.   **A.** IV, pt. I, 15
Printed: Writings of Washington (Ford) N. Y. 1890. 7, 191.

1778
SEP. 12

Washington, George. White Plains. To Henry Laurens [Philadelphia]. Gov. [George] Johnstone; Mons. Galvan; letters; Gérard [de Rayneval]. Auto. draft signed. 2 pp.   **P.** I, pt. II, 153
Printed: Writings of Washington (Ford) N. Y. 1890. 7, 193.

1778
SEP. 12

Continental Congress, President. Philadelphia. To [George] Washington, White Plains. Transmitting resolves; terms of Saratoga Convention and miscellaneous military matters. Letter-book copy with postscript in handwriting of Henry Laurens.   **C. C.** 13, II, 75

[1778]
[SEP. 12]

[Clark, John jr. and James **Johnston.]** Plan for settling back ration accounts. A. D. of Clark. 2 pp. Enclosed in preceding entry.   **95, 295**

1778
SEP. 12

Clark, John jr. and James **Johnston.** [Philadelphia.] To George Washington [White Plains]. Settlement of ration accounts. A. L. S. of Clark, signed also by Johnston. 1 p.   **95, 293**

1778
SEP. 14

Washington, George. White Plains. To the Board of War [Philadelphia]. Clothing, hats, shoes etc.; cartouche boxes; prisoners at Easton [Pennsylvania]. Draft. 5 pp. In handwriting of Robert Hanson Harrison.   **A.** IV, pt. I, 25

1778
SEP. 15

Continental Army, Board of General Officers. White Plains. Settlement of rank of artillery field officers. Contemporary copy. 2 pp. In handwriting of Tench Tilghman. Enclosed in Washington to the President of Congress, 1778, Sep. 23.
     C. C. 152, 6, 375

1778
SEP. 16

Continental Congress, President. [Philadelphia.] To [George] Washington [White Plains]. Magazines for projected winter expedition into Canada; clothing, snowshoes and other supplies. Letter-book copy.   **C. C.** II, 82

1778
SEP. 16

[Greene, Nathanael.] Boston. To [George] Washington [White Plains]. Exorbitant price of forage. [Extract of letter.] Contemporary copy. 1 p.

frame some general Regulations on this Head—they are unwilling they say to subject their Constituents to partial Restraints—

I once mentioned to Congress, that I thought a War-Office extremely necessary, & they seemed inclined to institute one for our doing, but the Affair seems to have been since dropt—give me Leave again to insist on the Utility and Importance of such an Establishment; the more I reflect upon the Subject, the more I am convinced of its Necessity, and that affairs can never properly be conducted without it—

'Tis with Pleasure I receive the Resolve inclosed in your Favour of the 8th Inst. one considerable Ground of Disaffaction in the Army is thereby removed—

I have employed Persons in building the Gondolas and Rafts, which the Congress thought necessary for the Defence of this Place; and in Conjunction with the Provincial Congress have determined to sink Chevaux de frize, one of which is already begun—

I am, with &c

G. W.

Hon'ble John Hancock Esq'r

WRITING OF ALEXANDER CONTEE HANSON.

In handwriting of Tench Tilghman. Enclosed in Washington to the President of Congress, 1778, Sep. 23. **C. C. 152, 6, 381**

1778
SEP. 19

Washington, George. West Point [New York]. To the Board of War [Philadelphia]. Enlistment of prisoners and deserters; clothing for cavalry. Draft. 2 pp. In handwriting of Robert Hanson Harrison. **A. IV, pt. I, 29**

1778
SEP. 22

Washington, George. Fredericksburg [New York]. To the several States. Need of forage; exorbitant prices demanded. Contemporary copy. 2 pp. In handwriting of James McHenry. Enclosed in Washington to the President of Congress, 1778, Sep. 23. **C. C. 152, 6, 373**

1778
SEP. 23

Washington, George. Fredericksburg. To [the President of Congress, Philadelphia]. Purchase of flour; expense of the horse troops; teams; claims against the Quartermaster; position of army. Draft. 3 pp. In handwriting of Robert Hanson Harrison. Read in Congress, Sep. 28. Referred to Committee on Col. Blaine's memorial and H. Hollingsworth's letter. **A. IV, pt. I, 33**
Printed in part: Writings of Washington (Ford) N. Y. 1890. 7, 197, note.

1778
SEP. 27

Continental Congress, President. Philadelphia. To [George] Washington [Fredericksburg]. Transmitting resolve; commission of Lt. Col. to John [Jean Baptiste] Ternant. Letter-book copy. **C. C. 13, II, 91**

1778
SEP. 29

Washington, George. Fredericksburg. To [the President of Congress Philadelphia]. French interest in exchange of prisoners; surprise of Col. [George] Baylor's troop; minor military maneuvers. Draft. 3 pp. In handwriting of Tench Tilghman. Read in Congress, Oct. 5. Referred to Board of War. **A. IV, pt. I, 35**

1778
SEP. 30

Continental Congress, Committee. Enlistment of prisoners and deserters; Pulaski's corps. A. L. S. of Joseph Reed. 4 pp. **27, 79**
Committee on arrangement of the army: Reed, Lovell, and Witherspoon.

[1778]
[SEP. ?]

[Armand-Tufin, Charles; Marquis de la Rouerie.] [White Plains.] Arrangement of officers in corps. A. D. 2 pp. Endorsed by Charles Thomson: "wch. Genl. Washington can not confirm." Referred to Board of War. Enclosed in Washington to the President of Congress, 1778, Sep. 23.   **C. C. 152, 6, 383**

1778
OCT. 2

Continental Congress, President. [Philadelphia] **To** [George] Washington [Fishkill]. Transmitting resolve. Letter-book copy.   **C. C. 13, II, 93**

1778
OCT. 3

Washington, George. Fishkill [New York]. To [the President of Congress, Philadelphia]. Movement of troops; surprise of Baylor's detachment. Draft, marked "Copy." 2 pp. In handwriting of George Baylor. Read in Congress, Oct. 7.   **A. IV, pt. I, 39**
Printed: Writings of Washington (Ford) N. Y. 1890. 7, 203.

1778
OCT. 3

Washington, George. Fishkill. To Henry Laurens [Philadelphia]. Intelligence of British plans; reasons operating against truth of same. Auto. draft signed. 3 pp.   **P. I, pt. II, 165**
Printed, in part: Writings of Washington (Ford) N. Y. 1890. 7, 205, note.

1778
OCT. 4

W[ashington,] G[eorge]. Fishkill. To [Gouverneur Morris, Philadelphia]. Queries as to the situation; extravagant prices; finances; temper of the army. Auto. draft signed. 4 pp.   **P. I, pt. II, 173**
Printed: Writings of Washington (Ford) N. Y. 1890. 7, 208.

1778
OCT. 5

Washington, George. [Fishkill.] To the Board of War [Philadelphia]. Clothing; lack of shoes. Draft. 2 pp. In handwriting of John Laurens.   **A. IV, pt. I, 41**

1778
OCT. 5

Lee, Richard Henry. Philadelphia. To [George] Washington [Fishkill]. Reenlisting army; depreciation of currency; designs of British; rise in price of flour. A. L. S. 2 pp.   **27, 62**

1778
OCT. 6

Washington, George. Fishkill. To [the President of Congress, Philadelphia]. Lafayette's request for a furlough to return to France. Draft. 3 pp. In handwriting of John Laurens. Read in Congress, Oct. 13. Referred to R. H. Lee, Witherspoon, S. Adams, and Drayton.   **A. IV, pt. I, 43**
Printed: Writings of Washington (Ford) N. Y. 1890. 7, 210.

1778
OCT. 6

Washington, George. Fishkill. To [Joseph Reed, Philadelphia]. Status of Count [Casimir] Pulaski's corps. Draft. 2 pp. In handwriting of Alexander Hamilton.   **A. IV, pt. 1, 47**

1778 Oct. 8	**Otis & Andrews.** Boston. To Timothy Pickering [jr.] [Fredericksburg.] Cloth for uniforms; high prices of everything.
Oct. 8	**Same** to Richard Peters [Philadelphia]. Clothing supplies. Contemporary copies. In handwriting of John Fitzgerald. Enclosed in Washington to the Board of War, 1778, Oct. 11. **C. C. 152, 6, 585**
1779 Oct. 9	**Continental Congress,** President. Philadelphia. To [George] Washington [Fredericksburg]. Transmitting resolve. Letter-book copy. **C. C. 13, II, 103**
1778 Oct. 10	**Washington, George.** Fredericksburg. To the Board of War [Philadelphia]. Clothing for Col. [John] Patton's regiment. Draft. 1 p. In handwriting of Tench Tilghman. **A. IV, pt. I, 49**
1778 Oct. 10	**Laurens,** Henry. Philadelphia. To [George] Washington [Fredericksburg]. Correspondence and minor matters; Britain's situation; danger to South Carolina and Georgia. A. L. S. 3 pp. **27, 160**
1778 Oct. 10	**Nicholas,** Samuel. Providence [Rhode Island]. To the Board of War, Philadelphia. Clothing from France; quality, color, etc. Contemporary copy. In handwriting of John Fitzgerald. Enclosed in Washington to the Board of War, 1778, Oct. 14. **C. C. 152, 6, 585**
1778 Oct. 11	**Washington, George.** Near Fredericksburg. To the Board of War [Philadelphia]. Want of clothing for officers; complaints of the Clothier General's Department. Draft. 4 pp. In handwriting of Robert Hanson Harrison. Read in Congress, Nov. 30. Referred to the Committee on Clothier Department, James Searle added. **A. IV, pt. I, 51**
1778 Oct. 13	**Continental Congress,** President. [Philadelphia.] To [George] Washington [Fredericksburg]. Transmitting resolves. Letter-book copy. **C. C. 13, II, 108**
1778 Oct. 14	**Washington, George.** Near Fredericksburg. To [the President of Congress, Philadelphia]. Account of naval engagement between D'Estaing and Keppel, July 27; designs of enemy; loss of the *Raleigh.* Draft. 1 p. In handwriting of

Robert Hanson Harrison. Read in Congress, Oct. 20. Ordered to lie on the table.

A. IV, pt. I, 55

Printed: Writings of Washington (Sparks) Boston. 1834. 6, 89.

1778
OCT. 16

Continental Congress, President. [Philadelphia.] To [George] Washington [Fredericksburg]. Transmitting resolves. Letter-book copy.

C. C. 13, II, 112

1778
OCT. 16

Connolly, John. Philadelphia. To George Washington [Fredericksburg]. Praying for release from confinement. A. L. S. 3 pp. Enclosed in Washington to Congress, 1778, Oct. 31.

C. C. 152, 6, 435

1778
OCT. 18

Washington, George. Fredericksburg. To [the President of Congress, Philadelphia]. Price of provisions; enemy's embarkation at New York. Draft. 2 pp. In handwriting of Tench Tilghman. Read in Congress, Oct. 27.   A. IV, pt. I. 57

1778
OCT. 18

Washington, George. [Fredericksburg.] To the Board of War, Philadelphia. Want of shoes; clothing and blankets. Draft. 1 p. In handwriting of Robert Hanson Harrison.   A. IV, pt. I, 59

1778
OCT. 21

Washington, George. Fredericksburg. To [the President of Congress, Philadelphia]. Request of Chevalier Mauduit du Plessis to return to France. Draft. 1 p. In handwriting of Alexander Hamilton.   A. IV, pt. I, 61

1778
OCT. 22

Washington, George. Fredericksburg. To [the President of Congress, Philadelphia]. Complaints of illicit commerce with enemy; gaining secret intelligence; Lt. Col. [William ?] Butler's expedition against Anaquaga; removal of Convention troops; seditious papers; fortifications; movements of troops; inhabitants of German Flats; want of money. Draft. 7 pp. In handwriting of Robert Hanson Harrison.   A. IV, pt. I, 63

Printed, in part: Writings of Washington (Ford) N. Y. 1890. 7, 223.

1778
OCT. 22

Continental Congress, President. Philadelphia. To [George] Washington [Fredericksburg]. Transmitting resolves and intelligence from New York. Letter-book copy.   C. C. 13, II, 125

1778
OCT. 22

Continental Congress, Resolve. Maj. Gen. [Horatio] Gates to take command at Boston. Contemporary copy attested by Richard Kidder Meade. 1 p. Transmitted to Washington.   **W**

1778
OCT. 22

Clinton, George, Ph[ilip John] **Schuyler**, and Edward **Hand**. Poughkeepsie [New York]. To [George Washington Fredericksburg]. Report on the expediency of an expedition against the Indians and their town of Chemung. Contemporary copy. 2 pp. In handwriting of Richard Kidder Meade. Enclosed in Washington to the President of Congress, 1778, Oct. 27. **C. C. 152**, 6, 423

1778
OCT. 23

Continental Congress, President. [Philadelphia.] To [George] Washington [Fredericksburg]. The Refugee petition to the British Peace Commissioners; Maj. Gen. [Horatio] Gates to command Eastern District. Letter-book copy.
C. C. 13, II, 127

1778
OCT. 24

Washington, George. Fredericksburg. To [the President of Congress, Philadelphia]. Reenlistments; clothing and bounties. Draft. 6 pp. In handwriting of Robert Hanson Harrison. Read in Congress, Oct. 31. Referred to the Committee to prepare a plan for procuring reinforcements etc.: Duer, Sherman, R. H. Lee and G. Morris.
A. IV, pt. I, 71
Printed: Writings of Washington (Ford) N. Y. 1890. 7, 226.

1778
OCT. 24

Continental Congress, Resolve. Attack on Canada. D. S. of Charles Thomson. 1 p. Enclosed in Committee of Foreign Affairs to Washington, 1778, Oct. 27.
28, 103

1778
OCT. 24

Dupui, Nicholas, John **Chambers** and Benjamin and John **Van Campen**. [Lower Smithfield, Northampton County, Pennsylvania.] To George Bryan [Philadelphia]. Defenceless condition of frontier; need of assistance. A. L. S. of Dupui, signed also by the others. 1 p. **91**, 216
Transmitted to Congress. Read, Oct. 30. Referred in President of Congress, 1778. Nov 1 to Washington "to take order thereon."

1778
OCT. 25

Continental Congress, President. [Philadelphia] To [George] Washington [Fredericksburg]. Case of Dominique L'Eglise. Letter book copy.
C. C. 13, II, 131

1778
OCT. 26

Washington, George. Fredericksburg. To [the President of Congress, Philadelphia]. Sailing of a fleet from New York. Draft. 2 pp. In handwriting of James McHenry. Read in Congress, Oct. 31.
A. IV, pt. I, 81

1778
Oct. 26
Continental Congress, Resolve. Rendezvous for Pulaski's cavalry. Contemporary copy. 1 p. In handwriting of George Bond. Enclosed in President of Congress to Washington, 1778, Oct. 30.

91, 215

1778
Oct. 26
Continental Congress, Orders. Plan of attack on Canada submitted to Washington; secrecy etc. D. S. of Charles Thomson. 1 p. Enclosed in Committee of Foreign Affairs to Washington, 1778, Oct. 27.

28, 104

[1778]
[Oct. 26]
Canada, Plan of attack on. Side expeditions against Detroit and Niagara; forces, rendezvous etc.; move against Quebec and Halifax; importance of project to France and America; other considerations; general plan of operations. D. S. of Henry Laurens, attested by Charles Thomson. 8 pp. Enclosed in Committee of Foreign Affairs to Washington, 1778, Oct. 27.   28, 105

1778
Oct. 26
Continental Congress, Resolves. Intelligence from Canada. D. S. of Charles Thomson. 1 p. Enclosed in Committee of Foreign Affairs, 1778, Oct. 27.

28, 111

1778
Oct. 26
Morris, Gouverneur. Philadelphia. To [George] Washington [Fredericksburg.] Designs of enemy; currency depreciation; memorial of officers of army to Congress; strictures thereon; discussion in Congress over [Maj] Gen. [Charles] Lee's courtmartial; [Maj.] Gen. [Thomas] Conway's application; support of cavalry horses. A. L. S. 3 pp.

28, 85

The above mentioned memorial, dated Sep. 13, 1778, was sent to Congress without Washington's knowledge Sep. 22, read before Congress, Oct. 20 and ordered to lie on the table. The original is in C. C. 41, 7: 195, 196, 200 and 202.

[1778]
Oct. 27
Washington, George. [Fredericksburg]. To [the President of Congress, Philadelphia]. Impracticability of the expedition against Chemung. Draft. 1 p. In handwriting of James McHenry.

A. IV, pt. I, 83

1778
Oct. 27
Washington, George. [Fredericksburg]. To the Board of War [Philadelphia]. Size of blankets procured. Draft. 1 p. In handwriting of Robert Hanson Harrison.   A. IV, pt. I, 85

1778
Oct. 27
Continental Congress, Committee for Foreign Affairs. To Washington. Plan for attacking Canada. A. L.

S. of James Lovell, signed also by Richard Henry Lee. 2 pp. **28**, 101

1778
Oct. 27

Continental Army. Return of number of men from the different regiments whose term of service will expire before spring. A. D. of Tench Tilghman. 1 p. **A.** IV, pt. I, 79

1778
Oct. 27

Continental Army. Expiration of enlistments. Return of numbers by states and brigades of expirations before the spring of 1779. Tabular statement. A. D. of Tench Tilghman. 1 p. Enclosed in Washington to the President of Congress, 1778, Oct. 31? **C. C.** 152, 6, 43

1778
Oct. 29

Washington, George. Fredericksburg. To [the President of Congress, Philadelphia]. Movements of enemy and of the Continental Army; Quartermaster General and flour magazines. Draft. 3 pp. In handwriting of Robert Hanson Harrison.
A. IV, pt. I, 87

1778
Oct. 30

Continental Congress, President. [Philadelphia.] To [George] Washington [Fredericksburg]. Transmitting correspondence and resolves; various commissions granted; money for Paymaster General. Letter-book copy. **C. C.** 13, II, 140

1778
Oct. 31

Washington, George. Fredericksburg. To [the President of Congress, Philadelphia]. [Dominique] L'Eglise; Dr. [John] Connolly; movements of enemy in New York bay. Draft. 2 pp. In handwriting of Robert Hanson Harrison. Read in Congress, Nov. 5. **A.** IV, pt. I, 91

1778
Oct. 31

Hamilton, James. Cambridge [Massachusetts]. To Maj. Gen. [William] Heath [Boston]. Request for transportation of sick and wounded by water to Virginia. Contemporary copy. 1 p. In handwriting of Caleb Gibbs. Enclosed in Washington to the President of Congress 1778, Nov. 12. **C. C.** 152, 6, 483

1778
Nov. 1

Continental Congress, President. [Philadelphia.] To [George] Washington, Fredericksburg. Committee to prepare plan for reenforcing army; Chemung expedition; minor matters and printed manifestoes to be' distributed among enemy. Letter-book copy. **C. C.** 13, II, 143

1778
Nov. 5

Washington, George. Fredericksburg. To Maj. [George Augustine] Washington near Bedford [New

York].   Orders to command dragoons at Bristol [Connecticut].   L. S.   1 p.   In handwriting of Tench Tilghman.   Enclosed in Washington to the President of Congress, 1778, Nov. 6?

C. C.   152, 6, 439

1778
Nov. 6

Washington, George.   [Fredericksburg.]   To [the President of Congress, Philadelphia].   Minor military matters; intelligence of the enemy.   Draft.   1 p. In handwriting of Robert Hanson Harrison. Read in Congress, Nov. 10.   A.   IV, pt. I, 93

1778
Nov. 6

Continental Congress, President.   Philadelphia.   To [George] Washington, Fredericksburg.   Dr. [John] Connolly's case; letter from State of New Jersey; minor military matters.   Letter-book copy.   C. C.   13, II, 151

1778
Nov. 10

Clinton, [Sir] H[enry].   New York.   To [George] Washington [Fredericksburg].   Exchange of Convention troops.   Contemporary copy.   1 p.   In handwriting of Richard Kidder Meade.   Enclosed in Washington to the President of Congress, 1778, Dec. 16.   C. C.   152, 6, 493

1778
Nov. 11

Washington, George.   [Fredericksburg.]   To [the President of Congress, Philadelphia].   Opinion of practicability of attempt against Canada, Detroit and Niagara.   Draft.   26 pp.   In handwriting of Robert Hanson Harrison.   Read in Congress, Nov. 19.   Referred to the Committee on the letters of the Marquis de Lafayette.

A.   IV, pt. I, 95

Printed: Writings of Washington (Ford) N. Y. 1890. 7, 239.
Committee: S. Adams, G. Morris and Drayton.

1778
Nov. 11

Washington, George.   Fredericksburg.   To the Board of War [Philadelphia].   Shoes and clothing.   Draft. 4 pp.   In handwriting of Tench Tilghman.

A.   IV, pt. I, 123

1778
Nov. 11

Fisher, Frederich.   Tryon County [New York].   To [Brig.] Gen. [Edward] Hand [Coughnawaga, New York]. Account of Indian attack on Cherry Valley.   Contemporary copy.   In handwriting of Richard Kidder Meade.   Enclosed in Washington to the President of Congress, 1778, Nov. 16.

C. C.   152, 6, 511

1778
Nov. 11

Morris, Gouveneur. Philadelphia. To [George] Washington [Fredericksburg]. Duties on committees; subsistence of army; location of army; suggestion as to disposition of troops for the winter; horses of the cavalry; Washington's visit to Congress. A. L. S. 4 pp.   **28, 310**

1778
Nov. 11

Webster, Alexander. Cambridge [New York]. To Brig. Gen. [Abraham] Ten Broeck [Albany]. British attack on Skeensborough. Contemporary copy. In handwriting of Tench Tilghman. Enclosed in Washington to the President of Congress, 1778, Nov. 21.   **C. C. 152, 6, 537**

1778
Nov. 12

Washington, George. Fredericksburg. To [the President of Congress, Philadelphia]. A request of Brig. Gen. [James] Hamilton. Draft. 1 p. In handwriting of Tench Tilghman. Read in Congress. Referred to Board of War.
       A. IV, pt. I, 127

1778
Nov. 12

Johnston, James [Philadelphia.] To [George Washington? Fredericksburg]. Ration, deficiency, etc. A. L. S. 1 p.   **95, 97**

1778
Nov. 12

Ten Broeck, Abraham. Albany [New York]. To [Brig.] Gen. [Edward] Hand [Coughnawaga, New York]. Ordering forward the militia. Contemporary copy. In handwriting of Tench Tilghman. Enclosed in Washington to the President of Congress, 1778, Nov. 21.   **C. C. 152, 6, 537**

1778
Nov. 12

Kloch, Jacob. Four miles from Cherry Valley [New York]. To [Brig.] Gen. [Edward] Hand [Coughnawaga, New York]. Report of Indian attack on Cherry Valley. Contemporary copy. In handwriting of Richard Kidder Meade. Enclosed in Washington to the President of Congress, 1778, Nov. 16.   **C. C. 152, 6, 511**

1778
Nov. 13

Washington, George. Fredericksburg. To [the President of Congress, Philadelphia]. Baron Steuben and the footing of the Inspectorship. Draft. 1 p. In handwriting of Alexander Hamilton. Read in Congress, Nov. 23.   **A. IV, pt. I, 129**

1778
Nov. 13

Hand, Edward. Conghnawaga [New York]. To [George] Washington [Fredericksburg]. Indian attack on Cherry Valley. Contemporary copy. In handwriting of Richard Kidder Meade. Enclosed in

Washington to the President of Congress, 1778,
Nov. 16.   C. C.   152, 6, 511

1778
Nov. 13

Whiting, Daniel.   Fort Alden [New York].   To Brig. Gen.
[Edward] Hand [Coughnawaga, New York].   At-
tack on the fort, pressing need of reenforcement.
Contemporary copy.   In handwriting of Tench
Tilghman.   Enclosed in Washington to the Presi-
dent of Congress, 1778, Nov. 21.

C. C.   152, 6, 541

1778
Nov. 14

Washington, George.   Fredericksburg.   To [the President
of Congress, Philadelphia].   Exchange of convention prisoners.   Draft.   1 p.   In handwriting
of Tench Tilghman.   Read in Congress, Nov. 18.
Referred to Board of War.   **A.**   IV, pt. I, 131

1778
Nov. 14

[Washington, George.]   Fred[ericksbur]g.   To [Henry
Laurens, Philadelphia].   The Canadian expedi-
tion; French motives and dangers therefrom.
Draft.   5 pp.   In handwriting of Alexander
Hamilton.   **P.**   I, pt. II, 207

Printed: Writings of Washington (Ford) N. Y. 1890. 7, 260.

1778
Nov. 14

Washington, George.   [Fredericksburg.]   To Sir Henry
Clinton [New York].   Exchange of Convention
troops. Contemporary copy.   1 p.   Enclosed in
Washington to the President of Congress, 1778,
Dec. 16.   C. C.   152, 6, 501

1778
Nov. 14

Continental Congress, President.   Fredericksburg.   To
[George] Washington, Fredericksburg.   Transmitting action of Congress on Dr. [John] Connolly's case.   Letter-book copy.   **C. C.**   13, II, 161

1778
Nov. 14

Whiting, Daniel.   Cherry Valley [New York].   To Col.
[Zebulon?] Butler [Tryon County? New York].
Account of massacre at Cherry Valley.   Con-
temporary copy.   1 p.   In handwriting of Caleb
Gibbs.   Enclosed in Washington to the President
of Congress, 1778, Nov. 23.   C. C.   152, 6, 553

1778
Nov. 14

Fonda, Jellis.   To Col. G[oose] Van Schaick [Mt. Johnson,
New York].   Attack on Fort Plank.   Contem-
porary copy.   In handwriting of Tench Tilghman.
Enclosed in Washington to the President of Congress, 1778, Nov. 21.   C. C.   152, 6, 541

1778
Nov. 14

Gordon, James.   Fort Plank [New York].   To Col. Goose
Van Schaick [Mt. Johnson, New York].   Capture
of Fort Alden.   Contemporary copy.   In hand-

writing of Tench Tilghman.   Enclosed in Washington to the President of Congress, 1778, Nov. 21.   C. C.   152, 6, 541

1778
Nov. 15
Continental Congress, President.   Philadelphia.   To [George] Washington, Fredericksburg.   Col. [Thomas] Hartley's letter to the Board of War. Letter-book copy.   C. C.   13, II, 164

1778
Nov. 15
Clyde, Samuel. [Cherry Valley, New York.] To Col. [Frederick] Fisher [Tryon County, New York]. Alarm at Cherry Valley.   Contemporary copy. 1 p.   In handwriting of Caleb Gibbs.   Enclosed in Washington to the President of Congress, 1778, Nov. 23.   C. C.   152, 6, 557

1778
Nov. 15
Hand, Edward.   Schenectady [New York].   To Gov. George Clinton [Poughkeepsie, New York.] Cherry Valley massacre and capture of Fort Alden.

[Nov. 15]
Van Schaick, Goose.   Mount Johnson [New York].   To [Brig.] Gen. [Edward] Hand.   Transmitting account of attack on Fort Plank.   Contemporary copies.   In handwriting of Tench Tilghman. Enclosed in Washington to the President of Congress, 1778, Nov. 21.   C. C.   152, 6, 541

1778
Nov. 16
Washington, George.   Fredericksburg.   To [the President of Congress, Philadelphia].   Du Portail's visit to Congress; his value to America; memorial on fortification system.   Draft.   2 pp.   In handwriting of Alexander Hamilton.   Read in Congress Nov. 21.   Letter referred to Board of War, memorial to Marine Committee.   A. IV, pt. I, 133

1778
Nov. 16
Washington, George.   Fredericksburg.   To [the President of Congress, Philadelphia].   Indian surprise in Cherry Valley; dispositions for protection of the frontier.   Draft.   2 pp.   In handwriting of Alexander Hamilton.   Read in Congress Nov. 21.   A. IV, pt. I, 135

1778
Nov. 17
Clinton, George.   Poughkeepsie [New York].   To [George] Washington [Fredericksburg].   Attack on Cherry Valley.   Contemporary copy.   1 p.   In handwriting of Tench Tilghman.   Enclosed in Washington to the President of Congress, 1778, Nov. 21.   C. C.   152, 6, 535

1778
Nov. 17

Stirling, [William Alexander, Lord].   Elizabethtown [New Jersey].   To [George] Washington [Fredericksburg].   British fleet at New York; condition, movements, etc.   Contemporary copy.   1 p.   In handwriting of Richard Kidder Meade.   Enclosed in Washington to the President of Congress, 1778, Nov. 23.   C. C.   152, 6, 559

1778
Nov. 18

Washington, George.   Fredericksburg.   To [the President of Congress, Philadelphia].   Introducing Count Kolkowski.   Draft.   1 p.   In handwriting of Richard Kidder Meade.   Read in Congress Nov. 25.   Referred to Board of War.

A.   IV, pt. I, 137

1778
Nov. 18

Washington, George.   Fredericksburg.   To the Board of War [Philadelphia].   March of the Convention troops to Virginia.   Draft.   2 pp.   In hand-writing of Tench Tilghman.   A.   IV, pt. I, 139

1778
Nov. 18

[Hand, Edward.]   Albany.   To [George Washington, Fredericksburg].   Enemy in Cherry Valley.   Extract of letter.   1 p.   In handwriting of Richard Kidder Meade.   Enclosed in Washington to the President of Congress, 1778, Nov. 23.

C. C.   152, 6, 555

1778
Nov. 18

Continental Congress, President.   Philadelphia.   To [George] Washington, Fredericksburg.   Receipt of certain letters.   Letter-book copy.

C. C.   13, II, 171

1778
Nov. 18

[Sullivan, John.]   [Providence, Rhode Island.]   To [George Washington, Fredericksburg].   British fleet at Rhode Island.   [Extract of letter.]   1 p. In handwriting of Caleb Gibbs.   Enclosed in Washington to the President of Congress, 1778, Nov. 23.   C. C.   152, 6, 561

[1778]
[Nov. 19]

Washington, George.   Fredericksburg.   To [the President of Congress, Philadelphia].   Arrangement and commissions for officers in Armand's corps. Draft.   2 pp.   In handwriting of Alexander Hamilton.   A.   IV, pt. I, 141

1778
Nov. 19

Washington, George.   Fredericksburg.   To [Col. Jeremiah] Wadsworth [Fredericksburg].   Magazine of sup-plies at Albany.   Transcript.   C. C.   169, 5, 510

1778
Nov. 19

Continental Congress, Resolves.   Empowering [George] Washington to effect an exchange of prisoners.

Contemporary copy. 2 pp. In handwriting of
Geo. Bond. C. C. 152, 6, 573

1778
Nov. 20

Washington, George. Fredericksburg. To [the President of Congress, Philadelphia]. Payment and
service of militia regiment in the Coos country
[New Hampshire]. Draft. 2 pp. In handwriting
of Robert Hanson Harrison. Read in Congress
Nov. 27. Ordered that the regiment be disbanded.
A. IV, pt. I, 143

1778
Nov. 20

Washington, George. Fredericksburg. Commission to
Lt. Cols. Robert Hanson Harrison and Alexander
Hamilton to negotiate exchange of prisoners.
Contemporary copy. 3 pp. Enclosed in Washington to the President of Congress, 1778,
Dec. 16. C. C. 152, 6, 519

1778
Nov. 20

Continental Congress, President. Philadelphia. To
[George] Washington, Fredericksburg. Referring of papers; transmitting resolves, treaty of
Amity and Commerce with France. Letter-book
copy. C. C. 13, II, 183

1778
Nov. 20

Laurens, Henry. Philadelphia. To [George] Washington
[Fredericksburg]. Invasion of Canada; relations
with France; loans and interest; debt; taxation;
jobbery of members of Congress; aspect of affairs.
A. L. S. 6 pp. 29, 122

1778
Nov. 20

Wheelock, John. Paulings Precinct [New York]. To
[George] Washington [Fredericksburg]. Principles on which Col. Timothy Bedel's regiment was
raised and reasons for its continuance. Contemporary copy. 3 pp. In handwriting of Richard
Kidder Meade. Enclosed in Washington to the
President of Congress, 1778, Nov. 20.
C. C. 152, 6, 527

1778
Nov. 21

Washington, George. Fredericksburg. To [the President of Congress, Philadelphia]. Attack on Fort
Alden [New York]; protection of frontiers; march
of the Convention troops. Draft. 1 p. In handwriting of James McHenry. Read in Congress,
Nov. 27. Referred to Board of War.
A. IV, pt. I, 147

1778
Nov. 21

Washington, George. Fredericksburg. To [the President of Congress, Philadelphia]. [Pierre] Penet's

request for a brevet commission. Draft. 1 p. In handwriting of Alexander Hamilton.
A. IV, pt. I, 149

1778
Nov. 23

Washington, George. [Fredericksburg.] To [the President of Congress, Philadelphia]. Introducing John Temple. Draft. 1 p. In handwriting of Robert Hanson Harrison. Read in Congress, Dec. 3.
A. IV, pt. I, 151

1778
Nov. 23

Washington, George. Fredericksburg. To the Board of War [Philadelphia]. Clothing; route of the Convention troops. Draft. 3 pp. In handwriting of Tench Tilghman.
A. IV, pt. I, 153
Printed: Writings of Washington (Sparks) Boston. 1834. 6, 121.

1778
Nov. 23

Washington, George. Fredericksburg. To Joseph Reed [Philadelphia]. Case of Col. [John] Cadwallader. D. S. 1 p. In handwriting of James McHenry.
A. IV, pt. I, 157

1778
Nov. 23

Washington, George. Fredericksburg. To [the President of Congress, Philadelphia]. Situation on the frontier; moves of enemy; payment and supplies for Maj. [Benjamin] Whitcomb's corps; need of cannon; march of the Convention troops. Draft. 5 pp. In handwriting of Robert Hanson Harrison. Read in Congress, Nov. 30.
A. IV, pt. I, 159

1778
Nov. 24

Continental Congress, Resolve. Pay for deranged officers. Broadside. Printed by Claypoole. Enclosed in President of Congress to Washington, 1779, May 25.
93, 167

1778
Nov. 26

Washington, George. Fredericksburg. To [the President of Congress, Philadelphia]. [John] Dodge's information of the Indian country. Draft. 3 pp. In handwriting of Robert Hanson Harrison. Read in Congress, Dec. 2. Referred to Board of War.
A. IV, pt. I, 165

1778
Nov. 26

Continental Congress, President. Philadelphia. To [George] Washington [Fredericksburg]. Transmitting resolves; Lt. Col's commission to Maj. [William Augustine] Washington; Col. [Moses] Hazen's regiment. Letter-book copy. C. C. 13, II, 188

1778
Nov. 27

Washington, George. Fredericksburg. To [the President of Congress, Philadelphia]. Exchange of prisoners; disposition of the various brigades in winter quarters. Draft. 3 pp. In handwriting of Alexander Hamilton. Read in Congress, Dec. 3. **A.** IV, pt. I, 169

Printed: Writings of Washington (Ford) N. Y. 1890. 7, 275.

[1778]
[Nov. 27]
Washington, George. Fredericksburg. To [the Board of War, Philadelphia]. Clothing for army. Draft. 1 p. In handwriting of James McHenry.
A. IV, pt. I, 173

1778
Nov. 27
Washington, George. Fredericksburg. To Joseph Reed [Philadelphia]. Inquiry into conduct of officer in charge of Baylor's dragoons; restoration of credit; paper money; factional spirit; conduct of enemy; arrangement of army. Auto. draft signed. 2 pp. **P.** I, pt. II, 215

1778
Nov. 27
[**Washington, George.**] Fredericksburg. To Gouverneur Morris [Philadelphia]. Disposition of army in winter quarters. Draft. 2 pp. In handwriting of Robert Hanson Harrison. **P.** I, pt. II, 219

Printed: Writings of Washington (Sparks) Boston. 1834. 6, 129.

1778
Nov. 27
Washington, George. Fredericksburg. To Sir Henry Clinton [New York]. Commissioners to arrange exchange of prisoners. Contemporary copy. 1 p. Enclosed in Washington to the President of Congress, 1778, Dec. 16. **C. C.** 152, 6, 571

1778
Nov. 27
Continental Congress, President. [Philadelphia.] To [George] Washington [Fredericksburg]. [Maj.] Gen. [William] Heath's letter. Letter-book copy. **C. C.** 13, II, 189

1778
Nov. 28
Continental Congress, President. [Philadelphia.] To [George] Washington [en route to Middlebrook, New Jersey]. Action of Congress on miscellaneous military matters; papers etc. transmitted. Letter-book copy. **C. C.** 13, II, 190

1778
Dec. 1
Washington, George. [Fredericksburg.] To Maj. Gen. [Philip John] Schuyler [Albany]. Magazines for supplies for northern operations. Transcript. Enclosed in Washington to the President of Congress, 1779, Aug. 15. **C. C.** 169, 5, 509

1778
Dec. 2
Clinton, [Sir] H[enry]. [New York.] To Gen. [George] Washington [Fredericksburg]. Arrangements for meeting of commissioners to effect an exchange of prisoners. Contemporary copy. 2 pp. Enclosed in Washington to the President of Congress, 1778, Dec. 16. **C. C.** 152, 6, 575

1778
Dec. 2

Continental Congress, President. Philadelphia. To [George] Washington [Fredericksburg]. Transmitting resolves. Letter-book copy.

C. C. 13, II, 193

1778
Dec. 4

Washington, George. Elizabethtown [New Jersey]. To [the President of Congress, Philadelphia]. Sick officers and men of the Convention troops. Draft. 2 pp. In handwriting of Robert Hanson Harrison. Read in Congress, Dec. 7. Referred to Board of War. A. IV, pt. I, 175

1778
Dec. 4

Washington, George. Elizabethtown. To [the Board of War, Philadelphia]. Movement of troops. Draft. 1 p. In handwriting of Tench Tilghman.

A. IV, pt. I, 177

1778
Dec. 5

Continental Congress, President. [Philadelphia.] To [George] Washington [Fredericksburg]. Transmitting resolves. Letter-book copy.

C. C. 13, II, 205

1778
Dec. 5

Harrison, Robert H[anson]. Elizabethtown [New Jersey]. To [the President of Congress, Philadelphia]. Movement of enemy up the North River; disposition of American troops. A. L. S. 3 pp. Read in Congress, Dec. 7. C. C. 152, 6, 593

1778
Dec. 6

Continental Congress, President. [Philadelphia.] To [George] Washington [Paramus, New Jersey]. Transmitting resolve; promotion of Lt. Henry P. Livingston; German Volunteer Corps; deserters; minor military matters. Letter-book copy.

C. C. 13, II, 207

1778
Dec. 7

Washington, George. Paramus. To [the President of Congress, Philadelphia]. Movements of enemy. Draft. 2 pp. In handwriting of Tench Tilghman. Read in Congress, Sept. 12.

A. IV, pt. I, 179

1778
Dec. 7

Clinton, [Sir] H[enry]. New York. Commission to Cols. Charles O'Hara and West Hyde to negotiate an exchange of prisoners. Contemporary copy. 1 p. In handwriting of Robert Hanson Harrison. Enclosed in Washington to the President of Congress, 1778, Dec. 16. C. C. 152, 7, 21

1778
Dec. 8

Continental Congress, President. [Philadelphia.] To [George] Washington [Paramus]. Intention to resign. Letter-book copy.

C. C. 13, II, 210

1778
Dec. 12

Continental Congress, President. Philadelphia. To [George] Washington, Middlebrook. Opening correspondence as President of Congress and transmitting resolve. Letter-book copy.

C. C. 14, 1

1778
Dec. 12

Harrison, Robert Hanson and Alexander Hamilton. To Charles O'Hara and West Hyde. See: Harrison and Hamilton to Washington. 1778. Dec. 15.

1778
Dec. 12

O'Hara, Charles and West Hyde. To Robert Hanson Harrison and Alexander Hamilton. See: Harrison and Hamilton to Washington. 1778. Dec. 15.

1778
Dec. 13

Washington, George. Middlebrook, [New Jersey]. To the President of Congress [Philadelphia]. Transmitting letter on report of Committee on Canadian Affairs [See: Washington to President of Congress this date]; exchange of prisoners. Draft. 1 p. In handwriting of Tench Tilghman. Read in Congress, Dec. 17. A. IV, pt. I, 181

1778
Dec. 13

Washington, George. Middlebrook. To the President of Congress [Philadelphia]. Lt. Col. Fleury's furlough. Draft. 2 pp. In handwriting of Tench Tilghman. Read in Congress, Dec. 17. Referred to Laurens, M. Smith, G. Morris, S. Adams, and Burke. A. IV, pt. I, 183

1778
Dec. 13

Washington, George. Middlebrook. To the President of Congress [Philadelphia]. Embarrassments in plan of Canadian expedition. Draft. 6 pp. In handwriting of James McHenry and Washington. Read in Congress, Dec. 17. Referred to Laurens, M. Smith, G. Morris, S. Adams, and Burke.

A. IV, pt. I, 185
Printed: Writings of Washington (Ford) N. Y. 1890. 7, 285.

1778
Dec. 13

Washington, George. Middlebrook. To the Board of War [Philadelphia]. Israel [John?] Dodge; leather breeches and clothing for troops. Draft. 1 p. In handwriting of Tench Tilghman.

A. IV, pt. I, 191

1778
Dec. 14

Connecticut, Danbury. Selectmen and others. To Congress. Memorial protesting against Dr. [Isaac] Foster. D. S. of Thaddeus Benedict and twenty-nine others. 2 pp. Read in Congress, Jan. 14, 1779. Referred to Medical Committee. Enclosed in Medical Committee to Washington, 1779, Nov. 15. 92, 307

1778
DEC. 15

Harrison, Robert Hanson and Alexander **Hamilton.** [Middlebrook.] To [George] Washington [Middlebrook]. Report of negotiations for an exchange of prisoners, containing copy of letter of Cols. O'Hara and Hyde, Dec. 12, respecting convention officers and soldiers and Harrison and Hamilton's answer to same, Dec. 12. Contemporary copy. 7 pp. In handwriting of Harrison. Enclosed in Washington to the President of Congress, 1778, Dec. 16.   C. C. **152, 7, 27**

1778
DEC. 16

Washington, George. Middlebrook. To the President of Congress, Philadelphia. Failure to secure an exchange of prisoners. Draft. 1 p. In handwriting of Robert Hanson Harrison.

A. **IV, pt. I, 193**
Printed, in part: Writings of Washington (Ford) N. Y. 1890. 7, 26, note.

1778
DEC. 16

Continental Congress, Resolve. Formation of the new 11th. Pennsylvania regiment. Contemporary copy, attested by Peter Scull. Enclosed in Board of War to Washington, 1779, May 21.   **94, 115.**

1778
DEC. 16

Continental Congress, Resolve. Composition of 11th. Pennsylvania regiment; troops incorporated therein. Contemporary copy, attested by Peter Scull. 2 pp. Transmitted to Washington.

Miscel.

1778
DEC. 18

Washington, George. Middlebrook. To the President of Congress [Philadelphia]. Compliments on his election as President of Congress. Draft. 2 pp. In handwriting of Robert Hanson Harrison.

A. **IV, pt. I, 195**
Printed: Writings of Washington (Sparks) Boston. 1834. 6, 141.

1778
DEC. 18

Washington, George. Middlebrook. To Charles Thomson [Philadelphia]. Election of John Jay as President of Congress. Draft. 1 p. In handwriting of Robert Hanson Harrison.

A. **IV, pt. I, 197**

1778
DEC. 18

W[ashington,] G[eorge]. Middlebrook. To Henry Laurens [Philadelphia]. Resignation of the Presidency of Congress. Draft. 2 pp. In handwriting of Robert Hanson Harrison. **P. I, pt. II, 237**

1778
DEC. 18

[**Washington,** George.] Middlebrook. To John Jay. Election to the Presidency of Congress. Draft. 2 pp. In handwriting of Robert Hanson Harrison.   **P. I, pt. II, 241**

1778
DEC. 18

Continental Congress, President.   Philadelphia.   To [George] Washington [Middlebrook].   Approaching interview of Washington and Congress.   Letter-book copy.   C. C.   14, 3

1778
DEC. 20

Washington, George.   Middlebrook.   To [the Board of War, Philadelphia].   Returns; terms of service; escort for Convention troops; military prisoners. Draft.   4 pp.   In handwriting of Tench Tilghman.   A. IV, pt. I, 199

1778
DEC. 28

[Livingston, William Smith.]   [Beverwyck, New Jersey]. To [Lt. Col. Ebenezer Huntington, Beverwyck]. Resignation.   [Extract of letter.]   Contemporary copy.   In handwriting of Jonathan Trumbull jr. Enclosed in Board of War to Washington, 1782, Oct. 10.   98, 215

1778
DEC. 29

Washington, George.   Philadelphia.   To Benjamin Franklin [Passy].   Introducing Lafayette.   Draft.   3 pp.   In handwriting of John Laurens.
                                                    A. IV, pt. I, 203
Printed: Writings of Washington (Sparks) Boston. 1834. 6, 148.

1778
DEC. 29

[Clinton, George.]   Poughkeepsie [New York].   To [George] Washington [Philadelphia].   Payment of inhabitants for supplies taken for the army. [Extract of letter.]   2 pp.   In handwriting of Tench Tilghman.   Enclosed in Washington to the President of Congress, 1779, Jan. 29.
                                                    C. C.   152, 7, 53

1778
DEC. 31

Washington, George.   Philadelphia.   To [the President of Congress, Philadelphia].   Case of Du Portail. Draft.   2 pp.   In handwriting of Alexander Hamilton.   Read in Congress, Jan. 1, 1779.
                                                    A. IV, pt. I, 207

1778

Order of Divine Providence.   List of officers and members. Printed pamphlet.   20 pp.   Enclosed in Washington to the President of Congress, 1783, Aug. 28.   C. C. 152, 11, 447

1779
JAN. 1

Washington, George.   Philadelphia.   To the President of Congress [Philadelphia].   Destruction of a barn by the Convention troops.   Draft.   1 p.   In handwriting of Robert Hanson Harrison.
                                                    A. IV, pt. I, 209

1779
JAN. 1

Bayley, Jacob.   Newbury [New Hampshire].   To Maj. Gen. [Horatio] Gates [Boston].   Intelligence from

Canada; strength of British etc. Contemporary
copy. 1 p. Transmitted to Washington.

93, 22

1779   **Bayley,** Jacob. Newbury [New Hampshire]. Situation in
JAN. 2   Canada. Contemporary copy. 1 p. Transmitted to Washington.   93, 21

1779   **MacPherson,** William. [Philadelphia]. Petition to Con-
JAN. 6   gress. Resignation from British army; applica-
tion for commission. Contemporary copy. 2
pp. In handwriting of Timothy Pickering, jr.
Enclosed in Board of War to Washington, 1779,
Mar. 25.   93, 57

1779   **Board of War.** [Philadelphia] To [George] Washington,
JAN. 7   Philadelphia. Mittens; officer's servants; horses
for dragoon officers. A. L. S. of Richard
Peters. 2 pp. Answered Jan. 9.*   93, 199

1779   **Pennsylvania Council.** Order recommending William
JAN. 7   MacPherson to Congress. Contemporary copy.
1 p. In handwriting of Timothy Pickering jr.
Enclosed in Board of War to Washington, 1779,
Mar. 25.   93, 59

1779   **Washington,** George. Philadelphia. To the Committee
JAN. 8   of Conference [Philadelphia]. Transmitting min-
utes of heads requiring attention. A. L. S. 1 p.
A. IV, pt. I, 211
Committee: Duane, Root, M. Smith, G. Morris and Laurens.

1779   **Washington,** George. [Philadelphia.] To [the Commit-
JAN. 8   tee of Conference]. Minutes of heads of matters
requiring attention: State of army; plans of campaign; supplies. D. S. 5 pp. In handwriting
of Alexander Hamilton. An A. D. of same,
6 pp., will be found in A, IV, pt. I, 213.
Printed: Writings of Washington (Ford) N. Y. 1890. 7, 309, note.
Miscel

1779   [**Livingston,** William Smith.] [Beverwyck, New Jersey.]
JAN. 8   To [Lt. Col. Ebenezer Huntington, Beverwyck].
Pay. [Extract of letter.] In handwriting of Jonathan Trumbull, jr. Enclosed in Board of War
to Washington, 1782, Oct. 10.   98, 215

1779   **Washington,** George. Philadelphia. To [the Board of
JAN. 9   War, Philadelphia]. Mittens for soldiers; officers' servants; horses. Draft. 2 pp. In handwriting of Tench Tilghman. A. IV, pt. I, 219

To Majr Genl Lee.

Sir

The late movement of the Enemy, (& the pro-
bability of their having designs upon the Jerseys
(confirm'd by sundry accounts from deserters and
prisoners) rendering it necessary to throw a body
of troops over the North river, I shall immediately
follow; and the command of the army (what remains
after General Heath's division marches to Peekskill)
devolving upon you, I have to request

⅟ That you will be particularly attentive
that all the intrenching & other tools (excepting
those in immediate use) be got together, &
delivered to the Quarter Master General, or
Majr Reed, who heretofore has been intrusted
with them.

That you will direct the commanding
officer of Artillery, to exert himself, in having
the Army well supplied with Musket Cartridges; for this purpose, a convenient place,
at a distance, should be fixed on, that the
business may go on uninterrupted.

That no troops who have been furnished with Arms, Accoutrements, or Camp
utensils be suffered to depart the Camp; before
they have delivered them, either to the Commissary
of Stores, or the Quarter Master General, (or his
Assistant) as the case may be, taking receipts
therefore, in exoneration of those which they
have passed. In a particular manner
let the tents be taken care of, & committed to
the Quarter Mr Genls care.

A little time now, must manifest

WRITING OF WILLIAM GRAYSON.

1779
JAN. 9

Continental Congress, Resolves.   Pay and supplies for American prisoners of war. Broadside. 1 p. Printed by Dunlap. Transmitted to Washington.
92, 320

1779
JAN. 9

Continental Congress, Resolve.   Raising an additional battalion in Virginia. Transmitted to Washington. D. S. of Charles Thomson. 2 p.   **W**

1779
JAN. 9

Continental Congress, Committee of Conference.   Philadelphia. To [George] Washington [Philadelphia]. Arrangement of army; preparation of a system. A. L. S. of James Duane. 2 pp.   30, 71
Committee appointed Dec. 24: Duane, Root, M. Smith, G. Morris and Laurens.

1779
JAN. 9

Board of War. [Philadelphia.] To [George] Washington [Philadelphia]. Reimbursement for deficiencies in clothing of Connecticut regiment for 1777; pay for North·Carolina dragoons. A. L. S. of Timothy Pickering, jr. 2 pp.   92, 321

1779
JAN. 10

Board of War. [Philadelphia.] To [George] Washington [Philadelphia]. Intelligence of [Brig.] Gen. [Lachlan] McIntosh's Indian Expedition. A. L. S. of Richard Peters. 2 pp.   92, 324

1779
JAN. 11

Washington, George. Philadelphia. To the Committee of Conference. Commissary of Prisoners department; proposed expedition against the Indian country. Draft. 6 pp. In handwriting of John Laurens.   **A.** IV, pt. I, 221
Printed: Writings of Washington (Ford) N. Y. 1890. 7, 309.

1779
JAN. 11

Continental Congress, Committee of Conference.   Philadelphia. To [George] Washington [Philadelphia]. Conference respecting an exchange of prisoners. A. L. S. of James Duane. 1 p.   92, 221

1779
JAN. 12

Washington, George. Philadelphia. To [the President of Congress]. Efforts of British to obtain exchange of the Convention troops. Draft. 1 p. In handwriting of Tench Tilghman.   **A.** IV, pt. I, 227

1779
JAN. 12

Homans, John. Durham [Connecticut]. To [George] Washington [Philadelphia]. Leave of absence for Capt. [Josiah] Stoddard. A. L. S. 1 p. Transmitted to Congress.   **C. C.** 152, 7, 39

1779
[JAN. 13]

Washington, George. [Philadelphia.] To [the Committee of Conference]. The situation; alternative plans

of campaign; reasons therefore. Draft. •12 pp.
In handwriting of Alexander Hamilton.

A. IV, pt. I, 231

Printed: Writings of Washington (Ford) N. Y. 1890. 7, 317.

1779
JAN. 13

Continental Congress, Resolve. Alteration of resolve [of
Dec. 16, 1778] establishing formation of the new
11th. Pennsylvania regiment. Contemporary
copy attested by Peter Scull. 2 pp. Enclosed in
Board of War to Washington, 1779, May 21.

94, 115

1779
JAN. 13

Bedel, Timothy. Haverhill [Massachusetts]. To Maj.
Gen. [Horatio] Gates [Boston]. Need of ammu-
nition and clothing. Contemporary copy. 2 pp.
Transmitted to Washington. 93, 20

1779
JAN. 14

Washington, George. Philadelphia. To [the Board of
Treasury, Philadelphia]. Want of money for pay
for troops in Northern Department. Draft. 1 p.
In handwriting of Tench Tilghman.

A. IV, pt. I, 243

1779
JAN. 14

Stoddard, Darius. Durham [Connecticut]. To George
Washington [Philadelphia]. Certifying to Capt.
Josiah Stoddard's condition. Transcript. Enclosed in · Washington to the President of Congress, 1779, Jan. 27. C. C. 169, 6, 306

1779
JAN. 14

Stoddard, Josiah. Durham [Connecticut]. To [George]
Washington [Philadelphia]. Application for
leave of absence. A. L. S. 2 pp. Enclosed in
Washington to the President of Congress, 1779,
Jan. 27. C. C. 152, 7, 41

1779
JAN. 16

Board of War. [Philadelphia.] To [George] Washington,
Philadelphia. Recovery of missing orderly books;
arrearages due troops for deficiencies of clothing. A. L. S. of Timothy Pickering, jr. 2 pp.
Answered Jan. 18*. 92, 322

1779
JAN. 18

Washington, George. Philadelphia. To [the Board of
War, Philadelphia]. Arrearages of clothing for
1777. Draft. 1 p. In handwriting of Tench
Tilghman. A. IV, pt. I, 245

[1779]
[JAN. 18]

Washington, George. [Philadelphia.] Plan for paying
arrearages of clothing to the troops. Draft.
2 pp. In handwriting of Alexander Hamilton
and Tench Tilghman. A. IV, pt. I, 247

1779
JAN. 18

[Washington, George.] [Philadelphia.] To [Maj.] Gen. [Philip John] Schuyler [Albany]. Curtailment of acquisition of supplies. [Extract of letter.] Transcript. Enclosed in Washington to the President of Congress, 1779, Aug. 15.

C. C. 169, 5, 510

1779
JAN. 18

Deane, James. Fort Schuyler [New York]. To [Maj.] Gen. [Philip John] Schuyler [Albany]. Councils of Oneidas; Onondagas; efforts for peace. Contemporary copy. 4 pp. Enclosed in President of Congress to Washington, 1779, Feb. 8.

92, 334

1779
JAN. 19

Arnold, B[enedict]. Philadelphia. To [the Board of War, Philadelphia]. Claim to rank superior to Maj. Gen. Arthur St. Clair. Contemporary copy, attested by Peter Scull. 2 pp. Enclosed in Board of War to Washington, 1779, Jan. 20.

92, 328

1779
JAN. 19

Coren, Isaac. Court martial of. Philadelphia. Proceedings and testimony; judgment and sentence of the court. Contemporary copy. 7 pp. In handwriting of the Judge Advocate, William Cross. Enclosed in Board of War to Washington, 1780, May 30.

95, 42

1779
JAN. 19

St. Clair, Arthur. Philadelphia. To the Board of War [Philadelphia]. Memorial on rank of Maj. Gen. [Benedict] Arnold. Contemporary copy, attested by Peter Scull. 3 pp. Enclosed in Board of War to Washington, 1779, Jan. 20.

92, 329

1779
JAN. 20

Washington, George. Philadelphia. To [the Committee of Congress]. Clothing for officers; half pay and pensions. Draft. 6 pp. In handwriting of Alexander Hamilton.

A. IV, pt. I, 249

Printed: Writings of Washington (Ford) N. Y. 1890. 7, 328.

1779
JAN. 20

Board of War. [Philadelphia.] To [George] Washington [Philadelphia]. Claim of rank of [Maj.] Genls. [Arthur] St. Clair and [Benedict] Arnold. A. L. S. of Richard Peters. 1 p.

92, 326

1779
JAN. 21

Washington, George. Philadelphia. To the President of Congress. Case of Col. [Moses] Rawlings. Draft. 2 pp. In handwriting of John Laurens. Read in Congress, Jan. 23. Order taken thereon.

A. IV, pt. I, 255

1779
JAN. 21

Continental Congress, Resolve. Paymasters and accounting officers station at headquarters. D. S. of Charles Thomson. 1 p. Transmitted to Washington.

95, 316

1779
JAN. 22

Continental Congress, President. Philadelphia. To [George] Washington [Philadelphia]. Transmitting resolve. Letter-book copy. C. C. 14, 23

1779
JAN. 22

Continental Congress, Resolve. Despatches for Comte D'Estaing. A. D. S. of Charles Thomson. 1 p. Enclosed in President of Congress to Washington, 1779, Jan. 27.

92, 341

1779
JAN. 23

Washington, George. Philadelphia. To [the Committee of Congress]. Methods and plan of furnishing clothing to the Army; color of cloth; officers' clothing. Draft. 7 pp. In handwriting of Alexander Hamilton and Tench Tilghman.

A. IV, pt. I, 257

1779
JAN. 23

Continental Congress, President. Philadelphia. To [George] Washington [Philadelphia]. Acknowledging letters and transmitting resolves. Letter-book copy.

C. C. 14, 30

1779
JAN. 23

Continental Congress, Resolve. Recruiting Col. [Moses] Rawlings's Corps. D. S. of Charles Thomson. 1 p. Transmitted to Washington.

30, 154

1779
JAN. 23

Continental Congress, Resolve. Refusing Maj. Gen. [William] Phillips permission to go into New York. D. S. of Charles Thomson. 1 p. Transmitted to Washington.

30, 155

1779
JAN. 23

Continental Congress, Resolves. Strength of army; recruiting battalions; enlistments; bounties; management of departments; Commissary of Prisoners; hospital arrangements. D. S. of Charles Thomson. 3 pp. Transmitted to Washington.

92, 331

1779
JAN. 25

[Washington, George.] [Philadelphia.] To [Maj.] Gen. [Philip John] Schuyler [Albany]. Queries as to proposed Expedition into the Indian Country. Transcript. Enclosed in Washington to the President of Congress 1779, Aug. 15.

C. C. 169, 5, 511

1779
JAN. 25

Dodge, John. Pittsburg. To [the President of Congress, Philadelphia] The situation in the northwest; Detroit, savages. Contemporary copy. 4 pp.

In handwriting of Timothy Pickering, jr. Enclosed in Board of War to Washington, 1779,
Feb. 19.   **93, 35**

1779   **Washington,** George. Philadelphia. To the President of
JAN. 27   Congress. Want of money; exchange of sick
Convention prisoners and minor military matters.
Draft. 1 p. In handwriting of Alexander Ham-
ilton.   **A. IV, pt. I, 265**

1779   **Continental Congress,** President. Philadelphia. To
JAN. 27   [George] Washington [Philadelphia]. Capt.
[Josiah] Stoddard's request; recruiting of army;
transmitting various resolves. L. S. of John
Jay. 2 pp.   **92, 338**

1779   **Continental Congress,** Resolve. Leave of absence to Capt.
JAN. 27   [Josiah] Stoddard. L. S. of Chas. Thomson.
1 p. Enclosed in President of Congress to
Washington, 1779, Jan. 27.   **92, 340**

1779   **Continental Congress,** Resolves. Commission to Marquis
JAN. 27   de Bretigny. A. D. S. of Charles Thomson.
Enclosed in President of Congress to Washing-
ton, 1779, Jan. 27.   **92, 341**

1779   **Anonymous.** Martinico [West Indies]. To [Anne César,
JAN. 27   Chevalier de La Luzerne, Philadelphia]. British
at San Lucia. Contemporary extract of letter.
1 p.   **93, 51**

1779   **Schuyler,** Ph[ilip John]. Albany. To [the President of
JAN. 27   Congress, Philadelphia]. Indian affairs; Onondagas espousal of cause of the States. Contemporary copy. 1 p. Enclosed in President of
Congress to Washington, 1779, Feb. 8.   **92, 333**

1779   **Continental Congress,** Resolves. Violations of paroles by
JAN. 28   American and British officers. D. S. of Charles
Thomson. 1 p. Transmitted to Washington.
92, 342

1779   **Duane,** James. Philadelphia. To [George Washington,
JAN. 28   Philadelphia]. The artillery and Armand's corps.
A. L. S. 2 pp.   **30, 142**

1779   **Glover,** John. Providence [Rhode Island]. To [George]
JAN. 28   Washington [Philadelphia]. Leave to resign.
L. S. 1 p. Enclosed in Washington to Con-
gress, 1779, Feb. 24.   **C. C. 152, 7, 131**

1779   **Knox,** H[enry]. Philadelphia. To [George] Washington
JAN. 28   [Philadelphia]. The artillery corps; state quo-

tas, enlistments. Transcript. Enclosed in Washington to the President of Congress, 1779, Apr. 7.
          C. C.   169, 6, 348

1779
JAN. 29

Washington, George. Philadelphia. To the President of Congress. Settlement of accounts. Draft. 1 p. In handwriting of Tench Tilghman. Read in Congress, Jan. 30. Ordered taken thereon.
          A.   IV, pt. I, 267

1779
JAN. 29

Washington, George. Philadelphia. To the President of Congress. Requesting permission to return to the army. Draft. 2 pp. In handwriting of John Laurens. Read in Congress, Jan. 29.
          A.   IV, pt. I, 269
Printed: Writings of Washington (Sparks) Boston. 1834. 6, 171.

1779
JAN. 29

Washington, George. Philadelphia. To the President of Congress. Transmitting letter of Du Portail on subject of fortifying Boston. Draft. 1 p. In handwriting of John Laurens. Referred to Marine Committee.   A.   IV, pt. I, 271

[1779]
[JAN. 29]

[Gates, Horatio.] Boston. To [the President of Congress, Philadelphia]. Supplies of British; return of prisoners; case of Ensign [John] Brown. [Extract of letter.] Contemporary copy. 1 p. Transmitted to Washington.   93, 18

1779
JAN. 30

Washington, George. Philadelphia. To the President of Congress. Supplies of provisions in the Western Department; Commissary General. L. S. 2 pp. In handwriting of Tench Tilghman. Read in Congress, Feb. 1. Acted on.   C. C.   152, 7, 97
Printed, in part: Writings of Washington (Ford) N. Y. 1890. 7, 315, note.

1779
JAN. 30

Washington, George. Philadelphia. To the Board of Treasury [Philadelphia]. Sum necessary to replenish the military chest. Draft. 2 pp. In handwriting of John Laurens.
          A.   IV, pt. I, 275

1779
JAN. 30

Continental Congress, President. Philadelphia. To [George] Washington [Philadelphia]. Transmitting resolves, etc. Letter-book copy.
          C. C.   14, 36

1779
JAN. 30

Continental Congress, Resolve. Commander in chief to return to the Army. A. D. S. of Charles Thomson. 1 p. Enclosed in President of Congress to Washington, 1779, Jan. 31.   93, 3

1779
JAN. 31

Continental Congress, President. Philadelphia. To
[George] Washington [Philadelphia]. Gov.
[George] Clinton's accounts; work of the Committee of Conference. L. S. of John Jay. 2 pp.
93, 1

1779
JAN. 31

Continental Congress, Committee of Conference. Report
on reenlisting of Cols. [John] Gibson's and
[Gregory] Smith's Virginia regiments. Contemporary copy, attested by Peter Scull. 2 pp.
Transmitted to Washington. 92, 344

1779
FEB. 1

Continental Congress, President. Philadelphia. To
[George] Washington [Philadelphia]. Commissary and Quartermaster's Departments to the
westward. L. S. of John Jay. 1 p. 93, 4

1779
FEB. 1

Continental Congress, Resolve. Arrangement of Quartermaster's and Commissary's departments to the
westward. A. L. S. of Charles Thomson. 1 p.
Enclosed in President of Congress to Washington, 1779, Feb. 1. 93, 6

1779
FEB. 2

Continental Congress, Resolves. Aids of troops, arms etc.
for South Carolina and Georgia. Contemporary
copy, attested by Charles Thomson. 2 pp. Enclosed in President of Congress to Washington,
1778, Feb. 3. 93, 9

1779
FEB. 2

Washington, George. Frankford [Pennsylvania]. To [the
Committee of Congress, Philadelphia]. Surveyor
of Ordnance. L. S. 2 pp. In handwriting of
Tench Tilghman. C. C. 152, 7, 101

1779
FEB. 3

Continental Congress, President. Philadelphia. To
[George] Washington [En route to Middlebrook].
Transmitting resolves. L. S. of John Jay. 1 p.
Answered Feb. 8.* 93, 7

1779
FEB. 4

Continental Congress, Resolves. Completion of Pulaski
and Armand's corps; arrangement of army and
settlement of rank. Contemporary copy, attested
by Charles Thomson. 1 p. Enclosed in President of Congress to Washington, 1778, Feb. 5.
93, 14

1779
Feb. 4

[Schuyler, Philip John.] [Albany.] To [George Wash-
ington, near Middlebrook]. Suggestions for man-
agement of expedition against the Six Nations.
[Extract of letter.] Transcript. Enclosed in
Washington to the President of Congress, 1779,
Aug. 15. C. C. 169, 5, 467

288

1779
FEB. 5

Continental Congress, President. Philadelphia. To [George] Washington [Middlebrook]. Transmitting resolves. L. S. of John Jay. 1 p. Answered Feb. 8.* 93, 12

1779
FEB. 5

Knox, H[enry]. Philadelphia. To [James] Duane [Philadelphia]. Duties of surveyor of artillery. Transcript. C. C. 169, 5, 191

1779
FEB. 7

[Washington, George.] Middlebrook. To [Brig. Gen. Edward Hand, Philadelphia?] Information of routes into the Indian country. Transcript. Enclosed in Washington to the President of Congress, 1779, Aug. 15. C. C. 169, 6, 12

1779
FEB. 8

Washington, George. Middlebrook [New Jersey]. To [the President of Congress, Philadelphia]. Enlistments in Pulaski's corps. Draft. 1 p. In handwriting of Tench Tilghman. Read in Congress, Feb. 10. Referred to the Board of War. A. IV, pt. I, 277
Printed: Writings of Washington (Sparks) Boston. 1834. 6, 172.

1779
FEB. 8

Washington, George. Middlebrook. To Col. [Charles] Armand [-Tufin, Middlebrook]. Recruiting his corps. L. S. 1 p. In handwriting of James McHenry. C. C. 152, 7, 107

1779
FEB. 8

Continental Congress, President. Philadelphia. To [George] Washington [Middlebrook]. Transmitting letters. L. S. of John Jay. 1 p. 92, 336

1779
FEB. 9

Board of War. [Philadelphia.] To [the President of Congress, Philadelphia]. Management of civil departments of the army; payment of certificates of officers. Contemporary copy. 6 pp. In handwriting of Timothy Pickering, jr. Enclosed in Board of War to Washington, 1779, Feb. 11. 93, 27

1779
FEB. 10

Board of War. [Philadelphia.] To [George] Washington [Middlebrook]. Transmitting arrangement of the army. A. L. S. of Peter Scull. 1 p. 93, 15

1779
FEB. 11

Washington, [George.] Middlebrook. To [Maj. Gen. Philip John Schuyler, Albany]. Information desired of the Indian country; routes etc. [Extract of letter.] Transcript. Enclosed in Washington to the President of Congress, 1779, Aug. 15. C. C. 169, 6, 13
Printed: Writings of Washington (Ford) N. Y. 1890. 7, 341.

1779
FEB. 11
Contir ntal Congress, Resolve. Ordering a court-martial as result of letters from Massachusetts. Contemporary copy. Attested by Charles Thomson. 1 p.   93, 31

1779
FEB. 11
Board of War. [Philadelphia.] To [George] Washington [Middlebrook]. Transmitting a report to Congress. A. L. S. of Richard Peters. 1 p. Answered Feb. 17.*   93, 26

1779
FEB. 14
W[ashington,]G[eorge]. Middlebrook. To[Col.]Jeremiah Wadsworth [Middlebrook?] Magazine of provision at Fort Pitt. Transcript. Enclosed in Washington to the President of Congress, 1779, Aug. 15.   C. C. 169, 5, 499

[1779]
[FEB. 14]
[Murray, John.] Memorandum of rank of Maj. Francis Nichols. A. D. 1 p. Enclosed in Board of War to Washington, 1779, Feb. 22.   93, 43

1779
FEB. 14
Murray, John. Waynesburg [Pennsylvania]. To Gov. [Joseph] Reed, Philadelphia. His seniority. A. L. S. 2 pp. Endorsed with memorandum respecting Maj. [Francis] Nichol's commission. Enclosed in Board of War to Washington, 1779, Feb. 22.   93, 41

1779
FEB. 15
Continental Congress, President. Philadelphia. To [George] Washington [Middlebrook]. Charges against officers conducting work at Springfield, Massachusetts. L. S. of John Jay. 1 p. 93, 32

1779
FEB. 15
Board of War. [Philadelphia]. To [George] Washington [Middlebrook]. Forwarding Virginia arrangement. A. L. S. of Peter Scull. 1 p.   93, 17

1779
FEB. 16
[Williamson, Andrew.] Near Adam's Ferry [Georgia]. To [Henry Laurens, Philadelphia]. Situation in Georgia; retreat of British; Indians. Extract of letter with auto. note by Laurens. Enclosed in Laurens to Washington, 1779, Mar. 16.   30, 390

1779
FEB. 17
Washington, George. [Middlebrook.] To the Board of War [Philadelphia]. Methods of accounting; granting of certificates. Draft. 2 pp. In handwriting of Alexander Hamilton.
A. IV, pt. I, 279

1779
FEB. 17
Washington, George. Middlebrook. To [the Board of War, Philadelphia]. Ordering papers sent to headquarters. Draft. 1 p. In handwriting of Tench Tilghman.   A. IV, pt. I, 283

1779
FEB. 17

[Washington, George.] Middlebrook. To Henry Laurens [Philadelphia]. His politeness during the Philadelphia visit; Spain and the French loan; British preparations. Auto. draft. 1 p.

P. I. pt. II, 283

Printed: Writings of Washington (Sparks) Boston. 1834. 6, 175.

1779
FEB. 17

Potter, James. Philadelphia. To the Board of War [Philadelphia]. Information, distances, waterways, etc., in the Indian country. Contemporary copy. 2 pp. In handwriting of Timothy Pickering, jr. Enclosed in Board of War to Washington, 1779, Feb. 19. 93, 37

1779
FEB. 19

Washington, George. Middlebrook. To the President of Congress [Philadelphia]. Court martial of officers in charge of public works at Springfield; [Maj.] Gen. [Alexander] McDougall; call for money. Draft. 1 p. In handwriting of Alexander Hamilton. Read in Congress, Feb. 22. Order taken thereon. A. IV, pt, I, 285

1779
FEB. 19

Board of War. [Philadelphia]. To [George] Washington [Pluckemin, New Jersey]. Transmitting papers. A. L. S. of Peter Scull. 1 p. Answered Feb. 26*. 93, 34

1779
FEB. 20

Continental Congress, Resolve. Brig. Gen. [Lachlan] McIntosh and the command at Fort Pitt. Contemporary copy, attested by Charles Thomson. 1 p. Enclosed in President of Congress to Washington, 1779, Feb. 22. 93, 50

1779
FEB. 20

Continental Congress, Resolve. Portmanteaus and valises of officers. Contemporary copy, attested by Charles Thomson. 1 p. Enclosed in President of Congress to Washington, 1779, Feb. 22. 93, 49

1779
FEB. 20

Continental Congress, Resolve. Convention troops at Charlottesville; confusion, troubles, etc. Contemporary copy. 2 pp. In handwriting of Timothy Pickering, jr. Enclosed in Board of War to Washington, 1779, Feb. 22. 93, 46

1779
FEB. 22

Continental Congress, President. Philadelphia. To [George] Washington [Middlebrook]. Transmitting resolves; extract from a letter to the French minister. L. S. of John Jay. 2 pp. 93, 47

1779
FEB. [22]

Continental Congress, Resolves. Explanation of Maj. Gen. [Charles] Lee's letters. Contemporary copy, attested by Charles Thomson. Transmitted to Washington. **93, 52.**

1779
FEB. 22

Board of War, Philadelphia. To George Washington, Middlebrook. Trouble with Convention troops [at Charlottesville]. A. L. S. of Richard Peters. 2 pp. Answered Feb. 28.* **93, 41**

1779
FEB. 22

Board of War. [Philadelphia.] To [George] Washington, Middlebrook. Transmitting papers. A. L. S. of Peter Scull. 1 p. **93, 39**

1779
FEB. 23

Continental Congress, President. Philadelphia. To [George] Washington [Middlebrook]. Money for [Maj.] Gen. [Alexander] McDougall. Letter-book copy. **C. C. 14, 53**

1779
FEB. 23

Gervais, John Lewis. [Charleston.] To Henry Laurens [Philadelphia]. Measures of the legislature; military situation; the Treason Act; minor matters. Extract of letter with auto. note by Laurens. Enclosed in Laurens to Washington, 1779, Mar. 16. **30, 390**

1779
FEB. 24

Washington, George. Middlebrook. To [the President of Congress, Philadelphia]. [Brig.] Gen. [John] Glover's and Col. [Edward] Wigglesworth's resignation; Maryland bills of credit as payment of bounty. Draft. 1 p. In handwriting of James McHenry. Read in Congress Feb. 27.

A. IV, pt. I, 287

1779
FEB. 24

Washington, George. [Middlebrook.] To Maj. Gen. [Nathanael] Greene [Middlebrook]. Magazine of provisions for Indian expedition. Transcript. [Extract of letter.] **C. C. 169, 5, 500**

1779
FEB. 24

Beatty, John. [Middlebrook.] To [George] Washington [Middlebrook]. Issues to prisoners; exchange of seaman. A. L. S. 4 pp. Enclosed in Washington to the President of Congress, 1779, Feb. 27. **C. C. 152, 7, 123**

1779
FEB. 25

Greene, Nath[anael]. Middlebrook. To [George Washington, Middlebrook]. Wagoners for the army. Contemporary copy. 3 pp. In handwriting of James McHenry. Enclosed in Washington to the President of Congress, 1779, Feb. 27. **C. C. 152, 7, 127**

[1779]　　　Lee, Charles.　Philadelphia.　To [the President of Con-
[FEB. 25?]　　　　gress, Philadelphia].　His correspondence with
　　　　　　　　[Lt.] Col. [William] Butler and [Brig.] Gen.
　　　　　　　　[Alexander] Leslie.　Contemporary copy.　3 pp.
　　　　　　　　Transmitted to Washington.　　　　　　93, 54

1779　　　[Maxwell, William.]　Elizabethtown [New Jersey].　At-
FEB. 25　　　　tempted surprise by the enemy at Elizabethtown.
　　　　　　　　[Extract of letter.]　2 pp.　In handwriting of
　　　　　　　　James McHenry.　Enclosed in Washington to the
　　　　　　　　President of Congress, 1779, Feb. 26.
　　　　　　　　　　　　　　　　　　　C. C.　152, 7, 119

1779　　　Pawling, A[lbert].　Haverstraw [New York].　To the
FEB. 25　　　　President of Congress [Philadelphia].　Resigna-
　　　　　　　　tion.　A. L. S.　1 p.　Read in Congress Mar. 5.
　　　　　　　　Accepted.　　　　　　　　C. C.　152, 7, 153

1779　　　Pawling, A[lbert].　Haverstraw.　To George Washington
FEB. 25　　　　[Middlebrook].　Resignation.　A. L. S.　1 p.
　　　　　　　　Enclosed in Pawling to the President of Congress.
　　　　　　　　1779, Feb. 25.　　　　　　C. C.　152, 7, 149

1779　　　Washington, George.　Middlebrook.　To the President of
FEB. 26　　　　Congress [Philadelphia].　Enemy's attempt on
　　　　　　　　Elizabethtown; trial of Quartermaster General
　　　　　　　　[Thomas] Mifflin.　Draft.　2 pp.　In handwriting
　　　　　　　　of Alexander Hamilton.　Referred, Mar. 1, to
　　　　　　　　committee composed of Plater, Ellery and Paca.
　　　　　　　　　　　　　　　　　　　A.　IV, pt. I, 289
　　　　　　　Printed in part: Writings of Washington (Ford) N. Y. 1890. 7, 346.

1779　　　Washington, George.　Middlebrook.　To the Board of
FEB. 26　　　　War [Philadelphia].　Corps of Sappers and
　　　　　　　　Miners; disputes of rank.　Draft.　1 p.　In
　　　　　　　　handwriting of Tench Tilghman.
　　　　　　　　　　　　　　　　　　　A.　IV, pt. I, 291

1779　　　Washington, G[eorge].　Middlebrook.　To [Brig. Gen.
FEB. 26　　　　Edward Hand? Philadelphia].　Information of
　　　　　　　　Indian country, map etc.　[Extract of letter.]
　　　　　　　　Transcript.　Enclosed in Washington to the Pres-
　　　　　　　　ident of Congress, 1779, Aug. 15.
　　　　　　　　　　　　　　　　　　　C. C.　169, 6, 15

1779　　　Continental Congress, President.　Philadelphia.　To
FEB. 26　　　　[George] Washington [Middlebrook].　Transmit-
　　　　　　　　ting resolves.　Letter-book copy.　C. C.　14, 55

1779　　　Continental Congress.　Resolve.　Explanation of Maj. Gen.
FEB. 26　　　　[Charles] Lee's letters.　Contemporary copy,

attested by Charles Thomson. Transmitted to Washington, 1779, Feb. 26. **93, 52**

1779
FEB. 27

Washington, George. Middlebrook. To [the Committee of Conference, Philadelphia]. Expense and exchanges of marine prisoners; bounty for waggoners; Clothier General's department; bounties. Draft. 3 pp. In handwriting of Alexander Hamilton. **A. IV, pt. I, 293**

1779
FEB. 27

Washington, George. Middlebrook. To [the Board of War, Philadelphia]. Establishment of an Engineer corps. Draft. 1 p. In handwriting of Alexander Hamilton. **A. IV, pt. I, 247**

[1779]
[FEB. 27]

Washington, George. [Middlebrook.] Remarks on establishment of Engineer corps and Sappers and Miners. Draft. 5 pp. In handwriting of Alexander Hamilton. **A. IV, pt. I, 299**

1779
FEB. 27

Continental Congress, Resolve. Money for Maj. Gen. [Charles] Lee. Contemporary copy, attested by Charles Thomson. Transmitted to Washington. **93, 52**

1779
FEB. 27

Elizabethtown, (New Jersey). Return of American troops killed, wounded and missing at. Contemporary copy. 1 p. In handwriting of Tench Tilghman. Enclosed in Washington to the President of Congress, 1779, Mar. 1. **C. C. 152, 7, 143**

1779
FEB. 27

Maxwell, William. Elizabethtown [New Jersey]. To [George Washington, Middlebrook]. Account of enemy's attempted surprise at Elizabethtown. A. L. S. 3 pp. Enclosed in Washington to the President of Congress, 1779, Mar. 1. **C. C. 152, 7, 139**

1779
FEB. 28

Washington, George. [Middlebrook.] To the Board of War [Philadelphia]. Col. [Theodorick] Bland to command Convention troops at Charlottesville [Virginia]. Draft. 1 p. In handwriting of John Laurens. **A. IV, pt. I, 305**

[1779]
[FEB.]

Continental Army. Arrangement. Memorandum of state of arrangement of the army. 2 pp. Enclosed in Board of War to Washington, 1779, Feb. 10. **93, 16**

1779
MAR 1.

Washington, George. Middlebrook. To [the President of Congress, Philadelphia]. Transmitting [Brig.] Gen. [William] Maxwell's account of the attack on Elizabethtown. Draft. 1 p. In handwriting of James McHenry. Read in Congress, Mar. 3. Referred to Committee of Intelligence: J. B. Smith, Lovell and J. Henry.   **A.** IV, pt. I, 307

1779
MAR. 1

[**Washington, George.**] Middlebrook. To John Jay. [Philadelphia]. Manner of communicating intelligence to the public. Draft. 2 pp. In handwriting of Alexander Hamilton. **P.** I, pt. II, 291
  Printed: Writings of Washington (Ford) N. Y. 1890. 7, 347.

1779
MAR. 1

Schuyler, Philip John. [Albany.] To [George Washington, Middlebrook]. Proposed Indian expedition; strength of enemy; routes etc. [Extract of letter.] Transcript. Enclosed in Washington to the President of Congress, 1779, Aug. 15. **C. C.** 169, 5, 469

1779
MAR. 2

W[ashington,] G[eorge]. [Middlebrook.] To [Col. Jeremiah Wadsworth, Middlebrook?]. Supplies for Western Expedition. Transcript.
                                              C. C. 169, 5, 501

1779
MAR. 2

Continental Congress, President. Philadelphia. To [George] Washington [Middlebrook]. Transmitting resolves. Letter-book copy. **C. C.** 14, 57

1779
MAR. 2

Jay, John. Philadelphia. To [George] Washington [Middlebrook]. British reenforcement from Rhode Island; European politics. **A. L. S.** 2 pp.
                                                          30, 270

1779
MAR. 2

Laurens, Henry. Philadelphia. To [George] Washington [Middlebrook]. Personal matters; British attempt on Elizabethtown; affairs to the Southward. **A. L. S.** 3 pp.   **30**, 272

1779
MAR. 2

[**Putnam, Israel.**] Redding [Connecticut]. To [George Washington, Middlebrook]. Incursion of enemy at Horse Neck. [Extract of letter.] 1 p. In handwriting of Caleb Gibbs. Enclosed in Washington to the President of Congress, 1778, Mar. 8.
                                              C. C. 152, 7, 167

1779
MAR. 2

Prisoners. British. List of those taken at Horse Neck [Connecticut]. 1 p. Enclosed in Washington to the President of Congress 1778, Mar. 8.
                                              C. C. 152, 7, 171

1779
MAR. 2

Sheriff, Charles. Middlebrook. Return of articles to be provided at Easton. List of quartermaster's stores with deficiencies noted. Contemporary copy. 4 pp. In handwriting of Peter Bryan Bruin. Transmitted to Washington. **93**, 260

1779
MAR. 3

Washington, George. Middlebrook. To [the President of Congress, Philadelphia]. The Western expedition; consolidation of regiments and question of officers. Draft. 1 p. In handwriting of Alexander Hamilton. Read in Congress, Mar. 8. Referred to the Board of War.

A. IV, pt. I, 309

1779
MAR. 3

Washington, George. [Middlebrook.] To [Joseph Reed, Philadelphia]. Troops for the Western expedition. Transcript. Enclosed in Washington to the President of Congress, 1779, Aug. 15.

C. C. 169, 5, 515

Printed: Writings of Washington (Ford) N. Y. 1890. 7,351.

1779
MAR. 3

Jay, John. [Philadelphia.] To [George Washington, Middlebrook]. Publishing of news; England's preparations; measures of public utility. A. L. S. 3 pp.   30, 283

1779
MAR. 4

Washington, George. Middlebrook. To [the Board of War, Philadelphia]. Arrangement of officers; disputes of rank etc. Draft. 2 pp. In handwriting of Tench Tilghman.   A. IV, pt. I, 311

1779
MAR. 4

W[ashington], G[eorge]. [Middlebrook.] To Gov. [George] Clinton [Poughkeepsie, New York]. The Western Expedition; secrecy; troops. Transcript. Enclosed in Washington to the President of Congress, 1779, Aug. 15.   C. C. 169, 6, 55

The same letter, with minor changes, sent to Prest. Joseph Reed, under date of Mar. 3.

1779
MAR. 4

Continental Congress, President. Philadelphia. To [George] Washington [Middlebrook]. Acknowledging letter. Letter-book copy.   C. C. 14, 58

1779
MAR 4.

Massachusetts, Council. [Boston.] Proceedings on Maj. Gen. [Israel] Putnam's request for cannon. Contemporary copy. 1 p. In handwriting of Richard Kidder Meade. Enclosed in Washington to the President of Congress, 1779, Apr. 28.

C. C. 152, 7, 279

1779
MAR. 6

Washington, George. Middlebrook. To [the President of Congress, Philadelphia]. Movement of the enemy. Draft. 2 pp. In handwriting of James McHenry. Read in Congress, Mar. 8.

A. IV, pt. I, 313

[1779]
[MAR. 6]

[Washington, George.] [Middlebrook.] To [Maj. Gen. John Sullivan, Providence, Rhode Island]. Command of expedition against the Six Nations. [Extract of letter.] Transcript. Enclosed in Washington to the President of Congress, 1779, Aug. 15. C. C. 169, 6, 64

Printed, in part: Writings of Washington (Ford) N. Y. 1890, 7, 356.

1779 [MAR. 6?]

Anonymous. [New York.] To [George Washington, Middlebrook]. Intelligence of a British fleet. [Extract of letter.] 1 p. In handwriting of Tench Tilghman. Enclosed in Washington to the President of Congress, 1779, Mar. 6. C. C. 152, 7, 161

1779 MAR. 8

Washington, George. Middlebrook. To [the President of Congress, Philadelphia]. Transmitting account of incursion of enemy to Horse Neck. Draft. 1 p. In handwriting of James McHenry. Read in Congress, Mar. 11. Referred to Committee of Intelligence. A. IV, pt. I, 315

1779 MAR. 8

Continental Congress, President. Philadelphia. To [George] Washington [Middlebrook]. Transmitting resolves. Letter-book copy. C. C. 14, 61

1779 MAR. 8

Continental Congress, Resolves. Method of making out military commissions. Contemporary copy, attested by Charles Thomson. 1 p. Enclosed in President of Congress to Washington, 1779, Aug. 6. 93, 288

1779 MAR. 9

Nelson, Thomas, jr. Philadelphia. To [George] Washington [Middlebrook]. Purchase of horses in Virginia. A. L. S. 1 p. 30, 334

1779 MAR. 10

Washington, George. Middlebrook. To [the President of Congress, Philadelphia]. Case of Brig. Gen. James Reid. Draft. 1 p. In handwriting of James McHenry. Read in Congress, Mar. 13. Referred to the Board of War.

A. IV, pt. I, 315

1779 MAR. 10

Washington, George. Middlebrook. To [the Board of War, Philadelphia.] Pay of supernumerary officers; shoes. Draft. 1 p. In handwriting of James McHenry. A. IV, pt. I, 315

1779 MAR. 10

[Maxwell, William.] [Elizabethtown, New Jersey.] To [George Washington, Middlebrook]. Intelligence of movements of British ships. [Extract of letter.] 1 p. In handwriting of Tench Tilghman. Enclosed in Washington to the President of Congress, 1779, Mar. 11. C. C. 152, 7, 181

1779
MAR. 11
Washington, George. Middlebrook. To [the President of Congress, Philadelphia]. Enemy's designs; Baron Steuben's regulations. Draft. 2 pp. In handwriting of James McHenry. Read in Congress, Mar. 15. A. IV, pt. I, 317

1779
MAR. 11
Washington, George. Middlebrook. To [the Board of War, Philadelphia.] Resolves of Congress respecting clothing due the army for the year 1777. Draft. 1 p. In handwriting of Tench Tilghman. A. IV, pt. I, 319

1779
MAR. 11
Continental Congress, Resolves. Establishment of Corps of Engineers. D. S. of Richard Peters. In handwriting of Timothy Pickering, jr. Enclosed in Board of War to Washington, 1779, Apr. 21. 93, 62

1779
MAR. 12
Continental Congress, President. Philadelphia. To [George] Washington [Middlebrook, New Jersey]. Transmitting resolves. Letter-book copy. C. C. 14, 66

1779
MAR. 13
Washington, George. Middlebrook. To [the Board of War, Philadelphia]. Disputes in 2d. Connecticut regiment. Draft. 1 p. In handwriting of Tench Tilghman. A. IV, pt. I, 321

1779
MAR. 14
Morris, Gouverneur. Philadelphia. To [George] Washington [Middlebrook]. Character of the former commander of the Western Department [Brig. Gen. Lachlan McIntosh]. A. L. S. 2 pp. 30, 376

1779
MAR. 15
Washington, George. Middlebrook. To the President of Congress [Philadelphia]. Recruiting; bounties; prosecution of war; clothing of army. Draft. 6 pp. In handwriting of Alexander Hamilton and Washington. Read in Congress, Mar. 18. A. IV, pt. I, 323
Printed: Writings of Washington (Ford) N. Y. 1890. 7, 363.

1779
MAR. 15
Washington, George. Middlebrook. To [Thomas Nelson, jr., Philadelphia]. Horses for personal use; crisis of affairs. Auto. draft. 3 pp. P. I, pt. II, 309

1779
MAR. 15
Continental Congress, President. Philadelphia. To [George] Washington [Middlebrook]. Transmitting resolve. Letter-book copy. C. C. 14, 68

1779
MAR. 15
 South Carolina, delegates to Continental Congress. Philadelphia. To [George] Washington [Middlebrook]. Exchange of prisoners; civilians; reenforcements for the South. L. S. of Thomas Burke and Henry Laurens. 2 pp. Answered Mar. 18.*
            30, 378

1779
MAR. 16
 Washington, George. Middlebrook. To [Brig. Gen. Edward Hand, Minisink, New York]. Information desired of the Indian country. [Extract of letter.] Transcript. Enclosed in Washington to the President of Congress, 1779, Aug. 15.
          C. C. 169, 6, 19

1779
MAR. 16
 Continental Congress, Committee of Conference. Philadelphia. Passage of recommended resolutions; provision for wagoners. A. L. S. of James Duane. 1 p.   **30, 383**
   Committee: Duane, Root, M. Smith, G. Morris, Drayton and Hutson.

1779
MAR. 16
 Laurens, Henry. Philadelphia. To [George] Washington [Middlebrook]. News from the South; forwarding papers. A. L. S. 2 pp.   **30, 388**

1779
MAR. 17
 Continental Congress, President. Philadelphia. To [George] Washington [Middlebrook]. Transmitting resolve. Letter-book copy. **C. C. 14, 68**

1779
MAR. 18
 Washington, George. Middlebrook. To [the South Carolina delegates in Congress, Philadelphia]. Exchange of prisoners; agreements. Draft. 5 pp. In handwriting of Alexander Hamilton.
         A. IV, pt. I, 329

1779
MAR. 19
 Continental Congress, President. Philadelphia. To [George] Washington [Middlebrook]. Transmitting resolves; regulations for Clothier's Department under consideration. Letter-book copy.   **C. C. 14, 69**

1779
MAR. 20
 Washington, George. Middlebrook. To [the President of Congress, Philadelphia]. Payment of certificates for supplies furnished by inhabitants. Draft. 1 p. In handwriting of Tench Tilghman.
         A. IV, pt. I, 333

[1779]
[MAR. 20]
 Washington, George. [Middlebrook.] To [the President of Congress, Philadelphia]. Memorial of officers and soldiers of Jackson's, Lee's and Henley's regiments; court martial at Fort Pitt. Draft.

2 pp.   In handwriting of Tench Tilghman.   Read in Congress Mar. 23.   Referred to Board of War.

A. IV, pt. I, 335

1779
MAR. 20

Washington, George. Middlebrook. To [the Board of War, Philadelphia]. Arrangements and clothing for the western expedition. Draft. 3 pp. In handwriting of Tench Tilghman.

A. IV, pt. I, 337

1779
MAR. 20

Washington, George. Middlebrook. To [the Board of War, Philadelphia]. Commissions for New Jersey, South Carolina and Virginia officers. Draft. 2 pp. In handwriting of Tench Tilghman.

A. IV, pt. I, 341

1779
MAR. 20

Washington, George. Middlebrook. To [Henry Laurens, Philadelphia]. Affairs in the South; arming of slaves. Auto. draft signed. 3 pp.

P. I, pt. II, 313

Printed: Writings of Washington (Ford) N. Y. 1890. 7, 370.

1779
MAR. 21

Washington, George. Middlebrook. To the Board of War [Philadelphia]. Col. [Moses] Rawlings ordered to Fort Pitt. Draft. 1 p. In handwriting of Tench Tilghman.   A. IV, pt. I, 343

1779
MAR. 21

[Washington, George.] [Middlebrook.] To [Brig. Gen. Edward Hand, Minisink, New York]. Swampy nature of country between Chemung and the Seneca Nation. [Extract of letter.] Transcript. Enclosed in Washington to the President of Congress, 1779, Aug. 15.   C. C. 169, 6, 20

1779
MAR. 21

W[ashington,] G[eorge]. Middlebrook. To [Maj. Gen. Philip John Schuyler, Albany]. The Western expedition; plan to be adopted; state of finances. Transcript. Enclosed in Washington to the President of Congress, 1779, Aug. 15.

C. C. 169, 5, 477

1779
MAR. 22

Burke, Thomas. Philadelphia. To [George] Washington [Middlebrook]. Reenlistment of North Carolina troops; state bounty. Recent copy. 1 p. 31, 37

1779
MAR. 23

Continental Congress. Ordinance for regulating the Clothier General's Department. Broadside. 1 p. Printed by Claypoole. Transmitted to Washington.

93, 303

1779
MAR. 23

Nelson, Thomas, jr. Philadelphia. To [George] Washington [Middlebrook]. Danger to America from condition of finances. A. L. S. 2 pp. 31, 72

1779
MAR. 24

Washington, George. Middlebrook. To [the President of Congress, Philadelphia]. Minor military matters; enlistment of wagoners. Draft. 1 p. In handwriting of Robert Hanson Harrison. Read in Congress Mar. 29. Referred to the Board of War.   **A.** IV, pt. I, 345

1779
MAR. 24

[Washington, George.] [Middlebrook.] To [Brig. Gen. Edward Hand, Minisink, New York]. Information desired of Indian country. [Extract of letter.] Transcript. Enclosed in Washington to the President of Congress, 1779, Aug. 15.
      C. C. 169, 6, 21

1779
MAR. 24

Continental Congress, President. Philadelphia. To [George] Washington [Middlebrook]. Transmitting resolves. Letter-book copy.   **C. C.** 14, 74

1779
MAR. 24

Continental Congress, President. Philadelphia. To [George] Washington [Middlebrook]. Provision supplies for Oneida and other friendly Indians. Letter-book copy.   **C. C.** 14, 75

1779
MAR. 24

Burke, Thomas. Philadelphia. To [George] Washington [Middlebrook]. Volunteer cavalry from Virginia to aid South Carolina. A. L. S. 2 pp. Answered Mar. 28.*   31, 64

1779
MAR. 25

Board of War [Philadelphia]. To [George] Washington [Middlebrook]. Petition of William MacPherson. L. S. of Richard Peters. 3 pp. In handwriting of Peter Scull. Answered Mar. 29.*
      93, 56

1779
MAR. 25

[White, Anthony Walton.] [Lancaster, Pennsylvania.] To [the Board of War, Philadelphia]. Blunderbusses for his dragoons. Contemporary extract of letter. 1 p. Enclosed in Board of War to Washington, 1779, Apr. 1.   93, 108

1779
MAR. 26

Washington, George. Middlebrook. To [the President of Congress, Philadelphia]. Movements of enemy's ships and troops. Draft. 2 pp. In handwriting of Caleb Gibbs. Read in Congress Mar. 30.   **A.** IV, pt. I, 347
Printed: Writings of Washington (Ford) N. Y. 1890. 7, 386, note.

1779
MAR. 26

Washington, George. Middlebrook. To the Board of War [Philadelphia]. Cartridges and hunting shirts. Draft. 1 p. In handwriting of Tench Tilghman.   **A.** IV, pt. I, 349

Morris Town Jan 11th 1777

Dear Sir,

From Mr Harrison you would know my Intention of offering you one of the 16 Regiments which the Congress have been pleas'd to leave to me to raise, & appoint the Officers of I have expressd my desire that Col: Levin Powell should be your Lieut. Col:, & if you have no objection, & Frazers Stomach comes to him it will be agreeable to me that he becomes your Major, as he is spoke very well of in that Character by the General & other Officers who Serv'd with him to the Northward

Instructions & Recruiting Orders (which you are to distribute to the Officers after your Arrangment is made) are inclos'd, as also a Warrant for 10,000 Dollars to begin your Recruiting with ——— After you have nominated your Officers & seen them fairly entered upon the Recruiting Service, repair yourself to Philadelphia, which is to be the General Rendezvous, in order that you may receive Form Cloath & provide for your Regiment

The Recruits are to be March'd by Fifty's or upwards as rais'd; & are to be sent on by the Lieut Col:, who is to use every means in his power to compleat the Regiment, & send the Men with all Imaginable dispatch ——— When you

WRITING OF JOHN FITZGERALD.

1779
MAR. 27

Harnage, Henry. Cambridge [Massachusetts]. To [George] Washington [Middlebrook]. Application to go to Charlottesville by sea. A. L. S. 3 pp. Enclosed in Washington to the President of Congress, 1779, Apr. 12.   C. C. 152, 7, 251

1779
MAR. 28

Washington, George. Middlebrook. To [the President of Congress, Philadelphia]. News in Rivington's Gazette. Draft. 1 p. In handwriting of Robert Hanson Harrison. Read in Congress, Apr. 1.
A. IV, pt. I, 351

1779
MAR. 28

Washington, George. Middlebrook. To Thomas Burke [Philadelphia]. [Col. George] Baylor's and [Col. Theodorick] Bland's dragoons; clothing and accoutrements; letters to go into New York. Draft. 2 pp. In handwriting of Tench Tilghman.   A. IV, pt. I, 353

1779
MAR. 28

Jay, John. Philadelphia. To [George] Washington, Middlebrook. Introducing a secret agent. A. L. S. 1 p.   31, 107

1779
MAR. 28

[Maxwell, William.] [Elizabethtown, New Jersey.] To [George Washington, Middlebrook]. Reports of British ships. [Extract of letter.] Contemporary copy. 1 p. In handwriting of Tench Tilghman. Enclosed in Washington to the President of Congress, 1779, Mar. 29.   C. C. 152, 7, 215

1779
MAR. 29

Washington, George. Middlebrook. To [the President of Congress, Philadelphia]. Transmitting letter from [Brig.] Gen. [William] Maxwell. Draft. 1 p. In handwriting of Tench Tilghman. Read in Congress, Apr. 5. Referred to Board of War.
A. IV, pt. I, 355

1779
MAR. 29

Washington, George. Middlebrook. To the Board of War [Philadelphia]. Proposed commission for [William] Macpherson. Draft. 2 pp. In handwriting of Robert Hanson Harrison.
A. IV, pt. I, 357

1779
MAR. 30

Board of War. Regulations for Engineer corps and Sappers and Miners; duties of engineers; plans, attacks, defense; composition of Sappers and Miners; duties. D. S. of Richard Peters. In handwriting of Timothy Pickering, jr. Enclosed in Board of War to Washington, 1779, Apr. 21.   93, 62

1779
APR. 1

Continental Congress, Resolves. New York militia for expedition against the Western Indians. Contemporary copy, attested by Charles Thomson. 2 pp. Enclosed in President of Congress to Washington, 1779, Apr. 4.   93, 70

1779
APR. 1

Board of War, Philadelphia. To [George] Washington, Middlebrook. Arming of Lt. Col. [Anthony Walton] White's dragoons. A: L. S. of Peter Scull. 1 p. Answered Apr. 4*   93, 106

1779
APR. 2

Washington, George. Middlebook. To [the President of Congress, Philadelphia]. Provisions for Oneida Indians; Clothier General's Department; arrangement of the cavalry. Draft. 3 pp. In handwriting of Robert Hanson Harrison. Read in Congress, Apr. 5. Reported to the Board of War.   A. IV, pt. I, 359

1779
APR. 2

Washington, George. Middlebrook. To [the Board of War, Philadelphia]. Contract for cannon. Draft. 1 p. In handwriting of Tench Tilghman.   A. IV, pt. I, 363

1779
APR. 3

Continental Congress, Resolve. Appointment of Pierre Charles L'Enfant as Captain of Engineers. Contemporary copy, attested by Charles Thomson. 1 p. Enclosed in President of Congress to Washington 1779, Apr. 12.   93, 90

1779
APR. 3

[Schuyler, Philip John.] [Albany.] To [George Washington, Middlebrook]. The Western Expedition; choice of routes. [Extract of letter.] Transcript. Enclosed in Washington to the President of Congress, 1779, Aug. 15.   C. C. 169, 5, 485

1779
APR. 4

Washington, George. Middlebrook. To [the Board of War, Philadelphia]. Rank of officers in the North Carolina line; blunderbusses for dragoons; arrangement of Engineer corps; Sappers and Miners; the German battalion. Draft. 4 pp. In handwriting of Robert Hanson Harrison.
     A. IV, pt. 1, 365

1779
APR. 4

Washington, George. Middlebrook. To [the Board of War, Philadelphia]. Arrangement of officers of Pennsylvania and Rhode Island regiments. Draft. 1 p. In handwriting of Tench Tilghman.
     A. IV, pt. 1, 369

1779
APR. 4

Washington, George. Middlebrook. To [the Board of War, Philadelphia]. Clothing, arms, etc. for troops ordered to Wyoming. Draft. 1 p. In handwriting of Tench Tilghman.
A. IV, pt. I, 371

1779
APR. 4

Washington, George. Middlebrook. To the Board of War [Philadelphia]. Clothing for troops at Wyoming. Contemporary copy. 1 p. In handwriting of James McHenry. Enclosed in Washington to the President of Congress, 1779, Aug. 21.
C. C. 152, 7, 611

1779
APR. 4

Washington, George. Middlebrook. To [Brig.] Gen. [Edward] Hand [Minisink, New York]. Clothing. Contemporary copy. 1 p. In handwriting of James McHenry. Enclosed in Washington to the President of Congress, 1779, Aug. 21.
C. C. 152, 7, 613

1779
APR. 4

Continental Congress, President. Philadelphia. To [George] Washington [Middlebrook]. Transmitting resolves. L. S. of John Jay. 1 p. 93, 68

1779
APR. 5

Washington, George. Middlebrook. To Thomas Burke [Philadelphia]. Plan of additional bounties. Draft. 1 p. In handwriting of Robert Hanson Harrison. A. IV, pt. I, 373

1779
APR. 5

Continental Congress, Resolve. Pay of army clothiers. Contemporary copy, attested by Charles Thomson. 2 pp. Enclosed in President of Congress to Washington, 1779, Apr. 7. 93, 73

1779
APR. 6

Continental Congress, Resolve. Election of deputy commissary generals of musters. Contemporary copy, attested by Charles Thomson. 1 p. Enclosed in President of Congress to Washington, 1779, Apr. 8 93, 80

1779
APR. 6

[Knox, Henry.] [Middlebrook.] To [George Washington, Middlebrook]. Completion of the artillery corps. Contemporary copy. 2 pp. In handwriting of Tench Tilghman. Enclosed in Washington to the President of Congress, 1779, Apr. 7.
C. C. 152, 7, 225

1779
APR. 7

Washington, George. Middlebrook. To [the Committee of Congress, Philadelphia]. Completion of the artillery regiment. Draft. 3 pp. In handwriting of Tench Tilghman. A. IV, pt. I, 375

[1779]
[APR. 7]

[Washington, George.] [Middlebrook.] Remarks to the Committee of Conference. Plan of campaign; militia on Western frontier; barrack-masters and commissaries; brigadiers; independent corps. Contemporary copy. 3 pp. In handwriting of Tench Tilghman. Enclosed in Washington to the President of Congress, 1779, Apr. 7.
C. C. 152, 7, 229

1779
APR. 7

Continental Congress, President. Philadelphia. To [George] Washington, [Middlebrook]. Transmitting resolves. L. S. of John Jay. 1 p.
93, 71

1779
APR. 7

Continental Congress, Resolve. Memorial of Capt. Job Sumner. Contemporary copy, attested by Charles Thomson. 2 pp. Enclosed in President of Congress to Washington, 1779, Apr. 8. 93, 79

1779
APR. 7

Continental Congress, Resolves. Road from Penobscot to St. Johns. Contemporary copy, attested by Charles Thomson. 2 pp. Enclosed in President of Congress to Washington, 1779, Apr. 8. 93, 77

1779
APR. 7

Board of War. [Philadelphia.] To [George] Washington, Middlebrook. Forwarding commissions for the Virginia line. A. L. S. of Peter Scull. 1 p.
31, 241

1779
APR. 8

Washington, George. Middlebrook. To the Board of War [Philadelphia]. Disputes of rank; hunting shirts. Draft. 1 p. In handwriting of Tench Tilghman. A. IV, pt. I, 379

1779
APR. 8

Continental Congress, President. Philadelphia. To [George] Washington [Middlebrook]. Transmitting resolves. L. S. of John Jay. 2 pp. Answered Apr. 15.* 93, 75

1779
APR. 9

Continental Congress, Resolve. Appointments of lieutenants in Col. [Charles] Harrison's artillery. Contemporary copy, attested by Charles Thomson. 1 p. Enclosed in President of Congress to Washington, 1779, Apr. 12. 93, 88

1779
APR. 9

Continental Congress, Resolve. Dismissal of Maj. de Bois. Contemporary copy, attested by Charles Thomson. 1 p. Enclosed in President of Congress to Washington, 1779, Apr. 12. 93, 89

1779
APR. 9

Board of War. [Philadelphia.] To [George Washington, Middlebrook]. Cartridges; clothing department;

cannon casting; Maryland men in the German battalion; cavalry. A. L. S. of Richard Peters. 4 pp. Answered Apr. 15.* 93, 81

1779
APR. 9

Board of War. [Philadelphia.] To [George] Washington, Middlebrook. The army shoe factory at Newark and establishment of others elsewhere. A. L. S. of Timothy Pickering, jr. 3 pp. Answered Apr. 15.* 93, 83

1779
APR. 10

Washington, George. Middlebrook. To the Board of War [Philadelphia]. Design of consolidating the Adjutant General and Inspector General Departments. Draft. 1 p. In handwriting of Alexander Hamilton. A. IV, pt. I, 381

1779
APR. 10

Washington, George. Middlebrook. To [the Board of War, Philadelphia]. Commissions for the Virginia line. Draft. 1 p. In handwriting of Tench Tilghman. A. IV, pt. I, 383

1779
APR. 10

Continental Congress, Resolve. Court martial of Col. [Archibald] Steel at Fort Pitt. Contemporary copy, attested by Charles Thomson. 1 p. Enclosed in President of Congress to Washington, 1779, Apr. 12. 93, 87

1779
APR. 12

Washington, George. Middlebrook. To [the President of Congress, Philadelphia]. Exchange of certain British officers. Draft. 1 p. In handwriting of Tench Tilghman. Read in Congress, April 14. A. IV, pt. I, 385

1779
APR. 12

Continental Congress, President. Philadelphia. To [George] Washington [Middlebrook]. Transmitting various resolves. L. S. of John Jay. 2 pp. 93, 85

1779
APR. 13

Washington, George. Middlebrook. To the Board of War [Philadelphia]. [Capt. Bartholomew] Von Heer's claim. Draft. 2 pp. In handwriting of Tench Tilghman. A. IV, pt. I, 387

1779
APR. 13

Board of War. [Philadelphia.] To [George] Washington [Middlebrook]. Promotion of Lt. Col. [Francis] Nichols; hunting shirts; proclamation pardoning deserters. A. L. S. of Richard Peters. 2 pp. Answered Apr. 22.* 31, 281

1779
APR. 13

Board of War. [Philadelphia.] To [George] Washington, Middlebrook. Ensigns commissions in the Vir-

ginia line. A. L. S. of Peter Scull. 2 pp. Answered Apr. 22.*   31, 283

1779   **Washington,** George. Middlebrook. To John Jay [Phil-
APR. 14   adelphia]. The Canada expedition and [Maj.]
                Gen. [Horatio] Gates's actions. Draft. 11 pp.
                In handwriting of Alexander Hamilton and
                Washington.   P. I, pt. II, 337
                Printed: Writings of Washington (Ford) N. Y. 1890. 7, 393.

1779   **Continental Congress,** President. Philadelphia. To
APR. 14   [George] Washington [Middlebrook]. Transmit-
                ting resolves; return of court-martial proceedings
                on officers at Springfield. L. S. of John Jay.
                2 pp.   93, 91

1779   **Continental Congress,** Resolves. Request of certain con-
APR. 14   vention officers; court-martial proceedings re-
                specting the Springfield laboratory. Contem-
                porary copy, attested by Charles Thomson. 1 p.
                Enclosed in President of Congress to Washington
                1779, Apr. 14.   93, 93

1779   **Continental Congress,** Resolves. Passports to enter enemy's
APR. 14   lines. Broadside. 1 p. Printed by Hall and
                Sellers. Enclosed in President of Congress to
                Washington, 1779, Apr. 18.   93, 100

1779   **Washington,** George. Middlebrook. To [the President of
APR. 15   Congress, Philadelphia.] Transmitting New York
                newspapers. Draft. 1 p. In handwriting of
                Tench Tilghman. Read in Congress, Apr. 19.
                                              A. IV, pt. I, 389

1779   **Washington,** George. Middlebrook. To [the Board of
APR. 15   War, Philadelphia]. Clothier General's depart-
                ment; need of cannon; the German battalion; re-
                duction of the cavalry; shoes. Draft. 4 pp. In
                handwriting of Alexander Hamilton.
                                              A. IV, pt. I, 391

1779   **Washington,** George. Middlebrook. To [the Board of
APR. 15   War, Philadelphia] Succession of officers in 2d
                New Jersey Regiment and other minor matters.
                Draft. 1 p. In handwriting of Tench Tilghman.
                                              A. IV, pt. I, 395

1779   **Board of War.** [Philadelphia.] To [George] Washington,
APR. 15   Middlebrook. Arrangement of the Rhode Island
                and Pennsylvania Lines; [Maj.] Gen. [Arthur]
                St. Clair's letter. A. L. S. of Peter Scull. 2
                pp. Answered Apr. 22.*   31, 320

1779
APR. 15
[Schuyler, Philip John.] [Livingston Manor, New York]. To [George Washington, Middlebrook]. Intelligence of enemy's movements in Canada. [Extract of letter]. Transcript. Enclosed in Washington to the President of Congress, 1779, Aug. 15.
C. C. 169, 6, 22

1779
APR. 16
Sullivan, John. Mill Stone [near Easton, Pennsylvania]. To [George] Washington [Middlebrook]. Force necessary for the Indian expedition. Transcript. Enclosed in Washington to the President of Congress, 1779, Aug. 15. C. C. 169, 5, 490

1779
APR. 17
Continental Congress, Resolves. Enlistment of wagoners. Contemporary copy, attested by Charles Thomson. 2 pp. Enclosed in President of Congress to Washington, 1779, Apr. 18. 93, 98

1779
APR. 17
New Jersey, Brigade Officers. Elizabethtown. To the Legislature of New Jersey. Remonstrance; lack of pay; necessities. Contemporary copy. 3 pp. In handwriting of Robert Hanson Harrison. Enclosed in Washington to the President of Congress, 1779, May 11. C. C. 152, 7, 325

1779
APR. 17
Sullivan, Daniel. Pittsburg. Charges against his conduct as Indian interpreter. Contemporary copy. 2 pp. In handwriting of Caleb Gibbs. Enclosed in Washington to the President of Congress, 1779, May 16. C. C. 152, 7, 357

1779
APR. 18
Continental Congress, President. Philadelphia. To [George] Washington [Middlebrook]. Transmitting resolves. L. S. of John Jay. 2 pp. 93, 96

1779
APR. 18
[Chaloner & White.] [Philadelphia.] To [Col. Jeremiah Wadsworth, Middlebrook?] Prospects of flour. [Extract of letter.] Transcript. Enclosed in Washington to the President of Congress, 1779, Aug. 15. C. C. 169, 5, 504

1779
APR. 19
Washington, George. Middlebrook. To Brig. Gen. James Clinton [Albany]. Batteaux for Western expedition. [Extract of letter.] Transcript. Enclosed in Washington to the President of Congress, 1779, Aug. 15. C. C. 169, 5, 512

1779
APR. 19
Washington, George. [Middlebrook.] To [Joseph Reed, Philadelphia]. Call for militia for the Western Expedition. Transcript. Enclosed in Washington to the President of Congress, 1779, Aug. 15.
C. C. 169, 5, 517

1779
APR. 19
[**Washington, George.**] Middlebrook. To [Maj. Gen. Philip John Schuyler, Albany]. Plans for the Western Expedition. [Extract of letter.] Transcript. Enclosed in Washington to the President of Congress, 1779, Aug. 15. C. C. 169, 5, 496
Printed: Writings of Washington (Ford) N. Y. 1890. 7, 406.

1779
APR. 19
Continental Congress, Resolve. Resignation of Capt. [Benjamin] Stoddert. Contemporary copy. 1 p.
93, 105

1779
APR. 19
Continental Congress, Resolve. Resignation of Maj. Gen. [Philip John] Schuyler. Contemporary copy attested by Charles Thomson. 1 p. Enclosed in President of Congress to Washington, 1779, Apr. 20.
93, 101

1779
APR. 19
Continental Congress, Resolve. Ration allowance of colonels acting as brigadiers. Contemporary copy attested by Charles Thomson. 1 p. Enclosed in President of Congress to Washington, 1779, Apr. 20.
93, 102

1779
APR. 19
Board of War. [Philadelphia.] To [George] Washington, Middlebrook. Transmitting commissions of Virginia subalterns; promotions in the Jersey Line. A. L. S. of Peter Scull. 1 p. Answered Apr. 22.*
31, 359

1779
APR. 20
Washington, George. Middlebrook. To [the President of Congress, Philadelphia]. Appointment of date for trial of Maj. Gen. [Benedict] Arnold. Draft. 1 p. In handwriting of Tench Tilghman. Read in Congress, Apr. 22. A. IV, pt. I, 397

1779
APR. 20
Continental Congress, President. Philadelphia. To [George] Washington [Middlebrook]. Transmitting resolves. L. S. of John Jay. 1 p. 93, 103

1779
APR. 21
Board of War. [Philadelphia.] To [George] Washington. Middlebrook. Regulations for government of Engineer Department; German battalion. A. L. S. of Richard Peters. 2 pp. Answered May 3.*
93, 60

1779
[APR. 21]
[**Gérard de Rayneval, Conrad Alexandre**]. To [the President of Congress, Philadelphia]. Cooperation of Comte D'Estaing with American forces. 3 pp. (In French.) Auto. note of Gérard that above was sent by Gouverneur Morris. Transmitted to Washington. 93, 336

1779
APR. 21

Jay, John. Philadelphia. To [George] Washington [Middlebrook]. Reflections [on the Conway Cabal]; the war. A. L. S. 4 pp.   **31, 367**

Printed, in part: Writings of Washington (Ford) N. Y. 1890, 7, 404 note.

1779
APR. 21

V[an] Schaick, G[oose]. Onondaga [New York]. Return of prisoners taken on Onondaga Expedition. Contemporary copy. 1 p. In handwriting of Richard Kidder Meade. Enclosed in Washington to the President of Congress, 1779, May 7.

C. C. 152, 7, 305

1779
APR. 22

Washington, George. Middlebrook. To the Board of War [Philadelphia]. Hunting shirts, blankets and shoes; rank; drums. Draft. 3 pp. In handwriting of Tench Tilghman.   **A. IV, pt. I, 401**

1779
APR. 22

Washington, George. Middlebrook. To William Ellery [Philadelphia]. Commissions for the Rhode Island regiments. Draft. 1 p. In handwriting of Tench Tilghman.   **A. IV, pt. I, 405**

1779
APR. 22 [?]

Washington, George. Middlebrook. To [the President of Congress, Philadelphia]. Need of money by Quartermaster General to provide for the Western Expedition. Draft. 1 p. In handwriting of Alexander Hamilton. Referred to Board of Treasury, Apr. 26.   **A. IV, pt. I, 399**

1779
APR. 23

Washington, George. Middlebrook. To the President of Congress [Philadelphia]. Reported embarkation of enemy for West Indies or Georgia. Draft. 1 p. In handwriting of Tench Tilghman. Read in Congress, Apr. 26.   **A. IV, pt. I, 407**

1779
APR. 23

W[ashingto]n, G[eorge]. Middlebrook. To John Jay [Philadelphia]. Queries respecting the Continental frigates; supplies for Bermuda and the currency. Draft. 3 pp. In handwriting of Alexander Hamilton.   **P. I, pt. II, 351**

Printed: Writings of Washington (Ford) N. Y. 1890. 7, 415.

1779
APR. 24

Washington, George. Middlebrook. To [the President of Congress, Philadelphia]. Reduction of pay of Captain-lieutenants of the artillery. Draft. 1 p. In handwriting of Tench Tilghman. Read in Congress, May 1. Referred to Board of War.

A. IV, pt. I, 409

1779
APR. 24

Flint, Royal. Raritan [New Jersey]. To [George] Washington [Middlebrook]. Prospects for supplies for

Western Expedition. Transcript. Enclosed in Washington to the President of Congress, 1779, Aug. 15.　　　　　　　　　　C. C.　169, 5, 503

1779
APR. 24

V[an] Schaik, G[oose]. Fort Schuyler [New York]. Account of the Onondaga Expedition. Contemporary copy. 3 pp. In handwriting of Caleb Gibbs. Enclosed in Washington to the President of Congress, 1779, May 7. C. C. 152, 7, 301

1779
APR. 25

Continental Congress, President. Philadelphia. To [George] Washington [Middlebrook]. Transmitting papers. L. S. of John Jay. 1 p.　　　32, 7

1779
APR. 25

Board of War. [Philadelphia.] To [George] Washington, Middlebrook. Clothing for troops; supply of shoes. A. L. S. of Timothy Pickering, jr. 2 pp.
93, 109

1779
APR. 26

Jay, John. Philadelphia. To [George] Washington [Middlebrook]. Marine and Commercial committees in Congress; Sieur Gérard [de Rayneval]; secrecy rules; state of currency. A. L. S. 3 pp. 32, 41

1779
APR. 26

Morris, Gouverneur. Philadelphia. To [George] Washington [Middlebrook]. Assistance from France; sketch of method of attack upon New York. A. L. S. 2 pp.　　　　　　　　　　　　32, 43

1779
APR. 26

Rhode Island, Council of War., Providence. To the President of Congress [Philadelphia]. Efforts of the state during the past; present situation; request for protection. Contemporary copy. 4 pp. Enclosed in President of Congress to Washington, 1779, May 10.　　　　　　　　　93, 111

1779
APR. 27

Washington, George. Middlebrook. To [Maj. Gen. Philip John Schuyler, Albany]. Intelligence from Canada. [Extract of letter.] Transcript. Enclosed in Washington to the President of Congress, 1779, Aug. 15.　　　　　　C. C.　169, 6, 23

1779
APR. 27

Washington, George. Middlebrook. To [Joseph Reed, Philadelphia]. Militia for the Western Expedition. [Extract of letter.] Transcript. Enclosed in Washington to the President of Congress, 1779, Aug. 15.　　　C. C.　169, 5, 519
Printed: Writings of Washington (Ford) N. Y. 1890. 7, 422.

1779
APR. 27

Board of War. [Philadelphia.] To [George] Washington [Middlebrook]. Commissions. A. L. S. of Peter Scull. 1 p.　　　　　　　　　　　32, 68

1779
APR. 27

Board of War. [Philadelphia]. To [George] Washington [Middlebrook]. Memorial of Capt. [Lawrence] Keene and minor matters. A. L. S. of Peter Scull. 1 p. **32, 68**

1779
APR. 27

Duane, James. Philadelphia. To George Washington, Raritan [Middlebrook]. Gov. [George] Clinton respecting exchange of prisoners. A. L. S. 1 p. **32, 63**

1779
APR. 27

[Schuyler, Philip John.] Albany. To [George Washington, Middlebrook]. Enclosing account of expedition against Onondaga. [Extract of letter.] Contemporary copy. 1 p. In handwriting of Robert Hanson Harrison. Enclosed in Washington to the President of Congress, 1779, May 7.
C. C. 152, 7, 299

1779
APR. 28

Washington, George. Middlebrook. To [the President of Congress, Philadelphia]. Cannon in Massachusetts; advance of enemy to Middletown [New Jersey]. Draft. 4 pp. In handwriting of James McHenry. Read in Congress, May 1.
A. IV, pt. I, 411

1779
APR. 28

Continental Congress, President. Philadelphia. To [George] Washington [Middlebrook]. Petition of Cols. [Philip] Van Cortlandt and [Peter] Gansevoort. Letter-book copy. **C. C. 14, 94**

1779
APR. 28

Continental Congress, Committee on defense of South Carolina and Georgia. To [George] Washington [Middlebrook]. Letter from South Carolina; troops raising in North Carolina and Virginia; plan proposed. A. L. S. of Richard Henry Lee. 2 pp. Answered Apr. 30.* **32, 87**
Committee: Lee, Burke and Laurens.

1779
APR. 29

Washington, George. Middlebrook. To [the President of Congress, Philadelphia]. Retreat of enemy from Middletown. D. S. 1 p. In handwriting of Alexander Hamilton and James McHenry. Read in Congress, May 3. **A. IV, pt. I, 415**

1779
APR. 30

Washington, George. Middlebrook. To [the President of Congress, Philadelphia]. Complaint of troops in Eastern Department as to pay. Draft. 1 p. In handwriting of James McHenry. Referred to Board of Treasury, May 4.
A. IV, pt. I, 417

1779
APR. 30

Washington, George. Middlebrook. To [Committee of Congress, Philadelphia]. Situation in Carolina; the Virginia levies; North Carolina troops. Draft. 2 pp. In handwriting of Alexander Hamilton.   A. IV, pt. I, 419

     Committee on defense of South Carolina and Georgia: R. H. Lee, Laurens and Burke.

1779
APR. 30

Flint, Royal. Raritan [New Jersey]. To [George] Washington [Middlebrook]. Abundance of flour. [Extract of letter.] Transcript. Enclosed in Washington to the President of Congress, 1779, Aug. 15.   C. C. 169, 5, 504

[1779]
[APR.]

[Washington, George.] [Middlebrook.] Observations on resolves of Congress respecting the Inspector-Generalship of the army. Contemporary copy. 9 pp. In handwriting of Tench Tilghman.
     C. C. 152, 7, 235

[1779]
[APR.]

Davies, William and Robert Hanson **Harrison.** [Middlebrook] To [George Washington, Middlebrook]. Report of conference with British Commissioners to arrange a general exchange; previous negotiations; defective powers of British Commissioners; liquidation of Convention troops' expenses; [Lt.] Gen. [John] Burgoyne's exchange status; definitive proposals of British; tariff; correspondence of Apr. 22 between Davies and Harrison and West Hyde and John [Lewis] André respecting proposals. Contemporary copy. 32 pp. In handwriting of Caleb Gibbs. Enclosed in Washington to the President of Congress, 1779, May 7. Endorsed: "Ordered to be printed."   C. C. 28, 1

1779
MAY 1

Continental Congress, Resolve. Cannon from Massachusetts for defense of the Highlands. Contemporary copy, attested by Charles Thomson. 1 p. Enclosed in President of Congress to Washington, 1779, May 4.   93, 123

1779
MAY 3

Washington, George. Middlebrook. To [the President of Congress, Philadelphia]. Peace with the Cayugas; British expedition from Canada. Draft. 2 pp. In handwriting of Alexander Hamilton. Read in Congress, May 7. Referred to the Board of War.   A. IV, pt. II, 1

     Printed: Writings of Washington (Ford) N. Y. 1890. 7, 429.

1779
MAY 3

Washington, George. Middlebrook. To the Board of War [Philadelphia]. Linen and blankets for troops; combining the Adjutant-General and Inspector-General's departments. Draft. 2 pp. In handwriting of James McHenry.

A. IV, pt. II, 3

1779
MAY 3

Washington, George. Middlebrook. To [the Board of War, Philadelphia]. Transmitting commissions and resignations in the Virginia line. Draft. 1 p. In handwriting of James McHenry.

A. IV, pt. II, 5

1779
MAY 3

[Washington, George.] [Middlebrook.] To [Gov. George Clinton, Poughkeepsie? New York]. Rendezvous and routes of troops on the Western Expedition. [Extract of letter.] Transcript. Enclosed in Washington to the President of Congress, 1779, Aug. 15.

C. C. 169, 5, 529

1779
MAY 3

Washington, George. Middlebrook. To James Duane [Philadelphia]. Exchange of civilians. Draft. 2 pp. In handwriting of Alexander Hamilton.

A. IV, pt. II, 7

1779
MAY 4

Washington, George. Middlebrook. To Maj. Gen. [John] Sullivan [Millstone? New Jersey]. Orders for preparations for the Western Expedition. Transcript. Enclosed in Washington to the President of Congress, 1779, Aug. 15.

C. C. 169, 5, 505

!779
MAY 4

Continental Congress, President. Philadelphia. To [George] Washington [Middlebrook]. Transmitting resolves; hard money for secret service. L. S. of John Jay. 2 pp. Answered May 11.*

93, 121

1779
MAY 4

Continental Congress, Resolve. Raising Rhode Island troops. Contemporary copy, attested by Charles Thomson. 1 p. Enclosed in President of Congress to Washington, 1779, May 5.

93, 126

1779
MAY 5

Washington, George. Middlebrook. To [the President of Congress, Philadelphia]. Britain's intentions of prosecuting the war; need of recruits. Draft. 2 pp. In handwriting of Alexander Hamilton. Read in Congress, May 8. Referred to Committee appointed to prepare an address to the several states, consisting of Morris, Drayton, Paca, S. Adams and Burke.

A. IV, pt. II, 9

Printed: Writings of Washington (Ford) N. Y. 1890. 7, 433.

1779
MAY 5

Washington, George. {Middlebrook.] To [a Committee of Congress, Philadelphia]. Orders for the Virginia levies; arms. Draft. 2 pp. In handwriting of Robert Hanson Harrison.

A. IV, pt. II, 17

Committee: R. H. Lee, Laurens and Burke.

1779
MAY 5

Washington, George. Middlebrook. To the Board of War [Philadelphia]. Need of clothing etc. in the Western Department. Draft. 3 pp. In handwriting of James McHenry.

A. IV, pt. II, 11

1779
MAY 5

Washington, George. Middlebrook. To the Board of War [Philadelphia]. Commission for Brig. Gen. [John] Glover. Draft. 1 p. In handwriting of James McHenry.   A. IV, pt. II, 15

1779
MAY 5

Continental Congress, President. Philadelphia. To [George] Washington [Middlebrook]. Transmitting resolve. L. S. of John Jay. 1 p. Answered May 11.*   **93, 124**

1779
MAY 6

Washington, George. Middlebrook. To [Brig.] Gen. [Alexander] McDougall [Peekskill, New York]. Pay and clothing for regiment of Poor's brigade. [Extract of letter.] Contemporary copy. 1 p. In handwriting of Richard Kidder Meade. Enclosed in Washington to the President of Congress, 1779, Aug. 21.   C. C. 152, 7, 617

1779
MAY 6

Maxwell, William. Elizabethtown [New Jersey]. To George Washington [Middlebrook]. Remonstrance of New Jersey officers. Contemporary copy. 2 pp. In handwriting of Richard Kidder Meade. Enclosed in Washington to the President of Congress, 1779, May 11.   **C. C.** 152, 7, 315

1779
MAY 6

Virginia, Delegates to Continental Congress. Philadelphia. To [George] Washington [Middlebrook]. Col. Alexander Spotswood's appointment. L. S.: Meriwether Smith, Richard Henry Lee, Cyrus Griffin and Wm. Fleming. 2 pp. Answered May 13.*   **92, 183**

1779
MAY 7

Washington, George. [Middlebrook.] To [the President of Congress, Philadelphia]. Sailing of a British expedition from New York; exchange negotiations. Draft. 3 pp. In handwriting of Robert Hanson Harrison. Read in Congress, May 10. Referred to Board of War.   A. IV, pt. II, 19

1779
MAY 7

Washington, George. Middlebrook. To Brig. Gen. [William] Maxwell [Elizabethtown]. Opinion of the remonstrance of the Jersey officers. Contemporary copy. 1 p. In handwriting of Richard Kidder Meade. Enclosed in Washington to the President of Congress, 1779, May 11.

C. C. 152, 7, 319

Printed: Writings of Washington (Ford) N. Y. 1891. 7, 445.

1779
MAY 7

Continental Congress, Resolves. Troops for the Southward; cavalry; clothing for Virginia levies. Contemporary copy, attested by Charles Thomson. 2 pp. Enclosed in President of Congress to Washington, 1779, May 10. 93, 115

1779
MAY 7

Continental Congress, Resolve. New England troops to be kept in Rhode Island. A. D. S. of Charles Thomson. 1 p. Enclosed in President of Congress to Washington, 1779, May 10. 93, 117

1779
MAY 7

Continental Congress, Resolve. The Rhode Island situation. Contemporary copy, attested by Charles Thomson. 1 p. Enclosed in President of Congress to Washington, 1779, May 10. 93, 118

1779
MAY 7

Board of War. Philadelphia. To [George] Washington, Middlebrook. Col. [Benjamin] Flower's rank and trouble between artillery and artificers at the laboratory. A. L. S. of Timothy Pickering, jr. 2 pp. Answered May 14.* 93, 127

1779
MAY 7

McHenry, James. Middlebrook. To [the Board of War, Philadelphia]. Changes among officers of the Virginia line. Auto. draft signed. 1 p.

A. IV, pt. II, 23

1779
MAY 8

[Washington, George.] Middlebrook. To [Gouverneur Morris, Philadelphia]. Morris's scheme [attack on New York]; campaign in the South; the civil and military situation. Draft. 3 pp. In handwriting of Alexander Hamilton.

P. I, pt. II, 377

Printed: Writings of Washington (Ford) N. Y. 1890. 7, 449.

1779
MAY 8

Continental Congress, Resolves. Appointing James Elliott and Thomas McIntire captains in Continental Army. Contemporary copy, attested by Benjamin Stoddert. 1 p. Enclosed in Board of War to Washington, 1779, May 10. Miscel.

1779
MAY 8

Webb, Samuel Blatchley. [Trenton, New Jersey.] Pay abstract of his regiment for April 1779, while commanded by Maj. Ebenezer Huntington. Attested copy, with explanatory note, by Paymaster General John Pierce, made Sept. 20, 1782. 2 pp. Enclosed in Board of War to Washington, 1782, Oct. 10.   98, 213

1779
MAY 8

Forman, Jonathan. Elizabethtown [New Jersey]. To [George] Washington [Middlebrook]. Reasons for the remonstrance of the Jersey officers. Contemporary copy. 1 p. In handwriting of Robert Hanson Harrison. Enclosed in Washington to the President of Congress, 1779, May 11.   C. C. 152, 7, 323

[1779]
[MAY 8]

[Pennsylvania, Executive Council.] [Philadelphia.] To [George Washington, Middlebrook]. Method of raising men for Western Expedition. [Extract of letter.] Transcript. Enclosed in Washington to the President of Congress, 1779, Aug. 15.   C. C. 169, 5, 520

1779
MAY 9

Gérard [de Rayneval, Conrad Alexandre]. Philadelphia. To [the President of Congress, Philadelphia]. Presenting his memorial on cooperation with Comte D'Estaing.

Gérard [de Rayneval, Conrad Alexandre]. Philadelphia. Memorial to Congress. D'Estaing's aid to Georgia; provisions for the fleet. Contemporary copy. 3 pp. In handwriting of Chas. Thomson. Enclosed in President of Congress to Washington, 1779, May 10.   32, 248

1779
MAY 9

Morgan, George. Princeton [New Jersey]. To [George Washington, Middlebrook]. Audience with Delaware Chiefs. Contemporary copy. 2 pp. In handwriting of James McHenry. Enclosed in Washington to the President of Congress, 1779, May 14.   C. C. 152, 7, 335

1779
MAY 10

Washington, George. Middlebrook. To [the Board of War, Philadelphia]. Return and commissions for 9th Virginia regiment. Draft. 1 p. In handwriting of Richard Kidder Meade.
    A. IV, pt. II, 25

1779
MAY 10

Washington, George. Middlebrook. To John Jay [Philadelphia]. Condition of affairs; the currency. Draft. 1 p. In handwriting of Alexander Hamilton.   P. I, pt. II, 381

1779
MAY 10

Washington, George. Middlebrook. To [Brig. Gen. William Maxwell, Elizabethtown, New Jersey]. Remonstrance of the Jersey officers; pay of soldiers. Contemporary copy. 1 p. In handwriting of Alexander Hamilton. Enclosed in Washington to the President of Congress, 1779, May 11.

C. C. 152, 7, 329

Printed, in part: Writings of Washington (Ford) N. Y. 1891. 7, 448, note.

1779
MAY 10

Continental Congress, President. Philadelphia. To [George] Washington [Middlebrook]. Transmitting resolves. L. S. of John Jay. 2 pp. Answered May 14.*

93, 113

1779
MAY 10

Continental Congress, President. Philadelphia. To [George] Washington [Middlebrook]. Letter of Minister of France [Gérard de Rayneval] to Congress; direction of military operations. A. L. S. of John Jay. 1 p.

32, 246

1779
MAY 10

Continental Congress, President. Philadelphia. To [George] Washington [Middlebrook]. Transmitting resolves. L. S. of John Jay. 2 pp.

93, 131

1779
MAY 10

Continental Congress, Resolve. Memorial of the Minister of France. A. D. S. of Charles Thomson. 1 p. Enclosed in President of Congress to Washington, 1779, May 10.

32, 250

1779
MAY 10

Continental Congress, Resolves. Thanks of Congress to Col. [Goose] Van Schaick and officers and soldiers; conduct of commissioners to arrange a cartel; report to be transmitted American prisoners. Contemporary copy, attested by Charles Thomson. 1 p. Enclosed in President of Congress to Washington 1779, May 10.

93, 133

1779
MAY 10

Board of War. [Philadelphia.] To [George] Washington [Middlebrook]. Trouble in Col. [Thomas] Proctor's regiment; drums and colors; supplies. A. L. S. of Richard Peters. 3 pp. Answered May 14.*

93, 129

1779
MAY 10

Board of War. [Philadelphia.] To [George] Washington [Middlebrook]. Transmitting commissions. A. L. S. of Peter Scull. 1 p.

32, 237

1779
MAY 10

Armstrong, John. Philadelphia. To [George] Washington [Middlebrook]. The situation, military and

in Congress; affairs on northern frontier; relief
of the Wyoming Valley from Fort Pitt.   A. L.
S.   2 pp.   **32, 253**

1779
MAY 11

Washington, George. Middlebrook. To [the President
of Congress, Philadelphia].   Remonstrance of
officers of 1st New Jersey regiment; lack of clothing; cattle for western expedition; secret intelligence.   Draft.   4 pp.   In handwriting of Alexander Hamilton and Robert Hanson Harrison.
Read in Congress, May 17.   Referred to Board
of War and Committee to Superintend Quartermaster and Commissary Departments: G. Morris,
Whipple and Armstrong.   **A. IV, pt. II, 27**
Printed: Writings of Washington (Sparks) Boston. 1834. 6, 254.

1779
MAY 11

Washington, George. Middlebrook. To [the President
of Congress, Philadelphia].   Brig. Gen. [Lachlan]
McIntosh and the Southern campaign.   L. S.   1 p.
In handwriting of Alexander Hamilton.   Read
in Congress, May 18.   **C. C.   152, 7, 307**
Draft dated May 12 is in A. IV, pt. II, 31.

1779
MAY 11

Henry, P[atrick]. Williamsburg [Virginia].   To the
President of Congress, Philadelphia.   British in
the Chesapeake; importance of Portsmouth.
Contemporary copy.   2 pp.   In handwriting of
Peter Scull.   Enclosed in President of Congress
to Washington 1779, May 22.   **32, 403**

1779
MAY 11

Continental Congress, Resolve. Pay and subsistance of
Engineers, Sappers and Miners: Duportail, commander in chief.   Contemporary copy, attested
by Charles Thomson.   1 p.   Enclosed in President of Congress to Washington, 1779, May 12.
                                       93, 139

1779
MAY 11

Continental Congress, Resolve. Pay of quarter-masters,
wagon-masters, commissaries and others.   Contemporary copy, attested by Charles Thomson.
2 pp.   Enclosed in President of Congress to
Washington, 1779, May 19.   **93, 158**

[1779]
MAY 12

Washington, George. Middlebrook. To the Delaware
Chiefs [Middlebrook].   Peace and friendship.
Contemporary copy.   5 pp.   In handwriting of
Caleb Gibbs.   Enclosed in Washington to the
President of Congress, 1779, May 14.
                              C. C.   152, 7, 339

1779
MAY 12
Continental Congress, President.   Philadelphia.   To [George] Washington [Middlebrook].   Transmitting resolves.   L. S. of John Jay.   2 pp.   Answered May 25.*   **93, 137**

1779
MAY 12
Continental Congress, Resolve.   Resignation of Lt. [David] Vallance and Ensign —— Brush.   Contemporary copy, attested by Charles Thomson.   1 p.   Enclosed in President of Congress to Washington, 1779, May 12.   **93, 135**

1779
MAY 12
Continental Congress, Resolve.   Election of Col. William Irvine to brigadier-general.   Contemporary copy, attested by Charles Thomson.   1 p.   Enclosed in President of Congress to Washington 1779, May 12.   **93, 156**

1779
MAY 12
McHenry, James.   Middlebrook.   To the Board of War [Philadelphia].   Retention of commissions by officers who resign.   Auto. draft signed.   1 p.
                                                A. IV, pt. II, 33

1779
MAY 12
Henry, Patrick.   Williamsburg.   To the President of Congress [Philadelphia].   British capture of Portsmouth.   Contemporary copy.   1 p.   Enclosed in President of Congress to Washington, 1779, May 22.   **32, 405**

1779
MAY 12
Jay, John.   Philadelphia.   To [George] Washington [Middlebrook].   Requesting passport for Mrs. [Margaret] De Lancey.   A. L. S.   2 pp.   **32, 257**

1779
MAY 12
Johnston, Thomas.   Annapolis [Maryland].   To Henry Hollingsworth [Head of Elk?].   British in the Chesapeake.   Contemporary copy.   1 p.   In handwriting of George Bond.   Enclosed in President of Congress to Washington, 1779, May 15.
                                                93, 146

[1779]
[MAY 12]
[Sullivan, John.]   Millstone [Pennsylvania].   To [George Washington, Middlebrook].   Clothing for troops.   [Extract of letter.]   Transcript.   Enclosed in Washington to the President of Congress, 1779, Aug. 15.   **C. C. 169, 6, 58**

1779
MAY 13
Washington, George.   [Middlebrook.]   To [the Virginia delegates to Congress, Philadelphia].   Reappointment of Col. [Alexander] Spotswood and trouble it would cause.   Draft.   4 pp.   In handwriting of Robert Hanson Harrison.   **A. IV, pt. II, 35**
Delegates: M. Smith, R. H. Lee, Griffin and Fleming.

[1779]   [Washington, George.] [Middlebrook.] To [Maj. Gen.
[MAY 13]   John Sullivan, Millstone, Pennsylvania]. Ren-
                     dezvous of troops. [Extract of letter.] Trans-
                     cript. Enclosed in Washington to the President
                     of Congress, 1779, Aug. 15.   C. C. 169, 5, 539

1779   Continental Congress, Resolve. Brig. Gen. [William]
MAY 13   Moultrie to command Southern army. Contem-
                     porary copy, attested by Charles Thomson. 1 p.
                     Enclosed in President of Congress to Washing-
                     ton, 1779, May 15.   93, 147

1779   Ford, Benjamin. Shrewsbury [South Carolina]. To
MAY 13   [George Washington, Middlebrook]. Intelli-
                     gence from Charleston. Contemporary copy.
                     2 pp. In handwriting of James McHenry. En-
                     closed in Washington to the President of Con-
                     gress, 1779, May 16.   C. C. 152, 7, 369

1779   Washington, George. Middlebrook. To [the President
MAY 14   of Congress, Philadelphia]. Position of troops;
                     visit of the Delaware chiefs. Draft, 1 p. In
                     handwriting of Alexander Hamilton. Read in
                     Congress May 17.   Referred to Committee on
                     Indian Affairs.   A. IV, pt. II, 39
                     Committee: Duane, Armstrong, Burke, Laurens and Sherman.

1779   Washington, George. Middlebrook. To the Board of
MAY 14   War [Philadelphia]. Lt. Col. [Benjamin] Flow-
                     ers' claim to advancement in the artillery; ap-
                     pointment of various officers. Draft. 4 pp.
                     In handwriting of Robert Hanson Harrison.
                                                 A. IV, pt. II, 41

1779   Washington, George. Middlebrook. To [Brig.] Gen.
MAY 14   [Alexander] McDougall [Peekskill, New York].
                     Ordering regiments of Poor's brigade to Easton.
                     Contemporary copy. 1 p. In handwriting of
                     James McHenry. Enclosed in Washington to
                     the President of Congress, 1779, Aug. 21.
                                                 C. C. 152, 7, 619

1779   Board of War. Philadelphia. To George Washington,
MAY 14   Middlebrook. Commission for Lt. Col. [Adam]
                     Hubley. A. L. S. of Richard Peters. 1 p.
                     Answered May 18.*   93, 140

1779   Hamilton, Alexander. [Middlebrook.] To [Brig. Gen.
MAY 14   Lachlan McIntosh, Middlebrook]. Inquiry into
                     his conduct. Contemporary copy. 1 p. In

Head quarters. Morris Town. 4. April 1777.

Dear Sr.

With this you will receive Two thousand Dollars, all in 30 dollar Bills — and a draft of the Recruiting Instructions to be delivered to the officers — His Excellency desires me to inform you that the Conveniencie of carrying the Money induced him to send it in such large Bills — In addition to the recruiting Instructions you will be pleased to order the officers to make Note of their Mens Size, fleshy Marks, places of their Nativity & where & by whom they were inlisted — and Ætherings appoint a place of genural Rendezvous, to which you will order the officers in the most peremptory manner to send their Recruits as fast as they are ~~so may they inlist a reasonable Number~~, equal to the trouble of sending them; in the mean time each Capth. ~~inlisted, that they may be in training while the Re~~ must fix upon some certain place for his Men to continue at, & not permit one to ~~a rutine Source is going on: for which purpose you~~ straggle about the Country, to the great Injury of the Source — ~~with appoint some experienced officer to attend there~~ you will be pleased to order some experienced Officer to remain, that he may be training the ~~constantly~~ men, while the recruiting Source is going on — Colo. Thruston has offered Captaincies,

& wrote Letters to that purpose, to Messrs. Edmund Taylor of Fredrick, Andrew Buchannan of Falmouth,

WRITING OF GEORGE JOHNSTON.

handwriting of Richard Kidder Meade. Enclosed
in Washington to the President of Congress,
1779, May 16.   C. C.   152, 7, 361

1779   `Henry, Patrick. Williamsburgh. Proclamation. Militia
MAY 14   to be held in readiness. Contemporary copy.
               In handwriting of John Jay. Enclosed in Presi-
               dent of Congress to Washington, 1779, May 22.
                                                   32, 406

1779   **McIntosh, Lachlan.** [Middlebrook.] To [George] Wash-
MAY 14   ington [Middlebrook]. Requesting an inquiry
               of his conduct; Col. George Morgan and the
               Delaware chiefs. Contemporary copy. 1 p.
               In handwriting of Richard Kidder Meade.
               Enclosed in Washington to the President of
               Congress, 1779, May 16.   C. C.   152, 7, 349

1779   **McIntosh, Lachlan.** [Middlebrook.] To [Lt. Col. Alex-
MAY 14   ander Hamilton, Middlebrook]. Investigation of
               affairs in the Western Department. Contempo-
               rary copy. 2 pp. In handwriting of James
               McHenry. Enclosed in Washington to the
               President of Congress, 1779, May 16.
                                        C. C.   152, 7, 365

[1779]   **Morgan, George.** His conduct in the Western Depart-
[MAY 14?]   ment. Contemporary copy. 1 p. In handwrit-
               ing of Richard Kidder Meade. Enclosed in
               Washington to the President of Congress, 1779,
               May 16.   C. C.   152, 7, 353

1779   **Pennsylvania,** Council. Resolve. Recommending Lt. Col.
MAY 14   Adam Hubley to the Board of War. A. D. S. of
               Timothy Matlack, marked "(copy)" 1 p. En-
               closed in Board of War to Washington, 1779,
               May 14.   93, 142

1779   **Continental Congress,** President. Philadelphia. To
MAY 15   [George] Washington [Middlebrook]. Maj. Gen.
               [Benjamin] Lincoln's retirement from South; let-
               ter of Gov. [Thomas] Johnston. L. S. of John
               Jay. 2 pp. Answered May 17.*   93, 143

1779   **[Cheever, Ezekiel.]** [Springfield, Massachusetts.] To [the
MAY 15   Board of War, Philadelphia]. Order for sup-
               plies from [Brig.] Gen. [James] Clinton. Extract
               in handwriting of Richard Peters. Enclosed in
               Board of War to Washington, 1778, May 25.
               Answered June 9.*   93, 147

1779
MAY 15

Duane, James. Philadelphia. To [George Washington, Middlebrook]. Coalescence of certain New York regiments. A. L. S. 1 p. Answered May 26.*
32, 329

1779
MAY 15

Irvine, William. Philadelphia. To the President of Congress [Philadelphia]. Claim to rank. Contemporary copy. 1 p. Enclosed in Board of War to Washington, 1779, May 17.   **Miscel.**

1779
MAY 15

[Lawson, Robert.] Smithfield [Virginia]. To Gov. [Patrick Henry, Williamsburgh]. British outrages in Virginia. [Extracts of two letters.] In handwriting of John Jay. Enclosed in President of Congress to Washington, 1779, May 22.   32, 406

1779
MAY 16

Washington, George. Middlebrook. To [the President of Congress, Philadelphia]. Case of Brig. Gen. [Lachlan] McIntosh; news from the South. Draft. 2 pp. In handwriting of James McHenry. Read in Congress May 17.
A. IV, pt. II, 45

1779
MAY 17

Washington, George. Middlebrook. To [the President of .Congress, Philadelphia]. British expedition from New York; Convention troops. 'Draft. 2 pp. In handwriting of Alexander Hamilton.
A. IV, pt. II, 47

Printed: Writings of Washington (Ford) N.Y. 1890. 7, 452.

1779
MAY 17

Washington, George. [Middlebrook.] To [the President of Congress, Philadelphia]. [Maj.] Gen. [Horatio] Gates's need of money to pay troops. Draft. 1 p. In handwriting of Robert Hanson Harrison. Referred to Board of Treasury.
A. IV, pt. II, 49

1779
MAY 17

Continental Congress, Resolve. Assistants and clerks to the Adjutant-General. Contemporary copy, attested by Charles Thomson. 1 p. Enclosed in President of Congress to Washington, 1779, May 19.   93, 151

1779
MAY 17

Continental Congress, Resolve. Indian affairs. Contemporary copy, attested by Charles Thomson. 1 p. Enclosed in President of Congress to Washington, 1779, May 19.   93, 153

1779
MAY 17

Board of War. [Philadelphia.] To George Washington, Middlebrook. Brig. Gen. [William] Irvine's claim to rank. A. L. S. of Richard Peters. 1 p.

Answered May 29. Endorsed as referred to Board of Genl. Officers July 4, 1780. **Miscel**

1779
MAY 17

Duane, James. Philadelphia. To [George Washington, Middlebrook]. Exchange of citizens. A. L. S. 1 p. Answered May 26.* **32, 327**

1779
MAY 17

Mason, Thompson. Leesburg [Virginia]. To the President of Congress [Philadelphia]. Descent of British on Portsmouth. Contemporary copy. 1 p. In handwriting of Peter Scull. Enclosed in President of Congress to Washington, 1779, May 22. **32, 402**

1779
MAY 18

Washington, George. Middlebrook. To [the Board of War, Philadelphia]. Promotion of Major [Thomas] Forrest; rank in the artillery; other promotions. Draft. 3 pp. In handwriting of Alexander Hamilton. **A. IV, pt. II, 51**

1779
MAY 18

W[ashingto]n, G[eorge]. Middlebrook. To [John Armstrong, Philadelphia]. Distresses of the present; conditions; need of exertion. Auto. draft signed. 4 pp. **P. I, pt. II, 387**

Printed: Writings of Washington (Ford) N. Y. 1890. 7, 454.

1779
MAY 18

Continental Congress, Resolve. Brig. Gen. [Lachlan] McIntosh ordered south. Contemporary copy, attested by Charles Thomson. 1 p. Enclosed in President of Congress to Washington, 1779, May 19. **93, 152**

1779
MAY 18–22

Continental Congress, Provision Committee. Extracts from letters and estimates to the Commissary General on the subject of supplies for the French. A. D. of Robert Hanson Harrison. 4 pp. **91, 243**

1779
MAY 18

Treasury Board. Philadelphia. To George Washington, Middlebrook. Resignation of army paymasters before settling accounts. L. S. of James Duane. Answered June 9.* **94, 350**

1779
MAY 18
MAY 18

Barnet, Ichabod B. Examination of [James] Hallett's actions in New York.

Brown, John. Report respecting Hallett. A. D. S. of Elias Boudinot. 1 p. Enclosed in Board of War to Washington, 1779, Aug. 31. **93, 335**

1779
MAY 19

Washington, George. Middlebrook. To Maj. Gen. [Nathanael] Greene. Wagons, tents, etc., for the Western Expedition. [Extract of letter.] Transcript. **C. C. 169, 5, 507**

[1779]   **Washington, George.** Middlebrook. To [Maj. Gen. John
[MAY 19]   Sullivan, Easton, Pennsylvania]. Overalls and
                  shirts. [Extract of letter.] Transcript. En-
                  closed in Washington to the President of Con-
                  gress, 1779, Aug. 15.   C. C.   169, 5, 523

1779   **Continental Congress,** President. Philadelphia. To
MAY 19   [George] Washington [Middlebrook]. Transmit-
                  ting resolve. L. S. of John Jay. 1 p. An-
                  swered May 25.*   93, 156

1779   **Continental Congress,** President. Philadelphia. To
MAY 19   [George] Washington [Middlebrook]. [Brig.]
                  Gen. [Lachlan] McIntosh's complaints; transmit-
                  ting resolves. L. S. of John Jay. 2 pp. An-
                  swered May 25.*   93, 149

1779   **Board of War.** [Philadelphia.] To [George] Washington
MAY 19   [Middlebrook]. Commissions for 9th Virginia
                  regiment; promotions in 6th Connecticut. A.
                  L. S. of Peter Scull. 1 p.   93, 154

1779   [Claiborne, Richard.] [Esthertown, Pennsylvania.] To
MAY 19   [Brig. Gen. Edward Hand, Wyoming]. Supplies
                  and boatmen. [Extract of letter.] Transcript.
                  Enclosed in Washington to the President of Con-
                  gress, 1779, Aug. 15.   C. C.   169, 5, 541

1779   **Claiborne,** R[ichard]. Esthertown [Pennsylvania]. To
MAY 19   [Maj. Gen. John Sullivan, Easton, Pennsylvania].
                  Provisions and boats for the Indian Expedition;
                  movement of troops, etc. Contemporary copy.
                  2 pp. In handwriting of Charles Morse. Trans-
                  mitted to Washington.   93, 258

1779   **Washington, George.** Middlebrook. To the [Executive]
MAY 20   Council of Pennsylvania [Philadelphia]. Inde-
                  pendent companies for the Western Expedition.
                  [Extract of letter.] Transcript. Enclosed in
                  Washington to the President of Congress, 1779,
                  Aug. 15.   C. C.   169, 5, 521

1779   **Johnson,** Thomas. Annapolis. To [the Maryland dele-
MAY 20   gates in Congress, Philadelphia]. British in Vir-
                  ginia; assistance for Maryland. A. L. S. 2 pp.
                  Enclosed in Maryland delegates to Washington,
                  1779, May 23.   92, 207

[1779]   [Purviance, Samuel.] [Baltimore.] To ——— ? Prepa-
[MAY 20]   rations for defense of Baltimore and Annapolis.
                  Contemporary extract of letter. 1 p. Enclosed in

Maryland delegates to Congress to Washington,
1779, May 23.   **92, 209**

1779
MAY 21

Board of War. [Philadelphia.] To [George] Washington
[Middlebrook]. Commissions and various arrange-
ment of matters among the Pennsylvania troops.
A. L. S. of Peter Scull. 2 pp.   **94, 117**

1779
MAY 21

Judd, William. Reading [Pennsylvania]. To the Board
of War [Philadelphia]. Petition respecting his
rank in the Army. A. L. S. 3 pp. Enclosed
in Board of War to Washington, 1779, June 18.
                                                93, 223

[1779]
[MAY 21]

Pennsylvania, Officers of the Line. Omissions in arrangement. A. D. S. of Peter Scull. 1 p. Enclosed
in Board of War to Washington, 1779, May 21.
                                                94, 119

1779
MAY 21

[**Schuyler,** Philip John.] [Saratoga.] To [George Wash-
ington, Middlebrook]. Intelligence from Canada.
[Extract of letter.] Transcript. Enclosed in
Washington to the President of Congress, 1779,
Aug. 15.   C. C. **169, 6, 24**

1779
MAY 21

[**Sullivan,** John.] Easton [Pennsylvania]. To [George
Washington, Middlebrook]. Delays in forwarding clothing. [Extract of letter.] Transcript.
Enclosed in Washington to the President of Congress, 1779, Aug. 15.   C. C. **169, 5, 524**

1779
MAY 21

[**Van Schaick,** Goose.] [Saratoga.] To [Brig. Gen. James
Clinton, Albany]. Intelligence from Oswego.
[Extract of letter.] Transcript. Enclosed in
Washington to the President of Congress, 1779,
Aug. 15.   C. C. **169, 6, 25**

1779
MAY 22

Washington, George. Middlebrook. To [the Board of
War, Philadelphia]. Dispute of rank between
Brig. Gens. [William] Irvine and [Edward] Hand;
far reaching consequences; minor matters of commissions. 6 pp. In handwriting of Robert Hanson Harrison.   **A. IV, pt. II, 55**

1779
MAY 22

Washington, George. Middlebrook. To the Board of War
[Philadelphia]. Orders to Col. [Theodorick]
Bland and Lt. Col. [William] Washington to join
the Southern army. Draft. 1 p. In handwriting of James McHenry.   **A. IV, pt. II, 61**

1779
MAY 22

Continental Congress, President. Philadelphia. To
[George] Washington [Middlebrook]. Enemy's

operations in Virginia.　L. S. of John Jay.　2 pp.
Answered May 25.*　　　　　　　　　　32, 400

| 1779
MAY 22 | Continental Congress, Resolve.　Rank of exchanged officers. Broadside.　Printed by Claypoole.　Enclosed in President of Congress to Washington, 1779, May 25.　　　　　　　　　　93, 167 |

1779
MAY 22　Continental Congress, Resolve.　Exchange of loyalists for
citizen prisoners.　Contemporary copy, attested
by Charles Thomson.　1 p.　Enclosed in President of Congress to Washington, 1779, May 25.
　　　　　　　　　　　　　　　　　93, 168

1779
MAY 22　Board of War.　[Philadelphia.]　To Gov. [William] Livingston and Caleb Camp [Trenton?].　State of the
New Jersey troops; numbers, deficiency etc.　Contemporary copy.　4 pp.　In handwriting of Timothy Pickering, jr.　Enclosed in Board of War to
Washington, 1779, May 27.　　　　　93, 173

1779
MAY 23　Washington, George.　Middlebrook.　To [the Board of
War, Philadelphia].　Need of shoes and overalls
for the Western Expedition.　Draft.　2 pp.　In
handwriting of Alexander Hamilton.
　　　　　　　　　　　A.　IV, pt. II, 63

1779
MAY 23　Washington, George.　Middlebrook.　To [Brig.] Gen. [Al-
exander] McDougall [Peekskill, New York].
Hunting shirts and shoes for the Western Expedition.　[Extract of letter.]　Contemporary copy.
2 pp.　In handwriting of Richard Kidder Meade.
Enclosed in Washington to the President of Congress, 1779, Aug. 21.　　　C. C.　152, 7, 623

1779
MAY 23　Washington, George.　Middlebrook.　To [George] Mea-
sam [Boston].　Supply of hunting shirts.　Contemporary copy.　1 p.　In handwriting of Tench
Tilghman.　Enclosed in Washington to the President of Congress, 1779, Aug. 21.
　　　　　　　　　　　C. C.　152, 7, 609

1779
MAY 23　Board of War.　[Philadelphia.]　To [George Washington,]
Middlebrook.　Movement of troops; Col. [Theo-
dorick] Bland; appointment of Capt. [Daniel?]
Topham.　A. L. S. of Richard Peters, with auto.
signed postscript of May 24 by T[imothy] Pickering, jr.　1 p.　Answered May 27.*　93, 160

1779
MAY 23　Maryland, Delegates to Continental Congress.　Philadelphia.　To [George Washington, Middlebrook].

British in Virginia; defense of Maryland. A. L. S.
of John Henry jr., signed also by George Plater,
Wm. Carmichael and Dan. of St. Thomas Jenifer.
2 pp. Answered May 25.* 92, 205

[1779]
[MAY 23]
[Sullivan, John.] [Easton, Pennsylvania.] To [George
Washington, Middlebrook]. The situation; want
of wagons. [Extract of letter.] Transcript. Enclosed in Washington to the President of Congress,
1779, Aug. 15. C. C. 169, 6, 59

1779
MAY 24
Washington, George. Middlebrook. To [the President
of Congress, Philadelphia]. Transmitting news-
papers. Draft. 1 p. In handwriting of Robert
Hanson Harrison. Read in Congress May 26.
A. IV, pt. II, 65

1779
MAY 24
W[ashington,] G[eorge]. Middlebrook. To Maj. Gen.
[John] Sullivan [Easton, Pennsylvania]. Shoes
and overalls for the Western Expedition. Transcript. Enclosed in Washington to the President
of Congress, 1779, Aug. 15. C. C. 169, 5, 525

[1779]
[MAY 24]
[Washington, George.] [Middlebrook.] To [Maj. Gen.
John Sullivan, Easton Pennsylvania]. Gov.
[George] Clinton's proposed expedition against
the Esopus Indians; the Western Expedition.
[Extract of letter.] Transcript. Enclosed in
Washington to the President of Congress, 1779,
Aug. 15. C. C. 169, 6, 65

1779
MAY 24
[Washington, George.] [Middlebrook.] To [Maj. Gen.
John Sullivan, Easton]. Wagons and powder.
[Extract of letter.] Transcript. Enclosed in
Washington to the President of Congress, 1779,
Aug. 16. C. C. 169, 6, 68

1779
MAY 24
Board of War. [Philadelphia.] To [George] Washington
[Middlebrook]. Supply of shoes; arms and ac-
coutrements. A. L. S. of Timothy Pickering, jr.
4 pp. 93, 163

[1779]
[MAY 24]
[Blaine, Ephraim.] [Carlisle, Pennsylvania]. To [Maj.
Gen. John Sullivan, Easton]. Abundance of provisions; lack of boots. [Extract of letter.] Transcript. Enclosed in Washington to the President
of Congress, 1779, Aug. 15. C. C. 169, 6, 60

[1779]
[MAY 25]
Washington, George. Middlebrook. To [the President
of Congress, Philadelphia]. Predatory warfare
of enemy; reenforcement of Southern army; de-

signs of enemy; lack of wagons for Western expedition. Draft. 2 pp. In handwriting of Alexander Hamilton. Read in Congress, May 28.

A. IV, pt. II, 67

Printed: Writings of Washington (Sparks) Boston. 1834. 6, 261.

1779
MAY 25

Washington, George. Middlebrook. To [the Board of War, Philadelphia]. Minor commissions and resignations. Draft. 1 p. In handwriting of James McHenry. A. IV, pt. II, 69

[1779]
[MAY 25]

Washington, George. Middlebrook. To [the Marine Committee, Philadelphia]. Proposition of destroying enemy's shipping in New York harbor. Draft. 2 pp. In handwriting of Alexander Hamilton. A. IV, pt. II, 71

1779
MAY 25

Washington, George. Middlebrook. To [the Maryland delegates to Congress, Philadelphia]. Impossibility of sending detachments to aid individual States. Draft. 3 pp. In handwriting of Robert Hanson Harrison. A. IV, pt. II, 73

Delegates: Plater, Carmichael, J. Henry, jr., and Daniel of St. Thomas Jenifer.

1779
MAY 25

Washington, George. Middlebrook. To [the Virginia delegates to Congress, Philadelphia]. Impossibility of detaching Lee's horse for service in Virginia; militia. Draft. 4 pp. In handwriting of Robert Hanson Harrison.

A. IV, pt. II, 77

Delegates: M. Smith, R. H. Lee, Griffen and Fleming.

1779
MAY 25

Washington, George. Middlebrook. To Brig. Gen. [Charles] Scott [Virginia]. Reenforcing the Southern army; aid to Virginia. Contemporary copy. 2 pp. In handwriting of Richard Kidder Meade. Enclosed in Washington to the President of Congress, 1779, May 28. C. C. 152, 7, 383

1779
MAY 25

Continental Congress, President. Philadelphia. To [George] Washington [Middlebrook]. Transmitting resolves. L. S. of John Jay. 2 pp. 93, 165

[1779]
[MAY 25.]

Board of War. Estimate of clothing necessary for army. Tabular statement giving style, colors, number of uniforms etc. A. D. of Peter Scull. 3 pp. Enclosed in Board of War to Washington, 1779, May 25. 93, 182

1779
MAY 25

Board of War. [Philadelphia.] To [George] Washington [Middlebrook]. Estimate of clothing for the army. A. L. S. of Peter Scull. 2 pp. 93, 184

1779
MAY 25
Board of War. [Philadelphia.] To [George] Washington, [Middlebrook]. [Brig.] Gen. [William] Irvine's rank; mistakes in commissions; complaints of Col. [Daniel] Brodhead; Baron de Woolfen. A. L. S. of Richard Peters. 3 pp. Answered May 27.*
93, 169

[1779]
MAY 25
Board of War. [Philadelphia.] To [Ezekiel Cheever, Springfield, Mass.]. Authority of order [of May 15]; compliance. Extract in handwriting of John Clark jr.

MAY 25
Board of War. To George Washington, Middlebrook. Transmitting above extract; decision of the Board. A. L. S. of Richard Peters. Answered June 9.*
93, 147

1779
MAY 26
Washington, George. Middlebrook. To [the President of Congress, Philadelphia]. News from Charleston [South Carolina]. Draft. 2 pp. In handwriting of James McHenry. Read in Congress, May 28.
A. IV, pt. II, 81

1779
MAY 26
Washington, George. Middlebrook. To [the Board of War, Philadelphia]. Promotion of Capt. Call of Bland's dragoons. Draft. 1 p. In handwriting of James McHenry.
A. IV, pt. II, 83

1779
MAY 26
Washington, George. Middlebrook. To [James Duane, Philadelphia]. Coalescing of New York regiments; confusion that would be caused thereby. Draft. 1 p. In handwriting of Alexander Hamilton.
A. IV, pt. II, 85

1779
MAY 26
Continental Congress, Resolve. Purchase of horses for Baylor's dragoons. Contemporary copy. 1 p. In handwriting of Richard Peters. Enclosed in Board of War to Washington, 1779, May 27.
93, 177

1779
MAY 26
Marine Committee. Philadelphia. To [George] Washington [Middlebrook]. Inability of Navy to cooperate. L. S. of Samuel Adams. 2 pp.
92, 211

[1779]
[MAY 26]
[Sullivan, John.] [Easton, Pennsylvania.] To [George Washington, Middlebrook]. Wagons and powder. [Extract of letter.] Transcript. Enclosed in Washington to the President of Congress, 1779, Aug. 15.
C. C. 169, 6, 59

1779
MAY 27
Washington, George. Middlebrook. To the Board of War [Philadelphia]. Wagons; arms for the west-

ern expedition and officers; shoes and overalls;
officers' clothing. Draft. 3 pp. In handwriting of Robert Hanson Harrison.

                                  A. IV, pt. II, 90

1779   **Board of War.** [Philadelphia.] To George Washington,
MAY 27   Middlebrook. State quotas of troops. A. L. S.
            of Richard Peters. 1 p. Answered June 9.*

                                              93, 171

1779   **Board of War.** [Philadelphia.] To George Washington,
MAY 27   Middlebrook. Purchase of horses for Baylor's
            regiment; station for unmounted men. A. L. S.
            of Richard Peters. 2 pp. Answered June 9.*

                                              93, 175

1779   **Burnet,** William. Philadelphia. Certificate of Dr. Isaac
MAY 27   Foster's management of Eastern Department,
            Continental Hospital. A. D. S. 1 p. Enclosed
            in Medical Committee to Washington, 1779, Nov.
            15.   92, 317

[1779]   **Cuyler,** Jacob. Albany. To [Maj. Gen. Philip John
[MAY 27]   Schuyler, Albany] Provision supplies. Tran-
            script. Enclosed in Washington to the President
            of Congress, 1779, Aug. 15.   C. C. 169, 5, 487

1779   **[Washington, George.]** [Middlebrook.] To [Maj. Gen.
MAY 28   John Sullivan, Easton, Pennsylvania]. Defi-
            ciency of supplies; troops. [Extract of letter.]
            Transcript. Enclosed in Washington to the
            President of Congress, 1779, Aug. 15.

                                  C. C.   169, 5, 531

1779   **Clinton,** James. Albany. To [George Washington, Mid-
MAY 28   dlebrook]. Supplies at Fort Schuyler; routes of
            march. [Extract of letter.] Transcript. En-
            closed in Washington to the President of Congress,
            1779, Aug. 15.   C. C.   169, 5, 514

1779   **Foster,** Isaac. Philadelphia. To the Medical Committee
MAY 28   of Congress [Philadelphia]. Memorial of the
            selectmen of Danbury; foundation of the com-
            plaints; conditions at Danbury. A. L. S. 4 pp.
            Enclosed in Medical Committee to Washington,
            1779, Nov. 15.   92, 315

1779   **Ryan,** M[ichael]. [Middlebrook?] To the Board of War
MAY 28   [Philadelphia]. His rank in the army. A. L. S.
            Enclosed in Board of War to Washington, 1779,
            May 29.   93, 180

1779
MAY 29

Washington, George. Middlebrook. To [the President of Congress, Philadelphia]. Acknowledging letter. Draft. 1 p. In handwriting of Robert Hanson Harrison.   A. IV, pt. II, 87

1779
MAY 29

Board of War. [Philadelphia.] To [George] Washington, Middlebrook. Inspectorship for Major [Michael] Ryan. A. L. S. of Timothy Pickering, jr. 1 p. Answered June 9.*   93, 178

1779
MAY 29

Continental Army, Board of General Officers. Middlebrook. Proceedings on Major [Joseph] Prowell's claim to his majority. Contemporary copy. 2 pp. In handwriting of Caleb Gibbs. Enclosed in Washington to the President of Congress 1779, June 3.   C. C. 152, 7, 397

1779
MAY 29-
JUNE 1

[McDougall, Alexander.] [Peekskill, New York.] To [George Washington, Middlebrook]. Intelligence of British advance up the Hudson [Extracts of letters.] In handwriting of Richard Kidder Meade. Enclosed in Washington to the President of Congress, 1779, June 3.
    C. C. 152, 7, 405

1779
MAY 29

Wayne, Anthony. [Middlebrook.] To the Board of War [Philadelphia]. Recommending Maj. [Michael] Ryan. A. L. S. 2 pp. Enclosed in Board of War to Washington, 1779, May 29.   93, 181

1779
MAY 30

Washington, George. Middlebrook. To [the Board of War, Philadelphia]. Commissions for officers in the Maryland line; Lt. Col. [Adam] Hubley's right to command; other promotions. Draft. 2 pp. In handwriting of Robert Hanson Harrison.   A. IV, pt. II, 93

1779
MAY 30

Thompson, William. Carlisle [Pennsylvania]. To Peter Scull, Philadelphia. Mistake in exchange. A. L. S. 1 p. Enclosed in Board of War to Washington, 1779, June 12.   93, 270

1779
MAY 31

[Washington, George.] [Middlebrook.] To Maj. Gen. [John] Sullivan [Easton, Pennsylvania]. Instructions for guidance of Western Expedition. Transcript. Enclosed in Washington to the President of Congress, 1779, Aug. 15.
    C. C. 169, 5, 532
Printed: Writings of Washington (Ford) N. Y. 1890. 7, 460.

1779
MAY 31

[Washington, George.] Middlebrook. To [Maj. Gen. John Sullivan, Easton, Pennsylvania]. Clothing and shoes for the Western Expedition. [Extract of letter.] Transcript. Enclosed in Washington to the President of Congress, 1779, Aug. 15.

C. C.   169, 5, 527

1779
MAY 31

Bland, Theodorick. Charlottesville [Virginia]. To the Board of War [Philadelphia]. Application of convention officers to go into New York. A. L. S. 1 p. Enclosed in Board of War to Washington 1779, June 8.   93, 221

1779
MAY 31-
JUNE 1

[Clark, Jonathan] [Paramus, New Jersey] To [George Washington, Middlebrook]. British advance up the Hudson. [Extract of letter.] In handwriting of Richard Kidder Meade. Enclosed in Washington to the President of Congress, 1779, June 3.   C. C.   152, 7, 405

1779
MAY 31

[Sullivan, John.] [Easton, Pennsylvania]. To [George Washington, Middlebrook]. Col. [Ephraim] Blaine's letter. [Extract of letter.] Transcript. Enclosed in Washington to the President of Congress, 1779, Aug. 15.   C. C.   169, 6, 60

[1779]
[MAY ?]

Anonymous. Report of repulse of British at Charleston [South Carolina]. Contemporary copy. 2 pp. Enclosed in President of Congress to Washington, 1779, June 7.   93, 204

[1779]
[MAY ?]

Pennsylvania, Captains of the Line. To [George] Washington [Middlebrook]. Memorial; majority of Capt. Joseph Prowell; promotions, seniority, etc. Contemporary copy. 3 pp. In handwriting of Robert Hanson Harrison. Enclosed in Washington to the President of Congress, June 3.

C. C.   152, 7, 393

1779
JUNE 1

Washington, George. Middlebrook. To the Board of War [Philadelphia]. Arrangement of New Hampshire officers; clothing for Pennsylvania troops; repairs to shoes. Draft. 3 pp. In handwriting of James McHenry.   A. IV, pt. II, 95

1779
JUNE 1

Washington, George. Middlebrook. To the Marine Committee [Philadelphia]. Recommending Maj. [William] Blodget. Draft. 2 pp. In handwriting of Alexander Hamilton.

A. IV, pt. II, 99

1779
JUNE 1

Blaine, Ephraim. Philadelphia. To [Col.] Jeremiah Wadsworth [Middlebrook]. Beef supply for the Western Expedition. [Extract of letter.] Transcript. Enclosed in Washington to the President of Congress, 1779, Aug. 15.   **C. C. 169**, 5, 508

1779
JUNE 2

Board of War, [Philadelphia.] To [George] Washington, Middlebrook. Arrangement of Proctor's artillery. A. L. S. of Peter Scull. 1 p. Answered June 6.   **93**, 186

1779
JUNE 2

Harnage, Henry. Cambridge [Massachusetts]. To [Maj. Gen. William Phillips, Charlottesville, Virginia]. His journey to Charlottesville. Contemporary copy. 1 p. Enclosed in President of Congress to Washington, 1779, Aug. 26.   **93**, 322

1779
JUNE 2

[St. Clair, Arthur.] [Pompton, New Jersey.] To [George Washington, Middlebrook]. Movements of British on the Hudson. [Extract of letter.] In handwriting of Richard Kidder Meade. Enclosed in Washington to the President of Congress, 1779, June 3.   **C. C. 152**, 7, 405

1779
JUNE 2

[Sullivan, John.] [Easton, Pennsylvania.] To [George Washington, Middlebrook]. Terms with the Indians. [Extract of letter.] Transcript. Enclosed in Washington to the President of Congress, 1779, Aug. 15.   **C. C. 169**, 5, 540

1779
JUNE 3

Washington, George. Middlebrook. To [the President of Congress, Philadelphia]. Movement of troops to check enemy; lack of wagons and forage; want of money to pay troops at Providence. Draft. 2 pp. In handwriting of Alexander Hamilton. Read in Congress, June 5.   **A. IV**, pt. II, 103
Printed: Writings of Washington (Ford) N. Y. 1890. 7, 463.

1779
JUNE 3

Washington, George. Middlebrook. To [the President of Congress, Philadelphia]. Disputes over rank in the Pennsylvania and New York line. Draft. 2 pp. In handwriting of Robert Hanson Harrison. Read in Congress, June 5. Acted on.   **A. IV**, pt. II, 101

1779
JUNE 3

Washington, George. [Middlebrook] [New Jersey]. To [the President of Congress, Philadelphia]. Return of British from Chesapeake Bay to New York. Draft. 1 p. In handwriting of Robert Hanson Harrison.   **A. IV**, pt. II, 105

1779
JUNE 3

Continental Congress, Resolve. Brig. Gen. [William] Thompson's and others petition; parole exchanges. Contemporary copy, attested by Charles Thom-

son. 1 p. Enclosed in President of Congress to
Washington, 1779, June 4.   93, 194

1779   Board of War. [Philadelphia.] To [George] Washington
JUNE 3   [Middlebrook]. Term of enlistment and minor
matters. A. L. S. of Peter Scull. 3 pp.
Answered June 9.*   93, 188

1779   [Washington, George.] [Middlebrook]. To [Maj. Gen.
JUNE 4   John Sullivan, Easton, Pennsylvania]. Terms
with Indians. [Extract of letter.] Transcript.
Enclosed in Washington to the President of Congress, 1779, Aug. 15.   C. C. 169, 5, 543

1779   Continental Congress, President. Philadelphia.   To
JUNE 4   [George] Washington [en route to the Highlands].
Transmitting resolves; victory at Charleston;
report of cartel commissioners. A. L. S. of John
Jay. 1 p. Answered June 11.*   93, 192

1779   Board of War. [Philadelphia.] To [George] Washington
JUNE 4   [Middlebrook]. Arrangement of the New Hamp-
shire Line, mistakes etc. A. L. S. of Peter
Scull. 2 pp. Answered June 9.*   93, 190

1779   Continental Congress, President. Philadelphia.   To
JUNE 5   [George] Washington [Middlebrook]. Receipt
of letters. A. L. S. 1 p. Answered June 11.*
93, 197

1779   Continental Congress, Resolves. Rank of Col. [Lewis]
JUNE 5   Dubois; Maj. [Joseph] Prowell's commission and
rank of Pennsylvania officers. Contemporary
copy, attested by Charles Thomson. 1 p. Enclosed in President of Congress to Washington
1779, June 7.   93, 203

1779   Board of War. [Philadelphia.] To [George] Washington,
JUNE 5   Middlebrook. Transmitting commissions for the
Maryland Line. A. L. S. of Peter Scull. 1 p.
Answered June 9.*   93, 195

1779   Phillips, W[illiam]. Charlottesville [Virginia]. To the
JUNE 5   President of Congress [Philadelphia]. Exchange
of Capt. [William] Featherstone. In handwriting of Timothy Pickering, jr.   93, 230

1779   Washington, George. Ringwood Iron Works [New Jer-
JUNE 6   sey]. To [the President of Congress, Philadel-
phia]. Enemy's works at Stony Point and capture of Fort Lafayette; maneuvers in the river.

Draft. 4 pp. In handwriting of Robert Hanson Harrison. Read in Congress June 10.

A. IV, pt. II, 107

Printed: Writings of Washington (Ford) N. Y. 1890. 7, 465.

1779
JUNE 6

Washington, George. Ringwood. To [the Board of War, Philadelphia]. Promotions in the artillery. Draft. 2 pp. In handwriting of Alexander Hamilton. **A.** IV, pt. II, 113

1779
JUNE 6

Hand, Edward. Wyoming [Pennsylvania]. To Maj. Gen. [John] Sullivan [Easton, Pennsylvania]. Movement of troops. Contemporary copy. 1 p. In handwriting of Charles Morse. Transmitted to Washington. **93, 255**

1779
JUNE 7

Continental Congress, President. Philadelphia. To [George] Washington [Smith's Clove, New York]. Transmitting resolves and other papers. Letter-book copy. **C. C. 14, 126**

1779
JUNE 7

Fallon, James. Philadelphia. Order to Dr. Jacob Ehrenseller to appear before Investigating Committee. Contemporary copy. Enclosed in President of Congress to Washington 1779, July 20. **93, 272**

1779
JUNE 9

Washington, George. Smith's Clove. To the Board of War. [Philadelphia.] Minor military matters; promotions, enlistments, bounties. Draft. 7 pp. In handwriting of Robert Hanson Harrison and Alexander Hamilton. **A.** IV, pt. II, 115

1779
JUNE 9

Washington, George. Smith's Clove. To the Board of Treasury [Philadelphia]. Officers leaving the service without settling their accounts. Draft. 1 p. In handwriting of Robert Hanson Harrison. **A.** IV, pt. II, 123

1779
JUNE 9

Washington, George. Middlebrook. To Col. [William] Malcolm, near Deans Furnace, [New Jersey]. Disbanding the militia. L. S. 1 p. In handwriting of Alexander Hamilton. Transmitted to Congress? **C. C. 152, 7, 435**

[1779]
[JUNE 9]

Washington, George. Smith's Clove. To [Maj. Gen. John Sullivan, Easton, Pennsylvania]. Cooperation with [Brig.] Gen. [James] Clinton. [Extract of letter.] Transcript. Enclosed in Washington to the President of Congress, 1779, Aug. 15. **C. C. 169, 5, 543**

[1779]
[JUNE 10]

Washington, George. [Smith's Clove.] To Brig. Gen. [James] Clinton [Albany]. Junction with [Maj.] Gen. [John] Sullivan. [Extract of letter.] Transcript. Enclosed in Washington to the President of Congress, 1779, Aug. 15. **C. C. 169, 5, 544**

1779
JUNE 10

Continental Congress, Resolve. Case of Messieurs Geranger. A. D. S. of Charles Thomson. 1 p. Enclosed in Board of War to Washington, 1779, June 11. **93, 206**

1779
JUNE 10

Anonymous. Montreal. To [Maj. Gen. Philip John Schuyler, Saratoga]. Intelligence of movement of troops to the Indian country. Transcript. Enclosed in Washington to the President of Congress, 1779, Aug. 15. **C. C. 169, 6, 26**

1779
JUNE 11

Washington, George. Smith's Clove. To [the President of Congress, Philadelphia]. Fortifications of enemy at Verplanks and Stony Point. Draft. 2 pp. In handwriting of Alexander Hamilton. Read in Congress, June 16. Referred to Gerry, Armstrong and Laurens. **A. IV, pt. II, 125**
Printed in part: Writings of Washington (Ford) N. Y. 1890. 7, 470, note.

1779
JUNE 11

Washington, George. Smith's Clove. To Michael Hillegas [Philadelphia]. Requesting hard money for secret service purposes. Draft. 1 p. In handwriting of Robert Hanson Harrison.
A. IV, pt. II, 127

1779
JUNE 11

Board of War. [Philadelphia.] To [George] Washington [Smith's Tavern]. Case of Messieurs Geranger. A. L. S. of Timothy Pickering, jr. 1 p. Answered June 23.* **93, 207**

1779
JUNE 12

Board of War. Philadelphia. Correction of an exchange mistake. A. L. S. of Timothy Pickering, jr. 1 p. Answered June 23.* **93, 209**

1779
JUNE 12

Smith, James. Philadelphia. Petition to Congress. Respecting his situation. A. D. 1 p. Read in Congress, June 14. Referred to the Commander in chief. Enclosed in President of Congress to Washington, 1779, June 12. **93, 218**

1779
JUNE 12

[Sullivan, John.] [Easton, Pennsylvania.] To [George Washington, Smith's Clove]. Preparations to commence march; delays. [Extract of letter.] Transcript. Enclosed in Washington to the President of Congress, 1779, Aug. 15.
C. C. 169, 6, 61

1779 June 14	Washington, George. Smith's Clove. To [the President of Congress, Philadelphia]. News from South Carolina. Draft. 1 p. In handwriting of Robert Hanson Harrison. **A.** IV, pt. II, 129
1779 June 14	Board of War. [Philadelphia.] To [George] Washington [Smith's Tavern]. Transmitting intelligence. A. L. S. of Timothy Pickering, jr. 1 p. 93, 212
1779 June 14	Board of War. [Philadelphia.] To Lt. Col. [Anthony Walton] White [New Jersey]. British spies from New York. L. S. of Timothy Pickering, jr. 2 pp. 93, 214
1779 June 15	Continental Congress, President. Philadelphia. To [George] Washington [Smith's Clove]. Case of Lt. [James] Smith. L. S. of John Hancock. 1 p. Answered June 23.* 93, 216
1779 June 15	Continental Congress, Resolve. Investigation of charges against Dr. William Shippen, jr. A. D. S. of Charles Thomson. 1 p. Enclosed in President of Congress to Washington, 1779, June 30. 93, 244
1779 June 15	Morgan, John. Philadelphia. To [the President of Congress, Philadelphia]. Charging Dr. William Shippen, jr. with mal-practices. Contemporary copy. 3 pp. Enclosed in President of Congress to Washington, 1779, June 30. 93, 245
1779 June 18	Continental Congress, Resolve. Exchange of Capt. [William] Featherstone. A. D. of Chas. Thomson. Transmitted to Washington. 93, 230
1779 June 18	Board of War. [Philadelphia.] To [George] Washington [Smith's Clove]. Exchange of Capt. [William] Featherstone and other minor matters. A. L. S. of Peter Scull. 2 pp. Answered June 25.* 93, 219
1779 June 19	Board of War. [Philadelphia.] To [George] Washington [Smith's Clove]. Transmitting sets of Journals of Congress. A. L. S. of Peter Scull. 1 p. Answered June 25.* 93, 225 Memo. of above vols. 1 p. 93, 227.
[1779] [June 19]	[Clinton, James.] [Conojaharie Creek, New York.] To [George] Washington [Smith's Clove]. Intelligence from Buck Island. [Extract of letter.] Transcript. Enclosed in Washington to the President of Congress, 1779, Aug. 15. C. C. 169, 6, 28

1779
JUNE 19   **Ehrenseller, J[acob].** Philadelphia. Certificate of collusion between Doctors James Fallon and William Shippen, jr. Contemporary copy. Enclosed in President of Congress to Washington, 1779, July 20.
     93, 272

1779
JUNE 21   **Washington, George.** Smith's Clove. To [the Board of War Philadelphia]. The military situation and minor matters. Draft. 1 p. In handwriting of Richard Kidder Meade.   A. IV, pt. II, 131

[1779]
[JUNE 21]   **[Washington, George.]** [Smiths Clove]. To [Maj. Gen. John Sullivan, Easton, Pennsylvania]. New York militia for the Western Expedition. [Extract of letter.] Transcript. Enclosed in Washington to the President of Congress, 1779, Aug. 15.
     C. C. 169, 6, 69

1779
JUNE 20   **Continental Congress, President.** Philadelphia. To [George] Washington [Smith's Clove]. Transmitting papers. L. S. of John Jay. 2 pp. Answered June 28.   93, 228

[1779]
JUNE [21]   **Harrison, Robert H[anson].** [Smith's Clove.] To the Board of War [Philadelphia]. Arrangement of officers in the New Hampshire line. Auto. draft signed. 1 p.   A. IV, pt. II, 133

1779
JUNE 22   **Continental Congress, Resolves.** Pay of brigade inspectors; gratuity to privates enlisted for the war. Contemporary copy, attested by Charles Thomson. 1 p. Enclosed in Board of War to Washington, 1779, July 28.   93, 232

1779
JUNE 22   **Continental Congress, Resolve.** Plundering of inhabitants. Contemporary copy, attested by Charles Thomson. 1 p. Enclosed in President of Congress to Washington, 1779, June 24. Published in Genl. Orders, July 1.   93, 239

1779
JUNE 23   **Washington, George.** New Windsor [New York]. To [the President of Congress, Philadelphia]. Removal of headquarters; enemy's news from South. Draft. 1 p. In handwriting of Alexander Hamilton. Read in Congress, June 28. Referred to Board of War.   A. IV, pt. II, 135

1779
JUNE 23   **Washington, George.** New Windsor. To the Board of War. [Philadelphia]. Arrangement and promotions of officers. Draft. 1 p. In handwriting of Robert Hanson Harrison.   A. IV, pt. II, 137

1779
JUNE 23

Board of War. [Philadelphia.] To [George] Washington [New Windsor]. Transmitting commission. A. L. S. of Peter Scull. 1 p. 93, 235

1779
JUNE 24

Continental Congress, President. Philadelphia. To [George] Washington [New Windsor]. Transmitting resolves. L. S. of John Hancock. 1 p. Answered July 1.* 93, 237

1779
JUNE 25

Washington, George. New Windsor. To the Board of War [Philadelphia] Arrangement, promotions and disputes of rank of officers. Draft. 3 pp. In handwriting of Robert Hanson Harrison.
A. IV, pt. II, 139

1779
JUNE 25

Armstrong, John. Philadelphia. To [George] Washington [New Windsor]. Expectation of return of Comte D'Estaing; finances and the depreciation; foreign affairs; the fisheries; half-pay; report of victory near Charleston; British inability to raise troops; land transfer. A. L. S. 5 pp. 33, 214

1779
JUNE 25

Gates, Horatio. Providence [Rhode Island]. To George Washington [New Windsor]. Sailing of a British fleet from Newport.

Topham, John. Little Compton [Rhode Island]. To [Brig.] Gen. [Ezekiel] Cornell [Tiverton, Rhode Island]. Sailing of British fleet from Newport.

Greene, C[hristopher]. East Greenwich [Rhode Island]. To Maj. Gen. Gates. Sailing of above fleet. Contemporary copies. 3 pp. In handwriting of Robert Hanson Harrison. Enclosed in Washington to the President of Congress, 1779, June 1.
C. C. 152, 7, 443

1779
JUNE 25

Sullivan, John. Wyoming [Pennsylvania]. To [George] Washington, [New Windsor]. Spoiled supplies; lack of troops. Transcript. Enclosed in Washington to the President of Congress, 1779, Aug. 15. C. C. 169, 6, 70

1779
JUNE 26

Clinton, James. Conojaharie Creek [New York]. To [George Washington, New Windsor]. Forwarding of batteaux and provisions. [Extract of letter.] Transcript. Enclosed in Washington to the President of Congress, 1779, Aug. 15.
C. C. 169, 6, 63

1779
JUNE 27

Washington, George. New Windsor. To [the President of Congress, Philadelphia]. Inefficiency of the

Clothier General's department; situation of the sixteen additional regiments; officers; supply of rum and minor military matters. Draft. 4 pp. In handwriting of Alexander Hamilton. Read in Congress July 6. Referred to Committee of Conference. **A.** IV, pt. II, 143

Printed: Writings of Washington (Ford) N. Y. 1890. 7,471.

1779
JUNE 27

Washington, George. New Windsor. To [Brig.] Gen. [James] Clinton [Albany]. Transportation of stores; rapidity and secrecy of movement. [Extract of letter.] Transcript. Enclosed in Washington to the President of Congress, 1779, Aug. 15. **C. C.** 169, 5, 545

1779
JUNE 27

[**Sullivan,** John.] Wyoming [Pennsylvania]. To [George Washington, New Windsor]. Spoiling of provisions; need of clothing. [Extract of letter.] Transcript. Enclosed in Washington to the President of Congress, 1779, Aug. 15.

C. C. 169, 5, 527

1779
JUNE 28

[**Washington,** George.] New Windsor. To [Gov. George Clinton, Poughkeepsie, New York]. New York troops for the Western expedition. Transcript. Enclosed in Washington to the President of Congress, 1779, Aug. 15. **C. C.** 169, 6, 71

1779
JUNE 28

Continental Congress, Resolve. Filling of State battalion. Contemporary copy, attested by Charles Thomson. 1 p. Enclosed in President of Congress to Washington, 1779, June 30. **93, 243**

1779
JUNE 28

Continental Congress, Resolves. Filling of State regiment vacancies in the Continental Line. Contemporary copy, attested by Charles Thomson. 1 p. Enclosed in President of Congress to Washington, 1779, June 30. **93, 243**

1779
JUNE 28

Board of War. [Philadelphia.] To [George] Washington [New Windsor]. Transmitting resolves. A. L. S. 1 p. Answered July 22.* **93, 233**

1779
JUNE 29

[**Sullivan,** John.] [Wyoming, Pennsylvania.] To [George Washington, New Windsor]. Boats and stores; New York troops; strength of expedition. [Extract of letter.] Transcript. Enclosed in Washington to the President of Congress, 1779, Aug. 15. **C. C.** 169, 6, 72

1779
JUNE 30

Washington, George. New Windsor. To the President of Congress, Philadelphia. Col. [Daniel] Mor-

3/

Head Quarters Army
at Middle Brook June 30. 1777

Sir,

I yesterday received your favour of the 28th instant with the inclosures. ——

Every proper measure has been already taken with respect to the Artillery, imported in the Amphitrite. The whole 52 pieces have been bought on to Springfield, and the 31 of the Swedish light construction is ordered on to Litchfield, from which place they will be forwarded to camp as fast as circumstances will permit. ... The other 21 are made upon an old plan exceedingly heavy and unmanageable, intended to be used principally in embrazures, and requiring so large a number of horses to carry them, and men to manœuvre them as must render them very inconvenient for field service, and the more liable to be lost in an unsuccessful action. —

— For these reasons, it has been judged expedient to have them cast over, and constructed upon a lighter plan, which besides making them more portable and convenient for use, will be attended with the advantage of increasing the number. ... Each of those heavy four pounders, will make nearly three six pounders, sufficiently substantial for any purpose whatever. ... Congress have directed the Council of Massa:-chusetts to establish a foundery, and have them new cast, and Springfield is the place designed for the purpose. — It were to be wished, that a matter of such importance, may meet with no delays, that can be avoided. ...

The light pieces, will all join the army as fast as the repairs they want can be completed, and the necessary horses and tackling provided to convey them — and

WRITING OF ALEXANDER HAMILTON.

gan's resignation. L. S. 1 p. In handwriting of Alexander Hamilton. Referred to Board of War.   C. C. 152, 7, 431

1779
June 30

Continental Congress, President. Philadelphia. To [George] Washington [New Windsor]. Charges against Dr. [William] Shippen [jr]. L. S. of John Jay. 2 pp. Answered July 9.*   93, 240

1779
June 30

Clinton, James. Conojaharie [New York]. To [George Washington, New Windsor]. Transportation of provisions. [Extract of letter.] Transcript. Enclosed in Washington to the President of Congress, 1779, Aug. 15.   C. C. 169, 6, 1

1779
June 30

[Schuyler, Philip John.] [Saratoga, New York.] To [George Washington, New Windsor]. Intelligence from Canada. [Extract of letter.] Transcript. Enclosed in Washington to the President of Congress, 1779, Aug. 15.   C. C. 169, 6, 26

[1779]
[May–
Juue?]

[Washington, George.] [Middlebrook?] Summary of intelligence from [Brig.] Gen. [Edward] Hand, Cols. [James] Cox, [Samuel] Patterson and [Charles] Stewart relative to the Indian country. A. D. 20 pp. Enclosed in Washington to the President of Congress, 1779, Aug. 15.   **W**

The nineteen questions propounded by Washington to these officers, with summaries of their replies, are arranged in parallel columns. The original answers to the questions are in the Force papers.

1779
July 1

Washington, George. New Windsor. To [the President of Congress, Philadelphia]. Prevention of plundering; movements of enemy; rations etc. to Inspectors. Draft. 2 pp. In handwriting of Robert Hanson Harrison. Read in Congress, July 5. Referred to Board of War.
                                   A. IV, pt. II, 147

1779
July 1

W[ashington,] G[eorge]. New Windsor. To [Maj.] Gen. [John] Sullivan [Wyoming, Pennsylvania]. Transportation of stores by [Brig.] Gen. [James] Clinton; embarrassments; men and clothing; rapidity of movement. Transcript. Enclosed in Washington to the President of Congress, 1779, Aug. 15.   C. C. 169, 6, 73

Printed in part: Writings of Washington (Ford) N. Y. 1890. 7, 477.

1779
July 1

Sullivan, John. Wyoming. To [George] Washington [New Windsor]. Intelligence of British reenforcement for the Indian country. [Extract of letter.] Transcript. Enclosed in Washington to the President of Congress, 1779, Aug. 15.

C. C.   169, 6, 29

1779
JULY 2

Hinman, John. Philadelphia. Certificate of conditions at general hospital at Bethlehem [Pennsylvania]. Affidavit of truth of above before Benjamin Paschall, July 3. Contemporary copy. 2 pp. In handwriting of George Bond. Enclosed in President of Congress to Washington, 1779, July 20.

93, 27

1779
JULY 2

Hubley, Adam, jr. [Sunbury, Pennsylvania]. To Maj. Gen. [John] Sullivan [Easton, Pennsylvania]. Forwarding supplies by boats; condition of salt beef, etc. Contemporary copy. 3 pp. In handwriting of Peter Bryan Bruin. Transmitted to Washington.

93, 256

1779
JULY 3

Sheldon, Elisha. Salem [New Jersey]. To [Maj. Gen. William Heath, Mandeville, New York.] Skirmish at Poundridge [New York]. Contemporary copy. 2 pp. In handwriting of Caleb Gibbs. Enclosed in Washington to the President of Congress, 1779, July 9.   C. C.   152, 7, 527

1779
JULY 3

Wadsworth, Jeremiah. New Windsor. To [George Washington? New Windsor]. Beef for the Western Expedition. Transcript.   C. C.   169, 5, 507

1779
JULY 4

Collier, Sir George and William **Tryon.** [Long Island] Sound. Address to Inhabitants of Connecticut recommending a return to British allegiance. Broadside. 1 p. Enclosed in Washington to the President of Congress, 1779, July 13.

C. C.   152, 7, 545

1779
JULY 5

Washington, George. New Windsor. To [the Executive Council of Pennsylvania, Philadelphia]. Pressing need of men for the Western Expedition. [Extract of letter.] Transcript. Enclosed in Washington to the President of Congress, 1779, Aug. 15.   C. C.   169, 5, 521

Printed in part: Writings of Washington (Ford) N. Y. 1890. 7, 479, note.

1779
JULY 5

Washington, George. New Windsor. To [Maj. Gen. John Sullivan, Wyoming]. [Brig.] Gen. [James] Clinton's supplies and manoeuvres of Western Expedition. Transcript. Enclosed in Washington to the President of Congress, 1779, Aug. 15.

C. C.   169, 6, 3

1779
JULY 7

Armstrong, John. Philadelphia. To [George Washington, New Windsor]. Reinstatement of Maj. [Francis] Nichols; news from Charleston. A. L. S. 2 pp. **33, 233**

1779
JULY 7

[Schuyler, Philip John.] Albany. To [George Washington, New Windsor]. Intelligence of Indian preparations. [Extract of letter.] Transcript. Enclosed in Washington to the President of Congress, 1779, Aug. 15. **C. C. 169, 6, 30**

1779
JULY 7

Trumbull, Jonathan. Lebanon [Connecticut]. To [George Washington, New Windsor]. Descent of enemy on New Haven. Contemporary copy. 3 pp. In handwriting of John Trumbull? Enclosed in Washington to the President of Congress, 1779, Aug. 6. **C. C. 152, 7, 489**

1779
JULY 7

Whiting, Samuel. [Near New Haven, Connecticut.] To Maj. Gen. [William] Tryon [New Haven]. Reply to his flag. Contemporary copy. 1 p. In handwriting of Robert Hanson Harrison. Enclosed in Washington to the President of Congress, 1779, July 13. **C. C. 152, 7, 493**

1779
JULY 9

Washington, George. New Windsor. To [the President of Congress, Philadelphia]. Movements of enemy; affair at Bedford [New York]; trials of Dr. [William] Shippen, [jr.] and [Maj.] Gen. [Benedict] Arnold; recruits; news of enemy. Draft. 6 pp. In handwriting of Robert Hanson Harrison. Read in Congress, July 13. Referred to Marchant, Huntington and Armstrong. Committee discharged Nov. 13. **A. IV, pt. II, 149**

Printed in part: Writings of Washington (Sparks) Boston. 1834. 6, 285.

1779
JULY 9

Continental Congress, President. Philadelphia. To [George] Washington [New Windsor]. Appointment of Peter Wickoff, clothier-general; transmitting papers. A. L. S. of John Jay. 1 p. Answered July 13.* **93, 246**

1779
JULY 10

Washington, George. New Windsor. To [Brig.] Gen. [Anthony] Wayne [near Stony Point]. Suggesting plan of attempt against enemy's works. Contemporary copy. 5 pp. In handwriting of Robert Hanson Harrison. Enclosed in Washington to the President of Congress, 1779, July 20. **C. C. 152, 7, 511**

Printed: Writings of Washington (Ford) N. Y. 1890. 7, 487.

1779
JULY 10

Parsons, Samuel H[olden]. Norwalk [Connecticut]. To [George] Washington [New Windsor]. Ravages of enemy in Connecticut; skirmishes at East Haven and Fairfield. Contemporary copy. 3 pp. In handwriting of Caleb Gibbs. Enclosed in Washington to the President of Congress, 1779, July 13.   C. C. **152, 7, 537**

1779
JULY 10

Sullivan, John. Wyoming [Pennsylvania] To [George Washington, New Windsor]. Failure of provision supplies; junction with [Brig.] Gen. [James] Clinton. Transcript. Enclosed in Washington to the President of Congress, 1779, Aug. 15.   C. C. **169, 6, 5**

1779
JULY 10

Trumbull, Jonathan. Lebanon [Connecticut]. To George Washington [New Windsor]. Ravages of enemy in Connecticut. Contemporary copy. 3 pp. In handwriting of Caleb Gibbs. Enclosed in Washington to the President of Congress, 1779, July 13.   C. C. **152, 7, 533**

1779
JULY 11

Washington, George. New Windsor. To [the Board of War, Philadelphia]. Cannon and carriages for works [at West Point]. Draft. 2 pp. In handwriting of Alexander Hamilton.

     A. IV, pt. II, 155

1779
JULY 11

Parsons, Samuel H[olden]. Wilton [Connecticut]. To [George] Washington [New Windsor]. Encounter with British at Norwalk. Contemporary copy. 3 pp. In handwriting of Caleb Gibbs. Enclosed in Washington to the President of Congress, 1779, July 13.   C. C. **152, 7, 541**

1779
JULY 11

Parsons, Samuel H[olden]. [Fort Arnold, Connecticut]. Return of buildings at Norwalk, destroyed by British. A. D. S. 1 p. Enclosed in Washington to the President of Congress, 1779, Aug. 6.

     C. C. **152, 7, 559**

1779
JULY 13

Washington, George. New Windsor. To [the President of Congress, Philadelphia]. Depredations of enemy in Connecticut; movement of troops; payment of bounties; lack of money. Draft. 4 pp. In handwriting of Robert Hanson Harrison. Read in Congress, July 19. Referred to Morris, Carmichael and Whipple.   **A.** IV, pt. II, 157

1779
JULY 13

Continental Congress, President. Philadelphia. To [George] Washington [New Windsor]. Transmitting intelligence. Letter-book copy..
C. C. 14, 148

1779
JULY 13

Hand, Edward. Kelso's Ferry [Pennsylvania]. To Maj. Gen. [John] Sullivan [Easton, Pennsylvania]. Forwarding of stores [for Indian Expedition; boats etc. Contemporary copy. 2 pp. In handwriting of Peter Bryan Bruin. Transmitted to Washington.   93, 253

1779
JULY 14

Hand, Edward. Kelso's Ferry [Pennsylvania]. To Maj. Gen. [John] Sullivan [Easton]. Forwarding stores [for the Indian Expedition]; transportation. Contemporary copy. 2 pp. In handwriting of Charles Morse. Transmitted to Washington.
93, 251

[1779]
[JULY 15]

Continental Congress, President. Philadelphia. To [George] Washington [New Windsor]. Receipt of letters; appointment of Lt. Col. Persifor Frazer, Clothier General, in place of Peter Wikoff; resolves transmitted. Letter-book copy.
C. C. 14, 150

1779
JULY 15

Steel, Alexander. Sunbury [Pennsylvania]. To [Maj. Gen. John Sullivan, Easton, Pennsylvania]. Stores [for the Indian Expedition]; flour, bread, cattle, packhorses. Contemporary copy. 2 pp. In handwriting of George Bond. Transmitted to Washington.   93, 249

1779
JULY 15

Wayne, Anthony. [Near Stony Point.] Orders for assault on Stony Point. Transcript. Enclosed in Washington to the President of Congress, 1776, July 21.   C. C. 169, 5, 407

1779
JULY 16

Washington, George. New Windsor. To [the President of Congress, Philadelphia]. Announcement [of capture of Stony Point]. Draft. 1 p. In handwriting of Robert Hanson Harrison
A. IV, pt. II, 161
Printed: Writings of Washington (Sparks) Boston. 1834. 6, 297.

1779
JULY 17

Rush, B[enjamin]. [Philadelphia.] To Dr. John Morgan [Philadelphia]. Charges against Dr. William Shippen, jr. Contemporary copy. 2 pp. In handwriting of Charles Morse. Enclosed in President of Congress to Washington, 1779, July 20.   93, 269

1779
JULY 18

Board of War. Philadelphia. To [George Washington, New Windsor]. Intelligence from Charleston; actions at Stono Ferry and other places. A. L. S. of Timothy Pickering, jr. 4 pp. 32, 333

1779
JULY 18

[Rice, John?] [Boston.] To [Maj. Gen. Horatio Gates, Providence]. Reports of British designs against Boston. [Extract of letter.] In handwriting of Alexander Hamilton. Enclosed in Washington to the President of Congress, 1779, July 29.

C. C. 152, 7, 459

1779
JULY 19

Morgan, John. Philadelphia. To the President of Congress [Philadelphia]. Charges against Dr. [William] Shippen, jr.; his removal from command. Contemporary copy. 5 pp. Enclosed in President of Congress to Washington, 1779, July 20.

93, 267

1779
JULY 19

Parsons, S[amuel] H[olden]. [Stamford, Connecticut]. Return of buildings burned by British at Fairfield. A. D. S. 1 p. Enclosed in Washington to the President of Congress, 1779, Aug. 6.

C. C. 152, 7, 557.

1779
JULY 20

Washington, George. [New Windsor.] To [the President of Congress, Philadelphia]. Plans of enemy. Draft. 1 p. In handwriting of Robert Hanson Harrison. Read in Congress, July 26.

A. IV, pt. II, 163

1779
JULY 20

Continental Congress, President. Philadelphia. To [George] Washington [New Windsor]. Transmitting papers; capture of Stony Point. L. S. of John Jay. 2 pp. Answered July 29.*

93, 265

[1779]
[JULY 20]

[Bingham, William.] [St. Pierre, Martinique.] To [the President of Congress, Philadelphia]. Capture of Grenada by French; naval engagement between D'Estaing and Byron. British reinforcements from West Indies; intelligence from Europe. Contemporary copy. 3 pp. Enclosed in President of Congress to Washington, 1779, Aug. 10. 34, 29

1779
JULY 21

Washington, George. [New Windsor.] To [the President of Congress, Philadelphia]. Particulars of the capture of Stony Point. In handwriting of

Alexander Hamilton. L. S. 8 pp. Referred to Morris, Huntington and Armstrong.

C. C. 152, 7, 503

(Draft. 7 pp. A. IV, pt. II, 165, is dated July 20.)
Printed: Writings of Washington (Ford) N. Y. 1890. 7, 493.

1779
JULY 21

Butler, Lord. Wyoming. Return of quartermaster's stores arrived at Wyoming since June 23. Tabular statement. Contemporary copy. 1 p. In handwriting of Peter Bryan Bruin. Transmitted to Washington. 93, 264

1779
JULY 21

Sullivan, John. List of letters and papers enclosed in letter to Congress, 1779, July 21. 1 p. In handwriting of Peter Bryan Bruin.

The list and documents themselves were transmitted to Washington.

93, 262

1779
JULY 22

Washington, George. West Point [New York]. To the Board of War [Philadelphia]. Exchange of Baron de Geisman; promotion of field officers of the 16 Additional Regiments. Draft. 4 pp. In handwriting of Robert Hanson Harrison.

A. IV, pt. II, 173

1779
JULY 22

Washington, George. West Point. To John Penn [Philadelphia]. Question of reinstatement of Major [Francis?] Taylor. Draft. 1 p. In handwriting of Robert Hanson Harrison.

A. IV, pt. II, 177

1779
JULY 22

Barber, F[rancis]. Return of men fit for duty at Wyoming. Tabular statement. Contemporary copy. 1 p. In handwriting of Peter Bryan Bruin. Transmitted to Washington. 93, 263

1779
JULY 22

Potbury, Henry. Boston. Affidavit as to British fleet from the West Indies. Contemporary copy. 1 p. In handwriting of Caleb Gibbs. Enclosed in Washington to the President of Congress, 1779, July 29. C. C. 152, 7, 463

1779
JULY 23

Washington, George. West Point. To [Maj. Gen. Philip John Schuyler, Albany]. Worth of intelligence from Canada. [Extract of letter.] Transcript. Enclosed in Washington to the President of Congress, 1779, Aug. 15. C. C. 169, 6, 31

1779
JULY 24

Washington, George. West Point. To [the President of Congress, Philadelphia]. Movements of enemy. Draft. 1 p. In handwriting of Alexander Hamilton. Read in Congress, July 30.

A. IV, pt. II, 179

1779   **Cook,** Lois.   New Haven [Connecticut].   Affidavit of mur-
JULY 24   der of Elisha Tuthill.   D. S.   1 p.   Enclosed in
                   Washington to the President of Congress, 1779,
                   Aug. 6.   C. C.   152, 7, 57

1779   **Washington,** George.   West Point.   To [the President of
JULY 25   Congress, Philadelphia].   Recommending Lt.
                   Col. de Fleury.   Draft.   1 p.   In handwriting
                   of Alexander Hamilton.   **A.**   IV, pt. II, 181
                   Printed: Writings of Washington (Sparks) Boston.   1834.   6, 304.

1779   **Washington,** George.   West Point.   To [the Board of War,
JULY 25   Philadelphia].   Repairing of clothes and shoes.
                   Draft.   1 p.   In handwriting of Alexander Ham-
                   ilton.   **A.**   IV, pt. II, 183

1779   **[Cornell,** Ezekiel.]   [Tiverton, Rhode Island.]   To [Maj.
JULY 25   Gen. Horatio Gates, Providence]   Reports of
                   British fleet.   [Extract of letter.]   In handwriting
                   of Alexander Hamilton.   Enclosed in Washing-
                   ton to the President of Congress, 1779, July 29.
                                                      C. C.   152, 7, 459

1779   **[Gates,** Horatio.]   [Providence, Rhode Island.]   To [George
JULY 25   Washington, West Point].   Intelligence of ene-
                   my; escape of prisoners of war from Boston.
                   [Extract of letter.]   In handwriting of Alexander
                   Hamilton.   Enclosed in Washington to the Presi-
                   dent of Congress, 1779, July 29.
                                                      C. C.   152, 7, 459

1779   **Continental Congress,** Resolves.   Thanks, medals, honors
JULY 26   and rewards for capture of Stony Point.   Con-
                   temporary copy, attested by Charles Thomson.
                   3 pp.   Enclosed in President of Congress to
                   Washington, 1779, July 27.   Published in Gen-
                   eral Orders, Aug. 7.   93, 278

1779   **Alling,** Charles.   New Haven.   Affidavit of appearance of
JULY 26   bodies of certain New Haven men.   A. D. S.   1 p.
                   Enclosed in Washington to the President of Con-
                   gress, 1779, Aug. 6.   C. C.   152, 7, 565

1779   **Beers,** Elias.   New Haven.   Affidavit of murder of his
JULY 26   father by British.
              Beers, Isaac.   Corroboration of above.   Ds. S.   2 pp.
                   Enclosed in Washington to the President of Con-
                   gress, 1779, Aug. 6.   C. C.   152, 7, 567

1779   **Collins,** John.   New Haven [Connecticut].   Affidavit of
JULY 26   brutality of British soldiers.   D. S.   2 pp.   En-

closed in Washington to the President of Congress, 1779, Aug. 6.   C. C.   152, 7, 547

1779
July 26

Gatter, Martin. New Haven. Affidavit of brutality of British. D. S. 1 p. Enclosed in Washington to the President of Congress, 1779, Aug. 6.
C. C.   152, 7, 561

1779
July 26

[Shippen, William, jr.] [Middlebrook.] To [George Washington, Middlebrook]. Memorials of physicians and surgeons to Congress. Contemporary copy. 1 p. In handwriting of Robert Hanson Harrison. Transmitted to Congress.   C. C.   152, 7, 233

1779
July 26

Townsend, Sarah. New Haven. Affidavit of brutality of British. D. S. 2 pp. Enclosed in Washington to the President of Congress, 1779, Aug. 6.
C. C.   152, 7, 551

1779
July 27

Washington, George. West Point. To the Board of War [Philadelphia]. Abuses at Springfield [laboratory]; Mons. Garanger and rank in the artillery. Draft. 1 p. In handwriting of Alexander Hamilton.   A.   IV, pt. II, 185

1779
July 27

Washington, George. West Point. To Col. [Theodorick] Bland [Charlottesville, Virginia]. Permission for Convention officers to go to Canada. [Extract of letter]. 1 p. In handwriting of Tench Tilghman. Enclosed in Washington to the President of Congress, 1779, Aug. 31.   C. C.   152, 7, 719

1779
July 27

Continental Congress, President. Philadelphia. To [George] Washington [West Point]. Success at Stony Point. A. L. S. of John Jay. 1 p. Answered Aug. 5.*   93, 276

1779
July 27

Hughes, Samuel. Annapolis [Maryland]. To [the Board of War,] Philadelphia. Introducing Capt. [John] Swan. A. L. S. 1 p. Enclosed in Board of War to Washington, 1779, Aug. 10.   93, 292

1779
July 28

Daggett, Naphtali. New Haven. Affidavit of brutality of British soldiers. D. S. 3 pp. Enclosed in Washington to the President of Congress, 1779, Aug. 6.   C. C.   152, 7, 553

1779
July 28

English, Abigail. [New Haven, Connecticut]. Affidavit of murder of Benjamin English by British. D. S. 1 p. Enclosed in Washington to the President of Congress, 1779, Aug. 6.   C. C.   152, 7, 549

1779
JULY 28

Gatter, Christiana. New Haven. Affidavit of brutality of British. Transcript. Enclosed in Washington to the President of Congress, 1779, Aug. 6.   C. C. 169, 5, 434

1779
JULY 29

Washington, George. West Point. To [the President of Congress, Philadelphia]. Trials of Dr. [William] Shippen, [jr.] and [Maj.] Gen. [Benedict] Arnold; arrival of troops and Lord Cornwallis. L. S. 3 pp. In handwriting of Robert Hanson Harrison. Read in Congress, Aug. 4.
C. C. 152, 7, 455

The draft A. IV, pt. II, 189, is dated July 30.

1779
JULY 29

Washington, George. West Point. To [the President of Congress, Philadelphia]. Movements of enemy; lack of powder; regimental vacancies. Draft. 1 p. In handwriting of Alexander Hamilton and Robert Hanson Harrison. Read in Congress, Aug. 3. Referred to Board of War.
A. IV, pt. II, 187

1779
JULY 29

Washington, George. West Point. To [Maj. Gen. John Sullivan, Wyoming, Pennsylvania]. Responsibility for failure of supplies; rapidity of movement; Col. [Daniel] Brodhead's projected expedition against the Mingoes. Transcript. Enclosed in Washington to the President of Congress, 1779, Aug. 15.   C. C. 169, 6, 10

1779
JULY 29

Continental Congress, President. Philadelphia. To [George] Washington, [New York]. Congress; demand for money from the British [on account of prisoners]. A. L. S. of John Jay. 1 p. Answered July 30. [29*]   11, 17

1779
JULY 29

Continental Congress, President. Philadelphia. To [George] Washington [West Point]. Transmitting papers and resolves; James Wilkinson appointed Clothier-General [in place of Lt. Col. Persifor Frazer]. Letter-book copy.
C. C. 14, 159

1779
JULY 30

Board of War. Proceedings. Transferring Capt. [John] Wilkie's Company to the 11th Pennsylvania regiment. Contemporary copy. 1 p. In handwriting of Robert Hanson Harrison.   93, 287

1779
JULY 30

Hopkins, D[avid]. Crompond [New York]. To Maj. [Thomas] Cartwright [Mandeville, New York]. Skirmish with enemy. Contemporary copy. 2

pp. In handwriting of James McHenry. Transmitted to Congress, 1779, Aug. ?

C. C. 152, 7, 481

1779
JULY 31

Parsons, Samuel H[olden]. [Stamford? Connecticut.] To George Washington [West Point]. Transmitting depositions of British barbarity in Connecticut. A. L. S. 1 p. Transmitted to Congress. Read, Aug. 16. Referred to Committee of Intelligence.

C. C. 152, 7, 487

Committee: J. B. Smith, Lovell and Henry.

1779
JULY 31

Powder. General return of powder on hand. Tabular statement of quantities and places where stored. 1 p. Enclosed in Board of War to Washington, 1779, Sep. 3.

93, 342

[1779]
[JULY ?]

[Continental Congress, Marine Committee?] [Philadelphia]. To [Benjamin Franklin? Passy]. Retaliatory measures against Great Britain; designs against London, Liverpool and elsewhere. Contemporary copy. 3 pp.

C. C. 152, 7, 495

Charles Thomson notes in C. C. 169, 5, 385, that above document was returned to Congress along with Washington's letter of July 13 and its enclosures by the committee to whom the latter had been referred, viz., Morris, Carmichael and Whipple.

1779
AUG. 1

Washington, George. To Edmund Randolph [Philadelphia]. Withholding of information by Congress; weak state of army; money. Auto. draft signed. 2 pp.

P. I, pt. II, 429

Printed: Writings of Washington (Ford) N. Y. 1890. 7, 506, note.

1779
AUG. 1

Washington, George. West Point. To [Maj. Gen. John Sullivan, Lackawanna, Pennsylvania]. Report of deserter of strength of Indians. [Extract of letter]. Transcript. Enclosed in Washington to the President of Congress, 1779, Aug. 15.

C. C. 169, 6, 32

1779
AUG. 1

Hayes, Samuel. Newark [New Jersey]. To [Maj. Gen. William Alexander], Lord Stirling [New Jersey]. Preparations on British fleet. Contemporary copy. 1 p. In handwriting of Robert Hanson Harrison. Enclosed in Washington to the President of Congress, 1779, Aug. 15.

C. C. 152, 7, 475

1779
AUG. 2

Washington, George. West Point. To [the President of Congress, Philadelphia]. Movements of enemy. Draft. 1 p. In handwriting of Robert Hanson Harrison. Referred to Committee to Correspond with Southern General: Laurens, Marchant and Holten.   **A.** IV, pt. II, 193

1779
AUG. 3

Washington, George. West Point. To the Board of War, Philadelphia. Arrangement of the 11th Pennsylvania regiment. Draft. 1 p. In handwriting of Robert Hanson Harrison.

A. IV, pt. II, 195

1779
AUG. 3

Board of War. [Philadelphia.] To [George] Washington [West Point]. Capt. [Archibald] Edmonstone's application to go into New York. A. L. S. of Peter Scull. 1 p. Answered Aug. 10.* **93,** 281.

[1779]
[AUG. 4]

Washington, George. [West Point.] To [Maj. Gen. John Sullivan, near Tuscarora, New York]. Junction [with Brig. Gen. James Clinton]. [Extract of letter.] Transcript. Enclosed in Washington to the President of Congress, 1779, Aug. 15.

C. C. 169, 6, 63

1779
AUG. 4

Board of War. [Philadelphia.] To the President of Congress[Philadelphia]. Maj. Gen. [John]Sullivan's complaints and supplies sent him. A. L. S. of Timothy Pickering, jr. 2 pp. Marked "copy."

93, ?83

1779
AUG. 5

Washington, George. West Point. To [the President of Congress, Philadelphia]. Filling of vacancies among officers; promotions, disputes, etc.; promotion of [Capt. Joseph?] Pettingill; enemy's movements; encounter between French and British fleets. Draft. 4 pp. In handwriting of Robert Hanson Harrison and Richard Kidder Meade. Read in Congress, Aug. 12. Referred to Board of War.   **A.** IV, pt. II, 199

1779
AUG. 5

Washington, George. West Point. To [the President of Congress, Philadelphia]. Acknowledging thanks of Congress respecting Stony Point. Draft. 1 p. In handwriting of Robert Hanson Harrison. Read in Congress, Aug. 16. **A.** IV, pt. II, 201

1779
AUG. 6

Washington, George. West Point. To [the President of Congress, Philadelphia]. Inquiry respecting the Western Expedition; depredations of British in Connecticut. Draft. 1 p. In handwriting of Robert Hanson Harrison. Read in Congress, Aug. 16.   **A.** IV, pt. II, 203

1779
Aug. 6

Continental Congress, President. Philadelphia. To [George] Washington [West Point]. Transmitting resolves. L. S. of John Jay. 1 p. Answered Aug. 16.*   **93,** 285

1779
Aug. 6

Howe, Robert. Salem [New Jersey]. To [George Washington, West Point]. Lt. Col. [Anthony Walton] White's raid. Contemporary copy. 3 pp. In handwriting of Tench Tilghman. Transmitted by Washington to the Committee of Intelligence.
C. C.   **152,** 7, 477

1779
Aug. 7

Continental Congress, President. Philadelphia. To [George] Washington [West Point]. Transmitting papers respecting military matters. Letterbook copy.   C. C.   **14,** 165

1779
Aug. 8

Washington, George. West Point. To the Board of War [Philadelphia]. Incorporation of Spencer's, Malcom's and Foreman's regiments; arrangement of officers. Draft. 2 pp. In handwriting of Robert Hanson Harrison.
A.   **IV,** pt. II, 205

1779
Aug. 8

Continental Congress, President. Philadelphia. To [George] Washington [West Point]. Leave of absence for [Lt.] Col. [Charles] Simms. Letterbook copy.   C. C.   **14,** 165

1779
Aug. 8

Continental Army, [West Point.] Board of General Officers. Settlement of rank of Colonels of Artillery. Contemporary copy. 4 pp. In handwriting of Tench Tilghman. Enclosed in Washington to Laurens, Spencer and Scudder, 1779, Sep. 13.   C. C.   **152,** 8, 13

1779
Aug. 8

Phillips, W[illiam]. Charlottesville [Virginia]. To [the President of Congress, Philadelphia]. Clothing for Convention troops; exchange of prisoners; Convention officers to go to New York. Contemporary copy. 4 pp. Enclosed in President of Congress to Washington, 1779, Aug. 26.
93, 321

1779
Aug. 9

Clark, Abraham. Elizabethtown [New Jersey]. To the [New Jersey] delegates [in Congress, Philadelphia]. Case of Nathaniel Randolph. Contemporary copy. 3 pp. In handwriting of Timothy Pickering, jr. Enclosed in Board of War to Washington, 1779, Aug. 17.   **93,** 306

1779
Aug. 10

Washington, George. West Point. To the Board of War [Philadelphia]. Exchange of Capt. [Archibald] Edmonstone. Draft. 1 p. In handwriting of Robert Hanson Harrison.   **A.** IV, pt. II, 207

1779
Aug. 10

Washington, George. West Point. To [John] Armstrong [Philadelphia]. Land in Virginia; news of British disasters. Auto. draft signed. 3 pp.

     P. I, pt. II, 443

1779
Aug. 10

Continental Congress, President. Philadelphia. To [George] Washington [West Point]. Transmitting intelligence. A. L. S. of John Jay. 1 p. Answered Aug. 16.*   **34,** 26

1779
Aug. 10

Board of War. Philadelphia. To [George] Washington [West Point]. Exchange of Capt. [John] Swan. A. L. S. of Peter Scull. 1 p. Answered Aug. 21.*   **93,** 291

1779
Aug. 11

Washington, George. West Point. To [the President of Congress, Philadelphia]. Reenforcement and designs of enemy; militia; lack of flour and transportation facilities. Draft. 5 pp. In handwriting of Robert Hanson Harrison and Washington.   **A.** IV, pt. II, 209

1779
Aug. 14

Continental Congress, Philadelphia. Circular letter to the States. British reenforcements; exertions necessary. Contemporary copy. 2 pp. Enclosed in President of Congress to Washington, 1779, Aug. 18.   **93,** 297

1779
Aug. 14

Board of War. [Philadelphia.] To [George] Washington [West Point]. Exchange of hides for officers' boots. A. L. S. of Timothy Pickering, jr. 2 pp. Answered Aug. 26.*   **93,** 294

1779
Aug. 15

Washington, George. West Point. To [the President of Congress, Philadelphia]. The Western Expedition; [Maj.] Gen. [John] Sullivan's misstatements; supplies, force employed. Draft. 9 pp. In handwriting of Alexander Hamilton and Washington. Referred to Atlee, Armstrong, Spencer, Dickinson and Mathews.   **A.** IV, pt. II, 219

     Printed: Writings of Washington (Ford) N. Y. 1890. 8, 8.

1779
Aug. 15

Sullivan, John. Tioga [New York]. To [George] Washington [West Point]. Account of destruction of Chemung. Contemporary copy. 4 pp. In handwriting of James McHenry. Enclosed in Wash-

ington to the President of Congress,1779, Aug. 27.
C. C. **152, 7, 687**

1779
AUG. 16

Washington, George. West Point. To [the President of Congress, Philadelphia]. Capt. [John] Wilkie's Pennsylvania troops and minor military matters. Draft. 2 pp. In handwriting of Robert Hanson Harrison. Read in Congress, Aug. 16. Referred to Board of War. **A. IV, pt. II, 215**

1779
AUG. 16

Washington, George. West Point. To [the Board of War, Philadelphia]. Hides for shoes; Mons. Garanger's wish for employment. Draft. 2 pp. In handwriting of Tench Tilghman. **A. IV, pt. II, 217**

1779
AUG. 16

[Washington, George.] West Point. To John Jay [Philadelphia]. England's actions respecting Spanish mediation; [Brig.] Gen. [Anthony] Wayne's report. Draft. 1 p. In handwriting of Alexander Hamilton. **P. I, pt. II, 447**

1779
AUG. 16

Continental Congress, Resolve. Pay to soldiers for deficiencies of clothing. Contemporary copy, attested by Charles Thomson. 1 p. Endorsed by Robert Hanson Harrison with memo. of the deficiencies. Enclosed in President of Congress to Washington, 1779, Aug. 18. Published in Genl. Orders, Aug. 29. **93, 296**

1779
AUG. 17

Washington, George. West Point. To the President of Congress [Philadelphia]. Officers nominated for the Sappers and Miners; Engineer corps; expenses of Baron Steuben. Draft. 3 pp. In handwriting of Alexander Hamilton. Read in Congress, Aug. 17. Referred to Board of Treasury and Board of War. **A. IV, pt. II, 229**
Printed: Writings of Washington (Sparks) Boston. 1834. 6, 324.

1779
AUG. 17

Continental Congress, Resolves. Recommendation to States to provide for officers and soldiers by pensions or otherwise; widows. Contemporary copy, attested by Charles Thomson. 3 pp. Enclosed in President of Congress to Washington, 1779, Aug. 20. Published in Genl. Orders, Aug. 29. **93, 311**

1779
AUG. 17

Board of War. [Philadelphia.] To [George] Washington [West Point]. Linen for officers; deficiency of clothing supplies; prospects for the winter; case of [Nathaniel] Randolph. A. L. S. of Richard Peters. 4 pp. **93, 304**

1779 AUG. 17	**Harrison**, Charles. Philadelphia. To the President of Congress [Philadelphia]. Memorial for settlement of rank. Contemporary copy. 1 p. In handwriting of Timothy Pickering, jr. Transmitted to Washington. **93**, 308
1779 AUG. 17	**Pierce**, John, jr. [West Point.] Account of warrants paid Baron von Steuben in 1779. A. D. S. 1 p. Enclosed in Washington to the President of Congress, 1779, Aug. 17. **C. C. 152**, 7, 589
1779 AUG. 17	**[Sullivan**, John.] Tioga [New York]. General Orders: Cloathing deficiency. [Extract.] A. D. S. of F[rancis] Barber. 1 p. Enclosed in Board of War to Washington, 1779, Aug. 28. **93**, 332
1779 AUG. 18	**Continental Congress**, President. Philadelphia. To [George] Washington [West Point]. Transmitting resolves. L. S. of John Jay. 1 p. Answered Aug. 24.* **93**, 299
[1779] [AUG. 18]	**Lee**, Henry, jr. [West Point?] Order of march and disposition of battle for attempt on Paulus Hook. Contemporary copy. 11 pp. In handwriting of James McHenry. Enclosed in Washington to the President of Congress, 1779, Aug. 23. **C. C. 152**, 7, 645
1779 AUG. 18	**Continental Congress**, Resolve. Subsistence money to officers and soldiers. Contemporary copy, attested by Charles Thomson. Enclosed in President of Congress to Washington, 1779, Aug. 20. Published in Genl. Orders, Aug. 29. **93**, 311
1779 AUG. 19	**Washington**, George. West Point. To [the President of Congress, Philadelphia]. Case of Lt. Col. [Charles] Simms. Draft. 2 pp. In handwriting of Robert Hanson Harrison. Read in Congress, Sep. 3. Referred to Mathews, Marchant and Armstrong. Returned. **A. IV**, pt. II, 233
1779 AUG. 19	**Continental Congress**, Resolve. Provision for the Commissary General. Contemporary copy, attested by Charles Thomson. Enclosed in President of Congress to Washington, 1779, Aug. 20. Published in Genl. Orders, Aug. 29. **93**, 311
1779 AUG. 20	**Washington**, George. West Point. To [Medical Committee of Congress, Philadelphia]. Question of

the Inspector and Mustering departments. Draft.
3 pp.   In handwriting of James McHenry.

A. IV, pt. II, 235
Committee: Laurens, Spencer and Scudder.

1779
Aug. 20

Continental Congress, President.   Philadelphia.   To
[George] Washington [West Point].   Transmit-
ting resolves; resolutions under consideration.
L. S. of John Jay.   1 p.   Answered Aug. 31.*

93, 309

1779
Aug. 21

Washington, George.   West Point.   To [the President of
Congress, Philadelphia].   [Maj.] Gen. [John]
Sullivan's complaint as to clothing for the Western
Expedition.   Draft.   3 pp.   In handwriting of
Alexander Hamilton.   Read in Congress Aug.
28.   Referred to Board of Treasury.

A. IV, pt. II, 239

1779
Aug. 21

Washington, George.   West Point.   To the Board of War
[Philadelphia].   Dispute between the Board and
[Maj.] Gen. [John] Sullivan.   Draft.   2 pp.   In
handwriting of Robert Hanson Harrison.

A. IV, pt. II, 243

1779
Aug. 21

Washington, George.   West Point.   To the Board of War
[Philadelphia].   Rule for exchange of prisoners.
Draft.   2 pp.   In handwriting of Robert Hanson
Harrison.   A. IV, pt. II, 245

1779
Aug. 21

Continental Congress, Resolves.   Treatment of Lt. Gov.
[Henry] Hamilton; favors to prisoners; Convention troops in Virginia.   Contemporary copy,
attested by Charles Thomson.   2 pp.   Enclosed
in President of Congress to Washington, 1779,
Aug. 26.   93, 315

1779
Aug. 21

Butler, Richard.   Fort Montgomery [New York].   To
[George] Washington [West Point].   Public
money stolen by a servant.   Contemporary copy.
3 pp.   In handwriting of Robert Hanson Harrison.   Enclosed in Washington to the President of
Congress, 1779, Aug. 23.   C. C. 152, 7, 673

1779
[Aug. 22?]

Forsyth, Robert.   [West Point?]   Return of prisoners
taken at Paulus Hook, Aug. 19.   Contemporary
copy.   1 p.   In handwriting of Alexander Hamilton.   Enclosed in Washington to the President
of Congress, 1779, Aug. 23.   C. C. 152, 7, 667

1779
Aug. 22

Lee, Henry, jr. Paramus [New Jersey]. To [George] Washington [West Point]. Account of the capture of Paulus Hook. 16 pp. Contemporary copy. In handwriting of Tench Tilghman. Enclosed in Washington to the President of Congress, 1779, Aug. 23.   C. C.   152, 7, 641

1779
Aug. 23

Washington, George. West Point. To [the President of Congress, Philadelphia.] Maj. [Henry] Lee's capture of Paulus Hook. Draft. 1 p. In handwriting of Alexander Hamilton. Read in Congress, Aug. 27. Referred to Paca, Atlee, and Dickinson.   A. IV, pt. II, 247
Printed: Writings of Washington (Ford) N. Y. 1890. 8, 27.

1779
Aug. 23

Washington, George. [West Point.] To [the President of Congress, Philadelphia]. Case of Col. [Richard] Butler. Draft. 1 p. In handwriting of Robert Hanson Harrison. Read in Congress Aug. 28. Referred to Board of Treasury. A. IV, pt. II, 247

1779
Aug. 23

Continental Congress, Resolve. Pay for Maj. Noirmont de la Neuville. Contemporary copy, attested by Charles Thomson. 1 p. Enclosed in President of Congress to Washington, 1779, Aug. 26.

93, 319

1779
Aug. 23

Anonymous. Boston. To [George Washington, West Point]. English newspaper account of Spain's manifesto, delivered June 16, 1779, and King's message to Parliament thereon, together with account of proceedings in the House of Commons. Copied from a London paper. 15 pp. In handwriting of James McHenry, Robert Hanson Harrison, Tench Tilghman and Caleb Gibbs. Enclosed in Washington to the President of Congress, 1779, Aug. 29.   C. C.   152, 7, 695

1779
Aug. 24

Washington, George. West Point. To the President of Congress [Philadelphia]. Circular letter to States on filling up the battalions and clothing the troops; scarcity of flour; exchange of British general officers. Draft. 6 pp. In handwriting of Robert Hanson Harrison. Read in Congress Sep. 2. Referred to committee for superintending the Quartermaster and Commissary Departments, and also to Board of War.

A. IV, pt. II, 249
Committee: Dickinson, Huntington and Burke.

1779
AUG. 24

Washington, George. West Point. To James Lovell [Philadelphia]. Minor matters. Draft. 1 p. In handwriting of Tench Tilghman.

A. IV, pt. II, 255

1779
AUG. 24

Continental Congress, President. Philadelphia. To [George] Washington [West Point]. Transmitting resolves; request for two Convention officers to go into Canada. L. S. of John Jay. 1 p. Answered Aug. 31.*

93, 313

1779
AUG. 25

Washington, George. West Point. To Joseph Hewes, Philadelphia. Release of Mr. Granberry. Draft. 1 p. In handwriting of Tench Tilghman.

A. IV, pt. II, 257

1779
AUG. 25

Jay, John. Philadelphia. To [George] Washington, West Point. European politics; Great Britain; a secret agent. A. L. S. 1 p. Marked "private."

94, 39

1779
AUG. 25

Wilkinson, James. Philadelphia. Estimate of price of clothing in Dec. 1778. Broadside. 1 p. Transmitted to Washington.

93, 338

1779
AUG. 26

Washington, George. West Point. To the Board of War [Philadelphia]. Hides and shoes; clothing supplies; disputes of rank in the artillery; exchange of prisoners; difficulties in the Virginia line. Draft. 8 pp. In handwriting of Robert Hanson Harrison.

A. IV, pt. II, 259

1779
AUG. 26

Continental Congress, President. Philadelphia. To [George] Washington [West Point]. Transmitting resolves; Major Noirmont de la Neuville. L. S. of John Jay. 1 p. Answered Sep. 5.*

93, 317

1779
AUG. 27

Washington, George. West Point. To the Board of War [Philadelphia]. Great want of powder. Draft. 2 pp. In handwriting of Alexander Hamilton and Tench Tilghman.

A. IV, pt. II, 267

1779
AUG. 27

Howe, Robert. Lower Salem [New York]. To [George Washington, West Point]. Arrival of a British fleet at New York. [Extract of letter.] 1 p. In handwriting of Robert Hanson Harrison. Enclosed in Washington to the President of Congress, 1779, Aug. 27.

C. C. 152, 7, 685

1779
Aug. 27

Continental Congress. Resolve. Approval of plan of the Western Expedition. Contemporary copy, attested by Charles Thomson. 1 p. Enclosed in President of Congress to Washington, 1779, Aug. 29.   **93, 327**

1779
Aug. 28

Board of War. [Philadelphia.] To [George] Washington [West Point]. Capt. [John] Swan's exchange; controversy with [Maj.] Gen. [John] Sullivan; regulations for prisoners. A. L. S. of Richard Peters. 2 pp. Answered Sep. 6.*   **93, 330**

1779
Aug. 28

Brisbane, Edward. New York. To Robert Burton, St Kitts [West Indies]. Intentions of British for next campaign. Extract in handwriting of Timothy Pickering, jr. Enclosed in Board of War to Washington, 1779, Oct. 5.   **34, 93**

1779
Aug. 29

Washington, George. West Point. To the President of Congress [Philadelphia]. Spain's declaration to Great Britain. Draft. 1 p. In handwriting of Alexander Hamilton. Read in Congress, Sep. 4.
                            A. IV, pt. II, 269

1779
Aug. 29

Continental Congress, President. Philadelphia. To [George] Washington [West Point]. Transmitting resolves. L. S. of John Jay. 1 p. Answered Sep. 5.*   **93, 328**

1779
Aug. 30

Armstrong, John [jr.] Boston. To [John Armstrong, Philadelphia]. Causes of failure of the Penobscot expedition. Contemporary copy. 4 pp. Enclosed in Armstrong to Washington, 1779, Oct. 15.   **34, 124**

1779
Aug. 30

Sullivan, John. Newtown [New York]. To [George Washington, West Point]. Account of engagement at Elmira. Contemporary copy. 7 pp. Enclosed in Washington to the President of Congress, 1779, Sep. 5. Referred to Committee of Intelligence.   **C. C. 152, 7, 731**
Committee: J. B. Smith, Lovell and Henry.

[1779]
[Aug. 30]

Sullivan, John. [Newtown, New York.] Address to the troops. Necessity of half rations. Contemporary copy. 2 pp. Enclosed in Washington to the President of Congress, 1779, Oct. 9.
                          C. C. 152, 8, 103

1779
Aug. 30

[Taylor, John.] Elizabethtown [New Jersey]. To [George] Washington [West Point]. Arrival of British fleet and troops. [Extract of letter.] 1 p. In handwriting of Caleb Gibbs. Enclosed in Washington to the President of Congress, 1779, Aug. 31. **C. C. 152, 7, 721**

1779
Aug. 31

Washington, George. West Point. To [the President of Congress, Philadelphia]. Money to soldiers for clothing and rations. Draft. 3 pp. In handwriting of Robert Hanson Harrison. Read in Congress, Sep. 6. **A. IV, pt. II, 271**

1779
Aug. 31

Board of War. Philadelphia. To [George] Washington, West Point. Case of [James] Hallett. A. L. S. of Timothy Pickering, jr. 2 pp. Answered Sep. 14.* **93, 333**

[1779]
[Aug. —]

Massachusetts, Field Officers. [West Point?] To George Washington [West Point]. Memorial complaining of promotion of Capt. Joseph Pettingill. Contemporary copy. 2 pp. In handwriting of Robert Hanson Harrison. Enclosed in Washington to the President of Congress 1779, Aug. 5. **C. C. 152, 7, 473**

[1779]
[Sep. 2?]

Sullivan, John. [Catherine's Town, New York.] Address to the Oneida Nation. Friendship and guides. Contemporary copy. 3 pp. Enclosed in Washington to the President of Congress, 1779, Oct. 9. **C. C. 152, 8, 105**

1779
Sep. 3

Continental Congress, Medical Committee. Philadelphia. To [George] Washington, West Point. Report to Congress on the Mustering Department. A. L. S. of Henry Laurens. 1 p. Answered Sep. 13.* **34, 43**

Committee: Laurens, Spooner and Scudder.

1779
Sep. 3

Board of War. [Philadelphia.] To [George] Washington [West Point]. Baron Steuben's regulations; standards for the army. A. L. S. of Richard Peters. 1 p. Answered Sep. 14.* **93, 339**

1779
Sep. 3

Board of War. [Philadelphia.] To [George] Washington [West Point]. Boots and shoes; Commissaries of Hides; continental and state supplies of clothing; deficiency regulation; want of powder and attempts to supply same. A. L. S. of Richard Peters. 4 pp. Answered Sep. 14.* **93, 340**

1779   Laurens, Henry.   Philadelphia.   To [George] Washing-
SEP. 3   ton [West Point].   Papers relating to mustering
                department.   Contemporary copy.   1 p.
                                         C. C.   152, 7, 603

1779   Washington, George.   West Point.   To [the President of
SEP. 5   Congress Philadelphia].   Exchange of prisoners;
                reports of British reenforcement.   Draft.   3 pp.
                In handwriting of Robert Hanson Harrison.
                Read in Congress, Sep. 13.   A.   IV, pt. II, 275

1779   Anonymous.   To [George] Washington [West Point].
SEP. 5   Movements of enemy's shipping; apparent
                intentions etc.   Contemporary copy.   3 pp.   In
                handwriting of James McHenry.   Enclosed in
                Washington to the President of Congress, 1779,
                Sep. 8.   C. C.   152, 7, 747

1779   Plombard, J——.   Charleston [South Carolina].   To Gér-
SEP. 5   ard [de Rayneval] Philadelphia.   Cooperation of
                Comte D'Estaing with Maj. Gen. [Benjamin] Lin-
                coln; supplies for the fleet.   Contemporary trans-
                lation.   2 pp.   In handwriting of George Bond.
                Transmitted to Washington.   94, 3

1779   Proud, John.   [Rhode Island.]   To [Maj.] Gen. [Horatio]
SEP. 5   Gates [Providence].   Report of French fleet from
                the West Indies.   Contemporary copy.   In hand-
                writing of Robert Hanson Harrison.   Enclosed
                in Washington to the President of Congress,
                1779, Sep. 12.   C. C.   152, 7, 759

1779   Western Expedition.   Return of troops employed upon.
[SEP. 5?]   Tabular statement.   D. S: "Alexd. Scammell
                Adjt. Genl."   2 pp.   Enclosed in Washington to
                the President of Congress, 1779, Sep. 5.
                                         C. C.   152, 7, 739

1779   Washington, George.   W[es]t P[oin]t.   To the Board of
SEP. 6   War [Philadelphia].   Regulation of the Depart-
                ment of Prisoners.   Draft.   1 p.   In handwriting
                of Alexander Hamilton and Tench Tilghman.
                                         A.   IV, pt. II, 279

[1779]   Washington, George.   Remarks on regulations for prison-
[SEP. 6]   ers of war.   Draft.   1 p.   In handwriting of
                Richard Kidder Meade.   Enclosed in Washing-
                ton to Board of War 1779, Sep. 6.
                                         A.   IV, pt. II, 281

1779
SEP. 7

Washington, George. West Point. To [the President of Congress, Philadelphia]. Reenforcements and intentions of enemy. Draft. 2 pp. In handwriting of Alexander Hamilton. Read in Congress, Sep. 13. Referred to committee to correspond with the Southern General.

A. IV, pt. II, 283

Committee: Laurens, Marchant, Holton; Harnett and Fitzhugh added. The L. S. sent is endorsed by Laurens with decision of Committee (Sep. 13) to recommend that North Carolina troops be sent to South Carolina in Continental frigates.

Printed: Writings of Washington (Ford) N. Y. 1890. 8, 39.

1779
SEP. 7

Washington, George. West Point. To John Jay [Philadelphia]. Britain and her European allies; a secret agent [Capt. Elijah Hunter]'s services. Draft. 4 pp. In handwriting of Robert Hanson Harrison.

P. I, pt. II, 467

Printed: Writings of Washington (Ford) N. Y. 1890. 8, 42.

1779
SEP. 7

Kemble, Stephen. New York. To Maj. Smith, St. Christopher [West Indies]. Trouble over [Francis,] Lord Rawdon's corps; movement of troops; gossip. Extract in handwriting of Timothy Pickering, jr. Enclosed in Board of War to Washington, 1779, Oct. 5.

34, 93

1779
SEP. 7

Van Dyke, Cornelius. Fort Schuyler [New York]. To Col. [Goose] Van Schaick [Albany, New York]. News of Sullivan's victories. Contemporary copy. 2 pp. In handwriting of Richard Kidder Meade. Enclosed in Washington to the President of Congress, 1779, Sep. 18.

C. C. 152, 8, 31

1779
SEP. 8

Washington, George. West Point. To [the President of Congress, Philadelphia]. Secret intelligence. Draft. 1 p. In handwriting of James McHenry. Read in Congress, Sep. 13.

A. IV, pt. II, 285

1779
SEP. 8

Mallet, J[onathan]. New York. To Dr. [William] Bruce, St. Kitts. Health of [British] troops. Extract in handwriting of Timothy Pickering, jr. Enclosed in Board of War to Washington, 1779, Oct. 5.

34, 93

1779
SEP. 8

Plombard, J——. Charleston [South Carolina]. To [Gérard de Rayneval, Philadelphia]. Comte D'Estaing's squadron. Contemporary translation. 2 pp. In handwriting of Charles Morse. Transmitted to Washington.

94, 1

1779
SEP. 9

Continental Army, White Plains. Committee of Arrangement. Rules for regulating rank in army. Contemporary copy. 4 pp. In handwriting of James McHenry. Enclosed in Washington to the Medical Committee, 1779, Sep. 13.

C. C. 152, 8, 9

1779
SEP. 11

Washington, George. West Point. To the President of Congress [Philadelphia]. Arrival of Comte de la Luzerne. Draft. 1 p. In handwriting of Tench Tilghman. Read in Congress, Sep. 16.

A. IV, pt. II, 287

1779
SEP. 11

Washington, George. West Point. To the Board of War [Philadelphia]. Exorbitant commission charges of certain Continental agents for prizes. Draft. 3 pp. In handwriting of Robert Hanson Harrison.

A. IV, pt. II, 289

1779
SEP. 11

Huntington, J[edediah]. [Peekskill, New York]. To [George] Washington [West Point]. Report of French fleet. Contemporary copy. 2 pp. In handwriting of Robert Hanson Harrison. Enclosed in Washington to the President of Congress, 1779, Sep. 12.

C. C. 152, 7, 759

1779
SEP. 12

Washington, George. West Point. To [the President of Congress Philadelphia]. News of a French fleet. Draft. 1 p. In handwriting of Tench Tilghman. Read in Congress, Sep. 17.

A. IV, pt. II, 293

1779
SEP. 12

Taylor, [John]. [Elizabethtown, New Jersey]. To Col. [John] Beatty [Elizabethtown?] Sailing of British regiments from New York. Contemporary copy. 1 p. In handwriting of Robert Hanson Harrison. Enclosed in Washington to the President of Congress, 1779, Sep. 14.

C. C. 152, 8, 25

1779
SEP. 13

Washington, George. West Point. To [Medical Committee of Congress, Philadelphia]. Transmitting papers. Draft. 1 p. In handwriting of Robert Hanson Harrison.

A. IV, pt. II, 295

Committee: Laurens, Spencer and Scudder.

1779
SEP. 14

Washington, George. West Point. To [the President of Congress Philadelphia]. Sailing of three British regiments from New York. Draft. 1 p. In handwriting of Robert Hanson Harrison. Read in Congress, Sep. 19. Referred to committee appointed to correspond with the Southern General. **A.** IV, pt. II, 297

Committee: Laurens, Marchant, Holton, Harnett and Fitzhugh.

1779
SEP. 14

Washington, George. West Point. To the Board of War [Philadelphia]. Case of [James] Hallet; design of flags; powder. Draft. 2 pp. In handwriting of Tench Tilghman. **A.** IV, pt. II, 299

1779
SEP. 15

Continental Congress, President. Philadelphia. To [George] Washington [West Point]. Transmitting resolve. Letter-book copy.

C. C. 14, 156

1779
SEP. 15

Campble, Robert. [New York?] To [Elizabeth] Burgin [New York]. Her request for a flag. A. L. S. 1 p. Enclosed in Washington to the President of Congress, 1779, Dec. 25. **C. C.** 152, 8, 312

1779
SEP. 15

Cliffe, William. Staten Island. To Brig. Gen. [Richard] Prescott, St. Christophers [West Indies]. Stony Point and Paulus Hook; [Charles,] Earl Cornwallis and southern expedition; minor military changes. Extract in handwriting of Timothy Pickering, jr. Enclosed in Board of War to Washington, 1779, Oct. 5. 34, 93

1779
SEP. 15

Cuyler, A——. New York. To Capt. [Garrett] Fisher, St. Kitts [West Indies]. The situation at New York.

SEP. 16

Cuyler to Lt. Col. [Cornelius] Cuyler, St. Kitts. Troops embarked for Quebec. Extracts in handwriting of Timothy Pickering, jr. Enclosed in Board of War to Washington, 1779, Oct. 5. 34, 93

1779
SEP. 16

[Brodhead, Daniel.] Pittsburg. To [George Washington, West Point]. Account of his expedition against the Muncy Indians on the Alleghany. [Extract of letter.] 3 pp. In handwriting of Richard Kidder Meade and Tench Tilghman. Enclosed in Washington to the President of Congress, 1779, Oct. 21. **C. C.** 152, 8, 135

1779
SEP. 18

Washington, George. West Point. To [the President of Congress, Philadelphia]. Departure of Luzerne for Philadelphia; news of the Western expedition. Draft. 2 pp. In handwriting of Robert Hanson Harrison. Read in Congress, Sep. 24.

A. IV, pt. II, 301

1779
SEP. 18

Washington, George. West Point. To the Board of War [Philadelphia]. Arrival of small supply of powder. Draft. 1 p. In handwriting of Tench Tilghman. **A.** IV, pt. II, 303

1779
SEP. 19

Washington, George. West Point. To [the President of Congress Philadelphia]. News of a French fleet; enemy fortifying New York. Draft. 2 pp. In handwriting of Tench Tilghman. Read in Congress, Sep. 25. **A.** IV, pt. II, 308

1779
SEP. 22

Washington, George. West Point. To the Board of War [Philadelphia]. Military stores to officers. Draft. 1 p. In handwriting of Tench Tilghman.
A. IV, pt. II, 305

1779
SEP. 22

Girard, William. New York. To Moore & Johnston, St. Kitts [West Indies]. Preparations for an expedition. Extract in handwriting of Timothy Pickering, jr. Enclosed in Board of War to Washington, 1779, Oct. 5. **34, 93**

1779
SEP. 23

Washington, George. West Point. To [the President of Congress, Philadelphia]. Marquis de Fleury's request for a furlough. Contemporary copy. 2 pp. In handwriting of de Fleury, with auto. note signed transmitting same to Charles Thomson. **C. C. 152, 8, 39**

1779
SEP. 23

Board of War. [Philadelphia.] To [George] Washington [West Point]. Powder and arms from France; clothing supplies. A. L. S. of Richard Peters. 1 p. Answered Sep. 29.* **93, 342**

1779
SEP. 23

Continental Congress, President. Philadelphia. To [George] Washington [West Point]. Transmitting resolve. Auto. draft of John Jay. 1 p.
C. C. 14, 1

1779
SEP. 23

Brisbane, Edward. New York. To Robert Burton, St. Kitts [West Indies]. Projected expedition; news from West Indies; forces etc. Extract in handwriting of Timothy Pickering, jr. Enclosed in Board of War to Washington, 1779, Oct. 5.
34, 93

1779
SEP. 24

Continental Congress, Resolves. Thanks of Congress for victory at Paulus Hook; honors and rewards. Contemporary copy, attested by Charles Thomson. 3 pp. Enclosed in President of Congress to Washington, 1779, Sep. 28. Published in Genl. Orders, Oct 8. **94, 7**

1779
SEP. 24

[Gates, Horatio.] [Providence, Rhode Island.] To [George Washington, West Point]. Pay for militia subsistence. [Extract of letter.] 1 p. In handwriting of Tench Tilghman. Enclosed in Washington to the President of Congress, 1779, Oct. 2.

C. C. 152, 8, 71

1779
SEP. 25

Washington, George. West Point. To [the President of Congress, Philadelphia]. Minor matters; secret intelligence of movements of British regiments, fleet etc. Draft. 4 pp. In handwriting of Tench Tilghman. Read in Congress, Sep. 30.

A. IV, pt. II, 309

1779
SEP. 26

Continental Congress. Resolve. Cooperation with French; Compt D'Estaing's fleet; exertions of the states. A. D. S. of Charles Thomson. 1 p. Transmitted to Washington.

93, 344

1779
SEP. 28

Continental Congress, President. Philadelphia. To [George] Washington [West Point]. Transmitting resolves; success at Paulus Hook; Convention troops. L. S. of Samuel Huntington. 2 pp.

94, 5

1779
SEP. 28

Marine Committee. Philadelphia. To [George] Washington [West Point]. Transmitting letter to Navy Board at Boston. L. S. of Jno. Mathews. 1 p. Answered Oct. 6.*

92, 296

1779
SEP. 28

Marine Committee. Philadelphia. To the Commissioners of the Navy Board at Boston. Continental frigates to prepare and await orders of Comte de Grasse and Gen. Washington. Contemporary copy. 2 pp. Enclosed in Marine Committee to Washington, 1779, Sep. 28.

92, 294

1779
SEP. 28

Frey, Charles, [Baron] de. West Point. To [George] Washington, West Point. Request for leave of absence. A. L. S. 1 p. Enclosed in Washington to the President of Congress, 1779, Sep. 29.

C. C. 152, 8, 53

1779
SEP. 28

Sullivan, John. Chemung [New York]. To [George] Washington [West Point]. Account of the expedition since leaving Newtown. Contemporary copy. 17 pp. In handwriting of James McHenry, Tench Tilghman, and Richard Kidder Meade. Enclosed in Washington to the President of Congress, 1779, Oct. 9.

C. C. 152, 8, 85

Cf: Sullivan to Congress. Sep. 30. In Amory, Life of Sullivan. Boston, 1838. 130.

1779
SEP. 29
Washington, George. [West Point.] To the President of Congress, Philadelphia. Leave of absence for Baron de Frey. L. S. 1 p. In handwriting of Alexander Hamilton. Read in Congress Oct. 4. Leave granted and petition referred to Board of Treasury.   C. C. 152, 8, 49

1779
SEP. 29
Washington, George. West Point. To the Board of War [Philadelphia]. Lack of clothing, shoes and blankets. Draft. 1 p. In handwriting of James McHenry.   A. IV, pt. II, 313

1779
SEP. 29
W[ashingto]n, G[eorge]. West Point. To [Henry Laurens, Philadelphia]. Letters for Carolina and news from Europe. Draft signed. 2 pp. In handwriting of James McHenry.

P. I, pt. II, 493

1779
SEP. 30
Washington, George. West Point. To [the President of Congress, Philadelphia]. March of the South Carolina troops southward; destination of the enemy's expedition. Draft. 3 pp. In handwriting of Tench Tilghman. Read in Congress Oct. 4.   A. IV, pt. II, 315

[1779]
[SEP.]
Anonymous. [New York?] To [George Washington, West Point]. Number of British troops on Sor'hern expedition. Contemporary copy. 1 p. In handwriting of Tench Tilghman. Enclosed in Washington to the President of Congress, 1779, Sep. 30.   C. C. 152, 8, 61

[1779]
[SEP. ?]
Leister, ———. Account of D'Estaing's fleet. Contemporary copy. 1 p. In handwriting of Tench Tilghman. Enclosed in Washington to the President of Congress, 1779, Sep. 19.

C. C. 152, 8, 37

[1779]
[SEP. ?]
Oneida Nation. Address to Maj. Gen. John Sullivan. Friendship and aid. Contemporary copy. 4 pp. Enclosed in Washington to the President of Congress, 1779, Oct. 9.   C. C. 152, 8, 109

[1779]
[SEP. ?]
Sullivan, John. Address to the Oneida Nation. The unfriendly Cayugas. Contemporary copy. 3 pp. In handwriting of Richard Kidder Meade. Enclosed in Washington to the President of Congress, 1779, Oct. 9.   C. C. 152, 8, 113

1779
OCT. 1
Washington, George. West Point. To [the President of Congress, Philadelphia]. Maj. Noirmont de la

Neuville's request for a furlough. Draft. 2 pp.
In handwriting of Alexander Hamilton. Read
in Congress Oct. 14. Referred to Board of
War. **A.** IV, pt. II, 319

1779
Oct. 1

Washi gton, George. West Point. To the Board of
War [Philadelphia]. Arrangement of the Virginia line; commissions, promotions, etc. Draft.
4 pp. In handwriting of Robert Hanson Harrison. **A.** IV, pt. II, 321

1779
Oct. 2

Washington, George. West Point. To [the President of
Congress, Philadelphia]. Claim of militia for
subsistence. Draft. 1 p. In handwriting of
Robert Hanson Harrison. Read in Congress
Oct. 9. **A.** IV, pt. II, 325

1779
Oct. 2

Washington, George. West Point. To the Board of
War [Philadelphia]. Deficiency of shoes; ex-
change of Maj. Gens. [William] Phillips and
[Friedrich Adolph, Baron] Riedesel. Draft.
3 pp. In handwriting of Tench Tilghman.
A. IV, pt. II, 327

1779
Oct. 4

Washington, George. West Point. To the President of
Congress [Philadelphia]. Measures for cooperation with Comte D'Estaing. Draft. 6 pp. In
handwriting of Tench Tilghman. Read in Congress Oct. 8. Referred to delegates of Delaware, Maryland and South Carolina to take order
thereon. **A.** IV, pt. II, 332
Printed: Writings of Washington (Ford) N. Y. 1890. 8, 73.

1779
Oct. 4

Continental Congress, Resolve. Halt of North Carolina
troops at Trenton. A. D. S. of Charles Thomson. 1 p. Enclosed in President of Congress to
Washington, 1779, Oct. 5. **94, 12**

1779
Oct. 5

Continental Congress, President. Philadelphia. To
[George] Washington [West Point]. North Carolina troops halted at Trenton; resolve transmitted. A. L. S. of Samuel Huntington. 1 p.
Answered Oct. 17.* **94, 10**

1779
Oct. 5

Continental Congress, President. Philadelphia. To Col.
[Thomas] Clarke [en route toward the South].
Halt at Trenton. A. L. S. of Samuel Huntington, marked "copy." 1 p. Enclosed in President of Congress to Washington, 1779, Oct. 5.
94, 11

1779
Oct. 5

Board of War. Philadelphia. To [George] Washington, West Point. Transmitting extracts of intelligence. A. L. S. of Timothy Pickering, jr. 1 p. Answered Oct. 12.* 34, 91

1779
Oct. 6

Washington, George. West Point. To the Marine Committee, Philadelphia. Plan of action; letter for Comte D'Estaing. Draft. 2 pp. In handwriting of Robert Hanson Harrison.
A. IV, pt. II, 337

1779
Oct. 6

Hamilton, Alexander. West Point. To [the Marine Committee, Philadelphia]. Pilots for Comte D'Estaing. Auto. draft signed. 1 p.
A. IV, pt. II, 339

1779
Oct. 7

Washington, George. West Point. To Charles Thomson [Philadelphia]. Acknowledging information of Samuel Huntington's election as President of Congress. Draft. 1 p. In handwriting of Tench Tilghman. A. IV, pt II, 341

1779
Oct. 7

Washington, George. West Point. To the Marine Committee [Philadelphia]. Introducing a pilot. Draft. 1 p. In handwriting of Richard Kidder Meade. A. IV, pt. II, 343

1779
Oct. 7

Washington, George. West Point. To John Jay [Philadelphia]. His appointment as minister to Spain. Auto. draft signed. 1 p. P. I, pt. II, 509
Printed: Writings of Washington (Sparks) Boston. 1834. 6, 377.

1779
Oct. 8

Washington, George. West Point. To the Board of War [Philadelphia]. Exchange of Major Francis Murray; return of artificers drafted from the army; the Clothier General's Department. Draft. 4 pp. In handwriting of Tench Tilghman.
A. IV, pt. II, 345

1779
Oct. 8

Continental Congress, President. Philadelphia. To [George] Washington [West Point]. March of the North Carolina troops. A. L. S. of Samuel Huntington. 1 p. 94, 13

1779
Oct. 9

Washington, George. West Point. To [the President of Congress, Philadelphia]. Movements of enemy; cooperation with D'Estaing; [Maj.] Gen. [John] Sullivan's success. Draft. 4 pp. In handwriting of James McHenry. Read in Congress, Oct. 14.
A. IV, pt. II, 349
Printed: Writings of Washington (Sparks) Boston. 1834. 6, 380.

1779
Oct. 9
Washington, George. West Point. To the Marine Committee [Philadelphia]. Case of John Springer, a deserter. Draft. 2 pp. In handwriting of Robert Hanson Harrison. A. IV, pt. II, 354

1779
Oct. 9
Continental Congress, President. Philadelphia. To [George] Washington [West Point]. Transmitting resolve. A. L. S. of Samuel Huntington. 1 p. Answered Oct. 17.* 94, 15

1779
Oct. 9
Continental Congress. Resolve. Subsistence money for Continental officers and soldiers. Contemporary copy, attested by Charles Thomson. 1 p. Enclosed in President of Congress to Washington, 1779, Oct. 9. 94, 16

1779
Oct. 9
Board of War. [Philadelphia.] To George Washington, West Point. Supply of shoes; Commissaries of Hides; transportation; Convention troops; exchange of hides for shoes. A. L. S. of Richard Peters. 3 pp. Answered Oct. 18.* 93, 289

1779
Oct. 10
Washington, George. West Point. To the Marine Committee [Philadelphia]. Transmitting letter for Brig. Gen. Du Portail and Lt. Col. [Alexander] Hamilton. Draft. 1 p. In handwriting of Robert Hanson Harrison. A. IV, pt. II, 355

1779
Oct. 10
Washington, George. [West Point.] To the Marine Committee [Philadelphia]. North River pilot for Comte D'Estaing. Draft. 1 p. In handwriting of James McHenry. A. IV, pt. II, 356

1779
Oct. 12
Washington, George. West Point. To the Board of War [Philadelphia]. Pressing need of shoes. Draft. 2 pp. In handwriting of Tench Tilghman. A. IV, pt. II, 359

1779
Oct. 12
Washington, George. West Point. To [the Board of War, Philadelphia]. Intelligence of condition of enemy. Draft. 1 p. In handwriting of Robert Hanson Harrison. A. IV, pt. II, 361

1779
Oct. 13
Board of War. [Philadelphia.] To [George] Washington [West Point]. Detention of artificers; officers' servants; clothing supply. L. S. of Richard Peters. 2 pp. 94, 17

1779
Oct. 14
Continental Congress, President. Philadelphia. To [George] Washington [West Point]. Sullivan's expedition. A. L. S. of Samuel Huntington. 1 p. 94, 19

1779
Oct. 14
Continental Congress, Resolve. Thanks of Congress for success of the Western Expedition. Contemporary copy, attested by Charles Thomson. 1 p. Enclosed in President of Congress to Washington, 1779, Oct. 14. Published to Army in orders of Oct. 22   **94, 21**

1779
Oct. 15
Armstrong, John. Philadelphia. To [George] Washington [West Point]. Approach of the French fleet; subsistence for general officers; U. S. ministers abroad; finance. A. L. S. 2 pp.   **34, 122**

1779
Oct. 15
Cochran, John. West Point. Certificate of condition of Capt-lt. John Van Dyke. A. L. S.

Knox, Henry. Endorsement of above. A. L. S. 2 pp. Enclosed in Washington to the President of Congress, 1779, Oct. 17.   **C. C.   152, 8, 121**

1779
Oct. 17
Washington, George. West Point. To the President of Congress [Philadelphia]. Movements and intentions of enemy. Draft. 2 pp. In handwriting of Tench Tilghman. Read in Congress, Oct. 22.
A.   IV, pt. II, 363

1779
Oct. 17
Washington, George. West Point. To the President of Congress, Philadelphia. Furlough for Capt-lt. [John] Van Dyke. L. S. 1 p. In handwriting of Tench Tilghman. Read in Congress, Nov. 5. Referred to Board of War.   **C. C.   152, 8, 117**

1779
Oct. 17
Continental Congress, President. Philadelphia. To [George] Washington [West Point]. Memorial of Capt. [Garret] Stediford and —— Baker. Letter-book copy.   **C. C.   14, 209**

1779
Oct. 18
Washington, George. West Point. To the Board of War [Philadelphia]. Shoes; clothing and stores for the Western Department. Draft. 1 p. In handwriting of Tench Tilghman. **A.   IV, pt. II, 365**

1779
Oct. 21
Washington, George. West Point. To [the President of Congress, Philadelphia]. Announcing evacuation [of Stony and Verplanck's Points by the enemy]. Draft. 1 p. In handwriting of James McHenry. Read in Congress, Oct. 25. Referred to Committee of Intelligence.
A.   IV, pt. II, 371
Committee: J. B. Smith, Lovell and Henry.

1779
Oct. 21
Washington, George. West Point. To [the President of Congress, Philadelphia]. Indian expeditions; enemy's evacuation of Stony and Verplanck's

Points and Rhode Island. Draft. 3 pp. In handwriting of James McHenry. Read in Congress, Oct. 25. Referred to Atlee, Houston and Marchant.   **A.** IV, pt. II, 367

Printed: Writings of Washington (Ford) N. Y. 1890. 8, 88.

1779
Oct. 21

Morris, Gouverneur. Philadelphia. To [George Washington, West Point]. Committee to report on making provision for hitherto unprovided officers; requests opinion; unity in Congress. A. L. S. 1 p.   **34, 126**

1779
Oct. 22

Lincoln, B[enjamin]. Charleston [South Carolina]. To the President of Congress [Philadelphia]. Account of siege and assault on Savannah; French cooperation. Contemporary copy. 4 pp. In handwriting of Charles Thomson and George Bond. Enclosed in President of Congress to Washington, 1779, Nov. 10.   **94, 29**

1779
Oct. 22

Lincoln, Benjamin. Charleston [South Carolina]. To [Henry?] Laurens and the Committee of Correspondence [South Carolina]. Failure of siege of Savannah; disposition of troops; weakness of State; supplies etc. Contemporary copy. 4 pp. Enclosed in President of Congress to Washington, 1779, Nov. 10.   **94, 31**

1779
Oct. 22

Massachusetts, Council. [Boston]. To [the President of Congress, Philadelphia]. Col. [Moses] Hazen's road to Canada; defense of the frontier. Contemporary copy. 1 p. Enclosed in President of Congress to Washington, 1779, Nov. 11.   **94, 39**

1779
Oct. 23

Van Rensselaer, Henry. Fort Herkimer [New York]. Advance of British and Indians. Contemporary copy. In handwriting of Richard Kidder Meade. Enclosed in Washington to the President of Congress, 1779, Oct. 30.   **C. C. 152, 8, 151**

1779
Oct. 24

Washington, George. West Point. To William Vernon and James Warren [Philadelphia]. Their request for powder. Draft. 1 p. In handwriting of Robert Hanson Harrison.   **A.** IV, pt. II, 373

1779
Oct. 25

Washington, George. West Point. To the Board of War [Philadelphia]. Supply of shoes; districts for Commissaries of Hides. Draft. 1 p. In handwriting of Tench Tilghman. **A.** IV, pt. II, 375

1779
Oct. 25

Van Dyke, Cornelius. Fort Schuyler [New York]. To Col. [Goose] Van Schaick [Albany]. Reports of advance of British and Indians from Oswego. Contemporary copy. In handwriting of Tench Tilghman. Enclosed in Washington to the President of Congress, 1779, Oct. 30.

C. C.　152, 8, 147

1779
Oct. 26

Benedict, Thaddeus. Danbury [Connecticut]. To the President of Congress, Philadelphia. Testimony in case of Dr. Isaac Foster. A. L. S? 1 p. Read in Congress Nov. 14. Referred to the Commander-in-chief. Enclosed in Medical Committee to Congress, 1779, Nov. 15.　92, 513

1779
Oct. 26

Bowen, Ephraim. Newport [Rhode Island]. To [Maj.] Gen. [Nathanael] Greene [West Point]. Evacuation of Rhode Island by British. Contemporary copy. 1 p. In handwriting of Tench Tilghman. Enclosed in Washington to the President of Congress, 1779, Oct. 30.　C. C.　152, 8, 153

1779
Oct. 26

Ten Broeck, Abraham. Stonearabia [New York]. To Gov. [George] Clinton [Fishkill, New York]. Troops ordered to frontier. Contemporary copy. In handwriting of Richard Kidder Meade. Enclosed in Washington to the President of Congress, 1779, Oct. 30.　C. C.　152, 8, 151

1779
Oct. 26

Van Schaick, G[oose]. Albany [New York]. To Gov. [George] Clinton [Fishkill]. Transmitting letters. Contemporary copy. In handwriting of Tench Tilghman. Enclosed in Washington to the President of Congress, 1779, Oct. 30.

C. C.　152, 8, 147

1779
Oct. 28

Clinton, G[eorge]. Fishkill [New York]. To [George] Washington [West Point]. Danger to the frontier. Contemporary copy. 1 p. In handwriting of John Clark, jr. Enclosed in Washington to the President of Congress, 1779, Oct. 30.

C. C.　152, 8, 143

1779
Oct. 29

Continental Congress, President. Philadelphia. To [George] Washington [West Point]. Transmitting resolve. Letter-book copy.　C. C.　14, 216

1779
Oct. 30.

Washington, George. West Point. To the President of Congress [Philadelphia]. Troops ordered to Albany; evacuation of Rhode Island. Draft. 1 p. In handwriting of Tench Tilghman. Read in Congress, Nov. 4.　A.　IV, pt. II, 377

1779
Oct. 30

McHenry, James. West Point. To [the Board of Treasury, Philadelphia]. Transmission of packet to Sir Henry Clinton. Auto. draft signed. 1 p.

A. IV, pt. II, 379

1779
Nov. 2

Washington, George. West Point. To the President of Congress [Philadelphia]. Movements of British. Draft. 2 pp. In handwriting of Tench Tilghman. Read in Congress, Nov. 8.

A. V, pt. I, 1

1779
Nov. 2

Washington, George. West Point. To the Board of War [Philadelphia]. Rank of officers in the Massachusetts Line. Draft. 2 pp. In handwriting of Tench Tilghman. A. V, pt. I, 3

1779
Nov. 3

Washington, George. West Point. To the President of Congress [Philadelphia]. The Abenaki Indians and a commission of major for their chief. Draft. 2 pp. In handwriting of Tench Tilghman. Read in Congress, Nov. 13. Referred to Board of War.

A. V, pt. I, 5

1779
Nov. 4

Continental Congress, Order. Case of Dr. [Isaac] Foster. D. S. of Charles Thomson. 1 p. Enclosed in Medical Committee to Congress, 1779, Nov. 15.

92, 310

1779
Nov. 4

Foster, Isaac. Philadelphia. To the President of Congress [Philadelphia]. Court of Inquiry on his conduct. A. L. S. 2 pp. Read in Congress, Nov. 5. Ordered transmitted to the Commander in Chief. Enclosed in Medical Committee to Washington, 1779, Nov. 15. 92, 311

1779
Nov. 5

Washington, George. West Point. To [the President of Congress, Philadelphia]. Brigade-majors and aides to brigadiers. Draft. 2 pp. In handwriting of Tench Tilghman. Read in Congress, Nov. 13. Referred to Board of War.

A. V, pt. I, 7

1779
Nov. 5

Washington, George. West Point. To [Henry Laurens, Philadelphia]. His appointment as minister to Holland; patriotism; clothing; the French fleet; [Lt.] Col. [John] Laurens. Auto. draft signed. 4 pp. P. I, pt. II, 547

Printed: Writings of Washington (Ford) N. Y. 1890. 8, 103.

1779
Nov. 6

Washington, George. West Point. To [the President of Congress, Philadelphia]. Northern frontier alarm premature. Draft. 1 p. In handwriting of James McHenry. Read in Congress, Nov. 13.

A. V, pt. I, 9

1779
Nov. 6

W[ashingto]n, G[eorge]. West Point. To Gouverneur Morris [Philadelphia]. Arrangement of officers; British fleets; alarm in England. Draft. 2 pp. In handwriting of Tench Tilghman.

P. I, pt. II, 551

1779
Nov. 6

Continental Congress, Resolve. Leave of absence to Capt-lt. [John] Van Dyke. Contemporary copy, attested by Charles Thomson. 1 p. Enclosed in President of Congress to Washington, 1779, Nov. 11.

94, 38

1779
Nov. 8

Continental Congress, Resolve. Letter from President of Massachusetts Council. Contemporary copy, attested by Charles Thomson. 1 p. Enclosed in President of Congress to Washington, 1779, Nov. 11.

94, 37

1779
Nov. 8

Board of War. [Philadelphia.] To [George] Washington, West Point. Arrangement of the Massachusetts Line; absentees; promotions. A. L. S. of Richard Peters. 2 pp. Answered Nov. 19* and 23.*

94, 22

[1779]
[Nov. 8?]

Board of War. Regulation governing return of absent officers. A. D. of Benjamin Walker. 1 p. Enclosed in Board of War to Washington, 1779, Nov. 8.

94, 24

1779
Nov. 10

Continental Congress, President. Philadelphia. To [George] Washington [West Point]. Disaster at Savannah. L. S. of Samuel Huntington. 2 pp. Answered Nov. 20.*

94, 27

1779
Nov. 10

Continental Congress, Resolve. Frigates ordered to Charleston, South Carolina. D. S. of Charles Thomson. 1 p. Enclosed in Marine Committee to Washington, 1779, Nov. 10.

34, 255

1779
Nov. 10

Board of War. [Philadelphia.] To [George] Washington [West Point]. Scarcity of military stores; casting of shells; guards for stores. A. L. S. of Richard Peters. 2 pp. Answered Nov. 19.*

94, 25

1779
Nov. 10

Marine Committee. [Philadelphia.] To [George Washington, West Point]. Frigates ordered to South Carolina. A. L. S. of John Mathews. 1 p.

34, 254

1779
Nov. 11
Continental Congress, President. Philadelphia. To [George] Washington [West Point]. Transmitting resolves; reenforcements for the South. L. S. 2 pp. Answered Nov. 20.* 94, 33

1779
Nov. 11
Continental Congress, Resolve. Reenforcement of [Maj.] Gen. [Benjamin] Lincoln; South Carolina and Georgia militia; Virginia and North Carolina troops; supplies. Contemporary copy, attested by Charles Thomson. 2 pp. Enclosed in President of Congress to Washington, 1779, Nov. 11. 94, 35

1779
Nov. 12
Continental Congress, Resolves. Subsistence of regimental paymasters; arrangement of Artificer corps. Contemporary copy, attested by Charles Thomson. 2 pp. Enclosed in President of Congress to Washington, 1779, Nov. 13. 94, 48

1779
Nov. 12
Continental Congress, Resolve. Arrangement of the Artificer corps. A. D. S. of Charles Thomson. Enclosed in President of Congress to Washington, 1779, Nov. 19. 94, 64

1779
Nov. 12
Board of War. [Philadelphia.] To [George] Washington [West Point]. Transmitting commissions for the Massachusetts Line. A. L. S. of Benjamin Stoddert. 2 pp. Answered Nov. 23.* 94, 92

1779
Nov. 12
Board of War. [Philadelphia.] To George Washington, West Point. Clothing for the Artillery; quality of coats delivered the Pennsylvania troops; applications for clothing; state purchases; needs of the ordnance department. A. L. S. of Richard Peters. 3 pp. Answered Nov. 23.* 94, 41

1779
Nov. 12
Massachusetts. Officers. List of those whose commissions are undated. 1 p. In handwriting of Benjamin Stoddert. Enclosed in Board of War to Washington, 1779, Dec. 3. 94, 91

1779
Nov. 13
Continental Congress, President. Philadelphia. To [George] Washington [West Point]. Transmitting resolves. L. S. of Samuel Huntington. 1 p. 94, 46

1779
Nov. 13
Continental Congress, Resolve. Permission to Maj. Gens. [William] Phillips and [Friedrich Adolph, Baron] Riedesel to go into New York. Contemporary copy. 1 p. Enclosed in Board of War to Washington, 1779, Nov. 15. 94, 55

1779
Nov. 13

Board of War. [Philadelphia.] To Joseph Reed [Philadelphia]. Trouble caused by delivery of coats to the Pennsylvania troops. Contemporary copy. 2 pp. In handwriting of Timothy Pickering, jr. Enclosed in Board of War to Washington 1779, Nov. 22.   **94, 73**

1779
Nov. 13

Board of War. [Philadelphia.] To [George] Washington, West Point. Transmitting commissions. A. L. S. of Benjamin Stoddert. Answered Nov. 23.* `

     94, 43

[1779]
[Nov. 13]

Warner, Seth. Arrangement of officers. Tabular statement. 1 p. Enclosed in Board of War to Washington, 1779, Nov. 13.   **94, 45**

1779
Nov. 14

Washington, George. West Point. To [the President of Congress Philadelphia]. Cooperation with the French; lack of supplies. Draft. 4 pp. In handwriting of Robert Hanson Harrison. Read in Congress, Nov. 18.   **A. V, pt. I. 11**

Printed: Writings of Washington (Ford) N. Y. 1890, 8, 107.

1779
Nov. 15

Continental Congress, Medical Committee. Philadelphia. To [George] Washington [West Point]. Transmitting papers relative to complaints against Dr. [Isaac] Foster. A. L. S. of Nathaniel Scudder. 1 p.   **92, 308**

1779
Nov. 15

Board of War. [Philadelphia.] To [George] Washington [West Point]. Permission to [Maj.] Gens. [William] Phillips and [Friedrich Adolph, Baron] Riedesel to go into New York. A. L. S. of Richard Peters. 1 p. Answered Nov. 23.*

     94, 50

1779
Nov. 15

Board of War. [Philadelphia.] To [Col. Robert Lettis Hooper jr., Easton, Pennsylvania]. Paroles of [Maj.] Gens. [William] Phillips and [Friedrich Adolph, Baron] Riedesel. Contemporary copy. 2 pp. In handwriting of Timothy Pickering, jr. Enclosed in Board of War to Washington 1779, Nov. 15.   **94, 52**

1779
Nov. 15

Board of War. [Philadelphia.] To [Col. Abraham Skinner, Elizabethtown, New Jersey]. [Maj.] Gen's. [William] Phillips and [Friedrich Adolph, Baron] Riedesel's journey to New York. Contemporary copy. 2 pp. In handwriting of Benjamin Stoddert. Enclosed in Board of War to Washington, 1779, Nov. 15.   **94, 53**

1779
Nov. 15

Board of War. [Philadelphia.] To [Maj. Gens. William Phillips and Friedrich Adolph, Baron Riedesel, Easton ? Pennsylvania]. Permission to continue their journey to New York. Contemporary copy. 2 pp. In handwriting of Timothy Pickering, jr. Enclosed in Board of War to Washington 1779, Nov. 15. **94, 54**

1779
Nov. 16

Continental Congress, Resolve. Allowances to Artificer officers. Contemporary copy, attested by Charles Thomson. 1 p. Enclosed in President of Congress to Washington, 1779, Nov. 19. **94, 60**

1779
Nov. 16

Continental Congress, Resolve. Provision for Spanish prisoner. A. D. S. of Charles Thomson. Enclosed in President of Congress to Washington, 1779, Nov. 19. **94, 64**

1779
Nov. 16

Continental Congress, Resolves. Witnesses before courts-martial; depositions as evidence. Contemporary copy, attested by Charles Thomson. 1 p. Enclosed in President of Congress to Washington, 1779, Nov. 19. **94, 62**

1779
Nov. 16

Continental Congress, Resolve. Subclothiers for army. Contemporary copy, attested by Charles Thomson. 1 p. Enclosed in President of Congress to Washington, 1779, Nov. 16. **94, 63**

1779
Nov. 16

Reed, Joseph. [Philadelphia.] To the Board of War [Philadelphia]. Clothing furnish for the Pennsylvania troops. Contemporary copy. 2 pp. In handwriting of Benjamin Stoddert. Enclosed in Board of War to Washington, 1777, Nov. 22.
94, 71

1779
Nov. 17

Steuben, [Frederich Wilhelm Augustus, Baron von] New Windsor [New York]. To [the President of] Congress [Philadelphia]. Recommending de Galvan. Contemporary copy. 2 pp. Enclosed in Board of War to Washington, 1779, Dec. 3.
94, 85

1779
Nov. 18

Washington, George. West Point. To the President of Congress [Philadelphia]. State of the army; annual draft; clothing; enlistments, supplies, etc. Draft. 13 pp. In handwriting of Robert Hanson Harrison. Referred to Mathews, Schuyler, Sherman, Gerry and Houston. A. V, pt. I, 15

Printed: Writings of Washington (Ford) N. Y. 1890. 8, 110.

1779
Nov. 18

Continental Congress, President. Philadelphia. To [George] Washington [West Point]. Transmitting resolves. L. S. of Samuel Huntington. 1 p. Answered Nov. 24.*   94, 56

1779
Nov. 18

Continental Congress, Resolve. Approval of Commander in chief's opinions. Contemporary copy, attested by Charles Thomson. 1 p. Enclosed in President of Congress to Washington, 1779, Nov. 18.   94, 58

1779
Nov. 18

Board of War. Philadelphia. To [President Joseph Reed, Philadelphia]. Return of coats by the council. Contemporary copy. 2 pp. In handwriting of Benjamin Stoddert. Enclosed in Board of War to Washington, 1779, Nov. 22.   94, 70

1779
Nov. 18

Schuyler, Ph[ilip John]. Philadelphia. To [George] Washington [West Point]. Suspension of co-operative measures with D'Estaing; depreciation of currency; De Grasse in the Chesapeake; new arrangement of Quartermaster and Commissary departments; inattention of Congress to business. A. L. S. 3 pp.   34, 362

1779
Nov. 19

Washington, George. West Point. To the Board of War [Philadelphia]. Loans and blast furnaces. Draft. 2 pp. In handwriting of James McHenry.   A. V, pt. I, 29

1779
Nov. 19

Continental Congress, President. Philadelphia. To [George] Washington [West Point]. Transmitting resolves. L. S. of Samuel Huntington. 1 p. Answered Nov. 23.*   94, 59

1779
Nov. 19

Board of War. [Philadelphia.] To George Washington, West Point. Clothing for Pennsylvania troops; march of troops to the southward; clothing, transportation etc. A. L. S. of Richard Peters. 1 p. Answered Nov. 23.*   94, 65

1779
Nov. 19

Pennsylvania, Council, Resolve. Returning clothing to the Board of War. Contemporary copy. In handwriting of Richard Peters. Transmitted to Washington with Board of War to Washington, 1779, Nov. 22.   93, 67

1779
Nov. 19

Burgin, Elizabeth. Elizabethtown [New Jersey]. To [George Washington, West Point]. Account of her escape from New York. A. L. S. 2 pp.

Sir

Morris Town 16. May 1777

Your letter of the 15th I had the Honor of receiving
last night at eleven o'Clock. The Commission enclos'd for Mon-
-sieur Armand, I shall deliver him as soon as I see him.

Agreeable to your request, I will give Commissions
to the Brigadiers, and will ascertain their Rank by their original
Commissions, when I obtain them. The inquiry directed, respec-
-ting Major Campbell, shall be made and that be done, which shall
shall appear right.

I fear it will be hardly possible to satisfy the views
& claims of some of the French Gent. The late promotion of
Monsieur Malmedy, I'd highly Honorable, and such as should be consider'd fully, if not more than adequate to his pretensions, taken upon
any principle, does not come up to his demands. He arriv'd here
yesterday morning, and has been writing some upon the subject.
From the high marks of distinction, but too readily conferred
upon those men, on many instances, they seem to have lost sight
of what is just and reasonable. It would have been happy for us
particularly for me, and for the Gent. themselves, if a too eager
of favors had not induced them to condemn all Rank in our Army,
under that of first Officers; nor is it in my Power to give commands having
Appointment. I shall inform Monsieur Armand, and reconcile him
to it in the best manner I can, that there is no Vacancy for him at pre-
-sent; and I would beg leave to suggest, that where promotions
are made in future, from Political and Honorary motives,
that it will be well for Congress to explain to the Gent. that it may
be some time before they can be put in actual Command. This
might prevent their entertaining suspicions of neglect on our part,
which the situation of the Army will not allow me to obviate. There
is no vacancy for Monsieur Malmody, of the Rank he now holds, un-
less the merits of many other officers, who have serv'd with reputation and
much longer here, are to be overlook'd to make way for him. Such a
measure will neither be practicable — nor prudent to attempt.

By a letter from Gen Heard, who is at Pompton, I am
inform'd that Colos. Barton & Buskirk with 300 Tory levies from Ber-
-gen on the morning of the 13th, attempted to surprize & cut off, about 70
of his Militia, Stationed at Pyramus. The officers happily had notice

Enclosed in Washington to the President of Congress, 1779, Dec. 25.   **C. C. 52, 8, 392**

1779
Nov. 20

Washington, George. West Point. To the President of Congress [Philadelphia]. Troops for the southward; northern frontier diversion; Col. Armand's enterprize. Draft. 3 pp. In handwriting of Caleb Gibbs. Referred to committee on letter of Nov. 18.   **A. V, pt. I, 31**

1779
Nov. 22

Board of War. [Philadelphia.] To George Washington, West Point. Return of clothing by the Pennsylvania council. A. L. S. of Richard Peters. Answered Dec. 6.*   **93, 67**

1779
Nov. 22

Morgan, John. Philadelphia. To the President of Congress [Philadelphia]. Charges against Dr. William Shippen, jr. A. L. S. 4 pp. Enclosed in President of Congress to Washington, 1779, Nov. 27.   **94, 77**

1779
Nov. 23

Washington, George. West Point. To the Board of War [Philadelphia]. Minor military matters; commissions and filling of vacancies. Draft. 3 pp. In handwriting of Tench Tilghman.

    A. V, pt. I, 35

1779
Nov. 23

Washington, George. West Point. To the Board of War [Philadelphia]. Clothing and jealousy of the Pennsylvania line. Draft. 3 pp. In handwriting of Tench Tilghman.   **A. V, pt. I, 39**

1779
Nov. 24

Washington, George. West Point. To the President of Congress [Philadelphia]. Military situation; militia; court martial witnesses; army in winter quarters. Draft. 3 pp. In handwriting of Caleb Gibbs. Read in Congress, Dec. 1.

    A. V, pt: I, 43

Printed in part: Writings of Washington (Sparks) Boston. 1834, 6, 408.

1779
Nov. 24

Continental Congress, Resolve. Dr. J[ohn] Morgan's letter. Contemporary copy, attested by Charles Thomson. 1 p. Enclosed in President of Congress to Washington, 1777, Nov. 27.   **94, 76**

1779
Nov. 27

Washington, George. West Point. To the President of Congress, Philadelphia. Arrangement of troops in winter quarters. Draft. 2 pp. In handwriting of James McHenry. Read in Congress, Dec. 4.   **A. V, pt. I, 49**

1779
Nov. 27

Continental Congress, President. Philadelphia. To [George] Washington [West Point]. Transmitting Dr. J[ohn] Morgan's letter. L. S. of Samuel Huntington. 1 p. Answered Dec. 4.*   **94, 74**

1779
Nov. 29

Washington, George. Peekskill [New York]. To the President of Congress [Philadelphia]. Virginia troops ordered to the southward; land and sea routes. Draft. 4 pp. In handwriting of Robert Hanson Harrison. Read in Congress, Dec. 4. Referred to Board of War.   **A. V, pt. I, 51**
Printed: Writings of Washington (Ford) N. Y. 1890. 8, 125.

1779
Nov. 30

Continental Congress, Resolves. Committee to confer with Commander in chief on Southern Department; paper submitted by French Minister and Don Juan Miralles; militia. Contemporary copy, attested by Charles Thomson. 2 pp. Enclosed in President of Congress to Washington, 1779, Dec. 2.   **94, 79**

1779
Nov. 30

Continental Congress, Resolves. Maj. Gen. [John] Sullivan's resignation. Contemporary copy, attested by Charles Thomson. 1 p. Enclosed in President of Congress to Washington, 1779, Nov. 30.
    94, 81

1779
Nov. 30

Board of War. [Philadelphia.] To [George] Washington [near Morristown, New Jersey]. Receipts of tanners for hides. A. L. S. of Timothy Pickering, jr. 2 pp. Answered Dec. 6.*   **94, 89**

1779
Nov. 30

Galvan, ——. Philadelphia. To the President of Congress [Philadelphia]. Request for commission. Contemporary copy. 2 pp. Enclosed in Board of War to Washington, 1779, Dec. 3.   **94, 83**

[1779]
[Nov.?]

Hay, Udny. Substance of several paragraphs in letter to [Maj.] Gen. [Nathanael] Greene. Great need of money. Contemporary copy. 1 p. In handwriting of John Fitzgerald? Enclosed in Washington to the President of Congress, 1779, Dec. 13.   **C. C. 152, 8, 235**

1779
Dec. 1

Board of War. [Philadelphia.] To [George] Washington [Morristown]. Preparation of an army register; resignations. A. L. S. of Benjamin Stoddert. 2 pp. Answered Dec. 6.*   **94, 94**

1779
Dec. 2

Washington, George. Morristown. To the President of Congress [Philadelphia]. Horses for Col.

[George] Baylor's dragoons. Draft. 3 pp. In handwriting of Tench Tilghman. Read in Congress, Dec. 6. **A. V, pt. I, 55**

1779
Dec. 2
Continental Congress, President. Philadelphia. To [George] Washington [Morristown]. Transmitting resolve. L. S. of Samuel Huntington. 1 p. Answered Dec. 7.* **94, 82**

1779
Dec. 3
Board of War. [Philadelphia.] To [George] Washington [Morristown]. Difficulties in granting a commission to Galvan. A. L. S. of Timothy Pickering, jr. 3 pp. Answered Dec. 12.* **94, 87**

1779
Dec. 3
Champion, Henry. Colchester [Connecticut]. To Col. [Jeremiah] Wadsworth [West Point]. Meat supply for army. Contemporary copy. 2 pp. In handwriting of John Clark, jr. Enclosed in Washington to the President of Congress, 1779, Dec. 13. **C. C. 152, 8, 231**

1779
Dec. 4
Washington, George. Morristown. To the President of Congress [Philadelphia]. Arrest of Dr. [William] Shippen [jr.]; winter quarters. Draft. 1 p. In handwriting of Robert Hanson Harrison. Read in Congress, Dec. 7. **A. V, pt. I, 59**

1779
Dec. 4
Washington, George. Morristown. To [Medical Committee of Congress, Philadelphia]. Trial of Dr. [Isaac] Foster. Draft. 1 p. In handwriting of James McHenry. **A. V, pt. I, 65**

1779
Dec. 4
Continental Congress, President. Philadelphia. To [George] Washington [Morristown]. Transmitting resolve. L. S. of Samuel Huntington. 1 p. Answered Dec. 8.* **94, 96**

1779
Dec. 4
Continental Congress, Resolve. Movement of Virginia troops. Contemporary copy, attested by Charles Thomson. 1 p. Enclosed in President of Congress to Washington, 1779, Dec. 4. **94, 98**

1773
Dec. 6
Washington, George. Morristown. To the Board of War [Philadelphia]. Poor quality of shoes; resignations and promotions; case of Lt. Col. [Peter] Adams; clothing. Draft. 3 pp. In handwriting of Richard Kidder Meade.
A. V, pt. I, 67

1779
Dec. 6
Continental Congress, Resolves. Baylor's dragoons ordered to South Carolina; court-martial of absent officers. Contemporary copy, attested by

Charles Thomson. 3 pp. Enclosed in President of Congress to Washington, 1779, Dec. 7. **94, 104**

1779
DEC. 6

Board of War. [Philadelphia.] To [George] Washington, Morristown. Forwarding commissions for the Virginia Line. A. L. S. of Benjamin Stoddert. 1 p. Answered Dec. 14.* **94, 99**

1779
DEC. 7

Washington, George. Morristown. To the President of Congress [Philadelphia]. Intentions of the enemy; counterfeiting; reenforcing the army. Draft. 4 pp. In handwriting of Alexander Hamilton. Read in Congress, Dec. 10.

A. V, pt. I, 71

Printed: Writings of Washington (Ford) N. Y. 1890. 8, 128.

1779
DEC. 7

Continental Congress, President. Philadelphia. **To** [George] Washington [Morristown]. Transmitting resolves. L. S. of Samuel Huntington. 1 p.

94, 101

1779
DEC. 7

Continental Congress, Committee to confer with Commander in chief. Morristown. Report [to Congress, Philadelphia]. Virginia troops sent to the southward; filling state quotas; cooperative measures with France and Spain. Contemporary copy attested by James McHenry. 4 pp.

A. V, pt. I, 61

Committee appointed Nov. 30 to confer with Commander in chief on state of Southern Department and other matters: Schuyler and Marchant.

1779
DEC. 8

Washington, George. Morristown. To the President of Congress [Philadelphia]. Right of challenges in court martial cases; Virginia troops ordered south. Draft. 2 pp. In handwriting of Robert Hanson Harrison. Read in Congress, Dec. 11. Referred to Livingston, Mathews and Sherman.

A. V, pt. I, 75

Printed in part: Writings of Washington (Ford) N. Y. 1890. 8, 131, note.

1779
DEC. 8

Board of War. [Philadelphia.] To George Washington [Morristown]. Transfer of Capts. [James] Lee and [Andrew] Porter's companies to Proctor's Artillery and troubles of rank that will be caused thereby. A. L. S. of Richard Peters. 1 p. Answered Dec. 12.* **94, 105**

1779
DEC. 10

Washington, George. Morristown. To [the President of Congress, Philadelphia]. March of the Virginia troops south; expiration of enlistments; bounties; scarcity of forage and flour. Draft. 6 pp. In handwriting of Robert Hanson Harrison. Read in Congress, Dec. 13. Referred to Board of War. **A.** V, pt. I, 79

1779
Dec. 10
Continental Congress, President. Philadelphia. To [George] Washington [Morristown]. Transmitting resolves; officer to succeed Col. [Theodorick] Bland. L. S. of Samuel Huntington. 1 p.
94, 113

1779
Dec. 10
Continental Congress, Resolve. Guards for Convention troops at Charlottesville; Col. [Theodorick] Bland's services and resignation. Contemporary copy, attested by Charles Thomson. 2 pp. Enclosed in President of Congress to Washington, 1779, Dec. 10. 94, 111

1779
Dec. 10
Board of War. [Philadelphia.] To [George] Washington [Morristown]. Forwarding commissions for the Maryland Line. A. L. S. of Benjamin Stoddert. 1 p. Answered Dec. 14.* 94, 109

1779
Dec. 10
Board of War. [Philadelphia.] To [George] Washington [Morristown]. March of Virginia troops to South Carolina. A. L. S. of Timothy Pickering, jr. 2 pp. Answered Dec. 14.* 94, 107

1779
Dec. 10
Ward, Joseph. Morristown. To [George] Washington [Morristown]. Subsistence of muster officers. Contemporary copy. 2 pp. In handwriting of Caleb Gibbs. Enclosed in Washington to the President of Congress, 1779, Dec. 13.
C. C. 152, 8, 239

1779
Dec. 11
Anonymous. New York. To [George Washington, West Point]. Embarkation of British at New York. Contemporary copy. 1 p. In handwriting of Tench Tilghman. Enclosed in Washington to the President of Congress, 1779, Dec. 10.
C. C. 152, 8, 223

1779
Dec. 12
Washington, George. Morristown. To the Board of War [Philadelphia]. Case of Galvan; inspectorships. Draft. 2 pp. In handwriting of Alexander Hamilton. **A.** V, pt. I, 85

1779
Dec. 12
Flint, Royal. Morristown [New Jersey]. To [George] Washington [Morristown]. Col. [Henry] Champion's difficulties; lack of money. Contemporary copy. 1 p. In handwriting of James McHenry.

Enclosed in Washington to the President of Congress, 1779, Dec. 13.   C. C.   152, 8, 237

1779
Dec. 12
Georgia, Council, Minutes.   Recommending Col. [Samuel] Elbert for a brigadiership.   Contemporary copy. 1 p.   Enclosed in President of Congress to Washington, 1780, Feb. 12.   94, 188

1779
Dec. 13
Washington, George.   Morristown.   To [the President of Congress, Philadelphia].   Supply of meat.   Draft. 1 p.   In handwriting of James McHenry.   Read in Congress, Dec. 13.   Referred to Sherman, Ellery, Livingston.   A.   V, pt. I, 87

1779
Dec. 14
Washington, George.   Morristown.   To [the President of Congress, Philadelphia].   Minor military matters. Auto. draft signed.   2 pp.   In handwriting of James McHenry.   Read in Congress, Dec. 17.
                     A.   V, pt. 1, 89

1779
Dec. 14
Washington, George.   Morristown.   To the Board of War [Philadelphia].   Movement of troops to the southward and kindred matters.   Draft.   3 pp.   In handwriting of Robert Hanson Harrison.   Referred to Board of War.   A.   V, pt. I, 91

1779
Dec. 14
Continental Congress, Resolve.   Credits for prices of supplies furnished by the States.   D. S. of Charles Thomson.   Enclosed in President of Congress to Washington, 1780, Jan. 25.   96, 20

1779
Dec. 14
Champion, Henry.   Colchester [Connecticut].   To Col. [Jeremiah] Wadsworth [West Point].   Inability to obtain cattle; lack of money.   Contemporary copy.   1 p.   In handwriting of Richard Kidder Meade.   Enclosed in Washington to the President of Congress, 1779, Dec. 24.
                     C. C.   152, 8, 265

1779
Dec. 15
Washington, George.   Morristown.   To [the President of Congress, Philadelphia].   Necessity of immediate supply of flour.   Draft.   2 pp.   In handwriting of Alexander Hamilton.   Read in Congress, Dec. 20.   Referred to Sherman, Forbes and Livingston.
                     A.   V, pt. I, 95
Printed: Writings of Washington (Ford) N. Y.   1890.   8, 138.

1779
Dec. 17
Washington, George.   Morristown.   To [the President of Congress, [Philadelphia].   Rev. Mr. de la Motte's qualifications as secret agent in Canada.   Draft. 2 pp.   In handwriting of Alexander Hamilton.

Read in Congress, Dec. 21. Referred to Board of
War.   **A.** V, pt. I, 97
Printed: Writings of Washington (Ford) N. Y.   1890.   8, 141.

1779
Dec. 17
    Continental Congress, Resolves.   Estimates of commissary
and quartermaster supplies; purchases.   D. S. of
Charles Thomson.   Enclosed in President of Congress to Washington, 1780, Jan. 25.   **96,** 20

1779
Dec. 17
    Board of War. [Philadelphia.] To [George] Washington,
Morristown. Powder for the Board of Admiralty.
A. L. S. of Timothy Pickering, jr. 1 p.   **94,** 120

1779
Dec. 20
    Phillips, W[illiam]. New York. To [Sir Henry Clinton,
New York]. Negotiations for exchange of prisoners. Contemporary copy. 4 pp. In handwriting of George Bond. Enclosed in Washington to
the President of Congress, 1780, Jan. 4.
                           C. C. 152, 8, 307

1779
Dec. 21
    Board of War. [Philadelphia.] To [George] Washington
[Morristown]. Clothing, horses etc. for Col.
[Elisha] Sheldon's troop; uneasiness over com-
missions; aides claim to command. A. L. S. of
Timothy Pickering, jr. 4 pp. Answered Jan. 15,
1780.*   **94,** 122

1779
Dec. 21
    Wayne, Anthony. Light Infantry Camp, Second River
[New Jersey]. To [George] Washington [Mor-
ristown]. Movement of British fleet. Contemporary copy. 1 p. In handwriting of Tench
Tilghman. Enclosed in Washington to the President of Congress, 1779, Dec. 23. **C. C.** 152, 8, 259

1779
Dec. 23
    Washington, George. Morristown. To the President of
Congress [Philadelphia]. Report of movement
of enemy fleet. Draft. 1 p. In handwriting
of Tench Tilghman. Read in Congress, Dec. 27.
Referred to Board of War.   **A.** V, pt. I, 99

1779
Dec. 23
    Washington, George. Morristown. To [the Board of
War, Philadelphia]. Horses and accoutrements
for Armand's corps. Draft. 1 p. In handwriting of Alexander Hamilton.
                           A. V, pt I, 101

1779
Dec. 23
    Wayne, Anthony. Second River [New Jersey]. To
[George] Washington [Morristown]. Sailing of
British fleet from New York. Contemporary
copy. 2 pp. In handwriting of Tench Tilghman. Enclosed in Washington to the President
of Congress, 1779, Dec. 24.   **C. C.** 152, 8, 267

1779
Dec. 23

Continental Congress, Resolve. Subsistence allowance to field commissaries of military stores. Contemporary copy, attested by Charles Thomson. 1 p. Enclosed in President of Congress to Washington, 1779, Dec. 24. Published in Genl. Orders, Dec. 31. **94, 126**

1779
Dec. 24

Washington, George. Morristown. To the President of Congress [Philadelphia]. Intelligence of the enemy; lack of supplies; want of flour. Draft. 1 p. In handwriting of Tench Tilghman. Read in Congress, Dec. 27. Referred to Board of War. **A. V, pt. I, 103**

1779
Dec. 24

Washington, George. Morristown. To the Board of War [Philadelphia]. Col. [John] Mitchell as a witness at trial of [Maj.] Gen. [Benedict] Arnold. Draft. 2 pp. In handwriting of Robert Hanson Harrison. **A. V, pt. I, 105**

1779
Dec. 24

Continental Congress, President. Philadelphia. To [George] Washington [Morristown]. Consideration of his letters; transmission of resolves. L. S. of Samuel Huntington. 1 p. **94, 124**

1779
Dec. 24

Continental Congress, Resolves. Witnesses at court martials; affidavits as evidence; expenses etc. Contemporary copy, attested by Charles Thomson. 2 pp. Enclosed in President of Congress to Washington, 1779, Dec. 24. **94, 125**

1779
Dec. 24

Clinton, [Sir] H[enry]. New York. To [Maj. Gen. William Phillips, New York]. Negotiation for an exchange of prisoners. Contemporary copy. 2 pp. Enclosed in Washington to the President of Congress, 1780, Jan. 4. **C. C. 152, 8, 311**

1779
Dec. 25

Washington, George. Morristown. To the President of Congress [Philadelphia]. Case of Elizabeth Burgin. Draft. 2 pp. In handwriting of James McHenry. Read in Congress, Dec. 30. Referred to Board of War. **A. V, pt. I, 107**

1779
Dec. 25

Phillips, W[illiam]. New York. To Cols. [Robert] Magaw, [George] Mathews, [John] Ely and Lt. Col. [Nathaniel] Ramsay [New York]. Negotiations for exchange of prisoners. Contemporary copy. 4 pp. Enclosed in Washington to the President of Congress, 1780, Jan. 4.
C. C. 152, 8, 313

1779
DEC. 26

Board of War. [Philadelphia.] To [George] Washington [Morristown]. Col. [Uriah] Mitchell's detention; need of his services. A. L. S. of Richard Peters. 2 pp.   **94, 127**

1779
DEC. 26

[Wayne, Anthony.] [Second River, New Jersey.] To [George Washington, Morristown]. Sailing of British fleet from New York. [Extract of letter.] Contemporary copy. 2 pp. Enclosed in Washington to the President of Congress, 1779, Dec. 27.   **C. C. 152, 8, 275**

1779
DEC. 27

Washington, George. Morristown. To the President of Congress [Philadelphia]. Sailing of enemy's fleet from New York. Draft. 1 p. In handwriting of Tench Tilghman. Read in Congress, Dec. 30.   **A. V, pt. I, 109**

1779
DEC. 27

Continental Congress, Resolve. Regulation of post office and discharge of express-riders. Contemporary copy attested by Charles Thomson. 2 pp. Enclosed in President of Congress to Washington, 1779, Dec. 29.   **94, 130**

1779
DEC. 28

Washington, George. Morristown. To the Board of War [Philadelphia]. Appointments in Armand's corps. Draft. 1 p. In handwriting of Tench Tilghman.   **A. V, pt. I, 111**

1779
DEC. 28

Continental Congress, Resolve. Postage rates and free letters. Contemporary copy, attested by Charles Thomson. 1 p. Enclosed in President of Congress to Washington, 1779, Dec. 29.   **94, 131**

1779
DEC. 29

Washington, George. Morristown. To the Board of War [Philadelphia]. Clothing for prisoners. Draft. 1 p. In handwriting of James McHenry.

A. V, pt. I, 113

1779
DEC. 29

Continental Congress, President. Philadelphia. To [George] Washington [Morristown]. Transmitting resolves; expectation of saving of express expenses. L. S. of Samuel Huntington. 1 p. Answered Jan. 4, 1780.* See also letter of Jan. 5.   **94, 129**

1779
DEC. 29

Henry, William. [Lancaster, Pennsylvania.] To [the Board of War, Philadelphia]. Mismanagement of commissary of hides. [Extract of letter.] Contemporary copy. 1 p. In handwriting of Benjamin Stoddert. Enclosed in Board of War to Washington, 1779, Jan. 2.   **94, 134**

1779
Dec. 30

Washington, George. Morristown. To [the President of Congress, Philadelphia]. Sailing of enemy's troops from New York. Draft. 1 p. In handwriting of James McHenry. Read in Congress, Jan. 4, 1780.   A. V, pt. I, 115

1779
Dec. 31

Washington, George. Morristown. To the Board of Treasury [Philadelphia]. Paymaster in the Highlands; low state of the military chest. Draft. 2 pp. In handwriting of James McHenry.
A. V, pt. I, 117

1779
Dec. 31

Continental Congress, Resolve. Plan for obtaining supplies [of blankets]; order to Board of War. A. D. S. of George Bond. 1 p. Enclosed in Board of War to Washington, 1780, Mar. 30.   96, 26

1779
Dec.

[Knox, Henry.] Return of four Pennsylvania companies of artillery. Tabular statement. 1 p. In handwriting of Samuel Shaw. Enclosed in Board of War to Washington, 1780, Aug. 14.   95, 260

1779
Dec.

[Knox, Henry.] Return of 4th Continental Artillery. Tabular statement. 1 p. In handwriting of Samuel Shaw. Enclosed in Board of War to Washington, 1780, Aug. 14.   95, 259

1780
Jan. 1

Board of War. [Philadelphia.] To the President of Congress [Philadelphia]. Clothing for British prisoners in Philadelphia. Contemporary copy. 2 pp. In handwriting of Benjamin Stoddert. Enclosed in Board of War to Washington, 1780, Jan. 3.   94, 160

1780
Jan. 2

Washington, George. Morristown. To [the President of Congress, Philadelphia]. Value of Duportail, la Radière, Laumoy and de Gouvion to the service. Draft. 2 pp. In handwriting of Alexander Hamilton. Read in Congress, Jan. 11. Referred to Board of War.   A. V, pt. I, 119
Printed: Writings of Washington (Ford) N. Y. 1890. 8, 148.

1780
Jan. 3

Board of War. [Philadelphia.] To George Washington, Morristown. Clothing for British prisoners. A. L. S. of Richard Peters. 1 p. Answered Jan. 11*   94, 156

1780
Jan. 3

Board of War. [Philadelphia.] To [George] Washington [Morristown]. [Richard] Howell and secret expedition of Capt. Nathaniel Bowman; measures adopted. A. L. S. of Richard Peters. 2 pp. Answered Jan. 11*   94, 158

1780
JAN. 3

Flint, Royal. Morristown. To [George] Washington
[Morristown]. Failure of meat supplies; want of
bread. Contemporary copy. 1 p. Enclosed in
Washington to the President of Congress, 1780,
Jan. 5.   C. C. 152, 8, 325

1780
JAN. 4

Washington, George. Morristown. To [the President of
Congress, Philadelphia]. Exchange of prisoners
proposed by the British. Draft. 4 pp. In
handwriting of Robert Hanson Harrison. Read
in Congress, Jan. 13.   A. V, pt. I, 121
Printed: Writings of Washington (Ford) N. Y. 1890. 8, 152.

1780
JAN. 4

Craig, I[saac], P[atrick] Duffy, John Webster and Matthew McGuire. Morristown. To [Brig.] Gen.
[Henry] Knox [Morristown]. Protesting against
annexing Pennsylvania companies to Proctor's
artillery. Contemporary copy. 1 p. In handwriting of Samuel Shaw. Addressed by Knox
to Prest. Jos. Reed. Enclosed in Board of War
to Washington, 1780, Aug. 14.   95, 256

1780
JAN. 4

Irvine, William. Crane's Mills [New Jersey]. To [Gen.
George Washington, Morristown]. Failure of
supplies; desertions. Contemporary copy. 2 pp.
Enclosed in Washington to the President of
Congress, 1780, Jan. 5.   C. C. 152, 8, 329

[1780]
[JAN. 4?]

Prisoners, Exchange of. Propositions advanced as result
of conference of Maj. Gen. William Phillips,
Cols. Robert Magaw, George Mathews, John Ely
and Lt. Col. Nathaniel Ramsay. Contemporary
copy. 11 pp. In handwriting of John Clark, jr?
Enclosed in Washington to the President of Congress, 1780, Jan. 4.   C. C. 152, 8, 291

[1780]
[JAN. 4?]

Prisoners. Statement of number in hands of enemy, Convention troops and balance struck; values of rank
etc. 2 pp. In handwriting of George Bond, Enclosed in Washington to the President of Congress, 1780, Jan. 4.   C. C. 152, 8, 307

1780
JAN. 5

Washington, George. Morristown. To [President of
Congress, Philadelphia]. Discharge of express
riders; method of paying troops; great want of
provisions. L. S. 4 pp. In handwriting of
Robert Hanson Harrison. Read in Congress,
Jan. 11.   C. C. 152, 8, 321

1780
JAN. 5

Board of War. [Philadelphia.] To [George] Washington
[Morristown]. Mismanagement of commissary

of hides.   A. L. S. of Richard Peters.   2 pp.
Answered Jan. 11.*   **94, 132**

1780   **Knox,** H[enry].   Morristown.   To [George] Washington.
JAN. 7   Statement of ammunition and apparatus necessary
                for certain specified pieces of ordnance.   D. S.
                2 pp.   In handwriting of Samuel Shaw.
                                          A.   V, pt. I, 187

1780   **Continental Congress,** Resolves.   Payment of officers for
JAN. 8   horses killed in battle; arrangement of Georgia
                regiments.   Contemporary copy, attested by
                Charles Thomson.   2 pp.   Enclosed in President
                of Congress to Washington, 1780, Jan 12.
                                                    94, 142

1780   **Continental Congress,** Resolve.   Dismissal of Maj. Gen.
JAN. 10   Charles Lee.   Contemporary copy, attested by
                Charles Thomson.   1 p.   Enclosed in President
                of Congress to Washington, 1780, Jan. 14.
                                                    94, 155

1780   **Safford,** Samuel.   Bennington [Vermont].   To President
JAN. 10   of Congress.   Memorial for permission to tem-
                porarily retire from the service.   A. D. S.   1 p.
                Read in Congress Feb. 3.   Referred to Board of
                War.   Enclosed in Board of War to Washington,
                1780, Feb. 7.   **94, 178**

1780   **Washington,** George.   Morristown.   To the Board of
JAN. 11   War [Philadelphia].   Col. [John] Mitchell as
                witness in court martial of [Maj.] Gen. [Bene-
                dict] Arnold; clothing for British prisoners.
                Draft.   1 p.   In handwriting of Robert Hanson
                Harrison.   **A.   V, pt. I, 129**

1780   **Washington,** George.   Morristown.   To the Board of
JAN. 11   War [Philadelphia].   Capt. [Nathaniel] Bowman's
                expedition.   Draft.   2 pp.   In handwriting of
                Robert Hanson Harrison.   **A.   V, pt. I, 131**

1780   **Continental Congress,** Committee on reduction of army.
JAN. 11   Philadelphia.   To [George] Washington, Mor-
                ristown.   Matters for consideration.   A. L. S.
                of E[lbridge] Gerry, signed also by Robt. R. Liv-
                ingston and Jno. Mathews.   1 p.   Answered
                Jan. 23.*   **94, 153**

[1780]   **Continental Congress.** Tentative resolves reducing army
[JAN. 11]   and providing for deranged officers.   Contem-
                porary copy.   1 p.   In handwriting of Elbridge

1780
JAN. 14

Board of Treasury. Philadelphia. To [George] Washington [Morristown]. Exchange of prisoners and liquidation of accounts of Convention troops. Contemporary copy. 3 pp. In handwriting of Caleb Gibbs. Enclosed in Washington to the President of Congress, 1780, Jan. 19.

C. C. 152, 8, 359

1780
JAN. 14

Continental Congress, Resolve. Retention of expresses in public service. Contemporary copy, attested by Charles Thomson. 1 p. Enclosed in President of Congress to Washington, 1780, Jan. 14.

94, 144

1780
JAN. 14

Continental Congress, Resolve. Retention of Duportail, Laumoy and Gouvion in service of the United States. Contemporary copy, attested by Charles Thomson. 2 pp. Enclosed in President of Congress to Washington, 1780, Jan. 14. 94, 145

1780
JAN. 14

Board of War. [Philadelphia.] To George Washington, Morristown. Col. [Uriah] Mitchell; troops ordered to Virginia. A. L. S. of Richard Peters. 2 pp. 94, 145

1780
JAN. 14

Board of Treasury. [Philadelphia.] To [George] Washington [Morristown]. Negotiations for exchange of prisoners; unsettled accounts of the Convention troops. A. L. S. of William Churchill Houston. 4 pp. Answered Jan. 20.* 92, 124

1780
JAN. 15

Washington, George. Morristown. To the Board of War [Philadelphia]. Clothing and horses for the dragoons; rank of aides and other officers. Draft. 3 pp. In handwriting of Tench Tilghman. A. V, pt. I, 133

Printed in part: Writings of Washington (Ford) N. Y. 1890, 8, 166.

1780
JAN. 15

Anonymous. Extract of letter from London to a British officer in Georgia. British plan for carrying on the war. Contemporary copy. 2 pp. Enclosed in President of Congress to Washington, 1780, Apr. 20. 94, 311

1780
JAN. 16

Duportail [Louis Le Bègue]. Morristown. To [George] Washington [Morristown]. Commission for Capt. [Daniel] Nevin; commissions for Sappers and Miners. Contemporary copy. 2 pp. In handwriting of Caleb Gibbs. Enclosed in Washington to the President of Congress, 1780, Jan. 26. C. C. 152, 8, 337

1780
JAN. 16

Stirling, [William Alexander, Lord].   Elizabethtown [New Jersey].   To [George Washington, Morristown]. Report of his expedition against Staten Island. Contemporary copy.   2 pp.   In handwriting of Richard Kidder Meade.   Enclosed in Washington to the President of Congress, 1780, Jan. 18.
C. C.   152, 8, 347

1780
JAN. 17

Georgia, General Assembly.   Committee report on conduct of Maj. Gen. [Robert] Howe in Dec. 1778.   Contemporary copy.   1 p.   In handwriting of George Bond.   Enclosed in President of Congress to Washington, 1781, Sep. 7.   97, 155

1780
JAN. 18

Washington, George.   [Morristown.]   To [the President of Congress, Philadelphia].   Baron Steuben and condition of army; the Virginia line arrangement.   Draft.   2 pp.   In handwriting of Robert Hanson Harrison.   Read in Congress, Jan. 24. Referred to Board of War to confer with Steuben and report to Congress.   A.   V, pt. I, 139

1780
JAN. 18

Washington, George.   Morristown.   To the President of Congress [Philadelphia].   Lord Stirling's expedition; intelligence of the enemy.   Draft.   In handwriting of Tench Tilghman.   Read in Congress, Jan. 20.   A.   V, pt. I, 137

1780
JAN. 18

Washington, George.   Morristown.   To [the President of of Congress, Philadelphia].   Respecting Lord Stirling's letter.   Draft.   1 p.   In handwriting of James McHenry.   Read in Congress, Jan. 22.
A.   V, pt. I, 141

1780
JAN. 18

Board of War.   [Philadelphia.]   To [the President of Congress, Philadelphia].   Col. Armand [-Tufin, Marquis de la Rouerie]'s] claim to promotion; his services.   Contemporary copy.   3 pp.   Enclosed in President of Congress to Washington, 1780, Jan. 21.   94, 164

1780
JAN. 19

Washington, George.   Morristown.   To [the President of Congress, Philadelphia].   Accounts of the Convention troops; exchanges.   Draft.   4 pp.   In handwriting of Robert Hanson Harrison.   Read in Congress, Jan. 25.   Referred to Sherman, Forbes and Mathews.   A.   V, pt. I, 143

1780
JAN. 19

Washington, George.   Morristown.   To Cols. [Robert] Magaw, [George] Mathews [John] Ely and [Nathaniel] Ramsay [Morristown]. Exchange of prisoners and settlement of accounts. Contemporary copy. 2 pp. In handwriting of Caleb Gibbs. Enclosed in Washington to the President of Congress, 1780, Jan. 23?   C. C.   152, 8, 317

1780
JAN. 20

Washington, George. Morristown. To the Board of Treasury [Philadelphia]. Settlement of accounts of the Convention troops. Draft. 2 pp. In handwriting of Tench Tilghman.   A. V, pt. I, 149

1780
JAN. 20

Washington, George. Morristown. To Dr. [John] Witherspoon [Philadelphia?]. Energy [of New Jersey] in furnishing supplies to the army. Draft. 2 pp. In handwriting of James McHenry.

A. V, pt. I, 147

Printed: Writings of Washington (Ford) N. Y. 1890. 8, 172, note.

1780
JAN. 20

Continental Congress, Resolve. Commission to investigate staff department; powers and duties. D. S. of Charles Thomson. Enclosed in President of Congress to Washington, 1780, Jan. 25.   96, 24

1780
JAN. 21

Continental Congress, Resolves. [Philip John] Schuyler, [Timothy] Pickering, [jr] and [Thomas] Mifflin appointed commissioners to investigate staff departments of the army. D. S. of Charles Thomson. Enclosed in President of Congress to Washington, 1780, Jan. 25.   96, 24

1780
JAN. 21

Continental Congress, President. Philadelphia. To [George] Washington [Morristown]. Col. Armand [-Tufin, Marquis de la Rouerie]'s] claim to promotion. L. S. of Samuel Huntington. 1 p. Answered Jan. 27.*   94, 163

1780
JAN. 21

Continental Congress, Resolve. Col. Armand [-Tufin]'s application. Contemporary copy, attested by Charles Thomson. 1 p. Enclosed in President of Congress to Washington, 1780, Jan. 21.

94, 162

1780
JAN. 22

Knox, Henry. Morristown. To Prest. [Joseph] Reed [Philadelphia]. Transmitting artillery returns and sentiments of officers on proposed incorporation. A. L. S. 1 p. Enclosed in Board of War to Washington, 1780, Aug. 14.   95, 258

1780
JAN. 23

Washington, George. [Morristown.] To [Committee on reduction of army,] Philadelphia. Expiration

of enlistments; consolidation of regiments; officers; filling the battalions, etc. Draft. 7 pp.
In handwriting of Robert Hanson Harrison.

A. V, pt. I, 153

Committee: Gerry, R. R. Livingston and Mathews.
Printed: Writings of Washington (Ford) N. Y. 1890. 8, 174.

1780
Jan. 25

Continental Congress, President. Philadelphia. To [George
Washington, Morristown]. Extravagance in staff
departments; investigating commission. L. S. of
Samuel Huntington. 1 p. Answered Feb. 8.*

96, 22

1780
Jan. 26

Washington, George. Morristown. To the President of
Congress [Philadelphia]. Commission for Capt.
[Daniel] Nevin; officers of the Sappers and
Miners. Draft. 3 pp. In handwriting of Alex-
ander Hamilton. Read in Congress, Jan. 31.
Referred to the Board of War. **A.** V, pt. I, 161

1780
Jan. 26

Washington, George. Morristown. To the President of
Congress [Philadelphia]. Col. [Theodorick]
Bland's expense account. Draft. 3 pp. In
handwriting of Tench Tilghman. Read in Congress, Jan. 31. Referred to Board of War.

A. V, pt. I, 165

1780
Jan. 26

Continental Congress, Resolve. Negotiation for exchange
of prisoners; liquidation of British accounts.
Contemporary copy, attested by Charles Thomson. 1 p. Enclosed in President of Congress to
Washington, 1780, Jan. 27. 94, 171

1780
Jan. 26

Arnold, Benedict. Court-martial of. Extract of proceedings. Opinion of court on the various charges.
Contemporary copy. 1 p. In handwriting of
Timothy Pickering, jr. Enclosed in President
of Congress to Washington, 1780, Mar. 14.

94, 193

1780
Jan. 26

[Hazen, Moses.] [Crane's Mills, New Jersey.] To [George
Washington, Morristown]. British attack on
Elizabethtown. [Extract of letter.] 1 p. In hand-
writing of Richard Kidder Meade. Enclosed in
Washington to the President of Congress, 1780,
Jan. 27. **C. C.** 152, 8, 383

1780
Jan. 27

Washington, George. Morristown. To [the President of
Congress, Philadelphia]. Col. Armand's claim to

promotion. Draft. 4 pp. In handwriting of
Tench Tilghman. Read in Congress, Jan. 31.

A. V, pt. I, 173

1780
JAN. 27

Washington, George. Morristown. To the President of
Congress [Philadelphia]. Enemy's surprise at
Elizabethtown [New Jersey]; exertions of county
magistrates to supply army with provisions.
Draft. 2 pp. In handwriting of Robert Hanson
Harrison. Read in Congress, Jan. 31.

A. V, pt. I, 171

Printed, in part: Writings of Washington (Ford) N. Y. 1890. 8, 183,
note.

1780
JAN. 27

Continental Congress, President. Philadelphia. To
[George] Washington [Morristown]. Exchange
of prisoners; payment of debt by British. L. S.
of Samuel Huntington. 3 pp. 94, 169

1780
JAN. 27

[Heath, William.] [West Point.] To [George Washington, Morristown]. Fire at West Point; return
of stores destroyed. [Extract of letter.] 2 pp.
In handwriting of Robert Hanson Harrison.
Enclosed in Washington to the President of Congress, 1780, Feb. 14. C. C. 152, 8, 409

1780
JAN. 29

[Washington, George.] To Elbridge Gerry [Philadelphia].
Reenforcing army; provisions. Draft. 3 pp. In
handwriting of Robert Hanson Harrison.

P. II, 17

Printed: Writings of Washington (Ford) N. Y. 1890. 8, 182.

1780
JAN. 30

Washington, George. Morristown. To [the President of
Congress Philadelphia]. Transmitting proceed-
ings of court martial of Maj. Gen. [Benedict]
Arnold and copy of letter from the Quartermaster
General. Draft. 1 p. In handwriting of Rob-
ert Hanson Harrison. A. V, pt. I, 177

1780
JAN. 31

Continental Congress, Resolve. Appreciation of efforts of
the State of New Jersey in supplying the Army.
Contemporary copy, attested by Charles Thomson. 1 p. Enclosed in President of Congress to
Washington, 1780, Feb. 1. 94, 174

1780
JAN. 31

Continental Congress, Resolves. Gratitude to France; cooperative measures; supplies; naval campaign;
British machinations. Contemporary copy, attested by Charles Thomson. 3 pp. Transmitted
to Washington. 95, 15

[1780] Washington, George. [Morristown.] Statement of times
[JAN.] of expiration of various troops. Draft. 1 p.
In handwriting of Tench Tilghman.
A. V, pt. I, 151

[1780] Campbell, Archibald. To the Council of Massachusetts
[JAN.?] [Boston]. Description of country around Penobscot; topography, number of inhabitants etc.
Contemporary copy, attested by Charles Thomson. 4 pp. Enclosed in President of Congress
to Washington, 1780, Apr. 9. 94, 336

1780 Greene, Nathanael. Morristown. To [George] Washing-
JAN. ton [Morristown]. Lack of money, facilities, etc.,
for obtaining supplies; the situation. Contem-
porary copy. 3 pp. In handwriting of Richard
Kidder Meade. Enclosed in Washington to the
President of Congress, 1780, Jan. 30.
C. C. 152, 8, 389

1780 Continental Congress, President. Philadelphia. To
FEB. 1 [George] Washington [Morristown]. Transmit-
ting resolves. L. S. of Samuel Huntington. 1 p.
Answered Feb. 8.* 94, 172

1780 Morris, Robert. Philadelphia. To [George Washington
FEB. 1 Morristown]. Wine; winter visit to Philadelphia. A. L. S. 2 pp. 35, 242

1780 [Heath, William.] [Highlands, New York.] To [George
FEB. 2 Washington, Morristown.] Second fire at West
Point. [Extract of letter.] 2 pp. In handwriting
of James McHenry. Enclosed in Washington to
the President of Congress, 1780, Feb. 14.
C. C. 152, 8, 413

1780 Stoddard, Orring. Young's Farm [Westchester County?
FEB. 3 New York]. Surprise of his detachment by Brit-
ish. [Extract of letter.] 1 p. In handwriting of
James McHenry. Enclosed in Washington to the
President of Congress, 1780, Feb. 14.
C. C. 152, 8, 415

1780 Washington, George. Morristown. To Robert Morris
FEB. 4 [Philadelphia]. Shipment of wine; invitation to
visit Philadelphia. Auto. draft signed. 3 pp.
P. II, 29

1780 [Heath, William.] [Highlands.] To [George Washington,
FEB. 4 Morristown]. The surprise at Young's Farm.
[Extract of letter.] 2 pp. In handwriting of

John Fitzgerald? Enclosed in Washington to the President of Congress, 1780, Feb. 14.

C. C. 152, 8, 417

1780
FEB. 5

Washington, George. Morristown. To [the President of Congress, Philadelphia]. Col. Armand [-Tufin]'s service in France. L. S. 1 p. In handwriting of Robert Hanson Harrison. Read in Congress, Feb. 10. C. C. 152, 8, 395

1780
FEB. 5

Armand, [-Tufin, Charles, Marquis de la Rouerie]. [Morristown.] To [George] Washington [Morristown] Length of service in the French army. A. L. S. 1 p. Enclosed in Washington to the President of Congress, 1780, Feb. 5.

C. C. 152, 8, 397

1780
FEB. 6

Washington, George. [Morristown.] To [the President of Congress, Philadelphia] Transmitting Col. Armand's statement of his length of service in French army. Draft. 1 p. In handwriting of Alexander Hamilton. Read in Congress, Feb. 2.

A. V, pt. I, 179

1780
FEB. 6

Washington, George. Morristown. To the Board of War [Philadelphia]. Incorporation of Pulaski's with Armand's corps; promotion of the latter. Draft. 1 p. In handwriting of Tench Tilghman.

A. V, pt. I, 181

1780
FEB. 7

Continental Congress, President. Philadelphia. To [George] Washington [Morristown]. Intelligence from the south. L. S. of Samuel Huntington. 1 p. Answered Feb. 14.* 94, 175

1780
FEB. 7

Board of War. [Philadelphia.] To [George] Washington, Morristown. Transmitting a memorial. A. L. S. of Benjamin Stoddert. 1 p. Answered Feb. 18.*

94, 177

1780
FEB. 8

Washington, George. Morristown. To the President of Congress [Philadelphia]. Exchange of prisoners. Draft. 2 pp. In handwriting of Robert Hanson Harrison. Read in Congress, Feb. 12.

A. V, pt. I, 183

1780
FEB. 8

Washington, George. Morristown. To the Board of War [Philadelphia]. Artillery and ordnance stores for a western expedition. Draft. 1 p. In handwriting of Tench Tilghman. A. V, pt. I, 185

objects— there are objects of the greatest
moment, as they may in their consequences
involve the fate of America— for I will
undertake to say that it is next to impof
=sible, when the season is so far advanced,
properly to accomplish those changes, ap=
=pointments and the dependent arrange=
=ments for the ensuing campaign— should
any convulsion happen, or move=ment
take place, they will be altogether im=
=practicable— Justice to my own
character as well as duty to the Public
constrain me to repeat these things— their
consequences are more easily conceived than
described—

It may be said by some his that
my wishes to see the officers of this army
upon a more respectable establishment,
is the cause of my Sollicitude— I carry; me too far—
I can declare, that my anxiety proceeds
from the causes abovementioned— if my
opinion is asked with respect to the necessity,
of making this provision for the officers,
I am ready to declare, that I, do most religiously believe the
Salvation of the cause depends upon
it— and without it your officers will
moulder to nothing, or be composed of

WRITING OF JOHN LAURENS.

1780
FEB. 9

Continental Congress, Resolves. Furnishing State quotas of troops; proportions, etc. Contemporary copy, attested by Charles Thomson. 2 pp. Enclosed in President of Congress to Washington, 1780, Feb. 10. **94,** 182

1780
FEB. 9

Continental Congress, Resolve. Reimbursement of states for expense of more than their quota of troops. Contemporary copy, attested by Charles Thomson. 1 p. Enclosed in President of Congress to Washington, 1780, Feb. 10. **94,** 183

1780
FEB. 9

Massachusetts, Council. Boston. Extract from Instructions to the delegates in Congress relative to proposed Penobscot expedition. Contemporary copy, attested by Charles Tomson. 2 pp. In handwriting of George Bond. Enclosed in President of Congress to Washington, 1780, Apr. 9.

94, 334

1780
FEB. 10

Washington, George. Morristown. To the Board of War [Philadelphia]. Arrangement of the regiment of Artificers; recruiting. 3 pp. In handwriting of Tench Tilghman. **A.** V, pt. I, 189

[1780]
[FEB. 10]

Washington, George. [Morristown.] Names, rank and pretensions of officers of the regiment of Artificers. Tabular statement. 2 pp. In handwriting of Tench Tilghman. Enclosed in Washington to the Board of War 1780, Feb. 10.

A. V, pt. I, 194

[1780]
[FEB. 10]

Washington, George. [Morristown.] Names and rank of officers recommended for retention in Artificer regiment, promotions etc. Tabular statement. 2 pp. In handwriting of Tench Tilghman. Enclosed in Washington to the Board of War 1780, Feb. 10. **A.** V, pt. I, 198

[1780]
[FEB. 10]

Washington, George. [Morristown.] A plan for enlisting a corps of Artificers to consist of ten companies. Draft. 1 p. In handwriting of Alexander Hamilton. Enclosed in Washington to the Board of War 1780, Feb. 10. **A.** V, pt. I, 201

1780
FEB. 10

Continental Congress, President. Philadelphia. To [George] Washington [Morristown]. Supplying deficiencies of State quotas of troops. L. S. of Samuel Huntington. 3 pp. Answered Feb. 17.*

94, 180

1780
FEB. 10

[Heath, William.] [Highlands.] To [George Washington, Morristown]. Account of the surprise at Young's Farm. [Extract of letter.] 3 pp. In handwriting of Robert Hanson Harrison. Enclosed in Washington to the President of Congress, 1780, Feb. 14.
C. C. 152, 8, 419

1780
FEB. 11

Continental Congress, Resolves   Georgia's exertions; quota of troops; arrangement; Col. [Samuel] Elbert's case. Contemporary copy, attested by Charles Thomson. 2 pp. Enclosed in President of Congress to Washington, 1780, Feb. 12.
94, 186

1780
FEB. 12

Continental Congress, President. Philadelphia. To [George] Washington [Morristown]. Exchange of Col. [Samuel] Elbert. L. S. of Samuel Huntington. 1 p. Answered Feb. 23.*   94, 183

1780
FEB. 12

Continental Congress, Resolve. Confirmation of court-martial sentence of Maj. Gen. [Benedict] Arnold. A. D. S. of Charles Thomson. 1 p. Enclosed in President of Congress to Washington, 1780, Mar. 14.   94, 189

1780
FEB. 14

Washington, George. Morristown. To [the President of Congress Philadelphia]. Fires at West Point; moves of enemy. Draft. 2 pp. In handwriting of Robert Hanson Harrison. Read in Congress, Feb. 19. Referred to Board of War.
A. V, pt. I, 203

1780
FEB. 15

Washington, George. Morristown. To the Board of War [Philadelphia]. Completing the States quotas of troops. Draft. 2 pp. In handwriting of Robert Hanson Harrison.   A. V, pt. I, 205

1780
FEB. 15

Greene, Ebenezer. To Congress. Memorial praying for relief from obligations of parole. D. S. 1 p. Endorsed on back in handwriting of Richard Peters and crossed out, is report of the Board of War on this memorial. Enclosed in President of Congress to Washington, 1780, Feb. 21.   94, 202

1780
FEB. 15

Board of War. [Philadelphia.] To [George] Washington [Morristown]. Combining certain troops with Armand's corps. A. L. S. of Benjamin Stoddert. 3 pp. Answered Feb 18.*   94, 197

1780
FEB. 15

Board of Admiralty. Philadelphia. To [George] Washington [Morristown]. Complaints of British

treatment of marine prisoners. L. S. of Francis
Lewis. 1 p. Answered Feb. 19.*   Miscel.

1780   Washington, George. Morristown. To the President of
FEB. 17   Congress [Philadelphia]. Returns of troops and
filling the States' quotas. Draft. 1 p. In handwriting of Robert Hanson Harrison. Referred
to Board of War.   A. V, pt. I, 209

1780   Washington, George. Morristown. To the North Caro-
FEB. 17   lina delegates in Congress [Philadelphia]. Clothing for North Carolina troops. Draft. 1 p. In
handwriting of James McHenry.
A. V, pt. I, 207

[1780]   Washington, George. [Morristown.] To [the Board of
[FEB. 18]   War, Philadelphia]. Reduction of Armand's
corps and minor matters. Draft. 2 pp. In
handwriting of James McHenry.
A. V, pt. I, 211

1780   [Board of War.] [Philadelphia.] To [Otis & Henley, Bos-
FEB. 18.   ton]. Clothing for dragoons. [Extract of letter.] Contemporary copy. 1 p. In handwrit-
ing of Benjamin Stoddert. Enclosed in Board of
War to Washington, 1780, Mar. 17.   94, 242

1780   Washington, George. Morristown. To the Board of
FEB. 19.   Admiralty [Philadelphia]. Marine prisoners of
war. Draft. 2 pp. In handwriting of Tench
Tilghman.   A. V, pt. I, 213

1780   Continental Congress. Resolve. Memorial of Capt. Eben-
FEB. 19.   ezer Greene and hostages of the Cedars. Contemporary copy, attested by George Bond. 1 p.
Enclosed in President of Congress to Washing
ton, 1780, Feb. 21.   94, 201

1780   Continental Congress, President. Philadelphia. To
FEB. 21.   [George] Washington [Morristown]. Transmitting resolves; hostages of the Cedars. L. S. of
Samuel Huntington. 1 p. Answered Mar. 6.*
94, 199

1780   Board of War. [Philadelphia.] To [George] Washington,
FEB. 21.   Morristown. Bounty for reenlistments in Bland's
troop; command of Eastern Department; retalia-
tion for treatment of [Maj.] Gen. [Charles] Lee.
A. L. S. of Richard Peters. 1 p. Answered
Mar. 3.   94, 203

1780 FEB. 22.	Continental Congress, President. Philadelphia. To [George] Washington [Morristown]. Fleet at Havana; report of British fleet off the Georgia Coast. L. S. of Samuel Huntington. 2 pp. Answered Mar 6.* 94, 207

1780 FEB. 22.	Board of War. [Philadelphia.] To [George Washington, Morristown]. Returns of the various cavalry troops; state quotas, embarrassments, delays, etc. L. S. of Richard Peters. 4 pp. In handwriting of Benjamin Stoddert. Answered Feb. 27.* 94, 205

1780 FEB. 22.	[Lincoln, Benjamin.] [Charleston, South Carolina]. To [the President of Congress, Philadelphia]. Movement of British at Stono Ferry. [Extract of letter.] Contemporary copy. 2 pp. Enclosed in President of Congress to Washington, 1780, Mar. 19. 94, 245

1780 FEB. 23.	Washington, George. Morristown. To [the President of Congress, Philadelphia]. Transmitting newspapers. Draft. 1 p. In handwriting of Tench Tilghman. A. V, pt. I, 215

1780 FEB. 23.	Washington, George. Morristown. To the President of Congress [Philadelphia]. Transmitting New York papers and acknowledging receipt of documents. L. S. 1 p. In handwriting of Tench Tilghman. C. C. 152, 8, 423

1780 FEB. 23	Washington, George. Morristown. To [the Board of War, Philadelphia]. Swords for non-commissioned officers; scarcity of drums, etc. Draft. 1 p. In handwriting of Alexander Hamilton. A. V, pt. I, 217

1780 FEB. 23	Lovell, James. Philadelphia. To [George] Washington [Morristown]. News from Europe; supplies from France; England and Holland. A. L. S. 3 pp. 36, 2

1780 FEB. 25	Biddle, Clement. Morristown. To [Maj. Gen. Nathanael Greene, Morristown]. Failure in forage and grain supplies and cause. Contemporary copy. 4 pp. In handwriting of James McHenry. Enclosed in Washington to the President of Congress, 1780, Mar. 6. C. C. 152, 8, 431

1780 FEB. 25	Continental Congress. Resolve. State quotas of supplies; ruling prices, general arrangements, etc. Con-

temporary copy. Attested by Charles Thomson. 5 pp. Enclosed in President of Congress to Washington, 1780, Feb. 29.   **94, 213**

1780
FEB. 25

[Blaine, Ephraim.] Boston. To [George] Washington [Morristown]. Purchase of supplies in Connecticut; beef, etc. Contemporary copy. 2 pp. In handwriting of James McHenry. Enclosed in Washington to the President of Congress, 1780, Mar. 17.   **C. C. 152, 8, 443**

[1780]
[FEB. 25]

[Laurens, Henry.] [Charleston, South Carolina.] To ———? Station and force of enemy; naval strength before Charleston; arrangement and force of American troops. Contemporary copy. 2 pp. Note by Samuel Huntington: "The Express who brings this says it is an Extract Taken from the late President Laurens in Charles Town which he saw copied off." Enclosed in President of Congress to Washington, 1780, Mar. 19.

94, 246

1780
FEB. 26

Washington, George. Morristown. To [the Board of War, Philadelphia]. Powers of the Board of War as respects courts-martial. Draft. 3 pp. In handwriting of Alexander Hamilton.

A. V, pt. I, 219

Printed: Writings of Washington (Ford) N. Y. 1890. 8, 203.

1780
FEB. 27

Washington, George. Morristown. To [the Board of War, Philadelphia]. State quota; exchange of prisoners. Draft. 1 p. In handwriting of Tench Tilghman.   **A. V, pt. I, 223**

1780
FEB. 28

Board of War. [Philadelphia.] Standards, drums and fifes, hangers, belts, etc., for troops, state of supplies. A. L. S. of Richard Peters. 2 pp. Answered Mar. 6.*   **94, 209**

1780
FEB. 29

Continental Congress, President. Philadelphia. To [George] Washington [Morristown]. [Brig.] Gen. [William] Irvine's claim to rank; resolves transmitted; exertions of states to furnish supplies. L. S. of Samuel Huntington. 2 pp. Answered Mar. 6* and 8.*   **94, 211**

1780
FEB. 29

Continental Congress. Resolve. Brig. Gen. [William] Irvine's claim to rank. D. S. of Charles Thomson. 1 p. Enclosed in President of Congress to Washington, 1780, Feb. 29.   **Miscel**

1780
MAR. 1

Fleury, [François] L[ouis Teisseydre, Marquis de]. Versailles. To the President of Congress, Philadelphia. Application for extension of leave. A. L. S. 2 pp. Enclosed in Washington to the President of Congress, 1780, May 17. C. C. 152, 8, 565

1780
MAR. 2

New York, Senate, Resolves. Raising of troops for defence of the frontier. Contemporary copy. 1 p. Enclosed in President of Congress to Washington, 1780, Apr. 6.   94, 279

1780
MAR. 3

Washington, George. Morristown. To the Board of War [Philadelphia]. Complaints of subalterns of the Massachusetts line. Draft. 1 p. In handwriting of Tench Tilghman.   A. V, pt. I, 225

1780
MAR. 4

Washington, George. Morristown. To James Lovell [Philadelphia]. Supplies from France; the King of England's speech. Draft. 2 p. In handwriting of James McHenry.   A. V, pt. I, 227

1780
MAR. 4

Board of War. [Philadelphia.] To [George Washington] Morristown. Supplies for Fort Pitt; prospective operations on the Western frontier. A. L. S. of Richard Peters. 2 pp. Answered Mar. 14.*
                                                                94, 217

1780
MAR. 6

Washington, George. Morristown. To [the President of Congress, Philadelphia]. British fleet; exchange of the hostages of the Cedars; Quartermaster General's department;]Brig.] Gen. [William] Irvine's rank; specific supplies from the states. L. S. 3 pp. In handwriting of Richard Kidder Meade. Read in Congress Mar. 16. Referred to Board of Treasury.   C. C. 152, 8, 427

The draft, A. V, pt. I, 229, is dated Mar. 7.
Printed in part: Writings of Washington (Ford) N.Y. 1890. 8, 213.

1780
MAR. 6

Washington, George. Morristown. To [the Board of War, Philadelphia]. Supplies from France; swords for non-commissioned officers. Draft. 1 p. In handwriting of Tench Tilghman.
                                                    A. V, pt. I, 223

1780
MAR. 6

Continental Congress, Resolve. Virginia, North and South Carolina troops. A. D. S. of Charles Thomson. 1 p. Enclosed in President of Congress to Washington, 1780, Mar. 9.   94, 222

1780
MAR. 6

Greene, Nathanael. Morristown. To [George] Washington. [Morristown.] State of affairs in Quartermaster General's Department. Contemporary copy. 3 pp. Enclosed in Washington to the President of Congress, 1780, Mar. 17.

C. C. 152, 8, 447

1780
MAR. 8

Washington, George. Morristown. To the Board of War [Philadelphia]. Accoutrements for the dragoons; clothing, etc. Draft. 3 pp. In handwriting of Tench Tilghman. **A.** V, pt. I, 235

1780
MAR. 8

Continental Congress, Resolves. Militia of Virginia, North and South Carolina; reenforcements for Southern army. Contemporary copy, attested by Charles Thomson. 1 p. Enclosed in President of Congress to Washington, 1780, Mar. 9.

94, 221

1780
MAR. 9

Continental Congress, President. Philadelphia. To [George] Washington [Morristown]. Transmitting resolves; discretionary power to make detachments. L. S. of Samuel Huntington. 2 pp. Answered Mar. 20.* 94, 219

1780
MAR. 10

Continental Congress, Resolves. Arrears due soldiers for clothing. Contemporary copy, attested by Charles Thomson. 2 pp. Enclosed in President of Congress to Washington, 1780, Mar. 11.

94, 192

1780
MAR. 10

Board of War. [Philadelphia.] To [George Washington] Morristown. Convening of a general court martial at Philadelphia. Capt. [Theophilus] Parke's case. A. L. S. of Richard Peters. 2 pp. Answered Mar. 25.* 94, 226

1780
MAR. 11

Continental Congress. Proclamation appointing Apr. 26 a day of fasting and prayer. D. S. of Samuel Huntington, countersigned by Charles Thomson. 2 pp. Enclosed in President of Congress to Washington, 1780, Mar. 14. 94, 229

1780
MAR. 11

Continental Congress, Resolves. Officers' servants. Contemporary copy, attested by Charles Thomson. 1 p. Enclosed in President of Congress to Washington, 1780, Mar. 11. 94, 190

1780
MAR. 11

Maryland, Council. Annapolis. To the Board of War [Philadelphia]. Furnishing supplies. Contemporary copy. 1 p. Enclosed in Board of War to Washington, 1780, Mar. 20. 94, 250

1780
MAR. 11

Pennsylvania, Council. Philadelphia. To the Board of War [Philadelphia]. Inability of Pennsylvania

to furnish supplies. Contemporary copy. 2 pp.
Enclosed in Board of War to Washington, 1780,
Mar. 20.   94, 252

1780
MAR. 12

Tilghman, T[ench]. Morristown. To the Board of War
[Philadelphia]. Col. [Oliver] Spencer's regiment.
Auto. draft signed. 1 p.   A. V, pt. I, 239

1780
MAR. 12

Continental Congress, President. Philadelphia. To
[George] Washington [Morristown]. Transmitting resolves; confirmation of court-martial sentence of Maj. Gen. [Benedict] Arnold. Letter-
book copy.   C. C. 14, 316

1780
MAR. 13

Schuyler, Ph[ilip John]. To [George] Washington [Mor-
ristown]. Plan for rearranging the finances; in-
delicacy of Congress in a personal matter; rumor
from Charleston. A. L. S. 3 pp.   36, 149$\frac{1}{2}$

1780
MAR. 14

Washington, George. Morristown. To the Board of War
[Philadelphia]. Supplies for Fort Pitt. Draft.
1 p. In handwriting of Robert Hanson Harrison
and Tench Tilghman.   A. V, pt. I, 241

1780
MAR. 14

Continental Congress, President. Philadelphia. To
[George] Washington [Morristown]. Transmit-
ting resolves. L. S. of Samuel Huntington. 1 p.
Answered Mar. 23.*   94, 228

1780
MAR. 14

Continental Congress, President. Philadelphia. To
[George] Washington [Morristown]. Transmitting resolves. L. S. of Samuel Huntington. 1 p.
                                   94, 232

1780
MAR. 15

Washington, George. Morristown. To the Board of
Admiralty [Philadelphia]. The proposed naval
expedition and [Maj.] Gen. [Benedict] Arnold's
desire to command. Draft. 2 pp. In handwriting of Robert Hanson Harrison.
                             A. V, pt. I, 243
Printed: Writings of Washington (Sparks) Boston. 1834. 6, 484.

1780
MAR. 15

Board of War. [Philadelphia.] To [George] Washington
[Morristown]. Transmitting arrangement of the
Massachusetts subalterns. A. L. S. of Benjamin
Stoddert. 1 p. Answered Mar. 25.*   94, 234

1780
MAR. 16

Hollingsworth, H[enry]. Head of Elk [Pennsylvania].
To the Board of War [Philadelphia]. Report on
gathering supplies. Contemporary copy. 1 p.
Enclosed in Board of War to Washington, 1780,
Mar. 20.   94, 251

1780
MAR. 17

Washington, George. Morristown. To [the President of Congress, Philadelphia]. Great scarcity of meal and grain. L. S. 3 pp. In handwriting of Robert Hanson Harrison. Read in Congress, Mar. 21. Referred to Board of War.

C. C. **152**, 8, 435

Draft, A. V, pt. I, 245, is dated Mar. 19.

1780
MAR. 17

Board of War. [Philadelphia.] To [George] Washington [Morristown]. Supplies for the cavalry, clothing, accoutrements, etc. L. S. of Richard Peters. 3 pp. Answered Mar. 25.* **94**, 240

1780
MAR. 17

Gamble, James. Morristown. Account of stores at magazine at Morristown. Contemporary copy. 1 p. In handwriting of Tench Tilghman. Enclosed in Washington to the President of Congress, 1780, Mar. 17. C. C. **152**, 8, 441

1780
MAR. 17

Grain. Estimate of amounts purchased by Azariah Dunham. Tabular statement. Contemporary copy. 1 p. In handwriting of Tench Tilghman. Enclosed in Washington to the President of Congress, 1780, Mar. 17. C. C. **152**, 8, 439

[1780]
[MAR. 18]

Continental Congress, Resolves. State quotas of money; emission of new continental bills, remission of old, interest, etc. Contemporary copy, endorsed with memo. of War Office: "This Resolve passed in Congress last Saturday." 5 pp. Transmitted to Washington. **94**, 236

1780
MAR. 18

Brodhead, Daniel. Fort Pitt. To Richard Peters, Philadelphia. Indian forays on the Western frontier; supplies; tents; forage; money for Quartermaster. Contemporary copy. 3 pp. Enclosed in Board of War to Washington, 1780, Apr. 17.

94, 301

1780
MAR. 19

Continental Congress, President. Philadelphia. To [George] Washington [Morristown]. Transmitting intelligence from Charleston [South Carolina]. L. S. of Samuel Huntington. 1 p.

94, 243

1780
MAR. 20

Washington, George. Morristown. To [the President of Congress, Philadelphia]. Directions of Congress respecting case of Maj. Gen. [Benedict] Arnold. Draft. 1 p. In handwriting of Robert Hanson Harrison. Read in Congress, Mar. 25.

A. V, pt. I, 249

1780
MAR. 20
: **Washington, George.** Morristown. To the Board of War [Philadelphia]. Arrangement of subalterns of the 8th Massachusetts regiment. Draft. 1 p. In handwriting of Tench Tilghman.

A. V, pt. I, 251

1780
MAR. 20
: **Board of War** [Philadelphia]. To [George] Washington, Morristown. Lack of supplies; prospects of obtaining them. A. L. S. of Benjamin Stoddert. 2 pp. Answered Mar. 25.* 94, 248

1780
MAR. 21
: **Continental Congress,** Resolve. Suspension of appointments of officers in State lines. Contemporary copy, attested by Charles Thomson. 1 p. Enclosed in President of Congress to Washington, 1780, Mar. 23. 94, 258

1780
MAR. 22
: **Continental Congress,** Resolve. Settlement of clothing accounts for 1777. Contemporary copy, attested by Charles Thomson. 1 p. Enclosed in President of Congress to Washington, 1780, Mar. 23. Published to Army in General Orders, Apr. 11.

94, 255

1780
MAR. 23
: **Washington, George.** Morristown. To [the President of Congress, Philadelphia]. Intelligence of enemy; scarcity of provisions. Draft. 2 pp. In handwriting of Robert Hanson Harrison. Read in Congress, Mar. 29. A. V, pt. I, 253

1780
MAR. 23
: **Continental Congress,** President. Philadelphia. To [George] Washington [Morristown]. Transmitting resolves. L. S. of Samuel Huntington. 1 p. Answered Mar. 28.* 94, 256

1780
MAR. 23
: **Board of Admiralty.** Philadelphia. To [George Washington, Morristown]. Lack of men for Maj. Gen. [Benedict] Arnold's proposed naval expedition. Recent copy. 1 p. 36, 244

1780
MAR. 24
: **Lincoln, Benjamin.** Charleston [South Carolina]. To [the President of Congress, Philadelphia]. British naval movements; reenforcements; advance of enemy. [Extract of letter.] Contemporary copy. 2 pp. Enclosed in President of Congress to Washington, 1780, Apr. 22. 94, 259

1780
MAR. 25
: **Washington, George.** Morristown. To the Board of War [Philadelphia]. General courts martial; saddles for dragoons; horses kept at public ex-

pense; provision supplies. Draft. 3 pp. In handwriting of Tench Tilghman.

A. V, pt. I, 255

[1780]
[MAR. 25?]
Washington, George. [Morristown.] Remarks on deficiency of supplies of flour and forage due from the different states. Draft. 3 pp. In handwriting of Tench Tilghman. Enclosed in: Washington to the President of Congress 1780, Mar. 26.

A. V, pt. I, 261

[1780]
[MAR. 25?]
Washington, George. [Morristown.] Estimate of forage necessary for 19,190 horses. Draft. 1 p. In handwriting of Tench Tilghman. Enclosed in Washington to the President of Congress 1780, Mar. 26. A. V, pt. I, 259

1780
MAR. 26
Washington, George. Morristown. To [the President of Congress, Philadelphia]. Failure of states to supply their quotas of provision and forage; forage from Massachusetts; salt and salt provisions; estimates of quantities needed; pasturage for horses of army. Draft. 8 pp. In handwriting of Robert Hanson Harrison. Read in Congress, Mar. 29. Referred to Sherman, Burke and Searle. A. V, pt. I, 265

Printed, in part: Writings of Washington (Ford) N. Y. 1890. 8, 224.

1780
MAR. 26
Washington, George. Morristown. To [Maj. Gen. Nathanael Greene, Philadelphia]. Detachment for the South; facilities for moving the army. Contemporary copy. 2 pp. In handwriting of Richard Kidder Meade. Enclosed in Washington to the President of Congress, 1780, Apr. 7.

C. C. 152, 8, 499

1780
MAR. 27
Washington, George. Morristown. To [the President of Congress, Philadelphia]. Suggesting sending Duportail to the southward. Draft. 1 p. In handwriting of Alexander Hamilton. Read in Congress, Mar. 29. A. V. pt. I, 273

1780
MAR. 27
Continental Congress, Commissioners for arranging the Staff Departments. Report: Establishment of magazines; duties of store-keepers, superintendents, etc.; provisioning detachments; rations; supplies; quartermasters department; wagon and forage masters; pay and accounts; wagons allowed officers; forage allowance; requisition for wagons; procuring supplies; Commissary Gen-

eral of Military Stores; money etc. Contemporary copy. 38 pp. Transmitted to Washington.
36, 135 and 282

Commissioners: Timothy Pickering, jr., and Thos. Mifflin. A Committee: Sherman, Jones and Schuyler, was chosen Mar. 10 to confer with them and approve the above report.
See: Journals of Congress, resolves of Jan. 20, 21, 22 and Mar. 10.

1780
MAR. 28

Washington, George. Morristown. To [the President of Congress, Philadelphia]. Indian attack on Skenesborough [New York]; encounter of British and Spanish fleets off Gibraltar; question of State and Continental bounties for reenlistments. Draft. 4 pp. In handwriting of Robert Hanson Harrison and Tench Tilghman. Read in Congress, Apr. 3. Referred to Board of War.
A. V, pt. I, 275

Printed in part: Writings of Washington (Ford) N. Y. 1890. 8, 223, note.

1780
MAR. 28

Schott, John Paul. Wyoming [Pennsylvania]. Muster roll of corps. Tabular statement. D. S. Attested by Zebulon Butler. 3 pp. Transmitted to Congress.
See: Weltner, Ludowick to Washington, 1780, May 16.

1780
MAR. 29

Continental Congress, President. Philadelphia. To [George] Washington [Morristown]. Transmitting papers, printed copy of Maj. Gen. [Benedict] Arnold's court martial, etc. L. S. of Samuel Huntington. 1 p. Answered Apr. 7.* 94, 261

1780
MAR. 29

Continental Congress, Resolve. Duportail ordered to Southern Army. Contemporary copy, attested by Charles Thomson. 1 p. Enclosed in President of Congress to Washington, 1780, Mar. 29.
94, 263

1780
MAR. 30

Washington, George. Morristown. To the Board of War [Philadelphia]. Dragoons ordered to the southward. Draft. 2 pp. In handwriting of Tench Tilghman. A. V, pt. I, 279

1780
MAR. 30

Washington, George. [Morristown.] To John Mathews [Philadelphia]. Situation of enemy. Draft. 2 pp. In handwriting of James McHenry.
A. V, pt. I, 281

Printed: Writings of Washington (Ford) N. Y. 1890. 8, 228.

1780
MAR. 30

Board of War, Philadelphia. To [George Washington, Morristown]. Importation of blankets from New York for army; secrecy, passport and difficulties; other supplies. L. S. of Richard

Peters. 4 pp. In handwriting of Timothy Pickering, jr. 96, 30

1780
MAR. 30

Clark, Abra[ham]. Philadelphia. To Gov. [William] Livingston [Morristown]. Blankets at Squan; threatened seizure; passport, etc. A. L. S. 1 p. Enclosed in Livingston to Washington, 1780, Apr. 3. 96, 31

1780
MAR.'31

Washington, George. Morristown. To [the President of Congress, Philadelphia]. Attempted exchange of prisoners. Draft. 3 pp. In handwriting of Alexander Hamilton. Read in Congress, Apr. 6. Referred to Scott, Houston and Ellery, who were discharged Oct. 13; then referred to Sullivan, Bland and Mathews.
A. V, pt. I, 283
Printed: Writings of Washington (Ford) N. Y. 1890. 8,229.

1780
MAR. 31

Board of War. [Philadelphia.] To [George] Washington, Morristown. Propriety of offering pardon to Virginia deserters. A. L. S. of Benjamin Stoddert. 1 p. Answered Apr. 9.* 94, 297

1780
MAR. —

Lawrance, John. Morristown. Memorandum of charges against [Maj. Gen. Benedict Arnold].

Lawrance, John. To [Lt.] Col. [Robert Hanson] Harrison [Morristown]. Transmitting above memorandum. 2 pp. Memo. in handwriting of Lawrance; letter an A. L. S. of same. 94, 195

[1780]
[MAR. ?]

Lane, Joseph jr. To the President of Congress [Philadelphia]. Exchanges effected in the Southern Department. A. L. S. 1 p. 94, 219

1780
APR. 1

Washington, George. Morristown. To the Board of Treasury, Philadelphia. Claims of soldiers that their enlistments have expired. Draft. 1 p. In handwriting of Robert Hanson Harrison.
A. V, pt. I, 287

1780
APR. 2

Washington, George. Morristown. To [the President of Congress, Philadelphia]. Embarkation of enemy for the South; weak state of American army. Draft. 5 pp. In handwriting of Robert Hanson Harrison. Read in Congress, Apr. 5. Referred to Board of War. A. V, pt. I, 289
Printed: Writings of Washington (Ford) N. Y. 1890. 8,234.

1780
APR. 2

Washington, George. Morristown. To Maj. Gen. [Nathanael] Greene. Detachment of troops to the Southward. Contemporary copy. 1 p. In handwriting of Alexander Hamilton. Enclosed in Washington to the President of Congress, 1780, Apr. 7.   C. C.   152, 7, 509

1780
APR. 2

Greene, Nathanael. Philadelphia. To [George] Washington [Morristown]. Want of cash; inability to supply needs of army. Contemporary copy. 2 pp. In handwriting of Richard Kidder Meade. Enclosed in Washington to the President of Congress, 1780, Apr. 7.   C. C.   152, 7,505

1780
APR. 3

Washington, George. [Morristown.] To [the President of Congress, Philadelphia]. Distresses of officers [of the 16 Additional Continental regiments]; dissatisfactions, hardships, etc. Draft. 6 pp. In handwriting of Alexander Hamilton. Read in Congress, Apr. 5.   A. V, pt. I, 295
Printed: Writings of Washington (Ford) N. Y. 1890. 8, 241.

1780
APR. 3

Washington, George. Morristown. To the Board of War [Philadelphia]. Passage up the Hudson of vessel with supplies for the army. Draft. 3 pp. In handwriting of Robert Hanson Harrison.
A. V, pt. I, 301

1780
APR. 3

Board of War. [Philadelphia.] To [George] Washington, Morristown. Augmenting Lee's corps; promotions therein. A. L. S. of Benjamin Stoddert. 2 pp.   Answered Apr. 9.*   94, 270

1780
APR. 3

Lee, Henry, jr. Philadelphia. To the Board of War [Philadelphia]. Promotions and field officers of the Light Horse. Contemporary copy. 2 pp. Enclosed in Board of War to Washington, 1780, Apr. 3.   94, 272

1780
APR. 3

Livingston, Wil[liam]. . Morristown. To [George] Washington [Morristown]. Blankets. A. L. S. 1 p.
96, 27

[1780]
[APR. 4?]

[Washington, George.] [Morristown.] To [Gov. William Livingston, Morristown]. Passport for blankets at Squan. Incomplete draft. 1 p. In handwriting of Robert Hanson Harrison.   96, 33

1780
APR. 4

Continental Congress, Resolve. Raising of New York militia. Contemporary copy, attested by Charles Thomson. 1 p. Enclosed in President of Congress to Washington, 1780, Apr. 6.   94, 278

1780
APR. 5

Continental Congress, Resolve. Approval of reenforcement of Southern Army. Contemporary copy,

attested by Charles Thomson. 1 p. Enclosed
in President of Congress to Washington, 1780,
Apr. 6.   94, 277

1780
APR. 6

Continental Congress, President. Philadelphia. To
[George] Washington [Morristown]. Transmit-
ting resolves of Congress and acts of the New
York legislature for raising militia. L. S. of
Samuel Huntington. 2 pp. Answered Apr. 17.*
                                                    94, 275

1780
APR. 6

Continental Congress, Resolve. Committee to confer
with Commander-in-chief. Contemporary copy,
attested by Charles Thomson. Enclosed in
President of Congress to Washington, 1780,
Apr. 18.   94, 307

1780
APR. 7

Washington, George. Morristown. To [the President of
Congress, Philadelphia]. Sailing of detachment
of enemy from New York; Maryland and Delaware troops under orders; provisions, etc. Draft.
2 pp. In handwriting of Robert Hanson Harrison. Read in Congress, Apr. 10.
                                        A. V, pt. I, 305

1780
APR. 7

Washington, George. Morristown. To the Board of War
[Philadelphia]. Want of meat for the army.
Draft. 3 pp. In handwriting of Robert Hanson
Harrison.   A. V, pt. I, 307

1780
APR. 7

Continental Congress, Resolves. Commission to Chief
Joseph Louis Gill; enlistment of St Francois Indians. Contemporary copy, attested by Charles
Thomson. 1 p. Enclosed in President of Congress to Washington, 1780, Apr. 13.   94, 285

1780
APR. 8

Continental Congress, Resolve. Papers referring to proposed expedition against Penobscot. Contemporary copy, attested by Charles Thomson. 1 p.
Enclosed in President of Congress to Washing-
ton, 1780, Apr. 9.   94, 333

1780
APR. 8

Maryland. Council. [Annapolis.] To the Board of War
[Philadelphia]. Exchange of Lt. Col. [Nathaniel]
Ramsay. Contemporary copy. 1 p. Enclosed
in President of Congress to Washington, 1780,
Apr. 25.   94, 280

1780
APR. 9

Washington, George. Morristown. To the Board of
War [Philadelphia]. Application for promotion
of Captains [Allen] McLane and [Henry] Peyton;

pardon for deserters in the Virginia line. Draft.
4 pp. In handwriting of Tench Tilghman.

A. V, pt. I, 311

1780
APR. 9

Continental Congress, President. Philadelphia. To
[George] Washington [Morristown]. Transmitting papers referring to proposed expedition
against Penobscot. L. S. of Samuel Huntington. 2 pp. Answered Apr. 17.*   94, 331

1780
APR. 9

Lincoln, B[enjamin]. Charleston. To Gov. [Richard]
Caswell [Newbern? North Carolina]. Military
situation. Contemporary copy. 1 p. In handwriting of Guilliame Aertsen, jr. Enclosed in
Board of War to Washington, 1780, May 9.

94, 345

1780
APR. 10

Washington, George. Morristown. To William Ellery
[Philadelphia]. Request of the Governor of
Rhode Island for troops. Draft. 2 pp. In
handwriting of Tench Tilghman.

A. V, pt. I, 315

1780
APR. 10

Washington, George. Morristown. To the President of
Congress [Philadelphia]. Intelligence of the
enemy. Draft. 1 p. In handwriting of Tench
Tilghman. Read in Congress, Apr. 11.

A. V, pt. I, 317

1780
APR. 10

Continental Congress, Resolves. Reimbursement to army
for pay depreciation. Contemporary copy,
attested by Charles Thomson. 1 p. Enclosed in
President of Congress to Washington, 1780,
Apr. 18. Published to army in General Orders,
Apr. 30.   94, 305

1780
APR. 10

St. Clair, Arthur, Edward Carrington, and Alexander
Hamilton. Morristown. To [George] Washington [Morristown]. Prisoners accounts in exchange negotiations. Contemporary copy. 1 p.
In handwriting of Tench Tilghman. Enclosed
in Washington to the President of Congress, 1780,
Apr. 17.   C. C. 152, 8, 523

[1780]
APR. 12

Virginia Delegates to Continental Congress. To [George]
Washington [Morristown]. Transmitting letter.
Recent copy. 1 p. Original was signed by Cyrus
Griffin and James Madison, jr.   36, 412

1780
APR. 13

Continental Congress, President. Philadelphia. To
[George] Washington [Morristown]. Transmit-

ting resolves and account of naval engagement [British and Dutch in the English channel, Dec. 31 and Jan. 1]. L. S. of Samuel Huntington, 2 pp. Answered Apr. 17.*   94, 283

1780
APR. 13
Continental Congress, Resolves. Selection of committee, Schuyler, Mathews and Peabody, to confer with Commander in chief; instructions for reorganizing army; general regulations etc. Contemporary copy, attested by Charles Thomson. Enclosed in President of Congress to Washington, 1780, Apr. 18.   94, 307

1780
APR. 13
Board of War. [Philadelphia.] To [George] Washington, Morristown. Sale of boats and building material. A. L. S. of Benjamin Stoddert. 1 p. Answered Apr. 23.*   94, 287

[1780]
[APR. 13]
Greene, Nathanael. Memorandum. Sale of boats and materials on the Susquehanna. Contemporary copy. 1 p. Enclosed in Board of War to Washington, 1780, Apr. 13.   94, 288

1780
APR. 15
Continental Congress, President. Philadelphia. To [George] Washington [Morristown]. Transmitting resolves. L. S. of Samuel Huntington. 1 p. Answered Apr. 28.*   94, 291

1780
APR. 15
Continental Congress, Resolve. Appointment of Col. Joseph Ward, Commissary-General of Prisoners. Contemporary copy, attested by Charles Thomson. 1 p. Enclosed in President of Congress to Washington, 1780, Apr. 15.   94, 293

1780
APR. 16
Hallet, Jonathan. Paramus [New Jersey]. To George Washington [Morristown]. Account of British attack on Paramus. Contemporary copy. 3 pp. Enclosed in Washington to the President of Congress, 1780, Apr. 17.   C. C.   152, 8, 519

1780
APR. 17
Board of War. [Philadelphia.] To [George] Washington [Morristown]. Supplies [for Fort Pitt]; commissions for Indians. A. L. S. of Benjamin Stoddert. 2 pp. Answered Apr. 23.*   94, 299

1780
APR. 17
Washington, George. Morristown. To [the President of Congress, Philadelphia]. March of Maryland troops to the Southward; enemy at Penobscot and necessity of a fleet; disaffected inhabitants at Paramus [New Jersey]. Draft. 4 pp. In hand-

writing of Alexander Hamilton. Read in Congress, Apr. 20. **A. V, pt. I, 319**

Printed, in part: Writings of Washington (Ford) N. Y. 1890. 8, 249.

1780
APR. 17

Washington, George. Morristown. To [the President of Congress, Philadelphia]. Establishment of the footing of officers of artillery battalions; promotions; South Carolina companies. Draft. 4 pp. In handwriting of Robert Hanson Harrison. Read in Congress, Apr. 20. Referred to Board of War. **A. V, pt. I, 323**

1780
APR. 17

Gervais, John Lewis. George Town, [South Carolina]. To Henry Laurens [Wilmington, South Carolina]. Attack on Charleston. Contemporary copy. 3 pp. Enclosed in Board of War to Washington, 1780, May 9. **94, 346**

1780
APR. 18

Washington, George. Morristown. To the Board of War [Philadelphia]. Rank of artillery officers; arrangement of corps. Draft. 4 pp. In handwriting of Robert Hanson Harrison.

A. V, pt. I, 327

1780
APR. 18

Continental Congress, President. Philadelphia. To [George] Washington [Morristown]. Transmitting resolves. L. S. of Samuel Huntington. 2 pp. Answered May 5.* **94, 303**

1780
APR. 19

Board of Treasury. [Philadelphia.] To [George] Washington [Morristown]. Forwarding muster-rolls. A. L. S. of John Gibson. 1 p. **92, 246**

1780
APR. 20

Continental Congress, President. Philadelphia. To [George] Washington [Morristown]. French fleet at Martinique; plan of British. L. S. of Samuel Huntington. 2 pp. Answered May 5.* **94, 309**

1780
APR. 21

Continental Congress, Resolve. British Commissary of Prisoners to reside within American lines. Contemporary copy, attested by Charles Thomson. 1 p. Enclosed in President of Congress to Washington, 1780, Apr. 22. **94, 313**

1780
APR. 22

Continental Congress, President. Philadelphia. To [George] Washington [Morristown]. Transmitting resolve and intelligence from Charleston. L. S. of Samuel Huntington. 1 p. Answered May 5.* **94, 314**

1780
APR. 23

Washington, George. Morristown. To the Board of War [Philadelphia]. Sale of articles; Col.

[Daniel] Brodhead's request for tents. Draft. 2 pp. In handwriting of Richard Kidder Meade and Robert Hanson Harrison. **A. V, pt. I, 331**

1780
APR. 24

Nash, A[bner]. Newburn [North Carolina]. To the President of Congress [Philadelphia]. Situation at Charleston; need of assistance. Contemporary copy. 1 p. In handwriting of Richard Peters. Enclosed in Board of War to Washington, 1780, May 9. **94, 344**

1780
APR. 25

Board of War. Philadelphia. To [George] Washington, Morristown. Exchange of Lt. Col. [Nathaniel] Ramsay for [Lt.] Col. [Dr. John] Connolly. A. L. S. of Benjamin Stoddert. 3 pp. Answered May 4.* **94, 281**

1780
APR. 27

Washington, George. Morristown. To the Board of War [Philadelphia]. Incorporation of companies of Captains [John Paul] Schott and [Anthony] Selin with the German battalion. Draft. 1 p. In handwriting of Tench Tilghman.
A. V, pt. I, 333

1780
APR. 28

Washington, George. Morristown. To [the President of Congress, Philadelphia]. Appointment of Col. [Joseph] Ward as Commissary of Prisoners; news from the southward. Draft. 2 pp. In handwriting of Robert Hanson Harrison. Read in Congress, May 1. **A. V, pt. I, 335**

1780
APR. 28

Washington, George. Morristown. To [the President of Congress, Philadelphia]. Announcing death of Don Juan de Miralles. Draft. 1 p. In handwriting of Robert Hanson Harrison. Read in Congress, May 1. **A. V, pt. I, 337**

1780
APR. 29

Board of War. Philadelphia. To George Washington, Morristown. Returns of provisions and military stores; regimental surgeon's mates. A. L. S. of Richard Peters. **94, 316**

1780
MAY 4

Washington, George. Morristown. To the Board of War [Philadelphia]. Exchange of prisoners. Draft. 2 pp. In handwriting of Robert Hanson Harrison. **A. V, pt. II, 1**

1780
MAY 4

Duane, James. Philadelphia. To [George Washington, Morristown]. Anxiety for Charleston; Virginia reenforcements; finances of the confederation; disaffection in Britain; reception of the new money. A. L. S. 4 pp. **37, 135**

1780
MAY 5

Washington, George. Morristown. To [the President of Congress, Philadelphia]. Making up the depreciation of pay to the army; French at Martinique; agent for prisoners; lack of money and supplies; rumor of [John] Paul Jones being on the American coast. Draft. 3 pp. In handwriting of Robert Hanson Harrison. Read in Congress, May 8. Part referred to Board of Treasury.

A. V, pt. II, 3

1780
MAY 5

Washington, George. Morristown. To the Board of War [Philadelphia]. Mistakes in dates of subalterns' commissions in Massachusetts line. Draft. 1 p. In handwriting of Tench Tilghman.

A. V, pt. II, 7

1780
MAY 5

Simpson, James. Charleston. To Rev. Mr. Wickman, North Carolina. Encouragement of loyalists. Contemporary copy. In handwriting of Charles Thomson. Enclosed in President of Congress to Washington, 1780, June 5.   95, 65

1780
MAY 6

Board of Admiralty. Philadelphia. To [George] Washington [Morristown]. Wine sent by order of Congress. Marine Committee Letter-book.

1780
MAY 8

Washington, George. Morristown. To the Board of War [Philadelphia]. Ordering muskets and cartouche boxes sent forward. Draft. 1 p. In handwriting of Tench Tilghman.   A. V, pt. II, 9

1780
MAY 9

Continental Congress, President. Philadelphia. To [George] Washington [Morristown]. Arrival of U. S. minister [John Jay] at Cadiz. L. S. of Samuel Huntington. 1 p. Answered May 13.*   37, 158

1780
MAY 9

Duane, James. Philadelphia. To [George] Washington [Morristown]. Situation at Charleston; new plan of finance. A. L. S. 3 pp.   37, 153

1780
MAY 9

Board of Admiralty. [Philadelphia]. To [George] Washington [Morristown]. Lemons taken from a prize. A. L. S. of Francis Lewis. 1 p. Answered May 12.*   Miscel

1780
MAY 9

Board of War. [Philadelphia.] To [George] Washington, Morristown. Transmitting intelligence from South Carolina. A. L. S. of Joseph Carleton. 1 p.   94, 342

Hd. Qr. Morristown
25 Octr. 1779

Sir

    I have the honor to lay before your Excellency the un representation of a certain Elizabeth Burgin late an inhabitant of New-York. From the testimony of different persons, and particularly ~~some~~ many of our own officers who have returned from captivity, it would appear that she has been indefatigable for the relief of the prisoners, and in measures for facilitating their escape. ~~They brought our few~~ In consequence of this conduct she incurred the suspicions of the enemy, and was finally compelled to make her escape, under the distressed circumstances which she describes. I could not ~~keep~~ forbear recommending to consideration a person who has risqued so much and been so friendly to our officers and privates, especially

WRITING OF JAMES McHENRY.

1780
MAY 12

Washington, George. Morristown. To [the Board of] Admiralty [Philadelphia]. Acknowledging lemons. Draft. 1 p. In handwriting of Tench Tilghman.

A. V, pt. II, 11

1780
MAY 13

Washington, George. Morristown. To [the President of Congress, Philadelphia]. Forwarding intelligence. Draft. 1 p. In handwriting of Tench Tilghman. Read in Congress, May 15.

A. V, pt. II, 15

1780
MAY 13

Washington, George. Morristown. To the President [of Congress, Philadelphia]. Return of the Marquis de Lafayette. Auto. draft signed. 2 pp. Read in Congress, May 16. A. V, pt. II, 13
Printed: Writings of Washington (Sparks) Boston. 1835. 7, 31.

1780
MAY 13

Washington, George. Morristown. To [the Board of Admiralty, Philadelphia]. Acknowledging Madeira. Draft. 1 p. In handwriting of Tench Tilghman.

A. V, pt. II, 17

1780
MAY 13

W[ashington,] G[eorge]. Morristown. To James Duane [Philadelphia]. The Confederation; alarm in New York caused by despatches from England. Auto. draft signed. 3 pp. P. II, 91
Printed: Writings of Washington (Ford) New York. 1890. 8, 262.

1780
MAY 14

Washington, George. Morristown. To [James] Duane [Philadelphia]. Aid from France; committee to sit at camp; its powers, etc.; suggested personnel. Draft. 3 pp. In handwriting of Alexander Hamilton. P. II, 95
Printed: Writings of Washington (Ford) N. Y. 1890. 8, 264.

1780
MAY 14

[Washington, George.] Morristown. To [the Board of Treasury, Philadelphia]. Hard money for secret service. Auto. draft. 1 p. P. II, 99

1780
MAY 15

Pennsylvania, Council. Philadelphia. To the Board of War [Philadelphia]. Complaints of [Lt.] Col. [Ludowick] Weltner. Contemporary copy. 1 p. Enclosed in Board of War to Washington, 1780, May 19. 95, 3

1780
MAY 16

Continental Congress, Resolve. Return of Marquis de Lafayette. Contemporary copy, attested by Charles Thomson. 1 p. Enclosed in President of Congress to Washington, 1780, May 20.

95, 14

1780
MAY 16

Hamilton, Henry. Lancaster [Pennsylvania]. To the Board of War, Philadelphia. Leave to go into New York. A. L. S. 1 p. 95, 21

1780
MAY 16

[La Luzerne, Anne César, Chevalier de.] Philadelphia. Memorial to Congress. Cooperation with the French; furnishing of supplies; intelligence; arms and clothing from France; zeal of America. Contemporary copy. 3 pp. Enclosed in President of Congress to Washington, 1780, May 29.   95, 39

1780
MAY 16

Rutledge, John. [South Carolina.] To [Abner] Nash [Newbern, North Carolina]. Surrender of Charleston; terms; the situation; James Simpson's intercepted letters. Contemporary copy. In handwriting of Charles Thomson. Enclosed in President of Congress to Washington, 1780, June 5.   95, 65

1780
MAY 16

Weltner, Ludowick. Northumberland [Pennsylvania]. To [George] Washington [Morristown]. Consolidation of Ottendorff's corps with his own; skirmish with Indians. A. L. S. 2 pp. Transmitted to Congress.   C. C. 152, 8, 553

1780
MAY 17

Washington, George. Morristown. To [the President of Congress, Philadelphia.] Extension of Lt. Col. Fleury's furlough. Draft. 1 p. In handwriting of Alexander Hamilton. Read in Congress, May 22.   A. V, pt. II, 19

1780
MAY 17

Continental Congress, Resolves. Memorial of Minister of France [Chevalier La Luzerne]. Contemporary copy, attested by Charles Thomson. Enclosed in President of Congress to Washington, 1780, May 29.   95, 37

1780
MAY 19

Washington, George. Morristown. To [the President of Congress Philadelphia]. Transmitting letters for Gov. [John] Rutledge; embarkation of troops at New York. Draft. 2 pp. In handwriting of Robert Hanson Harrison.   A. V, pt. II, 21

1780
MAY 19

Continental Congress, Resolves. States from Virginia northward to Massachusetts to furnish ten millions to the continental treasury; apportionment; bills to be drawn on [Benjamin] Franklin; preparation for campaign; duties and powers of committee of cooperation. A. D. of Robert Hanson Harrison. 3 pp. Transmitted to Washington.

W

1780
MAY 19

Board of Treasury. [Philadelphia.] To [George] Washington [Morristown]. Inability to furnish money required; sum sent. A. L. S. of Charles Lee. 1 p.   37, 222

1780
MAY 19

Board of War. [Philadelphia.] To [George] Washington [Morristown]. Transmitting petition against Lt. Col. [Ludowick] Weltner. A. L. S. of Joseph Carleton. 1 p. Answered June 5.* 95, 1

1780
MAY 20

Continental Congress, President. Philadelphia. To [George] Washington [Morristown]. Transmitting resolves; cooperation with French. L. S. of Samuel Huntington. 2 pp. 95, 10

1780
MAY 20

Continental Congress, Resolve. Forwarding of State quotas of troops. Contemporary copy attested by Charles Thomson. 1 p. Enclosed in President of Congress to Washington, 1780, May 20. 95, 12

1780
MAY 20

Continental Congress, Resolves. Cooperation with French. Contemporary copy, attested by Charles Thomson. 1 p. Enclosed in President of Congress to Washington, 1780, May 20. 95, 13

1780
MAY 20

Continental Congress, Resolve. Communications of Lafayette respecting cooperation with French. Contemporary copy attested by Charles Thomson. Enclosed in President of Congress to Washington, 1780, May 29. 95, 37

1780
MAY 21

Duane, James. Philadelphia. To [George Washington, Morristown]. Capt. [Allen] McLane's situation. A. L. S. 1 p. 37, 229

1780
[MAY 21?]

Shee, Johns. [Philadelphia.] To James Duane [Philadelphia]. Case of Capt. Allen McLane. A. L. S. 1 p. Enclosed in Duane to Washington, 1780, May 21. 37, 231

1780
MAY 22

Board of War. [Philadelphia.] To [George] Washington, Morristown. Salt meat for army. A. L. S. of Joseph Carleton. 2 pp. 95, 17

1780
MAY 23

Jones, Joseph. Philadelphia. To [George] Washington [Morristown]. Employment of Col. [William] Grayson; news from Charleston. A. L. S. 2 pp. 37, 285

1780
MAY 24

Washington, George. Morristown. To the Committee of Cooperation [Morristown]. Competency of their powers. Draft. 1 p. In handwriting of Alexander Hamilton. A. V, pt. II, 23
Committee: Schuyler, Mathews and Peabody.

1780
MAY 24

Board of War. [Philadelphia.] To [George] Washington [Morristown]. Passport for Surgeon Major Pausch; Ensign [Henry] Hamilton's request.

A. L. S. of Timothy Pickering, jr.　2 pp.　Answered June 5.*　　　　　　　　　　　　95, 19

1780
MAY 25

Washington, George. Morristown. To the Committee of Cooperation [Morristown]. Circular letter to the States; necessity of exertion. Draft. 5 pp. In handwriting of Alexander Hamilton.

A. V, pt. II, 25
Printed: Writings of Washington (Ford) N. Y. 1890. 8, 284.

1780
MAY 25

Continental Congress, Committee of Cooperation at Headquarters. Morristown. Circular letter to the States. Necessities of army; remedial measures; enlistments, supplies and transportation; cooperation with French.

MAY 25

——— Same. Supplying State quotas of troops. Contemporary copies, attested by Abraham Brasher. 6 pp. Transmitted to Washington.　　95, 25
Committee: Schuyler, Mathews and Peabody.

1780
MAY 25

Board of War. [Philadelphia.] To [George] Washington, Morristown. Negotiation of bills in New York for benefit of prisoners. L. S. of Joseph Carleton. 2 pp. Answered June 5.*　　　　95, 23

1780
MAY 25

Nash, A[bner]. Newbern [North Carolina]. To the President of Congress. [Philadelphia.] The situation in North Carolina. Contemporary copies. 3 pp. In handwriting of Charles Thomson. Enclosed in President of Congress to Washington, 1780, June 5.　　　　　　　　　　95, 65

1780
MAY 26

Continental Congress, Resolve. Mode of selection of Commissary of Prisoners. Contemporary copy, attested by Charles Thomson. 1 p. Enclosed in President of Congress to Washington, 1780, May 29.　　　　　　　　　　　95, 36

1780
MAY 26

Board of War. [Philadelphia.] To [George] Washington, Morristown. Exchange of Ensign [John?] Connolly. A. L. S. Timothy Pickering, jr. 1 p. Answered June 5.*　　　　　　　　　95, 29

1780
MAY 26

Buford, Abraham. Camden, South Carolina. To the Virginia Assembly. Loss of Charleston, movements of British and condition of affairs. Contemporary copy. 1 p. Enclosed in Henry, James to Washington, 1780, June 16.　　　38, 126

1780
MAY 26

Duane, James. Philadelphia. To [George Washington, Morristown]. The situation at Charleston; news from the West Indies. A. L. S. 2 pp. 38, 305

1780
MAY 27

Washington, George. Morristown. To the President of Congress, Philadelphia. Great distress from scarcity of meat; mutiny of Connecticut regiments; depreciation and pay; enemy's handbill. Draft. 7 pp. In handwriting of Robert Hanson Harrison. Read in Congress, May 31. Referred to Ellsworth, Armstrong and Duane.

A. V, pt. II, 33

Printed: Writings of Washington (Ford) N. Y. 1890. 8, 288.

1780
MAY 27

Washington, George. Morristown. To the Board of War [Philadelphia]. Distress of army for meat; mutiny of two regiments. Draft. 2 pp. In handwriting of Robert Hanson Harrison.

A. V, pt. II, 31

1780
MAY 27

Charleston, (South Carolina.) Extract of letter reporting surrender. (Taken from Williamsburg Gazette, June 3.) 1 p. Enclosed in President of Congress to Washington, June 12.

95, 76

1780
MAY 29

Washington, George. Morristown. To the Board of Admiralty [Philadelphia]. Recommending Capt. [Abraham] Van Dyke. Draft. 2 pp. In handwriting of Tench Tilghman. A. V, pt. II, 41

1780
MAY 29

Washington, George. Morristown. To the Board of Treasury [Philadelphia]. Cooperation with the French; need of services of Col. [Clement] Biddle. Draft. 2 pp. In handwriting of Robert Hanson Harrison. A. V, pt. II, 43

1780
MAY 29

Continental Congress, President. [Philadelphia.] To [George] Washington [Morristown]. Transmitting resolves and other papers. L. S. of Samuel Huntington. 2 pp.

95, 34

1780
MAY 30

Continental Congress, Resolve. Reduction of army. A. D. S. of Charles Thomson. 1 p. Enclosed in President of Congress to Washington, 1780, May 31.

95, 48

1780
MAY 30

Board of War. [Philadelphia.] To [George] Washington [Morristown]. Transmitting courts martial proceedings on Capt. [Isaac] Coren and Capt-lt. [William Egerton] Godfrey. A. L. S. of Benjamin Stoddert. 1 p. Answered June 5.* 95, 41

1780
MAY 30

Duane, James. Philadelphia. To [George Washington, Morristown]. Committee of Congress; failure of supplies; news from Charleston. A. L. S. 1 p.

37, 330

1780
MAY 31

Washington, George. Morristown. To [the Committee of Cooperation, Morristown]. Cooperation with the French; number of troops necessary; supplies from the states. Draft. 4 pp. In handwriting of Alexander Hamilton.

A. V, pt. II, 49

Printed: Writings of Washington (Ford) N. Y. 1890. 8, 299.

1780
MAY 31

Washington, George. Morristown. To the President of Congress [Philadelphia]. The surrender of Charleston. Draft. 1 p. In handwriting of Tench Tilghman. Read in Congress, June 5.

A. V, pt. II, 45

1780
MAY 31.

Washington, George. Morristown. To the President of Congress [Philadelphia]. Col. [Henry] Sherburne's services. Draft. 2 pp. In handwriting of Robert Hanson Harrison. A. V, pt. II, 47

1780
MAY 31

Washington, George. Morristown. To Joseph Jones [Philadelphia]. Transfer of power from Congress to States; [Brig.] Gen. [George] Weedon. Auto. draft signed. 2 pp. P. II, 115

Printed: Writings of Washington (Ford) N. Y. 1890. 8, 304.

1780
MAY 31

Continental Congress, President. Philadelphia. To [George] Washington [Morristown]. Transmitting resolves; reduction of army; distresses of present situation. L. S. of Samuel Huntington. 2 pp. 95, 46

[1780]
[MAY]

Anonymous. [New York.] To [George Washington, Morristown]. Intelligence of enemy; fortifying; French fleet; attempt against Charleston. Contemporary copy. 2 pp. In handwriting of Tench Tilghman. Enclosed in Washington to the President of Congress, 1780, May 13.

C. C. 152, 8, 547

1780
[MAY]

Anonymous. Address to the Soldiers of the Continental Army. Inducement to desert to British. Transcript. Enclosed in Washington to the President of Congress, 1780, May 27. C. C. 169, 7, 139

[1780]
[MAY?]

Pennsylvania. Northumberland County. Inhabitants. Petition to Supreme Executive Council of Pennsylvania. Supporting Lt. Col. [Ludowick] Weltner. Contemporary copy. 2 pp. Enclosed in Board of War to Washington, 1780, May 19.

95, 4

1780
JUNE 1

Continental Congress, Resolve. Establishment of post at Shokan [New York]; militia for defense of frontier; crediting States with overplus of supplies furnished. Contemporary copy, attested by Charles Thomson. 2 pp. Enclosed in President of Congress to Washington, 1780, June 3.   **95, 59**

[1780]
[JUNE 1]

Continental Congress, Committee to confer with Committee of Pennsylvania Council. Report of conference with Committee of Pennsylvania Council. Men, money and supplies to be furnished by the state. Contemporary copy, attested by Charles Thomson. 2 pp. Enclosed in President of Congress to Washington, 1780, June 3.   **95, 61**
Committee: Ellsworth, Armstrong and Duane.

1780
JUNE 2

Washington, George. Morristown. To Lt. Gen. [Wilhelm, Baron von] Knyphausen [New York]. Appointment of agents for prisoners to reside within the respective lines. Contemporary copy. 2 pp. In handwriting of Tench Tilghman. Enclosed in Washington to the President of Congress, 1780, Aug. 24.   **C. C. 152, 9, 119**

1780
JUNE 2

Continental Congress, Committee of Cooperation at Headquarters. Morristown. Circular letter to the States. Necessities of the army; quotas of supplies to be furnished by the different states; transportation; militia. Contemporary copy made and attested by Abraham Brasher. 12 pp. Transmitted to Washington.   **95, 49**
Committee: Schuyler, Mathews and Peabody.

1780
JUNE 2

Continental Congress, Committee of Cooperation. Tabular statement of supplies requested from the states from New Hampshire to Virginia inclusive. 2 pp. Transmitted to Washington.   **95, 55**

1780
JUNE 2

Woodford, William. Charleston [South Carolina]. To [the Board of War, Philadelphia]. Refusal of British to extend parole. [Extract of letter.] Contemporary copy. 1 p. In handwriting of William Grayson. Enclosed in Board of War to Washington, 1780, June 24.   **95, 126**

1780
JUNE 3

Continental Congress, President. Philadelphia. To [George] Washington [Morristown]. Pennsylvania's exertions to furnish supplies; transmitting resolves. L. S. of Samuel Huntington. 2 pp.   **95, 57**

1780
JUNE 5

Washington, George. Morristown. To [the Board of War, Philadelphia]. Minor military miscellany. Draft. 2 pp. In handwriting of Tench Tilghman.   A. V, pt. II, 53

1780
JUNE 5

Washington, George. To [James Duane, Philadelphia]. Capt. [Allen] McLane's promotion; news from Charleston and the West Indies. Draft signed. 3 pp. In handwriting of Tench Tilghman and Washington.   P. II, 117

1780
JUNE 5

Continental Congress, President. Philadelphia. To [George] Washington [Morristown]. Surrender of Charleston; capture of Mobile by the Spaniards. L. S. of Samuel Huntington. 2 pp. Answered June 20.*   95, 62

1780
JUNE 6

Continental Congress, President. Philadelphia. To [George] Washington [Morristown]. Ordering Lee's dragoons to the southward. L. S. of Samuel Huntington. 2 pp. Answered June 20.*
                                   95, 66

1780
JUNE 7

Board of War. [Philadelphia.] To [George] Washington [Springfield, New Jersey]. Order for Capt. [Nathaniel] Bowman. A. L. S. of Benjamin Stoddert. 1 p. Answered June 14.*   95, 68

1780
JUNE 8

Washington, George. Heights above Springfield [New Jersey]. To the Board of War [Philadelphia]. Need of Major [Henry] Lee's corps in the Jerseys. Draft. 1 p. In handwriting of Robert Hanson Harrison.   A. V, pt. II, 55

1780
JUNE 8

Board of War. [Philadelphia.] To [George] Washington [Springfield]. Complaints against [Lt.]Col. [Ludowick] Weltner; case of Capt. [Isaac] Coren. L. S. of Richard Peters. 1 p. Answered June 14.*
                                   95, 69

1780
JUNE 10

Washington, George. Springfield. To [the President of Congress, Philadelphia]. Advance of the British into New Jersey. Draft. 2 pp. In handwriting of Robert Hanson Harrison. Read in Congress, May 13.   A. V, pt. II, 57
Printed: Writings of Washington (Sparks) Boston. 1835. 7, 75.

1780
JUNE 11

Washington, George. Springfield. To [the Committee of Cooperation, Morristown]. Necessity of exertion on part of states. Draft. 3 pp. In handwriting of Alexander Hamilton. A. V, pt. II, 59
Printed: Writings of Washington (Ford) N. Y. 1890. 8, 310.

1780
JUNE 11

Connolly, John. [Lancaster? Pennsylvania.] To the Board of War [Philadelphia]. Requesting leave to go into New York. A. L. S. 1 p. Enclosed in Board of War to Washington, 1780, June 13.

94, 83

1780
JUNE 11

Knyphausen, Wilhelm, Baron von. [New York.] To George Washington [Springfield, New Jersey]. Appointment of Commissaries of Prisoners; Lewis Pintard. Contemporary copy. 1 p. In handwriting of Tench Tilghman. Enclosed in Washington to the President of Congress, 1780, Aug. 24.   C. C.   152, 9, 123

1780
JUNE 12

Washington, George. Springfield. To [the Committee of Cooperation, Morristown]. Action of states in filling their battalions. Draft. 1 p. In handwriting of Alexander Hamilton. A. V, pt. II, 63
Committee: Schuyler, Mathews and Peabody.

1780
JUNE 12

Continental Congress, President. Philadelphia. To [George] Washington [Springfield]. British in Jersey; Pennsylvania militia; intelligence. L. S. of Samuel Huntington. 2 pp. Answered June 20.*   95, 74

1780
JUNE 12

Continental Congress, Committee of Cooperation at Headquarters. Morristown. Circular letter to the States. Pressing need of troops. Contemporary copy. Attested by Abraham Brasher. Transmitted to Washington. 3 pp.   95, 72
Committee: Schuyler, Mathews and Peabody.

1780
JUNE 12

Board of War. [Philadelphia.] To [George] Washington [Springfield]. Lee's corps; Philadelphia city troop of cavalry. A. L. S. of Benjamin Stoddert. 2 pp. Answered June 16.*   95, 70

1780
JUNE 12

Continental Congress, Resolves. Curtailment of supply and forage issues; money value of ration. Contemporary copy. 1 p. Enclosed in President of Congress to Washington, 1780, June 12.   95, 88.

1780
JUNE 13

Washington, George. Springfield. To the Committee of Cooperation [Morristown]. System proposed for the Quartermaster's Department. Draft. 2 pp. In handwriting of Alexander Hamilton.

A. V, pt. II, 65

1780
JUNE 13

Continental Congress, President. Philadelphia. To [George] Washington [Springfield]. Transmitting resolve; surrender of Charleston. L. S. of Samuel Huntington. 2 pp. Answered June 20.*   95, 77

1780
JUNE 13

Continental Congress, Resolve. Maj. Gen. [Horatio] Gates to command Southern Department. A. D. S. of Charles Thomson. 1 p. Enclosed in President of Congress to Washington 1780, June 13.

95, 79

1780
JUNE 13

Board of War. [Philadelphia.] To [George] Washington [Springfield]. Exchange of Lt. Col. [John] Connolly. A. L. S. of Benjamin Stoddert. 1 p. Answered June 16.*   95, 81

1780
JUNE 14

Washington, George. Springfield. To the Board of War [Philadelphia]. Agent for prisoners and other minor military matters. Draft. 3 pp. In handwriting of Robert Hanson Harrison.

A. V, pt. II, 67

1780
JUNE 14

Continental Congress, Resolve. Powers of Maj. Gen. [Horatio] Gates in command of Southern Department. Contemporary copy, attested by Charles Thomson. 1 p. Enclosed in President of Congress to Washington, 1780, June 15.   95, 87

1780
JUNE 15

Continental Congress, President. Philadelphia. To [George] Washington [Springfield]. Transmitting resolves; despatches from Charleston. L. S. of Samuel Huntington. 2 pp. Answered June 20.*   95, 85

1780
JUNE 16

Washington, George. Springfield. To [the Board of War, Philadelphia]. Services of the city troop of horse; paroled marine prisoners. Draft. 1 p. In handwriting of Alexander Hamilton and Richard Kidder Meade.   A. V, pt. II, 71

1780
JUNE 16

Henry, James. Philadelphia. To [George] Washington [Springfield]. News from Virginia. A. L. S. 1 p. Answered June 29.*   38, 124

1780
JUNE 16

Continental Congress, Resolve. Recalling Brig. Gen. [William] Weedon and Col. [Daniel] Morgan into service. Contemporary copy attested by Charles Thomson. 1 p. Enclosed in President of Congress to Washington, 1780, June 18.   95, 110

1780
JUNE 16

Henry, James. Philadelphia. To [George] Washington [Springfield]. Transmitting intelligence. A. L. S. 1 p. Answered June 29.*   38, 124

1780
JUNE 17

Continental Congress, Resolves. Virginia and North Carolina militia. Contemporary copy attested by Charles Thomson. Enclosed in President of Congress to Washington, 1780, June 21. 95, 111

1780
JUNE 17

Board of War. [Philadelphia.] To [George] Washington [Springfield]. Supplies for West Point. A. L. S. of Timothy Pickering, jr. 1 p. Answered June 25.*   95, 93

1780
JUNE 18

Washington, George. Springfield. To [the President of Congress, Philadelphia]. Return of Sir Henry Clinton to New York; pressing necessity of exertions for men and supplies. Draft. 3 pp. In handwriting of Alexander Hamilton and Tench Tilghman. Read in Congress, June 20.

A. V, pt. II, 73

1780
JUNE 18

Continental Congress, President. Philadelphia. To [George Washington Springfield]. Transmitting a resolve. A. L. S. of Samuel Huntington. 1 p. Answered June 25*   95, 109

1780
JUNE 18

Schuyler, Ph[ilip John]. Philadelphia. To [George] Washington [Springfield]. Transportation for supplies; reenforcements; negligence of States; Pennsylvania; Robert Morris and the Philadelphia merchants; Congress and Virginia corn; command to the Southward and defeat of Col. [Abraham] Beaufort [Buford]. A. L. S. 7 pp.

38, 71

1780
JUNE 19

Washington, George. Springfield. To the Committee of Cooperation [Morristown]. Lack of information of aid to be given by States; cooperation with French. Draft. 3 pp. In handwriting of Robert Hanson Harrison.   A. V, pt. 77

Printed; Writings of Washington (Ford) N. Y. 1890, 8, 316, note.

1780
JUNE 19

Continental Congress, Committee of Cooperation at Headquarters. Morristown. Circular letter to the States. Urging men and supplies for cooperation with the French. Contemporary copy attested by Abraham Brasher. 2 pp. Transmitted to Washington.   95, 100

The original was signed by Mathews and Peabody.

1780
JUNE 19

Continental Congress, Resolves. Equipping and mounting Baylor's dragoons; Lee's infantry. Contemporary copy, attested by Charles Thomson. Enclosed in President of Congress to Washington, 1780, June 21.   95, 111

1780
JUNE 19

Board of War. [Philadelphia.] To [George] Washington [Springfield]. ·Imprisonment of Capt. [Benjamin?] Joel; agents for prisoners. A. L. S. of

Timothy Pickering, jr. 2 pp. Answered June
25.*   95, 98

1780
JUNE 20

Continental Congress, Committee of Cooperation at Headquarters. Morristown. To Gov. Jonathan Trumbull [Lebanon]. Brig. Gen. [Samuel Holden]
Parsons and recruiting in Connecticut. Contemporary copy, attested by Al. Brasher. 1 p.
Transmitted to Washington.   95, 106
The original was signed by Mathews and Peabody.

1780
JUNE 20

Washington, George. Springfield. To the President of
Congress [Philadelphia]. Cooperation with the
French; lack of supplies, clothing; mutiny at
Fort Schuyler; enemy's movements. Draft. 6
pp. In handwriting of Robert Hanson Harri-
son.   A. V, pt. II, 81
Printed: Writings of Washington (Ford) N. Y. 1890. 8, 315.

1780
JUNE 20

Washington, George. Springfield. To [the Committee of
Cooperation, Morristown]. Recruits from Connecticut. Draft. 1 p. In handwriting of Alexander Hamilton.   A. V, pt. II, 87

1780
JUNE 20

Board of War. [Philadelphia.] To [George] Washington
[Springfield]. Lt. Connolly Coan's application.
A. L. S. of William Grayson. 1 p. Answered
June 25.*   95, 104

1780
JUNE 21

Washington, George. Springfield. To [the Board of
War, Philadelphia]. Infantry of Maj. [Henry]
Lee's corps to be ordered to the army. Draft.
1 p. In handwriting of Alexander Hamilton.
                                     A. V, pt. II, 89

1780
JUNE 21

Continental Congress, President. Philadelphia. To
[George] Washington [Springfield]. Transmit-
ting resolves; affairs in the South. L. S. of
Samuel Huntington. 2 pp. Answered June 25.*
                                           94, 107

1780
JUNE 21

Continental Congress, Resolves. Fulfillment of requisitions
by the states. Contemporary copy, attested by
Charles Thomson. 2 pp. Enclosed in President of Congress to Washington, 1780, June 25.
                                           95, 133

1780
JUNE 21

Delaware, House of Representatives. Resolve respecting
supplies for the army. Contemporary copy, at-
Attested by Abraham Brasher. 1 p. Transmitted to Washington by the Committee of Cooperation.   95, 113

1780
JUNE 21

Loring, Joshua. New York. To [Abraham] Skinner [Springfield, New Jersey]. Exchange of prisoners. Contemporary copy. 3 pp. In handwriting of David Humphreys. Enclosed in Washington to the President of Congress, 1780, Aug. 24.   **C. C. 152,** 9, 105

1780
JUNE 22

Lincoln, Benjamin. Philadelphia. To [Congress?, Philadelphia]. Exchange of prisoners. Contemporary extract of letter. 1 p. Enclosed in President of Congress to Washington, 1780, June 22.   95, 135

1780
JUNE 22

Livingston, Robert R. Trenton. To [George] Washington [near Rockaway Bridge]. Supplies for army and means of forwarding same; command of West Point; [Maj.] Gens. [Robert] Howe and [Benedict] Arnold. A. L. S. 3 pp.   38, 191

1780
JUNE 22

Nicola, Lewis [Philadelphia.] To the Board of War [Philadelphia]. Information of Capt. [Benjamin?] Joel. Contempory copy. 1 p. Enclosed in Board of War to Washington, 1780, July 11.   95, 116

1780
JUNE 22

Rodney, Caesar. Dover [Delaware]. To the Committee of Congress [Morristown]. Efforts of State to comply with requisitions of Congress. Contemporary copy made and attested by Abraham Brasher. Transmitted to Washington by the Committee of Cooperation.   95, 114

1780
JUNE 23

Washington, George. Rockaway [New Jersey]. To [the Committee of Cooperation, Morristown]. Enemy's strength; need of wagons to remove stores; call for recruits from the states. Draft. 2 pp. In handwriting of Alexander Hamilton.
    A. V, pt. II, 91

1780
JUNE 23

Continental Congress, Resolve. Inquiry into loss of Charleston and Maj. Gen. [Benjamin] Lincoln's conduct. Contemporary copy, attested by Charles Thomson. 1 p. Enclosed in President of Congress to Washington 1780, June 25.   95, 131

1780
JUNE 23

Continental Congress, Committee of Cooperation at Headquarters. Morristown. Circular to States. Need of troops; [special paragraph to Pennsylvania and New Jersey on] need of teams to remove stores. Contemporary copy. 2 pp. Enclosed in Committee to Washington, 1780, June 24.

92, 239

The original letter was signed by Mathews and Peabody.

1780
June 23

Continental Congress, Committee of Cooperation at Headquarters. Morristown. Circular letter to the States. Urging sending forward of men and supplies; teams for removal of stores. Contemporary copy; attested by Abraham Brasher. 2 pp. Transmitted to Washington.   95, 121

The paragraph relating to teams was inserted only in letter sent to Pennsylvania and New Jersey. The original letter was signed by Mathews and Peabody

1780
June 24

Washington, George. Morristown. To the Board of War [Philadelphia]. Commissions for the Artificer regiment. Draft. 1 p. In handwriting of Tench Tilghman.   A. V, pt. II, 93

1780
June 24

Continental Congress, Committee of Cooperation. Morristown. To [George] Washington [Morristown]. Circular to states; removal of stores. A. L. S. of Jno. Mathews and Nathl. Peabody. 1 p.

92, 240

1780
June 24

Board of War. [Philadelphia.] To [George] Washington [Whippany, New Jersey]. Case of [Brig.] Gen. [William] Woodford. A. L. S. of Benjamin Stoddert. 1 p. Answered July 5.*   95, 124

1780
June 24

Clinton, George. Kingston [New York]. To the Committee [of Cooperation, Morristown]. Exertions of New York to comply with requisitions for men and supplies. Contemporary copy, 3 pp. Transmitted to Washington.   95, 127

Letter was addressed to Schuyler, Mathews and Peabody.

1780
June 25

Washington, George. Whippany [New Jersey]. To [the President of Congress, Philadelphia]. Burning of Springfield by the enemy; designs against West Point. Draft. 2 pp. In handwriting of Alexander Hamilton. Read in Congress, June 29. Referred to Committee of Intelligence.

A. V, pt. II, 95

Printed: Writings of Washington (Ford) N. Y. 1890. 8, 320.

1780
June 25

Washington, George. Whippany. To the Board of War [Philadelphia]. Stores at West Point and Fishkill; prisoners and minor matters. Draft. 3 pp. In handwriting of Robert Hanson Harrison.

A. V, pt. II, 97

1780
JUNE 25

Continental Congress, President. Philadelphia. To [George] Washington [Whippany, New Jersey]. Transmitting resolves and papers. L. S. of Samuel Huntington. 2 pp. Acknowledged July 6,* answered July 10.* 95, 129

1780
JUNE 25

Greene, W[illiam]. Providence. To Committee of Co-operation [Morristown]. Efforts of Rhode Island to furnish men and supplies. Contemporary copy made and attested by Abraham Brasher. 1 p. Transmitted to Washington. 95, 123

1780
JUNE 27

Washington, George. Ramapaugh [New Jersey]. To the Committee of Cooperation, Morristown. Maryland's attempt to raise an additional battalion; designs of the enemy. Draft. 2 pp. In handwriting of Robert Hanson Harrison.

1780
JUNE 28

A. V, pt. II, 101

Continental Congress, Committee of Cooperation at Headquarters. Morristown. To Daniel of St. Thomas Jenifer and Josiah Beall, Annapolis, Maryland. Maryland's propositions respecting the requisitions; necessities of the case. Contemporary copy, made and attested by Abraham Brasher. 2 pp. Transmitted to Washington. 95, 139

1780
JUNE 28

Livingston, William. Turkey [New Jersey]. To [the Committee of Congress, Morristown]. Measures of New Jersey to comply with the requisition for men and supplies. Contemporary copy, made and attested by Abraham Brasher. 1 p. Transmitted to Washington. 95, 137

1780
JUNE 29

Washington, George. Ramapaugh. To [Robert R. Livingston, Philadelphia]. Removal of stores; command of West Point. Auto. draft. 2 pp.
A. V, pt. II, 103
Printed: Writings of Washington (Ford) N. Y. 1890. 8, 326.

1780
JUNE 29

Washington, George. Ramapaugh. To James Henry [Philadelphia]. Impossibility of detaching troops to southward. Draft. 1 p. In handwriting of James McHenry. A. V, pt. II, 105

1780
JUNE 30

Continental Congress, Committee of Cooperation at Headquarters. Morristown. To [George] Washington [Ramapaugh]. The circular letter to States. L. S. of Jno. Mathews and Nathl. Peabody. 1 p.
92, 244

1780
JUNE 30

Ely, John and Others. Long Island. To [George] Washington [Ramapaugh, New Jersey]. Their exchange. Contemporary copy. 2 pp. In handwriting of David Humphreys. Enclosed in Washington to the President of Congress, 1780, Aug. 24.   C. C. 152, 9, 113

[1780]
[JUNE]

Jones, Joseph. [Philadelphia.] To [George Washington, Morristown]. State of the finances; new bills; relinquishment of power by Congress to the States; prevalent fear of offending States; exertions of the Philadelphia merchants and bankers to supply army; reinforcements for the south. A. L. S. 3 pp.   38, 308

1780
JULY 4

Washington, George. Bergen County [New Jersey]. To the Board of War [Philadelphia]. Brig. Gen. [Henry] Knox's estimate of artillery stores wanted for coming campaign. Draft. 2 pp. In handwriting of Alexander Hamilton. A. V, pt. II, 107

1780
JULY 4

Virginia, Officers of the Line. Return of Continental officers now in Virginia. Tabular statement. 2 pp. In handwriting of James McHenry. Enclosed in Washington to the President of Congress, 1780, July 22.   C. C. 152, 9, 51

1780
JULY 5

Washington, George. Near Passaic Falls [New Jersey]. To [the Board of War, Philadelphia]. Commissions in the New Jersey line; minor matters. Draft. 4 pp. In handwriting of Robert Hanson Harrison.   A. V, pt. II, 109

1780
JULY 5

Washington, George. [Near Passaic Falls.] To Sir Henry Clinton [New York]. Transmitting copy of his letter to Baron von Knyphausen. Contempocopy. 1 p. In handwriting of Robert Hanson Harrison. Enclosed in Washington to the President of Congress 1780, Aug. 24. C.C. 152, 9, 125

1780
JULY 5

Continental Congress, Committee of Cooperation at Headquarters. Morristown. To [George] Washington [near Passaic Falls]. Transmitting letters. L. S. of Jno. Mathews and Nathl. Peabody. 1 p.   92, 261

1780
JULY 6

Washington, George. Near Passaic Falls. To the President of Congress [Philadelphia]. Movements of enemy; failure of the recruiting; news from Europe. Draft. 2 pp. In handwriting of Robert Hanson Harrison.   A. V, pt. II, 113

1780
JULY 6

Washington, George. [Preakness, New Jersey.] To the Board of War [Philadelphia]. Need of arms. Draft. 1 p. In handwriting of Robert Hanson Harrison. **A. V, pt. II, 115**

1780
JULY 7

Anonymous. Martinique. Intelligence of French expedition against Jamaica. Contemporary copy. 1 p. Enclosed in President of Congress to Washington, 1780, Aug. 7. **95, 234**

1780
JULY 8

Washington, George. Col. Dey's, Bergen County [Preakness]. To [the Board of War, Philadelphia]. Need of shot and shells. Draft. 1 p. In handwriting of James McHenry. **A. V, pt. II, 117**

1780
JULY 8

Board of War. [Philadelphia.] To [George] Washington [Preakness]. Commission for Maj. [John] Jameson. A. L. S. of William Grayson. 2 pp. Answered July 15.* **95, 143**

1780
JULY 10

Washington, George. Near Passaic [Preakness]. To [the President of Congress, Philadelphia]. Inquiry into Maj. Gen. [Benjamin] Lincoln's conduct; exchange of prisoners. Draft. 4 pp. In handwriting of Robert Hanson Harrison. Read in Congress, July 17. Referred to Bee, Lovell and Scott. **A. V, pt. II, 119**
Printed: Writings of Washington (Ford) N. Y. 1890. 8, 338.

1780
JULY 10

Washington, George. [Preakness.] To the President of Congress [Philadelphia]. Association of merchants to supply the army; need of tents. Draft. 2 pp. In handwriting of Tench Tilghman. Read in Congress, July 13. Referred, part to Committee to confer with inspectors and directors of proposed bank, remainder to delegates New Hampshire, Massachusetts, Rhode Island and Connecticut. **A. V, pt. II, 123**
Printed: Writings of Washington (Ford) N. Y. 1890. 8, 336.

1780
JULY 10

Continental Congress, Committee of Cooperation at Headquarters. Preakness. To Philadelphia citizens. Need of flour and tents. Contemporary copy. 1 p. Transmitted to Washington. **95, 147**
The original letter was signed by Schuyler and Peabody.

1780
JULY 10

Continental Congress, Committee of Cooperation at Headquarters. Preakness. Circular letter to Delaware, Pennsylvania, Maryland and Virginia. Forming magazine of short forage in vicinity of Hudson river. Contemporary copy. 1 p. Transmitted to Washington. **95, 148**

1780
JULY 10

Continental Congress, Committee of Cooperation at Head-quarters. Preakness. To the President of Congress [Philadelphia]. Forage and tents; flour; sand bags and knapsacks; quartermaster general's department. Contemporary copy. 2 pp. Transmitted to Washington.   95, 149

The original letter of this and the preceding entry was signed by Schuyler and Peabody.

1780
JULY 11

Board of Admiralty. Philadelphia. To [George] Washington [Preakness]. Capt. [Abraham] Van Dyke to command marines; Madeira wine. L. S. of Francis Lewis. 2 pp. Answered July 18.*

     92, 265

1780
JULY 11

Board of War. [Philadelphia.] To [George] Washington [Preakness]. Difficulties in procuring ordnance supplies; shot, shell and powder. A. L. S. of Richard Peters. 3 pp. Answered July 18.*

     95, 117

1780
JULY 11

Board of War. [Philadelphia.] Return of ordnance stores on hand and demanded by [Brig.] Gen. [Henry] Knox. A. L. S. of Timothy Pickering, jr. 2 pp. Transmitted to Washington.   95, 119

1780
JULY 11

Board of War. Philadelphia. Proceedings. Report on a system of promotion in the Army. Contemporary copy, made and attested by Benjamin Stoddert. 2 pp. Enclosed in Board of War to Washington, 1780, July 28.   95, 208

1780
JULY 11

Continental Army, General officers. Preakness. Memorial to Congress [Philadelphia]. Distresses of army; depreciation of pay; pensions. Contemporary copy. 4 pp. Signed by Greene, Stirling and Wayne with copies of 12 other signatures. Transmitted to Washington.   95, 152

1780
JULY 11

[Greene, Nathanael and Others.] Preakness. To [Committee of Cooperation, Preakness]. Transmitting copy of memorial to Congress. A. L. of Greene. 1 p. Transmitted to Washington. Signatures are missing.   95, 151

1780
JULY 12

Washington, George. [Preakness.] To Abraham Skinner [Preakness]. Exchange of prisoners; officers, etc. Contemporary copy. 2 pp. In handwriting of Richard Kidder Meade. Enclosed in Washington to the President of Congress, 1780, Aug. 24.   C. C. 152, 9, 109

1780
JULY 13

Washington, George. [Preakness.] To the Committee of Cooperation [Preakness]. Report of arrival of the French; need of reenforcements. Draft. 2 pp. In handwriting of Alexander Hamilton.

A. V, pt. II, 125

Printed in part: Writings of Washington (Ford) N. Y. 1890. 8, 344, note.

1780
JULY 13

Continental Congress, Committee of Cooperation at Headquarters. Preakness. To Prest. Joseph Reed [Philadelphia]. Negligence of Pennsylvania; urging compliance with requisitions. Contemporary copy. 1 p. Transmitted to Washington.

95, 154

1780
JULY 13

Continental Congress, Committee of Cooperation at Headquarters. Preakness. To the President of Congress [Philadelphia]. Pennsylvania's inattention and negligence. Contemporary copy. 2 pp. Transmitted to Washington.

95, 156

1780
JULY 13

Continental Congress, Committee of Cooperation at Headquarters. Preakness. Circular letter to the States. Urging fulfilment of requisitions. Contemporary copy. 1 p. Transmitted to Washington.

95, 158

The originals of this and the two preceding entries were signed by Schuyler and Peabody.

1780
JULY 14

Washington, George. [Preakness.] To the President of Congress [Philadelphia]. Arrival of French at Newport; Inspector-General's department. Draft. 1 p. In handwriting of Alexander Hamilton. Read in Congress, July 17.

A. V, pt. II, 127

Printed: Writings of Washington (Ford) N. Y. 1890. 8, 343.

1780
JULY 14

Continental Congress, President. Philadelphia. To [George] Washington [Preakness]. Exchange of Brig. Gen. Duportail. Letter-book copy.

C. C. 15, 51

1780
JULY 15

Washington, George. [Preakness.] To [the President of Congress, Philadelphia]. Need of hospital supplies. Draft. 1 p. In handwriting of Tench Tilghman. Read in Congress, July 18. Referred to Medical Committee.

A. V, pt. II, 141

1780
JULY 15

Washington, George. [Preakness.] To [the President of Congress, Philadelphia]. Arrival of Admiral Graves's squadron; relative strength of

French and English. Draft. 1 p. In handwriting of Tench Tilghman. Read in Congress,
July 18.   A. V, pt. II, 139

1780   Washington, George. [Preakness.] To the President
July 15   of Congress [Philadelphia]. Result of court
                 martial of Dr. [William] Shippen [jr.]. Draft.
                 2 pp. In handwriting of Robert Hanson Har-
                 rison.   A. V, pt. II, 143

1780   Washington, George. [Preakness.] To the Board of
July 15   War [Philadelphia]. Promotion of Maj.
                 [John] Jameson. Draft. 1 p. In handwrit-
                 ing of Robert Hanson Harrison.
                                                    A. V, pt. II, 145

1780   Continental Congress, President. Philadelphia. To
July 15   [George] Washington [Preakness]. Arrival of
                 French fleet; tents. L. S. of Samuel Hunting-
                 ton. 1 p.   95, 159

1780   Putnam, Israel. Peekskill. To [the Board of War,
July 16   Philadelphia]. Returns of troops and stores.
                 Contemporary copy. Transmitted to Washing-
                 ton.   95, 194

1780   Washington, George. [Preakness.] To the Board of
July 17   War [Philadelphia]. Promotions in the Jersey
                 regiments. Draft. 1 p. In handwriting of
                 Robert Hanson Harrison.   A. V, pt. II, 147

1780   Board of War. [Philadelphia.] To [George] Washing-
July 17   ton [Preakness]. Brevet to Marquis de Vienne.
                 A. L. S. of Timothy Pickering, jr. · 1 p.

                                                         95, 164

1780   Board of War. [Philadelphia.] To [George] Washing-
July 17   ton [Preakness]. Application for arms and
                 cartouche boxes. A. L. S. of William Grayson.
                 2 pp.   95, 166

1780   Washington, George. [Preakness.] To the Committee
July 18   [of Cooperation], in camp. Claim of Connecti-
                 cut and Massachusetts to certain of the Addi-
                 tional Continental regiments. Draft. 2 pp.
                 In handwriting of Robert Hanson Harrison.
                                                    A. V, pt. II, 149

1780   Washington, George. Preakness. To the Board of
July 18   War [Philadelphia]. Danger of failure of co-
                 operative plans from lack of supplies. Draft.
                 2 pp. In handwriting of Alexander Hamilton.
                                                    A. V, pt. II, 151

Philadelphia 3d August 1777   461

Sir

Your favor of this date with its inclosures is now before me—

At the same time that I express my thanks for the high mark of confidence which Congress have been pleased to repose in me, by their Resolve authorizing me to send an Officer to command the northern Army, I should wish to be excused from making this appointment. For this, many Reasons might be mentioned, and which, I am persuaded will occur to Congress on reflection. ✗

The northern department, in a great measure, has been considered as separate, and more peculiarly under their direction, and the Officers commanding there always of their nomination. I have never interfered further than merely to advise, and to give such aids as were in my power on the requisitions of those Officers. ✗

It is certainly necessary that a Body of Militia should be immediately called out to rein force the northern Army. In the conference which your Committee honored me with yesterday Evening, I mentioned the Number which I thought sufficient. But my opinion on this point, and the apportioning

them

WRITING OF TENCH TILGHMAN.

1780
JULY 18

Washington, George. [Preakness.] To the Board of Admiralty [Philadelphia]. Case of Capt. [Abraham] Van Dyke. Draft. 1 p. In handwriting of Tench Tilghman. **A.** V, pt. II, 151a

1780
JULY 18

Continental Congress, Committee of Cooperation at Headquarters. Preakness. To the President [of Congress, Philadelphia]. Cooperation with the French; history of the Committee's efforts and exertions; efforts of the states; the present situation; stores; difficulties in the army; subsistence of officers; foreigners; estimates of supplies; forage; complaint of Pennsylvania; operations of commander in chief limited to United States. Contemporary copy by Abraham Brasher. 14 pp. Transmitted to Washington.

95, 168

The original letter was signed by Schuyler and Peabody.

1780
JULY 19

Washington, George. Bergen County. To Maj. Gen. [Nathanael] Greene [Preakness]. Arrival of French at Newport; supplies for campaign. Contemporary copy. 2 pp. Transmitted to Congress. **95, 175**

Printed: Writings of Washington (Ford) N. Y. 1890. 8, 349.

1780
JULY 19

Continental Congress, Resolve. Returns from Maj. Gen. [Israel] Putnam. Contemporary copy made and attested by Richard Peters. Transmitted to Washington. **95, 194**

1780
JULY 19

Clinton, [Sir] H[enry]. [New York.] To [George] Washington [Preakness]. Appointment of agents for prisoners. Contemporary copy. 1 p. In handwriting of George Lewis? Enclosed in Washington to the President of Congress, 1780, Aug. 24. **C. C. 152, 9, 127**

1780
JULY 19

Loring, Joshua. New York. To [Abraham] Skinner [Preakness, New Jersey]. Negotiations for exchange of prisoners. Contemporary copy. 2 pp. In handwriting of David Humphreys. Enclosed in Washington to the President of Congress, 1780, Aug. 24. **C. C. 152, 9, 111**

1780
JULY 20

Washington, George. [Preakness.] To [the President of Congress, Philadelphia]. Force of the French. Draft. 2 pp. In handwriting of James McHenry. Read in Congress, July 24.

A. V, pt. II, 155

1780
JULY 20

Washington, George. [Preakness.] To [the President of Congress, Philadelphia]. Resignation of Brig. Gen. [William] Maxwell. Draft. 1 p. In handwriting of Robert Hanson Harrison. Read in Congress July 25. Referred to Board of War.   **A.** V, pt. II, 153

1780
JULY 20

Continental Congress, Committee of Cooperation at Headquarters. Preakness. To [George] Washington [Preakness]. Clothing of troops. L. S. of Ph. Schuyler and Nathl. Peabody. 1 p.
     92, 270

[1780]
[JULY 20]

Greene, Nathanael. Estimate of teams necessary for transportation between Trenton and Dobbs Ferry. D. S. 2 pp. Transmitted to Washington by the Committee of Cooperation at Headquarters. Copy sent Congress July 23. **95, 179**

1780
JULY 20

Greene, Nathanael. Preakness. To the Committee of Cooperation [Preakness]. Teams required for transporting stores; money necessary. L. S. 3 pp. Transmitted to Washington, and copy sent Congress.   **95, 181**

1780
JULY 20

Maxwell, William. Preakness. To [George] Washington [Preakness]. Resignation. Contemporary copy. 2 pp. In handwriting of Robert Hanson Harrison. Enclosed in Washington to the President of Congress, 1780, July 20.
     C. C. 152, 9, 37

1780
JULY 21

Continental Congress, Committee of Cooperation at Headquarters. Preakness. To Maj. Gen. [Nathanael] Greene [Preakness]. Problem of transportation of stores; requisitions on the States. Auto. draft signed by Schuyler and signed also by him for Peabody. 6 pp. Transmitted to Washington and copy sent Congress, July 23. **95, 183**

1780
JULY 21

Greene, Nath[anael]. Preakness. To Committee of Cooperation [Preakness]. Transportation of supplies. L. S. 2 pp. Transmitted to Washington, and copy sent Congress.   **95, 186**

1780
JULY 22

Washington, George. Preakness. To [the President of Congress, Philadelphia]. Necessity of exertion on part of States in furnishing supplies, forage and transportation. Draft. 3 pp. In handwriting of Alexander Hamilton. Read in Congress July 31.   Referred to S. Adams, McKean, Sherman, Laurens, and Clark.   **A.** V, pt. II, 161

Printed: Writings of Washington (Ford) N. Y. 1890. 8, 354.

1780
JULY 22

Washington, George. [Preakness.] To [the President of Congress, Philadelphia].   Troops to be raised by Virginia and arrangement of officers; exchange of Duportail. Draft. 3 pp. In handwriting of Robert Hanson Harrison. Read in Congress, July 26. Referred to Board of War. " Nothing to be done by the Board."

A. V, pt. II, 157

[1780]
[JULY 22?]

[Washington, George.] [Preakness.] Arrangement of Virginia officers for the 5,000 drafts to be raised. 4 pp. In handwriting of Richard Kidder Meade. Enclosed in Washington to the President of Congress, 1780, July 22. **C. C.** 152, 9, 53

1780
JULY 22

Washington, George. To Joseph Jones [Philadelphia]. Promotion [of Col. Daniel Morgan]; case of [Maj. Gen. Adam] Stephen [Britain's naval power and resources compared with France and Spain's]. Auto. draft signed. 3 pp.

P. II, 135

The part in brackets was supplied, in accordance with note in the above entry, from a letter to Joseph Reed, 1780, May 25, not included in this calendar.

Printed: Writings of Washington (Ford) N. Y. 1890. 8, 356 and 294.

[1780]
[JULY 22?]

Gist, Nathaniel. [Preakness?] Return of officers of regiment. 1 p. In handwriting of David Humphreys. Enclosed in Washington to the President of Congress, 1780, July 22. **C. C.** 152, 9, 57

1780
JULY 23

Continental Congress, Committee of Cooperation at Headquarters. Preakness. To [the President of Congress, Philadelphia]. Memorial of General Officers to Congress; papers respecting transportation of stores; exertions of New Jersey, New Hampshire, and Maryland; miscellaneous arrangements. Auto. draft signed of Schuyler and signed also by him for Mathews and Peabody. 5 pp. Transmitted to Washington.

95, 188

1780
JULY 24

[Washington, George.] [Preakness.] To [Abraham Skinner, Preakness]. Negotiations and basis for exchange of prisoners. Contemporary copy. 2 pp. In handwriting of Richard Kidder

Meade. Enclosed in Washington to the President of Congress, 1780, Aug. 24.

C. C.   152, 9, 115

1780
JULY 24

Continental Congress, Resolve. Procuring shot and shell. Contemporary copy, attested by Charles Thomson. 1 p. Enclosed in President of Congress to Washington, 1780, July 26.   95, 203

1780
JULY 24

Continental Congress, Resolve. Procuring shot and shell. A. D. S. of George Bond. Enclosed in Board of War to Washington, 1780, July 27.   95, 207

1780
JULY 24

Board of War. Estimate of supplies for service of cannon and mortars. 1 p. Enclosed in Board of War to Washington, 1780, July 27.   95, 209

1780
JULY 24

Board of War. Return of shells, shot and powder in possession the United States; deficiencies. Tabular statement. A. D. of Richard Peters. 1 p. Enclosed in Board of War to Washington, 1780, July 27.   95, 210

1780
JULY 25

Continental Congress, Resolve. Money for procuring shot and shell. A. D. S. of George Bond. Enclosed in Board of War to Washington, 1780, July 27.

95, 207

1780
JULY 25

Continental Congress, Resolve. Election of Charles Pettit Asst. Quartermaster-General; resignation of Brig. Gen. William Maxwell. Contemporary copy attested by Charles Thomson. 1 p. Enclosed in President of Congress to Washington, 1780, July 26.   95, 201

1780
JULY 26

Washington, George. [Preakness.] To [the President of Congress, Philadelphia]. Wayne's attack on block house at Bergen Point. Draft. 2 pp. In handwriting of Tench Tilghman. Referred to Committee of Intelligence. A.   V, pt. II, 165

1780
JULY 26

Washington, George. [Preakness.] To Maj. Gen. Nathanael Greene [Preakness]. Transmitting plan for conducting the Quartermaster-General's Department. Contemporary copy. 1 p. In handwriting of George Lewis? Transmitted to Congress.   C. C.   152, 9, 59

1780
JULY 26

Washington, George. [Preakness.] To Sir Henry Clinton [New York]. Appointment of agents for prisoners. Contemporary copy. 1 p. In handwriting of Tench Tilghman. Enclosed in

Washington to the President of Congress, 1780, Aug. 24.   C. C. **152,** 9, 129

1780
JULY 26

Washington, George. [Preakness.] Propositions respecting agents to be appointed for prisoners; duties, powers. Contemporary copy. 2 pp. In handwriting of Robert Hanson Harrison. Enclosed in Washington to the President of Congress, 1780, Aug. 24.   C. C. **152,** 9, 131

1780
JULY 26

Continental Congress, President. Philadelphia. To [George] Washington [Preakness]. Transmitting resolves; naval cooperation with the French. L. S. of Samuel Huntington. 2 pp. Answered Aug. 3.*   **95,** 197

1780
JULY 26

Continental Congress, Resolves. Naval cooperation with the French. Contemporary copy, attested by Charles Thomson. 2 pp. Enclosed in President of Congress to Washington, 1780, July 26.

95, 199

1780
JULY 27

Washington, George. Preakness. To the President of Congress [Philadelphia]. Enemy's intentions against the French at Rhode Island. Draft. 1 p. In handwriting of Tench Tilghman. Read in Congress, July 29.   **A.** V, pt. II, 167

1780
JULY 27

Continental Congress, Committee of Cooperation at Headquarters. Preakness. To the President of Congress [Philadelphia]. Resignation of the Quartermaster-General [Maj. Gen. N a t h a n a e l Greene]. Contemporary copy of L. S. of Schuyler, Matthews and Peabody. 1 p. Transmitted to Washington.   **95,** 204

1780
JULY 27

Board of War. [Philadelphia.] To [George] Washington [Preakness]. Ordnance stores; furnaces; powder supply; stores for French. A. L. S. of Timothy Pickering, jr. 3 pp. Answered Aug. 3.*   **95,** 206

1780
JULY 28

Board of War. [Philadelphia.] To [George Washington, Preakness]. Difficulties in arrangement of the Jersey Line. A. L. S. of Richard Peters. 1 p. Answered Aug. 14.*   **95,** 204

1780
JULY 28

Forrest, U[riah]. Annapolis [Maryland]. Court-martial of a recruiting officer. A. L. S. 1 p. Enclosed in Board of War to Washington, 1780, Aug. 9.   **95,** 245

1780
JULY 30

Washington, George. Paramus [New Jersey]. To [the President of Congress, Philadelphia]. Difficulties in the Quartermaster-General's Department. Draft. 1 p. In handwriting of Alexander Hamilton. Read in Congress, Aug. 1. Referred to Henry, McKean, Ward, J. Jones and Ingersol.   **A. V, pt. II, 169**
Printed: Writings of Washington (Ford) N. Y. 1890. 8, 363.

1780
JULY

Washington, George. [Preakness.] Plan for establishment of the Inspector-General's Department. Officers and their duties. Draft. 10 pp. In handwriting of Alexander Hamilton. Enclosed in Washington to the President of Congress, 1780, July 14. Read in Congress, July 17. " To be considered on Thursday next."
     A. V, pt. II, 133

1780
AUG. 2

Continental Congress, Resolve. Removing restriction on Commander-in-chief. Contemporary copy, attested by Charles Thomson. 1 p. Enclosed in President of Congress to Washington, 1780, Aug. 3.   **95, 221**

1780
AUG. 2

Board of War. [Philadelphia.] To [George] Washington [Peekskill, New York]. Location of magazines. A. L. S. of William Grayson. 1 p. Answered Aug. 14.*   **95, 218**

1780
AUG. 2

Pennsylvania, Council. Proceedings on case of sundry artificers of Capt. [Isaac] Coren's company; recommendations. A. D. S. of James Trimble. 4 pp. Enclosed in Board of War to Washington, 1780, Aug. 14.   **95, 254**

1780
AUG. 3

Washington, George. Peekskill [New York]. To the President of Congress [Philadelphia]. Movements of army in consequence of Sir Henry Clinton's actions. Draft. 1 p. In handwriting of Alexander Hamilton. Read in Congress, Aug. 7.   **A. V, pt. II, 171**

1780
AUG. 3

Washington, George. Peekskill. To the Board of War [Philadelphia]. Great need of shot, shells and artillery stores. Draft. 2 pp. In handwriting of Tench Tilghman.   **A. V, pt. II, 173**

1780
AUG. 3

Continental Congress, President. Philadelphia. To [George] Washington [Peekskill]. Transmitting resolve. L. S. of Samuel Huntington. 1 p. Answered Aug. 20.*   **95, 219**

1780
AUG. 4

Loring, Joshua. New York. To [Abraham] Skinner [Peekskill?]. Exchange of Duportail; Maj. Gen. [Benjamin] Lincoln's case; negotiations. Contemporary copy. 1 p. In handwriting of Tench Tilghman. Enclosed in Washington to the President of Congress, 1780, Aug. 24.

C. C.   152, 9, 133

1780
AUG. 5

Continental Congress, President. Philadelphia. To [George] Washington [Peekskill]. Transmitting resolves; cooperative measures with the French; requisitions on States. L. S. of Samuel Huntington. 2 pp. Answered Aug. 20.*

95, 228

1780
AUG. 5

Continental Congress, Resolve. Election of Timothy Pickering [jr.] Quartermaster General. Contemporary copy, attested by Charles Thomson. 1 p. Enclosed in President of Congress to Washington, 1780, Aug. 5.   95, 224

1780
AUG. 5

Continental Congress, Resolves. Attempt on British in South Carolina and Georgia; cooperation with French or Spanish; Virginia recruits. Contemporary copy, attested by Charles Thomson. 2 pp. Enclosed in President of Congress to Washington 1780, Aug. 5.   95, 226

1780
AUG. 6

Washington, George. [On march toward Kings bridge, New York.] To [the Board of Admiralty, Philadelphia]. Command of the Continental frigates. Draft. 2 pp. In handwriting of Alexander Hamilton.   A. V, pt. II, 175

1780
AUG. 6

Board of War. [Philadelphia.] To [George] Washington [en route to Tappan]. Supplies to be furnished by James White; field armourer. A. L. S. of Richard Peters. 1 p.   95, 230

1780
AUG. 6

Prisoners, American. State of, at Charleston, South Carolina. Transcript. Enclosed in Washington to the President of Congress, 1780, Dec. 8.

C. C.   169, 7, 357

1780
AUG. 7

Continental Congress, President. Philadelphia. To [George] Washington [near Clarkstown, New York]. Transmitting intelligence of French troops from Martinique. L. S. of Samuel Huntington. 1 p. Answered Aug. 20.*   95, 232

1780
AUG. 7

Continental Congress, Resolve. Exchange of officers; subsistence and clothing for officers in hands of the enemy; commissary of prisoners within enemy's lines; volunteer cavalry in the south. Contemporary copy, attested by Charles Thomson. 3 pp. Enclosed in President of Congress to Washington 1780, Aug. 9. **95, 241**

1780
Aug. 7

Reed, Joseph. Philadelphia. To the President of Congress [Philadelphia]. Transmitting papers respecting artificers. L. S. 1 p. Read in Congress, Aug. 9. Referred to Board of War. Enclosed in Board to Washington, 1780, Aug. 14.
95, 252

1780
Aug. 8

Board of War. [Philadelphia.] To [George] Washington [Tappan, New York]. Supplies for the army; clothing. A. L. S. of Richard Peters. 2 pp. Answered Aug. 14.* **95, 236**

1780
Aug. 8

Board of War. [Philadelphia.] To [George] Washington [Tappan]. Case of Lts. [Samuel] Leonard, [John] Thompson and Ensign [John] Lawrence. A. L. S. of Benjamin Stoddert. 1 p. Answered Aug. 14.* **95, 237**

1780
Aug. 8

Continental Congress, Resolves. Report of Board of War on pensioning of officers. Contemporary copy, attested by Charles Thomson. 2 pp. Enclosed in President of Congress to Washington, 1780, Aug. 9. **95, 243**

1780
Aug. 9

Continental Congress, President. Philadelphia. To [George] Washington [Tappan]. Transmitting resolves; exchange of officers; subsistence of American prisoners; volunteer light-horse in the south. L. S. of Samuel Huntington. 3 pp. Answered Aug. 24.* **95, 239**

1780
Aug. 9

Board of War. [Philadelphia.] To [George] Washington [Tappan]. Transmitting letter of Lt. Col. U[riah] Forrest. A. L. S. of Benjamin Stoddert. 1 p. Answered Aug. 31.* **95, 245**

1780
Aug. 9

Skinner, Abraham. [Tappan, New York.] To [George] Washington [Tappan]. Exchange negotiations. Contemporary copy. 1 p. In handwriting of Tench Tilghman. Enclosed in Washington to the President of Congress, 1780, Aug. 24.
C. C. 152, 9, 117

1780
Aug. 12

Continental Congress, Resolve. Reimbursement of officers' depreciated pay. A. D. S. of George Bond. 1 p. Transmitted to Washington. **95, 247**

1780
AUG. 12

Continental Congress, Resolve. Memorial of the General Officers. Reimbursement for depreciated pay; rations; land gratuities. Contemporary copy, attested by Charles Thomson. 2 pp. Enclosed in President of Congress to Washington, 1780, Aug. 28. Published to Army in General Orders of Sept. 5.   95, 249

1780
AUG. 13

W[ashingto]n, G[eorge]. Orangetown [New Jersey]. To [Joseph Jones, Philadelphia]. [Maj.] Gen. [Nathanael] Greene's resignation as Quartermaster General; contemplated action of Congress. Auto. draft signed. 3 pp. Part in handwriting of Robert Hanson Harrison.

P. II, 141

Printed: Writings of Washington (Ford) N. Y. 1890. 8, 378.

1780
AUG. 14

Washington, George. Orangetown. To the Board of War [Philadelphia]. Supplies needed and minor matters. Draft. 2 pp. In handwriting of Tench Tilghman.   A. V, pt. II, 177

1780
AUG. 14

Board of Admiralty. Philadelphia. To [George] Washington [Newburgh]. Movements of the Continental frigates. L. S. of Francis Lewis. 1 p.
92, 280

1780
AUG. 14

Board of War. [Philadelphia.] Return of military stores furnished the 2d Delaware Regiment. A. D. S. of Joseph Carleton. 1 p. Enclosed in Board of War to Washington, 1780, Aug. 14.   95, 261

1780
AUG. 14

Board of War. [Philadelphia.] To George Washington [Orangetown]. Annexing companies to Procter's regiment; arms of Delaware levies. L. S. of William Grayson. 1 p.   95, 251

1780
AUG. 15

Washington, George. Orangetown. To the Board of Admiralty [Philadelphia]. Frigates for use of the French. Draft. 1 p. In handwriting of Tench Tilghman.   A. V, pt. II, 179

1780
AUG. 15

Blaine, Ephraim. Tappan [New York]. To [George] Washington [Orangetown]. Exhausted magazines; lack of supplies; new commissaries. Contemporary copy. 2 pp. In handwriting of Tench Tilghman. Enclosed in Washington to the President of Congress, 1780, Aug. 17.
C. C. 152, 9, 73

1780
Aug. 15

Sumter, Thomas. Wateree Ferry [South Carolina]. **To** [Maj.] Gen. [Horatio] Gates [near Camden]. Seizure of the Wateree fords. Contemporary copy by Charles Thomson. 2 pp. Enclosed in President of Congress to Washington, 1780, Aug. 31.   **95, 289**

1780
Aug. 17

Washington, George. Orangetown. To [the Committee of Cooperation, in camp]. Deficiencies of states in supplying troops; lack of provisions, forage. Draft. 6 pp. In handwriting of Alexander Hamilton.   **A. V, pt. II, 181**
Printed: Writings of Washington (Ford) N.Y. 1890. 8, 383.

1780
Aug. 18

Continental Congress, Order. Release of Dr. W[illiam] Shippen [jr.] from arrest. A. D. S. of Charles Thomson. 1 p. Enclosed in President of Congress to Washington, 1780, Aug. 24.   **95, 275**

1780
Aug. 19

Continental Congress, Committee of Co-operation at Headquarters. Tappan. Circular letter to the States. Urging action; deficiency in men, supplies etc. Contemporary copy. 5 pp. In handwriting of Abraham Brasher. Transmitted to Washington.
                                          95, 267

1780
Aug. 20

Washington, George. Orangetown. To [the President of Congress, Philadelphia]. Lack of supplies; militia; necessity of a draft; Continental money; promotions, half pay, etc. Draft. 13 pp. In handwriting of Alexander Hamilton. Read in Congress, Aug. 28. Referred to Adams, J. Jones, McKean, Scott and Cornell. **A. V, pt. II, 187**
Printed: Writings of Washington (Ford) N.Y. 1890. 8, 386.

1780
Aug. 20

Gates, Horatio. Hillsborough [North Carolina]. **To** [the President of Congress, Philadelphia]. Defeat at Camden. Contemporary copy, by Charles Thomson. 4 pp. Enclosed in President of Congress to Washington, 1780, Aug. 31.   **95, 287**

1780
Aug. 22

Continental Congress, Resolve. Punishment for destruction, embezzlement etc. of military stores. Contemporary copy, attested by Charles Thomson. 1 p. Enclosed in President of Congress, 1780, Aug. 24. Published in Genl. Orders, Sept. 6.
                                          95, 273

[1780]
[Aug. 23]

[Adams, John.] [Amsterdam.] To [the President of Congress, Philadelphia]. Prosecution of War on the part of Britain. [Extract of letter.]

1 p. In handwriting of Charles Thomson. Endorsed by Charles Morse: "For Genl. Washington." Enclosed in President of Congress to Washington, 1781, Jan. 2. 97, 278

1780
Aug. 24
Washington, George. "Miles from F. Lee." [Teaneck, New Jersey.] To [the President of Congress, Philadelphia]. Exchange of officers; Commissary of prisoners in New York; lack of meat. Draft. 4 pp. In handwriting of Robert Hanson Harrison. Read in Congress, Sept. 4.
A. V, pt. II, 201

1780
Aug. 24
Continental Congress, President. Philadelphia. To [George] Washington [Teaneck, New Jersey]. Transmitting resolves. L. S. of Samuel Huntington. 1 p. 95, 271

1780
Aug. 24
Continental Congress, Resolves. Ration allowance of officers; half-pay and pensions. Contemporary copy, attested by Charles Thomson. 1 p. Enclosed in President of Congress to Washington, 1780, Aug. 28. Published in Genl. Orders, Sept. 5. 95, 283

1780
Aug. 25
Board of War. [Philadelphia.] To [George] Washington [Teaneck]. Commissions for Moylan's and Webb's regiments. A. L. S. of Benjamin Stoddert. 1 p. Answered Sept. 5.* 95, 277

1780
Aug. 27
Washington, George. Near Liberty Pole [Tavern, Teaneck]. Circular letter to the States. Failure of supplies; distress of army; urgency of case. Contemporary copy. 3 pp. In handwriting of David Humphreys. Enclosed in Washington to the President of Congress, 1780, Aug. 28.
C. C. 152, 9, 143
Printed: Writings of Washington (Ford) N. Y. 1890. 8, 410.

1780
Aug. 28
Washington, George. Liberty Pole [Tavern, Teaneck]. To the President of Congress [Philadelphia]. Lack of provisions; no hope of accomplishing anything this campaign. Draft. 2 pp. In handwriting of Alexander Hamilton. Read in Congress Sept. 4. Referred to Committee on letter of Aug. 20. A. V, pt. II, 205
Printed: Writings of Washington (Ford) N. Y. 1890. 8, 416.

1780
Aug. 28
Washington, George. Liberty Pole. To Col. [William] Malcom, Dobbs Ferry. Ordering New York brigade to Albany. L. S. 2 pp. In handwrit-

ing of David Humphreys. Transmitted to Congress.   C. C.   152, 9, 135

1780
AUG. 28

Continental Congress, President. Philadelphia. To [George] Washington [Teaneck]. Transmitting resolves; intelligence from the Southward. L. S. of Samuel Huntington. 1 p. Answered Sept. 6.*   95, 281

1780
AUG. 28

Board of War. [Philadelphia.] To [George] Washington [Teaneck]. Lack of list of officers of the army. A. L. S. of Benjamin Stoddert. 2 pp. Answered Sept. 5.*   95, 279

1780
AUG. 29

Harrison, R[obert] H[anson]. Liberty Pole [Teaneck]. To [the Board of War, Philadelphia]. Commissions for officers. Auto draft. Signed. 1 p.   A. V, pt. II, 207

1780
AUG. 31

Washington, George. " In the vicinity of Fort Lee " [Teaneck]. To the Board of War [Philadelphia]. Minor military matters. Draft. 2 pp. In handwriting of Robert Hanson Harrison.   A. V, pt. II, 209

1780
AUG. 31

Continental Congress, President. Philadelphia. To [George] Washington [Teaneck]. Defeat of Maj. Gen. [Horatio] Gates. L. S. of Samuel Huntington. 2 pp. Answered Sep. 6.*   95, 285

1780
AUG. 31

Board of Admiralty. [Philadelphia.] To [George] Washington [Teaneck]. Movements of Continental frigates. Marine Committee Letter-book.

1780
AUG. 31

Armstrong, John. Philadelphia. To [George] Washington [Teaneck]. News from the West Indies and the defeat at Camden. A. L. S. 2 pp.   41, 182

[1780]
[AUG.]

Jones, Joseph. [Philadelphia.] To [George Washington, Teaneck?]. Necessity of exertion in cooperating with the French; campaign in the south; conditions in that quarter; [Maj.] Gen. [Nathanael] Greene and the Quartermaster's Department; promotion matters. A. L. S. 4 pp.   41, 192

[1780]
[AUG?]

Prisoners, British. Plan proposed for exchanging two divisions of Convention troops. Transcript. Enclosed in Washington to the President of Congress, 1780, Dec. 8.   C. C.   169, 7, 357

1780
SEP. 5

Washington, George. Hackensack Bridge [New Jersey]. To [the Board of War, Philadelphia]. Resolution of Congress of Aug. 12 respecting pay for officers, land grants etc. Draft. 2 pp. In handwriting of Robert Hanson Harrison.

A. V, pt. II, 211

1780
SEP. 6

Washington, George. Near Hackensack Bridge. To the President of Congress [Philadelphia]. Reimbursement of depreciated pay of officers; want of meat. Draft. 2 pp. In handwriting of Robert Hanson Harrison. Read in Congress, Sep. 11. Referred to Committee on letter of Aug. 20. A. V, pt. II, 213

Printed: Writings of Washington (Ford) N. Y. 1890. 8, 421.

1780
SEP. 6

Washington, George. [Hopper House,] Bergen County [New Jersey]. To the Board of War [Philadelphia]. Maryland regiment ordered to the Southward. Draft. 1 p. In handwriting of Tench Tilghman. A. V, pt. II, 215

1780
SEP. 6

Continental Congress, President. Philadelphia. To [George] Washington [Hopper House]. Transmitting resolve. Letter-book copy.

C. C. 15, 96

1780
SEP. 6

Jones, Joseph. Philadelphia. To [George Washington, Hopper House]. Resignation [of Maj. Gen. Nathanael Greene] and affairs of the Quartermaster's Department; operations against New York on the South; permanent army; Virginia's Ohio lands. A. L. S. 4 pp. 41, 303

1780
SEP. 7

Board of War. [Philadelphia.] To [George] Washington [Hopper House]. Permission from British to send shirts and provisions to American prisoners at Charleston. A. L. S. of Richard Peters. 1 p. Miscel.

1780
SEP. 7

[André, John Lewis.] New York. To Col. [Elisha] Sheldon [New Salem, New York]. Requesting permission to enter American lines. Signed: John Anderson. In proceedings of trial of André 1780, Sep. 29.

Printed: Writings of Washington (Sparks) Boston. 1835. 7, 522.

1780
SEP. 8

Washington, George. "Liberty Pole, Bergen County." To [the President of Congress, Philadelphia]. Powers granted by resolution of Aug. 5; cooperation with French. Draft. 2 pp. In handwriting of Alexander Hamilton. Read in Con-

gress Aug. 12.   Referred to Committee on letter
of Aug. 20.   **A. V, pt. II, 217**

Printed: Writings of Washington (Ford) N. Y. 1890. 8, 425.

1780   Continental Congress, President.   Philadelphia.   To
SEP. 8   [George] Washington [Hopper. House].   Transmitting intelligence from the South.   Letter-
book copy.   **C. C. 15,96**

1780   Howe, R[obert].   New Bridge [near Hackensack, New
SEP. 8   Jersey].   To [George Washington, Tappan, New
York].   Resignation of Brig. Gen. [John]
Nixon.   A. L. S.   Enclosed in Washington to
the President of Congress, 1780, Sep. 9.   Dated
in error Aug. 8.   **C. C. 152, 9, 159**

1780   Nixon, John.   New Bridge.   To Maj. Gen. [Robert]
SEP. 8   Howe [New Bridge].   Resignation.   A. L. S.
1 p.   Enclosed in Washington to the President
of Congress, 1780, Sep. 9.   **C. C. 152, 9, 161**

1780   Washington, George.   [Hopper House,] Bergen County.
SEP. 9   To the President of Congress [Philadelphia].
Clothing for troops, and minor matters.   Draft.
2 pp.   In handwriting of Tench Tilghman.
Read in Congress Sep. 12.   " What relates to
clothing Referred to the board of War."

1780   Washington, George.   [Hopper House.]   To John Ma-
SEP. 9   thews [Philadelphia].   New arrangement of the
Medical Line; names recommended.   Draft. 2
pp.   In handwriting of Robert Hanson Harrison.   **P. II, 151**

Printed: Writings of Washington (Ford) N. Y. 1890. 8, 428.

1780   Board of War.   [Philadelphia.]   To [George] Washing-
SEP. 9   ton [Hopper House].   Papers to be sent to British in New York; Lt. Connolly Coan.   A. L. S.
of Benjamin Stoddert. 1 p.   Answered Sep.
15.*   **Miscel.**

1780   Washington, G[eorge].   " Near Hackensac New Bridge."
SEP. 10   To the President of Congress [Philadelphia].
Salt beef taken in the Quebec ships.   Auto. draft
signed. 1 p.   Read in Congress, Sep. 14.   Referred to Board of War.   **A. V, pt. II, 221**

1780   Continental Congress, President.   Philadelphia.   To
SEP. 12   [George] Washington [Hopper House].   Trans-
mitting resolves: reenforcing Southern army.
Letter-book copy.   **C. C. 15, 98**

1780
SEP. 13

Washington, George. [Hopper House] Bergen County. To [the President of Congress, Philadelphia]. Capt. Hendricks Solomon and the Stockbridge Indians. Draft. 1p. In handwriting of Tench Tilghman. Referred to Board of War to take order. **A. V, pt. II, 223**

Printed: Writings of Washington (Sparks) Boston. 1837. 7, 203.

17 0
SEP. 14

Washington, George. [Hopper House.] To Nathaniel Peabody [Philadelphia]. News of sailing of a French fleet for America. Draft. 2 pp. In handwriting of David Humphreys.
A. V, pt. II, 225

1780
SEP. 14

Forman, David. Freehold [New Jersey]. To [George Washington, Hackensack Bridge]. Arrival of Admiral [George Bridges] Rodney at Sandy Hook; troops for North Carolina. Contemporary copy. 1 p. In handwriting of Caleb Gibbs. Enclosed in Washington to the President of Congress, 1780, Sep. 16.
C. C. 152, 9, 179

1780
SEP. 15

Washington, George. New Bridge [Hackensack]. To [the President of Congress, Philadelphia]. Defeat in Carolina [Camden]; militia; supplies; conference with Comte de Rochambeau. Draft. 3 pp. In handwriting of Alexander Hamilton. Read in Congress, Sep. 18. Referred to Committee on letter of Aug. 20. **A. V, pt. II, 227**

Printed: Writings of Washington (Ford) N.Y. 1890. 8, 440.

1780
SEP. 15

Washington, George. [Hackensack Bridge.] To [the Board of War, Philadelphia]. Clothing for American prisoners of war; minor matters. Draft. 2 pp. In handwriting of Robert Hanson Harrison. **A. V, pt. II, 231**

1780
SEP. 15

Washington, George. [Hackensack Bridge] Bergen County. To the Georgia delegates in Congress [Philadelphia]. Exchange of Lt. Thomas Morris. Draft. 1 p. In handwriting of Tench Tilghman. **A. V, pt. II, 233**

Delegates: Walter, Telfair and Few.

1780
SEP. 15

Mathews, John. Philadelphia. To [George Washington, Hackensack]. New arrangement of Hospital department; criticism of Congressional action; character of members; dilatory tactics of committee on Washington's letter. A. L. S. 4 pp. **42, 357**

1780
SEP. 16

Washington, George. New Bridge [Hackensack]. To the President of Congress [Philadelphia]. Transmitting intelligence. Draft. 1 p. In handwriting of Caleb Gibbs. Read in Congress, Sep. 18. **A. V, pt. II, 235**

1780
SEP. 16

Washington, George. Bergen County. To Col. [William] Malcom, Albany. Supplies for Fort Schuyler. L. S. 2 pp. In handwriting of Tench Tilghman. Transmitted to Congress.
C. C. 152, 9, 181

1780
SEP. 16

Contingent Congress, President. [Philadelphia.] To [George] Washington [Hopper House]. Transmitting resolves; beef supply for army. Letterbook copy. **C. C. 15, 108**

1780
SEP. 17

W[ashington,] G[eorge.] [Hackensack Bridge]. To Abraham Skinner [Hackensack Bridge]. Instructions governing his negotiations for exchange of prisoners; Massachusetts officers prisoners in Canada. Contemporary copy. 5 pp. In handwriting of Tench Tilghman. Enclosed in Washington to Congress, 1780, Oct. 7.
C. C. 152, 9, 185

1780
SEP. 18

Tilghman, T[ench]. [Hackensack Bridge] Bergen County. To the Board of War [Philadelphia]. Enclosing passports for schooner *Blazing Star*. Auto. draft signed. 1 p. **A. V, pt. II, 237**

1780
SEP. 19

Duane, James. Philadelphia. To [George Washington, en route to Hartford]. Hospital department; permanent army; disaster in the South and conduct of regular troops; centralization of government. A. L. S. 2 pp. **42, 120**

1780
SEP. 24

Continental Congress, President. Philadelphia. To [George] Washington [Litchfield, Connecticut]. Transmitting resolve. Letter-book copy.
C. C. 15, 115

1780
SEP. 24

Mathews, John. Philadelphia. To [George Washington, Litchfield]. Action of Congress to fill up the army; Mathews's plan, its benefits and rejection. A. L. S. 4 pp. **43, 2**

1780
SEP. 24

André, John [Lewis]. Salem [New Jersey]. To George Washington [Robinson House, Highlands]. Declaring his identity and explaining his position. In proceedings of trial of Maj. André. 1780, Sep. 29.
Printed: Writings of Washington (Sparks) Boston. 1835. 7, 531.

1780
SEP. 25

Continental Congress, Resolves. Plan for conducting the Inspector's Department of the Army. Printed pamphlet. 6 pp. and title page. Printed by Claypoole, Phila. Transmitted to Washington.
43, 47

1780
SEP. 25

Arnold, B[enedict]. On board [H. M. S.] *Vulture*. To [George] Washington [Robinson House]. Protection for Mrs. Arnold; exculpation of Lt. Col. [Richard] Varick, Maj. [David S.] Franks, and Joshua [Hett] Smith. Contemporary copy. 2 pp. In handwriting of Richard Kidder Meade. Enclosed in Washington to the President of Congress, 1780, Oct. 7. C. C.´ 152, 9, 225
Printed: Writings of Washington (Sparks) Boston. 1835. 7,533.

1780
SEP. 25

Lincoln, Benjamin. [Tappan, New York.] To [George] Washington [Robinson House, Highlands]. Exchange of prisoners; rights of privates. Contemporary copy. 4 pp. In handwriting of Tench Tilghman. Enclosed in Washington to the President of Congress, 1780, Oct. 7.
C. C. 152, 9, 195

1780
SEP. 25

Robinson, Beverly. [H. M. S.] *Vulture*, off Sinsinck [Sing Sing]. To George Washington [Robinson House]. André's release. In proceedings of trial of André, 1779, Sep. 29.
Printed: Writings of Washington (Sparks) Boston. 1835. 7,533.

1780
SEP. 26

Washington, George. Robinson's House, Highlands [New York]. To [the President of Congress, Philadelphia]. Arnold's treason; capture of André. Draft. 4 pp. In handwriting of Robert Hanson Harrison. Read in Congress, Sep. 30. Referred to Lovell, Van Dyke, and Duane.
A. V, pt. II, 239
Printed: Writings of Washington (Ford) N. Y. 1890. 8,455.

1780
SEP. 26

Arnold, B[enedict]. New York. To Sir Henry Clinton [New York]. Release of André. In proceedings of trial of André. 1780, Sep. 29.
Printed: Writings of Washington (Sparks) Boston. 1835. 7,534.

1780
SEP. 26

Clinton, [Sir] H[enry]. New York. To [George] Washington [Robinson House]. Release of André. In proceedings of trial of André. 1780, Sep. 29.
Printed: Writings of Washington (Sparks) Boston. 1835. 7,534.

1780
SEP. 26

Prisoners, British and Hessian. State of, at Charlottesville Barracks [Virginia]. Tabular statement.

Transcript. Enclosed in Washington to the President of Congress, 1780, Dec. 8.

C. C.   169, 7, 355

1780
SEP. 28

Morris, Robert. Philadelphia. To [George] Washington [Tappan]. Obligations to Andrew Elliot; exchange of Capt. [William] Muir. A. L. S. 2 pp. Answered Oct. 11.   **42, 213**

1780
SEP. 29

Washington, George. Tappan. To the Board of General Officers, Tappan. Instructions regarding Maj. [John Lewis] André. In proceedings of trial of André. 1780, Sep. 29.

Printed: Writings of Washington (Sparks) Boston. 1835. 7, 535.

1780
SEP. 29

Continental Congress, President. Philadelphia. To [George] Washington [Tappan]. Arnold's desertion; seizure of his papers and effects in Philadelphia. Letter-book copy.   **C. C.**   **15,** 119

1780
SEP. 29

André, John [Lewis]. Tappan. To Sir Henry Clinton [New York]. Capture; probable fate; his commission, mother and sisters. Contemporary copy. 2 pp. In handwriting of Robert Hanson Harrison. Enclosed in Washington to the President of Congress, 1780, Oct. 7.   **C. C.**   **152,** 9, 229

Printed: Writings of Washington (Sparks) Boston. 1835. 7, 537.

1780
SEP. 29

Continental Army. Board of General Officers, Tappan, New York. Trial of Maj. [John Lewis] André. Proceedings, evidences, etc. Documents submitted:

Sep. 7. André to Col. [Elisha] Sheldon.
Sep. 24. André to Washington.
Sep. 25. Robinson, Beverly, to Washington.
Sep. 26. Clinton, Sir Henry, to Washington.
Sep. 26. Arnold to Clinton.
Sep. 29. Washington to the Board.

Contemporary copy. 10 pp. In handwriting of Robert Hanson Harrison, and endorsed by him: "Major André was executed Monday the 2d of Octbr. at Tappan at 12 o'clock." Enclosed in Washington to the President of Congress, 1780, Oct. 7.   **C. C.**   **152,** 9, 213

1780
SEP. 29

Robertson, James. New York. To [George] Washington [Tappan]. Complaint of treatment of flags; necessaries for Maj. André. Contemporary copy. 1 p. In handwriting of Robert Hanson Harrison. 1780, Oct. 7.

C. C.   **152,** 9, 233

Printed: Writings of Washington (Sparks) Boston. 1835. 7, 537.

1780
SEP. 30

Washington, George. Tappan. To Sir Henry Clinton [New York]. Maj. [John Lewis] André's case. Contemporary copy. 1 p. In handwriting of Robert Hanson Harrison. Enclosed in Washington to the President of Congress, 1780, Oct. 7.

C. C. **152**, 9, 231

Printed: Writings of Washington (Sparks) Boston. 1835. 7, 538.

1780
SEP. 30

Washington, George. Tappan. To Lt. Gen. [James] Robertson, New York. His complaint; necessaries for Maj. André. Contemporary copy. I p. In handwriting of Robert Hanson Harrison. Enclosed in Washington to the President of Congress, 1780, Oct. 7.   C. C. **152**, 9, 235

Printed: Writings of Washington (Sparks) Boston. 1835. 7, 538.

1780
SEP. 30

Board of War. [Philadelphia.] To George Washington [Tappan]. Troops from the south; forage scarcity at Winchester; Virginia troops; arrangement of officers, Jan. 1 [1781]; A. L. S. of Benjamin Lincoln. 4 pp.   **98,** 179

1780
SEP.30

Clinton, Sir H[enry]. New York. To [George] Washington [Tappan]. Maj. André's case; request to hear Lt. Gen. [James] Robertson, Andrew Elliott, and Chief Justice William Smith in the matter. Contemporary copy. 2 pp. In handwriting of Robert Hanson Harrison. Note of result of interview between Robertson and Maj. Gen. Nathanael Greene. Enclosed in Washington to the President of Congress, 1780, Oct. 7.

C. C. **152**, 9, 237

Printed: Writings of Washington (Sparks) Boston, 1835. 7, 539.

1780
SEP. 30

Stewart, Charles. Tappan. To [George] Washington [Tappan]. Failure of flour supply. Contemporary copy. 1 p. In handwriting of Tench Tilghman. Enclosed in Washington to the President of Congress, 1780, Oct. 1.

C. C. **152**, 9, 207

[1780]
[SEP.]

Continental Congress. Memorandum of information for [George] Washington. Ability of North Carolina to furnish flour, meat, forage, etc., to the army. 2 pp.   C. C. **152**, 9, 173

1780
OCT. 1

Washington, George. Orangetown [Tappan, New York]. To the President of Congress [Philadelphia]. Supply of flour and forage. Draft. 2 pp. In handwriting of Tench Tilghman. Read in Congress, Oct. 3. Referred to Committee appointed to confer with the Director of the U. S. Bank: Scott, Adams, Van Dyke and Sullivan.

A.   V, pt. II, 243

1780
Oct. 1

André, John [Lewis]. Tappan. To [George] Washington [Tappan]. Requesting to be shot instead of hung. Contemporary copy. 2 pp. In handwriting of Richard Kidder Meade. Note by Harrison of reasons for refusing above request. Enclosed in Washington to the President of Congress, 1780, Oct. 7.   C. C.   152, 9, 245

Printed: Writings of Washington (Sparks) Boston. 1835. 7, 543.

1780
Oct. 1

Arnold, B[enedict]. New York. To [George] Washington [Tappan]. Foreswearing his allegiance. Contemporary copy. 1 p. In handwriting of Tench Tilghman. Enclosed in Washington to the President of Congress, 1780, Oct. 7.

C. C.   152, 9, 239

Printed: Writings of Washington (Sparks) Boston. 1835. 7, 540.

1780
Oct. 1

Arnold, B[enedict]. New York. To [George] Washington [Tappan]. Maj. André's case; threats of retaliation. Contemporary copy. 3 pp. In handwriting of Tench Tilghman. Enclosed in Washington to the President of Congress, 1780, Oct. 7.   C. C.   152, 9, 243

Printed: Writings of Washington (Sparks) Boston. 1835. 7, 541.

1780
Oct. 2

Robertson, James. H. M. S. *Greyhound*, Dobbs Ferry [New York]. To George Washington [Tappan]. Interview with Maj. Gen. [Nathanael] Greene; André's case; efforts for his release. Contemporary copy. 2 pp. In handwriting of Robert Hanson Harrison. Enclosed in Washington to the President of Congress, 1780, Oct. 7.

C. C.   152, 9, 241

Printed: Writings of Washington (Sparks) Boston. 1835. 7, 541.

1780
Oct. 2

Jones, Joseph. [Richmond] Virginia. To [George Washington, Tappan]. A recommendation for the Medical Department; disappearance of factional spirit in Congress; Virginia and the Federal Union; control of the seas. A. L. S. 3 pp.

42, 241

1780
Oct. 4

W[ashingto]n, G[eorge]. Tappan. To John Mathews [Philadelphia]. Permanent force; bounties; expense and waste of short enlistments; reception of the Committee of Cooperation by Congress. Auto. draft signed. 4 pp.   P. II, 157

Printed: Writings of Washington (Ford) N. Y. 1890. 8, 461.

④ Head Quarters Newburgh

Dear Sir,   Jany 7th 1782

        I have to acknowledge the
receipt of the Letter, your Excellency did
me the honor to write on the 25th of Decr.
                    you
and to assure ^ of the great satisfaction
I experienced from the agreeable commu=
nications you had the goodness to make

        Enclosed your Excellency will
find the original Certificate which was
given by Mr Chittendon to the bearer
of your Letter of the 11th Ult.—

        Nothing very interesting has
happened since my last—a fleet sailed
a few days after from New York for
Europe, and I am informed the Enemy
are under apprehensions lest the french
                      two   after
Fleet which sailed the days before
should have fallen in with it.—I am
extremely anxious to hear from Charles=
Town; and still more so, to hear the
                                      result

WRITING OF DAVID HUMPHREYS.

1780
Oct. 4

Washington, George. Tappan. To James Duane [Philadelphia]. Permanent force and short enlistments; supineness, false hopes, etc.; interview at Hartford. Draft signed. 2 pp. In handwriting of Alexander Hamilton. **P. II**, 161

Printed: Writings of Washington (Ford) N. Y. 1780. 8, 464.

1780
Oct. 4

Continental Congress, President. Philadelphia. To [George] Washington [Tappan]. New arrangement of army; considerations weighing in establishment of a permanent army; recruiting. Letter-book copy. **C. C.** **15**, 122

1780
Oct. 6

Continental Congress, President. Philadelphia. To [George] Washington [Tappan]. Transmitting resolves. Letter-book copy. **C. C.** **15**, 126

1780
Oct. 6

Mathews, John. Philadelphia. To [George Washington, Paramus]. Request of Southern delegates to 'Congress that Maj. Gen. [Nathanael] Greene be appointed to command the Southern Army. A. L. S. 1 p. Answered by letter to Congress, Oct. 15.* **42**, 273

1780
Oct. 7

Washington, George. Paramus [New Jersey]. To [the President of Congress, Philadelphia]. Proceedings of the André court martial; names of his captors; movement of troops; list of papers enclosed with certain comment. Draft. 5 pp. In handwriting of Caleb Gibbs and Robert Hanson Harrison. Read in Congress, Sep. 12. Referred to Sullivan, Bland, and Mathews.

A. **V, pt. II**, 245

Printed in part: Writings of Washington (Ford) N. Y. 1890. 8, 472.

1780
Oct. 7

Washington, George. Paramus. To Sir Henry Clinton [New York]. Acceding to exchange of prisoners. Contemporary copy. 1 p. Enclosed in Washington to the President of Congress, 1780, Oct. 16. **C. C.** **152, 9**, 303

1780
Oct. 7

Washington, George. Paramus. To Abraham Skinner [Paramus?]. Instructions for exchange of prisoners. Contemporary copy. 2 pp. In handwriting of Robert Hanson Harrison. Enclosed in Washington to the President of Congress, 1780, Oct. 16. **C. C.** **152, 9**, 305

1780
Oct. 7

Washington, George. [Paramus.] [Memorandum to accompany letter of André to Col. Elisha Sheldon, 1780, Sep. 7, transmitted to Congress.] Shel-

don's ignorance of Arnold's treasonable designs.
Contemporary copy. 1 p. In handwriting of
Robert Hanson Harrison. Enclosed in Wash-
ington to the President of Congress, 1780, Oct. 7.

C. C.   152, 9, 227

1780
Oct. 8

Harrison, Rob[ert] H[anson]. Paramus. To the Board
of War [Philadelphia]. Commission for New
Hampshire officers. Auto. draft signed. 1 p.

A. V, pt. II, 251

1780
Oct. 9

Continental Congress, President. Philadelphia. To
[George] Washington [Preakness, New Jersey].
Transmitting papers at request of [Maj.] Gen.
[Horatio] Gates. Letter-book copy.

C. C.   15, 129

1780
Oct. 10

Washington, George. Preakness. To Lt. Col. Dubuysson
[Philadelphia?]. Death of Baron de Kalb; Du-
buysson's exchange. Contemporary copy. 2 pp.
In handwriting of Caleb Gibbs. Enclosed in
Washington to the President of Congress, 1780,
Oct. 29.   C. C.   152, 9, 337

> Preakness is near Passaic Falls and Washington's letters from this
> date to Nov. 27 are indifferently dated from either place.

1780
Oct. 10

Continental Congress, President. Philadelphia. To
[George] Washington [Preakness]. Transmitting resolves. Letter-book copy. C. C.   15, 132

1780
Oct. 10

Duane, James. Philadelphia. To [George Washington,
Preakness]. Arrangement of army; permanent
force; difficulties in Congress; need of men and
supplies. A. L. S. 3 pp.   42, 310

1780
Oct. 11

Washington, George. Near Passaic Falls [New Jersey].
To [the President of Congress, Philadelphia].
Reorganization of army; members, officers, etc.
Draft. 11 pp. In handwriting of Alexander
Hamilton and Robert Hanson Harrison. Read
in Congress, Oct. 16. Referred to Committee
on letter of Aug. 20.   A. V, pt. II, 253

> Extract of above made on occasion of the Newburgh Addresses, in
> handwriting of Jonathan Trumbull, jr., 7 pp. Enclosed in Washington
> to the President of Congress, 1783, May 18. C. C. 152, 11, 167.
> Printed in part: Writings of Washington (Ford) N. Y. 1890. 8, 481.

1780
Oct. 11

Malcom, William. Albany [New York]. To Gov.
[George] Clinton [Poughkeepsie]. Incursion
of enemy from Canada; capture of Fort Ann.
Contemporary copy. In handwriting of Caleb
Gibbs. Enclosed in Washington to the Presi-
dent of Congress, 1780, Oct. 16. C. C.   152, 9, 313

1780
Oct. 12

Washington, George. [Passaic Falls.] To the Board of War [Philadelphia]. Delays in forwarding officers' commissions. Draft. 2 pp. In handwriting of Robert Hanson Harrison.

A. V, pt. II, 265

1780
Oct. 12

Livingston, H[enry]. Fort Edward [New York]. To [Gov. George Clinton, Poughkeepsie]. Surrender of Forts George and Ann to British and Indians; depredations; situation at Fort Edward. Contemporary copy. 3 pp. In handwriting of David Humphreys. Enclosed in Washington to the President of Congress, 1780, Oct. 16.   C. C. 152, 9, 309

1780
Oct. 12

Lush, Stephen. Albany. To Gov. [George] Clinton [Poughkeepsie]. Strength of enemy; surrender of Forts Ann and George and investure of Fort Edward; reenforcements; lack of provisions; militia etc. Contemporary copy. 1 p. In handwriting of Richard Kidder Meade. Enclosed in Washington to the President of Congress, 1780, Oct. 16.   C. C. 152, 9, 315

1780
Oct. 12

Malcom, William. Albany. To Gov. [George] Clinton [Poughkeepsie]. Surrender of Fort George; the frontier situation. Contemporary copy. In handwriting of Caleb Gibbs. Enclosed in Washington to the President of Congress, 1780. Oct. 16.   C. C. 152, 9, 313

1780
Oct. 13

Washington, George. [Passaic Falls.] To the President of Congress [Philadelphia]. The Inspector General's department. Draft. 1 p. In handwriting of Alexander Hamilton. Read in Congress, Oct. 16.   A. V, pt. II, 267

1780
Oct. 13

Washington, George. [Passaic Falls.] To Sir Henry Clinton [New York]. Propositions for government of agents for prisoners. L. S. 2 pp. In handwriting of Tench Tilghman. Enclosed in Washington to the President of Congress, 1780, Oct. 15.   C. C. 152, 9, 283

[1780]
[Oct. 13]

Washington, George. [Passaic Falls.] Articles of agreement proposed for government of agents of prisoners. Contemporary copy. 3 pp. In handwriting of Robert Hanson Harrison. Enclosed in Washington to the President of Congress, 1780, Oct. 15.   C. C. 152, 9, 287

1780
Oct. 13

Clinton, [Sir] H[enry]. New York. To [George] Washington [Passaic Falls]. Exchange of prisoners. Contemporary copy. 1 p. In handwriting of Robert Hanson Harrison. Enclosed in Washington to the President of Congress, 1780, Oct. 16. **C. C. 152, 9, 307**

1780
Oct. 14

Continental Congress, President. Philadelphia. To [George] Washington [Passaic Falls]. Col. [Daniel] Morgan's promotion to a brigadiership; intelligence from the South; publication of proceedings relative to Maj. [John Lewis] André. Letter-book copy. **C. C. 15, 135**

1780
Oct. 14

Clinton, George. Poughkeepsie. To [George] Washington [Passaic Falls]. Enemy's attack on frontier; disposition of troops; reenforcements etc. Contemporary copy. 2 pp. In handwriting of David Humphreys. Enclosed in Washington to the President of Congress, 1780, Oct. 16.
  C. C. 152, 9, 317

1780
Oct. 14

Mathews, John. Philadelphia. To [George Washington, Preakness]. Flag for Mrs. Mathews to go to Carolina; reasons; affairs in South; need of commander and reenforcements. A. L. S. 4 pp. **42, 338**

1780
Oct. 15

Washington, George. " Prackness " [New Jersey]. To [the President of Congress, Philadelphia]. American Commissary of Prisoners to reside in New York City; resignations in Massachusetts Line. Draft. 1 p. In handwriting of Alexander Mamilton. Read in Congress, Oct. 19.
  A. V, pt. II, 273

1780
Oct. 15

Washington, George. Preakness. To [the President of Congress, Philadelphia]. Capture of [Henry] Laurens; Cork fleet on the coast. Draft. 1 p. In handwriting of Robert Hanson Harrison. Read in Congress, Oct. 19. **A. V, pt. II, 275**

1780
Oct. 15

Washington, George. Passaic Falls. To the President of Congress [Philadelphia]. Court of Inquiry of Maj. Gen. [Horatio] Gates; [Maj.] Gen. [Nathanael] Greene to command in the South; Arnold's proclamation; embarkation of enemy at New York. Draft. 3 pp. In handwriting of Tench Tilghman. Read in Congress, Oct. 19.
  A. V, pt. II, 269

[1780]
[Oct. 15] Massachusetts, Officers. Resignations in October. 1 p. In handwriting of Tench Tilghman. Enclosed in Washington to the President of Congress, 1780, Oct. 15. C. C. 152, 9, 291

1780
Oct. 16 Washington, George. [Near Passaic Falls.] To [the President of Congress, Philadelphia]. Correspondence with Sir Henry Clinton respecting civil prisoners of South Carolina; exchanges; enemy's incursions from Canada. Draft. 2 pp. In handwriting of Robert Hanson Harrison. Read in Congress, Oct. 23. Referred to Bee, Livingston, Duane and Sullivan.
A. V, pt. II, 277

1780
Oct. 17 Washington, George. Passaic Falls. To the President of Congress [Philadelphia]. Sailing of enemy's detachment from New York. Draft. 1 p. In handwriting of Tench Tilghman. Read in Congress, Oct. 20. A. V, pt, II, 279

1780
Oct. 17 Mathews, John. Philadelphia. To [George Washington, near Passaic Falls]. Plan for reorganizing army; dilatory attitude of Congress; [Maj.] Gen. [Nathanael] Greene's appointment. A. L. S. 2 pp. 42, 355

1780
Oct. 18 Board of War. [Philadelphia.] To George Washington [Passaic Falls]. Capt. [B. Edgar] Joel's charge against Maj. Gen. [Robert] Howe. A. L. S. of Richard Peters. 2 pp. Miscel.

1780
Oct. 19 Continental Congress, President. Philadelphia. To [George] Washington [Preakness]. Transmitting resolves and printed plan for conducting Hospital Department. Letter-book copy.
C. C. 15, 138

1780
Oct. 19 Board of War. [Philadelphia.] To [George] Washington [Preakness]. Officers to whom depreciation of pay is to be made up. L. S. of Richard Peters. 2 pp. Answered Oct. 21.* Miscel.

1780
Oct. 21 Washington, George. Near Passaic Falls. To the President of Congress [Philadelphia]. Enemy's reenforcement; lack of provisions at Fort Pitt; dismissal of Lt. Col. [David] Mason; incursions from Canada. Draft. 3 pp. In handwriting of Tench Tilghman. Referred to Matlack, Hanson and Walker. A. V, pt. II, 281

1780 Oct. 21	Washington, George. Preakness. To the Board of War [Philadelphia]. Question as to what is "the line of the army"; minor matters. Draft. 1 p. In handwriting of Alexander Hamilton. A. V, pt. II, 285
1780 Oct. 22	Washington, George. Preakness. To the President of Congress [Philadelphia]. Maj. Gen. [Nathanael] Greene to command Southern Department; need of Baron Steuben's services. Draft. 2 pp. In handwriting of Alexander Hamilton. Read in Congress, Oct. 27. Referred to Sharpe, Bland, Cornell, Sullivan and Walton. A. V, pt. II, 287 Printed in part: Writings of Washington (Ford) N. Y. 1890. 9, 11, note.
1780 Oct. 22	Washington, George. Preakness. To the Board of War [Philadelphia]. Major [Henry] Lee's corps to be sent to the Southward. Draft. 1 p. In handwriting of Tench Tilghman. A. V, pt. II, 289
1780 Oct. 22	[Washington, George.] Preakness. To Maj. Gen. [Horatio] Gates [Hillsboro, North Carolina]. Maj. Gen. [Nathanael] Greene to command the Southern Army; court of inquiry for Gates. Contemporary copy. 1 p. In handwriting of Alexander Hamilton. Enclosed in Washington to the President of Congress, 1780, Oct. 22. C. C. 152, 9, 327
1780 Oct. 22	[Washington, George.] Preakness. To Maj. Gen. [Nathanael] Greene [Preakness]. Instructions for his command of Southern Army; trial of Maj. Gen. [Horatio] Gates. Contemporary copy. 3 pp. In handwriting of Alexander Hamilton. Enclosed in Washington to the President of Congress, 1780, Oct. 22. C. C. 152, 9, 229 Printed: Writings of Washington (Ford) N. Y. 1891. 9, 9.
1780 Oct. 23	Washington, George. To John Mathews [Philadelphia]. Request for Mrs. Mathews; affairs in the South; [Maj. Gen. Nathanael Greene]. Draft signed. 2 pp. In handwriting of Alexander Hamilton. P. II, 195
1780 Oct. 23	Continental Congress, President. Philadelphia. To [George] Washington [Preakness]. Transmitting news of defeat of Col. [Patrick] Ferguson [battle of King's Mountain]. L. S. of Samuel Huntington. 1 p. Answered Oct. 29.* 43, 44½

1780
Oct. 23

Continental Congress, President. Philadelphia. To [George] Washington [Preakness]. Chevalier Dubuysson's request; transmitting printed proceedings of the board of general officers respecting Maj. [John Lewis] André. Letter-book copy.   **C. C. 15, 143**

1780
Oct. 24

Board of Treasury. Philadelphia. To [George] Washington [Preakness]. Waste of public flour at various posts through negligence. A. L. S. of William Denning. 3 pp. Answered Nov. 2.*
                                                    42, 59

1780
Oct. 25

Washington, George. [Preakness.] To [the Board of War, Philadelphia]. Suspicions of treasons; character of a deserter. Draft. 2 pp. In handwriting of Alexander Hamilton.
                                          ·A. V, pt. II, 291
Printed: Writings of Washington (Ford) N. Y. 1891. 9, 16.

1780
Oct. 26

Continental Congress, President. Philadelphia. To [George] Washington [Preakness]. Transmitting resolves. Letter-book copy.   **C. C. 15, 145**

1780
Oct. 28

Board of War. [Philadelphia.] To [George] Washington [Preakness]. Transmitting commissions for Col. [Henry] Jackson's regiment. A. L. S. of Benjamin Stoddert. 1 p.   **Miscel.**

1780
Oct. 29

Washington, George. Near Passaic Falls. To the President of Congress [Philadelphia]. Intelligence from Southward, parole, exchange etc. of prisoners; Arnold's proclamation. Draft. 2 pp. In handwriting of Tench Tilghman. Read in Congress, Nov. 1. Part referred to Board of War.   **A. V, pt. II, 293**

1780
Oct. 30

Board of War. [Philadelphia.] To [George] Washington [Preakness]. Transmitting papers. A. L. S. of William Jackson. 1 p. Answered Nov. 7.*
                                                    98, 233

1780
Oct. 30

Mathews, John. Philadelphia. To [George Washington, Preakness]. Flag for Mrs. Mathews's return to Carolina; adoption of plan for army; news from the South. A. L. S. 1 p.   **43, 119**

1780
Oct. 31

Washington, George. Passaic Falls. To the Board of War [Philadelphia]. Exchange of Brigadiers von Speck and von Gall of the Convention troops. Draft. 1 p. In handwriting of Tench Tilghman.   **A. V, pt. II, 295**

1780
Oct. 31

Board of War [Philadelphia]. To [George] Washington [Passaic Falls]. Meaning of words of resolve of Apr. 10 [1780]. A. L. S. of Richard Peters. 1 p. Answered Nov. 7.* **Miscel.**
See: Board of War to Washington, 1780, Aug. 28.

[1780]
[Oct.]

[**Clinton**, Sir Henry.] [New York.] Articles proposed for government of agents for prisoners. Contemporary copy. 3 pp. In handwriting of Tench Tilghman. Enclosed in Washington to the President of Congress, 1780, Oct. 15.

C. C. 152, 9, 279

[1780]
[Oct.]

Continental Army, Officers. Resignations since Jan. 1, 1780. Names by states, artillery, dragoons etc. 6 pp. In handwriting of Robert Hanson Harrison. Transmitted to Congress. C. C. 152, 9, 193

1780
Nov. 1

Washington, George. Preakness. To the President of Congress [Philadelphia]. Sufferings of Canadians who have espoused the cause of the United States; Capt. [Joseph] Traversie's claim. Draft. 2 pp. In handwriting of Alexander Hamilton. Read in Congress, Nov. 6. Referred to Duane, Howley and Sharp. A. V, pt. II, 297

1780
Nov. 1

Continental Congress, President. Philadelphia. To [George] Washington [Preakness]. Transmitting resolve. Letter-book copy. C. C. 15, 150

1780
Nov. 2

Washington, George. Preakness. To [the Board of Treasury, Philadelphia]. Waste of public stores in magazines. Draft. 3 pp. In handwriting of Tench Tilghman. A. V, pt. II, 299

1780
Nov. 4

Washington, George. [Preakness.] To the President of Congress [Philadelphia]. Sailing of fleets from New York; establishment of the army. Draft. 1 p. In handwriting of Alexander Hamilton. Read in Congress, Nov. 8. A. V, pt. II, 303

1780
Nov. 4

Washington, George. Preakness. To the Board of War [Philadelphia]. Exchanged officers. Draft. 1 p. In handwriting of Tench Tilghman.

A. V, pt. II, 305

1780
Nov. 4

Continental Army. Hospital Department. Officers. Totaway [New Jersey]. To [George] Washington [Passaic Falls]. Salaries. D. S.: John Cochran, James Craik, Hy. Latimer, Francis Hagan. 3 pp. Enclosed in Washington to the President of Congress, 1780, Nov. 5. C. C. 152, 9, 351

1780
Nov. 4

Phillips, W[illiam]. New York. Propositions for exchange of prisoners. Transcript. Enclosed in Washington to the President of Congress, 1780, Dec. 8.   C. C. 169, 7, 352

1780
Nov. 5

Washington, .G[eorge]. Passaic Falls. To the President of Congress [Philadelphia]. Half-pay for the Hospital Department. Auto. draft signed. Read in Congress, Nov. 11. Referred to Clark, Bland and Cornell.   A. V, pt. II, 307

1780
Nov. 5

Wright, George and Others. Long Island. To Congress. Petitioning for exchange.   D. S.: George Wright, Jno. Wm. Annis, Jacob Sommer, Garret J. Van Wagener, Duke Wikoff, Matthias Ward, Robert Hondgson, Silas Snow.   2 pp. Read in Congress, Dec. 9.   Referred to Sullivan, Clark and Atlee.   Jan. 27, 1781, Referred to the Commander in chief.   Enclosed in President of Congress to Washington 1781, Jan. 27.   96, 64

1780
Nov. 7

Washington, George. Passaic Falls. To the President of Congress [Philadelphia]. Recruiting, supplies etc. for the partisan corps; establishment of the Engineer Department; enemy's destruction of grain on northern frontier; necessity of flour; supplies of enemy through inhabitants; exchange of prisoners; embarkation at New York; scarcity of supplies at the North. Draft. 7 pp. In handwriting of Tench Tilghman. Read in Congress, Nov. 13. Referred to Duane, Henry and Cornell. . A. V, pt. II, 311
Printed, in part: Writings of Washington (Ford) N. Y. 1891. 9, 21.

1780
Nov. 7

Washington, George. Passaic Falls. To the Board of War [Philadelphia]. Minor military matters; forwarding letters to the southward. Draft. 1 p. In handwriting of Tench Tilghman.
A. V, pt. II, 319

1780
Nov. 7

Board of War. [Philadelphia.] To [George] Washington [Passaic Falls]. Transportation for provisions and clothing for American prisoners at Charleston. A. L. S. of Richard Peters. 1 p. Answered Nov. 16.*   Miscel.

1780
Nov. 7

[Heath, William.] [West Point, New York.] To [George Washington, Passaic Falls]. British on Lake George; lack of provisions for troops on the frontier. [Extract of letter.] 2 pp. In handwriting of Tench Tilghman. Enclosed in Washington to the President of Congress, 1780, Nov. 7.   C. C.   152, 9, 361

1780
Nov. 8

Continental Congress, President. Philadelphia. To [George] Washington [Preakness]. Transmitting resolve. Letter-book copy.   C. C.   **15, 153**

1780
Nov. 9

Sullivan, John. Philadelphia. To [George] Washington [Preakness]. System of promotion in army. A. L. S.   2 pp.   **43, 184**

1780
Nov. 12

Washington, George. Passaic Falls. To Col. William Malcom, Wallkill [New York]. News from the frontiers; scarcity of supplies. L. S. 1 p. In handwriting of Tench Tilghman. Transmitted to Congress.   C. C.   **152, 9, 365**

1780
Nov. 12

Continental Congress, President. Philadelphia. To [George] Washington [Preakness]. Transmitting resolves; precedence in exchange of prisoners; purchase of horses on public account and reduction of number in camp. Letter-book copy.   C. C.   **15, 154**

1780
Nov. 12

Sullivan, John. Philadelphia. To [George] Washington [Preakness]. Difficulties in Congress; reforms introduced; danger to Southern states. A. L. S. 2 pp.   **43, 230**

1780
Nov. 14

Washington, George. Preakness. To the President of Congress [Philadelphia]. Enemy's fleet destined for the Southward. Draft. 1 p. In handwriting of Caleb Gibbs. Read in Congress, Nov. 17.   A.   V, pt. II, 321

1780
Nov. 16

Washington, George. Passaic Falls. To the Board of War [Philadelphia]. Passport for sloop. Draft. 1 p. In handwriting of Tench Tilghman.   A.   V, pt. II, 323

1780
Nov. 16

Continental Congress, President. Philadelphia. To [George] Washington [Preakness]. Transmitting resolves; retention of Engineer officers. Letter-book copy.   C. C.   **15, 161**

1780
Nov. 16

Board of War. [Philadelphia.] To [George] Washington [Passaic Falls]. Letters forwarded. A. L. S. of Richard Peters. 1 p.   **Miscel.**

1780
Nov. 16

Scammell, Alexander. Totaway [New Jersey]. To [George] Washington [Passaic Falls]. Resignation. Contemporary copy. 1 p. In handwriting of Tench

Tilghman.   Enclosed in Washington to the President of Congress, 1781, Jan. 2.   **C. C.   152,** 9, 429

1780
Nov. 17

Continental Congress, President.   Philadelphia.   To [George] Washington [Passaic Falls].   Transmitting intelligence of British in Virginia.   Letterbook copy.   **C. C.   15, 162**

1780
Nov. 19

Washington, George.   Passaic Falls.   To George Walton [Philadelphia].   Exchange of certain officers.   Draft.   2 pp.   In handwriting of Tench Tilghman.   **A.   V, pt. II, 325**

1780
Nov. 20

Washington, George.   Passaic Falls.   To [the President of Congress, Philadelphia].   Exchange of prisoners; reward of Paulding, Van Wart and Williams.   Draft.   3 pp.   In handwriting of Alexander Hamilton.   Read in Congress, Nov. 24.

A.   V, pt. II, 327

1780
Nov. 20

[**Washington,** George.]   To [Arthur Lee, Philadelphia].   Loan from France.   Draft.   2 pp.   In handwriting of Alexander Hamilton.   **P.   II, 219**

1780
Nov. 20

W[ashingto]n, G[eorge].   To [John] Sullivan [Philadelphia].   Reestablishment of the army; specific supplies; multiplicity of business in Congress; remedy; clothing; foreign loan; situation in Southern states.   Auto. draft signed.   4 pp.

P.   II, 215

Printed: Writings of Washington (Ford) N. Y.   1891.   9, 32.

1780
Nov. 20

Washington, George.   Passaic Falls.   To Sir Henry Clinton [New York].   Exchange of prisoners.   Contemporary copy.   2 pp.   In handwriting of Tench Tilghman.   Enclosed in Washington to the President of Congress, 1780, Dec. 8.   **C. C.   152,** 9, 389

1780
Nov. 20

Board of War.   [Philadelphia.]   To [George] Washington [Passaic Falls].   Capt. [Thomas] McIntire's case.   A. L. S. of Richard Peters.   1 p.   **Miscel**

1780
Nov. 23

Board of War.   [Philadelphia.]   To [George] Washington [Preakness].   Returns of cavalry.   A. L. S. of Benjamin Stoddert.   2 pp.   Answered Dec. 7.*

Miscel.

1780
Nov. 25

W[ashingto]n, G[eorge].   Preakness [New Jersey].   To [John] Sullivan [Philadelphia].   [Brig.] Gen. [Henry] Knox; the Inspector's Department.   Draft signed.   2 pp.   In handwriting of Alexander Hamilton and Washington.   **P.   II, 221**

Printed. Writings of Washington (Ford) N. Y.   1891.   9, 39.

1780 Nov. 25	Continental Congress, President. Philadelphia. To [George] Washington [Preakness]. Transmitting resolves. Letter-book copy. C. C. 15, 166

1780
Nov. 26

Washington, George. Preakness. To [the President of Congress, Philadelphia]. Minor matters; pay of Inspectors; the marechausée corps; death of William Erskine. L. S. 3 pp. In handwriting of Caleb Gibbs. Read in Congress, Nov. 30. Referred to Cornell, Sullivan and Ward.

C. C. 152, 9, 377

Draft, A. V, pt. II, 331, is dated Nov. 25.

Printed, in part: Writings of Washington (Ford) N. Y. 1891. 9, 40, note.

1780
Nov. 26

Sullivan, John. Philadelphia. To [George] Washington [Preakness]. Correspondence; regulations for army; requisitions and clothing; new loan solicited; Clothier's department. A. L. S. 2 pp.

44, 57

1780
Nov. 27

W[ashingto]n, G[eorge]. Preakness. To the President of Congress [Philadelphia]. Introducing Chevalier de Chastellux. Draft signed. 1 p. In handwriting of Alexander Hamilton.   P. II, 223

1780
Nov. 27

W[ashingto]n, G[eorge]. Preakness. To the President of Congress [Philadelphia]. Introducing Viscomte de Noailles. Draft signed. 1 p. In handwriting of Alexander Hamilton.   P. II, 225

1780
Nov. 27

W[ashingto]n, G[eorge]. Preakness. To the President of Congress [Philadelphia]. Introducing Comte de Damas. Draft signed. 1 p. In handwriting of Alexander Hamilton.   P. II, 227

1780
Nov. 27

W[ashingto]n, G[eorge]. Preakness. To the President of Congress [Philadelphia]. Introducing Chevalier Du Plessis. Draft signed. 1 p. In handwriting of Alexander Hamilton.   P. II, 229

1780
Nov. 28

Washington, George. Morristown. To the President of Congress [Philadelphia]. Cantonment of troops in winter quarters; Col. [Alexander] Scammell's resignation of the Adjutant Generalship; Maj. [Benjamin] Tallmadge's destruction of forage on Long Island. Draft signed. 3 pp. In handwriting of Tench Tilghman. Read in Congress Dec. 24. Referred to Sullivan, Cornell, and Mathews.   A. V, pt. II, 335

Printed: Writings of Washington (Ford) N. Y. 1891. 9, 40.

1780
Nov. 28

Morris, Gouverneur; Philadelphia. To [George Washington, New Windsor]. Suggesting an attempt against New York. A. L. S. 1 p. Answered Dec. 10.*   **44**, 160

1780
Nov. 29

Continental Congress, President. Philadelphia. To [George] Washington [Morristown]. Transmitting resolves. Letter-book copy. **C. C. 15**, 168

1780
Nov. 29

[Clinton, Sir Henry.] New York. To [George Washington, Morristown, New Jersey]. Exchange of prisoners and adjustment of accounts of Convention troops. [Extract of letter.] 4 pp. In handwriting of David Humphreys. Enclosed in Washington to the President of Congress, 1780, Dec. 8.   **C. C. 152**, 9, 393

1780
Nov. 30

Phillips, W[illiam]. New York. To Brig. Gen. [William] Irvine and Cols. [George] Matthews and [John] Ely [New York]. Propositions for exchange of Convention troops. Transcript. Enclosed in Washington to the President of Congress, 1780, Dec. 8.   **C. C. 169**, 7, 353

1780
Dec. 4

Continental Congress, President. Philadelphia. To [George] Washington [en route to New Windsor]. Transmitting resolve; news from the South. Letter-book copy.   **C. C. 15**, 171

1780
Dec. 6

Continental Congress, President. Philadelphia. To [George] Washington [New Windsor]. Transmitting resolves; prohibition of officers purchasing articles intended for troops. Letter-book copy.   **C. C. 15**, 173

1780
Dec. 7

[Washington, George.] New Windsor [New York]. To [the President of Congress, Philadelphia]. Introducing Comte de Custine. Draft. 1 p. In handwriting of Tench Tilghman.   **P. II**, 231

1780
Dec. 7

[Washington, George.] New Windsor. To [the President of Congress, Philadelphia]. Introducing Marquis de Laval. Draft. 1 p. In handwriting of Tench Tilghman.   **P. II**, 233

1780
Dec. 7

Washington, George. New Windsor [New York]. To the Board of War [Philadelphia]. Minor military matters. Draft. 1 p. In handwriting of Tench Tilghman.   **A. V**, pt. II, 339

1780
Dec. 8

Washington, George. New Windsor. To the President of Congress [Philadelphia]. Laboratory at Carlisle [Pennsylvania]; exchange of Convention troops.

Draft. 2 pp. In handwriting of Tench Tilghman. Read in Congress Dec. 18. Referred to Sullivan, Mathews, and Bland.   **A.** V, pt. II, 341

1780
DEC. 9

Continental Congress, President. Philadelphia. To [George] Washington [New Windsor]. Transmitting resolve. Letter-book copy.

    C. C. 15, 179

1780
DEC. 9

Board of War. [Philadelphia.] To [George] Washington [New Windsor]. Vessel with supplies for prisoners at Charleston. A. L. S. of Richard Peters. 1 p. Answered Dec. 19.*   **Miscel**

1780
DEC. 9

Duane, James. Philadelphia. To [George] Washington [New Windsor]. Contingencies of success of the war; Congress; speculators; money; trouble with France; possible plan of meeting the situation; estimates for coming year; European aid; Spain; British reenforcements; internal trouble with Ireland and political condition. A. L. S. 3 pp.

    44, 149

1780
DEC. 10

Washington, George. New Windsor. To Gouverneur Morris, Philadelphia. His suggestions of attempt against New York; weak state of army; want of clothing and supplies; impossibility of accomplishing anything under present conditions. Auto. draft signed. 3 pp.   **44, 158**

1780
DEC. 12

Continental Congress, Resolve. Garrison at Wyoming. D. S. of Charles Thomson. 1 p. Enclosed in President of Congress to Washington, 1780, Dec. 16.   **45, 136**

1780
DEC. 13

Washington, George. New Windsor. To the President of Congress [Philadelphia]. Payment for officers' horses killed or disabled in action; embarkation of enemy at New York. Draft. 2 pp. In handwriting of Tench Tilghman. Read in Congress Dec. 18. Referred to Board of War.

    A. V, pt. II, 343

1780
DEC. 15

Washington, George. New Windsor. To [the President of] Congress [Philadelphia]. Maj. [Benjamin] Tallmadge's exploit; British reenforcements; urgency of recruiting; European politics; route of the post through Connecticut. Draft. 3 pp. In handwriting of Tench Tilghman. Read in Congress Dec. 22.   **A.** V, pt. II, 343

1780
Dec. 15

Continental Congress, President. Philadelphia. To [George] Washington [New Windsor]. Transmitting resolve and papers connected therewith. Letter-book copy. **C. C. 15**, 182

1780
Dec. 15

[Clinton, George.] Poughkeepsie. To [George Washington New Windsor]. Impress of flour for army. [Extract of letter.] 2 pp. In handwriting of David Humphreys. Enclosed in Washington to the President of Congress, 1780, Dec. 22. **C. C. 152**, 9, 419

1780
Dec. 16

Continental Congress, President. Philadelphia. To [George] Washington [New Windsor]. Transmitting resolve. Letter-book copy.
C. C. 15, 186

1780
Dec. 16

Board of War. [Philadelphia.] To [George] Washington [New Windsor]. Transmitting resolve of Congress. L. S. of Benjamin Stoddert. 1 p. Answered Dec. 24.* **Miscel.**

1780
Dec. 17

Washington, George. New Windsor. To [John] Sullivan [Philadelphia]. Promotions to general officerships; lack of system; case of New Jersey; brigadiers. Auto. draft signed. 6 pp.
P. II, 243
Printed: Writings of Washington (Ford) N. Y. 1891. 9, 63.

1780
Dec. 18

Sullivan, John. Philadelphia. To [George] Washington [New Windsor]. Dispute between Connecticut and Pennsylvania over the garrison at Wyoming. A. L. S. 1 p. **44**, 217

1780
Dec. 19

Washington, George. New Windsor. To the Board of War [Philadelphia]. Returns of the various troops of horse. Draft. 1 p. In handwriting of Tench Tilghman. **A. V, pt. II**, 347

1780
Dec. 19

Batterman, George. Boston. Deposition respecting treatment received from British; prison-ships. Sworn to before S. Holten. Contemporary copy. 3 pp. Enclosed in President of Congress to Washington. 1781, Jan. 12. **96**, 39

1780
Dec. 20

Washington, G[eorge]. To the President of Congress [Philadelphia]. Promotions of officers; system, seniority etc. Auto. draft signed. 6 pp. Read in Congress Jan. 1, 1781. Referred to Sullivan, Varnum, and Bland. Reported May [Mar.] 9. Acted on May [Mar.] 25. **A. V, pt. II**, 349
Printed: Writings of Washington (Ford) N. Y. 1891. 9, 68.

1780
DEC. 21

Continental Congress, President. Philadelphia. To [George] Washington [New Windsor]. Leave of absence of Brig. Gen. John Stark. Letter-book copy.   C. C. 15, 190

1780
DEC. 22

Washington, George. New Windsor. To the President of Congress [Philadelphia]. Lack of flour and energy of Gov. [George] Clinton. Draft. 2 pp. In handwriting of Tench Tilghman. Read in Congress, Dec. 24. Referred to Floyd, Root, Clymer, Clark, and Adams.   A. V, pt. II, 355

1780
DEC. 23

Board of War. [Philadelphia.] To [the President of Congress, Philadelphia]. Case of four Swedish officers. Contemporary copy. 2 pp. Read in Congress, Jan. 1, 1781. Referred to Board of War. Enclosed in Board of War to Washington, 1781, Jan. 2.   97, 267

1780
DEC. 24

Washington, George. New Windsor. To the Board of War [Philadelphia]. Lt. Col. [Thomas] Forrest [to command Artificers at Carlisle]. Draft. 1 p. In handwriting of Tench Tilghman.
     A. V, pt. II, 357

1780
DEC. 26

W[ashingto]n, G[eorge]. New Windsor. To James Duane [Philadelphia]. Increase of powers of Congress; mode of obtaining supplies; promotions; cases of [Brig.] Gen. [Henry] Knox and Lt. Col. [William Stephens] Smith. Auto. draft signed. 3 pp.
     P. II, 357

Printed in part: Writings of Washington (Ford) N. Y. 1891. 9, 75.

1780
DEC. 26

Skinner, Abraham. "Commissary of Prisoners Office." [Elizabeth? New Jersey.] To Thomas Bradford [Philadelphia]. Exchanges; American prisoners sent to England; treatment on prison ships. Contemporary copy. 2 pp. Enclosed in President of Congress to Washington, 1781, Jan. 6.
     97, 285

1780
DEC. 27

Washington, George. New Windsor. To the President of Congress [Philadelphia]. Sailing of a fleet from New York. Draft. 1 p. In handwriting of Tench Tilghman. Read in Congress, Jan. 1, 1781.   A. V, pt. II, 359

1780
DEC. 28

Continental Congress, President. Philadelphia. To [George] Washington. Transmitting resolve. Letter-book copy.   C. C. 15, 191

1780
DEC. 28

Lyman, George and Others. "Provost Condemned Room" [New York]. To Congress. Harsh treatment received from British; prayer for relief. Contemporary copy of D. S.: George Lyman, James Hallet, Peter Foster, Thomas Selus, Thomas Clark, Daniel Lawrence and Simon Tylor. 2 pp. Enclosed in President of Congress to Washington, 1781, Jan. 6. **97, 284**

1780
DEC. 29

Continental Congress, Resolve. Exchange of prisoners. D. S. of Charles Thomson. 1 p. Enclosed in President of Congress to Washington, 1781, Jan. 2. **97, 277**

1780
DEC. 29

Board of War. [Philadelphia.] To the President of Congress [Philadelphia]. Artificers ordered to Carlisle [Pennsylvania]; affairs at Springfield [Massachusetts]; preparations for the campaign; need of money. Contemporary copy. 2 pp. In handwriting of Joseph Carleton. Enclosed in Board of War to Washington, 1781, Mar. 3. **96, 103**

1780
DEC. 30

Sproat, David. New York. To Capt. —— Griffin. Exchange of prisoners. Contemporary copy. 1 p. Enclosed in President of Congress to Washington, 1781, Jan. 6. **97, 283**

1781
JAN. 1

Continental Congress, Resolves. British intentions against the south; Lt. Col. William [Stephens] Smith; arrangement of officers, prisoners of enemy. D. S. of Charles Thomson. 1 p. Enclosed in President of Congress to Washington, 1781, Jan. 2. **97, 282**

1781
JAN. 2

Washington, George. New Windsor. To the President of Congress [Philadelphia]. Retirement of [Brig.] Gen. [John] Stark and resignation of Col. [Alexander] Scammell as Adjutant General; enemy's southern expedition under command of Arnold. Draft. 2 pp. In handwriting of Tench Tilghman. Read in Congress, Jan. 8.

A. V, pt. II, 361

Printed: Writings of Washington (Ford) N. Y. 1891. 9, 85.

1781
JAN. 2-3

Washington, G[eorge]. [New Windsor.] Amount of the National debt. Money; taxes; supplies; war expenses; estimate of expense for campaign of 1781. "Taken from Mr. Duane's estimates, &c., furnished Colo. Jno. Laurens." A. D. S. 3 pp.

A. V, pt. II, 385

1781
JAN. 2

Continental Congress, President. Philadelphia. To [George] Washington [New Windsor]. Transmitting resolves and other papers; cooperation with French in southern movement. L. S. of Samuel Huntington. 2 pp. Answered Jan. 15.*
97, 280

1781
JAN. 2

Continental Congress, Resolve. Completion of Armand's corps by volunteers from the line. D. S. of Charles Thomson. 1 p. Enclosed in President of Congress to Washington, 1781, Jan. 6. 97, 293

1781
JAN. 2

Continental Congress, Resolve. Completion of Armand's corps from line of army. A. L. S. of Charles Thomson. 1 p. Transmitted to Washington.
53, 22

1781
JAN. 2

Board of War. [Philadelphia.] To [George] Washington [New Windsor]. Transmitting papers. A. L. S. of Benjamin Stoddert. 1 p. Answered Jan. 10.*
97, 269

Dated in error, 1780.

1781
JAN. 2

Board of War. Proceedings. Case of four Swedish officers. A. D. S. of Benjamin Stoddert. 1 p. Enclosed in Board of War to Washington, 1781, Jan. 2. 97, 271

1781
JAN. 2

Sullivan, John. Philadelphia. To [George] Washington [New Windsor]. System of promotion in army; [Lt.] Col. [William Stephens] Smith; news from the South. A. L. S. 2 pp. 45, 8

1781
JAN. 2

Wayne, Anthony. Mount Kimball [New Jersey]. Negotiations with mutineers; conference, grievances, etc., and a copy of the Propositions of Committee of Sergeants, Jan. 4. [Same as C. C. 152, 9, 443.] Endorsed: "Genl. Wayne's first orders." Contemporary copy. 2 pp. In handwriting of and attested by Richard Butler. Enclosed in Wayne, Butler and Stewart to the President of Congress, 1781, Jan. 8. C. C. 152, 9, 477

1780
JAN. 3

Washington, George. New Windsor. To Brig. Gen. [Anthony] Wayne. Mutiny of the Pennsylvania line; advice as to action, etc. Contemporary copy. 3 pp. In handwriting of Henry Latimer. Enclosed in Wayne, Butler and Stewart to the President of Congress, 1781, Jan. 8.
C. C. 152, 9, 505

[1781]
[JAN. 3?]

[Washington, George.] [New Windsor.] Extracts and substance of papers of John Laurens. Commission; Instructions of Dec. 23 & 27, 1780; Instructions to [Benjamin] Franklin Nov. 28, 1780; letters to King of France Nov. 22 & Dec. 23, 1780; estimate of supplies wanted. A. D. 4 pp.
A. V, pt. II, 389

1781
JAN. 3

Continental Congress, Order. Resignation of Dr. William Shippen [jr]. D. S. of Charles Thomson. 1 p. Enclosed in President of Congress to Washington, 1781, Jan. 6. 97, 291

1781
JAN. 4

Continental Congress, Order. To the Board of War. Warrants for the Invalid and Artificers regiments. Contemporary copy. 1 p. Transmitted to Washington. Published in Genl. Orders, Jan. 16. 96, 35

[1781]
[JAN. 4]

Pennsylvania, Troops. Committee of Sergeants. [Princeton, New Jersey]. Propositions [to Brig. Gen. Anthony Wayne]. Demands of mutineers for pay and clothing and discharges to which they are entitled. Contemporary copy. 2 pp. Transmitted to Congress. C. C. 152, 9, 443

1781
JAN. 4

Pennsylvania, Troops, Committee of Sergeants. Princeton. To [Brig.] Gen. [Anthony] Wayne [Princeton]. Men entitled to discharge. Contemporary copy. 1 p. In handwriting of and attested by Benjamin Fishbourn. Enclosed in Wayne, Butler and Stewart to the President of Congress, 1781, Jan. 8. C. C. 152, 9, 481

1781
JAN. 4

St. Clair, Arthur. Trenton [New Jersey]. To the President of Congress, Philadelphia. March of the mutineers toward Philadelphia; efforts to negotiate with them. A. L. S. 3 pp. Read in Congress, Jan 6. C. C. 152, 9, 439

1781
JAN. 4

Wayne, Anthony. Princeton. To the Sergeants of the Pennsylvania Line [Princeton]. Answer to propositions of the Serjeants. Contemporary copy. 2 pp. Transmitted to Congress.
C. C. 152, 9, 445

1781
JAN. 4

Wayne, Anthony. Princeton. To Committee of Sergeants [Princeton]. Right to discharges. (2 copies of same.)

Sergeants to Wayne. Negotiations and threats. Contemporary copies. 3 pp. In handwriting of and attested by Benjamin Fishbourn. Enclosed in Wayne, Butler and Stewart to the President of Congress, 1781, Jan. 8.   C. C. 152, 9, 483

1781
JAN. 4

Wayne, Anthony; Richard. Butler and Walter Stewart. [Princeton.] To [Prest. Joseph Reed, Trenton?] Revolt of the Pennsylvania line; disposition of troops, situation of affairs. Contemporary copy. 2 pp. In handwriting of Henry Latimer? Enclosed in Wayne, Butler and Stewart to the President of Congress, 1781, Jan. 8.
C. C. 152, 9, 501

1781
JAN. 4

Wayne, Anthony; Richard Butler and Walter Stewart. Princeton. To [George] Washington [New Windsor]. The mutiny situation. Contemporary copy. 2 pp. In handwriting of Henry Latimer?   C. C. 152, 9, 509

1781
JAN. 5

Washington, George. New Windsor. To the Board of War [Philadelphia]. Transmitting return of Col. [Elisha] Sheldon's regiment of cavalry. Draft. 1 p. In handwriting of Tench Tilghman.   A. V, pt. II, 363

1781
JAN. 5

Washington, George. New Windsor. Circular letter to Governors of Connecticut, Rhode Island, Massachusetts and New Hampshire. Mutiny of the Pennsylvania troops; distresses and hardships of army; need of money and supplies. Contemporary copy. 3 pp. In handwriting of Tench Tilghman. Enclosed in Washington to the President of Congress, 1781, Jan. 6.
C. C. 152, 9, 435
Printed: Writings of Washington (Ford) N. Y. 1891. 9, 91.

1781
JAN. 5

Continental Congress, Resolves. British treatment of prisoners; retaliation authorized. D. S. of Charles Thomson. 2 pp. Enclosed in President of Congress to Washington, 1781, Jan. 6.   97, 289

1781
JAN. 6

Washington, George. New Windsor. To the President of Congress [Philadelphia]. Revolt of the Pennsylvania line. Draft. 3 pp. In handwriting of Tench Tilghman. Read in Congress, Jan. 15.
A. V, pt. II, 365
Printed: Writings of Washington (Ford) N. Y. 1891. 9, 93.

Head Quarters Newburgh
Feb'y 12/1783

Gentlemen

I do inclose You a Letter & Memorial
of the 13th of January last from B. Gen'l Hazen
in behalf of himself & 24 Officers of his
Regiment remonstrating generally on
the Want of System & some general esta-
-blished Rules in the Proceedings of Courts
Martial, by which Means the innocent
have been at some Times injured and the
guilty escaped the Punishment due to their
Crimes; And then pointing out Cases in
which they conceive that for Want of some
certain uniform Rules, the Proceedings of
General Courts Martial have on different
Occasions been diametrically opposite, to
the Exclusion of themselves from Redress
for supposed Injuries received from Major
Reid; And praying that for some supposed Misconduct
& Partiallity in Mr Edwards the Judge Advocate
the Proceedings of a late Gen'l Court Martial of

WRITING OF RICHARD VARICK.

1781
JAN. 6

Continental Congress, President. Philadelphia. To [George] Washington [New Windsor]. Correspondence relating to prisoners; retaliation; transmitting resolves. L. S. of Samuel Huntington. 2 pp. Answered Jan. 15.* 97, 287

1781
JAN. 6

Pennsylvania, Troops. Committee of Sergeants. [Princeton] To [Brig.] Gen. [Anthony] Wayne [Princeton]. Procuring of clothing. Contemporary copy. 1 p. In handwriting of and attested by Benjamin Fishbourn. Enclosed in Wayne, Butler and Stewart to the President of Congress, 1781, Jan. 8. C. C. 152, 9, 487

1781
JAN. 6

Pennsylvania, Troops. Committee of Sergeants. [Princeton] To [Brig.] Gen. [Anthony] Wayne [Princeton]. Refusal to agree to propositions. Contemporary copy. 1 p. In handwriting of and attested by Henry Latimer. Enclosed in Wayne, Butler and Stewart to the President of Congress, 1781, Jan. 8. C. C. 152, 9, 493

1781
JAN. 6

Pennsylvania, Troops. Committee of Sergeants. [Princeton.] To [Brig.] Gen. [Anthony] Wayne [Princeton]. Request for orders issued at Mount Kimball. Contemporary copy. 1 p. In handwriting of and attested by Henry Latimer. Enclosed in Wayne, Butler and Stewart to the President of Congress, 1781, Jan. 8.
C. C. 152, 9, 495

1781
JAN. 6

[Wayne, Anthony.] Princeton. To [the Committee of Sergeants, Princeton]. Compliance with propositions; supply of clothing. Contemporary copy. 1 p. In handwriting of Benjamin Fishbourn. Enclosed in Wayne, Butler and Stewart to the President of Congress, 1781, Jan. 8.
C. C. 152, 9, 489

1781
JAN. 6

Wayne, Anthony. Princeton. To [Prest. Joseph Reed, Trenton]. The situation. L. S. marked "Copy." 1 p. In handwriting of Benjamin Fishbourn. Enclosed in Wayne, Butler and Stewart to the President of Congress, 1781, Jan. 8.
C. C. 152, 9, 491

1781
JAN. 7

Continental Congress, Committee of Conference with Pennsylvania Executive. Trenton. To [George] Washington [New Windsor]. Surrender of Brit-

ish emissaries by the mutineers. L. S. of John
Sullivan. 1 p. In handwriting of Samuel John
Atlee.   **45, 56**
Committee: Sullivan, Matthews and Witherspoon.

1781
JAN. 7
Pennsylvania, Commissioners to treat with Pennsylvania
Line. Princeton. Proposals of terms granted by
the State to the mutineers; enlistments, bounty,
clothing. Broadside issued under authority of
Joseph Reed and James Potter. 1 p. Enclosed
in Committee to Washington, 1781, Jan. 15.
                       45, 173

1781
JAN. 7
St. Clair, Arthur. Morristown. To the President of Congress, [Philadelphia]. Situation and aspect of the
mutiny; conference with sergeants. A. L. S.
4 pp. Read in Congress, Jan. 11.
                 C. C.   **152, 9, 451**

1781
JAN. 7
Witherspoon, John. Trenton. To [the President of Congress, Philadelphia]. Situation as regards the
mutiny; seizure of British Emissaries. A. L. S.
1 p. Read in Congress, Jan. 8.
                 C. C.   **152, 9, 447**

1781
JAN. 8
Continental Congress, Resolve. States quotas of money to be
furnished American prisoners. D. S. of Charles
Thomson. 1 p. Enclosed in President of Con-
gress to Washington, 1781, Jan. 12.   **96, 40**

1781
JAN. 8
Continental Congress, Resolve. Election of Brig. Gen.
[Edward] Hand as Adjutant General. D. S. of
Charles Thomson. 1 p. Enclosed in President of
Congress to Washington, 1781, Jan. 12.   **96, 41**

1781
JAN. 8
Continental Congress, Committee of Conference with Pennsylvania Executive. Trenton. Resolves. Boun-
ties of soldiers enlisted for the war; discharges;
settlement of grievances as to pay, clothing;
delivery of the British emissaries; pardons. A. D.
of John Witherspoon. 2 pp. Enclosed in Committee to Washington, 1781, Jan. 9.   **45, 96**

1781
JAN. 8
Livingston, Robert R. Clermont [New York]. To [George
Washington, New Windsor]. Discontent in New
York state; scarcity of money; prejudice of Penn-
sylvania; New York's inability to furnish supplies;
invasion from Canada; representation of situation
and its dangers to Congress. A. L. S. 11 pp.
                       45, 74

1781
JAN. 8

Pennsylvania, Troops. Committee of Sergeants. [Princeton.] To [Brig. Gen. Anthony Wayne, Princeton]. Agreements and understandings of [Gov. Joseph Reed's] proposals. Contemporary copy. 2 pp. In handwriting of John Sullivan. Enclosed in Wayne, Butler and Stewart to the President of Congress, 1781, Jan. 8.

C. C.   152, 9, 497

1781
JAN. 8

Reed, Joseph. Maidenhead [New Jersey.] To the Committee of Congress [Trenton]. Progress of the mutiny; [Brig.] Gen. [Anthony] Wayne. Contemporary copy. 2 pp. In handwriting of John Sullivan. Transmitted to Congress.

C. C.   152, 9, 459

1781
JAN. 8

Sullivan, John. Trenton. To the President of Congress, [Philadelphia.] Aspect of the mutiny; demands of mutineers; British emissaries. A. L. S. 2 pp. Read in Congress, Jan. 10.

C. C.   152, 9, 455

1781
JAN. 8

Wayne, Anthony; Richard Butler and Walter Stewart. Princeton. To the President of Congress [Philadelphia]. Report of mutiny; disposition of soldiery; British emissaries. L. S. 2 pp. Read in Congress, Jan. 10.   C. C.   152, 9, 473

1781
JAN. 9

Continental Congress, Committee of Conference with Pennsylvania Executive. Trenton. To [George] Washington [New Windsor]. Transmitting papers relating to negotiations with the Pennsylvania mutineers. A. L. S.   1 p.   45, 94

1781
JAN. 9

Reed, Joseph. [Princeton.] To [the Committee of Congress, Trenton]. Negotiations with the mutineers. Contemporary copy. 2 pp. In handwriting of John Mathews. Enclosed in Committee to Washington, 1781, Jan. 9.   45, 95

1781
JAN. 9

Sullivan, John. Trenton. To the President of Congress [Philadelphia]. Arrival of mutineers at Trenton. A. L. S.   1 p.   Read in Congress, Jan. 10.

C. C.   152, 9, 461

1781
JAN. 10

Washington, George. New Windsor. To the Board of War [Philadelphia]. Leather caps for army; Swedish officers. Draft. 2 pp. In handwriting of Tench Tilghman.   A.   V, pt. II, 369

1781
JAN. 10   Continental Congress, Committee of Conference with Penn-
           sylvania Executive. Near Trenton. To [George]
           Washington [New Windsor]. Negotiations with
           mutineers; execution of British spies. L. S. of
           John Sullivan and partly in his handwriting.
           1 p.   45, 99

1781
JAN. 10   Sullivan, John. Trenton. To the President of Congress
           [Philadelphia]. Conference of mutineers with
           President Joseph Reed. A. L. S. 1 p. Read
           in Congress, Jan. 11.   C. C. 152, 9, 465

1781
JAN. 11   Sullivan, John. Trenton. To the President of Congress
           [Philadelphia]. Trial and conviction of British
           emissaries; approaching finish of the mutiny.
           A. L. S. 1 p. Read in Congress, Jan. 12.
                                          C. C. 152, 9, 469

1781
JAN. 12   Washington, George. New Windsor. To the Board of
           War [Philadelphia]. Officers for Armand's
           Corps. Draft. 1 p. In handwriting of Alex-
           ander Hamilton.   A. V, pt. II, 371

1781
JAN. 12   Continental Congress, President. Philadelphia. To
           [George] Washington [West Point]. Transmit-
           ting resolves and papers respecting British treat-
           ment of prisoners. L. S. of Samuel Huntington.
           2 pp. Answered Jan. 23.*   96, 36

1781
JAN. 12   Continental Congress, Resolves. Establishing pay in the
           commissary department and artillery and ord-
           nance; aides-de-camp, paymasters, etc. D. S. of
           Charles Thomson. 3 pp. Enclosed in President
           of Congress to Washington, 1781, Jan. 13.   96, 49

1781
JAN. 13   Continental Congress, President. Philadelphia. To
           [George] Washington [West Point?]. Establish-
           ment of pay of certain officers. L. S. of Samuel
           Huntington. 1 p. Answered Jan. 23.*
                                                        96, 42

1781
JAN. 13   Continental Congress, Committee of Conference with Penn-
           sylvania Executive. Trenton. To [George]
           Washington [New Windsor]. Execution of
           British spies; adjusting grievances of Pennsyl-
           vania troops. A. L. S. of John Sullivan. 1 p.
                                                        45, 146
           Committee: Sullivan, Witherspoon and Mathews.

1781
JAN. 15   Washington, G[eorge]. New Windsor. To the President
           of Congress [Philadelphia]. Expediency of mov-
           ing French troops to Virginia; lack of supplies;

mutiny of Pennsylvania troops. Auto. draft signed. 3 pp. Read in Congress, Jan. 23.

A. V, pt. II, 373

Printed: Writings of Washington (Ford) N. Y. 1891. 9, 110.

1781
JAN. 15

Washington, George. New Windsor. To [John] Laurens [New Windsor]. State of affairs; aid from France; money and men; credit and resources of America. Draft. 7 pp. In handwriting of Alexander Hamilton. **A. V, pt. II, 377**

1781
JAN. 15

Continental Congress, Circular letter to the States. Finances; progress of states in collecting supplies; returns; pay of army; collection of taxes; cooperation with French; specie and a foreign loan. Contemporary copy. 4 pp. Enclosed in President of Congress to Washington, 1781, Jan. 16. **96, 46**

[1781]
[JAN. 15]

Continental Congress, Estimate of sums to be furnished by the several states. Apportioned by states. Contemporary copy. 1 p. Enclosed in Congress, Circular to the States 1781, Jan. 15. **96, 48**

1781
JAN. 15

Continental Congress, Committee of Conference with Pennsylvania Executive. Trenton. To [George] Washington [New Windsor]. Settlement of matters with Pennsylvania troops; execution of the British spies; terms granted by Pennsylvania; authority of the Board of Sergeants. L. S. of John Sullivan. 1 p. **45, 171**

1781
JAN. 16

Washington, George. New Windsor. To John Sullivan [Philadelphia]. Mutiny of the Pennsylvania line; distress of soldiers; pay. Draft. 2 pp. In hand-writing of David Humphreys. **A. V, pt. II, 393**

1781
JAN. 16

Continental Congress, President. Philadelphia. To [George] Washington [New Windsor]. Circular to the States; funds; British in the James River. L. S. of Samuel Huntington. 2 pp. Answered Jan. 23.* **96, 45**

1781
JAN. 16

Knox, H[enry]. Boston. To [John] Lowell [Boston]. Grievances of the Massachusetts troops; pay, clothing; bounty and hard money. Contemporary copy. 3 pp. In handwriting of George Lewis. Enclosed in Washington to the President of Congress, 1781, Feb. 13.

C. C. 152, 9, 557

1781
JAN. 16
Massachusetts, House of Representatives [Boston]. Resolves reimbursing Massachusetts soldiers for stoppages; bounties, gratuities, hard money, clothing. Contemporary copy. 3 pp. In handwriting of George Lewis? Enclosed in Washington to the President of Congress, 1781, Feb. 13.
C. C. 152, 9, 561

1781
JAN. 17
Continental Congress, Resolves. Electing Dr. John Cochran, Director of Military Hospital and John Pierce, Paymaster General; regulations governing the hospital department, half-pay. D. S. of Charles Thomson. 3 pp. Enclosed in President of Congress to Washington, 1781, Jan. 18.
96, 53

1781
JAN. 18
Continental Congress, President. Philadelphia. To [George] Washington [New Windsor]. Transmitting resolves. L. S. of Samuel Huntington. 1 p. Answered Feb. 13.* 96, 52

1781
JAN. 19
Board of War. [Philadelphia.] Report recommending Lt. Col. [Jean Baptiste] Ternant to command in Armand's Legion. Contemporary extract. 1 p. Enclosed in President of Congress to Washington, 1781, Jan. 27. 96, 66

1781
JAN. 21
Washington, George. New Windsor. To [John Sullivan, Philadelphia]. Mutiny of the New Jersey troops. Draft. 1 p. In handwriting of Alexander Hamilton. Endorsed: "To General Sullivan or Committee of Congress." A. V, pt. II, 395

1781
JAN. 23
Washington, George. New Windsor. To the President of Congress [Philadelphia]. Revolt of the Jersey regiments; need of money, provisions and forage. Draft. 2 pp. In handwriting of Alexander Hamilton. Read in Congress Jan. 29.
A. V, pt. II, 397

1781
JAN. 23
Board of War. [Philadelphia.] To [George Washington, New Windsor]. Return of officers remaining in service and those retired. A. L. S. of Benjamin Stoddert. 1 p. Answered Feb. 19.* 96, 55

1781
JAN. 23
Continental Congress, Resolve. Equipment for Col. Armand's legion; remounts; Lt. Col. [Jean Baptiste] Ternant's appointment. D. S. of Charles Thomson. 2 pp. Enclosed in President of Congress to Washington, 1781, Jan. 27.
96, 63

1781
JAN. 24

W[ashingto]n, G[eorge]. New Windsor. To the President of Congress [Philadelphia]. Introducing Comte de Charlus. Auto. draft signed.

———. To same. Introducing Comte de Dillon. Auto. draft.

———. To same. Introducing Mons. Dumat [Comte de Damas?]. Auto. draft. 3 pp.

P. II, 267

1781
JAN. 24

Continental Congress, President. Philadelphia. To [George] Washington. [New Windsor]. Approving measures respecting mutiny of the Pennsylvania line and removal of French troops. L. S. of Samuel Huntington. 1 p. Answered Feb. 13.*

96, 56

1781
JAN. 25

Washington, George. New Windsor. To the officer commanding the British fleet in New York harbor [Capt. George Dawson]. Treatment of American prisoners on the prison ship [*Jersey*]; inspection. Transcript. Enclosed in Washington to the President of Congress, 1781, Feb. 13.

C. C.   169, 8, 48

Printed: Writings of Washington (Ford) N. Y. 1891. 9, 119.

1781
JAN. 25

Hull, William. Crompond [New York]. To Maj. Gen. [Samuel Holden] Parsons [Highlands]. Account of enterprize against Morrisania [New York]. Contemporary copy. 8 pp. In handwriting of David Humphreys. Enclosed in Washington to the President of Congress, 1781, Jan. 31.

C. C.   152, 9, 525

1781
JAN. 25

Lee, Henry, jr. Sampit River [North Carolina]. Report of enterprize against Georgetown. Contemporary copy. 1 p. Enclosed in President of Congress to Washington, 1781, Feb. 21.

95, 93.

1781
JAN. 25

Parsons, Samuel Holden. Highlands. To Maj. Gen. [William] Heath [Highlands]. Account of expedition against Morrisania. Contemporary copy. 6 pp. In handwriting of David Humphreys. Enclosed in Washington to the President of Congress, 1781, Jan. 31.

C. C.   152, 9, 533

1781
JAN. 26

Continental Congress, Resolve. Ration allowance; additional pay of aides-de-camp and others. D. S. of Charles Thomson. Enclosed in President of Congress to Washington, 1781, Jan. 27.

96, 62

1781
JAN. 27

Continental Congress, President. Philadelphia. To [George] Washington [New Windsor]. Transmitting resolves and papers; Armand's corps; additional pay. L. S. 2 pp. Answered Feb. 13.*

          96, 60

1781
JAN. 27

Continental Congress, Order. On petition of George Wright and others. D. S. of Charles Thomson. 1 p. Enclosed in President of Congress to Washington, 1781, Jan. 27.   **96, 58**

1781
JAN. 27

Howe, Robert. Ringwood [New Jersey]. To [George Washington, New Windsor]. Report of suppression of revolt of the Jersey troops. Contemporary copy. 4 pp. In handwriting of Alexander Hamilton. Enclosed in Washington to the President of Congress, 1781, Jan. 23. **C. C.** **152, 9, 521**

1781
JAN. 29

Duane, James. Philadelphia. To [George] Washington [New Windsor]. Clothing for army; important measures before Congress; centralization of power of government; distresses of army and the Pennsylvania mutiny; Virginia's cession of western lands and Maryland's endorsement of the Confederation; public credit; political situation and news from the South. A. L. S. 3 pp. **46, 15**

1781
JAN. 29

Rochambeau, Comte de. Newport [Rhode Island]. To [George] Washington [New Windsor]. Effect of storm; naval arrangements. Transcript. Enclosed in Washington to the President of Congress, 1781, Feb. 3. **C. C.** **169, 8, 36**

1781
JAN. 29

Sullivan, John. Philadelphia. To [George] Washington [New Windsor]. Disbanding the Pennsylvania Line; revolt of the New Jersey troops; the political outlook; new loan from individuals; paper money; prospects; late disturbances among the troops. A. L. S. 3 pp.   **46, 10**

1781
JAN. 31

Washington, George. New Windsor. To [the President of Congress, Philadelphia]. Suppression of the Jersey revolt. [Maj.] Gen. [Samuel Holden] Parsons's exploit [at Morrisania, New York]. Draft. 1 p. In handwriting of Alexander Hamilton. Read in Congress, Feb. 5. **A. V, pt. II, 399**

1781
JAN. 31

Washington, George. New Windsor. To the Board of War [Philadelphia]. Remount for the dragoons. Draft. 1 p. In handwriting of David Humphreys.   **A. V, pt. II, 401**

1781
JAN. 31

Greene, Nathanael. Sherard's Ford, Catawba River [North Carolina]. To [the President of Congress, Philadelphia]. The military situation; militia; strength of enemy; supplies. Contemporary copy. 4 pp. Enclosed in President of Congress to Washington 1781, Feb. 21. **96, 92**

1781
JAN. 31

North and South Carolina, Officers. Resolutions requesting changes in uniform. Contemporary copy. 1 p. Enclosed in Board of War to Washington, 1781, May 14. **96, 258**

[1781]
[JAN.]

[Clinton, Sir Henry] [New York.] To the Pennsylvania troops. Offer of British protection, pay etc. Contemporary copy. 1 p. In handwriting of and attested by John Witherspoon. Transmitted to Congress. **C. C. 152, 9, 449**

[1781]
[JAN.]

Rhode Island. Memorandum of money ordered paid to the Rhode Island troops; depreciation. Contemporary copy. 2 pp. In handwriting of Tench Tilghman. Enclosed in Washington to the President of Congress, 1781, Feb. 13.
C. C. 152, 9, 565

1781
FEB. 1

Continental Congress, Resolve. Discontinuance of allowance to officers on command. D. S. of Charles Thomson. 1 p. Transmitted to Washington. Published in Genl. Orders, Feb. 12. **96, 67**

1781
FEB. 2

Continental Congress, President. Philadelphia. To [George] Washington [New Windsor]. Transmitting resolve. Letter-book copy.
C. C. 15, 226

1781
FEB. 2

Dawson, G[eorge]. [H. M. S.] *Iris,* off New York. To [George] Washington [New Windsor]. Treatment of American prisoners on the prison-ship [*Jersey*]. Transcript. Enclosed in Washington to the President of Congress, 1781, Feb. 13.
C. C. 169, 8, 50

1781
FEB. 2

"Jersey" [Prison-ship.] New York harbor. Report of British Board of Inquiry as to treatment of American prisoners thereon. Testimony of prisoners; findings. Transcript. Enclosed in Washington to the President of Congress, 1781, Feb. 13. **C. C. 169, 8, 50.**

1781
FEB. 2

Nash, A[bner]. Halifax [North Carolina]. To [the President of Congress, Philadelphia]. British in North Carolina; want of arms and military supplies; successes of militia and spirit of people. Contemporary copy. 2 pp. Read in Congress, Feb. 20. Enclosed in President of Congress to Washington, 1781, Feb. 20. 96, 83

1781
FEB. 3

Washington, George. New Windsor. To [the President of Congress, Philadelphia]. Corporal punishment in the army; furloughs and discharges. Draft. 5 pp. In handwriting of Alexander Hamilton. Referred, Feb. 9, to J. Jones, McDougall and Sullivan. Reported, June 15. Acted on June 16. A. V, pt. II, 407
Printed: Writings of Washington (Ford) N. Y. 1891. 9, 126.

[1781]
[FEB. 3]

Continental Army. Form of honorable discharge. Draft. 1 p. In handwriting of Alexander Hamilton. Enclosed in Washington to the President of Congress 1781, Feb. 3. A. V, pt. II, 403

[1781]
[FEB. 3]

Continental Army. Form of furlough. Draft. 1 p. In handwriting of Alexander Hamilton. Enclosed in Washington to the President of Congress 1781, Feb. 3. A. V, pt. II, 405

1781
FEB. 4

W[ashingto]n, G[eorge]. New Windsor. To [John] Sullivan [Philadelphia]. [Lt.] Col. [Alexander] Hamilton as a financier; mismanagement; finance; traffic with enemy. Auto. draft signed. 4 pp.
P. II, 283
Printed: Writings of Washington (Ford) N. Y. 1891. 9, 131.

1781
FEB. 5

Continental Congress, Order. Publication of report of enterprise against Morrisania and thanks of Congress to Maj. Gen. [Samuel Holden] Parsons. D. S. of Charles Thomson. 1 p. Enclosed in President of Congress to Washington, 1781, Feb. 9. 96, 73

1781
FEB. 6

Pennsylvania, Officers of the Line. Philadelphia. Memorial to [George] Washington [New Windsor]. Services in 1776 and disarrangement in 1779; resolves of Congress of Jan. 1, 1781 and injury sustained thereby. D. S. of John Richardson, Danl. Brodhead, John Lawrence, John Morgan, John Helm, Danl. Topham, Robert Caldwell, Bernard Ward, Matths. Weiderman. 1 p. Enclosed in Atlee to Washington, 1781, Feb. 10. 46, 151

1781
FEB. 7

Germain to Sir Henry Clinton. See: President of Congress to Washington, 1781, July 17.

1781
FEB. 7

Knox, H[enry]. New Windsor. To [George] Washington [New Windsor]. Report of visit to New England States in effort to raise recruits. Contemporary copy. 4 pp. Enclosed in Washington to the President of Congress, 1781, Feb. 13.
C. C. 152, 9, 553

1781
FEB. 8

Jefferson, Thomas. Richmond. To [the President of Congress, Philadelphia]. British in Cape Fear River; want of arms. Contemporary copy. 1 p. Enclosed in President of Congress to Washington, 1781, Feb. 20.
95, 82

1781
FEB. 9

Washington, George. New Windsor. To [the President of Congress, Philadelphia] Col. [Peter] Gansevoort's claim to command at Fort Schuyler. Draft. 1 p. In handwriting of Alexander Hamilton.
A. V, pt. II, 413

1781
FEB. 9

Continental Congress, President. Philadelphia. To [George] Washington [New Windsor]. British fleet at Gardiner's Bay [Long Island]; success at Cowpens; Chevalier de Chastellux and other Frenchmen. L. S. of Samuel Huntington. 1 p. Answered Feb. 17.*
96, 68

1781
FEB. 9

Continental Congress, President. Philadelphia. To [George] Washington [New Windsor]. Delay in transmitting thanks to Maj. Gen. [Samuel Holden] Parsons. Answered Feb. 17.* L. S. of Samuel Huntington. 1 p.
96, 71

[1781]
[FEB. 9?]

Sharpe, William [Philadelphia]. To [George] Washington [New Windsor]. Description of country in vicinity of the Cowpens. A. L. S. 1 p. Enclosed in President of Congress to Washington, 1781, Feb. 9.
96, 70

1781
FEB. 10

Atlee, Samuel John. Philadelphia. To [George] Washington [New Windsor]. Address of officers who were prisoners in 1776; disarrangement and half-pay. A. L. S. 2 pp.
46, 150

1781
FEB. 12

Jefferson, Thomas. Richmond. To the President of Congress [Philadelphia]. British in Virginia; affairs in the Carolinas. Contemporary copy. 1 p. Enclosed in President of Congress to Washington, 1781, Feb. 20.
96, 81

1781
FEB. 13

Washington, George. New Windsor. To [the President of Congress, Philadelphia]. Approbation of Congress; civilians prisoners of enemy; recruiting

measures in the Eastern States; conference with
Rochambeau; British treatment of prisoners
Draft. 3 pp. In handwriting of Tench Tilghman. Read in Congress, Feb. 19. Part referred
to Board of Admiralty. A. V, pt. II, 415

1781
FEB. 13

Washington, George. New Windsor. To the President
of Congress [Philadelphia]. Mistake in transmitting letters. Draft. 1 p. In handwriting of
Tench Tilghman. A. V, pt. II, 419

1781
FEB. 13

Board of War. [Philadelphia.] To [George] Washington
[New Windsor]. Distress of British prisoners
through British neglect. A. L. S. of Richard
Peters. 1 p. Answered Feb. 19.* 96, 74

1781
FEB. 14

Washington, George. New Windsor. To John Mathews
[Philadelphia]. Completion of the Confederation;
Virginia's reliquishment of claim to Western lands.
Auto. draft signed. 2 pp. P. II, 287

1781
FEB. 14

Continental Congress, President. [Philadelphia.] To
[George] Washington [New Windsor]. British
at Portsmouth [Virginia] and in the Chesapeake
Bay. L. S. of Samuel Huntington. 1 p. Answered Feb. 26.* 96, 75

1781
FEB. 15

Mathews, John. Philadelphia. To [George] Washington
[New Windsor]. [Brig.] Gen. [Daniel] Morgan's
victory [at the Cowpens]; exchange of prisoners
in Southern Department. Recent copy. 1 p.
46, 184

1781
FEB. 17

Washington, George. New Windsor. To the President
of Congress [Philadelphia]. Col. [Daniel] Mor-
gan's victory in the South [Cowpens]; supplies
for an operation against New York. Draft. 2 pp.
In handwriting of Tench Tilghman. Read in
Congress, Feb. 26. Referred to Board of War.
A. V, pt. II, 421
Printed: Writings of Washington (Ford) N. Y. 1891. 9, 145.

1781
FEB. 17

Board of War. [Philadelphia.] To George Washington,
New Windsor. Food and clothing for friendly
Oneidas and Tuscaroras. A. L. S. of Richard
Peters. 2 pp. Answered Feb. 23.* 96, 77

1781
FEB. 17

Jefferson, Thomas. Richmond. To [the President of Congress, Philadelphia]. Greene and Cornwallis in
North Carolina; prisoners; British naval force in
Elizabeth River [Virginia]; expedition against
the Cherokees; reenforcements. Contemporary

copy. 3 pp. Enclosed in President of Congress to Washington 1781, Feb. 25.   **96, 97**

1781
FEB. 17
Knox, H[enry]. Near New Windsor. To [George] Washington [New Windsor]. Estimate of ordnance supplies necessary for an operation against New York. Transcript. Enclosed in Washington to the President of Congress, 1781, Feb. 17.
C. C. 169, 8, 55

1781
FEB. 19
Washington, George. New Windsor. To the Board of War [Philadelphia]. Arrangements of officers and minor matters. Draft. 3 pp. In handwriting of Tench Tilghman.   **A. V, pt. II, 423**

1781
FEB. 19
Washington, George. New Windsor. To the Board of War [Philadelphia]. Preparation of a battering train for a secret expedition. Draft. 1 p. In handwriting of Samuel Shaw. **A. V, pt. II, 427**

1781
FEB. 19
Washington, George. New Windsor. To James Duane [Philadelphia]. Changes made by Congress [establishment of Secretaries]; increased powers; the Confederacy and Virginia relinquishment of Western lands. Auto. draft signed. 2 pp.
P. II, 289

1781
FEB. 20
Washington, George. New Windsor. To Elbridge Gerry, Boston. [James] Lovell's embarrassing letter. Auto. draft. 1 p.   **P. II, 299**
Printed: Writings of Washington (Ford) N. Y. 1891. 9, 152.

1781
FEB. 20
Continental Congress, President. Philadelphia. To [George] Washington [New Windsor]. Transmitting resolves; Pennsylvania line ordered to the southward; French troops. L. S. of Samuel Huntington. 2 pp. Answered Feb. 26.* **96, 87**

1781
FEB. 20
Continental Congress, President. Philadelphia. To [George] Washington [New Windsor]. Conditions in North Carolina; aid of the French. L. S. of Samuel Huntington. 3 pp. Answered Feb. 26.*   **96, 79**

1781
FEB. 20
Continental Congress, Resolves. Troops to compose Southern Army; supplies and payment for same; provisions from contiguous states. D. S. of Charles Thomson. 4 pp. Enclosed in President of Congress to Washington, 1781, Feb. 20.   **96, 85**

1781
FEB. 21
Continental Congress, President. Philadelphia. To [George] Washington [New Windsor]. Intelli-

gence from [Maj.] Gen. [Nathanael] Greene.
L. S. of Samuel Huntington. 1 p. Answered
Feb. 27.*   96, 89

1781
FEB. 21

Jones, Joseph. Philadelphia. To [George Washington,
New Windsor]. Dr. John Lewis's parole; mili-
tary situation in the South; arrival of [Capt.
John] P[aul] Jones; Virginia and navigation of
the Mississippi; [Robert] Morris and the finances;
War office. A. L. S. 4 pp.   46, 107

1781
FEB. 23

Washington, George. New Windsor. To the Board of
War [Philadelphia]. Clothing and supplies for
Oneida Indians. Draft. 1 p. In handwriting
of Tench Tilghman.   **A.** V, pt. II, 429

1781
FEB. 25

Continental Congress, President. Philadelphia. To
[George] Washington [New Windsor]. Intelli-
gence from the Southward. L. S. of Samuel
Huntington. 2 pp. Answered Mar. 1.* **96, 95**

1781
FEB. 26

Washington, George. New Windsor. To [the President
of Congress, Philadelphia]. Situation in the
South; cooperation of the French; attempt
against Arnold. Draft. 3 pp. In handwriting
of Alexander Hamilton. Read in Congress, **Mar.**
2. Part referred to Board of Admiralty.
                          A. V, pt. II, 431
Printed: Writings of Washington (Ford) N. Y. 1891. 9, 168.

1781
FEB. 26

Washington, George. New Windsor. To [John Mathews,
Philadelphia]. Exchange of Southern prisoners.
Draft. 2 pp. In handwriting of Tench Tilgh-
man: **A.** V, pt. II, 435
Printed: Writings of Washington (Ford) N. Y. 1891. 9, 168.

1781
FEB. 26

Jefferson, Thomas. Richmond. To the President of Congress [Philadelphia]. Military situation in Virginia. Contemporary copy. 1 p. Enclosed in
President of Congress to Washington, 1781,
Mar. 5.   96, 108

1781
FEB. 27

Washington, George. New Windsor. To [the President
of Congress, Philadelphia]. Danger in the South;
equipping Col. [Stephen] Moylan's dragoons;
[Lt. Col. Henry Lee's] surprise of Georgetown.
Draft. 1 p. In handwriting of Tench Tilghman. Read in Congress, Mar. 5. Referred to
Board of War.   **A.** V, pt. II, 437

1781
FEB. 27

Jones, Joseph. Philadelphia. To [George Washington, New Windsor]. Cornwallis in the South; [Maj.] Gen. [Nathanael] Greene's ability; Maryland and the Confederation; British affairs in the South. A. L. S. 3 pp. **47, 21**

1781
FEB. 27

Sharpe, William. Philadelphia. To [George] Washington [New Windsor]. Cornwallis in North Carolina; topographic notes of the country; probable movements of British; death of [Brig.] Gen. [William Lee] Davidson. A. L. S. 3 pp. Answered Mar. 23.* **47, 29**

1781
MAR. 1

Washington, George. New Windsor. To the President of Congress [Philadelphia]. Conference with Rochambeau; Cornwallis in the South. Draft. 1 p. In handwriting of Tench Tilghman. Read in Congress, Mar. 6. Referred to Ward, Sullivan and Motte, Mar. 23. Acted on Apr. 20. **A. VI, pt. I, 3**

1781
MAR. 1

Washington, George. New Windsor. To the President of Congress [Philadelphia]. Memorial of Col. [Moses] Hazen. Draft. 1 p. In handwriting of Alexander Hamilton. Read in Congress, Mar. 23. Referred to Ward, Sullivan and Motte. **A. VI, pt. I, 1**

1781
MAR. 1

Continental Congress, Extract from the Minutes. Ratification by Maryland delegates of the Articles of Confederation. D. S. of Charles Thomson. 1 p. Enclosed in President of Congress to Washington, 1781, Mar. 5. **96, 107**

1781
MAR. 1

Hazen, Moses. Fishkill [New York]. To George Washington [New Windsor]. Memorial recounting his services, praying payment for his regiment and promotion to a brigadiership. D. S. 4 pp. Enclosed in Washington to the President of Congress, 1781, Mar. 1. **C. C. 152, 10, 13**

1781
MAR. 2

Continental Congress, President. Philadelphia. To [George] Washington [New Windsor]. British in Virginia. L. S. of Samuel Huntington. 2 pp. Answered Mar. 11.* **96, 99**

1781
MAR. 3

Board of War. [Philadelphia.] To [George] Washington [near Hartford, Connecticut]. Leather caps; wants of the cavalry; commissions for certain officers; command of the German regiment; stoppage of work at Springfield; lack of money for

Department of Military Stores; stores for the
artillery and Indians; business of the War Department. A. L. S. of Richard Peters. 4 pp. Answered Mar. 23.* 96, 102

1781 Continental Congress, President. Philadelphia. To
MAR. 5 [George] Washington [Lebanon, Connecticut].
Transmitting intelligence and resolve. L. S. of
Samuel Huntington. 2 pp. Answered Mar 21.*
96, 105

1781 Mathews, John. Philadelphia. To [George] Washington
MAR. 6 [New Windsor]. Status of militia, prisoners at
St. Augustine; exchange. A. L. S. 2 pp. An-
swered Mar. 23.* 47, 85

1781 Sullivan, John. Philadelphia. To [George] Washington
MAR. 6 [New Windsor]. Election of Secretaries of the
different Departments; [Lt.] Col. [Alexander]
Hamilton, Robert Morris and the Superintendency
of Finance; Sullivan, the Secretaryship of War
and New England jealousy; slowness of Congress
traffic with enemy; news from South; settlement
of his accounts. A. L. S. 2 pp. 47, 83

1781 Germain, Lord George, to Sir Henry Clinton. See: Presi
MAR. 7 dent of Congress to Washington, 1781, July 17.

1781 Germain to Peace Commissioners. See: President of Con
MAR. 7 gress to Washington, 1781, July 17.

[1781] Continental Congress, Committee Report on Washington's
[MAR. 9] letter of Dec. 20 [1780]; system of army promo-
tions; half pay etc. Contemporary copy. 6 pp.
Enclosed in Sullivan to Washington, 1781, Mar. 9.
96, 145
Committee: Sullivan, Varnum and Bland.

1781 Sullivan, John. Philadelphia. To [George Washington,
MAR. 9 Newport, Rhode Island]. Transmitting report
of Committee on promotions etc. and comment-
ing on same. A. L. S. 2 pp. 96, 147

1781 Sullivan, John. Philadelphia. To [George] Washington
MAR. 9 [Newport, Rhode Island]. Case of [Lt.] Col.
[Jacob Gerhard] Derick. A. L. S. 1 p. 47, 101

1781 Washington, George. Newport [Rhode Island]. To the
MAR. 11 President of Congress [Philadelphia]. Sailing of
detachment of the French; embarkation of British for the Chesapeake. Draft. 1 p. In handwriting of Tench Tilghman. Read in Congress,
Mar. 19. A. VI, pt. I, 5

1781
MAR. 11
Continental Congress, Resolves. Officers' servants. Contemporary copy. 2 pp. Enclosed in Board of War to Washington, 1782, Jan. 8. **97, 325**

1781
MAR. 12
Board of War. Proceedings. Discontinuing post at Fishkill. Contemporary copy. 1 p. In handwriting of Samuel Shaw. Enclosed in Knox to Washington, 1781, Apr. 23. **47, 125**

1781
MAR. 14
Prisoners, British. "New Prison," Philadelphia. To [Sir Henry Clinton, New York]. Petitioning for clothing, subsistence and relief. Tabulated statement of numbers by regiments. A. D. of Thomas Quartermon. 2 pp. Enclosed in Board of War to Washington, 1781, Mar. 17. **96, 112**

1781
MAR. 17
Board of War. [Philadelphia.] To [George] Washington [Hartford]. Transmitting papers from British prisoners. A. L. S. of Joseph Carleton. 1 p. Answered Mar. 23.* **96, 111**

1781
MAR. 17
Prisoners, British. "New Prison" [Philadelphia]. To the Board of War, Philadelphia. Petitioning for sergeant to go into New York to obtain clothing etc. for prisoners. A. L. S. of Sergt. Thomas Quartermon. 1 p. Enclosed in Board of War to Washington, 1781, Mar. 17. **96, 109**

1781
MAR. 19
Continental Congress, Proclamation, designating the last Thursday in April as a day of fasting and prayer. D. S. of John Hanson. Countersigned by Charles Thomson. 3 pp. **Miscel.**

1781
MAR. 19
Clinton, George. [Albany.] To [the President of Congress, Philadelphia]. Raising of two new regiments by New York. Contemporary extract of letter. 1 p. Enclosed in President of Congress to Washington, 1781, Apr. 4. **96, 152**

[1781]
[MAR. 19]
Destouches, Chevalier [*Duc de Bourgogne*, at sea.] To George Washington [New Windsor]. Account of engagement between French and English fleets, 16th inst. L. S. 6 pp. (In French.) Enclosed in Washington to the President of Congress, 1781, Mar. 31. **C. C. 152, 10, 31**

1781
MAR. 20
Barron, James. Hampton [Virginia]. To [Gov.] Thomas Jefferson [Richmond]. Arrival of British ships in the Chesapeake. Contemporary copy. 1 p. Enclosed in President of Congress to Washington, 1781, Mar. 26. **96, 131**

1781
MAR. 20

Dubuysson, Le Chevalier. Philadelphia. To [the President of Congress, Philadelphia]. Leave to go to France in return for permission to Lt. Col. [John] Hill to go to England. L. S. 1 p. Read in Congress, Mar. 21. Referred to the Commander in chief.   96, 133

1781
MAR. 20

Stanbery, Joseph. Essex County, New Jersey. Examination respecting actions of John Adam.

Frazee, Isaac. Essex County. Same.

Stanbery, Peter. Same. Ds. S. Before Mathias Halsted. 2 pp. In handwriting of Halsted. Enclosed in President of Congress to Washington, 1781, Mar. 20.   96, 240

1781
MAR. 21

Washington, George. New Windsor. To the President of Congress [Philadelphia]. Completion of the Confederation of the United States. Draft. 1 p. In handwriting of Tench Tilghman. Read in Congress, Mar. 26.   **A.** VI, pt. I, 7
Printed: Writings of Washington (Sparks) Boston. 1835. 7, 456.

1781
MAR. 21

[Jefferson, Thomas.] Richmond. To [the President of Congress, Philadelphia]. Report of battle of Guilford Court House. Contemporary extract of letter. 2 pp. Enclosed in President of Congress to Washington, 1781, Mar. 26.   96, 130

1781
MAR. 21

Wood, James. Philadelphia. To the President of Congress [Philadelphia]. Application of Lt. Col. [John] Hill to go to England. A. L. S. 1 p. Enclosed in President of Congress to Washington, 1781, Mar. 26.   96, 135

1781
MAR. 22

Continental Congress, Committee. Report on Convention and other prisoners; desertions, rations etc.; resolutions for quartering prisoners; officers, German troops, transportation etc. A. D. of Joseph Carleton. 7 pp. Enclosed in Board of War to Washington, 1781, Mar. 26.   96, 140
Above report considered Mar. 23 and referred to Board to take action thereon. Committee on report of Board of War of Mar. 17: Bland, Duane and Varnum.

1781
MAR. 22

Continental Congress, Resolve. Act of Connecticut Legislature respecting debt contracted by the United States; discharge of principal and interest; import tax. D. S. of George Bond. 3 pp. Transmitted to Washington.   96, 114

1781
MAR. 22

Board of War. Philadelphia. To [George] Washington [New Windsor]. Proposed alteration of the Provision departments. A. L. S. of Richard Peters. 1 p. Answered Mar. 30.* **96, 116**

[1781]
[MAR. 22?]

Board of War. Plan of reorganization of Provision departments; abolishment of departments of Commissary General of Purchases and that of Issues; duties of quartermasters. 10 pp. In handwriting of Nathan Jones. Enclosed in Board of War to Washington 1781, Mar. 22. **96, 120**

1781
MAR. 23

Washington, George. New Windsor. To the Board of War [Philadelphia]. Supply of shoes and accoutrements; hides; horses for cavalry; Lt. Col. [Ludowick] Weltner's claim; want of money; rank in cavalry; British prisoners etc. Draft. 4 pp. In handwriting of Tench Tilghman.
A. VI, pt. I, 9

1781
MAR. 23

Washington, George. New Windsor. To William Sharpe [Philadelphia]. His information as to distances etc. of places in the South. Draft. 1 p. In handwriting of Tench Tilghman.
A. VI, pt. I, 13

1781
MAR. 23

Washington, George. New Windsor. To [John] Mathews [Philadelphia]. Exchange of southern prisoners. Draft. 2 pp. In handwriting of Tench Tilghman. **A. VI, pt. I, 15**

1781
MAR. 23

Continental Congress, President. Philadelphia. To [George] Washington [New Windsor]. Exchange of [Lt.] Gen. [John] Burgoyne. L. S. of Samuel Huntington. 2 pp. Answered May 1.* **96, 124**

1781
MAR. 23

Continental Congress, Resolve. Authorizing exchange of Lt. Gen. [John] Burgoyne. A. D. of James Duane, attested by Charles Thomson. 1 p. Enclosed in President of Congress to Washington, 1781, Mar. 23. **96, 126**
Inadvertently dated by Thomson Apr. 23.

1781
MAR. 23

Blaine, Ephraim. Newburgh [New York]. To [George] Washington [New Windsor]. State of supplies; prospects. Transcript. Enclosed in Washington to the President of Congress, 1781, Mar. 24.
C. C. 169, 8, 79

1781
MAR. 23

Greene, Nathanael. Buffalo Creek [North Carolina]. To [the President of Congress, Philadelphia]. Results of battle of Guilford Court House; condition of army; [Brig.] Genls. [Thomas] Sumter and [Francis] Marion in South Carolina. Contemporary copy. 2 pp. Enclosed in President of Congress to Washington, 1781, Apr. 5.

96, 156

1781
MAR. 24

Washington, George. New Windsor. To the President of Congress [Philadelphia]. Want of money for elaboratory work; complaint of conduct of Clothier General [James] Wilkinson; flour from Pennsylvania. Draft. 3 pp. In handwriting of Tench Tilghman. Read in Congress, Apr. 2. Referred to Board of War.   A. VI, pt. I, 17

1781
MAR. 24

Board of War. [Philadelphia.] To Col. James Wood [Philadelphia]. Instructions relative to treatment and management of the Convention prisoners. A. D. of Joseph Carleton. 4 pp. Enclosed in Board of War to Washington, 1781, Mar. 26.

96, 138

1781
MAR. 26

Continental Congress, President. Philadelphia. To [George Washington, New Windsor]. Leaves of absence for certain officers; intelligence from the south. L. S. of Samuel Huntington. 2 pp. Answered Mar. 31.*   96, 128

1781
MAR. 26

Board of War. [Philadelphia.] To [George] Washington [New Windsor]. Instructions respecting Convention troops. A. L. S. of Richard Peters. 1 p. Answered Mar. 30.*   96, 137

1781
MAR. 27

Knox, H[enry]. New Windsor. To George Washington [New Windsor]. Promotions in the artillery. Contemporary copy. 3 pp. Enclosed in Washington to Committee of Congress, 1781, Apr. 3.

C. C.   152, 10, 39

1781
MAR. 29

Continental Congress, Resolves. Arrangement of artificer companies. Contemporary copy. 1 p. Transmitted to Washington.   97, 211

1781
MAR. 29

Fowler, A[lexander]. Pittsburg. To Prest. Joseph Reed, Philadelphia. Charges of mal-administration, fraud etc. at Pittsburg. Contemporary copy by Charles Thomson. 6 pp. Enclosed in President of Congress to Washington, 1781, Apr. 20.

96, 191

Head Quarters 29th Sepd 1782

Sir

On the 25th instant a boat [Skiled] of
Mrs Beck, from Lancaster, arrived at Dobbs Ferry, with Genl
Hazens passport to go into N York — agreeable
[the] to Genl Orders, they were stopped & reported
at Head Quarters — The Genl has ordered them
to be detained ~~at~~ until information can be had from you respecting them

As these people are very impatient
to go in, you will be so good as to give them
as soon as possible
Genl Notice whether it is with your knowledge,
or with your Approbation, they are come on

His Excellency being absent when
this opportunity presented — is the Reason
of my writing to you in my own Name

With great Respect & Regard
I am Dear Sir
Your Obt [J. T.]

Secretary at War

WRITING OF JONATHAN TRUMBULL, Jr.

1781
MAR. 30

Washington, George. New Windsor. To [the Board of War, Philadelphia]. Proposed consolidation of the different Commissary departments with that of the Quartermaster General's. Draft. 4 pp. In handwriting of Tench Tilghman.

A. VI, pt. I, 21

Printed: Writings of Washington (Ford) N. Y. 1891. 9, 198.

1781
MAR. 31

Washington, George. New Windsor. To [the President of Congress, Philadelphia]. Encounter between French and English fleets on the 16th inst.; exchange of Lt. Col. Dubuysson. Draft. 2 pp. In handwriting of Tench Tilghman. Read in Congress, Apr. 5. A. VI, pt. I, 25

1781
MAR. 31

Washington, George. New Windsor. To [Alexander] McDougall [Philadelphia]. Suggesting thanks of Congress to French, on account of expedition against Arnold. Auto. draft signed. 1 p.

P. II, 329

Same sent to Sullivan and Mathews.

1781
MAR. 31

Balfour, N[esbitt]. [Before] Charleston [South Carolina]. To [Brig.] Gen. [William] Moultrie [Charleston]. Exchange of prisoners; shipment to West Indies and treatment of British. Contemporary copy. 1 p. Enclosed in Mathews, John to Washington, 1781, May 2. 48, 341

[1781?]
[MAR. ?]

[**Pickering,** Timothy, jr.] Memorandum of resolves of Congress of 12th and 16th of Nov. 1779 respecting the Artificer corps. A. D. 1 p. Transmitted to Washington. 97, 210

1781
APR. 1

Hand, Edward. [New Windsor.] Return of recruits that have joined the army since Jan. 1, 1781. Tabular statement. D. S. 1 p. Enclosed in Washington to the President of Congress, 1781, Apr. 8.

A. VI, pt. I, 47

1781
APR. 2

Continental Congress, Resolve. Status of two new regiments to be raised by New York. D. S. of Charles Thomson. 1 p. Enclosed in President of Congress to Washington, 1781, Apr. 4. 96, 150

1781
APR. 2

Forman, David. Freehold, New Jersey. To [the President of Congress, Philadelphia]. Robbery of mail; intelligence of British embarkation for the Delaware. Contemporary copy. 2 pp. Enclosed in President of Congress to Washington, 1781, Apr. 7. 96, 161

1781
APR. 2

Greene, Nathanael. Deep River, North Carolina. 'To the Board of War [Philadelphia]. Uniforms of North and South Carolina officers. Contemporary copy. 1 p. Enclosed in Board of War to Washington, 1781, May 14.   **96, 257**

1781
APR. 3

Washington, George. New Windsor. To [Committee of Congress, Philadelphia]. Remarks on report on system of promotion in Army. D. S. 10 pp. Report in handwriting of Tench Tilghman and remarks in that of Washington arranged in parallel columns.   **C. C. 152, 10, 43**
Committee on Washington's letter of Dec. 20, 1780: Sullivan, Varnum and Bland.

[1781]
[APR. 3]

[Washington, George.] [New Windsor.] To [Committee of Congress Philadelphia]. Inspector-General's department, organization, needs etc.; Barons Steuben, Arendt and Holtzendorf. Draft. 3 pp. In handwriting of Alexander Hamilton.
     C. C. 152, 10, 53
Committee on letter of Dec. 20. See preceding entry.

1781
APR. 3

Continental Congress, Resolve. Recall of all British officers absent from America on parole. D. S. of Charles Thomson. 1 p. Enclosed in President of Congress to Washington, 1781, Apr. 5.   **96, 155**

1781
APR. 4

Washington, George. New Windsor. To the President of Congress [Philadelphia]. Preservation of records; employment of a secretary. Auto. draft. 1 p. Read in Congress, Apr. 9. Acted on.
     A. VI, pt. I, 27
Printed: Writings of Washington (Sparks) Boston. 1835. 7, 467.

1781
APR. 4

Washington, George. New Windsor. To the Board of War [Philadelphia]. Powder at Lancaster. Draft. 1 p. In handwriting of Tench Tilghman.
     A. VI, pt. I, 29

1781
APR. 4

[Washington, George.] New Windsor. To [John] Sullivan [Philadelphia]. Transmitting ideas on the committee report; news from [Maj.] Gen. [Nathanael] Greene. Auto. draft. 1 p.
     A. VI, pt. I, 31

1781
APR. 4

Washington, George. New Windsor. To [John Sullivan, Philadelphia]. Remarks on report of the Committee of Congress respecting promotions in the Army. Draft. 10 pp. In handwriting of Tench Tilghman. Enclosed in Washington to Sullivan, same date.   **A. VI, pt. I, 33**

1781
APR. 4

Continental Congress, President. Philadelphia. To [George] Washington [New Windsor]. Transmitting resolve; New York regiments. L. S. of Samuel Huntington. 2 pp. Answered Apr. 16.*
96, 148

1781
APR. 5

Continental Congress, President. Philadelphia. To [George] Washington [New Windsor]. Transmitting resolve; treatment of Henry Laurens; robbery of mail; intelligence from South. L. S. of Samuel Huntington. 2 pp. Answered Apr. 16.*
96, 153

1781
APR. 5

Continental Congress, Resolve. Thanks of Congress to Rochambeau and Destouches. D. S. of Charles Thomson. 2 pp. Enclosed in President of Congress to Washington, 1781, Apr. 6.
96, 165

1781
APR. 5

Livingston, William. Trenton. To the President of Congress [Philadelphia]. Report of British embarkation from New York for the Delaware. Contemporary copy. 1 p. Enclosed in President of Congress to Washington, 1781, Apr. 5.
96, 159

1781
APR. 5

Sullivan, John. Philadelphia. To [George] Washington [New Windsor]. Naval action between French and British [Mar. 16 off Capes Charles and Henry]. A. L. S. 2 pp.
47, 327

1781
APR. 6

Continental Congress, President. Philadelphia. To [George] Washington [New Windsor]. Transmitting resolve. L. S. of Samuel Huntington. 1 p.
96, 163

1781
APR. 7

Continental Congress, President. Philadelphia. To [George] Washington [New Windsor]. Transmitting letters. L. S. of Samuel Huntington. 1 p. Answered Apr. 12.*
96, 157

1781
APR. 7

Miller, David. Essex County, New Jersey. Affidavit of goods brought from British lines by John Adam. D. S. 1 p. Enclosed in President of Congress to Washington, 1781, May 1.
96, 239

1781
APR. 8

Washington, George. New Windsor. To [the President of Congress, Philadelphia]. Failure of States to furnish men; Lafayette's detachment ordered south; pay for troops. Auto. draft. 1 p. Read in Congress, Apr. 12.   A. VI, pt. I, 43

Printed: Writings of Washington (Ford) N. Y. 1891. 9, 207.

1781
APR. 10

Washington, George. New Windsor. To [the President of Congress, Philadelphia]. Introducing Col. Menonville; cannon for works at Newport. Draft. 2 pp. In handwriting of Tench Tilghman. A. VI, pt. I, 49

1781
APR. 10

Continental Congress, Resolve. Additional confidential secretary and writers for the Commander in chief. D. S. of Charles Thomson. 1 p. Enclosed in President of Congress to Washington, 1781, Apr. 14. 96, 169

1781
APR. 12

Washington, George. New Windsor. To [the President of Congress, Philadelphia]. Feeble state of army; want of money and provisions; defense of Philadelphia. Draft. 2 pp. In handwriting of Tench Tilghman. Read in Congress, Apr. 16.
A. VI, pt. I, 51

1781
APR. 13

Washington, George. New Windsor. To [the Board of War, Philadelphia.] Need of money by exchanged American officers on Long Island. Draft. 1 p. In handwriting of Alexander Hamilton.
A. VI, pt. I, 53

1781
APR. 13

Continental Congress, Resolves. Pay accounts of levies; settlement of pay and other army accounts. D. S. of Charles Thomson. 2 pp. Enclosed in President of Congress to Washington, 1781, Apr. 14.
96, 173

1781
APR. 14

Washington, George. New Windsor. To [the President of Congress, Philadelphia]. Expectation of Indian outrages on Northern frontier; magazines of provisions. Draft. 2 pp. In handwriting of David Humphreys. A. VI, pt. I, 55

1781
APR. 14

Continental Congress, President. Philadelphia. To [George] Washington [New Windsor]. Transmitting resolve. L. S. of Samuel Huntington. 1 p. Answered Apr. 16.* 96, 167

1781
APR. 14

Continental Congress, President. Philadelphia. To [George] Washington [New Windsor]. Transmitting resolves; payment of levies. L. S. of Samuel Huntington. 1 p. Answered April 21.*
96, 171

1781
APR. 16

Washington, George. New Windsor. To [the President of Congress, Philadelphia]. Exchange of [Lt.] Gen. [John] Burgoyne. Draft. 3 pp. In handwriting of Alexander Hamilton. Read in Congress, April 23.   **A.** VI, pt. I, 57

Printed: Writings of Washington (Ford) N. Y. 1891. 9, 218.

1781
APR. 16

Clinton, James. Albany. To [George] Washington [New Windsor]. Enemy about Fort Schuyler; lack of provisions. Contemporary copy. 3 pp. In handwriting of David Humphreys. Enclosed in Washington to the President of Congress, 1781, April 18.   **C. C.** 152, 10, 85

1781
APR. 16

Mathews, John. Philadelphia. To [George] Washington [New Windsor]. Actual condition of affairs; weakness of army; lack of supplies, money, etc.; aid from Europe; money needed and prospects of obtaining it; general situation. A. L. S. 4 pp.   48, 338

1781
APR. 16

Morris, Robert. Philadelphia. To [George] Washington [New Windsor]. Forwarding commission of [Maj.] Gen. [James] Robertson to New York. A. L. S. 2 pp. Answered May 12.*   48, 159

1781
APR. 17

Continental Congress, Resolve. Bond for Clothier-General; election of John Moylan to that office. D. S. of Charles Thomson. 1 p. Enclosed in President of Congress to Washington, 1781, Apr. 29. Published in Genl. Orders, May 5.   96, 225

1781
APR. 18

Washington, George. New Windsor. To [the President of Congress, Philadelphia]. Want of flour; certificates valueless; Pennsylvania's remissness. Draft. 3 pp. In handwriting of Alexander Hamilton and Tench Tilghman. Read in Congress Apr. 23.   **A.** VI, pt. I, 61

1781
APR. 18

Continental Congress, Committee. Report on state of national debt. Statement of debt; history of its incurrence, management, etc., from 1775 to date; army and military expenses; estimate of current expense and means of meeting same. D. S. of Charles Thomson. 24 pp. Enclosed in President of Congress to Washington, 1781, Apr. 26.   96, 175

Committee: Duane, Sharpe and Wolcott.

1781
APR. 18

Pennsylvania, Supreme Executive Council. Philadelphia. To the President of Congress [Philadelphia]. Supplies furnished Fort Pitt; charges of maladministration. Contemporary copy by Charles Thomson. 2 pp. Enclosed in President of Congress to Washington, 1781, Apr. 20.   96, 190

1781
APR. 19

Continental Congress, Resolve. Directing inquiry into abuses complained of in letter from the Supreme Executive Council of Pennsylvania. A. D. S. of Charles Thomson. 1 p. Enclosed in President of Congress to Washington, 1781, Apr. 20. **96, 189**

1871
APR. 19

Continental Congress, Committee. Report on representation of March 10 of Massachusetts General Court. Complaints of undue proportion of money being assigned as the State's quota unfounded; commercial and financial conditions. D. S. of George Bond. 6 pp. Transmitted to Washington. **96, 229**
Committee: Adams, Duane and Wolcott.

1781
APR. 19

Knox, H[enry]. [New Windsor.] Estimate of ordnance stores necessary to be sent to Fort Pitt. D. S. 4 pp. In handwriting of Samuel Shaw. Enclosed in Washington to the President of Congress, 1781, Apr. 20. **A. VI, pt. I, 65**

1781
APR. 20

Washington, George. New Windsor. To the Board of War [Philadelphia]. Supplies for Col. [George Rogers] Clark's proposed Detroit expedition; shoes, shirts and other clothing. Draft. 2 pp. In handwriting of Tench Tilghman.
A. VI, pt. I, 69

1781
APR. 20

Continental Congress, President. Philadelphia. To [George] Washington [New Windsor]. Transmitting resolves and papers respecting difficulties in the Western department. L. S. of Samuel Huntington. 2 pp. Answered May 1.* **96, 187**

1781
APR. 20

Continental Congress, Resolves. Pay due Col. Moses Hazen's regiment; depreciation. D. S. of George Bond. 2 pp. Enclosed in President of Congress to Washington, 1781, Apr. 20.
96, 194

1781
APR. 21

Washington, George. New Windsor. To the President of Congress [Philadelphia]. Barrack-master for the French Army. Draft. 2 pp. In handwriting of Alexander Hamilton. Read in Congress Apr. 26. Request granted. **A. VI, pt. I, 71**

1781
APR. 21

Board of War. [Philadelphia.] To [George] Washington [New Windsor]. Exchange of Capt. James Willing. A. L. S. of Richard Peters. 1 p. Answered May 1.* **96, 196**

1781
APR. 21

Halsted, Matthias. Elizabethtown [New Jersey]. To Abraham Clark, Philadelphia. Charges against John Adam. A. L. S. 2 pp. Read in Congress Apr. 27 and transmitted to the Commander in chief, May 1.   96, 236

1781
APR. 21

[Marion, Francis.] [Near Camden, South Carolina.] To [Maj. Gen. Nathanael Greene, before Camden]. Reports of minor operations. [Extract of letter.] Contemporary copy. 2 pp. Enclosed in President of Congress to Washington, 1781, May 23.   96, 213

1781
APR. 22

Greene, Nathanael. Camden [South Carolina]. To the President of Congress [Philadelphia]. The situation in South Carolina; supplies, weakness of army, strength of enemy. Contemporary copy. 7 pp. Enclosed in President of Congress to Washington, 1781, May 23.   96, 209

1781
APR. 23

Continental Congress, President. Philadelphia. To [George] Washington [New Windsor]. Exchange of [Lt.] Gen. [John] Burgoyne. Letter-book copy.   C. C. 15, 276

1781
APR. 23

Continental Congress, Resolves. Removal of cattle and stores from between Delaware and Chesapeake Bays. D. S. of Charles Thomson. 1 p. Enclosed in President of Congress to Washington, 1781, Apr. 26.   96, 203

1781
APR. 23

Fort Watson (South Carolina). Capitulation. Terms agreed between Capt. Patrick Carns and Lt. James McKay. List of surrendered officers with number of men. Contemporary copy. 2 pp. In handwriting of Charles Morse. Enclosed in President of Congress to Washington, 1781, May 23.   96, 215

1781
APR. 23

Jefferson, Thomas. [Richmond.] To [the President of Congress, Philadelphia]. Inability of Virginia to support the Convention troops. Contemporary copy. 2 pp. Enclosed in Board of War to Washington, 1781, May 25.   96, 287

1781
APR. 23

Knox, H[enry]. New Windsor. To [George] Washington [New Windsor]. Discontinuance of post at Fishkill; objections to such proceeding; dismissal of John Ruddock. L. S. 5 pp. In handwriting of Samuel Shaw. Noted by Tilghman: "Copy of above (except the paragraph relating to the dismission of Mr. Ruddock) transmitted to Board of War the 26th of April, 1781."   47, 126

1781
APR. 23

Marion, Francis. Fort Watson. [South Carolina]. To [Maj. Gen. Nathanael Greene, near Camden]. Report of reduction of Fort Watson. Contemporary copy. 4 pp. Enclosed in President of Congress to Washington, 1781, May 23.   96, 217

1781
APR. 24

Gates, Horatio. Philadelphia. To [the President of Congress, Philadelphia]. Injury to his character; court of inquiry. A. L. S. 2 pp. Read in Congress Apr. 25. Ordered to be transmitted to the Commander in chief. Enclosed in President of Congress to Washington, 1781, Apr. 26.   96, 201.

1781
APR. 24

Hay, Udny. [Philadelphia.] To the Board of War [Philadelphia]. Suggestion of exchange of salt for shad. Contemporary copy. 1 p. Enclosed in Board of War to Washington, 1781, Apr. 25.   96, 197

1781
APR. 25

Washington, George. New Windsor. To the President of Congress [Philadelphia]. Intended attack on Fort Pitt by British and Indians. Draft. 2 pp. In handwriting of Tench Tilghman. Read in Congress, Apr. 30.   **A.** VI, pt. I, 73

1781
APR. 25

Board of War. [Philadelphia]. To [George] Washington [New Windsor]. Proposition of Udny Hay. A. L. S. of Joseph Carleton. 1 p.   96, 197

1781
APR. 26

Washington, George. New Windsor. To [the Board of War, Philadelphia]. Discontinuance of military store post at Fishkill. Draft. 1 p. In handwriting of Tench Tilghman.   **A.** VI, pt. I, 75

1781
APR. 26

Continental Congress, President. Philadelphia. To [George] Washington [West Point]. Transmitting sundry papers and resolves. L. S. of Samuel Huntington. 2 pp. Answered May 8.*   96, 199

1781
APR. 26

Continental Congress, Resolves. Barrack-master to French Army; pay of captain-lieutenants of artillery and lieutenants and sergeants of infantry. D. S. of Charles Thomson. 1 p. Enclosed in President of Congress to Washington, 1781, Apr. 29. Published in Genl. Orders, May 5.   96, 224

1781
APR. 26

Williams, O[tho] H[olland]. Camp before Camden, South Carolina. Returns of killed, wounded and missing of infantry, cavalry and artillery after battle of Hobkirk's Hill. Tabular statements. Contemporary copies. 2 pp. In handwriting of Charles Morse. Enclosed in President of Congress to Washington 1781, May 23. **96, 218**

1781
APR. 27

Continental Congress, Resolve. Depreciated pay of Col. [Loammi] Baldwin's regiment. D. S. of Charles Thomson. 1 p. Enclosed in President of Congress to Washington, 1781, May 1. **96, 238**

1781
APR. 27

Board of War. Proceedings. Extra rations to be drawn by officers. A. D. S. of Joseph Carleton. 1 p. Enclosed in Board of War to Washington, 1781, Apr. 28. **96, 221**

1781
APR. 27

Greene, Nathanael. Saunders Creek [South Carolina]. To [the President of Congress, Philadelphia]. Report of the battle of Hobkirk's Hill. Contemporary copy. 4 pp. Enclosed in President of Congress to Washington 1781, May 23. **96, 205**

1781
APR. 28

Board of War. [Philadelphia.] To [George] Washington [New Windsor]. Transmitting act of the Board of War. A. L. S. of Joseph Carleton. 1 p. **96, 220**

1781
APR. 28

Hay, Udny. Philadelphia. To Congress. Memorial of his services and treatment; prayer for relief. D. S. 1 p. Read in Congress, Apr. 30. Referred to: Ward, Bland and Varnum. May 10 referred to the Commander in chief to appoint board of inquiry. Enclosed in President of Congress to Washington, 1781, May 20. **96, 272**

1781
APR. 29

Continental Congress, President. Philadelphia. To [George] Washington [New Windsor]. Transmitting resolves. L. S. of Samuel Huntington. 2 pp. Answered May 8.* **96, 222**

1781
APR. 30

Board of War. [Philadelphia.] To [George] Washington, New Windsor. Scarcity of supplies; stores for Western department; lead and artillery for the Southern army; Marquis de Lafayette's purchases in Baltimore; shoes; Clothier-General's department; Lt. Col. [Edward] Carrington's commission. A. L. S. of Richard Peters. 2 pp. Answered May 8.* **96, 226**

1781
APR. 30

Board of War. Return of military stores sent to Western Department. Contemporary copy. 1 p. Enclosed in Board of War to Washington, 1781, Apr. 30.   **96, 227**

1781
APR. 30

Clinton, James. Albany. To [George] Washington [New Windsor]. Failure of provision supplies; desertions; Canadian families. Contemporary copy. 2 pp. Enclosed in Washington to the President of Congress, 1781, May 8.

           C. C. 152, 10, 105

[1781]
[APR.]

Pittsburg, Inhabitants. To the President and Council of Pennsylvania. Petition to remove Col. [Daniel] Brodhead from command at Fort Pitt; charges of usurping the civil power. Contemporary copy of petition signed by twenty-six names. 4 pp. Enclosed in President of Congress to Washington, 1781, June 2.   **96, 307**

[1781]
[APR.]

Pittsburg, Inhabitants. To the President and Council of Pennsylvania. Petition and remonstrance reciting charges against and praying for removal of Col. [Daniel] Brodhead and David Duncan. Contemporary copy of D. S. of 420 signatures. 6 pp. Enclosed in President of Congress to Washington, 1781, June 2.   **96, 304 and 310**

1781
APR. —

Tait, David. Pittsburg. Affidavit of conduct of Asst. Deputy Quartermaster David Duncan at Fort Pitt. Contemporary copy. 2 pp. Enclosed in President of Congress to Washington 1781, June 2.

           96, 309

1781
MAY 1

Washington, George. New Windsor. To the President of Congress [Philadelphia]. Col. [Daniel] Brodhead's conduct at Fort Pitt; application of Massachusetts money to purchase provisions; impress; expense at West Point. Draft. 3 pp. In handwriting of Tench Tilghman. Read in Congress, May 7. Referred to Board of War. Acted upon.   **A. VI, pt. I, 79**

Printed, in part: Writings of Washington (Ford) N. Y. 1891. 9, 241, note.

1781
MAY 1

Washington, George. New Windsor. To the Board of War [Philadelphia]. Exchange of Capt. [James] Willing, of the Navy. Draft. 1 p. In handwriting of Tench Tilghman.   **A. VI, pt. I, 83**

1781
MAY 1

Continental Congress, President. Philadelphia. To [George] Washington [New Windsor]. Conduct of John Adam; transmitting resolve. L. S. of Samuel Huntington. 2 pp. Answered May 11.*

96, 234

1781
MAY 1

Board of War. [Philadelphia.] To [George Washington, New Windsor]. Number of field officers in artillery and cavalry regiments. A. L. S. of Richard Peters. 1 p. Answered May 8.* 96, 233

1781
MAY 2

Continental Congress, Committee. Report on transporting tobacco to Charleston for benefit of American prisoners. D. S. of Charles Thomson. 1 p. Enclosed in Board of War to Washington, 1781, May 2. 96, 242

Committee: Mathews, Atlee and Walton.

1781
MAY 2

Board of War. [Philadelphia.] To [George] Washington [New Windsor]. Sending tobacco to Charleston for use of American prisoners. L. S. of William Grayson. 2 pp. Answered May 16.* 96, 248

1781
MAY 2

Mathews, John. Philadelphia. To [George Washington, New Windsor]. News from Europe; Spain, Holland, Russia and Germany; prisoners in the south. A. L. S. 2 pp. 48, 337

1781
MAY 2

Sullivan, John. Philadelphia. To [George] Washington [New Windsor]. Aid from France; diversion against Canada; suggestion of objects of campaign. A. L. S. 3 pp. Answered May 29.

48, 333

1781
MAY 3

Lafayette, [Marquis de]. Pamunky River [Virginia]. To Maj. Gen. [Nathanael] Greene [near Camden]. Situation in Virginia; manœuvers of the two forces. Contemporary copy. 3 pp. Enclosed in Board of War to Washington, 1781, May 13.

96, 253

1781
MAY 3–8

Anonymous. [Martinique.] West Indies. To ————? Arrival of French fleet; encounter with British; expedition against St. Lucia etc. Contemporary extract. 2 pp. Enclosed in President of Congress to Washington, 1781, June 3. 96, 315

1781
MAY 4

Continental Congress, Resolve. Appointment of Thomas Hutchins, Geographer for Southern Army. D. S. of Charles Thomson. 1 p. Published in Genl. Orders, May 30. Enclosed in Secretary of Congress to Washington, 1781, May 10. 96, 249

1781
MAY 4

Clinton, James. Albany. To [George] Washington [New Windsor]. Lack of provisions; intentions of enemy. Contemporary copy. 2 pp. Enclosed in Washington to the President of Congress, 1781, May 8.   C. C. 152, 10, 103

1781
MAY 6

Heath, W[illiam]. West Point. To [George] Washington [New Windsor]. Failure of supplies; dispersion of troops. Contemporary copy. 2 pp. Enclosed in Washington to the President of Congress, 1781, May 8.   C. C. 152, 10, 101

1781
MAY 7

Board of War. [Philadelphia.] Proceedings. Maintenance of post at Fishkill. A. D. S. of Nathan Jones. 1 p. Enclosed in Board of War to Washington, 1781, May 8.   96, 244

1781
MAY 8

Washington, George. New Windsor. To the President of Congress [Philadelphia]. The Gates court of inquiry; lack of beef and flour; supplies for the French Army. Draft. 4 pp. In handwriting of Tench Tilghman. Read in Congress, May 14. Referred to Sullivan, Varnum and Montgomery. May 15, referred to Witherspoon, Bland and Carroll. May 18, referred to Sullivan, Varnum and Atlee. Reported and acted on May 21.
A. VI, pt. I, 85
Printed: Writings of Washington (Ford) N. Y. 1891. 9, 240.

1781
MAY 8

Washington, George. New Windsor. To the Board of War [Philadelphia]. Clothing and supplies to the southward; promotions. Draft. 2 pp. In handwriting of Tench Tilghman.   A. VI, pt. I, 89

1781
MAY 8

Continental Congress, Resolves. Chaplains, retained and supernumerary; extra allowance to commander at West Point; remounting and equiping Sheldon's dragoons. D. S. of Charles Thomson. 2 pp. First two resolves published in Genl. Orders, May 30. Enclosed in Secretary of Congress to Washington, 1781, May 10.   96, 246

1781
MAY 8

Board of War. [Philadelphia.] To [George] Washington [New Windsor]. Continuance of the post at Fishkill. A. L. S. of Richard Peters. 2 pp. 96, 243

1781
MAY 8

Lafayette, [Marquis de.] Richmond. To the President of Congress [Philadelphia]. News from [Maj.] Gen. [Nathanael] Greene and the Virginia situation. Contemporary copy. 2 pp. Enclosed in Board of War to Washington, 1781, May 13.
96, 253

[1781] **Continental Congress,** Committee. [Philadelphia.] Report
[MAY 9] to Congress establishing rank and system of promotion in the army. Draft. 5 pp. Partly in
handwriting of John Sullivan. Delivered May
9, read and part debated; passed May 25.

C. C. 152, 10, 57

This is the report on Washington's letter of Dec. 20, 1780. Committee: Sullivan, Varnum and Bland.

1781 [Dayton, Elias.] [Chatham, New Jersey.] To [George]
MAY 9 Washington [New Windsor]. Sailing of British
fleet from New York. [Extract of letter.] Transcript. Enclosed in Washington to the President
of Congress, 1781, May 11. C. C. 169, 8, 118

1781 **Fowler,** A[lexander] and Others. Pittsburg. To the
MAY 9 President of Congress [Philadelphia]. Col.
Daniel Brodhead's conduct. A. L. S. of Fowler,
signed also by Edw. Ward, Robert Campbell,
Tho. Smallman Devereux Smith and John Irwin.
2 pp. Enclosed in President of Congress to
Washington, 1781, June 2. 96, 301

1781 **Jefferson,** Thomas. Richmond. To the President of Con-
MAY 9 gress [Philadelphia]. The military situation in
Virginia; British movements; skirmishes; need
of reenforcements. Contemporary copy. 2 pp.
Enclosed in Board of War to Washington, 1781,
May 13. 96, 252

1781 **Continental Congress,** Secretary. Philadelphia. To
MAY 10 [George Washington, New Windsor]. Case of
Thomas Hutchins. L. S. of Charles Thomson.
2 pp. Answered May 29.* 96, 245

1781 **Continental Congress.** Order. Referring memorial of
MAY 10 Udny Hay to Commander in chief. D. S. of
George Bond. Enclosed in President of Con-
gress to Washington, 1781, May 10. 96, 269

1781 [Greene, Nathanael.] [Near Camden, South Carolina.] To
MAY 10 [the President of Congress, Philadelphia]. En-
listment of American prisoners in the British
Army. Contemporary extract. 1 p. In hand-
writing of Nathan Jones. Enclosed in Board of
War to Washington, 1781, June 22. 97, 23

1781 **Washington,** George. New Windsor. To [the President
MAY 11 of Congress, Philadelphia]. Sailing of a British
fleet. Draft. 1 p. In handwriting of David

Humphreys and Tench Tilghman. Read in Congress, May 17.   A.   VI, pt. I, 91

1781
MAY 11

W[ashingto]n, G[eorge]. To [John] Sullivan [Philadelphia]. Necessity of a principle of promotion; [Lt.] Col. [Tench] Tilghman; appointment of Ministers of Departments. Auto. draft signed. 3 pp.   P.   II, 371

Printed: Writings of Washington (Ford), N. Y. 1891. 9, 244.

1781
MAY 12

Washington, George. New Windsor. To Robert Morris, Philadelphia. Minor matters. Draft. 1 p. In handwriting of Tench Tilghman and Washington.
A.   VI, pt. I, 93

1781
MAY 13

Board of War. [Philadelphia.] To B[rig]. Gen. [Anthony] Wayne [Philadelphia]. Ordering him to join Lafayette with all possible despatch. Contemporary copy. 2 pp. Enclosed in Board of War to Washington, 1781, May 13.   96, 250

1781
MAY 13

Board of War. [Philadelphia.] To [George] Washington [New Windsor]. Delay in [Brig.] Gen. [Anthony] Wayne's march. A. L. S. of William Grayson. 1 p. Answered May 29.*   96, 251

1781
MAY 14

Continental Congress, Resolve. Forwarding supplies to the army. D. S. of Charles Thomson. 1 p. Enclosed in President of Congress to Washington, 1781, May 20.   96, 271

1781
MAY 14

Board of War. [Philadelphia.] To [George] Washington [New Windsor]. Uniforms of North and South Carolina officers. A. L. S. of Joseph Carleton. 1 p. Answered May 29.*   96, 256

1781
MAY 14

Amboy, John. Allentown [New Jersey]. To [the President of Congress, Philadelphia]. Intelligence of British naval movements. Contemporary copy. 2 pp. Enclosed in President of Congress to Washington, 1781, May 17.   95, 262

1781
MAY 14

Hand, Edward. [New Windsor.] Return of killed, wounded and missing of detachment on Crotan River. Tabular statement. D. S. 1 p. Enclosed in Washington to the President of Congress, 1781, May 17.   C. C.   152, 10, 113

1781
MAY 15

Continental Congress, Resolves. Arrangements and appointments in Medical corps of the Southern Department. D. S. of Charles Thomson. 2 pp. Enclosed in President of Congress to Washington, 1781, May 20.   96, 266

1781
MAY 15

Continental Congress, Order. To the Board of Admiralty to deliver heavy cannon to the Commander in chief. D. S. of Charles Thomson. Enclosed in President of Congress to Washington, 1781, May 20. **96, 267**

1781
MAY 16

Washington, George. New Windsor. To the Board of War [Philadelphia]. Tobacco for Charleston. Draft. 1 p. In handwriting of Tench Tilghman. **A. VI, pt. I, 95**

1781
MAY 16

Jones, Joseph. Philadelphia. To [George Washington, New Windsor]. Loss of opportunity in Virginia; British ravages; object of enemy. A. L. S. 3 pp. **49, 177**

1781
MAY 16

Riedesel, [Frederich Adolph, Baron de]. Brooklyn. To Maj. [Peter] Van Alstine [Fort Slongo, Long Island] Approbation of conduct; a spy system. Contemporary copy. 1 p. In handwriting of Charles Thomson and George Bond. Enclosed in McKean to Washington, 1781, Oct. 15. **53, 10**

1781
MAY 17

Washington, George. New Windsor. To the President of Congress [Philadelphia]. Conference with Rochambeau; surprise and death of Col. [Christopher] Greene at Croton River. Draft. 2 pp. In handwriting of Tench Tilghman. Read in Congress, May 21. **A. VI, pt. I, 97**
Printed: Writings of Washington (Ford) N. Y. 1891. 9, 250.

1781
MAY 17

Continental Congress, President. Philadelphia. To [George] Washington [New Windsor]. Enclosing intelligence. L. S. of Samuel Huntington. 1 p. Answered May 27.* **96, 260**

1781
MAY 17

Board of War. [Philadelphia.] To [George Washington New Windsor]. Increase of pay of deputy judge advocates. A. L. S. of Richard Peters. 1 p. Answered May 29.* **96, 259**

1781
MAY 17

Sullivan, John. Philadelphia. To [George] Washington [New Windsor]. Report on promotions; delay in appointing a Secretary of War. A. L. S. 2 pp. Answered May 29. **49, 189**

1781
MAY 17

Wood, James. Frederick [Maryland]. To the Board of War [Philadelphia]. Convention troops; need of provisions and money; removal to Fort Frederick; officers. Contemporary copy. 2 pp. Enclosed in Board of War to Washington, 1781, May 25. **96, 288**

1781
MAY 19

Hamilton, James. Frederick [Maryland]. To the Board of War [Philadelphia]. Exchange of Lt. Col. [John] Hill. Contemporary copy. 1 p. Enclosed in Board of War to Washington, 1781, June 4.   96, 320

1781
MAY 20

Continental Congress, President. Philadelphia. To [George] Washington [Weathersfield, Connecticut]. Transmitting resolves. L. S. of Samuel Huntington. 1 p. Answered May 27.*   96, 263

1781
MAY 21

Continental Congress, Resolve. Maj. Gen. Horatio Gates and court of inquiry. A. D. S. of George Bond. 1 p. Transmitted to Washington.   49, 253

1781
MAY 21

Continental Congress, Resolve. Explaining resolution of Oct. 5 [1780] removing Maj. Gen. [Horatio] Gates from command of southern army; orders to Gates. D. S. of Charles Thomson. 1 p. Enclosed in President of Congress to Washington 1781, May 28.   96, 296

1781
MAY 21

Lafayette, [Marquis de.] [Richmond, Virginia] To [Charles,] Earl Cornwallis [Petersburg]. Transmitting papers. Contemporary copy. 1 p. Enclosed in President of Congress to Washington, 1781, July 26.   97, 83

1781
MAY 22

Continental Congress, Order. Supply of army by contract. Contemporary copy. 1 p. In handwriting of Joseph Carleton. Enclosed in Board of War to Washington, 1781, June 7.   96, 333

1781
MAY 22

Continental Congress, Resolve. Funding of the public debt; recommended repeal of paper-money acts; Continental Treasurer's drafts on States; ration for northern and southern army. D. S. of Charles Thomson. 2 pp. Enclosed in President of Congress to Washington, 1781, May 24.   96, 277

1781
MAY 22

Board of War. [Philadelphia.] To [George] Washington [Weathersfield, Connecticut]. Capt. [Joshua?] Swan's claim to rank. A. L. S. of Joseph Carleton. 1 p. Answered May 30.*   96, 274

1781
MAY 23

Continental Congress, President. Philadelphia. To [George] Washington [Weathersfield, Connecticut]. Intelligence from the South. L. S. of Samuel Huntington. 1 p. Answered May 30.*   96, 207

1781
MAY 23

Continental Congress, Resolve.   Ordering removal of Convention troops from Virginia.   D. S. of Charles Thomson.   1 p.   Enclosed in President of Congress to Washington, 1781, May 28.   96, 295
<small>D. S., of same of George Bond.   1 p.   96, 286, Enclosed in Board of War to Washington, 1781, May 25.</small>

1781
MAY 23

Blaine, Ephraim.   Philadelphia.   To the Board of War [Philadelphia].   Ration for army.   Contemporary copy.   2 pp.   Enclosed in Board of War to Washington, 1781, June 7.   96, 332

1781
MAY 24

[Washington, George.]   Weathersfield [Connecticut].   Circular letter to Connecticut, Rhode Island, Massachusetts and New Hampshire.   Cooperative measures with the French; state quotas of troops.   Contemporary copy.   6 pp.   In handwriting of Peregrine Fitzhugh.   Enclosed in Washington to the President of Congress, 1781, Aug. 2.
C. C.   152, 10, 191
<small>Printed: Writings of Washington (Ford) N. Y. 1891.   9, 251.</small>

1781
MAY 24

Continental Congress, President.   Philadelphia.   To [George] Washington [Weathersfield].   Transmitting resolve.   L. S. of Samuel Huntington. 1p.   Answered May 30.*   93, 274

1781
MAY 24

Bayley, Jacob and Others.   On Connecticut River.   To the President of Congress [Philadelphia].   Petitioning for protection of the frontier and an expedition into Canada.   A. D. S. of Bayley, signed by twelve others.   2 pp.   Read in Congress, June 16.   Referred to the Commander in chief.   Enclosed in President of Congress to Washington 1781, June 20.   97, 9

1781
MAY 25

Continental Congress, Resolve.   System of promotion in line of army; brigadiers; certain appointments; aides-de-camp and others; hostages etc.   D. S. of Charles Thomson.   3 pp.   Enclosed in President of Congress to Washington, 1781, May 28.   Published in Genl. Orders, June 5.   96, 279

1781
MAY 25

Board of War.   [Philadelphia.]   To Col. [James] Wood [Frederick ?, Maryland].   Removal of Convention troops from Virginia to Rutland, Massachusetts.   Contemporary copy.   2 pp.   In handwriting of Nathan Jones.   Enclosed in Board of War to Washington, 1781, May 25.   96, 281

1781
MAY 25

Board of War. [Philadelphia.] To Col. [Ephraim] Blaine [Philadelphia]. Supplies for Convention troops on their march from Virginia to Massachusetts. Contemporary copy by Richard Peters. 2 pp. Enclosed in Board of War to Washington, 1781, May 25. **96, 283**

1781
MAY 25

Board of War. [Philadelphia] To John Hancock [Boston]. Convention troops ordered to Rutland, Massachusetts; supplies and guards. Contemporary copy. 2 pp. Enclosed in Board of War to Washington, 1781, May 25. **96, 283**

1781
MAY 25

Board of War. [Philadelphia.] To [George] Washington [New Windsor]. Transmitting papers relative to removal of Convention troops from Virginia to Massachusetts; reasons for the removal; advice desired. L. S. of William Grayson. 3 pp. Answered June 6.* **96, 284**

1781
MAY 25

Lafayette, [Marquis de.] [Richmond.] To [Charles,] Earl Cornwallis [Petersburg]. Transmitting letter; Mr. Maury. Contemporary copy. 1 p. Enclosed in President of Congress to Washington 1781, July 26. **97, 82**

1781
MAY 26

Continental Congress, Order. Transmitting Maj. Gen. [Nathanael] Greene's letter of Apr. 22 to the states. D. S. of Charles Thomson. 1 p. Enclosed in President of Congress to Washington, 1781, May 28. **96, 292**

1781
MAY 26

Board of War. [Philadelphia.] To [George Washington, New Windsor]. Transmitting letters. A. L. S. of Richard Peters. 1 p. Answered May 30.* **96, 289**

1781
MAY 26.

Cornwallis, [Charles, Earl] [Petersburg.] To Marquis de Lafayette [Richmond?]. Passport for supplies for Convention troops; exchange of prisoners with [Maj.] Gen. [Nathanael] Greene. Contemporary copy. 1 p. Enclosed in President of Congress to Washington 1781, July 26. **97, 81**

1781
MAY 27.

Washington, George. New Windsor. To [the President of Congress, Philadelphia]. Cooperative measures with the French against New York; enemy on the Northern frontier. Draft. 6 pp. In handwriting of Tench Tilghman. Referred to Board of War, June 1. **A. VI, pt. I, 99**
Printed: Writings of Washington (Ford) N. Y. 1891. 9, 259.

1781
May 27.

Lafayette, [Marquis de.] [Richmond.] To [Charles,] Earl Cornwallis [Petersburg]. Exchange negotiations. Contemporary copy. 1 p. Enclosed in President of Congress to Washington 1781, July 26.
97, 80

1781
May 28.

Continental Congress, President. Philadelphia. To [George] Washington [New Windsor]. Transmitting resolves; plan of army promotions. L. S. of Samuel Huntington. 2 pp. Answered June 6.*
96, 290

1781
May 28.

Continental Congress, President. Philadelphia. To [George] Washington [New Windsor]. Removal of Convention troops; possibility of exchange; case of Maj. Gen. [Horatio] Gates. L. S. of Samuel Huntington. 2 pp. Answered June 6.*
96, 293

1781
May 28.

Jefferson, Thomas. Charlottesville [Virginia]. To [the President of Congress, Philadelphia]. Force of British in Virginia; the military situation. Contemporary copy. 1 p. Enclosed in Board of War to Washington, 1781, June 5.
96, 324

1781
May 28.

Sullivan, John. Philadelphia. To [George] Washington [New Windsor]. The situation; aids from France; European interest; adoption of plan of promotions. A. L. S. 3 pp.
49, 300

1781
May 29.

Washington, George. New Windsor. To the Secretary of Congress [Philadelphia]. Pay of Geographer to the army. Draft. 1 p. In handwriting of Tench Tilghman.
A. VI, pt. I, 107

1781
May 29.

Washington, George. New Windsor. To the Board of War [Philadelphia]. Uniforms of Carolina troops; salaries in Judge Advocate General's department; tobacco for Charlestown; medical sergeant for British prisoners. Draft. 2 pp. In handwriting of Tench Tilghman.
A. VI, pt. I, 105

1781
*May 29.

Continental Congress, Order. Transmitting papers respecting conduct of commanding officer at Pittsburg to the Commander in chief. D. S. of Charles Thomson. 1 p. Enclosed in President of Congress to Washington, 1781, June 2.
96, 303

1781
May 29.

Morris, Robert. Philadelphia. To [George Washington, New Windsor]. Appointment as Superintendent of Finance; difficulties and reliances. A. L. S. 3 pp.
49, 309

1781
MAY 29

Morris, Robert. Philadelphia. To [George] Washington
[New Windsor]. Measures to supply bread to
army; reports respecting provisions; inspection
of rations. A. L. S. 3 pp.   **49, 311**

1781
MAY 30

Washington, George. New Windsor. To [the President
of Congress, Philadelphia]. [Maj.] Gen. [Na-
thanael] Greene's perseverance; movements of
enemy. Draft. 2 pp. In handwriting of Tench
Tilghman. Read in Congress, June 12. Note
by David Humphreys: "Duplicate The Original
was intercepted by the Enemy."

A. VI, pt. I, 109

1781
MAY 30

Washington, George. New Windsor. To the Board of
War [Philadelphia]. Minor matters. Draft.
1 p. In handwriting of Tench Tilghman. Note
by Humphreys: "The Original was intercepted
in the last mail * * *"   **A.** VI, pt. I, 111

1781
MAY 30

Brodhead, Daniel. Philadelphia. To [the President of
Congress, Philadelphia]. Weakness of garrison
at Fort Pitt; expected British advance; Indian
allies; lack of provisions and supplies. Contemporary copy. 2 pp. Enclosed in Board War to
Washington, 1781, June 1.   **96, 298**

1781
MAY 30

Lee, Thomas. Annapolis. To Maryland delegates [in
Congress, Philadelphia]. Need of state in arms
and clothing. Contemporary copy. 1 p. Enclosed in Board of War to Washington, 1781,
June 5.   **96, 325**

1781
MAY 31

Continental Congress, Resolve. Raising of troops by Pennsylvania, Maryland and Delaware. D. S. of
Charles Thomson. 2 pp. Enclosed in President
of Congress to Washington, 1781, June 3. 2d
D. S. 49, 353.   **96, 317**

1781
MAY 31

Continental Congress, Resolve. Recommending raising of
troops by Pennsylvania, Delaware and Maryland
for operations in Virginia. D. S. of Charles
Thomson. 2 pp. Transmitted to Washington.

49, 353

1781
MAY 31

Jones, Joseph. Philadelphia. To [George] Washington
[New Windsor]. Aid for the South; necessity of
exertion; selfishness of the North; suggestion of
movement to Virginia. A. L. S. 2 pp. **49, 342**

and I should do injustice to the Officers
of this Army, was I not to declare, that
as far as my opportunities have gone
(and I have conversed freely on the subject
from the General to the Ensign) they
seem equally well disposed to carry it
into execution; but they can see no
reason why the Contractors should poc-
-ket the benefits which flow from their
distresses. —

If the Officers could receive their pay,
or even their subsistence regularly, more
especially, if they could, as I am told is
the Custom with the British Service,
have always a month of the latter in
advance; it is possible they would renounce
both Sands & his Issues; but having none
of the former, & with difficulty come at
the latter, it is both inconvenient and
mortifying to them to be tyed up as they
are, when it does not appear that the
public interest is advanced by it. —
but admitting it is so in a small degree,
we may spin the thread of Œconomy 'till
it breaks. —— Minds sowered by distresses
are

WRITING OF DAVID COBB.

1781
[MAY]

Sullivan, John. [Philadelphia.] To [Congress, Philadelphia]. Proposing the invasion of Canada. D. S. 4 pp. Enclosed in Sullivan to Washington, 1781, May 2. **48, 335**

1781
JUNE 1

Continental Congress, President. [Philadelphia.] Circular to the States. European pressure for peace; exertions necessary. L. S. 3 pp. "For His Exy. Genl. Washington." Enclosed in President of Congress to Washington, 1781, June 3. **96, 313**

1781
JUNE 1

Board of War. [Philadelphia.] To [George Washington, New Windsor]. Clothing and provisions for the Western Department; pardoning of deserters. A. L. S. of Richard Peters. Answered June 8.* **96, 297**

1781
JUNE 1

Plater, George and William Bruff. To Maryland delegates in Congress [Philadelphia]. Movements of British in Virginia; reenforcements needed. Contemporary copy. 1 p. Enclosed in Board of War to Washington, 1781, June 5. **96, 323**

1781
JUNE 2

Continental Congress, President. Philadelphia. To [George] Washington [New Windsor]. Complaints of Pittsburg inhabitants against Col. [Daniel] Brodhead. L. S. of Samuel Huntington. 1 p. Answered June 7.* **96, 299**

1781
JUNE 2

Continental Congress, Resolve. Issuance of bill of credit. D. S. of Charles⁻Thomson. 1 p. Enclosed in President of Congress to Washington, 1781, June 5. **96, 328**

1781
JUNE 2

Lafayette, [Marquis de] [Malvern Hill, Virginia]. To [Charles, Earl] Cornwallis [Portsmouth]. Application for passport for tobacco to Charleston. Contemporary copy. 1 p. Enclosed in President of Congress to Washington, 1781, July 26. **97, 79**

1781
JUNE 3

Continental Congress, President. Philadelphia. To [George] Washington [New Windsor]. Raising of troops by Pennsylvania, Maryland and Delaware; circular to states; Virginia and other intelligence. L. S. of Samuel Huntington. 2 pp. Answered June 7.* **96, 311**

1781
JUNE 4

Washington, George. To Robert Morris [Philadelphia]. His appointment as Superintendent of Finance. Auto. draft signed. 1 p. **P. II, 383**
Printed: Writings of Washington (Sparks) Boston. 1835. 8, 66.

1781
JUNE 4

Continental Congress, Resolve. Superintendent of Finance to dispose of the specific supplies. Contemporary copy. 1 p. Enclosed in Morris to Washington, 1781, July 5.   **49,** 372

1781
JUNE 4

Board of War. [Philadelphia.] To [George] Washington [New Windsor]. Letter of [Brig.] Gen. [James] Hamilton. A. L. S. of Richard Peters. 1 p. Answered June 21.*   **96,** 319

1781
JUNE 4

Cornwallis, [Charles, Earl]. [Portsmouth, Virginia.] To Marquis de Lafayette [Malvern Hill]. Tobacco for American prisoners at Charleston; correspondence. Contemporary copy. 3 pp. Enclosed in President of Congress to Washington, 1781, July 26.   **97,** 77

1781
JUNE 5

Board of War. [Philadelphia.] To [George Washington,] New Windsor. Arms for Southern states. A. L. S. of Richard Peters. 1 p. Answered June 21.*
  96, 321

1781
JUNE 6

Washington, George. New Windsor. To [The President of Congress, Philadelphia]. Exchange of Convention troops; [Maj.] Gen. [Horatio] Gates's case; rules for promotions. Draft. 4 pp. In handwriting of Tench Tilghman. Read in Congress, June 12.   **A.** VI, pt. I, 113
Printed. Writings of Washington (Ford) N. Y. 1891. 9, 271.

1781
JUNE 6

Washington, George. New Windsor. To the Board of War [Philadelphia]. Reasons for Convention prisoners being kept in Pennsylvania. Draft. 1 p. In handwriting of Tench Tilghman.
  A. VI, pt. I, 115

1781
JUNE 6

Continental Congress, President. Philadelphia. To [George] Washington [New Windsor]. Transmitting resolves; intelligence from South Carolina. L. S. of Samuel Huntington. 2 pp. **96,** 326

1781
JUNE 6

Continental Congress, President. Philadelphia. To [George] Washington [New Windsor]. Transmitting papers relating to complaints against Col. [Daniel] Brodhead. L. S. 1 p.   **50,** 6

1781
JUNE 6

Boudinot, Elias. Baskingridge [New Jersey]. To the Board of Treasury [Philadelphia]. Transmitting protested bills of British officers and papers relating thereto. Contemporary copy, attested by John Lavinius Clarkson. 3 pp. Enclosed in Board of Treasury to Washington, 1781, Aug. 22.
  92, 290

1781
JUNE 7

Washington, George. New Windsor. To [the President of Congress Philadelphia]. Complaints against Col. [Daniel] Brodhead; necessity of exertions by the States; few recruits and strength of the army. Draft. 2 pp. In handwriting of Tench Tilghman. Read in Congress, June 12.

A. VI, pt. I, 125

1781
JUNE 7

Washington, George. New Windsor. To [the Maryland delegates to Congress, Philadelphia]. General matters; equipment of troops, interruption of mail etc. Draft. 1 p. In handwriting of Tench Tilghman.   A. VI, pt. I, 127

Delegates, Daniel of St Thomas Jenifer and Charles Carroll.

1781
JUNE 7

Washington, George. New Windsor. To John Mathews [Philadelphia]. Condition of affairs; prospects; prisoners and Convention troops. Auto. draft signed. 2 pp.   P. II, 387

Printed in part: Writings of Washington (Ford) N. Y. 1891. 9, 273.

1781
JUNE 7

W[ashingto]**n,** G[eorge]. New Windsor. To [Arthur] Lee [Philadelphia]. Information respecting peace. Auto. draft signed. 1 p.   P. II, 389

1781
JUNE 7

Washington, George. New Windsor. To Joseph Jones [Philadelphia]. Delay in writing; ability to aid the South. Auto. draft signed. 2 pp.

P. II, 391

1781
JUNE 7

Board of War. [Philadelphia.] To the President of Congress [Philadelphia]. Establishment and estimate of ration; contracts for supplying the army. Contemporary copy. 3 pp. Enclosed in Board of War to Washington, 1781, June 7.   96, 329

1781
JUNE 7

Board of War. [Philadelphia.] To [George] Washington [New Windsor]. Supplying army by contract. L. S. of Richard Peters. 1 p. Answered June 21.*   96, 331

[1781]
[JUNE 7?]

Board of War. Estimate of number and cost of ration for Northern and Southern armies from July 1, 1781 to Jan. 1, 1782. Tabular statements. A. D. of Nathan Jones. 2 pp. Enclosed in Board of War to Washington, 1781, June 7.   96, 334

1781
JUNE 7

Greene, William. Providence [Rhode Island]. To [the President of Congress, Philadelphia]. Asking for assistance. Contemporary extract. 2 pp. Enclosed in President of Congress to Washington, 1781, July 8.   97, 50

1781
JUNE 7

Hand, Edward. New Windsor. Return of recruits from the several states from Jan. 1 to June 1. Tabular statement. D. S. 1 p. Enclosed in Washington to the President of Congress, 1781, June 7.

C. C.   152, 10, 137

1781
JUNE 8

Washington, George. New Windsor. To the Board of War [Philadelphia]. Supplies for troops on the Western frontier; Col. [George Rogers] Clark's proposed expedition against Detroit. Draft. 1 p. In handwriting of Tench Tilghman.

A. VI, pt. I, 119

1781
JUNE 9

Washington, George. New Windsor. To the Board of War [Philadelphia]. Promotions in the artillery. Draft. 1 p. In handwriting of Tench Tilghman.

A. VI, pt. I, 123

1781
JUNE 11

Continental Congress, Resolves. Depreciation of pay in Hospital and Medical department. D. S. of Charles Thomson. 1 p. Enclosed in President of Congress to Washington, 1781, June 15. Published in Genl. Orders, June 21.   97, 4

1781
JUNE 11

Sullivan, John. Philadelphia. To [George] Washington [New Windsor]. The intercepted letter; attack on New York; British in the Chesapeake. A. L. S. 2 pp.   50, 38

1781
JUNE 12

Continental Congress, Resolves. Halting Convention prisoners in Pennsylvania; depreciation of pay of Armand's legion; cavalry for Southern army to be raised by Pennsylvania and Maryland. D. S. of Charles Thomson. 2 pp. Enclosed in President of Congress to Washington, 1781, June 15.

97, 2

1781
JUNE 13

Continental Congress, Resolve. Col. [Isaac] Nicola's battalion to garrison West Point. D. S. of Charles Thomson. 1 p. Enclosed in President of Congress to Washington, 1781, June 15.   96, 337

1781
JUNE 13

Continental Congress, Resolve. Settlement by States of depreciated pay of Hospital and Medical corps officers. D. S. of Charles Thomson. 1 p. Enclosed in President of Congress to Washington, 1781, June 15.   97, 1

1781
JUNE 14

Continental Congress, Resolve. Exchange of Lt. Gen. [John] Burgoyne for Henry Laurens. D. S. of Charles Thomson. Enclosed in President of Congress to Washington, 1781, Aug. 23.   97, 132

1781
JUNE 15

[Washington, George.] New Windsor. Circular letter to Connecticut, Rhode Island, Massachusetts and New Hampshire. Additional men needed. Contemporary copy. 2 pp. In handwriting of Peregrine Fitzhugh. Enclosed in Washington to the President of Congress, 1781, Aug. 2.

C. C. 152, 10, 199

1781
JUNE 15

Continental Congress, President. Philadelphia. To [George] Washington [New Windsor]. Transmitting resolves. L. S. of Samuel Huntington. 2 pp. Answered June 21.*

96, 335

1781
JUNE 15

Morris, Robert. Philadelphia. To [George] Washington [New Windsor]. Effect of Pennsylvania Tender and Penal laws on credit; State taxation; general ideas respecting office of Superintendant of Finance. A. L. S. 4 pp.

50, 82

1781
JUNE 16

Washington, George. New Windsor. To the President of Congress [Philadelphia]. Charges against Col. [Daniel] Brodhead; intelligence from the South. Draft. 1 p. In handwriting of Jonathan Trumbull, jr. Read in Congress June 25.

A. VI, pt. I, 129

1781
JUNE 16

Continental Congress, Resolve. Furloughs and discharges. D. S. of Charles Thomson. 1 p. Enclosed in President of Congress to Washington, 1781, June 21.

97, 18

1781
JUNE 16

Hazard, Ebenezer. Philadelphia. To the President of Congress [Philadelphia]. Case of one, Vernon, British Commissary of Prisoners at Elizabethtown. Contemporary copy. 1 p. Enclosed in Board of War to Washington, 1781, June 17.

97, 6

1781
JUNE 17

Board of War. [Philadelphia.] To [George] Washington [New Windsor]. British Commissary of Prisoners at Elizabethtown. L. S. of Richard Peters. 1 p. Answered June 28.*

97, 5

1781
JUNE 18

Continental Congress, Resolves. Regulations of the Clothier-General's department. D. S. of Charles Thomson. 7 pp. Enclosed in President of Congress to Washington, 1781, June 21. 97, 14

1781
JUNE 19

Board of War. Proceedings. Plan for filling vacancies in Hospital Department. Contemporary copy. 1 p. Enclosed in Board of War to Washington, 1781, July 17.

97, 71

1781
JUNE 19

Bland, Theodorick. Philadelphia. To [George Washington, New Windsor]. Tarleton's raid on Charlottesville and other reports of British in Virginia. A. L. S. 2 pp.   **50, 104**

1781
JUNE 20

Continental Congress, President. Philadelphia. To [George] Washington [New Windsor]. Petition of [Brig.] Gen. [Jacob] Bailey and others; exchange of Henry Laurens. A. L. S. of Samuel Huntington. 2 pp. Answered June 28.*   **97, 7**

1781
JUNE 20

Continental Congress, Resolve. Resignation of Charles Pettit and abolition of office of Asst. quartermaster general. D. S. of Charles Thomson. 1 p. Enclosed in President of Congress to Washington, 1781, June 21.   **96, 13**

1781
JUNE 20

Jones, Joseph. Philadelphia. To [George Washington, New Windsor]. Impracticability of aiding Virginia; British horse in that State; raid at Charlottesville; need of cavalry; Baron Steuben and the command in Virginia. A. L. S. 4 pp.
     50, 115

1781
JUNE 20

Lafayette, [Marquis de]. [Malvern Hill, Virginia.] To [Charles, Earl Cornwallis, Portsmouth]. Exchange negotiations; tobacco for American prisoners and British bills of exchange. Contemporary copy. 2 pp. Enclosed in President of Congress to Washington, 1781, June 26.
     97, 75

1781
JUNE 20

Schuyler, Ph[ilip John]. Poughkeepsie [New York]. To [George] Washington [New Windsor]. Building batteaux on personal credit. Contemporary copy. 2 pp. In handwriting of Jonathan Trumbull, jr. Enclosed in Washington to the President of Congress, 1781, June 28.
     C. C.   **152, 10, 155**

1781
JUNE 21

Washington, George. New Windsor. To the President of Congress [Philadelphia]. March of French troops to the North River. Draft. 2 pp. In handwriting of Jonathan Trumbull, jr. Read in Congress, June 25.   A. VI, pt. I, **131**

1781
JUNE 21

Washington, George. New Windsor. To the Board of War [Philadelphia]. Estimate of rations; supplies of beef and flour; vinegar and salt; weight of beef; new contracts and salt provision; maga-

zines in the southward; clothing.   Draft.   9 pp.
In handwriting of Tench Tilghman.

A. VI, pt. I, 133

1781
JUNE 21

Continental Congress, President.   Philadelphia.   To
[George] Washington [New Windsor].   Transmitting resolves.   L. S.   1 p.   Answered June
28.*   **96, 11**

1781
JUNE 21

Board of War. [Philadelphia.]   To the President of Congress [Philadelphia].   Establishment of ration;
alterations of same.   Contemporary copy.   1 p.
Enclosed in Board of War to Washington, 1781,
June 26.   **97, 29**

1781
JUNE 21

Bache, Richard.   [Philadelphia.]   To the Board of War
[Philadelphia].   Escort for mail-riders between
Pompton and New Windsor.   Contemporary
copy.   1 p.   Enclosed in Board of War to Wash-
ington, 1781, June 22.   **97, 22**

1781
JUNE 21

Morris, Robert.   [Philadelphia.]   To George Washington
[New Windsor].   Furnishing flour to army.
L. S.   1 p.   Answered June 28.*   **50, 124**

1781
JUNE 22

Board of War. [Philadelphia.]   To [George] Washington,
New Windsor.   Enlistment of prisoners in British army; lack of money in forwarding supplies;
clothing, lead; Convention troops; escort for
post-riders.   L. S. of William Grayson.   2 pp.
Answered June 28.*   **97, 20**

1781
JUNE 24

Washington, George.   New Windsor.   To the President
of Congress [Philadelphia].   Requisition on Pennsylvania for a corps of riflemen.   Draft.   1 p.
In handwriting of Jonathan Trumbull, jr.   Read
in Congress, July 2.   A. VI, pt. I, 143

1781
JUNE 25

Pennsylvania, Delegates in Congress.   Motion respecting
[Capt. Bartholomew] von Heer's corps.   Contemporary copy.   1 p.   Enclosed in Board of War
to Washington, 1781, June 26.   **97, 25**

1781
JUNE 25

Whitwell, S[amuel] and S[amuel] **Adams.** Boston.   Certificate of Lt. [Abijah] Hammond's health.   D. S.
1 p.   Enclosed in Peters, Richard, to Washing-
ton, 1781, Aug. 13.   **97, 131**

1781
JUNE 26

Board of War. [Philadelphia.]   To [George] Washington
[Peekskill].   Incorporation of [Capt. Bartholo-
mew] von Heer's corps into the Pennsylvania line.
A. L. S. of Richard Peters.   1 p.   Answered
July 9.*   **97, 24**

1781
JUNE 26

Board of War. [Philadelphia.] To [George Washington, Peekskill]. Ration report; transportation of clothing to south; Convention troops in Pennsylvania. A. L. S. of Richard Peters. 1 p. Answered July 9.*   **97, 26**

1781
JUNE 26

Board of War. [Philadelphia.] To the President of Congress [Philadelphia]. Contracts for supplies for Army; salt. Contemporary copy. 1 p. Enclosed in Board of War to Washington, 1781, June 26.   **97, 27**

[1781]
[JUNE 26]

Board of War. Estimates of the component parts of a ration. Four variations. 2 pp. In handwriting of Joseph Carleton. Enclosed in Board of War to Washington, 1781, June 26.   **97, 28**

1781
JUNE 27

Knox, H[enry]. New Windsor. To the Board of War [Philadelphia]. Collection and transportation of artillery stores. Contemporary copy. 2 pp. Enclosed in Board of War to Washington, 1781, July 16.   **97, 61**

1781
JUNE 28

Washington, George. Peekskill [New York]. To the President of Congress [Philadelphia]. Exchange of Burgoyne; Canadian expedition; clothing supply; Maj. Gen. [Philip John] Schuyler's boats. Draft. 2 pp. In handwriting of Jonathan Trumbull, jr.   **A. VI, pt. I, 145**

1781
JUNE 28

Washington, George. Peekskill. To the Board of War [Philadelphia]. Conduct of British Commissary of Prisoners; transportation of stores from the southward; post-riders. Draft. 3 pp. In handwriting of Tench Tilghman.   **A. VI, pt. I, 147**

1781
JUNE 28

Washington, George. Peekskill. To Robert Morris [Philadelphia]. New issue of paper money; lack of flour and source of supply. Draft. 2 pp. In handwriting of Tench Tilghman.
A. VI, pt. I, 151

1781
JUNE 28

Cornwallis, [Charles, Earl.] [Portsmouth, Virginia.] To Marquis de Lafayette [Malvern Hill]. Tobacco for prisoners at Charleston; exchange negotiations, etc. Contemporary copy. 2 pp. Enclosed in President of Congress to Washington, 1781, July 26.   **97, 76**

1781
JUNE 29

Hammond, A[bijah]. Boston. To James Lovell, [Philadelphia.] Leave of absence. A. L. S. 1 p. July 18, referred to Board of War. Aug. 13, referred to Commander-in chief. Enclosed in President of Congress to Washington, 1781, Aug. 18. **97, 123**

1781
JUNE 29

Hammond, A[bijah]. Boston. To Congress. Petition for leave of absence. A. L. S. 1 p. Enclosed in President of Congress to Washington, 1781, Aug. 18. **97,125**

1781
JUNE 29

Kohler, John August Leonard, and John Christian Timotheus **Tegel**. Lancaster [Pennsylvania]. To Col. [James] Wood, Lancaster. Petition for parole. Contemporary copy. In handwriting of Nathan Jones. Enclosed in Board of War to Washington, 1781, July 5. **97, 41**

1781
JUNE 29

Pennsylvania. Artillery. Captains and subalterns. Philadelphia. To Congress. Memorial respecting promotions. Contemporary copy. 2 pp. Enclosed in Board of War to Washington, 1781, July 3. **97, 34**

1781
JUNE 30

West, Jeremiah. Peekskill. Certificate of Capt. David Parsons's fitness for the Invalid corps. A. L. S. 1 p. Enclosed in Peters, Richard, to Washington, 1781, Aug. 13. **97, 116**

1781
JUNE 30

Wood, James. Lancaster [Pennsylvania]. To the Board of War [Philadelphia]. Request of Hessian chaplains; reasons for granting same. Contemporary copy. In handwriting of Nathan Jones. Enclosed in Board of War to Washington, 1781, July 5. **97, 41**

1781
JULY 2

Continental Congress, President. Philadelphia. To [George] Washington [en route to Valentine's Hill, New York]. Rumor of Pensacola prisoners being sent to New York. A. L. S. of Samuel Huntington. 1 p. Answered July 10.* **97, 30**

1781
JULY 2

Continental Congress, Resolve. Table of the Commander-in-chief. Contemporary copy. 1 p. In handwriting of Nathan Jones. Enclosed in Board of War to Washington, 1781, July 3. **97, 33**

1781
JULY 2

Continental Congress, Resolves. Raising of rifle corps by Pennsylvania; table of the Commander-in-chief. D. S. of Charles Thomson. 2 pp. Enclosed in President of Congress to Washington, 1781, July 3. **97, 38**

1781
JULY 2

Bland, Theodorick. Fairy Hill near Schuylkill Falls. To [George Washington, near Tarrytown, New York]. Pennsylvania opposition to raising riflemen; news from the Carolinas; British in Virginia. A. L. S. 2 pp. 50, 243

1781
[JULY 2]

Lewis, [Francis.] [Philadelphia.] To the President of Congress [Philadelphia]. Pensacola prisoners sent to New York. A. L. S. in 3d person. 1 p. Enclosed in President of Congress to Washington, 1781, July 2. 97, 31

1781
JULY 2

Morris, Robert. [Philadelphia.] To George Washington [near Tarrytown]. Contracts for rations; result of removal of embargo; abundance of flour and supplies; prices, etc.; principles of commerce; industry of the people; money and clothing. A. L. S. 4 pp. Answered July 13.* 50, 241

1781
JULY 2

Sullivan, John. Philadelphia. To [George] Washington [near Tarrytown]. Personal matters; Roger Sherman; court-martial penalties. A. L. S. 2 pp. Answered July 9. 50, 235

1781
JULY 3

Continental Congress, President. Philadelphia. To [George] Washington [Valentine's Hill, New York]. Transmitting resolves. L. S. of Samuel Huntington. 1 p. 97, 35

1781
JULY 3

Board of War. [Philadelphia.] To [George] Washington [Valentine's Hill]. Preparations of the Commissary General of Military Stores; table of the Commander-in-chief. L. S. of Ezekiel Cornell. 1 p. Answered July 9.* 97, 39

1781
JULY 3

Board of War. [Philadelphia.] To [George Washington, Valentine's Hill]. Promotions in Pennsylvania artillery. A. L. S. of Richard Peters. 1 p. Answered July 9.* 97, 32

1781
JULY 3

Board of War. Proceedings. Measures for supplying table of the Commander-in-chief. D. S. of Joseph Carleton. 2 pp. Enclosed in Board of War to Washington, 1781, July 5. 97, 45

1781
JULY 3

Jones, Joseph. Philadelphia. To [George Washington, Valentine's Hill]. Moylan's dragoons for Virginia; spirit of the State. A. L. S. 2 pp. 50, 251

1781
JULY 5

Board of War. [Philadelphia.] To [George] Washington [Phillipsburg, New York]. Letters from German chaplains. A. L. S. of Joseph Carleton. 1 p. Answered July 9.* 97, 40

1781
JULY 5

Board of War. [Philadelphia.] To [George] Washington [Phillipsburg]. Table supplies of the Commander-in-chief. A. L. S. of Joseph Carleton. 1 p. Answered July 16.*   **97, 44**

1781
JULY 5

Morris, Robert. Philadelphia. To [George] Washington [near Dobbs Ferry, Phillipsburg]. Disposal of the specific supplies; failure of states to furnish said supplies; Pennsylvania's action; the contract system. L. S. 6 pp. Answered July 13.* **49, 373**

1781
JULY 6

Washington, George. Near Dobbs Ferry. To the President of Congress [Philadelphia]. Engagement at Kingsbridge, New York. Draft. 4 pp. In handwriting of Tench Tilghman. Read in Congress, July 10.   **A. VI, pt. I, 153**
Printed: Writings of Washington (Ford) N. Y. 1891. 9, 295.

1781
JULY 6

Continental Congress, President.   Philadelphia.   To [George] Washington [Phillipsburg]. Intelligence from the South. L. S. of Samuel Huntington. 2 pp. Answered July 10.*   **97, 43**

1781
JULY 6

Knox, H[enry]. New Windsor. To the Board of War [Philadelphia]. Forwarding of artillery stores. Contemporary copy. 1 p. Enclosed in Board of War to Washington, 1781, July 16.   **97, 60**

1781
JULY 7

Continental Congress. Resolve. Call for militia for defense of Rhode Island. D. S. of Charles Thomson. 1 p. Enclosed in President of Congress to Washington, 1781, July 8.   **97, 49**

1781
JULY 8

Continental Congress, President.   Philadelphia.   To [George] Washington [Phillipsburg]. Transmitting papers; defense of Rhode Island. L. S. of Samuel Huntington. 2 pp. Answered July 16.*   **97, 47**

1781
JULY 9

Washington, George. Near Dobbs Ferry. To the Board of War [Philadelphia]. Need of hard money to purchase supplies; [Capt. Bartholomew von] Heer's corps; resignations and promotions; release of chaplains. Draft. 4 pp. In handwriting of Tench Tilghman.   **A. VI, pt. I, 157**

1781
JULY 9

Washington, George. Near Dobbs Ferry. To [John] Sullivan [Philadelphia]. His services to army in Congress; general situation. Draft. 1 p. In handwriting of Jonathan Trumbull, jr.
          A. VI, pt. I, 161

1781
JULY 10

Washington, George. Near Dobbs Ferry. To the President of Congress [Philadelphia]. Need of riflemen; minor matters; news of fall of Pensacola. Draft. 1 p. In handwriting of Jonathan Trumbull, jr. Read in Congress, July 17. July 23 referred to Mathews, Sullivan and Madison.

A. VI, pt. I, 163

1781
JULY 10

Washington, George. Near Dobbs Ferry. To Robert Morris, Philadelphia. Purchase of flour. Draft. 1 p. In handwriting of Tench Tilghman.

A. VI, pt. I, 165

1781
JULY 10

Continental Congress, Secretary. Philadelphia. To George Washington [Phillipsburg]. Resignation of Samuel Huntington and election of Thomas McKean as president of Congress. L. S. of Charles Thomson. 1 p. Answered July 21.*   97, 52

1781
JULY 10

Huntington, Samuel. Philadelphia. To [George] Washington [near Dobbs Ferry]. Retirement from Presidency of Congress; the general situation. L. S. 1 p. Answered July 25.*   50, 327

1781
JULY 10

Parsons, Samuel H[olden]. Near Dobb's Ferry. To Richard Peters, Philadelphia. Invalid officers in the Connecticut Line and filling of vacancies. A. L. S. 1 p. Enclosed in Peters, Richard to Washington, 1781, Aug. 13.   97, 113

1781
JULY 11

Continental Congress. Resolve. Title of Geographer to the United States of America. D. S. of Charles Thomson. 1 p. Enclosed in President of Congress to Washington, 1781, July 14.   97, 55

1781
JULY 12

Continental Congress, Proceedings. Election of Samuel Hodgdon, Commissary General of Military Stores. D. S. of Charles Thomson. 1 p. Enclosed in President of Congress to Washington, 1781, July 14.   97, 53

1781
JULY 13

Washington, George. Near Dobbs Ferry. To Robert Morris [Philadelphia]. Supplies and magazines. Draft. 4 pp. In handwriting of Tench Tilghman.   A. VI, pt. I, 167
Printed: Writings of Washington (Ford) N. Y. 1891. 9, 301.

1781
JULY 14

Continental Congress, President. Philadelphia. To [George] Washington [Phillipsburg]. Transmitting resolves; comment; crops and condition of the country. L. S. of Thomas McKean. 3 pp. Answered July 21.*   97, 57

1781
JULY 14
Board of War. Proceedings. Promotions and appoint-ments in the Hospital Department. Contempo-rary copy. 1 p. In handwriting of Guilliame Aertsen, jr. Enclosed in Board of War to Wash-ington, 1781, July 17. 97, 70

[1781]
[JULY 14?]
Board of War. Resolves. Promotions and appointments in the Hospital Corps. A. D. of Guilliame Aert-sen, jr. 1 p. Submitted to Congress. Enclosed in Board of War to Washington, 1781, July 17.
97, 72

1781
[JULY 14?]
Board of War. Estimate of sundries wanting for use of Gen. Washington's table. Tabular statement. Contemporary copy. 1 p. Enclosed in Board of War to Washington, 1781, July 26. 97, 90

1781
JULY 14
Blaine, Ephraim. Philadelphia. To the Board of War [Philadelphia]. Return of articles sent to head-quarters for use of Gen. Washington. Contem-porary copy. 1 p. Enclosed in Board of War to Washington, 1781, July 26. 97, 88

1781
JULY 16
Washington, George. Near Dobbs Ferry. To the Presi-dent of Congress [Philadelphia]. Receipt of letters; Rhode Island militia. Draft. 1 p. In handwriting of Jonathan Trumbull, jr. Read in Congress, July 23. **A.** VI, pt. I, 169

1781
JULY 16
Washington, George. Near Dobbs Ferry. To the Board of War [Philadelphia]. Choice of a steward. Draft. 2 pp. In handwriting of Tench Tilgh-man. **A.** VI, pt. I, 171

1781
JULY 16
Continental Congress, Resolve. Rations to officers on pa-role. D. S. of Charles Thomson. 1 p. Enclosed in President of Congress to Washington, 1781, July 17. 97, 62

1781
JULY 16
Continental Congress, Resolve. Repealing resolution re-specting Brig. Gen. [Lachlan] McIntosh. D. S. of Charles Thomson. 1 p. Enclosed in President of Congress to Washington, 1781, July 28. 97, 66

1781
JULY 16
Board of War. [Philadelphia.] To [George] Washington [Phillipsburg]. Transportation of stores. D. S. of William Grayson. 1 p. Answered July 21.*
97, 59

1781
JULY 17
Continental Congress, President. Philadelphia. To [George] Washington [Phillipsburg]. Transmit-ting resolve. L. S. of Thomas McKean. 1 p. Answered July 21.* 97, 64

1781
JULY 17

Continental Congress, President. Philadelphia. To George Washington [Phillipsburg]. Capture of British mail; extracts of letters as follows:

FEB. 7

Germain, [Lord George.] Whitehall. To Sir Henry Clinton [New York]. British troops in Virginia; Vermont and Canada; reenforcements from England.

MAR. 7

Germain to Peace Commissioners [New York]. Peace measures.

Germain to Clinton. Revolt of the Pennsylvania Line; Cornwallis in Virginia; loyalists and projected settlement at Penobscot; enlistment of American prisoners; delay in sailing of reenforcements from England.

Amount of Arnold's bribe. L. S. of Thomas McKean. 7 pp. Answered July 21.*   **97, 95**

The Arnold paragraph is in McKean's handwriting.

1781
JULY 17

Board of War. [Philadelphia.] To [George] Washington [Phillipsburg]. Plans for promotion of officers in Hospital Department. A. L. S. of Joseph Carleton. 1 p. Answered Aug. 5.*   **97, 69**

1781
JULY 21

Washington, George. [Near Dobbs Ferry.] To the President of Congress [Philadelphia]. His election to the Presidency; value of intelligence received. Draft. 2 pp. In handwriting of Jonathan Trumbull, jr. Read in Congress, July 25.

A. VI, pt. I, 181

1781
JULY 21

Washington, George. Near Dobbs Ferry. To the Board of War [Philadelphia]. Forwarding stores to camp. Draft. 1 p. In handwriting of Jonathan Trumbull, jr.   **A. VI, pt. I, 183**

1781
JULY 21

Washington, George. Near Dobbs Ferry. To Charles Thomson [Philadelphia]. Acknowledging receipt of information. Draft. 1 p. In handwriting of Jonathan Trumbull, jr.   **A. VI, pt. I, 185**

1781
JULY 21

Lafayette, [Marquis de.] Malvern Hill [Virginia]. To the President of Congress [Philadelphia]. Transmitting letters. Contemporary copy. 1 p. Enclosed in President of Congress to Washington, 1781, July 26.   **97, 73**

1781
JULY 21

Lafayette, [Marquis de.] To Maj. Gen. [Nathanael] Greene [High Hills of the Santee]. British manoevers in Virginia; prisoners. Contemporary copy. 1 p. Enclosed in President of Congress to Washington, 1781, July 26.   **97, 74**

1781
July 23

Morris, Robert. [Philadelphia.] To [George] Washington [Near Dobbs Ferry]. Flour supply; disposal of the specific supplies; Pennsylvania's action; paper money; contract system of supplying army; ration and cost thereof; draft for hard money; visit to camp. A. L. S. 6 pp. Answered Aug. 2.* 51, 69

1781
July 25

Washington, George. Dobbs Ferry. To Samuel Huntington, Norwich [Connecticut]. His resignation from Congress; need of recruits. Draft. 2 pp. In handwriting of Tench Tilghman.

A. VI, pt. I, 187
Printed: Writings of Washington (Sparks) Boston. 1835. 8, 114.

1781
July 26

Continental Congress, President. [Philadelphia.] To [George] Washington [Phillipsburg]. Transmitting papers; Cornwallis's probable intention. L. S. of Thos. McKean. 2 pp. Answered July 30.* 97, 84

1781
July 26

Continental Congress, Resolve. Committee: Carroll, Bland and Varnum, to confer with the Commander in chief, Board of War and Superintendent of Finance on number and arrangement of army. A. D. of Carroll. 1 p. 51, 199

1781
July 26

Board of War. Philadelphia. To [George] Washington [Phillipsburg]. Supplies for his table; steward; exchange of chaplains; forwarding of stores; lack of money. L. S. of Ezekiel Cornell. 2 pp. Answered Aug. 5.* 97, 86

1781
July 28

Continental Congress, President. Philadelphia. To [George] Washington [Phillipsburg]. Transmitting resolve; intelligence from [Lt.] Col. [John] Laurens. L. S. of Thomas McKean. 2 pp. Answered Aug. 13.* 97, 67

1781
July 29

Sullivan, John. Philadelphia. To [George] Washington [Dobbs Ferry]. Recommending Capt. [Anthony] Selin. A. L. S. 1 p. 51, 119

1781
July 30

Washington, George. Dobbs Ferry. To the President of Congress [Philadelphia]. Enemy in Virginia; reenforcements in New York. Draft. 1 p. In handwriting of Jonathan Trumbull, jr. Read in Congress, Aug. 3. A. VI, pt. I, 189

1781
July 31

Continental Congress. Order. Leave of absence to member of Board of War to repair to Headquarters. D. S. of Charles Thomson. 1 p. Enclosed in President of Congress to Washington, 1781, Aug. 3. 97, 92

1781
JULY 31

Continental Congress. Order. Member of Board of War and the Superintendant of Finance to confer with Commander-in-Chief on arrangement of army. D. S. of George Bond. 1 p. Enclosed in Peters, Richard, to Washington, 1781, Aug. 13.   **97, 113**
Peters was the member chosen.

1781
AUG. 1

Hand, Edward. Dobbs Ferry. Return of recruits from the several states from Jan. 1, to July 31. Tabular statement. D. S. 2 pp. Enclosed in Washington to the President of Congress, 1781, Aug. 2.   **C. C. 152, 10, 203**

1781
AUG. 2

Washington, George. Dobbs Ferry. To [the President of Congress, Philadelphia]. Weak state of army; failure of states to furnish men; general condition. Draft. 7 pp. In handwriting of Tench Tilghman. Read in Congress Aug. 6. Referred to Bland, Boudinot and Varnum. Reported Aug. 9, acted on Sep. 29.   **A. VI, pt. I, 191.**
Printed: Writings of Washington (Ford) N. Y. 1891. 9, 324.

1781
AUG. 2

Washington, George. Dobbs Ferry. To Robert Morris [Philadelphia]. Supply of flour; sale of specific supplies; contemplated move against enemy in Virginia; shipping necessary for transportation. Draft. 4 pp. In handwriting of Tench Tilghman.   **A. VI, pt. I, 199**
Printed in part: Writings of Washington (Ford) N. Y. 1891. 9, 330.

1781
AUG. 2

Washington, George. Dobbs Ferry. Circular letter to Connecticut, Rhode Island, Massachusetts and New Hampshire. Pressing need of recruits to carry on the campaign. Contemporary copy. 3 pp. In handwriting of Peregrine Fitzhugh. Enclosed in Washington to the President of Congress, 1781, Aug. 2.   **C. C. 152, 10, 187.**
Printed: Writings of Washington (Ford) N. Y. 1891. 9, 329.

1781
AUG. 2

Board of Treasury. [Philadelphia.] To the Board of War [Philadelphia]. Case of [Lt.] Philip Steubing [Strauben?]. A. L. S. of John Gibson. 1 p. Enclosed in Peters, Richard to Washington, 1781, Aug. 13.   **97, 120**

1781
AUG. 3

Continental Congress, President. Philadelphia. To [George] Washington [Phillipsburg]. British embarkation in Virginia; committee on arrangement of army. L. S. of Thomas McKean. 4 pp. Answered Aug. 13.*   **97, 94**

1781
Aug. 3

Continental Congress, Resolve. Condition of prisoners on the prison ships. D. S. of Charles Thomson. 2 pp. Enclosed in President of Congress to Washington, 1781, Aug. 7. 97, 99

1781
Aug. 3

Board of War. Order. Submitting various matters to the Commander-in-chief. A. D. S. of Joseph Carleton. 1 p. Enclosed in Peters, Richard to Washington, 1781, Aug. 13. 97, 111

1781
Aug. 3

Board of War. Proceedings. Appointment of Richard Peters to confer with Commander-in-chief. A. D. S. of Joseph Carleton. 1 p. Enclosed in Peters, Richard to Washington, 1781, Aug. 13. 97, 112

1781
Aug. 4

Board of War. Proceedings. Essay of plan for Hospital Department to be laid before the Commander-in-chief. A. D. S. of Joseph Carleton. 1 p. Enclosed in Peters, Richard to Washington, 1781, Aug. 13. 97, 110

[1781]
[Aug. 4]

Board of War. Essay of plan for Hospital Department. Duties of officers; expense; contracts for supplies; deaths; medicines etc. A. D. of Nathan Jones. 2 pp. Enclosed in Peters, Richard to Washington, 1781, Aug. 13. 97, 117

1781
Aug. 5

Washington, George. Dobbs Ferry. To the Board of War [Philadelphia]. Plan for filling vacancies and making promotions in the Medical line. Draft. 2 pp. In handwriting of Tench Tilghman. A. VI, pt. I, 203

1781
Aug. 5

Washington, George. Dobbs Ferry. To Robert Morris [Philadelphia]. Sale of salt beef to procure pork. Draft. 1 p. In handwriting of Tench Tilghman. A. VI, pt. I, 205

1781
Aug. 6

Jones, Joseph. Philadelphia. To [George Washington, Phillipsburg]. News from Europe; British in South Carolina; Vermont; British in the Chesapeake. A. L. S. 3 pp. 51, 180

1781
Aug. 7

Continental Congress, President. Philadelphia. To [George] Washington [Phillipsburg]. Treatment of American prisoners; retaliation; British movement toward Annapolis. L. S. of Thomas McKean. 3 pp. Answered Aug. 13 * 97, 101

1781
Aug. 7

Continental Congress, Resolve. Abuse of commissions granted by Connecticut to suppress commerce with British. D. S. of Charles Thomson. 2 pp.

Enclosed in President of Congress to Washington 1781, Aug. 9.   **97, 102**

1781
AUG. 7

Continental Congress, Committee of Conference with Commander-in-chief. Philadelphia. To [George Washington, Dobbs Ferry]. Resolve of Congress submitted for consideration. A. L. S. of Daniel Carroll.   **51, 199**

Committee: Carroll, Bland and Varnum.

1781
AUG. 7

Continental Congress, Resolves. Claim of Vermont to admission into the Federation. A. D. S. of George Bond. 3 pp. Enclosed in President of Congress to Washington, 1781, Aug. 23.   **97, 127**

1781
AUG. 7

Georgia, Delegates to Congress. Philadelphia. To [George] Washington [Dobbs Ferry]. Exchange of Col. [Samuel] Elbert; aspect of affairs in the South. A. L. S. of Geo. Walton, signed also by Richard Howley. 2 pp. Answered Aug. 13.*
     51, 197

1781
AUG. 8

Washington, George. Dobbs Ferry. To [the President of Congress, Philadelphia]. Exchange of Burgoyne and other prisoners. Draft. 3 pp. In handwriting of Tench Tilghman. Read in Congress, Aug. 17. Referred to Boudinot, Varnum and Sherman. Reported Aug. 20, acted on Aug. 21.   **A. VI, pt. I, 207**

Printed: Writings of Washington (Ford) N. Y. 1891. 9, 332.

1781
AUG. 9

Washington, George. Dobbs Ferry. To [Robert Morris, Philadelphia]. Distress of troops at Wyoming for supplies. Draft. 1 p. In handwriting of Tench Tilghman.   **A. VI, pt. I, 211**

1781
AUG. 9

Continental Congress, President. Philadelphia. To [George] Washington [Phillipsburg]. Transmitting resolve; intelligence of British fleet from Virginia. L. S. of Thomas McKean. 1 p.   **97, 104**

1781
AUG. 9

Board of War. [Philadelphia.] To [George] Washington [Phillipsburg]. Appointment of John Loviday as steward to the Commander-in-chief. A. L. S. of Joseph Carleton. 1 p.   **97, 107**

1781
AUG. 12

McKean, Thomas. Philadelphia. To [George] Washington [Dobbs Ferry]. Spain's actions; aid from France; prospects of peace; the Congress at Vienna; Rodney's losses; preparations at Cadiz; Cornwallis in Virginia and other intelligence. L. S. 4 pp.   **51, 244**

1781
Aug. 13

Washington, George. Dobbs Ferry. To the President of Congress [Philadelphia]. Plans for next campaign; marine prisoners. Draft. 2 pp. In handwriting of Tench Tilghman. Read in Congress, Aug. 16. **A.** VI, pt. I, 213

1781
Aug. 13

Washington, George. Dobbs Ferry. To [the Georgia delegates to Congress, Philadelphia]. Exchange of Col. [Samuel] Elbert; Maj. Gen. [Nathanael] Greene's abilities. Draft. 2 pp. In handwriting of Tench Tilghman. **A.** VI, pt. I, 215
Delegates: Walton and Howley.

1781
Aug. 13

Continental Congress, Committee of Conference with Commander-in-chief. [Dobbs Ferry.] To [George] Washington [Dobbs Ferry]. Necessity for economy in expenditures; decrease of army; queries as to extent of reduction; officers and noncommissioned officers, length of enlistments, servants, brevets etc. A. L. S. of Richard Peters, signed also by Robert Morris. 4 pp. **51,** 258

1781
Aug. 13

Continental Congress, Order. Referring case of [Lt.] A[bijah] Hammond to Commander-in-chief. A. D. S. of George Bond. 1 p. Transmitted to Washington. **97,** 121

1781
Aug. 13

Peters, Richard. [Phillipsburg.] To [George Washington, Phillipsburg]. [Brig.] Gen. [Samuel Holden] Parsons's letter respecting Invalid corps; pay of convalescent and retired officers; essay of plan for Hospital Department; Lt. [Philip] Strauben's pay. A. L. S. 2 pp. **97,** 108

1781
Aug. 15

Parsons, Samuel H[olden] and Others. [Dobbs Ferry.] To [George Washington, Dobbs Ferry]. Col. [John] Durkee's retirement and consequent promotions. Contemporary copy. 2 pp. Enclosed in: Washington to the President of Congress 1781, Aug. 18. In handwriting of David Cobb.
A. VI, pt. I, 225

1781
Aug. 16

Continental Army, Board of General Officers. Dobbs Ferry. Opinion on rank of Udny Hay. Contemporary copy. 1 p. In handwriting of Tench Tilghman. Enclosed in Washington to the President of Congress, 1781, Aug. 18.
C. C. 152, 10, 219

1781   **Washington, George.** Dobbs Ferry. To Robert Morris
Aug. 17   [Philadelphia]. Provisions and boats for move
                of army south; need of money. Draft. 2 pp.
                In handwriting of Tench Tilghman.
                                                A. VI, pt. I, 217

1781   **Washington, George.** [Dobbs Ferry.] To [the President
Aug. 18   of Congress, Philadelphia]. Memorial of the
                field officers of the Connecticut and Rhode Island
                Lines respecting promotions. Draft. 2 pp. In
                handwriting of David Humphreys.
                                                A. VI, pt. I, 225
                Transcript, C. C. 169, 8, 171, is dated, Aug. 17.
                For memorial see: Parsons, Samuel Holden and Others to Washing-
                ton, 1781, Aug. 15.

1781   **Washington, George.** Dobbs Ferry. To the President of
Aug. 18   Congress [Philadelphia]. Transmitting report on
                memorial of Col. Udny Hay. Draft. 1 p. In
                handwriting of Tench Tilghman. Read in Con-
                gress, Aug. 27.   A. VI, pt. I, 229

1781   **Continental Congress,** President. Philadelphia. To
Aug. 18   [George] Washington [Phillipsburg]. Transmit-
                ting resolve. L. S. of Thomas McKean. 1 p.
                                                97, 139

1781   **Z[eisberger,]** D[avid]. "Topecking" [Ohio?] To [Col.
Aug. 18   Daniel Brodhead, Fort Pitt]. Advance of Indians
                against the Western frontier. Contemporary
                copy. 1 p. Enclosed in Board of War to Wash-
                ington, 1781, Sep. 3.   97, 144

1781   **Gibson,** John and Others. Fort Pitt. To [Col. Daniel
Aug. 19   Brodhead, Fort Pitt]. Refusing to serve under
                his command. Contemporary copy. 1 p. En-
                closed in President of Congress to Washington,
                1781, Sep. 25.   97, 172

1781   **Varnum,** J[ames] M[itchell]. Philadelphia. To [George]
Aug. 20   Washington [Kings Ferry]. Committee to re-
                form the military establishment; permanent force;
                finance; British strength; proportion of American
                troops to population; ability of various states to
                raise men; over-supply of officers; composition of
                battalions; artillery; cavalry; general officers;
                possibilities for the Secretary-ship of War.
                A. L. S. 8 pp. Endorsed by Jonathan Trum-
                bull, jr.: "Conference held upon it."   48, 225

Dear General

Upon a visit to my Father some little time ago I was informed by him you wanted number of Ewe Lambs and as there was prospect of my being able to make a considerable collection in my neighbourhood I promised to make enquiry on my return and address you upon the subject - this letter is to comply with my promise to my Father and to execute a pleasing duty to you - If I had fortunately been acquainted with your desire a fortnight sooner it would have been in my power to have purchased for you an hundred Ewe lambs at 10/ each, this was done in my absence by a Butcher from Baltimore who I found upon the Island at my return and who had purchased upwards of an hundred and fifty - This draught on the inhabitants has made my attempt to accomplish your wishes not so successful as I could wish. from 20 to 30 are

WRITING OF PEREGRINE FITZHUGH.

1781
Aug. 21

Washington, George. Kings Ferry [New York]. To Robert Morris and Richard Peters [Philadelphia]. Opinion on proposed reduction of the army. Draft. 8 pp. In handwriting of David Humphreys.   A. VI, pt. I, 231

> Morris and Peters were Commissioners appointed by Congress to confer with Commander in chief on arrangement and reduction of army.

> Printed: Writings of Washington (Ford) N. Y. 1891. 9, 347.

1781
Aug. 21

Continental Congress, Resolve. Remonstrance to British Commander-in-chief on protest of bills drawn by British officers. Contemporary copy. 1 p. Enclosed in Board of Treasury to Washington, 1781, Aug. 22.   92, 289

1781
Aug. 21

Continental Congress, Resolves. Exchange of prisoners; Lt. Gen. [John] Burgoyne; Cedar hostages; protested British bills of exchange. D. S. of Charles Thomson. 3 pp. Enclosed in President of Congress to Washington, 1781, Aug. 23.   97, 129

1781
Aug. 21

Continental Congress, Resolve. Boundaries of Vermont. A. D. of Daniel Carroll. 1 p. Enclosed in President of Congress to Washington, 1781, Aug 23.   97, 126

1781
Aug. 21

Varnum, J[ames] M[itchell]. [Philadelphia.] To [George] Washington [Kings Ferry]. Reduction of officers; recalls to the service; promotions; corps of artillery and horse; changes. A. L. S. 3 pp.   48, 229

1781
Aug. 21

Z[eisberger,] D[avid]. "Tuppaking." [Ohio?] To Col. [Daniel] Brodhead, Fort Pitt. Intelligence of Indian designs; [Col. George Rogers] Clark's expedition against Detroit. Contemporary copy. 3 pp. Enclosed in Board of War to Washington, 1781, Sep. 3.   97, 145

1781
Aug. 22

Continental Congress, Resolve. Exchange of Lt. Gen. [John] Burgoyne for Henry Laurens. D. S. of Charles Thomson. Enclosed in President of Congress to Washington, 1781, Aug. 23.   97, 132

1781
Aug. 22

Board of Treasury. Philadelphia. To George Washington [Kings Ferry]. Protest of bills drawn by British officers. L. S. of John Lavinius Clarkson. 2 pp. Endorsed by Jonathan Trumbull, jr.: "Letter written to Sir Guy Carleton—& Bills with protests transmitted."   92, 287

1781
Aug. 22

Morris, Robert. [Philadelphia.] To [George] Washing-ington [Kings Ferry]. The financial situation; exchange; Pennsylvania paper currency. L. S. 1 p. In cipher.   51, 302

Translation in handwriting of Jonathan Trumbull, jr. 51, 299.

1781
Aug. 22

Morris, Robert. [Philadelphia.] Circular to the States. Specific supplies; information necessary. L. S. with auto. foot note transmitting the circular to Washington. 1 p.   51, 300

1781
Aug. 23

Continental Congress, President. Philadelphia. To [George] Washington [King's Ferry]. Trans-mitting resolves; Cornwallis at Yorktown; action [at Quinby's Bridge?] in South Carolina; British naval movements. L. S. of Thomas McKean. 2 pp.   97, 134

1781
Aug. 23

Varnum, J[ames] M[itchell]. [Philadelphia.] To [George] Washington [Kings Ferry]. Memorial of Rhode Island and Connecticut officers on promotion. A. L. S. 1 p.   48, 223

1781
Aug. 24

Washington, George. Kings Ferry. To Robert Morris [Philadelphia]. Flour for French troops; the march south; boats in the Chesapeake and Dela-ware. Draft. 2 pp. In handwriting of Tench Tilghman.   A. VI, pt. I, 239

1781
Aug. 24

Brodhead, Daniel. Fort Pitt. To the President of Con-gress [Philadelphia]. Situation on Western fron-tier. Contemporary copy. 1 p. Enclosed in Board of War to Washington, 1781, Sep. 3.
    97, 143

1781
Aug. 27

Washington, George. Chatham [New Jersey]. To the President of Congress [Philadelphia]. Change of plan of campaign. Draft. 1 p. In handwriting of Jonathan Trumbull, jr. Read in Congress, Aug. 28.   A. VI, pt. I, 241

1781
Aug. 27

Washington, George. Chatham. To Robert Morris [Philadelphia]. Boats and supplies for march of the army south; pay for troops. Draft. 4 pp. In handwriting of Tench Tilghman.
    A. VI, pt. I, 241

Printed: Writings of Washington (Ford) N. Y. 1891. 9, 353.

1781
Aug. 28

Morris, Robert. Philadelphia. To [George] Washington [New Brunswick]. Difficulty in obtaining craft for transportation of army down the Chesapeake; supplies and pay, etc. L. S. 2 pp.   52, 6

1781
AUG. 30

Affleck, Edmund. New York. To [George] Washington [Philadelphia]. Treatment of prisoners on the prison ships. Contemporary copy. 4 pp. In handwriting of David Humphreys. Enclosed in Washington to the President of Congress, 1781, Sep. 4.   **C. C.** **152, 10, 233**

1781
AUG. 31

Continental Congress, Resolve. Forwarding arms in Philadelphia to Southern Army. D. S. of Charles Thomson. 1 p. Enclosed in President of Congress to Washington, 1781, Sep. 4.   **97, 138**

[1781]
[AUG.]

[**Morris**, Robert.] [Philadelphia]. To [George Washington, Dobbs Ferry]. Questions respecting financial administration of the army. Draft. 2 pp. In handwriting of Tench Tilghman.
                                        A. VI, pt. I, 223

[1781]
[AUG.]

Washington, George. [Dobbs Ferry.] To [Robert Morris, Philadelphia]. Answers to questions respecting financial administration of the army. Draft. 3 pp. In handwriting of Tench Tilghman.
                                        A. VI, pt. I, 219

1781
SEP. 1

Washington, George. Philadelphia. To the President of Congress [Philadelphia]. Referring exchange of French Engineer officers to Congress. Draft. 2 pp. In handwriting of Tench Tilghman. Read in Congress Sep. 3. Referred to Board of War.
                                        A. VI, pt. I, 247

1781
SEP. 1

Sharpe, William. Philadelphia. To [George] Washington [Philadelphia]. Arms for North Carolina. A. L. S. 3 pp.   **52, 36**

1781
SEP. 3

Board of War. [Philadelphia.] To George Washington, Philadelphia. Intelligence from Western frontiers. A. L. S. of Joseph Carleton. 1 p.
                                        97, 141

1781
SEP. 4

Washington, George. Philadelphia. To the President of Congress [Philadelphia]. British treatment of marine prisoners. Draft. 1 p. In handwriting of David Humphreys. Read in Congress, Sep. 4. Acted on.   **A. VI, pt. I, 249**

1781
SEP. 4

Continental Congress, President. Philadelphia. To [George] Washington [Philadelphia]. Transmitting resolve. L. S. of Thomas McKean. 1 p.
                                        97, 135

1781
SEP. 4

Continental Congress, President. Philadelphia. To George Washington [Philadelphia]. Transmitting resolve. L. S. of Thomas McKean. 1 p. 97, 149

1781
SEP. 4

Continental Congress, Resolve. Prisoners on prison ship in New York harbor. A. D. S. of Charles Thomson. 1 p. Enclosed in President of Congress to Washington, 1781, Sep. 4. 97, 147

1781
SEP. 4

Continental Congress, Resolves. Lt. Col. le Chev. Dubuysson. D. S. of Charles Thomson. Enclosed in President of Congress to Washington, 1781, Sep. 7. 97, 153

1781
SEP. 4

Gist, M[ordecai]. Baltimore. To [George] Washington [Philadelphia]. Arrival of French fleet in the Chesapeake; list of number and rates. Contemporary copy. 3 pp. In handwriting of William Stephens Smith. Enclosed in Washington to the President of Congress, 1781, Sep. 5.
C. C. 152, 10, 241

1781
SEP. 5

Washington, George. Chester [Pennsylvania]. To the President of Congress [Philadelphia]. Arrival of De Grasse in the Chesapeake; march of the army. Draft. 1 p. In handwriting of Jonathan Trumbull, jr. Read in Congress, Sep. 6.
A. VI, pt. I, 251
Printed: Writings of Washington (Sparks) Boston. 1835. 8, 153.

1781
SEP. 5

Continental Congress, Resolve. Inquiry into conduct of Maj. Gen. Robert Howe in Georgia, Dec. 1778. D. S. of Charles Thomson. 1 p. Enclosed in President of Congress to Washington, 1781, Sep. 7. 97, 151

1781
SEP. 5

Continental Congress, Resolves. Approving conduct of Lt. Col. J[ohn] Laurens in Europe. D. S. of George Bond. 1 p. Enclosed in Duane to Washington, 1781, Sept. 9. 52, 110

1781
SEP. 6

Washington, George. Head of Elk [Pennsylvania]. To Robert Morris [Philadelphia]. Urgent necessity of pay for the army. Draft. 1 p. In handwriting of Jonathan Trumbull, jr.
A. VI, pt. I, 353

1781
SEP. 6

Washington, George. Christiana [Delaware]. To Robert Morris [Philadelphia]. Expenses for pursuit of deserters. Draft. 1 p. In handwriting of David Cobb. A. VI, pt. I, 255

1781
SEP. 6
Morris, Robert [Philadelphia.] To [George] Washington [Head of Elk, Maryland]. Hard money for secret service; payment of troops. L. S. 1 p. **52, 77**

1781
SEP. 6
Morris, Robert. Chester [Pennsylvania]. To [George] Washington [Head of Elk]. Payment of army; supineness of states. L. S. 1 p. **52, 83**

1781
SEP. 6
Morris, R[obert]. Chester. To [George] Washington [Head of Elk]. Plea for deserter under sentence of death. A. L. S. 1 p. **52, 85**

1781
SEP. 6
Morris Robert. Philadelphia. To George Washington [Head of Elk]. Transmitting letters; payment of troops; loan from Comte de Rochambeau. L. S. 1 p. **52, 86**

1781
SEP. 6
[Morris, Robert.] [Philadelphia.] To Philip Audibert [Philadelphia]. Instructions for loan from Comte de Rochambeau and payment of army. Contemporary copy. 1 p. Enclosed in Morris to Washington, 1781, Sep. 6. **52, 89**

1781
SEP. 6
[Morris, Robert.] [Philadelphia.] To Comte de Rochambeau [Head of Elk]. Loan to the United States. Contemporary copy. 1 p. Enclosed in Morris to Washington, 1781, Sep. 6. **52, 90**

1781
SEP. 7
Washington, George. Head of Elk. To the Board of War [Philadelphia]. Transmitting paper relating to Hospital appointments. Draft. 1 p. In handwriting of Jonathan Trumbull, jr.
A. VI, pt. I, 257

1781
SEP. 7
Washington, George. Head of Elk. To Robert Morris [Philadelphia]. Payment of troops; haste of movement. Draft. 1 p. In handwriting of Jonathan Trumbull, jr. **A. VI, pt. I, 259**

1781
SEP. 7
Continental Congress, President. Philadelphia. To [George] Washington [Head of Elk]. Transmitting resolves. L. S. of Thomas McKean. 1 p.
97, 161

1781
SEP. 9
Duane, James. Philadelphia. To [George Washington, Mt Vernon]. Arrival of de Grasse; news from the North; changes of Marine and Treasury Boards; success of [Lt.] Col. [John] Laurens's mission. A. L. S. 3 pp. **52, 108**

1781
SEP. 10
Morris, Robert. [Philadelphia.] To [George] Washington [Mt Vernon]. Pay of troops; scarcity of money etc. L. S. 1 p. **52, 114**

1781
SEP. 11

Continental Congress, Resolve. Escort for mail between Morristown and Fishkill. Contemporary copy. 1 p. 53, 254

1781
SEP. 12

Washington, George. Dumfries [Virginia]. To the President of Congress [Philadelphia]. Progress of march. Draft. 1 p. In handwriting of Jonathan Trumbull, jr. Read in Congress, Sep. 17.
A. VI, pt. I, 261

1781
SEP. 12

Brodhead, Daniel. Fort Pitt. To the President of Congress [Philadelphia]. Charges against him; conditions at Fort Pitt. Contemporary copy. 2 pp. Enclosed in President of Congress to Washington, 1781, Sep. 25. 97, 170

1781
SEP. 13

Morris, Robert. [Philadelphia.] To [George] Washington [en route to Williamsburg]. Non-payment of a draft; bills for table expenses. L. S. 1 p.
52, 130

1781
SEP. 15

Washington, George. Williamsburg [Virginia]. To the President of Congress [Philadelphia]. Defeat of the British fleet off the Capes; lack of provisions for army. Draft. 1 p. In handwriting of Jonathan Trumbull, jr. Read in Congress, Sep. 27. A. VI, pt. I, 263
Printed: Writings of Washington (Ford) N. Y. 1891. 9, 359.

1781
SEP. 15

Continental Congress, President. Philadelphia. To [George] Washington [Williamsburg]. Intelligence of British fleets; expedition preparing at New York; [Brig. Gen. Benedict] Arnold in Connecticut; militia etc. L. S. of Thomas McKean. 4 pp. Answered, Sep. 23.* 97, 176

1781
SEP. 17

Washington, George. [Williamsburg.] To [Comte de Grasse, In the Chesapeake]. Queries and answers as to cooperation with land forces at Yorktown. D. S. 4 pp. In handwriting of David Cobb. Enclosed in Washington to the President of Congress, 1781, Oct. 27. C. C. 152, 10, 319
Printed: Writings of Washington (Ford) N. Y. 1891. 9, 364.

1781
SEP. 18

Continental Congress, Resolves. Murder of Col. [Isaac] Hayne; British barbarity toward prisoners; American prisoners sent to England; retaliations planned. D. S. of Charles Thomson. 2 pp. Enclosed in President of Congress to Washington, 1781, Sep. 21. 97, 163

1781
SEP. 22

Continental Congress, Order. Appointment of hospital mates. D. S. of Charles Thomson. Enclosed in President of Congress to Washington, 1781, Sep. 25. Published in Genl. Orders. Oct. 5.   **97, 167**

1781
SEP. 20

Continental Congress, Resolves. Promotions in Hospital Department; certain appointments. D. S. of Charles Thomson. Enclosed in President of Congress to Washington, 1781, Sep. 25. Published in Genl. Orders Oct. 5.   **97, 167**

1781
SEP. 21

Continental Congress, President. Philadelphia. To [George] Washington [Williamsburg, Virginia]. Transmitting resolves; the French and British fleets; Cornwallis; defense of Philadelphia; arrival of [Rear] Admiral [Thomas] Graves at Sandy Hook. L. S. of Thomas McKean. 4 pp. Answered Oct. 1.*   **97, 165**

1781
SEP. 21

Board of War. Philadelphia. To Captains and Commanders of the French frigates, Boston. Delivery of stores to the U. S. Clothier General. Contemporary copy. 1 p. Enclosed in Board of War to Washington, 1781, Oct. 13.   **97, 191**

1781
SEP. 23

Washington, George. Williamsburg. To the President of Congress [Philadelphia]. Interview with Comte de Grasse; arrival of troops etc. Draft. 1 p. In handwriting of Jonathan Trumbull, jr. Read in Congress, Oct. 1.   **A. VI, pt. I, 265**
Printed: Writings of Washington (Sparks) Boston. 1835. 8, 163.

1781
SEP. 23.

Washington, George. Williamsburg. To [the President of Congress, Philadelphia]. Reenforcement of British fleet. Draft. 1 p. In handwriting of Tench Tilghman. Marked "(private)"
   A. VI, pt. I, 267

1781
SEP. 23.

Washington, George. Williamsburg. To the Board of War [Philadelphia]. Strength of enemy's works; necessity of supply of ammunition. Draft. 1 p. In handwriting of Tench Tilghman.
   A. VI, pt. I, 269

1781
SEP. 24.

Continental Congress, Resolve. Brig. Gen. [William] Irvine and the command at Fort Pitt. D. S. of Charles Thomson. 2 pp. Enclosed in President of Congress to Washington, 1781, Sep. 25.
   97, 169

1781   Board of War. [Philadelphia.] To [Col.] John Moylan
SEP. 24.   [Philadelphia]. Instructions for transporting
                   stores from Boston. Contemporary copy. 3 pp.
                   Enclosed in Board of War to Washington, 1781,
                   Oct. 13.   97, 189

1781   Board of War. [Philadelphia.] To the President of Con-
SEP. 25.   gress [Philadelphia]. Salaries in the Clothier
                   General's Department. A. L. S. of Benjamin
                   Lincoln. 1 p. Enclosed in Board of War to
                   Washington, 1781, Dec. 3.   97, 227

[1781]   Continental Congress, President. [Philadelphia] To
[SEP. 26.]   [George] Washington [Williamsburg]. Trans-
                   mitting resolves; troops in Philadelphia. L. S.*
                   of Thomas McKean. 1 p. Answered Oct. 6.*
                                                              97, 173

1781   McKean, Thomas. Philadelphia. To [George] Washington
SEP. 26.   [Williamsburg]. Brief account of political hap-
                   penings in Europe; France, Spain and Russia;
                   proposed congress at Vienna; French aids; sug-
                   gestions as to campaign; siege of New York etc.
                   L. S. 5 pp. Marked: "Private."   52, 213

1781   Washington, George. Williamsburg. To R[obert] Mor-
SEP. 27.   ris [Philadelphia]. Need of rum. Draft. 2 pp.
                   In handwriting of David Humphreys.
                                                       A. VI, pt. I, 271

1781   Washington, George. Williamsburg. To the Board of
SEP. 28.   War [Philadelphia]. Needs of the Hospital.
                   Draft. 1 p. In handwriting of Jonathan Trum-
                   bull, jr.   A. VI, pt. I, 273

1781   Continental Congress, Resolve. Depreciation of pay of
SEP. 28.   officers. D. S. of Charles Thomson. 1 p. En-
                   closed in President of Congress to Washington,
                   1781, Oct. 10.   97, 184

1781   Washington, George. Camp near Yorktown [Virginia].
OCT. 1   To the President of Congress [Philadelphia]. In-
                   vesture of Yorktown. Draft. 2 pp. In hand-
                   writing of Jonathan Trumbull, jr. Read in Con-
                   gress, Oct. 12.   A. VI, pt. I, 285
                   Printed: Writings of Washington (Ford) N. Y. 1891. 9, 372.

1781   Washington, George. Before Yorktown. To Robert Mor-
OCT. 1   ris [Philadelphia]. Introducing Col. Charles
                   Harrison; pay for [Maj.] Gen. [Benjamin] Lin-
                   coln. Draft. 1 p. In handwriting of Jonathan
                   Trumbull, jr.   A. VI, pt. I, 287

1781
Oct. 1

Washington, George. Before Yorktown. To Robert Morris [Philadelphia]. Return of bill of exchange. Draft. 1 p. In handwriting of Jonathan Trumbull, jr.

A. VI, pt. I, 289

1781
Oct. 1

Mathews, John. Philadelphia. To George Washington [Before Yorktown]. Spain's demand for U. S. representative at Vienna Congress; necessity of vigorous exertion on part of America; Great Britain's attitude; effect of demonstration toward Charleston; Charles Fox's motion in Parliament. A. L. S. 5 pp. 52, 246

1781
Oct. 2

Board of War. Philadelphia. To [George] Washington [Before Yorktown]. Capt. [Allan] McLane and the vacant majority in Armand's Corps. A. L. S. of Richard Peters. 1 p. Answered Oct. 27.*

97, 177

1781
Oct. 2

Varnum, J[ames] M[itchell]. Philadelphia. To [George] Washington [Before Yorktown]. Suggesting conquest of Bermuda; Secretary-ship of War. A. L. S. 3 pp. 51, 257

1781
Oct 4

Anonymous. To ———? Intelligence of British movements at New York. Contemporary copy. 1 p. Enclosed in President of Congress to Washington, 1781, Oct. 13. 97, 179

1781
Oct. 6

Washington, George. Before Yorktown. To the President of Congress [Philadelphia]. Progress of the siege; Maj. Gen. Greene's victory [Eutaw Springs]. Draft. 1 p. In handwriting of Tench Tilghman. Read in Congress, Oct. 16.

A. VI, pt. I, 291

Printed, in part: Writings of Washington (Ford) N. Y. 1891. 9, 380, note.

1781
Oct. 6

Washington, George. Before Yorktown. To [the President of Congress, Philadelphia]. Dependence of America upon her own exertions; prospects of success of the siege. Draft. 3 pp. In handwriting of Tench Tilghman. A. VI, pt. I, 393

1781
Oct. 6

Washington, George. Before Yorktown. To James Lovell [Philadelphia]. Ciphers of the enemy. Draft. 1 p. In handwriting of Jonathan Trumbull, jr. A. VI, pt. I, 297

1781
Oct. 6

Lytle, Archibald. Wilmington [North Carolina]. To
Maj. Anderson Craig [Wilmington]. Seizure of
effects and treatment received. A. L. S. Enclosed in Board of War to Washington, 1782,
Nov. 22.   **98, 309**

1781
Oct. 7

Heath, W[illiam]. "Continental Village" [near Peekskill].
To the President of Congress [Philadelphia]. In-
telligence of British at New York. Contempo-
rary copy. 2 pp. In handwriting of Charles
Thomson. Enclosed in President of Congress to
Washington, 1781, Oct. 13.   **97, 178**

1781
Oct. 8

Continental Congress, Resolve. Exchange of Robert
Starke and authorizing retaliation. D. S. of
Charles Thomson. 1 p. Enclosed in President
of Congress to Washington, 1781, Oct. 10.

97, 182

1781
Oct. 9

Heath, W[illiam]. [Newburgh, New York.] To [the President of Congress, Philadelphia] Reward for captors of Fort Slongo [Smithtown, Long Island];
letter of Baron Riedesel; relief of Cornwallis.
Contemporary copy. 2 pp. In handwriting of
Charles Thomson. Enclosed in McKean to Washington, 1781, Oct. 15.   **53, 9**

1781
Oct. 9

Lytle, Archibald. Wilmington [North Carolina]. To Maj.
Anderson Craig [Wilmington]. Parole. A. L. S.
Enclosed in Board of War to Washington, 1782,
Nov. 22.   **98, 309**

1781
Oct. 10

Continental Congress, President. Philadelphia. To
[George] Washington [Before Yorktown]. Case
of Robert Starke; depreciation of pay. L. S. of
Thomas McKean. 2 pp. Answered Oct. 27.*

97, 186

1781
Oct. 12

Washington, George. Before Yorktown. To the President of Congress [Philadelphia]. Progress of the
siege; opening parallels and trenches etc. Draft.
3 pp. In handwriting of Tench Tilghman.
Read in Congress, Oct. 22.

A. VI, pt. I, 299

Printed: Writings of Washington (Ford) N. Y. 1891. 9, 380.

1781
Oct. 12

Washington, George. Before Yorktown. To James Lovell [Philadelphia] Acknowledging letters for
Maj. Gen. [Nathanael] Greene. Draft. 1 p. In
handwriting of Jonathan Trumbull, jr.

A. VI, pt. I, 303

1781
OCT. 12

McKean, Thomas. Philadelphia. To George Washington [Before Yorktown]. Arrival of British fleet at New York; intended attempt to relieve Cornwalls; capture of Clinton's despatches; Armand's Corps; arrival of clothing and money from France. A. L. S. 5 pp. 52, 333

1781
OCT. 13

Continental Congress, President Philadelphia. [Before Yorktown]. To [George] Washington Relief of Cornwallis. Letter-book copy. C. C. 16, 95

1781
OCT. 13

Board of War. [Philadelphia.] To [George] Washington [Before Yorktown]. Transportation of clothing and stores from Boston; artillery supplies. L. S. of Richard Peters. 1 p. 97, 188

1781
OCT. 14

Continental Congress, President. Philadelphia. To [George] Washington [Before Yorktown]. Intercepted British letters; intelligence disclosed; British force at New York. L. S. of Thomas McKean. 5 pp. Answered Oct. 27.* 97, 222

1781
OCT. 14

Lovell, James. [Philadelphia.] To [George] Washington [Before Yorktown]. Cyphers used by British. A. L. S. 2 pp. 51, 314

1781
OCT. 14

Yorktown, Siege. Continental Army. Return of Killed and wounded since Sep. 28. Tabular statement. Transcript. Enclosed in Washington to the President of Congress, 1781, Oct. 27–29.
C. C. 169, 8, 253

1781
OCT. 15

Hamilton, A[lexander]. Before Yorktown. To Marquis de Lafayette [Before Yorktown]. Report of capture of redoubt; special cases of valor; behavior of troops; losses etc. Contemporary copy. 4 pp. In handwriting of David Cobb. Enclosed in Washington to the President of Congress, 1781, Oct. 16. C. C. 152, 10, 281

[1781]
[OCT. 15]

Yorktown, Siege. French troops. Return of killed and wounded of French Army from beginning of siege. Addressed to Washington. 2 pp. Enclosed in Washington to the President of Congress, 1781, Oct. 16. C. C. 152, 10, 285

1781
OCT. 16

Washington, George. Before Yorktown. To the President of Congress [Philadelphia]. Progress of the siege; capture of two redoubts. Draft. 3 pp. In handwriting of Tench Tilghman. Read in Congress, Oct. 25. Referred to Randolph, Boudinot, Varnum and Carroll.
A. VI, pt. I, 305

1781
Oct. 16

Lafayette, [Marquis de]. Before Yorktown. To [George] Washington [Before Yorktown]. Report of capture of redoubt. Contemporary copy. 2 pp. In handwriting of Tench Tilghman. Enclosed in Washington to the President of Congress, 1781, Oct. 16.   C. C.   152, 10, 277

[1781]
[Oct. 16]

[Rochambeau, Comte de] [Before Yorktown]. To [George Washington, Before Yorktown]. Report of capture of redoubts; casualties. Contemporary copy. 3 pp. In handwriting of Tench Tilghman. Enclosed in Washington to the President of Congress, 1781, Oct. 16.

C. C.   152, 10, 273

1781
Oct. 17

Morris, Robert. [Philadelphia.] To [George] Washington [Before Yorktown]. Rum for army; bills and minor matters; lukewarmness of states. L. S. 2 pp.   52, 331

1781
Oct. 17

Cornwallis, [Charles, Earl] Yorktown. To [George] Washington [Before Yorktown]. Cessation of hostilities to arrange for surrender.

Washington to Cornwallis. Willingness to grant terms.

Cornwallis to Washington. Basis of conditions.

Oct. 18   Washington to Cornwallis. Terms that will be granted.

Cornwallis to Washington. Agreement to treat. Contemporary copies. 7 pp. In handwriting of Jonathan Trumbull, jr. Enclosed in Washington to the President of Congress, 1781, Oct. 19.

C. C.   152, 10, 297

Printed: Writings of Washington (Sparks) Boston. 1835. 8, 530.

1781
Oct. 18

McKean, Thomas. Philadelphia. To [George] Washington [Before Yorktown]. Intelligence of British; resignation from Congress. L. S. 2 pp. 53, 7

1781
Oct. 19

Washington, George. Before Yorktown. To the President of Congress [Philadelphia]. Announcing the surrender of Cornwallis; harmony among the allied troops. Draft. 4 pp. In handwriting of Jonathan Trumbull, jr Read in Congress, Oct. 24. Referred to Randolph, Boudinot, Varnum and Carroll. Reported and acted on Oct. 29.

A. VI, pt. I, 309

Printed: Writings of Washington (Ford) N. Y. 1891. 9, 386.

1781
Oct. 19

Board of War. [Philadelphia] To [George Washington, Yorktown]. Secret agent in New York; British fleet signals; blankets and hospital supplies. A. L. S. of Richard Peters. 1 p. Answered Oct. 27.*   **97, 209**

1781
Oct. 19

Knox, H[enry]. [Yorktown.] Return [to George Washington, Yorktown]. of ordnance and military stores taken at York and Gloucester. D. S. 6 pp. Enclosed in Washington to the President of Congress, 1781, Oct. 27.   **C. C. 152, 10, 339**

1781
Oct. 19

Yorktown, Surrender. Articles settled between Washington, Rochambeau, De Grasse and Cornwallis and Symonds. Contemporary copy. 9 pp. In handwriting of Jonathan Trumbull, jr. Enclosed in Washington to the President of Congress, 1781, Oct. 19.   **C. C. 152, 10, 299**
Printed: Writings of Washington (Sparks) Boston. 1835. 8, 532.

1781
Oct. 19

Yorktown, Surrender. British naval force. Return of vessels surrendered. 2 pp. (In French). Enclosed in Washington to the President of Congress, 1781, Oct. 27–29.   **C. C. 152, 10, 353**

1781
Oct. 20

Washington, George. [Before Yorktown.] To Comte de Grasse [In the Chesapeake]. Propositions for operations against Charleston or Wilmington.
[**Grasse,** Comte de.] To Washington. Agreeing to Wilmington plan. Contemporary copies. 4 pp. In handwriting of Jonathan Trumbull, jr. Transmitted to Congress.   **C. C. 152, 10, 323**
Printed: Writings of Washington (Ford) N. Y. 1891. 9, 389.

1781
Oct. 21

Jones, Thomas. Yorktown. Return to George Washington, [Yorktown,] of provisions and stores surrendered at York and Gloucester. Tabular statement. D. S. 1 p. Signed also by Jacob Weed and Adam Dolmage. Enclosed in Washington to the President of Congress, 1781, Oct. 27–29.
                C. C. 152, 10, 357

1781
Oct. 22

Washington, George. Near Yorktown. To [Benjamin] Franklin [Passy]. Transmitting accounts of surrender at Yorktown and victory of Eutaw Springs. Contemporary copy. 1 p. In handwaiting of Jonathan Trumbull, jr. Enclosed in Washington to the President of Congress, 1781, Oct. 27–29.   **C. C. 152, 10, 329**
Printed: Writings of Washington (Sparks) Boston. 1835. 8, 188.

1781
Oct. 24

Anspach, Peter. Yorktown. Receipt to British paymaster for cash surrendered at Yorktown. Contemporary copy. 1 p. Note by Jonathan Trumbull, jr. that the British military chest was turned over to the Quartermaster General. Enclosed in Washington to the President of Congress 1781, Oct. 27–29.   **C. C.** 152, 10, 351

1781
Oct. 24

Duportail, [Louis Le Bègue]. Before Yorktown. To [George] Washington [Before Yorktown]. Application for furlough; claim to advancement. A. L. S. 2 pp. Enclosed in Washington to the President of Congress, 1781, Oct. 31.

     C. C. 152, 10, 369

1781
Oct. 26

Grasse, Comte de. [In the Chesapeake.] To [Marquis de Lafayette, near Yorktown]. Convoy and transportation of troops to Wilmington. Contemporary copy. 2 pp. In handwriting of David Cobb. Enclosed in Washington to the President of Congress, 1781, Oct. 27–29. **C. C.** 152, 10, 327.

1781
Oct. 26

Continental Congress, Proclamation establishing a day of Thanksgiving and Prayer. D. S. of Thomas McKean, attested by Charles Thomson. 3 pp. In handwriting of Charles Morse. Enclosed in President of Congress to Washington, 1781, Oct. 31.   **97, 194**

1781
Oct. 27

Washington, George. Near Yorktown. To [the President of Congress, Philadelphia]. Transmitting extract of letter from Maj. Gen. [William] Heath. Draft. 1 p. In handwriting of Jonathan Trumbull, jr. Referred, Nov. 5, to delegates from Georgia. Reported Nov. 7. "part passed 7. rem^r postron^d.—22"   **A.** VI, pt. I, 321

1781
Oct. 27

Washington, George. Near Yorktown. To the Board of War [Philadelphia]. Clothing and ordnance stores. Draft. 1 p. In handwriting of Jonathan Trumbull, jr.   **A.** VI, pt. I, 323

1781
Oct. 27

Washington, George. [Near Yorktown]. To Robert Morris [Philadelphia]. Education of his sons; rum for the army etc. Draft. 2 pp. In handwriting of Jonathan Trumbull, jr.

     A. VI, pt. I, 327

1781
Oct. 27–29

Washington, George. [Near Yorktown.] To the President of Congress [Philadelphia]. Returns of the surrender; future operations. L. S. 5 pp. In

handwriting of Jonathan Trumbull, jr. Read
in Congress, Nov. 3. Referred to Randolph,
Boudinot, Varnum and Carroll.

C. C.   **152**, 10, 309

Draft. 5 pp. A. VI, pt. I, 315, iş dated Oct. 26.
Printed: Writings of Washington (Ford) N. Y. 1891. 9, 393.

1781
OCT. 27

Amerman, D——. Near Yorktown. Invoice [sent to
George Washington, Yorktown,] of clothing surrendered by British. Tabular statement. D. S.
1 p. Endorsed by Jonathan Trumbull, jr. as
having been in a cartel ship that had violated
rights of a flag and so adjudged forfeited.
Above return stated as inaccurate but best obtainable. Enclosed in Washington to the President of Congress, 1781, Oct. 27–29.

C. C.   **152**, 10, 361

1781
OCT. 27

Amerman, D——. Near Yorktown. Invoice [sent to
George Washington, Yorktown,] of clothing received from British. A. D. S. 1 p. Enclosed
in Washington to the President of Congress,
1781, Oct. 27–29.   C. C.   **152**, 10, 343

1781
OCT. 27

Durie, Thomas. Near Yorktown. Return [to George
Washington, Yorktown] of British troops surrendered. Tabular statement. A. D. S. 2 pp.
Enclosed in Washington to the President of Congress, 1781, Oct. 27–29.   C. C.   **152**, 10, 331

[1781]
[OCT. 27]

Pickering, Timothy [jr.] [Near Yorktown.] Return [to
George Washington, Yorktown] of wagons,
horses and quartermaster's stores taken at York
and Gloucester. Contemporary copy. 2 pp.
Enclosed in Washington to the President of Congress, 1781, Oct. 27–29.   C. C.   **152**, 10, 347

1781
OCT. 28

Amerman, D——. Near Yorktown. Return [to George
Washington, Yorktown] of British clothing surrendered Oct. 19. Tabular statement. D. S.
1 p. Enclosed in Washington to the President
of Congress, 1781, Oct. 27–29.   C. C.   **152**, 10, 343

1781
OCT. 29

Continental Congress, Resolves. Thanks of Congress to
Washington, Rochambeau and others on surrender of Yorktown. D. S. of Chas. Thomson. 3 pp.
Enclosed in President of Congress to Washington, 1781, Oct. 31.   **97**, 192

1781
OCT. 29

Continental Congress, Resolves. Thanks of Congress to
Maj. Gen. [Nathanael] Greene and others on occasion of battle of Eutaw Springs. D. S. of Charles

Thomson. 2 pp. Enclosed in President of Congress to Washington, 1781, Oct. 31. 97, 196

1781
Oct. 29

Frey, [Charles,] Baron de. [Before Yorktown.] To George Washington [Before Yorktown]. Application for command or a furlough. A. L. S. 2 pp. Enclosed in Washington to the President of Congress, 1781, Oct. 31. C. C. 152, 10, 379

1781
Oct. 29

Duportail, [Louis Le Bègue]. Before Yorktown. To [George] Washington [Before Yorktown]. Recommending [Major Jean Baptiste] Gouvion and [Capt. Bichet de] Rochefontaine. A. L. S. 1 p. Enclosed in Washington to the President of Congress, 1781, Oct. 31. C. C. 152, 10, 373

1781
Oct. 30

Greene, Nathanael. Hills of Santee [South Carolina]. To [George] Washington [near Yorktown]. Recommending Col. [Otho Holland] Williams for promotion. Contemporary copy. 2 pp. In handwriting of Tench Tilghman. Enclosed in Washington to the President of Congress, 1781, Dec. 4.
C. C. 152, 10, 409

1781
Oct. 31

Washington, George. Near York. To [the President of Congress Philadelphia]. Abilities of Duportail and Knox. Draft. 3 pp. In handwriting of John Laurens. Read in Congress, Nov. 9. Referred to Varnum, Montgomery and Lovell. Reported Nov. 12. A. VI, pt. I, 329
Printed: Writings of Washington (Ford), N. Y. 1891. 9, 403.

1781
Oct. 31

Continental Congress, President. Philadelphia. To [George] Washington [Yorktown]. Thanks of Congress on surrender of Yorktown. L. S. of Thomas McKean. 3 pp. Answered Nov. 15.*
97, 198

1781
Nov. 1

Provaux, Adrian. Williamsburg [Virginia]. To [George] Washington [near Yorktown]. Permission to go to Cape François. Contemporary copy. 2 pp. In handwriting of Tench Tilghman. Enclosed in Washington, 1781, Dec. 4. C. C. 152, 10, 411

1781
Nov. 2

Washington, George [Near Yorktown.] To the President of Congress [Philadelphia]. Baron de Frey's application for furlough. Draft. 1 p. In handwriting of John Laurens. Read in Congress, Nov. 21. Referred to Board of War.
A. VI, pt. I, 333

1781
Nov. 4
Washington, George. [Near Yorktown.] To the President of Congress [Philadelphia]. Proposition of Capt. [Allen] McLane for reentering the service. L. S. 2 pp. In handwriting of David Cobb. Read in Congress, Nov. 19. Referred to Board of War.   **C. C. 152,** 10, 383
Draft, A. VI, pt. I. 335 is dated Nov. 5.

1781
Nov. 5
Continental Congress, Secretary. Philadelphia. To [George] Washington [Yorktown]. Election of · John Hanson, President of Congress. L. S. of Charles Thomson. 1 p. Answered Nov. 15.*
                                                            97, 200

1781
Nov. 6
Washington, George. "Col. Bassett's, near Ruffens Ferry" [Virginia]. To the President of Congress [Philadelphia]. Forwarding of troops. Auto. draft signed. 1 p. Read in Congress, Nov. 22.
                                               A. VI, pt. I, 337

1781
Nov. 7
Continental Congress, Resolve. Sword to [Lt.] Col. [David] Humphreys. D. S. of Charles Thomson. 1 p. Enclosed in President of Congress to Washington, 1781, Nov. 10.   97, 201

1781
Nov. 8
Heath, W[illiam]. Continental Village. [Near Peekskill.] To the President of Congress [Philadelphia]. Return of British fleet to New York; Col. [Marinus] Willett's expedition; rumor of attempt on the Highlands. Contemporary copy. 2 pp. Enclosed in President of Congress to Washington, 1781, Nov. 13.   97, 205

1781
Nov. 9
Board of War. [Philadelphia.] To [George] Washington [Eltham? Virginia]. Continental regiment to be quartered in Philadelphia; clothing supplies, sick etc. L. S. of Richard Peters. 2 pp.   97, 208

1781
Nov. 10
Continental Congress, President. Philadelphia. To [George] Washington [Eltham, Virginia]. Transmitting resolve; state of affairs. L. S. of John Hanson. 2 pp. Answered Nov. 30.*   97, 203

1781
Nov. 13
Continental Congress, President. Philadelphia. To [George] Washington [Fredericksburg, Virginia]. Transmitting copy of letter. L. S. of John Hanson. 1 p. Answered Nov. 30.*   97, 206

1781
Nov. 14
Chittenden, Thomas. Arlington [Vermont]. To George Washington [Mt Vernon]. Vermont's policy and actions; rights etc. Transcript. Enclosed in Washington to the President of Congress, 1783, Feb. 11.   **C. C. 169,** 9, 111

1781 Nov. 15	**Washington, George.** Mt Vernon [Virginia]. To [the President of Congress, Philadelphia]. Receipt of resolutions of approbation. Draft. 1 p. In handwriting of Jonathan Trumbull, jr. Read in Congress Nov. 21. **A.** VI, pt. I, 339
1781 Nov. 15	**Washington, George.** Mt Vernon. To Thomas McKean [Philadelphia]. Proclamation of Congress; his retirement from the Presidency. Draft. 1 p. In handwriting of Jonathan Trumbull, jr. **A.** VI, pt. I, 341 Printed: Writings of Washington (Ford), N. Y. 1891. 9, 409.
1781 Nov. 15	**Washington, George.** Mt Vernon. To Charles Thomson [Philadelphia]. Receipt of announcement of election of a new President of Congress. Draft. 1 p. In handwriting of Jonathan Trumbull, jr. **A.** VI, pt. I, 343
1781 Nov. 16	**Continental Congress,** Resolves. Promotion of Duportail and other French officers. D. S. of Charles Thomson. 1 p. Enclosed in President of Congress to Washington 1781, Nov. 24. **97, 214**
1781 Nov. 16	**Board of War.** Proceedings. Report to Congress on retention of General officers in service. Contemporary copy. 2 pp. Enclosed in Board of War to Washington, 1781, Dec. 3. **97, 231**
1781 Nov. 19	**Washington, George.** Mt. Vernon. To the Board of War [Philadelphia]. Furnishing clothing to troops; supply of same. Draft. 1 p. In handwriting of Jonathan Trumbull, jr. **A.** VI, pt. I, 345
1781 Nov. 19	**Washington, George.** Mt Vernon. To R[obert] Morris [Philadelphia]. Goods taken at Yorktown for relief of officers; sale of public stores. Draft. 2 pp. In handwriting of Jonathan Trumbull, jr. **A.** VI, pt. I, 347
1781 Nov. 19	**Board of War.** Philadelphia. To the Oneida Nation [New York]. Friendship; victory at Yorktown etc. [Peters, Richard.] [Philadelphia.] Report to Congress on letter of Washington [1781, Nov. 4] respecting Capt. [Allen] McLane. [Incomplete.] Drafts in handwriting of Peters. 2 pp. **C. C.** 152, 10, 387
1781 Nov. 22	**Continental Congress,** Resolve. Approving Washington's actions. D. S. of Charles Thomson. 1 p. Enclosed in President of Congress to Washington, 1781, Nov. 24. **97, 212**

| 1781 Nov. 24 | Continental Congress, President. Philadelphia. To [George Washington, Baltimore]. Transmitting resolves. L. S. of John Hanson. 1 p. An swered Nov. 30.* 97, 216 |

| [1781] [Nov. 28] | Washington, George. [Philadelphia.] Reply in Congress to address of the President. Exertions of states, committee of conference etc. A. D. 2 pp. En closed in Washington to Thomson, 1781, Nov. 30. C. C. 152, 10, 397 |

| [1781] [Nov. 28] | Continental Congress, President. Philadelphia. To [George] Washington [Philadelphia]. Address of Congress; his services; stay in Philadelphia etc. A. D. of John Hanson. 1 p. 97, 296 |

| 1781 Nov. 28 | Continental Congress, Secretary. [Philadelphia.] To George Washington [Philadelphia]. Audience with Congress. A. L. S. of Charles Thomson. 1 p. 97, 298 |

| 1781 Nov. 28 | Continental Congress, Resolve. Resignation of Capt. [Charles, Baron] de Fry. D. S. of Charles Thom son. 1 p. Transmitted to Washington. 97, 218 |

| [1781] [Nov. 28] | Washington, George. [Philadelphia.] To the President [of Congress, Philadelphia]. Thanks for their favors etc. A. D. 1 p. 97, 297 |

| 1781 Nov. 28 | Continental Congress, Committee of Conference on Estab lishment of Army. Philadelphia. To [George Washington, Philadelphia]. Requesting attend ance; points to be considered. A. L. S. of Dan iel Carroll. 1 p. 53, 227 |

Committee: Carroll, Cornell, Atlee, Randolph, and Eveleigh.

| 1781 Nov. 29 | Lytle, A[rchibald]. Charleston. To Dr. [James] Fraser [Charleston]. Parole. A. L. S. 1 p. Enclosed in Secretary of War to Washington, 1782, Nov. 22. 98, 308 |

| 1781 Nov. 30 | Washington, George. Philadelphia. To [the President of Congress, Philadelphia]. His accession to office of President; necessity of vigorous exertions to maintain the advantages gained. Draft. 1 p. In handwriting of Jonathan Trumbull, jr. A. VI, pt. I, 349 |

Printed: Writings of Washington (Sparks), Boston. 1835. 8, 214.

| 1781 Nov. 30 | Washington, George. Philadelphia. To [the Committee of Conference]. Extensive nature of his queries. Draft. 1 p. In handwriting of Jonathan Trum bull, jr. A. VI, pt. I, 351 |

Committee: Carroll, Cornell, Atlee, Randolph, and Eveleigh.

1781
Nov. 30

Washington, George. [Philadelphia] To [Charles] Thomson [Philadelphia]. Enclosing reply to address of Congress. A. L. S. 1 p.   **C. C. 152,** 10, 399

1781
Nov. 31

Continental Congress, President. Philadelphia. To [George] Washington [Philadelphia]. Transmitting resolves. L. S. of John Hanson. 1 p.
                                    97, 220

1781
Nov. —

Lytle, Archibald. Beaufort [North Carolina]. To Lt. Col. [Nesbitt] Balfour [Beaufort]. His case; supplies for prisoners. A. L. S. 2 pp. Enclosed in Secretary at War to Washington, 1782, Nov. 22.   **98,** 310

[1781]
[Nov?]

Continental Congress, Committee [of Conference]. Report. Pay and depreciation to be made to discharged and retired army officers. A. D. of Nathan Jones. 1 p. Enclosed in Secretary at War to Washington, 1781, Dec. 3?   **97,** 230
           Cf. Journals of Congress, 1781, Dec. 31.

1781
Dec. 1

Continental Congress, Committee of Conference. [Philadelphia]. To [George Washington, Philadelphia]. Appointing time of conference. Recent copy. 1 p.   **53,** 258

1781
Dec. 3

Washington, George. Philadelphia. To the President of Congress [Philadelphia]. British proposal of exchange of prisoners; Cornwallis. Draft. 1 p. In handwriting of Tench Tilghman. Read in Congress, Dec. 3. Referred to Carroll, Cornell, Atlee, Randolph and Eveleigh. Reported Dec. 28. "negatived Jany. 2, 1782." **A.** VI, pt. I, 353

1781
Dec. 3

Secretary at War. [Philadelphia.] To [George] Washington [Philadelphia]. Transmitting papers. A. L. S. of Benjamin Lincoln. 1. p.   **97,** 226
       The Board of War was discontinued by resolve of Congress, Oct. 30, 1781 and its powers and duties vested in a Secretary at War. Gen. Lincoln accepted the appointment Nov. 26 on which date the Board was dissolved.

1781
Dec. 3

Irvine, William. Fort Pitt. To the President of Congress [Philadelphia]. Arrangement of troops at Fort Pitt; failure of [Brig.] Gen. [George Rogers] Clark's expedition; fortification below Fort Pitt; leaves of absence. A. L. S. 3 pp. Enclosed in President of Congress to Washington, 1781, Dec. 19.   **97,** 255

1781
Dec. 4

Washington, George. [Philadelphia.] To the President of Congress [Philadelphia]. Promotion of Col. [Otho Holland] Williams. Draft. 1 p. In hand-

Camp 4th Novr 1781 —

Dear Sir —

Your application is not a little distressing to me; and if complyd with must have an unhappy influence on the mind of the detachment which is going to the southward — Col. Stewart is already gone — and Col. Butler on account of his Health is going — three of the first officers then in rank and consequence in the Pensylvania line, to be away from their Troops when an important & interesting Service is in View (independant of the ——— succure intended by it to the Army of Major General Greene) will discourage that line; and must subject me to censure for yielding to it

But of the two alternatives proposed by you I shall prefer the first as more consonant to military propriety, if your wound does not render the March too obnox -ious to it. —

Under this exposition of my sentiments I leave you at liberty to follow the dictates of your own Judgement being with much esteem & regard Dr Sir

Yr Most Obedt Servt

G. W.

WRITING OF WILLIAM STEPHENS SMITH.

writing of Jonathan Trumbull, jr and Tench Tilghman. Read in Congress, Dec. 6. Referred to Secretary at War.   A. VI, pt. I, 355

1781
DEC. 4

Washington, George. Philadelphia. To [the Secretary at War, Philadelphia]. Accoutrements for the dragoons. Draft. 2 pp. In handwriting of Tench Tilghman.   A. VI, pt. I, 359

1781
DEC. 5

Continental Congress, President. Philadelphia. To [George] Washington [Philadelphia]. Directing a exchange of officers. L. S. of John Hanson. 1 p.   97, 233

1781
DEC. 5

Washington, George. Philadelphia. To [the Secretary at War, Philadelphia]. [Brig.] Gen. [Henry] Knox's recommendation. Auto. draft. signed. 1 p.
          A. VI, pt. I, 357
Printed: Writings of Washington (Sparks) Boston. 1835. 8, 214.

1781
DEC. 5

Secretary at War. [Philadelphia.] To [George] Washington [Philadelphia]. Ordering Yorktown prisoners to Lancaster [Pennsylvania]. L. S. of Benjamin Lincoln. 1 p.   97, 237

1781
DEC. 5

Lincoln, B[enjamin]. Philadelphia. To George Washington [Philadelphia]. Maj. Gen. Duportail's promotion and [Brig.] Gen. [Henry] Knox. A. L. S. 2 pp.   97, 235

1781
DEC. 8

Washington, George. Philadelphia. To Robert Morris [Philadelphia]. Bills for sale of goods at Yorktown. Draft. 2 pp. In handwriting of Tench Tilghman.   A. VI, pt. I, 361

1781
DEC. 10

Continental Congress, Resolves. Filling state quotas of army. D. S. of Charles Thomson. 2 pp. Enclosed in President of Congress to Washington, 1781, Dec. 14.   97, 239

1781
DEC. 14

Continental Congress, President. Philadelphia. To [George] Washington [Philadelphia]. Transmitting resolve. L. S. of John Hanson. 2 pp. Answered Dec. 17.*   97, 241

1781
DEC. 14

Continental Congress, Resolve Warrants for pay and subsistence of officers. D. S. of Charles Thomson.

Secretary at War. Report of secretary on advance of pay to officers. Extract in handwriting of Joseph Carleton. 2 pp in all. Transmitted to Washington.   97, 243

1781
DEC. 17

Washington, George. Philadelphia. To the President of Congress [Philadelphia]. Deficiencies in State quota's of troops. Draft. 1 p. In handwriting of Tench Tilghman. **A.** VI, pt. I, 363

1781
DEC. 17

Continental Congress, President. Philadelphia. To [George] Washington [Philadelphia]. Resolutions transmitted to [Maj.] Gen. [Nathanael] Greene; returns. L. S. of John Hanson. 1 p. 97, 247

1781
DEC. 18

Secretary at War. [Philadelphia.] To the President of Congress [Philadelphia]. Defense of Fort Pitt; erection of fortifications etc. L. S. of Benjamin Lincoln. 5 pp. In handwriting of Joseph Carleton. Endorsed by Charles Thomson: "Referred to the Commander in chief to take order" Enclosed in President of Congress to Washington, 1781, Dec. 19. 97, 251

1781
DEC. 18

Continental Congress, Resolve. Mustering of recruits for the army. Contemporary copy. Enclosed in President of Congress to Washington, 1781, Dec. 20. 97, 245

1781
DEC. 19

Continental Congress, President. Philadelphia. To [George] Washington [Philadelphia]. Transmitting papers. L. S. of John Hanson. 1 p. 97, 249

1781
DEC. 19

Secretary at War. [Philadelphia.] To [George] Washington [Philadelphia]. West Point provision contract; transfer of powers of Secretary at War to the Commander in chief. L. S. of Benjamin Lincoln. 3 pp. In handwriting of Joseph Carleton. 97, 265

1781
DEC. 19

Continental Congress, Resolve. Supplies for recruits before joining the army. Contemporary copy. Enclosed in President of Congress to Washington, 1781, Dec. 20. 97, 245

1781
DEC. 19

Continental Congress, Resolves. Retention of General officers in the service. D. S. of Charles Thomson. 1 p. Enclosed in President of Congress to Washington, 1781, Dec. 21. 97, 259

1781
DEC. 20

Continental Congress, President. Philadelphia. To [George] Washington [Philadelphia]. Transmitting resolve. Letter-book copy. **C. C.** 16, 135

1781
Dec. 20

Continental Congress, Resolve. Exchange of Gov. Thomas Burke. A. D. S. of Charles Thomson. 1 p. Transmitted to Washington. 97, 261

1781
Dec. 20

Continental Congress, Resolve. Inquiry as to the Board of Associated Loyalists. A. D. S. of Charles Thomson. 1 p. Transmitted to Washington. 97, 262

1781
Dec. 20

Secretary at War. [Philadelphia.] To [George] Washington [Philadelphia]. Requesting opinion on letter to be submitted to Congress. A. L. S. of Benjamin Lincoln. 1 p. 97, 274

1781
Dec. 21

W[ashingto]n, G[eorge]. Philadelphia. To [the Secretary at War, Philadelphia]. Queries respecting the provision contract for West Point and its dependencies. Auto. draft signed. 2 pp.
A. VI, pt. I, 365

1781
Dec. 21

Continental Congress, President. Philadelphia. To [George] Washington [Philadelphia]. Transmitting resolve. L. S. of John Hanson. 1 p.
97, 257

1781
Dec. 21

Wales, Ebenezer, and Caleb **Davis.** Boston. To Maj. Gen. William Heath [Highlands]. Clothing for Massachusetts troops. Contemporary copy. 1 p. In handwriting of Benjamin Walker. Enclosed in Washington to the President of Congress, 1782, Jan. 30. C. C. 152, 10, 441

1781
Dec. 22

Secretary at War. [Philadelphia.] To [George] Washington [Philadelphia]. Answers to queries regarding contract for supplies at West Point. L. S. of Benjamin Lincoln. 2 pp. In handwriting of Joseph Carleton. 97, 264

1781
Dec. 23

Skinner, Abraham. Philadelphia. To [George] Washington [Philadelphia]. Exchange of Lord Cornwallis. Contemporary copy. 2 pp. In handwriting of William Stephens Smith. Enclosed in Washington to the President of Congress, 1781, Dec. 24. C. C. 152, 10, 421

1781
Dec. 23

Skinner, Abraham. Philadelphia. To [George] Washington [Philadelphia]. Exchange of naval prisoners. Transcript. Enclosed in Washington to the President of Congress, 1781, Dec. 27.
C. C. 169, 8, 272

1781
Dec. 24

Washington, George. Philadelphia. To the President of Congress [Philadelphia]. Exchange of prisoners. Draft. 1 p. In handwriting of Tench Tilghman. Read in Congress, Dec. 24. Referred to Committee appointed to confer with Commander in chief.   A. VI, pt. I, 367
Committee: Carroll, Cornell, Atlee, Randolph and Eveleigh.

1781
Dec. 24

Washington, George. Philadelphia. To [the Committee of Conference, Philadelphia]. Complaint of New Jersey as to prisoners. Draft. 1 p. In handwriting of Tench Tilghman. Addressed to Daniel Carroll [as chairman]. A. VI, pt. I, 369
Committee: Carroll, Cornell, Atlee, Randolph and Eveleigh.

1781
Dec. 24

Skinner, Abraham. Philadelphia. To [George] Washington [Philadelphia]. Exchange of naval prisoners; difficulties etc. Transcript. Enclosed in Washington to the President of Congress, 1781, Dec. 27.   C. C.   169, 8, 272

1781
Dec. 26

Secretary at War. [Philadelphia.] To [George] Washington [Philadelphia]. [Lt. ?] Col. [John ?] Connolly's breach of parole. A. L. S. of Benjamin Lincoln. 1 p.   97, 273

1781
Dec. 27

Washington, George. Philadelphia. To the President of Congress [Philadelphia]. Exchange of prisoners; complaints regarding marine prisoners. Draft. 3 pp. In handwriting of Tench Tilghman. Read in Congress, Dec. 28. Referred to Clymer, Cornell and Law.   A. VI, pt. I, 371
Printed: Writings of Washington (Ford), N. Y 1891. 9, 421.

1781
Dec. 27

Lytle, Archibald. Charleston. To Maj. Gen. [Nathanael] Greene [High Hills of the Santee]. Narration of treatment received from British while prisoner. A. L. S. 2 pp. Enclosed in Secretary at War to Washington, 1782, Nov. 22.   98, 299

1781
Dec. 28

W[ashingto]n, G[eorge]. Philadelphia. To [the Secretary at War, Philadelphia]. Comment on plan of inspection of army. Auto. draft signed. 4 pp.
A. VI, pt. I, 375

1781
Dec. 28

Secretary at War. [Philadelphia.] To [George] Washington [Philadelphia]. Transmitting standards presented by Congress. A. L. S. of Benjamin Lincoln. 2 pp.   97, 275

1781
Dec. 29

Washington, George. Philadelphia. To [the Secretary at War, Philadelphia]. Pay of the army; prisoners. Auto. draft. 2 pp. A. VI, pt. I, 379

1781
Dec. 30

Washington, George. Philadelphia. To [the Secretary at War, Philadelphia]. Trophies presented by Congress. Draft. 1 p. In handwriting of Tench Tilghman. **A.** VI, pt. I, 381

1781
Dec. 31

Continental Congress, Resolves. Pay and depreciation of officers, below brigadiers, retained in service; retirements; State settlement of depreciation. Contemporary copy. 2 pp. Transmitted to Washington. 97, 294

1781
Dec. —

Lytle, Archibald. [Charleston.] To Lewis H. De Rossett [Charleston]. Complaint of treatment received. **A. L. S.** 1 p. Enclosed in Secretary at War to Washington, 1782, Nov. 22. 98, 307

1781
[Dec. ?]

Duane, James. [Philadelphia.] To [George Washington, Philadelphia]. Objection of Congress to plan of Inspector General's department; miscellany. **A. L. S.** 2 pp. 53, 240

1782
Jan. 1

Washington, George. Philadelphia. To Thomas Chittenden [Arlington, Vermont]. Vermont's claim to territory; effect of her negotiations with the British. Transcript. Enclosed in Washington to the President of Congress, 1783, Feb. 11.
C. C. 169, 9, 123
Printed: Writings of Washington (Ford), N. Y. 1891. 9, 424.

1782
Jan. 2

Washington, George. Philadelphia. To the President of Congress [Philadelphia]. Sailing of detachment of the enemy for Charlestown. Draft. 1 p. In handwriting of William Stephens Smith. Read in Congress, Jan. 2. **A.** VI, pt. II, 1

1782
Jan. 4

Continental Congress, President. Philadelphia. To [George] Washington [Philadelphia]. Referring case of [Ensign] William Connor to Washington. Letter-book copy. **C. C.** 16, 136

1782
Jan. 8

Washington, George. Philadelphia. To the Secretary at War [Philadelphia]. • Referring letter to him. Draft. 1 p. In handwriting of Tench Tilghman.
A. VI, pt. II, 3

1782
Jan. 8

Secretary at War. [Philadelphia]. To [George] Washington [Philadelphia]. Transmitting resolve respecting officers' servants. L. S. of Benjamin Lincoln. 1 p. In handwriting of Joseph Carleton. 97, 326

1782
JAN. 10

Washington, George. Philadelphia. To the Secretary at War [Philadelphia]. Officers' servants and other minor matters. Draft. 1 p. In handwriting of Tench Tilghman. A. VI, pt. II, 5

1782
JAN. 10

Secretary at War. Philadelphia. To [George] Washington [Philadelphia]. Money for British prisoners; officers of Hospital Department; retirements. A. L. S. of Benjamin Lincoln. 3 pp. 97, 299

1782
JAN. 11

Secretary at War. [Philadelphia.] To [George] Washington [Philadelphia]. Request for names of officers below brigadiers who should be retained. A. L. S. of Benjamin Lincoln. 2 pp. 97, 301

1782
JAN. 14

Washington, George. Philadelphia. To the President of Congress [Philadelphia]. Interception of mail by the enemy. Draft. 1 p. In handwriting of David Humphreys. A. VI, pt. II, 7

1782
JAN. 18

Continental Congress, Resolve. Repeal of resolve of May 25, 1781. Contemporary copy. 1 p. 97, 303

1782
JAN. 19

[Heath, William.] [Highlands.] To [George] Washington [Philadelphia]. Massachusetts Legislature's order respecting clothing. [Extract of letter.] 1 p. In handwriting of Tench Tilghman. Enclosed in Washington to the President of Congress, 1782, Jan. 30. C. C. 152, 10, 439

1782
JAN. 20

Washington, George. Philadelphia. To [the Secretary at War, Philadelphia]. Measures for filling up and supporting the army; clothing for troops and officers; provisions for field operations; deserters. Draft. 7 pp. In handwriting of Tench Tilghman. A. VI, pt. I, 9

1782
JAN. 21

Secretary at War. [Philadelphia.] To [George] Washington [Philadelphia]. Relief of detachment at Wyoming; drums and fifes. L. S. of Benjamin Lincoln. 2 pp. In handwriting of Joseph Carleton. 97, 304

1782
JAN. 23

Washington, George. Philadelphia. To the President of Congress [Philadelphia]. Forwarding proceedings of court martial of Maj. Gen. [Robert] Howe. Draft. 1 p. In handwriting of Tench Tilghman. Read in Congress, Jan. 24. A. VI, pt. II, 17

1782
JAN. 23

Secretary at War. [Philadelphia.] To [George] Washington [Philadelphia]. Officer to incite New England States to raise troops; clothing; contract system; salt provisions; forage; transportation; tents etc.; deserters; supplies for coming campaign. A. L. S. of Benjamin Lincoln. 11 pp.

97, 306

1782
JAN. 23

Morris, Robert. [Philadelphia]. To [George] Washington [Philadelphia]. Capt. [Thomas] Hutchins employment by Pennsylvania. L. S. 2 pp.

54, 117

1782
JAN. 24

Continental Congress, Resolve. Approval of court martial acquittal of Maj. Gen. [Robert] Howe. Contemporary copy. 1 p. Transmitted to Washington.

97, 312

1782
JAN. 25

Washington, George. Philadelphia. To [Robert] Morris [Philadelphia]. Officers to go to the Eastern States to urge filling up of the battalions. Draft. 2 pp. In handwriting of Tench Tilghman.

A. VI, pt. II, 19

Printed: Writings of Washington (Sparks) Boston. 1835. 8, 230.

1782
JAN. 25

Sproat, David. New York. To Abraham Skinner [Philadelphia]. Exchange of naval for army prisoners. Contemporary copy. 2 pp. In handwriting of Tench Tilghman. Enclosed in Washington to the President of Congress, 1782, Feb. 18.

C. C. 152, 10, 457

1782
JAN. 26

Morris, Robert [Philadelphia.] To [George Washington, Philadelphia]. Plan for providing clothing for officers. L. S. 2 pp. Answered Feb. 2.*

54, 137

1782
JAN. 26

Morris, Robert. [Philadelphia.] To [George] Washington [Philadelphia]. Ideas for officers recruiting in the New England States; recruiting expense and states' quotas of money; food, clothing, equipment etc. of army; early and vigorous campaign etc. L. S. 5 pp. 54, 139

1782
JAN. 29

Washington, George. [Philadelphia.] To Robert Morris [Philadelphia]. Value of Capt. [Thomas] Hutchins's services in the south. Draft. 1 p. In handwriting of Benjamin Walker. A. VI, pt. II, 21

1782
JAN. 30

Washington, George. Philadelphia. To the President of Congress. Clothing of Massachusetts troops. L. S. 1 p. In handwriting of Benjamin Walker. Read in Congress Feb. 1. Referred to Clymer, Osgood and Madison. Reported and acted on Feb. 11. C. C. 152, 10, 435

Draft, A, VI, pt. II, 23, is dated Jan. 28.

1782
JAN. 31
Washington, George. Philadelphia. To Robert Morris [Philadelphia]. Maj. [William] McPherson's claim to depreciated pay. Draft. 1 p. In handwriting of Tench Tilghman.   **A.** VI, pt. II, 25

1782
FEB. 1
Continental Congress, President. Philadelphia. To [George] Washington [Philadelphia]. Maj.[John.] Porter. **L. S.** of John Hanson. 2 pp.   **97, 313**

1782
FEB. 1
Wayne, Anthony. Ebenezer [Georgia]. Speech to Creek and Choctaw chiefs. Friendship; the British, etc. **A. D. S.** 7 pp. Enclosed in Wayne to Washington, 1783, Nov. 1.   **C. C.** 152, 11, 567

1782
FEB. 2
Washington, George. Philadelphia. To [Robert] Morris [Philadelphia]. Clothing for officers. Draft. 1 p. In handwriting of Tench Tilghman.
    A. VI, pt. II, 27

1782
FEB. 9
Skinner, Abraham and Joshua **Loring.** New York. Agreement to exchange of certain officers for Lt. Gen. [John] Burgoyne.

Same. Agreement for exchange of Brig. Genls. [Lachlan] McIntosh and Charles O'Hara and Lt. Cols. Archibald Lyttle and [Robert] Abercromby. Contemporary copies. In handwriting of David Humphreys. Enclosed in Washington to the President of Congress, 1782, Feb. 18.
    C. C. 152, 10, 451

1782
FEB. 11
Continental Congress, Resolve. Purchase of clothing from Massachusetts. Contemporary copy. Transmitted to Washington.   **97, 315**

1782
FEB. 11
Clinton, H[enry]. New York. To [George] Washington [Philadelphia]. Exchange of Cornwallis for [Henry] Laurens. Contemporary copy. In handwriting of Benjamin Walker. Enclosed in Washington to the President of Congress, 1782, Feb. 18.   **C. C.** 152, 10, 447

1782
FEB. 12
Cornell, E[zekiel]. [Philadelphia.] To [George] Washington [Philadelphia]. Resolves, on promotion and half-pay to general officerships, to be proposed for consideration in Congress. A. L. S. 1 p. Answered Feb. 13.   **54, 233**

1782
FEB. 12
Loring, Joshua. New York. To [Abraham] Skinner [New York]. Reservation of American officers against Lord Cornwallis in exchange account. Memorandum of Skinner respecting same. Contempo-

rary copy. In handwriting of David Humphreys. Enclosed in Washington to the President of Congress, 1782, Feb. 18.　　　**C. C. 152, 10, 451**

1782 FEB. 13	**Washington, George.** Philadelphia. To [Brig.] Gen. [Ezekiel] Cornell [Philadelphia]. Plan for promotion of general officers. Draft. 3 pp. In handwriting of Tench Tilghman. **A. VI, pt. II, 29**

1782
FEB. 13

Continental Congress, Resolves. Supplies for Southern army; men and beef from Virginia for Maj. Gen. Nathanael Greene. Contemporary copy. Transmitted to Washington.　　　**97, 315**

1782
FEB. 14

Secretary at War. Boston. To [George] Washington [Philadelphia]. New Hampshire troops; stores for the campaign. L. S. of Benjamin Lincoln. 5 pp. In handwriting of William Jackson.　　　**97, 317**

1782
FEB. 14

[South Carolina,] House of Representatives, Resolve. Flags from British for return of inhabitants to the State. Concurred in by Senate, Feb. 19. Contemporary copy. 1 p. Transmitted to Washington.　　　**98, 5**

1782
FEB. 18

Washington, George. Philadelphia. To the President of Congress [Philadelphia]. Exchange of Cornwallis for [Henry] Laurens; marine prisoners. Draft. 3 pp. In handwriting of Tench Tilghman. Read in Congress, Feb. 20. Referred to Boudinot, Cornell and Bee.

A. VI, pt. II, 33

Printed: Writings of Washington (Ford) N. Y. 1891. 9, 443.

1782
FEB. 18

Continental Congress, Resolves. Exchange and treatment of prisoners of war; settlement of accounts; exchange of [Charles,] Earl Cornwallis. Contemporary copy. 1 p. Transmitted to Washington.

97, 321

Resolve respecting Cornwallis is marked secret.

1782
FEB. 18

Skinner, Abraham. Philadelphia. To George Washington [Philadelphia]. Exchange of Cornwallis. Contemporary copy. 1 p. In handwriting of Benjamin Walker. Enclosed in Washington to the President of Congress, 1782, Feb. 18.

C. C. 152, 10, 449

1782
FEB. 18

Skinner, Abraham. Philadelphia. To [George] Washington [Philadelphia]. ·Exchange of military for naval prisoners. Contemporary copy. 1 p. In handwriting of Tench Tilghman. Enclosed in Washington to the President of Congress, 1782, Feb. 18.   C. C. 152, 10, 455

1782
FEB. 20

Washington, George. Philadelphia. To [the President of Congress, Philadelphia]. Public and secret resolves of Congress respecting exchange of prisoners; Cornwallis's case. Draft. 4 pp. In handwriting of Tench Tilghman. Read in Congress, Feb. 21. Referred to Boudinot, Cornell and Bee.   A. VI, pt. II, 37
Printed: Writings of Washington (Ford) N. Y. 1891. 9, 449.

1782
FEB. 23

Continental Congress, Resolve. Exchange of [Charles,] Earl Cornwallis and Henry Laurens. D. S. of Charles Thomson. 1 p. Transmitted to Washington.   97, 323

1782
FEB. 25

Washington, George. Philadelphia. To the President of Congress [Philadelphia]. Sailing of enemy's transports for Charleston. Draft. 1 p. In handwriting of David Humphreys. Read in Congress, Feb. 25.   A. VI, pt. II, 41

1782
FEB. 28

Washington, George. Philadelphia. To [Robert] Morris [Philadelphia]. Accoutrement of Capt. [Bartholomew] von Heer's dragoons. Draft. 1 p. In handwriting of Tench Tilghman.
     A. VI, pt. II, 43

1782
MAR. 2

Washington, George. Philadelphia. To the Asst. Secretary at War [Philadelphia]. Petition of Ezekiel Addams[?]. Draft. 1 p. In handwriting of David Humphreys.   A. VI, pt. II, 45

1782
MAR. 4

Washington, George. Philadelphia. To [Robert] Morris [Philadelphia]. Baron Steuben's claim for arrearages of pay. Draft. 1 p. In handwriting of Tench Tilghman.   A. VI, pt. II, 45

1782
MAR. 7

Washington, George. Philadelphia. To the Secretary at War [Philadelphia]. Regulations for the Adjutant General's Department. Draft. 1 p. In handwriting of David Humphreys.
     A. VI, pt. II, 47

1782
MAR. 8

Washington, George. Philadelphia. To [Thomas] Bee [Philadelphia]. Opinion as to certain resolves of Congress; [Brig.] Gen. [Henry] Knox's ability. Auto. draft signed. 3 pp.   A. VI, pt. II, 49

1782
MAR. 11   **Washington**, George.   Philadelphia.   To Brig. Gen.
            Henry Knox and Gouverneur Morris [Philadel-
            phia].   Instructions for negotiating an exchange
            of prisoners.   Transcript.   Enclosed in Wash-
            ington to the President of Congress, 1782, Apr. 30.
            See: Knox and Morris to Washington, 1782,
            Mar. 31–Apr. 19.   **C. C.   169**, 8, 382

1782
MAR. 11   **Washington**, George.   Commission to Henry Knox and
            Gouverneur Morris.   See: Knox and Morris to
            Washington, 1782, Mar. 31–Apr. 19.

1782
MAR. 12   **Livingston**, Robert R.   Philadelphia.   To [George] Wash-
            ington [Philadelphia].   Peace negotiations; pre-
            liminary articles agreed to; French negotiations;
            withdrawal of British troops.   L. S.   3 pp.
                                                       62, 66

1782
MAR. 15   **Washington**, George.   Philadelphia.   To R[obert] Morris.
            [Philadelphia].   Baron Steuben's case.   Draft.
            1 p.   In handwriting of Benjamin Walker.
                                             A.   VI, pt. II, 53

1782
MAR. 16   **Knox** and **Morris** to Sir Henry Clinton.   See: Knox and
            Morris to Washington, 1782, Apr. 22.

1782
MAR. 16   **Knox** and **Morris** to Courtlandt Skinner.   See: Knox and
            Morris to Washington, 1782, Apr. 22.

1782
MAR. 18   **[Washington**, George.]   Philadelphia.   To the President
            of Congress [Philadelphia].   Preparation for de-
            parture to the army.   Auto. draft.   1 p.   Read
            in Congress, Mar. 18.   **A.   VI**, pt. II, 55

1782
MAR. 18   **Clinton**, Sir Henry, to Knox and Morris.   See: Knox and
            Morris to Washington, 1782, Apr. 22.

1782
MAR. 18   **Digby**, Robert.   Commission to Dalrymple and Elliott.
            See: Knox and Morris to Washington, 1782, Mar.
            31–Apr. 19.

[1782]
[MAR. 19]   **Continental Congress**, President.   [Philadelphia.]   To
            [George Washington, Philadelphia].   Speech of
            the President on Washington's audience of leave-
            taking.   A. D. of John Hanson.   1 p.
                                             A.   VI, pt. II, 59

1782
MAR. 19   **Continental Congress**, Resolve.   Repealing portion of re-
            solve of Sep. 30, 1780; pay and rations of regi-
            mental surgeons and mates.   Contemporary copy,
            attested by Joseph Carleton.   1 p.   Transmitted
            to Washington.   Published in General Orders,
            Apr. 4.   **97**, 329

[1782]   [**Washington**, George.] [Philadelphia.] To [the President
[MAR. 20]   of Congress, Philadelphia]. Reply to speech.
     Auto. draft. 1 p.   **A. VI, pt. II, 57**

1782   **Washington**, George. Philadelphia. To [Robert] Morris
MAR. 20   [Philadelphia]. Negotiation of bills. Draft.
     1 p. In handwriting of Tench Tilghman.
     A. VI, pt. II, 61

1782   **Morris**, Robert. [Philadelphia.] To [George]Washington
MAR. 20   [Philadelphia]. Method of supplying money to
     support the Commander-in-chief's table. L. S.
     1 p. Answered Mar. 20.*   **55, 62**

1782   **Washington**, George. Philadelphia. To the Secretary at
MAR. 21   War [Philadelphia]. Calculation of general offi-
     cers required for the coming campaign. Draft.
     5 pp. In handwriting of Tench Tilghman.
     A. VI, pt. II, 63

1782   **Knox** and **Morris** to Sir Henry Clinton. See: Knox and
MAR. 21   Morris to Washington, 1782, Apr. 22.

1782   **Continental Congress**, Resolves. Brig. Gen. [Henry] Knox
MAR. 22   to be Major General. D. S. of Charles Thomson.
     1 p. Transmitted to Washington.   **97, 330**

1782   **Continental Congress**, Resolve. Repealing portion resolve
MAR. 22   of Jan. 12, 1780, respecting de Galvan. D. S. of
     Charles Thomson. 1 p. Transmitted to Con-
     gress.   **97, 328**

1782   **Clinton**, Sir Henry. Commission to Dalrymple and
MAR. 25   Elliott. See: Knox and Morris to Washington,
     1782, Mar. 31–Apr. 19.

1782   **Continental Congress**, Resolve. Pioneer corps for South-
MAR. 26   ern Army. D. S. of Charles Thomson. 1 p.
     97, 331

1782   **Secretary at War**. [Philadelphia.] To [George] Wash-
MAR. 26   ington [Morristown, New Jersey]. Officers' serv-
     ants. L. S. of Benjamin Lincoln. 2 pp. In
     handwriting of William Jackson. Answered
     Apr. 1.*   **97, 332**

1782   **Washington**, George. Morristown [New Jersey]. To
MAR. 28   Robert Morris [Philadelphia]. Supplies by con-
     tract for the Jersey troops. Draft. 2 pp. In
     handwriting of David Humphreys.
     A. VI, pt. II, 69

1782   [**Lafayette**, Marquis de.] [Versailles?] To [Robert R.
MAR. 30   Livingston, Philadelphia]. Attitude of Spain;

advances of Britain toward peace; loans; necessity of exertion on part of America. [Extract of letter.] Contemporary copy. 4 pp. Enclosed in Livingston to Washington, 1732, May 27.

56, 353

1782

MAR. 31–
APR. 19

Knox, Henry, and Gouverneur **Morris**. Baskingridge [New Jersey]. To [George Washington, Newburgh, New York]. Report of proceedings of Commissioners to negotiate exchange of prisoners. Minutes of proceedings. Papers submitted:

Mar. 11. Washington. Commission to Knox and Morris.

Mar. 18. Digby, Robert. Commission to Dalrymple and Elliott.

Mar. 25. Clinton, Sir Henry. Commission to Maj. Gen. William Dalrymple and Andrew Elliott.

Apr. 2. Knox and Morris. Tariff of exchange proposed.

Apr. 2. Knox and Morris. Ration proposed.

Apr. 3. Dalrymple and Elliott. Counterpropositions.

Apr. 3. Knox and Morris. Liquidation of prisoners accounts.

Apr. 4. Knox and Morris. Classification of prisoners.

Apr. 5. Dalrymple and Elliott. Liquidation of accounts.

Apr. 5. Dalrymple and Elliott. Extent of exchange.

Apr. 6. Knox and Morris. Exchange of citizens.

Apr. 6. Dalrymple and Elliott. Extent of exchange; ransom.

Apr. 7. Dalrymple and Elliott. Marine prisoners.

Apr. 8. Dalrymple and Elliott. Reduction of propositions to writing.

Apr. 8. Knox and Morris. Refusal of propositions; failure of negotiations; liquidation of accounts.

Apr. 13. Dalrymple and Elliott. Counterpropositions as to liquidation of accounts; rations; extent of exchange etc.

Apr. 16. Dalrymple and Elliott. Provisions for prisoners.

Apr. 16. Knox and Morris. Maintenance of prisoners.

Apr. 16. Dalrymple and Elliott. Supplying provisions to prisoners.

Apr. 17. Knox and Morris. Estimated cost of ration; payment of balances etc.

Apr. 19. Dalrymple and Elliott. Refusal of propositions; end of negotiations.

Apr. 19. Knox and Morris. Statement of position; end of negotiations.

Transcript. Enclosed in Washington to the President of Congress, 1782, Apr. 30.

C. C.   169, 8, 320

1782
APR. 1

Washington, George. Newburgh [New York]. To [the Secretary at War, Philadelphia]. Question of servants for line and staff officers; pay for men on duty as artificers. Draft. 4 pp. In handwriting of Benjamin Walker. **A.** VI, pt. II, 71

1782
APR. 2

Knox and Morris to Dalrymple and Elliott. See: Knox and Morris to Washington, 1782, Mar. 31–Apr. 19.

1782
APR. 3

Continental Congress, Resolve. Referring resolve of South Carolina House of Representatives of Feb. 14, 1782 to the Commander in chief. D. S. of Charles Thomson. 1 p. Transmitted to Washington. Endorsed: "Sir Guy Carleton written to 21st May."   98, 6

1782
APR. 3

Morris, Robert. Philadelphia. To [George] Washington [Newburgh]. Extra expense of magazines of provisions requested by [Maj.] Gen. [William] Heath. L. S. 1 p.   55, 124

1782
APR. 3

Dalrymple and Elliott to Knox and Morris. See: Knox and Morris to Washington, 1782, Mar. 31–Apr. 19.

1782
APR. 3

Knox and Morris to Dalrymple and Elliott. See: Knox and Morris to Washington, 1782, Mar. 31–Apr. 19.

1782
APR. 4

Knox and Morris to Dalrymple and Elliott. See: Knox and Morris to Washington, 1782, Mar. 31–Apr. 19.

1782
APR. 5

Dalrymple and Elliott to Knox and Morris. See: Knox and Morris to Washington, 1782, Mar. 31–Apr. 19.

1782
APR. 6

Knox and Morris to Dalrymple and Elliott. See: Knox and Morris to Washington, 1782, Mar. 31–Apr. 19.

1782
APR. 6

Morris, Robert. [Philadelphia.] Articles of Agreement with Tench Frances, Comfort Sands & Co., Thomas Lowry, Oliver Phelps, Timothy Edwards, and Walter Livingston to supply the moving army with provisions. Contemporary copy. 6 pp. Enclosed in Morris to Washington, 1782, Apr. 15.
                                                                    55, 152

1782
APR. 7

Dalrymple and Elliott to Knox and Morris. See: Knox and Morris to Washington, 1782, Mar. 31–Apr. 19.

1782
APR. 7

Duane, James. Manor Livingston [New York]. To Gen. [George] Washington [West Point]. Efforts for next campaign; Superintendent of Finance's demands of New York; British at Charleston. A. L. S. 1 p.   55, 235

1782
APR. 8

Continental Congress, Resolves. For better regulating the pay of the Army; accounts, warrants, paymasters. Contemporary copy, attested by William Jackson. 2 pp. Enclosed in Secretary at War to Washington, 1782, Apr. 10.   97, 334

1782
APR. 8

Secretary at War. [Philadelphia.] To [George] Washington [West Point]. Contractors for supplying army. L. S. of Benjamin Lincoln. 4 pp. In handwriting of William Jackson.   97, 335

1782
APR. 8

Secretary at War. [Philadelphia.] To [George] Washington [West Point]. Troops for the south; horses for Armand's corps. L. S. of Benjamin Lincoln. 3 pp. In handwriting of William Jackson. Answered Apr. 12.*   98, 1

1782
APR. 8

Dalrymple and Elliott to Knox and Morris. See: Knox and Morris to Washington, 1782, Mar. 31–Apr. 19.

1782
APR. 8

Knox and Morris to Dalrymple and Elliott. See: Knox and Morris to Washington, 1782, Mar. 31–Apr. 19.

1782
APR. 9

Secretary at War. [Philadelphia.] To [George] Washington [West Point]. Pay of servants; clothing for Maryland troops; horses for Sheldon's dragoons. L. S. of Benjamin Lincoln. 2 pp. In handwriting of William Jackson. Answered in part, Apr. 17,* in full, Apr. 23.*   98, 3

1782
APR. 10

Washington, George. Newburgh. To the Secretary at War [Philadelphia]. Clothing, hats and shoes. Draft. 4 pp. In handwriting of David Humphreys.   **A.** VI, pt. II, 75

1782
APR. 10

Secretary at War. [Philadelphia.] To [George] Washington [West Point]. Transmitting resolve of Congress. L. S. of Benjamin Lincoln. 1 p. Answered Apr. 23.*   **98, 9**

1782
APR. 12

Washington, George. [Newburgh.] To the Secretary at War [Philadelphia]. Nature of future operations; Armand's corps and war in the South. Draft. 1 p. In handwriting of Jonathan Trumbull, jr   **A. VI, pt. II, 79**

[1782]
[APR. 12]

Huddy, Joshua. Death of. Placard pinned to Huddy's body by Loyalists. Contemporary copy. In handwriting of Jonathan Trumbull, jr. Enclosed in Washington to the President of Congress, 1782, Apr. 20.   **C. C. 152, 10, 507**

1782
APR. 12

Logan, John and James Thompson. Philadelphia. To Slough & Co. [New Jersey.] Conflict of contracts for moving army and stationary posts in New Jersey; deficiency in supplies; lack of money; compliance with terms of contract etc. Contemporary copy. 3 pp. Enclosed in Morris to Washington, 1782, Apr. 22.   **56, 37**

1782
APR. 13

Dalrymple and Elliott to Knox and Morris. See: Knox and Morris to Washington, 1782, Mar. 31–Apr. 19.

1782
APR. 13

Logan, John. Philadelphia. To Robert Morris [Philadelphia]. Explanatory of letter to the Commander in chief reflecting upon Morris's exertions. Contemporary copy. 1 p. Enclosed in Morris to Washington, 1782, Apr. 22.   **56, 35**

1782
APR. 14

Monmouth County, [New Jersey]. Inhabitants. To [George] Washington [Newburgh]. Account of murder of Capt. Joshua Huddy; death of Philip White; retaliation. Contemporary copy. 7 pp. In handwriting of Benjamin Walker. Enclosed in Washington to the President of Congress, 1782, Apr. 20.   **C. C. 152, 10, 483**

1782
APR. 15

Washington, George. Newburgh. To Arthur Lee [Philadelphia]. European intelligence. Auto. draft signed. 1 p.   **P. II, 483**

1782
APR. 15

Morris, Robert. [Philadelphia.] To [George] Washington [Newburgh]. Contract to supply the moving army; settlement of disputes; economy. L. S. 2 pp. Answered Apr. 23.*   **55, 297**

1782
APR. 15

North, John. Monmouth County [New Jersey]. Deposition respecting death of Philip White. Contemporary copy. 3 pp. Enclosed in Washington to the President of Congress, 1782, Apr. 20.

C. C. 152, 10, 493

1782
APR. 15

Randolph, Daniel. Monmouth County, New Jersey. Deposition respecting capture and hanging of Capt. Joshua Huddy. 8 pp. Contemporary copy. Enclosed in Washington to the President of Congress, 1782, Apr. 20. C. C. 152, 10, 485

1782
APR. 15

Russel, John. Monmouth County [New Jersey]. Deposition respecting death of Philip White.

Borden, William. Monmouth County. Deposition respecting death of Philip White.

Contemporary copies. 2 pp. Partly in handwriting of Jonathan Trumbull, jr. Enclosed in Washington to the President of Congress, 1782, Apr. 20. C. C. 152, 10, 501

1782
APR. 15

White, Aaron. Monmouth County [New Jersey]. Deposition respecting death of Philip White. Contemporary copy. 3 pp. In handwriting of David Humphreys. Enclosed in Washington to the President of Congress, 1782, Apr. 20.

C. C. 152, 10, 497

1782
APR. 16

Washington, George. Newburgh. To Robert Morris [Philadelphia]. [William?] Duer's ability; Lt. Col. [Richard] Varick's needs. Draft. 1 p. In handwriting of Jonathan Trumbull, jr.

A. VI, pt. II, 81

1782
APR. 16

Dalrymple and Elliott to Knox and Morris. See: Knox and Morris to Washington, 1782, Mar. 31–Apr. 19.

1782
APR. 16

Knox and Morris to Dalrymple and Elliott. See: Knox and Morris to Washington, 1782, Mar. 31–Apr. 19.

1782
APR. 16

Livingston, Robert R. Philadelphia. To [George Washington, Newburgh]. Reception of Cornwallis in England; continuation of war; changes in British cabinet; [Vice-Adm'l George Brydges] Rodney in the West Indies. A. L. S. 2 pp. Answered Apr. 23.* 55, 312

1782
APR. 17

Washington, George. Newburgh. To the Secretary at War [Philadelphia]. Equipment of Col. [Elisha] Sheldon's corps. Draft. 1 p. In handwriting of Jonathan Trumbull, jr. A. VI, pt. II, 83

1782 APR. 17	**Knox and Morris** to Dalrymple and Elliott. See: Knox and Morris to Washington, 1782, Mar. 31–Apr. 19.
1782 APR. 19	**Borden,** William. [Monmouth County, New Jersey.] Deposition respecting death of Philip White.

Walton, John.   Certificate respecting Borden.

Forman, David.   Deposition respecting appearance of corpse of Philip White.   Contemporary copies. In handwriting of John Fitzgerald.   Enclosed in Washington to the President of Congress, 1782, Apr. 20.   C. C.   152, 10, 507

1782 APR. 19	**Dalrymple and Elliott** to Knox and Morris. See: Knox and Morris to Washington, 1782, Mar. 31–Apr. 19.
1782 APR. 19	**Knox and Morris** to Dalrymple and Elliott. See: Knox and Morris to Washington, 1782, Mar. 31–Apr. 19.
1782 APR. 20	**Washington,** George. [Newburgh.] To the President of Congress [Philadelphia]. Murder of Capt. [Joshua] Huddy; retaliation necessary. Draft. 2 pp. In handwriting of Jonathan Turnbull, jr. Read in Congress, Apr. 29. Referred to Boudinot, Scott and Bee. Reported Apr. 29 and acted on same day. **A.** VI, pt. II, 85
1782 APR. 20	**Secretary at War.** [Philadelphia.] To [George] Washington [Newburgh]. Purchase of clothing; objects of the campaign. L. S. of Benjamin Lincoln. 1 p. Answered Apr. 27.* **98, 7**
1782 APR. 21	**[Washington,** George.] Newburgh. To Sir Henry Clinton [New York]. Demanding murderers of Capt. [Joshua] Huddy. Contemporary copy. 2 pp. In handwriting of Benjamin Walker. Enclosed in Washington to the President of Congress, 1782, May 10. C. C. 152, 10, 513

Printed: Writings of Washington (Ford) N. Y. 1891.   9, 478.

1782 APR. 21	**Knox,** Henry and Gouverneur **Morris.** Baskingridge [New Jersey]. To [George] Washington [Newburgh]. Report of negotiations; Board of Directors of Associated Loyalists; feeling of loyalists against the British; liquidation of prisoners accounts; Convention troops, marine prisoners etc. Transcript. Enclosed in Washington to the President of Congress, 1782, Apr. 30. C. C. 169, 8, 389
1782 APR. 22	**Washington,** George. Newburgh. To the Secretary at War [Philadelphia]. Transmitting list of staff

officers who were not allowed servants. Draft.
3 pp. In handwriting of David Humphreys.

A. VI, pt. II, 87

1782
APR. 22

Continental Congress, Resolves. Establishment of ration
allowance of the various officers of the army.
D. S. of George Bond. 3 pp. Transmitted to
Washington. 98, 15

1782
APR. 22

Clinton, [Sir] H[enry]. New York. To [George] Washington [Newburgh]. Recent exchange negotiations; arguments etc. Transcript. Enclosed in
Washington to the President of Congress, 1782,
Apr. 30. C. C. 169, 8, 396

1782
APR. 22

Knox, Henry and Gouverneur Morris. Baskingridge [New
Jersey]. To George Washington [Newburgh].
Report of proceedings in negotiating an exchange
of prisoners. Papers submitted:
Mar. 16. Knox and Morris to Sir Henry Clinton. Meeting of Commissioners.
Mar. 16. Knox and Morris to Brig. Gen.
[Courtlandt] Skinner. Forwarding of letters.
Mar. 18. Clinton to Knox and Morris. Meeting of commissioners.
Mar. 21. Knox and Morris to Clinton. Meeting at Elizabethtown.
Transcript. Enclosed in Washington to the
President of Congress, 1782, Apr. 30.

C. C. 169, 8, 365

1782
APR. 22

Morris, Robert. Philadelphia. To [George] Washington
[Newburgh]. Trouble with contractors for supplying the army; contracts for fixed posts and
the moving army. L. S. 4 pp. 56, 33

1782
APR. 23

Washington, George. [Newburgh.] To the Secretary at
War [Philadelphia]. Settlement of accounts.
Draft. 2 pp. In handwriting of Jonathan
Trumbull, jr. A. VI, pt. II, 91

1782
APR. 23

[Washington, George.] Newburgh. To R[obert] R. Livingston [Philadelphia]. Lafayette's letter on
Britain's intentions as to prosecution of war; necessary policy. Draft. 3 pp. In handwriting
of David Humphreys. P. II, 507

1782
APR. 23

Washington, George. [Newburgh.] To [Robert Morris,
Philadelphia]. Intendant to settle contractors
disputes. Draft. 2 pp. In handwriting of
Jonathan Trumbull, jr. A. VI, pt. II, 93

1782
APR. 23

Clinton, George. Poughkeepsie. To [George] Washington [Newburgh]. Subsistence for the levies; measures adopted. Contemporary copy. 2 pp. In handwriting of Benjamin Walker. Enclosed in Washington to Lincoln, 1782, Apr. 24.
C. C.   152, 10, 521

1782
APR. 23

Continental Congress, Resolves. Discharge and pension of disabled soldiers. Contemporary copy, attested by John M. Lovell. 2 pp. Transmitted to Washington.   98, 11

1782
APR. 23

Continental Congress, Resolve. Retirement of lieutenants; their employment in Staff Department. D. S. of George Bond. Enclosed in Secretary at War to Washington, 1782, July 16. Published in Genl. Orders, July 30.   98, 98

1782
APR. 24

Washington, George. Newburgh. To [the Secretary at War, Philadelphia]. Col. [Goose] Van Schaick's leave of absence. Draft. 1 p. In handwriting of Benjamin Walker.   A. VI, pt. II, 95

The Secretary reported on this matter by letter to Congress Apr. 29, which letter was referred to Cornell, Clark and Montgomery, same date.

1782
APR. 24

Washington, George [Newburgh.] To the Secretary at War [Philadelphia]. Gov. [George] Clinton's letter respecting feeding of New York troops. Draft. 1 p. In handwriting of Jonathan Trumbull, jr.   A. VI, pt. II, 97

1782
APR. 24

Washington, George. Newburgh. To Gov.' [George] Clinton [Poughkeepsie]. Subsistence of the levies. Contemporary copy. 2 pp. Enclosed in Washington to Lincoln, 1782, Apr. 24.
C. C.   152, 10, 523

1782
APR. 24

Washington, George. Newburgh. To Maj. Gen. [Benjamin] Lincoln [Philadelphia]. Transmitting letter of Gov. George Clinton respecting subsistence of levies. L. S. 2 pp. In handwriting of Jonathan Trumbull, jr.   C. C.   152, 10, 517

1782
APR. 25

Clinton, [Sir] H[enry]. New York. To [George] Washington [Newburgh]. Retaliation and Capt. [Joshua] Huddy's case. Contemporary copy. 3 pp. In handwriting of Benjamin Walker. Enclosed in Washington to the President of Congress, 1782, May 10.   C. C.   152, 10, 537

Head Quarters

Newburgh Mass 1 April 1782

Dr Sir,

I have to reply to your favor
of the 26 March which was handed
me on my way to this place

When the matter respecting the
number of servants to be allowed to the
Officers of the Army, was taken up by the
General Officers, If I am not mistaken,
it was the general sentiment that the
indulgence ought to be confined to the
Officers of the Line, & that as the Staff
were in general allowed a pay superior to them they ought to provide
themselves with servants & receiving therefor
the allowance of Cloathing & regulated
by Congress — It was upon this
principle the regulation was made
and I cannot help thinking that
if we depart from it instead of

assuring

WRITING OF BENJAMIN WALKER.

1782
APR. 26

Mullock, William. New York. Deposition as to hanging of Daniel Current. Contemporary copy. 2 pp. In handwriting of Hodijah Baylies? Enclosed in Washington to the President of Congress, 1782, May 10.   C. C. 152, 10, 547

1782
APR. 27

Washington, George. Newburgh. To the Secretary at War. Enlistment of German prisoners into the army. Draft. 3 pp. In handwriting of David Humphreys.   A. VI, pt. II, 99

Printed: Writings of Washington (Ford) N. Y. 1891. 9, 483.

The Secretary's letter of May 3, transmitting above to Congress, was referred, same date, to Boudinot, Atlee and Rutledge. On May 15, Scott, Madison and Rutledge reported on Washington's letter and on June 5 reported finally on both when the Commander in chief, Secretary at War and Superintendent of Finance were directed by Congress to take order thereon.

1782
APR. 27

Alyay, Isaac. New York. Deposition respecting hanging of Daniel Current. Contemporary copy. 2 pp. Enclosed in Washington to the President of Congress, 1782, May 10.   C. C. 152, 10, 551

1782
APR. 27

Clinton, [Sir] H[enry]. New York. To [George] Washington [Newburgh]. Release of a flag officer. Contemporary copy. 1 p. In handwriting of William Stephens Smith. Enclosed in Washington to the President of Congress, 1782, May 10.   C. C. 152, 10, 541

1782
APR. 27

White, Aaron. New York. Deposition respecting death of Aaron White. Contemporary copy. 3 pp. Enclosed in Washington to the President of Congress, 1782, May 10.   C. C. 152, 10, 555

1782
APR. 29

Continental Congress, Resolve. Supporting the Commander-in-chief in retaliating for murder of Capt. [Joshua] Huddy. A. D. S. of Chas. Thomson. 1 p. Transmitted to Washington.   98, 17

1782
APR. 30

Washington, George. [Newburgh.] To the President of of Congress [Philadelphia]. Negotiations for exchange of prisoners; refugees. Draft. 2 pp. In handwriting of Jonathan Trumbull, jr. Referred to Boudinot, Atlee and Rutledge. June 11, Lowell in place of Rutledge.
    A. VI, pt. II, 103

Printed: Writings of Washington (Ford) N. Y. 1891. 9, 488.

1782
APR. 30

Secretary at War. [Philadelphia.] To [George] Washington [Newburgh]. Letters transmitted to Congress. L. S. of Benjamin Lincoln. 1 p.   98, 20

1782
APR. 30

[Irvine, William.] Fort Pitt. To [the Board of War, Philadelphia]. Introducing Capt. [John] Montour, an Indian chief. Contemporary copy. Enclosed in Secretary at War to Washington, 1781, May 16.   **98, 39**

1782
APR. 30

Livingston, Robert R. Philadelphia. To [George Washington, Newburgh]. Projected campaign with the French against Charleston; reply of Great Britain to powers respecting America; British on Northern frontier; torpidity of states. A. L. S. 5 pp.   **56, 117**

1782
MAY 1)

Washington, George. Newburgh. To the Secretary at War [Philadelphia]. Demand of Col. [David] Hall for a court martial. Draft. 1 p. In handwriting of William Stephens Smith.
     A. VI, pt. II, 105

1782
MAY 1

Washington, George. [Newburgh.] To the Secretary at War [Philadelphia]. Right of challenge in courts-martial. Adjutant General's Department; officers' rations; Paymaster General at camp. Draft. 4 pp. In handwriting of Jonathan Trumbull, jr.   A. VI, pt. II, 107

1782
MAY 1

Washington, George. Newburgh. To Robert Morris [Philadelphia]. Contracts for supplies; embarrassment of contractors. Draft. 2 pp. In handwriting of David Humphreys.
     A. VI, pt. II, 111

1782
MAY 1

Loyalists of New Jersey. Extracts from information laid before Sir Henry Clinton of acts of cruelty committed upon certain loyalists. Contemporary copy. 4 pp. In handwriting of Benjamin Walker. Enclosed in Washington to the President of Congress, 1782, May 10.
     C. C. 152, 10, 543

1782
MAY 1

Robertson, James. New York. To [George] Washington [Newburgh]. Recriminating complaints of barbarity; seizure of [John Smith] Hatfield and [Abner] Badgely; court martial ordered [on Capt. Richard Lippincott]. Contemporary copy. 3 pp. In handwriting of William Stephens Smith. Enclosed in Washington to the President of Congress, 1782, May 10.   C. C. 152, 10, 529

1782
MAY 3

Continental Congress, Committee report. Letter of the Commander-in-chief to the Board of War of Apr. 27; enlistment of German prisoners into the army. In handwriting of George Bond. Transmitted to Washington.   **98, 18**
Committee: Boudinot, Atlee and Rutledge.

1782
MAY 3

[Wayne, Anthony.] [Near Savannah.] Address to British soldiery urging desertion to American cause; bounty offered. Contemporary copy. 3 pp. In Wayne's handwriting. Enclosed in Wayne to Washington, 1783, Nov. 1.   C. C.   **152, 11, 575**

1782
MAY 4

Washington, George. Newburgh. To the Secretary at War [Philadelphia]. Retaliatory measures for murder of Capt. Joshua Huddy; scarcity of drums and fifes. Draft. 4 pp. In handwriting of David Humphreys.   **A. VI, pt. II, 113**
Printed in part: Writings of Washington (Ford) N. Y. 1891. 10, 4.

1782
MAY 4

Washington, George. [Newburgh.] To [Lt.] Gen. [James] Robertson [New York]. Retaliation [for Capt. Joshua Huddy]; Robertson's complaints; [John Smith] Hatfield and [Abner] Badgely. Contemporary copy. 3 pp. In handwriting of David Humphreys. Enclosed in Washington to the President of Congress, 1781, May 10.
C. C.   **152, 10, 533**

1782
MAY 5

Secretary at War. [Philadelphia.] To [George] Washington [Newburgh]. Challenges and Adjutant-General's Department; ration allowance to officers; deputy-paymaster at camp; secret matter. L. S. of Benjamin Lincoln. 4 pp. In handwriting of William Jackson.   **98, 24**

1782
MAY 6

Secretary at War. [Philadelphia.] To [George] Washington [Newburgh]. Removal of the Rhode Island regiment from the city. L. S. of Benjamin Lincoln. 2 pp. Answered, May 15.*   **98, 22**

1782
MAY 6

Laurens, Henry. London. Passport for William Blake. A. D. S. 1 p. Transmitted to Congress.
C. C.   **152, 10, 675**

1782
MAY 7

Secretary at War. [Philadelphia.] To [George] Washington [Newburgh]. Case of Majors [James Randolph] Reid and [Tarleton] Woodson. L. S. of Benjamin Lincoln. 2 pp. Answered May 15.*
98, 26

1782
May 7

Carleton, [Sir] Guy. New York. To [George] Washington [Newburgh]. Softening the miseries of war; excesses in New Jersey; letter to Congress. Contemporary copy. 3 pp. In handwriting of William Stephens Smith. Enclosed in Washington to the President of Congress, 1782, May 10.

C. C. 152, 10, 559

Printed: Writings of Washington (Sparks) Boston. 1835. 8, 536.

1782
May 8

Montour, John. [Philadelphia.] To [the Board of War, Philadelphia]. Petition for relief; recital of services; want of money and clothes. Contemporary copy. 1 p. Enclosed in Secretary at War to Washington, 1782, May 16.

98, 40

1782
May 10

Washington, George. [Newburgh.] To the President of Congress, [Philadelphia]. Correspondence in the Huddy case; effect of expected peace. Draft. 3 pp. In handwriting of Jonathan Trumbull, jr and David Humphreys. Read in Congress, May 13.

A. VI, pt. II, 117

Printed: Writings of Washington (Ford) N. Y. 1891. 10, 9.

1782
May 10

Washington, George. [Newburgh.] To Sir Guy Carleton [New York]. Severities of war; messenger to Congress; flags. Contemporary copy. 2 pp. In handwriting of Jonathan Trumbull, jr. Reported May 14 and acted on same day. Enclosed in Washington to the President of Congress, 1782, May 10.

C. C. 152, 10, 563

1782
May 13

Washington, George. Newburgh. To the Secretary at War [Philadelphia]. Investigation of contractors' disputes. Draft. 2 pp. In handwriting of Jonathan Trumbull, jr.

A. VI, pt. II, 121

1782
May 13

Livingston, Robert R. Philadelphia. To [George] Washington [Newburgh]. Announcement of birth of a Dauphin of France. L. S. 2 pp. Answered May 22.*

53, 238

1782
May 13

Secretary at War. [Philadelphia.] To [George] Washington [Newburgh]. Miscellaneous military matters; sick and hospitals. L. S. of Benjamin Lincoln. 5 pp. In handwriting of William Jackson. Answered May 18.*

98, 28

1782
May 14

Continental Congress, Resolve. Refusal of passport to [Maurice] Morgann. D. S. of Charles Thomson. 1 p. Enclosed in Secretary at War to Washington, 1782, May 15.

98, 32

1782
MAY 14

Secretary at War [Philadelphia.] To the President of Congress [Philadelphia]. Case of Capt. [John] Montour. Enclosed in Secretary at War to Washington, 1782, May 16.　　　　98, 39

1782
[MAY 14]

Livingston, William. [Trenton, New Jersey.] To [George] Washington [Newburgh]. Chief Justice [David] Brearly's opinion in case of [John Smith] Hatfield and [Abner] Badgely.

[MAY 14?]

Brearly, David. [Trenton.] To Gov. Livingston. Opinion respecting Hatfield and Badgely. Contemporary copies. In handwriting of Benjamin Walker. Enclosed in Washington to the President of Congress, 1782, July 9.

C. C.　152, 10, 613

1782
MAY 15

Washington, George. Newburgh. To [the Secretary at War, Philadelphia]. Complaint of Col. [Timothy] Pickering [jr]. Auto. draft signed. 2 pp.

A.　VI, pt. II, 123

1782
MAY 15

Washington, George. Newburgh. To [the Secretary at War, Philadelphia]. Ration; Rhode Island regiment to join the army. Draft. 2 pp. In handwriting of David Humphreys.

A.　VI, pt. II, 125

1782
MAY 15

Washington, George. Newburgh. To [Robert Morris, Philadelphia]. Contract business. Draft. 1 p. In handwriting of Jonathan Trumbull, jr.

A.　VI, pt. II, 127

1782
MAY 15

Secretary at War. [Philadelphia.] To [George] Washington [Newburgh]. Transmitting certain papers. L. S. of Benjamin Lincoln. 2 pp. Answered May 22.*　　　　98, 33

1782
MAY 16

Secretary at War. [Philadelphia.] To [George] Washington [Newburgh]. Establishment of hospital in Virginia; Captain [John] Montour, an Indian chief. L. S. of Benjamin Lincoln. 4 pp. In handwriting of William Jackson. Answered May 28.*　　　　98, 37

1782
MAY 17

Washington, George. Newburgh. To Robert Morris [Philadelphia]. Difficulty with contractors and rations. Draft. 9 pp. In handwriting of Jonathan Trumbull, jr. and David Cobb.

A.　VI, pt. II, 129

1782
MAY 17

Secretary at War. [Philadelphia.] To [George] Washington [Newburgh]. Introducing Capt. [John] Montour. L. S. of Benjamin Lincoln. 2 pp.

98, 41

1782
MAY 18

Washington, George. [Newburgh.] To the Secretary at War [Philadelphia]. Selection of a British officer for retaliation; aides and the hospital. Draft. 1 p. In handwriting of Jonathan Trumbull, jr.

A. VI, pt. II, 139

1782
MAY 20

Anspach, Peter. New Windsor. To Maj. Samuel Hodgdon, Philadelphia. Arms forwarded to Philadelphia. A. L. S. 2 pp. Enclosed in Secretary at War to Washington, 1782, May 28. 98, 50

1782
MAY 21

Washington, George. [Newburgh.] To [Sir Guy Carleton, New York]. Refusal of passport for [Maurice] Morgann; return of South Carolina inhabitants. Contemporary copy. 1 p. In handwriting of David Cobb. Enclosed in Washington to the President of Congress, 1782, June 6.

C. C. 152, 10, 585

1782
MAY 21

Anonymous. Elizabethtown [New Jersey]. To [George Washington, Newburgh]. Assembling of shipping and preparation of the British army for review. [Extract of letter.] 1 p. In handwriting of David Cobb. Enclosed in Washington to the President of Congress, 1782, May 28.

C. C. 152, 10, 575

1782
MAY 22

Washington, George. [Newburgh.] To the Secretary at War [Philadelphia]. South Carolina inhabitants; provision for Indians. Draft. 1 p. In handwriting of Jonathan Trumbull, jr.

A. VI, pt. II, 141

1782
MAY 22

Washington, George. [Newburgh.] To the Secretary at War [Philadelphia]. Difficulties in the contract supply of provisions for the army; Sir Guy Carleton and South Carolina inhabitants; hospitals; officers pay. Draft. 3 pp. In handwriting of Jonathan Trumbull, jr. A. VI, pt. II, 147

1782
MAY 22

Washington, George. Newburgh. [Philadelphia]. To Robert R. Livingston. Stupor into which the country has fallen; rumor of naval action off Guadaloupe. Auto. draft signed. 2 pp.

P. II, 511

1782
MAY 22

Washington, George. [Newburgh]. To [Robert R. Livingston, Philadelphia]. Birth of the Dauphin of France. Draft. 1 p. In handwriting of Jonathan Trumbull, jr. **A.** VI, pt. II, 143

1782
MAY 23

Secretary at War. [Philadelphia.] To [George] Washington [Newburgh]. Discharge of a disabled soldier [Charles King]. A. L. of Jno. M. Lovell. 1 p.
98, 43

1782
MAY 23

Anonymous. [New York.] To [George] Washington [Newburgh]. Intentions [of Sir Guy Carleton]; preparations for embarkation. Contemporary copy. 1 p. In handwriting of Jonathan Trumbull, jr. Enclosed in Washington to the President of Congress, 1782, May 28.
C. C. 152, 10, 577

1782
MAY 23

Anonymous. [New York.] To [George] Washington [Newburgh]. Fleet for transporting garrison from Charleston and Savannah; militia and review of British army. Contemporary copy. 1 p. In handwriting of David Cobb. Enclosed in Washington to the President of Congress, 1782, May 28. C. C. 152, 10, 579

1782
MAY 23

Carleton, [Sir] Guy. New York. To [George] Washington [Newburgh]. Return of South Carolina inhabitants in British transports. Contemporary copy. 1 p. In handwriting of David Cobb. Enclosed in Washington to the President of Congress, 1782, June 6. C. C. 152, 10, 587

1782
MAY 24

Secretary at War. [Philadelphia.] To [George] Washington [Newburgh]. Transmitting papers. A. L. S. of Benjamin Lincoln. 1 p. 98, 45

1782
MAY 24

Wayne, Anthony. Ebenezer [Georgia]. To [Maj.] Gen. [Nathanael] Greene [near Bacon's Bridge, South Carolina]. Account of battle of Ogechee Road. A. L. S. Marked by Wayne "Copy." 6 pp. Enclosed Wayne to Washington, 1783, Nov. 1.
C. C. 152, 11, 579

1782
MAY 27

Livingston, Robert R. Philadelphia. To [George Washington, Newburgh]. British manoevers for peace; aids from France; plan of campaign; prospects of peace; European news. A. L. S. 6 pp.
56, 349

1782
MAY 28
Washington, George. Newburgh. To the President of Congress [Philadelphia]. Transmitting intelli-.gence. Draft. 1 p. In handwriting of Jonathan Trumbull, jr. Read in Congress, June 3.
A. VI, pt. II, 145

1782
MAY 28
[Washington, George.] [Newburgh.] To [the Board of War, Philadelphia]. Contract supplies for army; discontents; Sir Guy Carleton's compliance with request respecting South Carolina inhabitants; hospital in Virginia; Capt. [John] Montour. Draft. 3 pp. In handwriting of Jonathan Trumbull, jr.   A. VI, pt. II, 147

1782
MAY 28
Secretary at War. [Philadelphia.] To [George] Washington [Newburgh]. Detention of arms at Philadelphia; prohibition of removal of public stores to magazines. L. S. of Benjamin Lincoln. 2 pp. Answered June 5.*   98, 48

1782
MAY 28
Hodgdon, Samuel. Philadelphia. To [the Board of War, Philadelphia]. Arms ordered from North River. A. L. S. 1 p. Enclosed in Secretary at War to Washington, 1782, May 28.   98, 46

1782
MAY 29
Washington, George. Newburgh. To [the Secretary at War, Philadelphia]. Resignation of Judge Advocate General John Lawrance. Draft. 2 pp. In handwriting of David Humphreys.
A. VI, pt. II, 151

1782
MAY 29
Washington, George. Newburgh. To Robert Morris [Philadelphia]. Money due Lt. Col. [Richard] Varick. Draft. 1 p. In handwriting of Jonathan Trumbull, jr.   A. VI, pt. II, 153

1782
MAY 29
[Secretary at War.] [Philadelphia.] To Comfort Sands & Co. [Philadelphia]. Responsibility for vouchers for supplies. Extract in handwriting of Nathan Jones. Enclosed in Board of War to Washington, 1782, Aug. 19.   98, 138

1782
MAY 30
Secretary at War. [Philadelphia.] To [George] Washington [Newburgh]. Respecting Capt. [Charles] Asgill; feeling between Tories and British. L. S. of Benjamin Lincoln. 2 pp.   98, 52

1782
MAY 31
Hand, Edward. [Newburgh.] Return of recruits from the several States from Jan. 1 to May 31. Tabular statement. D. S. 1 p. Enclosed in Washington to the President of Congress, 1782, June 24.   C. C. 152, 10, 593

[1782]
JUNE 4

Washington, George. Newburgh. To the Secretary at War [Philadelphia]. Capt. [Charles] Asgill and Lt. [Tompkins Hilgrove?] Turner. Draft. 1 p. In handwriting of Jonathan Trumbull, jr.

A. VI, pt. II, 155

1782
JUNE 4

Continental Congress, Committee. To [George] Washington [Newburgh]. Application to Sir Guy Carleton respecting exiled South Carolinians. A. L. S. of John Morin Scott. 3 pp. Answered June 10.*

57, 63

Committee: Scott, Boudinot and Ramsay.

1782
JUNE 4

Morris, Robert. Philadelphia. To [George] Washington [Newburgh]. Great want of money; trouble over contracts; officers' complaints; the West Point contract; general expense. L. S. 5 pp.

57, 65

1782
JUNE 4

Parsons, Samuel H[olden]. Middletown [New Jersey]. To [the President of Congress, Philadelphia]. Requesting leave of absence. A. L. S. 2 pp. Read in Congress, July 11. Referred to Secy. at War. C. C. 152, 10, 609

1782
JUNE 4

Morris, Robert. ·[Philadelphia.] To [George] Washington [Newburgh]. State of finances and measures adopted by Congress. L. S. 2 pp. 57, 69

1782
JUNE 5

Washington, George. Newburgh. To the Secretary at War [Philadelphia]. Address of officers on birth of the Dauphin. Draft. 1 p. In handwriting of Jonathan Trumbull, jr. A. VI, pt. II, 157

1782
JUNE 5

Washington, George. Newburgh. To the Secretary at War [Philadelphia]. Arrest of Ensign [Reuben?] Johnson. Draft. 1 p. In handwriting of Benjamin Walker. A. VI, pt. II, 159

1782
JUNE 5

Washington, George. Newburgh. To the Secretary at War [Philadelphia]. Detention of arms; British treatment of marine prisoners. Draft. 2 pp. In handwriting of Jonathan Trumbull, jr.

A. VI, pt. II, 161

1782
JUNE 5

Washington, George. Newburgh. To Robert R. Livingston [Philadelphia]. Lafayette's letters; prosecution of war by Britain. Auto. draft signed. 2 pp. P. II, 517

1782
JUNE 5

Continental Congress, President. Order. To George Washington [Newburgh]. Referring report of Committee [May 3] on enlistment of German prisoners to the Commander in chief, Secretary at War and Superintendent of Finance. A. D. S. of Charles Thomson. 98, 18

1782
JUNE 5

Secretary at War. [Philadelphia.] To [George] Washington [Newburgh]. Appointment of a Judge-Advocate; contract system and minor matters. L. S. of Benjamin Lincoln. 1 p. 98, 54

1782
JUNE 6

Washington, George. Newburgh. To the President of Congress [Philadelphia]. Refusal of passport for [Maurice] Morgann. Draft. 2 pp. In handwriting of Jonathan Trumbull, jr. Read in Congress, June 13. Referred to Scott, Boudinot and Ramsay. A. VI, pt. II, 163

1782
JUNE 7

Continental Congress, Resolve. Recall of British prisoners working for inhabitants. Contemporary copy. 1 p. In handwriting of Nathan Jones. Transmitted to Washington. 98, 56

1782
JUNE 8

Washington, George. [Newburgh.] To Robert Morris [Philadelphia]. Settlement of complaints concerning contractors. Draft. 2 pp. In handwriting of Jonathan Trumbull, jr. A. VI, pt. II, 165

1782
JUNE 9

Washington, George. Newburgh. To thé Secretary at War [Philadelphia]. Prisóners and their horses; minor matters. Draft. 2 pp. In handwriting of Benjamin Walker and Jonathan Trumbull, jr. A. VI, pt. II, 167

1782
JUNE 10

Washington, George. Newburgh. To [the Secretary at War, Philadelphia]. Countermanding order for forwarding a prisoner. Draft. 1 p. In handwriting of Jonathan Trumbull, jr. A. VI, pt. II, 169

1782
JUNE 10

Washington, George. Newburgh. To [a Committee of Congress, Philadelphia]. Request made of Sir Guy Carleton in favor of South Carolina inhabitants. Draft. 2 pp. In handwriting of Jonathan Trumbull, jr. A. VI, pt. II, 171

Committee: Scott, Boudinot and Ramsay.

1782
JUNE 10

Washington, George. [Newburgh.] To [Sir] Guy Carleton [New York]. Chief Justice David Brearly's opinion in case of [John Smith] Hatfield and [Abner] Badgely. [Extract of letter.] In handwriting of Benjamin Walker. Enclosed in Washing to the President of Congress, 1782, July 9. C. C. 152, 10, 613

1782
JUNE 12

Secretary at War. [Newburgh.] To [George] Washington [Newburgh]. Case of Col. [Goose] Van Schaick. L. S. of Benjamin Lincoln. 2 pp. 98, 57

1782
JUNE 12

Secretary at War. [Newburgh.] To [George] Washington [Newburgh]. Detention of arms; naval prisoners; minor military matters. L. S. of Benjamin Lincoln. 3 pp. 98, 58

1782
JUNE 12

Secretary at War. [Newburgh.] To [George] Washington [Newburgh]. Reduction of the army. A. L. S. of Benjamin Lincoln. 2 pp. 98, 60

1782
JUNE 12

Morris, Robert. [Philadelphia.] To [George] Washington [Newburgh]. Action of New York as regards taxes; money for wheat and flour. L. S. 2 pp. 57, 128

1782
JUNE 12

[Skinner, Abraham.] Newburgh. To [the Secretary at War, Philadelphia]. Fish and wood for marine prisoners; their distress etc. Contemporary copy. In handwriting of John M. Lovell. Enclosed in Secretary at War to Washington, 1782, July 5. 98, 87

1782
JUNE 13

Secretary at War. [Philadelphia.] To [George] Washington [Newburgh]. Clothier-General's lack of money and miscellaneous matter. A. L. S. of William Jackson. 3 pp. 98, 62

1782
JUNE 14

Continental Congress, Resolve. British transportation of South Carolina inhabitants to their homes. D. S. of Charles Thomson. 1 p. Enclosed in Secretary at War to Washington, 1782, June 19. 98, 71

[1782]
[JUNE 14]

South Carolina, Georgetown Inhabitants. List of persons desirous returning in the British transports to Georgetown. A. D. of Nathan Jones. 1 p. Enclosed in Secretary at War to Washington, 1782, June 19. 98, 73

[1782]
[JUNE 14]

North Carolina, Edenton Inhabitants. List of persons desirous of returning in the British transports to Edenton. A. D. of Nathan Jones. 1 p. Enclosed in Secretary at War to Washington, 1782, June 19. 98, 72

1782
JUNE 15

Secretary at War. [Philadelphia]. To [George] Washington [Newburgh]. Retention of letter for [Brig.] Gen. [Moses] Hazen. A. L. S. of William Jackson. 1 p. 98, 64

1782
JUNE 16

Washington, George. Newburgh. To Robert Morris [Philadelphia]. [Comfort] Sands actions; officers' ration etc. Draft. 7 pp. In handwriting of Benjamin Walker.   **A.** VI, pt. II, 173
Printed: Writings of Washington (Ford) N.Y. 1891. 10, 31.

1782
JUNE 17

Washington, George. [Newburgh.] To the Secretary at War [Philadelphia]. Reduction of the army. Draft. 4 pp. In handwriting of Jonathan Trumbull, jr.   **A.** VI, pt. II, 181
Printed: Writings of Washington (Ford) N.Y. 1891. 10, 35.

1782
JUNE 17

Washington, George. Newburgh. To [the Secretary at War, Philadelphia]. Promotions to Brigadiers. Draft. 2 pp. In handwriting of Jonathan Trumbull, jr.   **A.** VI, pt. II, 185

1782
JUNE 17

Danforth, Samuel and John **Warren.** Boston. Certificate of health of [Brig.] Gen. [John] Glover. Contemporary copy. 1 p. In handwriting of David Cobb. Enclosed in Washington to the President of Congress, 1782, July 10.
     C. C. 152, 10, 607

1782
JUNE 17

Sands, Comfort & Co. and Walter **Livingston.** Fishkill [New York]. To [Robert Morris, Philadelphia]. Disappointment of specie payments; difficulties of supplies of beef and flour; the situation. Contemporary copy. 3 pp. Enclosed in Morris to Washington, 1782, June 22.   **57, 212**

1782
JUNE 18

Secretary at War. [Newburgh.] To [George] Washington [Newburgh]. Excellent appearance of the troops. L. S. 2 pp. In handwriting of David Cobb.
     98, 65

1782
JUNE 18

Secretary at War. [Philadelphia.] To [George] Washington [Newburgh]. Dr. [William] Cleland's return to New York. A. L. S. of William Jackson. 2 pp. Answered July 3.*   **98, 67**

1782
JUNE 18

Glover, John. Marblehead [Massachusetts]. To [George Washington, Newburgh]. Resignation on account of health. Contemporary copy. 4 pp. In handwriting of David Cobb. Enclosed in Washington to the President of Congress, 1782, July 10.   **C. C.** 152, 10, 603

1782
JUNE 19

Washington, George. Newburgh. To the Secretary at War [Philadelphia]. Alterations in the Invalid corps. Draft. 2 pp. In handwriting of David Humphreys.   VI, pt. II, 187

1782
JUNE 19

[Washington, George.] [Newburgh.] To Robert R. Livingston [Philadelphia]. Sentiments conveyed by [Maj.] Gen. [Benjamin] Lincoln. Draft. 1 p. In handwriting of Benjamin Walker. P. II, 523

1782
JUNE 19

Secretary at War. [Philadelphia.] To [George] Washington [Newburgh]. Transmitting resolve of Congress. A. L. S. of William Jackson. 2 pp. Answered July 3.*   98, 69

1782
JUNE 20

Carleton, [Sir] Guy. New York. To [George] Washington [Newburgh]. Chief Justice [David] Brearly's opinion in case of [John Smith] Hatfield and [Abner] Badgely; treason laws in the states; retaliations; passport for Lt. Gen. [James] Robertson. Contemporary copy. 4 pp. In handwriting of Hodijah Baylies. Enclosed in Washington to the President of Congress, 1782, July 9.   C. C. 152, 10, 621
Printed: Writings of Washington (Sparks) Boston. 1835. 8, 537.

1782
JUNE 21

Morris, Robert. [Philadelphia.] To [George] Washington [Newburgh]. Debts of American officers, recent prisoners with the enemy. L. S. 2 pp. Answered July 3.*   57, 205

1782
JUNE 22

Washington, George. [Newburgh.] To Sir Guy Carleton [New York]. Proposed meeting; civil powers of states. Contemporary copy. 3 pp. In handwriting of David Cobb. Enclosed in Washington to the President of Congress, 1782, July 9.
                                  C. C. 152, 10, 625

1782
JUNE 22

Morris, Robert. [Philadelphia.] To Comfort Sands & Co. and Walter Livingston [Fishkill]. Requiring performance of contract. Contemporary copy. 1 p. Enclosed in Morris to Washington, 1782, June 22.   57, 208

1782
JUNE 22

Morris, Robert. [Philadelphia.] To [George] Washington [Newburgh]. Attitude of the contractors for supplying the army. L. S. 1 p. Answered July 3.*   57, 210

1782
JUNE 23

Washington, George. Newburgh. To the Secretary at War [Philadelphia]. Court martial of Capt. [William] McCurdy on charges of Capt. [Charles] Asgill. Draft. 3 pp. In handwriting of David Humphreys.   A. VI, pt. II, 189

1782
JUNE 23

Secretary at War. Philadelphia. To [George] Washington [Newburgh]. Officers rations; contractors and flo**u**r contract. L. S. of Benjamin Lincoln. 4 pp. Answered July 3.*   **98, 74**

1782
JUNE 24

Washington, George. Newburgh. To [the President of Congress, Philadelphia]. Inaction of States in furnishing men. Draft. 1 p. In handwriting of Jonathan Trumbull, jr. Read in Congress, June 27.   **A. VI, pt. II, 193**

1782
JUNE 24

Washington, George. [Newburgh]. To [the President of Congress, Philadelphia] Application of officers to join combined armies in the West Indies. Draft. 1 p. In handwriting of David Cobb.
    A. VI, pt. II, 195

1782
JUNE 25

Wayne, Anthony. Sharon [Georgia]. To Maj. Gen. [Nathanael] Greene [Sharon]. Account of battle with the Creeks at Ebenezer. A. L. S. 5 pp. Marked by Wayne "Copy." Enclosed in Wayne to Washington, 1783, Nov. 1.
    C. C. 152, 11, 587

A copy of above in handwriting of John Hanson had been enclosed in President of Congress to Washington, 1782, Aug. 13.

1782
JUNE 25

Fishbourne, Benjamin. Sharon. Return of killed and wounded in action of June 24. Contemporary copy. 1 p. In handwriting of John Hanson. Enclosed in President of Congress to Washington, 1782, Aug. 13.   **98, 129**

1782
JUNE 25

Linder, John, jr. St. Augustine [Florida]. To [Brig.] Gen. [Anthony] Wayne [Sharon, Georgia]. Attachment to the American cause; information etc. Contemporary copy. 2 pp. In handwriting of Wayne. Enclosed in Wayne to Washington, 1783, Nov. 1.   **C. C. 152, 11, 599**

1782
JUNE 26

Secretary at War. [Philadelphia.] To [George] Washington [Albany]. Case of Dr. [Robert] Smith; [Maj.] Gen. [Nathanael] Greene's letter. L. S. of Benjamin Lincoln. 1 p. Answered July 3.*
    98, 76

1782
JUNE 27

Continental Congress, President. Philadelphia. To [George] Washington [Albany]. Acknowledging receipt of papers. L. S. of John Hanson. 1 p.
    98, 78

1782
JUNE 27

[Cobb, David.] [Newburgh.] To [the Secretary at War, Philadelphia]. Alteration in mode of issuing rations. Auto. draft. 2 pp. **A. VI, pt. II, 197**

1782
JUNE 28

Secretary at War. [Philadelphia.] To [George Washington, Albany]. Case of Capt. [William] McCurdy. L. S. of Benjamin Lincoln. 1 p. Answered July 3.* 98, 80

1782
JUNE 28

Secretary at War. [Philadelphia.] To the President of Congress [Philadelphia]. Fish and fire-wood for American marine prisoners in New York; policy of indulgences toward prisoners. Contemporary copy. In handwriting of John M. Lovell. Enclosed in Secretary at War to Washington, 1782, July 5. 98, 87

1782
JUNE 29

Morris, Robert. [Philadelphia.] To [George] Washington [Newburgh]. Alterations in issues to army; difficulty between officers and contractors; the civil and military salaries. L. S. 3 pp.

57, 262

1782
JULY 1

Continental Congress, Resolve. Commander-in-chief to take order on letter of Secretary at War [June 28] respecting fish and fire-wood for American marine prisoners. Contemporary copy. In handwriting of John M. Lovell. Enclosed in Secretary at War to Washington, 1782, July 5. 98, 87

1782
JULY 3

Washington, George. [Newburgh.] To [the Secretary at War, Philadelphia]. Establishment of troops; Judge-Advocate and Adjutant-General; reduction of lieutenants. Draft. 3 pp. In handwriting of Benjamin Walker. A. VI, pt. II, 199

1782
JULY 3

W[ashingto]n, G[eorge]. Newburgh. To Robert Morris [Philadelphia]. American prisoners' debts; difficulty with contractors; West Point as a place of deposit for supplies. In part, auto. draft signed. 3 pp. In handwriting of David Humphreys. A. VI, pt. II, 205

1782
JULY 4

Secretary at War. [Philadelphia.] To [George] Washington [Newburgh]. Building of magazine at West Point; employment of soldiers. L. S. of Benjamin Lincoln. 5 pp. Answered July 30. 98, 81

1782
JULY 5

Secretary at War. [Philadelphia.] To [George] Washington [Newburgh]. Indulgences to American prisoners in New York. A. L. S. of Benjamin Lincoln. 2 pp. Answered July 30.* 98, 85

| 1782
JULY 6 | **Morris,** Robert. [Philadelphia.] To [George] Washington [Newburgh]. Plunder of flag by British privateers. A. L. S. 1 p. 　　　　57, 292 |

| 1782
JULY 7 | **Carleton,** [Sir] Guy. New York. To [George Washington, Newburgh]. Objects of conference; civil and military power; [Richard] Lippincott's court martial; exchange of prisoners. Contemporary copy. 4 pp. In handwriting of David Cobb. Enclosed in Washington to the President of Congress, 1782, July 9.
　　　　　　　　　　C. C. 152, 10, 629
Printed: Writings of Washington (Sparks) Boston. 1835. 8, 539. |

| 1782
JULY 9 | **Washington,** George. Newburgh. To [the President of Congress, Philadelphia]. Enemy's raid on Northern frontier; correspondence with Sir Guy Carleton. Draft. 3 pp. In handwriting of David Humphreys. Read in Congress, July 15. Referred to Witherspoon, Madison and Rutledge. Recommitted July 19 to Lowell, Cornell and Madison who reported July 29 and were finally discharged Aug. 8.
　　　　　　　　　A. VI, pt. I, 209
Printed: Writings of Washington (Ford) N. Y. 1891. 10, 41. |

| 1782
JULY 9 | **[Washington,** George.] Newburgh. To [James] Duane and Col. [Theodorick] Bland [Philadelphia]. Baron Steuben's case. Auto. draft. 2 pp.
　　　　　　　　　A. VI, pt. II, 213 |

| 1782
JULY 9 | **Secretary at War.** [Philadelphia.] To [George] Washington [Newburgh]. Judge Advocate and Adjutant Generalship; lieutenants' and ensigns' duties; a British subaltern; plans for magazine at West Point. L. S. of Benjamin Lincoln. 2 pp. Answered July 30.*　　　　　98, 89 |

| 1782
JULY 9 | **Morris,** Robert. [Philadelphia.] To [George] Washington [Newburgh]. Magazine at West Point; financial news from Virginia; distress of his position. L. S. 2 pp.　　　　　57, 312 |

| 1782
JULY 10 | **Washington,** George. [Newburgh.] To [the Secretary at War, Philadelphia]. Retirement of Brig. Genls. [John] Glover and [Samuel Holden] Parsons. Draft. 2 pp. In handwriting of Benjamin Walker.　　　A. VI, pt. II, 215 |

| 1782
JULY 10 | **Secretary at War.** [Philadelphia.] To [George] Washington [Newburgh]. Provision for Invalid Officers; |

dispute of rank in southern cavalry. L. S. of
Benjamin Lincoln. 2 pp. Answered July 30.*
98, 91

1782
JULY 11   **Continental Congress**, Resolve. Release of Henry Laurens.
D. S. of George Bond. 1 p. Enclosed in Secre-
tary at War to Washington, 1782, July 16.
"Transmitted to Sir Guy Carleton . . . , 30th
July." 98, 93

1782
JULY 11   **Continental Congress**, Resolve. Lieutenants and vacant en-
signcies. D. S. of George Bond. Enclosed in
Secretary at War to Washington, 1782, July 16.
Published in Gen¹. Orders, July 30. 98, 98

1782
JULY 11   [**Greene**, Nathanael.] [Ashley Hill, South Carolina.] To
[the·President of Congress, Philadelphia]. Re-
cruiting of Lee's Partizan corps. Contemporary
copy. 1 p. Enclosed in Secretary at War to
Washington, 1782, Sep. 17. 98, 170

1782
JULY 11   [**Wayne**, Anthony.] Savannah. General Orders. Posting
of troops; civil authority; invoice of stores etc.
Contemporary extract. 2 pp. Enclosed in President of Congress to Washington, 1782, Aug. 13.
98, 125

1782
JULY 12   **Wayne**, Anthony. Savannah. To Maj. Gen. [Nathanael]
Greene [Ashley River, South Carolina]. Evacu-
ation of Savannah; measures adopted. Contem-
porary copy. 3 pp. In handwriting of Charles
Morse. Enclosed in President of Congress to
Washington, 1782, Aug. 13. 98, 123

1782
JULY 13   [**Barclay**, Thomas.] Amsterdam. To [Robert R. Livingston? Philadelphia]. Continuance of the war;
naval movements; Geneva; U. S. ministers at
Paris. [Extract of letter.] Contemporary copy.
2 pp. Enclosed in Livingston to Washington,
1782, Sep. 11. 59, 98

1782
JULY 13   **Greene**, Nath[anael]. Ashley River. To the President of
Congress [Philadelphia]. [Brig.] Gen. [Anthony]
Wayne's engagement with Creeks; clothing for
troops; health of army; intentions of enemy;
strength of army. Contemporary copy. 2 pp.
In handwriting of John Hanson. Enclosed
in President of Congress to Washington, 1782,
Aug. 13. **98, 121**

1782
JULY 13
  Wayne, Anthony. Savannah [Georgia]. Speech to the Factor and other Creek chiefs. Defeat of British and killing of their warriors; peace and friendship. A. D. S. 4 pp. Marked by Wayne: "Copy" Enclosed in Wayne to Washington, 1783, Nov. 1.   C. C.   152, 11, 595

1782
JULY 14
  Greene, Nath[anael]. Ashly Hill, South Carolina. To the President of Congress [Philadelphia]. Evacuation of Savannah by British; [Brig.] Gen. [Anthony] Wayne's merit. Contemporary copy. 1 p. Enclosed in President of Congress to Washington, 1782, Aug. 13.   98, 119

1782
JULY 15
  Washington, George. Philadelphia. To the President of Congress [Philadelphia]. Conference with Rochambeau. Draft. 1 p. In handwriting of Jonathan Trumbull, jr.   A.   VI, pt. II, 217

1782
JULY 15
  Connecticut, Governor and Council of Safety. Lebanon. Minutes of meeting. Memorial of Lt. Col. Ebenezer Gray on promotion of Lt. Col. Ebenezer Huntington. Contemporary copy. 2 pp. In handwriting of Nathan Jones. Enclosed in Board of War to Washington, 1782, Sep. 2.   98, 154

     The A. D. S. of John Porter, clerk of council sent to the Secretary at War by Connecticut, 5 pp., is in 98, 211.

1782
JULY 16
  Secretary at War. [Philadelphia.] To [George] Washington [Philadelphia]. Removal of military stores from Virginia. L. S. of Benjamin Lincoln. 2 pp. Answered July 30.*   98, 95

1782
JULY 17
  Lincoln, B[enjamin]. Philadelphia. To [George] Washington [Philadelphia]. Reasons for not halting the French army at Baltimore. A. L. S.   4 pp.   57, 372

1782
JULY 17
  Wayne, Anthony. Savannah. To Maj. Gen. [Nathanael] Greene [Ashley River, South Carolina]. Movements of British in East Florida; probable evacuation of St. Augustine. Contemporary copy. Transmitted to Washington.   98, 191

1782
JULY 18
  Asgill, [Lady Charles]. London. To [Comte de Vergennes, Versailles]. Praying his interposition to save the life of her son [Capt. Charles Asgill]. Contemporary copy. 3 pp. In handwriting of Hodijah Baylies. Enclosed in Washington to the President of Congress, 1782, Oct. 25.   C. C.   152, 11, 13

1782
JULY 19

Washington, George. Philadelphia. To the Secretary at War [Philadelphia]. Ordnance stores in Virginia. Draft. 1 p. In handwriting of Jonathan Trumbull, jr.   **A.** VI, pt. II, 219

1782
JULY 22

Continental Congress, Resolve. Retiring Maj. Gen. [Samuel Holden] Parsons and Brig. Gen. [John] Glover. D. S. of William Jackson. 1 p. Recorded in the War Office July 23. Transmitted to Washington.   **98,** 97

1782
JULY 23

Continental Congress, Resolve. Regulations of Hospital Department. Broadside. 1 p. Enclosed in Secretary at War to Washington, 1782, July 26.
        98, 100

1782
JULY 24

Continental Congress, Resolves. Department of Commissary General of Military Stores. D. S. of Charles Thomson. 1 p. Enclosed in Secretary at War to Washington, 1782, July 26.   **98,** 101

1782
JULY 24

Continental Congress, Resolves. Regulating Department of Commissary General of Prisoners. D. S. of Charles Thomson. 2 pp. Enclosed in Secretary at War to Washington, 1782, July 26.   **98,** 102

1782
JULY 24

Wayne, Anthony. Savannah [Georgia]. Proclamation to citizens and soldiery of East Florida to pledge allegiance to the United States. A. D. S. 4 pp. Marked by Wayne: "Copy" Enclosed in Wayne to Washington, 1783, Nov. 1.
        C. C. 152, 11, 607

1782
JULY 25

Carleton, [Sir] Guy. New York. To [George] Washington [Bethlehem, Pennsylvania]. Transmission of minutes of [Capt. Richard] Lippincott's trial; transportation of South Carolinians. Contemporary copy. 2 pp. In handwriting of Jonathan Trumbull, jr. Enclosed in Washington to the President of Congress, 1782, Aug. 2.
        C. C. 152, 10, 637

1782
JULY 26

Secretary at War. [Philadelphia.] To [George] Washington [Bethlehem, Pennsylvania]. Transmitting resolves of Congress. L. S. of Benjamin Lincoln. 1 p. Answered Aug. 6.*   **98,** 106

1782
JULY 29

Vergennes,[Charles Gravier,Comte]de. Versailles[France]. To [George] Washington [Newburgh]. Pleading for Capt. [Charles] Asgill. Contemporary translation. 3 pp. In handwriting of Hodijah

Baylies. Enclosed in Washington to the President of Congress, 1782, Oct. 25.

C. C. 152, 11, 9

Printed: Writings of Washington (Ford) N. Y. 1891. 10, 105, note.

1782
JULY 30

Washington, George. [Newburgh.] To the Secretary at War [Philadelphia]. Invalid corps; disputes of rank. Draft. 1 p. In handwriting of Jonathan Trumbull, jr. **A. VI, pt. II, 221**

1782
JULY 30

Washington, George. Newburgh. To Robert Morris [Philadelphia]. Failure of contractors to supply provisions. Draft. 3 pp. In handwriting of David Humphreys. **A. VI, pt. II, 223**

1782
JULY 30

Washington, George. [Newburgh.] To Sir Guy Carleton [New York]. Appointing officers for proposed conference; propositions submitted to Congress. Contemporary copy. 2 pp. In handwriting of Jonathan Trumbull, jr. Enclosed in Washington to the President of Congress, 1782, Aug. 2. **C. C. 152, 10, 633**

1782
JULY 30

Washington, George. [Newburgh.] To Sir Guy Carleton [New York]. Earl Cornwallis and release of Henry Laurens. Contemporary copy. 2 pp. In handwriting of Jonathan Trumbull, jr. Enclosed in Washington to the President of Congress, 1782, Aug. 2. **C. C. 152, 10, 645**

[1782]
[JULY]

Leake, ——. [Savannah, Georgia.] To [Brig. Gen. Anthony Wayne, Savannah]. Information respecting East Florida. A. L. ? 3 pp. Enclosed in Wayne to Washington, 1782, Nov. 1.

C. C. 152, 11, 603

[1782]
[JULY?]

Board of Treasury. Clerks of Accounts. Observations on accounts of contractors for supplying army. Overdraw of rations. Contemporary copy. In handwriting of Nathan Jones. Enclosed in Board of War to Washington, 1782, Aug. 19. **98, 138**

[1782]
[JULY?]

[Mathews, John.] [Uxbridge ? South Carolina]. To [South Carolina delegates to Congress, Philadelphia]. Situation in South Carolina; disaffected; dangers in withdrawal of Continental troops. Extract. 7 pp. In handwriting of John Rutledge. Enclosed in South Carolina delegates to Washington, 1782, Aug. 17. **92, 283**

Taunton, March 1st 1783.

Sir,

I was not till yesterday honoured with your Excellency's Favour of the 8th of January. The amazing Length of Time it has taken to reach me, can only be accounted for upon the Blunders of the Post-master; who, probably, as he has heretofore done with others, gave it a circuitous Route to Boston, via Philadelphia.

Your Letter relieved me from a painful Anxiety, founded on an Apprehension that mine had miscarried, and that, in Consequence, my Conduct might be ascribed to other than the true Motives.

When I begged an Extension of your Indulgence, the Idea did not enter my Mind, that your Excellency could be properly attended by two Gentlemen only, with any Convenience to yourself or to them; or that, by consenting to my Request, the Number would be reduced to two. Upon the Departure of Colo. Tilghman

WRITING OF HODIJAH BAYLIES.

1782
Aug. 1

Treasury, Comptroller. [Philadelphia.] To [Robert Morris, Philadelphia]. Conflict of contracts for supplying posts and the moving army; settlement of the accounts. A. L. S. of James Milligan. 2 pp. Enclosed in Morris to Washington, 1782, Aug. 5
58, 98

1782
Aug. 1

Carleton, [Sir] Guy. New York. To [George] Washington [Newburgh]. Passports for Chief Justice Frederick Smyth; exchange of prisoners. Contemporary copy. 2 pp. In handwriting of Benjamin Walker. Enclosed in Washington to the President of Congress, 1782, Aug. 2.
C. C. 152, 10, 649

1782
Aug. 1

Pickering, Timothy, [jr.] Schuylkill Falls [Pennsylvania]. To Richard Sands [Philadelphia]. Ration issue in Quartermaster's department. Contemporary copy. In handwriting of Nathan Jones. Enclosed in Board of War to Washington, 1782, Aug. 19.
98, 138

1782
Aug. 2

Washington, George. Newburgh. To [the Secretary at War, Philadelphia]. Need of colors, drums and fifes. Draft. 1 p. In handwriting of Hodijah Baylies.
A. VI, pt. II, 231

1782
Aug. 2

Secretary at War. [Philadelphia.] To [George] Washington [Newburgh]. Transmitting Congressional establishment of the Adjutant-General's Department. A. L. S. of William Jackson. 1 p. Answered Aug. 16.*
98, 104

1782
Aug. 2.

Carleton, Sir Guy and Robert Digby. New York. To George Washington [Newburgh]. Peace negotiations at Paris; liberation of [Henry] Laurens; return of prisoners from England. Contemporary copy. 3 pp. In handwriting of David Cobb. Enclosed in Washington to the President of Congress, 1782, Aug. 5. C. C. 152, 10, 669
Printed: Writings of Washington (Sparks) Boston. 1835. 8, 540.

1782
Aug. 3

Washington, George. Newburgh. To the President of Congress [Philadelphia]. Transmitting correspondence with Sir Guy Carleton. Draft. 1 p. In handwriting of Jonathan Trumbull, jr. Read in Congress, Aug. 7. Referred to Scott, Bland and Madison. Aug. 9. Committee discharged and letter referred to Lee, Witherspoon and Rutledge who reported Aug. 12 on this and Washington's letter of Aug. 5. A. VI, pt. II, 227

1782
Aug. 3
Washington, George. Newburgh. To the President of Congress [Philadelphia]. Transmitting proceedings of court martial of Maj. Gen. [Alexander] McDougall. Draft. 1 p. In handwriting of Jonathan Trumbull, jr. Read in Congress, Aug. 7.   A. VI, pt. II, 229

1782
Aug. 3
Francis, Tench, Comfort Sands & Co. and Others. Account current with U. S. for supplying the moving army from May 1 to Aug. 2. A. D. S. of Joseph Nourse. 2 pp. Enclosed in Morris to Washington, 1782, Aug. 5.   58, 105

1782
Aug. 3
Sands, Comfort & Co. Account current with the United States. Tabular statement from Dec. 1781 to July 1782. Contemporary copy from records of the Register's office. 4 pp. In handwriting of James Milligan. Enclosed in Morris to Washington, 1782, Aug. 5.   58, 101

1782
[Aug. 3?]
Treasury. Account of issues made to the moving army and West Point by the contractors; note of payments made. 1 p. Enclosed in Morris to Washington, 1782, Aug. 5.   58, 103

1782
Aug. 5
Washington, George. [Newburgh.] To the President of Congress [Philadelphia]. Transmitting correspondence with Sir Guy Carleton; minor matters. Draft. 1 p. In handwriting of Jonathan Trumbull, jr. Referred to Lee, Witherspoon and Rutledge. Reported Aug. 12.   A. VI, pt. II, 233

1782
Aug. 5
Washington, George. Newburgh. To the Secretary at War [Philadelphia]. Release of a Rhode Island soldier from confinement. Draft. 1 p. In handwriting of David Cobb.   A. VI, pt. II, 235

1782
Aug. 5
Washington, George. Newburgh. To Robert Morris [Philadelphia]. Complaint of [Comfort] Sands's negligence in supplying the army. Draft. 2 pp. In handwriting of Jonathan Trumbull, jr.
                              A. VI, pt. II, 237

1782
Aug. 5
Morris, Robert. [Philadelphia.] To [George] Washington [Newburgh]. Accounts with the contractors; advances, settlements etc.; analysis of the accounts etc. L. S. 6 pp. Answered Aug. 11.*
                              58, 94

1782
Aug. 6
Washington, George. Newburgh. To [the Secretary at War, Philadelphia]. Horses for Armand's corps; Indians; equipment of levies. Hazen's regiment.

Draft. 2 pp. In handwriting of David Humphreys. **A.** VI, pt. II, 239

1782
AUG. 6

Cochran, John. Fishkill [New York]. To George Washington [Newburgh]. Needs of the hospital and field service. A. L. S. 2 pp. Enclosed in Washington to the Secretary at War, 1782, Aug. 7. **A.** VI, pt. II, 245

1782
AUG. 6

Swanwick, J[ohn]. [Philadelphia.] Certificate of payment to the army contractors. A. D. S. 1 p. Enclosed in Morris to Washington, 1782, Aug. 5.
58, 100

1782
AUG. 7

Washington, George. Newburgh. To the Secretary at War [Philadelphia]. Supplies for hospital. Draft. 1 p. In handwriting of Hodijah Baylies.
A. VI, pt. II, 243

1782
AUG. 7

Washington, George. Newburgh. To Gouverneur Morris [Philadelphia]. Gen. [William] Dalrymple's departure for England. Auto. draft signed. 1 p.
P. II, 541

1782
AUG. 7

Continental Congress, Resolves. Arrangement of army. Contemporary copy. 2 pp. In handwriting of Nathan Jones. Enclosed in Secretary at War to Washington, 1782, Aug. 8. **98, 108**

The original report on which these resolves were founded, delivered to Congress, July 29, 1782, was submitted to Washington for suggestions and his suggestions are in The Papers of the Continental Congress, 21, 287-95.

1782
AUG. 7

Govett, William. Philadelphia. Observations upon accounts of contractors for supplying army. Contemporary copy. 3 pp. In handwriting of Nathan Jones. Enclosed in Secretary at War to Washington, 1782, Aug. 19. **98, 136**

1782
AUG. 8

Continental Congress, Resolves. Reenforcement and supplies for Fort Pitt. Contemporary copy. 1 p. In handwriting of Nathan Jones. Enclosed in President of Congress to Washington, 1782, Aug. 16. **98, 110**

1782
AUG. 8

Secretary at War. [Philadelphia.] To [George] Washington [Newburgh]. Complaint of Dr. [John Francis] Vache; dispute of rank in cavalry; colors etc.; transmission of resolves. L. S. of Benjamin Lincoln. 2 pp. **98, 111**

1782
AUG. 9

Continental Congress, Resolve. Retirement of Capt. Seth Phelps. A. D. S. of Benjamin Lincoln. 1 p. Transmitted to Washington. **98, 113**

1782
Aug. 9

Morris, Robert. [Philadelphia.] To [George] Washington [Newburgh]. Contract matters; appointment of an Inspector. L. S. 1 p. Answered Aug. 23.*   58, 133

1782
Aug. 10

Secretary at War. [Philadelphia.] To [George] Washington [Newburgh] Exchange of foreigners, prisoners with enemy; status of surgeons and hospital officers. L. S. of Benjamin Lincoln. 2 pp. Answered Aug. 16.*   98, 133

1782
Aug. 10

Livington, William. Trenton [New Jersey]. To Sir Guy Carleton [New York]. Case of Ezekiel Tilton. Contemporary copy. 6 pp. In handwriting of David Cobb. Enclosed in Washington to the President of Congress, 1782, Sep. 30.

1782
Aug. 11

C. C. 152, 10, 687

Washington, George. Newburgh. To the Secretary at War [Philadelphia]. Command for Maj. Gen. [Horatio] Gates; Hazen's regiment. Draft. 2 pp. In handwriting of David Humphreys.

A. VI, pt. II, 247

Printed, in part: Writings of Washington (Ford) N. Y. 1891. 10, 62.

1782
Aug. 11

Washington, George. Newburgh. To Robert Morris [Philadelphia]. Trouble with [Comfort] Sands and the other contractors. Draft. 2 pp. In handwriting of Jonathan Trumbull, jr.

A. VI, pt. II, 249

1782
Aug. 12

Continental Congress, Resolves. Prospects for peace; general exchange of prisoners; treason acts of the several states. D. S. of Charles Thomson. 1 p. Transmitted to Washington. Sent to Sir Guy Carleton, Aug. 19.   98, 114

1782
Aug. 12

Secretary at War. [Philadelphia.] To [George] Washington [Newburgh]. Armand's troop; supplies for Indians and clothing for New York troops; arrangements for department of Field Commissary of Military Stores; hospital supplies; lack of money; shirts; Hazen's regiment. L. S. of Benjamin Lincoln. 4 pp. In handwriting of William Jackson. Answered Aug. 18.*   98, 115

1782
Aug. 13

Washington, George. Newburgh. To the Secretary at War [Philadelphia]. Public teams for use of contractors. Draft. 2 pp. In handwriting of Jonathan Trumbull, jr.   A. VI, pt. II, 253

1782
Aug. 13

Continental Congress, President. Philadelphia. To [George] Washington [Newburgh]. Sir Guy Carleton's and [Rear] Admiral [Robert] Digby's letters; transmitting letters of [Maj.] Gen. [Nathanael] Greene and [Brig.] Gen. [Anthony] Wayne. A. L. S. of John Hanson. 1 p. Answered Aug. 28.* **98, 117**

1782
Aug. 13

Carleton, [Sir] Guy. New York. To [George] Washington [Newburgh]. Transmitting minutes of court martial of Capt. [Richard] Lippincott; retaliation; New Jersey loyalists; responsibility etc. Contemporary copy. 8 pp. In handwriting of Jonathan Trumbull, jr. Enclosed in Washington to the President of Congress, 1782, Sep. 30.
C. C. 152, 10, 693

1782
Aug. 13

Leslie, Alexander. [Charleston, South Carolina]. To Maj. Gen. [Nathanael] Greene [Ashley Hill]. British foraging parties; payment for provisions. Contemporary copy. 2 pp. Transmitted to Washington. **98,.190**

1782
Aug. 13

Morris Robert. [Philadelphia.] To [George] Washington [Newburgh]. Money from New York. L. S. 1 p. Answered Aug. 23.* **58, 175**

1782
Aug. 14

Washington, George. Newburgh. To Robert R. Livingston [Philadelphia]. [Ensign Lewis R.] Morris's furlough; correspondence with Sir Guy Carleton and [Rear] Adml. [Robert] Digby; meaning of British actions and statements. Auto. draft signed. 3 pp. **P. II, 563**

1782
Aug. 14

Continental Congress, Resolve. Repealing resolve of Oct. 5, 1780, ordering court of inquiry on Maj. Gen. [Horatio] Gates. D. S. of George Bond. Enclosed in Secretary at War to Washington, 1782, Aug. 16. **98, 130**

1782
Aug. 15

Washington, George. [Newburgh.] To the Secretary at War [Philadelphia]. Arrangement of army. Draft. 1 p. In handwriting of Jonathan Trumbull, jr. **A. VI, pt. II, 251**

1782
Aug. 15

Continental Congress, Resolve. Approving sentence of court martial of Maj. Gen. [Alexander] McDougall. D. S. of George Bond. Enclosed in Secretary of War to Washington, 1782, Aug. 16. **98, 130**

1782
AUG. 16
Washington, George. Newburgh. To the Secretary at War [Philadelphia]. Resolves of Congress respecting the Orderly Department; exchange of prisoners; status of chaplains and hospital officers. Draft. 3 pp. In handwriting of David Humphreys.
A. VI, pt. II, 255

1782
AUG. 16
Secretary at War. [Philadelphia.] To [George] Washington [Newburgh]. Transmitting resolves. L. S. of Benjamin Lincoln. 2 pp. 98, 131

1782
AUG. 17
Morris, Robert. [Philadelphia.] To [George] Washington [Newburgh]. Money from New York. L. S. 1 p. (In cipher.) Answered Sep. 2.* 58, 320
Translation in Washington's handwriting, 58, 322.

1782
AUG. 17
South Carolina. Delegates to the Continental Congress. Philadelphia. To [George] Washington [Newburgh]. Protest against withdrawing [Maj.] Gen. [Nathanael] Greene and troops from South Carolina. A. L. S. of J[ohn] Rutledge, Ra[lph] Izard, David Ramsay, A[rthur] Middleton and John Lewis Gervais. 3 pp. Answered Sep. 2.*
92, 281

1782
AUG. 18
Washington, George. [Newburgh.] To the Secretary at War [Philadelphia]. Arrangement of department of field commissary of military stores. Draft. 1 p. In handwriting of Tench Tilghman.
A. VI, pt. II, 259

1782
AUG. 18
W[ashingto]n, G[eorge]. Newburgh. To [Benjamin] Lincoln [Philadelphia]. Exchange of Cornwallis; authorization of cartel; former negotiations. Draft signed. 3 pp. In handwriting of Tench Tilghman.
Printed: Writings of Washington (Ford) N Y. 1891. 10, 66

1782
AUG. 18
Washington, George. Newburgh. To Gouverneur Morris [Philadelphia]. Commission to arrange a cartel with British. Draft. 1 p. In handwriting of Tench Tilghman. A. VI, pt. II, 261

1782
AUG. 18
Washington, George. [Newburgh.] To Sir Guy Carleton [New York]. Transmitting resolves of Congress; commissioners for cartel; status of surgeons, clergymen etc. Contemporary copy. 2 pp. In handwriting of Jonathan Trumbull, jr. Enclosed in Washington to the President of Congress, 1782, Aug. 19? C. C. 152, 10, 673

1782
Aug. 19

Washington, George. Newburgh. To the President of Congress [Philadelphia]. Capt. [Richard] Lippincott's case. Draft. 3 pp. In handwriting of Tench Tilghman. Read in Congress, Aug. 26. Referred to Rutledge, McKean and Duane. Oct. 15 Witherspoon and Wright added. Reported Oct. 17 recommitted and committee augmented. See letter of Oct. 25. **A. .VI, pt. II, 263**
Printed: Writings of Washington (Ford) N. Y. 1891. 10, 69.

1782
Aug. 19

Continental Congress, Resolve. Clothing for New York troops. Contemporary copy. In handwriting of Nathan Jones. Enclosed in Secretary at War to Washington, 1782, Aug. 22. **98, 142**

1782
Aug. 19

Secretary at War. [Philadelphia.] To [George] Washington [Newburgh]. Trouble with contractors. L. S. of Benjamin Lincoln. 2 pp. Answered Sep. 1. **98, 134**

1782
Aug. 20

Morris, Robert. [Philadelphia.] To [George] Washington [Newburgh]. Payments made to the contractors. L. S. 2 pp. Answered Sep. 2.* **58, 234**

1782
Aug. 21

Washington, George. [Newburgh.] To the Secretary at War [Philadelphia]. Brig. Gen. [Edward] Hand's ability; the Adjutant Generalship; issuance of rations. Draft. 3 pp. In handwriting of Jonathan Trumbull, jr. Referred Aug. 26 to Cornell, Osgood, Izard, Bland and Duane. **A. VI, pt. II, 267**
Printed in part: Writings of Washington (Ford) N. Y. 1891. 10, 69, note.

1782
Aug. 22

Secretary at War. [Philadelphia.] To [George] Washington [Newburgh]. Transmitting resolves of Congress. L. S. of Benjamin Lincoln. 1 p. Answered Sep. 1.* **98, 140**

1782
Aug. 22

Secretary at War. [Philadelphia.] To [John Moylan, Philadelphia]. Order to furnish clothing to New York troops. Contemporary copy. In handwriting of Nathan Jones. Enclosed in Secretary at War to Washington, 1782, Aug. 22. **98, 142**

1782
Aug. 22

Morris, Robert. [Philadelphia.] To [George] Washington [Newburgh]. Transmission of letters into New York. L. S. 1 p. **58, 262**

1782
Aug. 23

Washington, George. [Newburgh.] To Robert Morris [Philadelphia]. Inspector to supply department of the army; contractors. Draft. 2 pp. In handwriting of Jonathan Trumbull, jr and Tench Tilghman. **A. VI, pt. II, 271**

1782
AUG. 23

Carleton, [Sir] Guy. New York. To [George] Washington [Newburgh]. Appointment of Commissioners to settle a cartel. Contemporary copy. 2 pp. In handwriting of Hodijah Baylies. Enclosed in Washington to the President of Congress, Aug. 28.   C. C.   152, 10, 751

1782
AUG. 26

M[orris,] R[obert]. Philadelphia. To [George] Washington [Newburgh]. Minor matters; inability to comply with a request. Letter-book copy.

Morris. D, 132

1782
AUG. 27

Call, Richard. [Near Chehaw Ferry, South Carolina]. To [Brig.] Gen. [Mordecai] Gist. [Chehaw Ferry]. Frustration of attack on British. Contemporary copy. 1 p. Transmitted to Washington. 98, 192

1782
AUG. 27

Gist, M[ordecai]. Chehaw Neck [South Carolina]. To Maj. Gen. [Nathanael] Greene [Ashley Hill]. Movements of British; skirmish at Chehaw Neck; death of [Lt.] Col. [John] Laurens; list of killed and wounded. Contemporary copy. 3 pp. Transmitted to Washington.   98, 186

1782
AUG. 28

Washington, George. [Newburgh.] To the President of Congress [Philadelphia]. Instructions looking to arranging a cartel with British. Draft. 2 pp. In handwriting of Tench Tilghman. Read in Congress, Sep. 3. Referred to Bland, Duane and Cornell. Reported Sep. 5.

A.   VI, pt. II, 273
Printed: Writings of Washington (Sparks) Boston. 1835. 8, 338.

1782
AUG. 28

Washington, George. [Newburgh.] To the Secretary of War [Philadelphia]. Consolidating offices of Brigade Conductor and Brigade Quartermaster. Draft. 1 p. In handwriting of Tench Tilghman.
A.   VI, pt. II, 275

1782
AUG. 28

Secretary at War. [Philadelphia.] To [George] Washington [Newburgh]. South Carolinians wishing to return home in British transports. A. L. S. of Benjamin Lincoln. 1 p. Answered Sep. 2.* List sent to Sir Guy Carleton Sep. 3.   98, 143

1782
AUG. 28

Secretary at War. Philadelphia. To [George Washington, Newburgh]. Exchange of [Henry] Laurens; Congress on the Adjutant General's Department; officers' rations. A. L. S. of Benjamin Lincoln. 3 pp. Answered Sep. 2.*   98, 147

1782
AUG. 28

Greene, Nath[anael]. Ashley Hill, South Carolina. To [the President of Congress, Philadelphia]. British preparations to evacuate Charleston; contemplated West India operations; provisions; raids of enemy; evacuation of St Augustine; East Florida and [Brig.] Gen. [Anthony] Wayne. Contemporary copy. 3 pp. Transmitted to Washington.

98, 188

1782
AUG. 28

South Carolina, Inhabitants. List of families desiring to return home in British transports. A. D. of Benjaman Stoddert. 3 pp. Enclosed in Secretary at War to Washington, 1782, Aug. 28.

98, 145

[1782]
AUG. 29

Washington, George. [Newburgh.] To [the Secretary at War, Philadelphia]. Derangement of Dr. [John Francis] Vache. Draft. 1 p. In handwriting of Benjamin Walker. **A.** VI, pt. II, 277

1782
AUG. 29

Carleton, [Sir] Guy. New York. To [George] Washington [Newburgh]. Persecution of loyalists in New Jersey; Indian depredations on Northern frontier. Contemporary copy. 2 pp. In handwriting of David Cobb. Enclosed in Washington to the President of Congress, 1782, Sep. 30.

C. C. 152, 10, 683

Printed in part: Writings of Washington (Ford) N. Y. 1891. 10, 77, note.

1782
AUG. 29

Greene, Nathanael. Ashley Hill [South Carolina]. To [the President of Congress, Philadelphia]. Operations of Brig. Gen. [Mordecai] Gist; death of Lt. Col. [John] Laurens. Contemporary copy. 1 p. Transmitted to Washington. **98,** 185

1782
AUG. 29

M[orris,] R[obert]. [Philadelphia.] To [George] Washington [Newburgh]. Approaching necessity of dissolving contracts for supplying army; monthly expense; attitude of Congress. Letter-book copy. **Morris.** D, 153

1782
AUG. 29

Morris, Robert. [Philadelphia.] To [George] Washington [Newburgh]. Disbursements. L. S. 1 p. Endorsed by Jonathan Trumbull, jr.: "Not to be done—no money." **58,** 366

1782
AUG. 30

M[orris,] R[obert]. [Philadelphia.] To [George] Washington [Newburgh]. Application to States; necessity of secrecy. Letter-book copy.

Morris. D, 159

1782 Aug. 30	**Posey**, Thomas and Samuel **Finley**. Ashley Hill [South Carolina]. To [Brig.] Gen. [Anthony] Wayne [Ashley Hill]. Sentiments of the Virginia detachment. Contemporary copy. 2 pp. In handwriting of Wayne. Enclosed in Wayne to Washington, 1783, Nov. 1. C. C. **152, 11, 611**
1782 Aug. 30	**Wayne**, Anthony. Drayton Hall [Ashley Hill, ? South Carolina]. To Lt. Col. [Thomas] Posey and Maj. Samuel Finley [Ashley Hill]. Thanks for their sentiments. A. L. S. 2 pp. Marked by Wayne: "Copy." Enclosed in Wayne to Washington, 1783, Nov. 1. C. C. **152, 11, 615**
[1782] [Aug. ?]	**Huddy**, Joshua. Schedule of papers relative to murder of, transmitted to Congress. 2 pp. A. D. of Jonathan Trumbull, jr. C. C. **152, 10, 701**
1782 Sep. 1	**Washington**, George. Verplancks Point. [New York.] To the Secretary at War [Philadelphia]. Promotions; rumor of evacuation of Southern states; recall of troops. Draft. 4 pp. In handwriting of Tench Tilghman. Reported by Secretary of War, Sep. 9, and acted on by Congress same day. A. VI, pt. II, 279 <div align="center">Printed in part: Writings of Washington (Ford) N. Y. 1891. 10, 73.</div>
1782 Sep. 1	**Continental Congress**, President. Philadelphia. To [George Washington, Verplancks Point]. Letters laid before Congress. A. L. S. of John Hanson. 1 p. Answered Sep. 5.* **98, 151**
1782 Sep. 2	**Washington**, George. Verplancks Point. To the Secretary at War [Philadelphia]. Request of South Carolina delegates for retention of army in the state; Pennsylvania's proposed expedition; supplies, men and money for same. Draft. 4 pp. In handwriting of Tench Tilghman. A. VI, pt. II, 283
1782 Sep. 2	**Washington**, George. Verplanck's Point. To Robert Morris [Philadelphia]. Difficulties with contractors; arrangements for negotiations for a cartel. Draft. 2 pp. In handwriting of Tench Tilghman. A VI, pt. II, 287
1782 Sep. 2	**Washington**, George Verplancks Point. To [South Carolina delegates to Congress, Philadelphia]. Withdrawal of troops from the Southern states. Draft. 3 pp. In handwriting of Tench Tilghman. A. VI, pt. II, 289 <div align="center">Delegates. Rutledge, Izard, Ramsay, Middleton and Gervais.</div>

1782
SEP. 2

Secretary at War. [Philadelphia.] To [George] Washington [Verplanck's Point]. Case of Lt. Col. [Ebenezer] Huntington. L. S. of Benjamin Lincoln. 1 p. Answered Sep. 11* and more fully Sep. 13.* 98, 153

1782
SEP. 3

Washington, George. [Newburgh.] To Sir [Guy] Carleton [New York]. List of South Carolinians desiring transportation. Contemporary copy. 1 p. In handwriting of Jonathan Trumbull, jr. Enclosed in Washington to the President of Congress, 1782, Sep. 30. C. C. 152, 10, 705

1782
SEP. 3

Secretary at War. Philadelphia. To [George] Washington [Verplanck's Point]. Cannon presented to Comte de Rochambeau. A. L. S. of Benjamin Lincoln. 1 p. Answered Sep. 11.* 98, 155

1782
SEP. 4

Washington, George. Verplancks Point. To the President of Congress [Philadelphia]. Move of army to Verplancks Point; enemy's transports sent to Halifax. Draft. 1 p. In handwriting of Tench Tilghman. Read in Congress, Sep. 9.
A. VI, pt. II, 293

1782
SEP. 4

Washington, George. [Newburgh.]ˑ To the Secretary at War [Philadelphia]. Passport for a British Commissary. Draft. 2 pp. In handwriting of Jonathan Trumbull, jr. A. .VI, pt. II, 295

1782
SEP. 4

Washington, George. Verplancks Point. To Robert Morris [Philadelphia]. Commissioners to arrange a cartel; expense. Draft. 1 p. In handwriting of Tench Tilghman. A. VI, pt. II, 299

1782
SEP. 4

Washington, George. [Newburgh.] To [Robert] Morris [Philadelphia]. Trouble with contractors over flour and rum; [Comfort] Sand's conduct. Draft. 2 pp. In handwriting of Tench Tilghman.
A. VI, pt. II, 301

1782
SEP. 4

Secretary at War. [Philadelphia.] To [George] Washington [Verplanck's Point]. Field Commissary of Military Stores. L. S. of Benjamin Lincoln. 1 p. Answered Sep. 11.* 98, 157

1782
SEP. 5

Washington, George. [Newburgh.] To the President of Congress [Philadelphia]. Arrival of a British fleet at New York. Draft. 1 p. In handwriting of Tench Tilghman. Read in Congress, Sep. 9.
A. VI, pt. II, 303

1782
SEP. 5

Continental Congress, Resolve. Employment of Pennsylvania troops. D. S. of Charles Thomson. Enclosed in Secretary at War to Washington, 1782, Sep. 17.   **98, 158**

1782
SEP. 5

Hand, Edward. Verplancks Point [New York]. Return of recruits from the various states from Jan. 1 to Aug. 31. Tabular statement. D. S. 1 p. Enclosed in Washington to the President of Congress, 1782, Sep. 11.   C. C. 152, 10, 723

1782
SEP. 8

Washington, George. [Newburgh.] To the President of Congress[Philadelphia]. Transmitting New York newspapers. Draft. 1 p. In handwriting of Jonathan Trumbull, jr. Read in Congress, Sep. 11.   A. VI, pt. II, 305

1782
SEP. 8

Washington, George. [Newburgh.] To [Sir] Guy Carleton [New York]. Commissioners for a cartel; suspension of hostilities; Indian depredations. Contemporary copy. 3 pp. In handwriting of Jonathan Trumbull, jr. Enclosed in Washington to the President of Congress, 1782, Sep. 30.   C. C. 152, 10, 719

Printed: Writings of Washington (Ford) N. Y. 1891. 10, 75.

1782
SEP. 9

Continental Congress, Resolves. Exchange of prisoners; liquidation of subsistence accounts of same; exchange of sailors for soldiers etc.; powers of exchange commissions; Maryland recruits; Maj. Gen. [Nathanael] Greene; force in the South. D. S. of Charles Thomson. Enclosed in Secretary at War to Washington, 1782, Sep. 17.   **98, 158**

1782
SEP. 9

M[orris,] R[obert]. [Philadelphia.] To [George] Washington [Newburgh]. Distress of his situation; exhaustion of resources; taxation. Letter-book copy.   Morris. D, 181

1782
SEP. 9

Morris, Robert. [Philadelphia.] To [George] Washington [Verplanck's Point]. Purchase of flour for army. L. S. 1 p.   59, 55

1782
SEP. 10

Continental Congress, Resolve. Capt. [Patrick] Carnes; recruiting service. D. S. of Charles Thomson. Enclosed in Secretary at War to Washington, 1782, Sep. 17.   **98, 158**

1782
SEP. 10

Beers, Nathan. Verplanck's Point. Certificate respecting William S[mith] Livingston's pay. Contemporary copy. In handwriting of Jonathan Trumbull, jr. Enclosed in Board of War to Washington, 1782, Oct. 10.   **98, 215**

1782
SEP. 10

Huntington, Ebenezer. [Verplanck's Point]. To [George] Washington [Verplanck's]. Claim to rank; Lt. Col. [William Smith] Livingston's case. Contemporary copy. 3 pp. In handwriting of Benjamin Stoddert. Enclosed in Secretary at War to Washington, 1782, Oct. 10.   98, 219

1782
SEP. 11

Washington, George. [Newburgh.] To the President of Congress [Philadelphia]. Transmitting returns of recruits. Draft. 1 p. In handwriting of Jonathan Trumbull, jr. Read in Congress, Sep., 14.
A. VI, pt. II, 307

1782
SEP. 11

Washington, George. [Newburgh.] To the Secretary at War [Philadelphia]. Appointment of a Judge Advocate; engraving for cannon for Rochambeau. Draft. 2 pp. In handwriting of Jonathan Trumbull, jr.   A. VI, pt. II, 309

1782
SEP. 11

Washington, George. [Newburgh.] To Gouverneur Morris [Philadelphia]. Prisoners subsistence accounts. Draft. 1 p. In handwriting of Tench Tilghman.   A. VI, pt. II, 311

1782
SEP. 11

Washington, George. [Newburgh.] To Robert Morris [Philadelphia]. [Lt.] Col. [Richard] Varick's demand [for money]. Draft. 1 p. In handwriting of Tench Tilghman. A. VI, pt. II, 313

1782
SEP. 11

Livingston, R[obert] R. Philadelphia. To George Washington [Verplanck's Point]. News from Europe; peace negotiations. A. L. S. 1 p.   59, 97

1782
SEP. 12

Carleton, [Sir] Guy. New York. To [George] Washington [Newburgh]. Commissioners for a cartel; suspension of hostilities; Indians on Northern frontier. Contemporary copy. 3 pp. In handwriting of Hodijah Baylies. Enclosed in Washington to the President of Congress, 1782, Sep. 30.   C. C. 152, 10, 725

1782
SEP. 12

Morris, Robert. [Philadelphia.] To [George] Washington [Verplanck's. Point]. Appointment of Inspector of Contracts; conference on settling the accounts. L. S. 1 p. Answered Sep. 22.*
59, 102

1782
SEP. 13

Washington, George. [Newburgh.] To [the Secretary at War, Philadelphia]. Lt. Col. [William Smith] Livingston's resignation; inscription for cannon presented to Rochambeau; passports for British officers. Draft. 3 pp. In handwriting of Tench Tilghman and Jonathan Trumbull, jr.

A. VI, pt. II, 315

1782
SEP. 13

Continental Congress, Resolve. Proposed [Pennsylvania] expeditions [against Indians towns of Sandusky and Genesee]. D. S. of Charles Thomson. Enclosed in Secretary at War to Washington, 1782, Sep. 17. **98, 158**

See letter of Secretary at War to Congress, 1782, Sept. 11. C. C. 149, 1, 679.

1782
SEP. 14

Secretary at War. Philadelphia. To [George] Washington [Verplanck's Point]. Retirement of Lieuts. [François] Guilemat, [Alexandre] Ferriol and [Pierre] Boileau. L. S. of Benjamin Lincoln. 1 p. **98, 166**

1782
SEP. 16

Washington, George. [Newburgh.] To the President of Congress [Philadelphia]. Delay of Congress in forwarding powers for commissioners for settling a cartel. Draft. 1 p. In handwriting of Tench Tilghman. Read in Congress, Sep. 18.

A. VI, pt. II, 319

1782
SEP. 16

Continental Congress. Commission to George Washington to establish a general cartel for the exchange of prisoners. D. S. of John Hanson, countersigned by Charles Thomson. Seal of the U. S. attached. 1 p. parchment. 57.5×41.3 cm. Enclosed in Secretary at War to Washington, 1782, Sep. 17. **98, 181**

1782
SEP. 16

Washington, George. [Newburgh.] To [Sir] Guy Carleton [New York]. Postponing meeting of cartel commissioners. Contemporary copy. 1 p. In handwriting of Jonathan Trumbull, jr. Enclosed in Washington to the President of Congress, 1782, Sep. 30. **C. C. 152, 10, 729**

1782
SEP. 16

Washington, George. [Newburgh.] To the Secretary at War [Philadelphia]. Disagreeable situation as to negotiations for cartel; troops being sent north by [Maj.] Gen. [Nathanael] Greene. Draft. 1 p. In handwriting of Tench Tilghman.

A. VI, pt. II, 321

1782
SEP. 16

Washington, George. [Newburgh.] To [Robert] Morris [Philadelphia]. Postponed meeting of Commissioners for arranging a cartel; contractor's receipts. Draft. 1 p. In handwriting of Tench Tilghman and Jonathan Trumbull, jr.

A. VI, pt. II, 325

1782
SEP. 17
Secretary at War. [Philadelphia.] To [George] Washington [Verplanck's Point] Judge Advocate for army; general cartel; recruiting Lee's Partizan Corps. L. S. of Benjamin Lincoln. 1 p. Answered Sep. 24.*   98, 168

1782
SEP. 18
Continental Congress, Proceedings. Election of Maj. Richard Howell, Judge Advocate. D. S. of Charles Thomson. 1 p. Transmitted to Washington.
                                98, 175

1782
SEP. 18
Secretary at War. [Philadelphia.] To [George] Washington [Verplanck's Point]. Passports to enter New York; exchange of [Charles,] Earl Cornwallis and other matters in Congress. A. L. S. of Benjamin Lincoln. 2 pp. Answered Sep. 24.*
                                98, 171

1782
SEP. 18
Anonymous. [Newburgh.] To [George Washington, Newburgh]. Preparation of British shipping; Charleston garrison; rumored evacuation of New York. Contemporary copy. 2 pp. In handwriting of David Cobb. Enclosed in Washington to the President of Congress, 1782, Sep. 22.
                                C. C.   152, 10, 739

1782
SEP. 18
Lytle, Archibald. [Ashley Hill? South Carolina.] To [the Board of War, Philadelphia]. Treatment received from British while a prisoner. A. L. S. 5 pp. Enclosed in Secretary at War to Washington, 1782, Nov. 22.   98, 303

1782
SEP. 19
Washington, George. [Newburgh.] To the Secretary at War [Philadelphia]. Magazine at Constitution Island. Draft. 2 pp. In handwriting of Jonathan Trumbull, jr.   **A.** VI, pt. II, 327

1782
SEP. 19
Washington, George. Newburgh. To Robert R. Livingston [Philadelphia]. News from Europe; death of Rockingham and change in British ministry; military intelligence. Auto. draft signed. 2 pp.
                                P. II, 591
Printed in part: Writings of Washington (Ford) N. Y. 1891. 10, 82.

1782
SEP. 19
Morris, Robert. [Philadelphia.] To [George] Washington [Verplanck's Point]. Arrangement of contract matters. L. S. 1 p. Answered Oct. 3.*
                                59, 176

1782
SEP. 19
Morris, Robert. [Philadelphia.] To [George] Washington [Verplanck's Point]. Ezekiel Cornell appointed Inspector of Contracts for the army. L. S. 1 p. Answered Oct. 3.*   59, 178

1782
SEP. 19

Morris, Robert. [Philadelphia.] To [George] Washington [Verplanck's Point]. Notes for payment of [Lt.] Col. [Richard] Varick. L. S. 1 p. Answered Oct. 3.*   59, 180

1782
SEP. 21

George III. Westminster. Commission to Richard Oswald to treat for peace with Commissioners of the United States of America. Contemporary copy. 4 pp. Enclosed in President of Congress to Washington, 1782, Dec. 25.   98, 297

1782
SEP. 22

Washington, George. [Newburgh.] To the President of Congress [Philadelphia]. Transmitting intelligence from New York. Draft. 1 p. In handwriting of Jonathan Trumbull, jr. Read in Congress, Sep. 26.   A. VI, pt. II, 329

1782
SEP. 22

Washington, George. [Newburgh.] To the Secretary at War [Philadelphia]. Transmitting muster rolls. Draft. 1 p. In handwriting of Tench Tilghman.   A. VI, pt. II, 331

1782
SEP. 22

Washington, George. [Newburgh.] To [Robert] Morris [Philadelphia]. Appointment of [Brig.] Gen. [Ezekiel] Cornell as Inspector of Contracts; lack of instruction from Congress as to cartel. Draft. 1 p. In handwriting of Tench Tilghman.   A. VI, pt. II, 333

1782
SEP. 22

Washington, George. [Newburgh.] To [Robert Morris, Philadelphia]. Application to the States; change of system of obtaining supplies. Draft signed. 2 pp. In handwriting of Tench Tilghman and Washington.
Printed in part: Writings of Washington (Ford) N. Y. 1891. 10. 83.
        P. II, 595

1782
SEP. 23

Washington, George. [Newburgh.] To the Secretary at War [Philadelphia]. The proposed Pennsylvania expedition against the savages. Draft. 2 pp. In handwriting of Jonathan Trumbull, jr.   A. VI, pt. II, 335

1782
SEP. 24

Washington, George. [Newburgh.] To the Secretary at War [Philadelphia]. Minor matters; Armand's Corps. Draft. 2 pp. In handwriting of Tench Tilghman.   A. VI, pt. II, 337

1782
SEP. 25

Morris, Robert. [Philadelphia.] To [George] Washington [Verplanck's Point]. Meaning of Morris's letters; feeding the army; lack of money; tax-dodgers. L. S. 3 pp. Answered Oct. 3*   55, 85

1782
SEP. 26

Washington, George. Newburgh. To the President of Congress [Philadelphia]. Enemy's condition in Canada; Indians. Draft. 3 pp. In handwriting of Jonathan Trumbull, jr. Read in Congress Sep. 30. Referred to Boudinot, Duane and Williamson. Reported Oct. 11 and acted on same day.   A. VI, pt. II, 339

1782
SEP. 26

Washington, George. [Newburgh.] To the Secretary at War [Philadelphia]. Application to Sir Guy Carleton in behalf of South Carolina inhabitants. Draft. 2 pp. In handwriting of Jonathan Trumbull, jr.   A. VI, pt. II, 343

1782
SEP. 27

Secretary at War. [Philadelphia.] To [George] Washington [Verplanck's Point]. Return of troops from the South; abandonment of [Sandusky and Genesee] expeditions against Indians; suggested station of troops at Lancaster, York and other places. L. S. of Benjamin Lincoln. 2 pp. Answered Oct. 3*   **98,** 173

1782
SEP. 27

T[rumbu]ll, J[onathan, jr.] [Newburgh.] To the Secretary at War [Philadelphia]. Passports for persons to go into New York. Auto. draft signed. 1 p.   A. VI, pt. II, 345

1782
SEP. 30

Washington, George. [Newburgh.] To the President of Congress [Philadelphia]. Transmitting correspondence with Sir Guy Carleton. Draft. 1 p. In handwriting of Jonathan Trumbull, jr. Read in Congress, Oct. 10.   A. VI, pt. II, 347

1782
SEP. 30

Washington, George. [Newburgh.] To the Secretary at War [Philadelphia]. Transmitting returns. Draft. 1 p. In handwriting of Jonathan Trumbull, jr.   A. VI, pt. II, 349

1782
SEP. 30

Washington, George. [Newburgh.] To the Secretary at War [Philadelphia]. Result of conference of Commissioners to arrange a cartel; exchange of Cornwallis and his military family. Draft. 3 pp. In handwriting of Jonathan Trumbull, jr.
A. VI, pt. II, 351

1782
SEP. 30

Washington, George. Newburgh. To James Duane [Philadelphia]. Delay of Congress in acting in the Huddy and Asgill case. Auto. draft signed. 2 pp.   P. II, 603

1782
SEP. 30
Secretary at War. Philadelphia. To J[onathan] Trumbull [jr., Verplanck's Point]. British officers desiring to go into New York. A. L. S. of Benjamin Lincoln. 1 p. Answered by Washington Oct. 7.*   98, 176

1782
SEP. 30
Secretary at War. [Philadelphia]. To [George] Washington [Verplanck's Point]. Capt. [Charles] Asgill's request; British officers allowed to go into New York. [Oct. 1.] Appointment of [Thomas] Edwards Judge Advocate in room of [Richard] Howell. L. S. of Benjamin Lincoln. 2 pp. Answered Oct. 7.*   98, 177

1782
SEP. 30
Bayley, Jacob. Newbury [New Hampshire]. To Gov. [George] Clinton [Poughkeepsie]. Intelligence from Canada; intentions of British. Contemporary copy. 2 pp. Enclosed in Secretary at War to Washington, 1782, Oct. 28.   98, 228

1782
OCT. 1
Continental Congress, Resolves. Representation of New Jersey respecting payment of troops by other states; infringement of the Confederation; states' quotas of money. D. S. of Charles Thomson. 1 p. Enclosed in Morris to Washington, 1782, Oct. 5.
59, 256

1782
OCT. 1
Continental Congress, Resolves. State of New Jersey's application of taxes to pay of troops; system of pay of Army etc. Contemporary copy. 2 pp. In handwriting of Nathan Jones. Enclosed in Secretary at War to Washington, 1782, Oct. 9.
98, 182

1782
OCT. 2
[Washington, George.] Newburgh. To Robert Morris. Temper and disposition of the army; clothing from Amsterdam. Draft. 2 pp. In handwriting of David Humphreys.   P. II, 613

1782
OCT. 2
[Washington, George.] Newburgh. To the Secretary at War [Philadelphia]. Sufferings and distress of the army. Draft. 5 pp. In handwriting of David Humphreys and Washington.   P. II, 607
Printed Writings of Washington (Ford) N Y. 1891, 10, 90

1782
OCT. 2
Continental Congress, Proceedings. Appointment of Thomas Edwards, Judge Advocate. A. D. S. of Benjamin Lincoln. 1 p. Enclosed in Secretary at War to Washington, 1782, Oct. 5.   98, 203

1782
Oct. 2

Continental Congress, Order. Copies of [Maj.] Gen. [Nathanael] Greene's letters of Aug. 28 and 29 be transmitted to the Commander in chief. Contemporary copy. 1 p. Transmitted to Washington.   98, 184

1782
Oct. 3

Washington, George. [Newburgh.] To the Secretary at War [Philadelphia]. Transmitting copy of letter to Sir Guy Carleton respecting payment for maintenance of British prisoners. Draft. 1 p. In handwriting of Jonathan Trumbull, jr.

A. VI, pt. II, 355

1782
Oct. 3

Washington, George. [Newburgh.] To the Secretary at War [Philadelphia]. Troops ordered from the South; irregularity in granting passports to go into New York. Draft. 3 pp. In handwriting of Jonathan Trumbull, jr.   A. VI, pt. II, 357

1782
Oct. 3

Washington, George. [Newburgh.] To [Robert] Morris [Philadelphia]. Army contractors; subsistence of British prisoners. Draft. 2 pp. In handwriting of Tench Tilghman. A. VI, pt. II, 361

1782
Oct. 4

Continental Congress, Resolve. Cooperation with France in negotiating peace. Contemporary copy. 1 p. In handwriting of Nathan Jones. Enclosed in Secretary at War to Washington, 1782, Oct. 9.

98, 201

1782
Oct. 4

Secretary at War. Philadelphia. To [George] Washington [Verplanck's Point]. Expediency of a partial exchange of prisoners; foreign officers. A. L. S. of Benjamin Lincoln, marked "private." 2 pp.   Answered Oct. 7.*   98, 193

1782
Oct. 4

Secretary at War. [Philadelphia.] To [George] Washington [Verplanck's Point]. Return of prisoners taken at Yorktown; numbers etc. L. S. of Benjamin Lincoln. 2 pp. Answered Oct. 7.*

98, 195

[1782]
[Oct. 4]

Prisoners, British. Statement of numbers taken at Yorktown, where confined etc. A. D. of Nathan Jones. 1 p. Enclosed in Secretary at War to Washington, 1782, Oct. 4.   98, 197

[1782]
[Oct. 4]

Prisoners, British. Account as by return of Sep. 1781, also of those captured at Yorktown; numbers, where confined, etc. A. D. of Nathan Jones. 2 pp. Enclosed in Secretary at War to Washington, 1782, Oct. 4.   98, 199

1782
Oct. 4

Sullivan, John.   Keene, [New] Hampshire.   To Maj. Gen. [William Alexander,] Lord Stirling [Albany]. Intelligence from Canada of intentions of British. Contemporary copy.   2 pp.   Enclosed in Secretary at War to Washington, 1782, Oct. 28.

98, 227

1782
Oct. 5

Secretary at War.   [Philadelphia].   To [George] Washington [Verplanck's Point].   Transmitting appointment of Judge Advocate Thomas Edwards. A. L. S. of Benjamin Lincoln.   1 p.   98, 202

1782
Oct. 5

Morris, Robert.   [Philadelphia.]   To [George] Washington [Verplanck's Point].   Transmitting papers relating to payment of army.   L. S.   1 p. Answered Oct. 14.*   59, 254

1782
Oct. 5

[Morris, Robert.]   [Philadelphia.]   To the Continental Receivers in the different States.   State evasion of payment of taxes into the U. S. Treasury; resolve of Congress respecting same.   Contemporary copy.   2 pp.   Enclosed in Morris to Washington 1782, Oct. 5.   59, 257

1782
Oct. 5

[Morris, Robert.] · [Philadelphia.]   Circular to Governors of the States.   Resolve of Congress calling for means with which to pay the Army.   Contemporary copy.   1 p.   Enclosed in Morris to Washington, 1782, Oct. 5.   59, 259

1782
Oct. 7

Washington, George.   Newburgh.   To the Secretary at War [Philadelphia].   Troops in Virginia; exchange of prisoners; Capt. [Charles] Asgill's case. Draft.   4 pp.   In handwriting of Jonathan Trumbull, jr.   A.   VI, pt. II, 36

1782
Oct. 7

Washington, George.   [Newburgh.]   To Robert Morris [Philadelphia].   Exchange of marine prisoners. Draft.   2 pp.   In handwriting of Jonathan Trumbull, jr.   A.   VI, pt. II, 367

1782
Oct. 7

Continental Congress, Proclamation.   Appointing Nov. 28 a day of Thanksgiving.   D. S. of John Hanson, countersigned by Charles Thomson.   2 pp.   Enclosed in President of Congress to Washington, 1782, Oct. 11.   98, 239

1782
Oct. 7

Snyder, Jeremiah.   Examination of.   Report of situation in Canada, British expeditions preparing against Schenectady and Albany.   Contemporary copy. 2 pp.   Enclosed in Secretary at War to Washington, 1782, Oct. 28.   98, 226

1782
Oct. 8

Secretary at War. [Philadelphia.] To [George] Washington [Verplanck's Point]. Transmitting sketches of posts in Canada. A. L. S. of Benjamin Lincoln. 1 p. Answered Oct. 14.* 98, 204

1782
Oct. 9

Continental Congress, Order. Rank of Lt. Cols. [Ebenezer] Huntington and [Ebenezer] Gray. A. D. S. of Benjamin Lincoln. 1 p. Enclosed in Secretary at War to Washington, 1782, Oct. 10. 98, 206

1782
Oct. 9

Secretary at War. [Philadelphia.] To [George] Washington [Verplanck's Point]. Letters of Sir Guy Carleton; permission to British officers to go into New York. L. S. of Benjamin Lincoln. 1 p. Answered Oct. 14.* 98, 207

1782
Oct. 10

Secretary at War. [Philadelphia.] To [George] Washington [Verplanck's Point]. Cases of Capt. [Seth] Phelps and Lt. Cols. [Ebenezer] Huntington and [Ebenezer] Gray. L. S. of Benjamin Lincoln. 2 pp. Answered Oct. 14.* 98, 209

1782
Oct. 14

Washington, George. [Newburgh.] To the Secretary at War [Philadelphia]. Intelligence from Canada and minor matters. Draft. 1 p. In handwriting of Tench Tilghman. A. VI, pt. II, 369

1782
Oct. 14

Washington, George. [Newburgh.] To [Robert] Morris [Philadelphia]. Morris's circular letter to States. Draft. 1 p. In handwriting of Tench Tilghman. A. VI, pt. II, 371

1782
Oct. 14

Secretary at War. [Philadelphia.] To [George] Washington [Verplanck's Point]. Partial exchanges; case of Capt. [Charles] Asgill. A. L. S. of Benjamin Lincoln. 2 pp. 98, 221

1782
Oct. 14

Lincoln, B[enjamin]. Philadelphia. To [George] Washington [Verplanck's Point]. Sufferings of the army; half-pay; feeling of Congress; taxation to provide funds; application of officers to Congress; European loans to pay army; delays in Congressional action. A. L. S. 9 pp. 59, 314

1782
Oct. 15

Morris, Robert. [Philadelphia.] To [George] Washington [Verplanck's Point]. Inability to relieve distress of army; debts and disputes; his strained credit. L. S. 1 p. 59, 329

1782
Oct. 16

Continental Congress, Resolves. Commission; approval of exchange negotiations; subsistence accounts against British prisoners; exchange; chaplains, physicians etc. Contemporary copy. 2 pp. Transmitted to Washington.   98, 237

1782
Oct. 16

Morris, Robert. [Philadelphia.] To [George] Washington [Verplanck's Point]. Plan to obtain money by selling bills in Havana; secrecy; peace and war as fund producers. L. S. 2 pp. (In cipher.)   59, 343
    Translation in handwriting of Tench Tilghman, 59, 345.

1782
Oct. 17

Washington, George. [Newburgh.] To the Secretary at War [Philadelphia]. Rank dispute and return of recruits. Draft. 1 p. In handwriting of Jonathan Trumbull, jr.   A. VI, pt. II, 373

1782
Oct. 18

Washington, George. [Newburgh.] To [Robert Morris, Philadelphia]. Expense of supplying Marquis de Vaudreuil with information. Draft. 2 pp. In handwriting of Jonathan Trumbull, jr.
                                     A. VI, pt. II, 377

1782
Oct. 18

Continental Congress, Resolve. Retention of military post at Wyoming [Pennsylvania]. Contemporary copy. 1 p. In handwriting of Joseph Carleton. Enclosed in Secretary at War to Washington, 1782, Oct. 28.   98, 223

1782
Oct. 18

T[rumbull,] J[onathan, jr.] [Newburgh.] To the Secretary at War [Philadelphia]. Transmitting monthly return of the Army. Auto. draft signed. 1 p.
                                     A. VI, pt. II, 375

1782
Oct. 22

Washington, George. [Newburgh.] To the Secretary at War [Philadelphia]. [Lt. Col. James] McHenry's depreciated pay. Draft. 2 pp. In handwriting of Tench Tilghman.   A. VI, pt. II, 379

1782
[Oct. 23]

Sprout, E[benezer] and Others. [Camp, New Windsor, New York]. To [the Secretary at War, Philadelphia]. Rank and authority of Lieutenant-colonel's Commandant; injustice suffered etc. Contemporary copy of original signed by Sprout, Colvin Smith, Isaac Sherman, Jeremiah Olney and Thomas Grosvenor. 2 pp. In handwriting of Joseph Carleton. Enclosed in Secretary at War to Washington, 1782, Nov. 8.   98, 247

1782
Oct. 24

Warren, Samuel. [Ashely Hills, South Carolina]. To Lt. Col. [William] Hamilton [Charleston?] Granting letter of service. Contemporary copy. 1 p. In handwriting of Nathan Jones. Enclosed in Secretary at War to Washington, 1783, Feb. 12.
                                               92, 299

1782
OCT. 25

Washington, George. [Newburgh.] To the President of Congress [Philadelphia]. British fleet ready for sea; evacuation of Charleston. L. S. 2 pp. In handwriting of Jonathan Trumbull, jr. Read in Congress, Oct. 29.   C. C. 152, 11, 1

1782
OCT. 25

Washington, George. [Newburgh.] To the President of Congress [Philadelphia]. Letters from Comte de Vergennes pleading for Capt. [Charles] Asgill. Draft. 2 pp. In handwriting of Jonathan Trumbull, jr. Read in Congress, Oct. 29. Referred together with letter of Aug. 19 and report thereon to Rutledge, Osgood, Montgomery, Boudinot and Duane. Reported and acted on Nov. 7.

A. VI, pt. II, 38

Printed: Writings of Washington (Sparks) Boston. 1835. 8, 361.

1782
OCT. 25

Washington, George. [Newburgh.] To the Secretary at War [Philadelphia]. Baron Steuben's ideas as to number of officers to a regiment. Draft. 1 p. In handwriting of Tench Tilghman.

A. VI, pt. II, 383

1782
OCT. 25

Anonymous. Cadiz [Spain]. To ———? Siege of Gibraltar; reenforcements of British; destruction of Hudson Bay Company's property by French. Contemporary extract. 2 pp. Enclosed in President of Congress to Washington, 1782, Dec. 11.

98, 282

1782
OCT. 25

Carleton, [Sir] Guy. New York. To [George] Washington [Newburgh]. Liquidation of prisoners accounts; exchanges. Contemporary copy. 4 pp. In handwriting of Jonathan Trumbull, jr. Enclosed in Washington to the President of Congress, 1782, Nov. 1.   C. C. 152, 11, 25

Printed: Writings of Washington (Sparks) Boston. 1835. · 8, 541.

[1782]
[OCT. 25]

[Steuben, Baron von.] [Newburgh.] Arrangement of officers to a regiment. Draft. 2 pp. Enclosed in Washington to the Secretary at War, 1782, Oct. 25.   A. VI, pt. II, 385

1782
OCT. 28

Secretary at War. [Philadelphia.] To [George] Washington [Newburgh]. Information from Canada and minor military matters; case of Capt. [Charles] Asgill under debate; servants for Adjutant General. L. S. of Benjamin Lincoln. 2 pp. Answered Nov. 6.*   98, 224

1782
Oct. 28

La Luzerne, [Anné César,] Chevalier de. Philadelphia. To [the President of Congress, Philadelphia]. Reporting existence of a clandestine trade with British; supplies furnished New York from Jersey. Contemporary translation. 2 pp. Enclosed in Secretary at War to Washington, 1782, Oct. 30.   **98, 232**

1782
Oct. 29

Continental Congress, President. Philadelphia. To [George] Washington [Newburgh]. Acknowledging letters; intelligence from Europe and West Indies. L. S. of John Hanson. 1 p.   **98, 229**

1782
Oct. 29

Secretary at War. [Philadelphia.] To the President of Congress [Philadelphia]. State of the Invalid Corps; its usefulness and expense; investigation etc. Contemporary copy. 2 pp. Enclosed in Secretary at War to Washington, 1782, Nov. 7.   **98, 246**

1782
Oct. 30

Washington, George. [Newburgh.] To the President of Congress [Philadelphia]. Winter quarters for the Army; movements of enemy. Draft. 2 pp. In handwriting of Jonathan Trumbull, jr. Read in Congress, Nov. 4.   **A. VI, pt. II, 387**

1782
Oct. 30

Continental Congress, Resolve. Clandestine trade with enemy. D. S. of George Bond. 1 p. Enclosed in Secretary at War to Washington, 1782, Oct. 30.   **98, 231**

1782
Oct. 31

Washington, George. [Newburgh.] To Robert Morris [Philadelphia]. Contracts for provisioning the army. Draft. 3 pp. In handwriting of Tench Tilghman.   **A. VI, pt. II, 389**

1782
Oct. 31

Secretary at War. [Philadelphia.] To [George] Washington [Newburgh]. Clothing and blankets for troops; resolves respecting Quartermaster's department. L. S. of Benjamin Lincoln. 3 pp. Answered Nov. 11.*   **98, 235**

1782
Nov. 1

Washington, George. [Newburgh.] To the President of Congress [Philadelphia]. Transmitting letter of Sir Guy Carleton. Draft. 1 p. In handwriting of Jonathan Trumbull, jr. Read in Congress, Nov. 8.   **A. VI, pt. II, 393**

1782
Nov. 4

Continental Congress, Secretary. [Philadelphia.] To [George] Washington [Newburgh]. Election of Elias Boudinot, President. L. S. of Charles Thomson. 1 p.   **98, 241**

1782
Nov. 5

Morris, Robert. [Philadelphia.] To [George] Washington [Newburgh]. Acknowledging receipt of letter. L. S. 1 p. 54, 352

1782
Nov. 6

Washington, George. [Newburgh.] To the Secretary at War [Philadelphia]. The company at Wyoming; illicit trade with enemy; clothing etc. Draft. 3 pp. In handwriting of Tench Tilghman.
A. VI, pt. II, 395

1782
Nov. 7

Continental Congress, Resolve. Capt. [Charles] Asgill to be set at liberty. D. S. of Charles Thomson. 1 p. Enclosed in Secretary at War to Washington, 1782, Nov. 7. 98, 243

1782
Nov. 7

Secretary at War. [Philadelphia.] To [George] Washington [Newburgh]. Invalid Regiment. L. S. of Benjamin Lincoln. 2 pp. Answered Nov. 19.*
98, 244

1782
Nov. 8

Continental Congress, Resolve. Call for justice on murderers of Capt. [Joshua] Huddy; authorizing retaliations. Contemporary copy. 1 p. In handwriting of Nathan Jones. Enclosed in Secretary at War to Washington, 1782, Nov. 11. 98, 248

1782
Nov. 8

Secretary at War. Philadelphia. To [George] Washington [Newburgh]. Letter of Lieutenant colonels Commandant before Congress. A. L. S. of Benjamin Lincoln, marked "private." 2 pp. Answered Nov. 19.* 98, 246½

1782
Nov. 9

Secretary at War. [Philadelphia.] To [George] Washington [Newburgh]. Information of flags to be furnished by British to South Carolina citizens. L. S. of Benjamin Lincoln. 3 pp. Answered Nov. 19.* 98, 249

1782
Nov. 11

Washington, George. [Newburgh.] To the Secretary at War [Philadelphia]. Blankets; Col. [Elias] Dayton's claim to promotion. Draft. 1 p. In handwriting of Tench Tilghman. A. VI, pt. II, 399

1782
Nov. 11

Secretary at War. [Philadelphia.] To [George] Washington [Newburgh]. Post at Wyoming [Pennsylvania]; retaliation resolve; report of committee on complaints of army; purchase of clothing etc. L. S. of Benjamin Lincoln. 3 pp. Answered Nov. 19.* 98, 251

1782
Nov. 12

Continental Congress, Resolves. Pay of Geographers and assistants. D. S. of Charles Thomson. 1 p. Enclosed in Secretary at War to Washington, 1782, Nov. 20. Published in Genl. Orders, Nov. 27.

98, 255

1782
Nov. 13

Osgood, Christopher. Providence [Rhode Island]. Information of Vermont correspondence with the enemy; account of letters carried etc. Contemporary copy. 4 pp. In handwriting of Tench Tilghman. Endorsed by Charles Thomson: "Nov. 25, 1782. To be kept secret. Referred to Mr. Osgood Mr. Carroll Mr. Rutledge Dec. 13, 1782 Injunction of secrecy taken off" Enclosed in Washington to the President of Congress, 1782, Nov. 19.   **C. C. 152, 11, 33**

1782
Nov. 18

[Morris, Robert.] A general view of receipts and expenditures of public money by authority of the Superintendent of Finance to Dec. 31, 1781. Tabular statement from records of the Registers Office. Broadside. 1 p. Enclosed in Morris to Washington, 1782, Apr. 7.   **62, 243**

1782
Nov. 19

Washington, George. [Newburgh.] To the President of Congress [Philadelphia]. Vermont matters; sailing of enemy's fleet from New York. Draft. 1 p. In handwriting of Tench Tilghman. Read in Congress Nov. 28. Referred to Osgood, Carroll and Rutledge. Reported Nov. 27.

A. VI, pt. II, 401

1782
Nov. 19

Washington, George. [Newburgh.] To the Secretary at War [Philadelphia]. Lieutenant-colonels commandant; correspondence with Sir Guy Carleton. Draft. 1 p. In handwriting of Tench Tilghman.

A. VI, pt. II, 403

1782
Nov. 19

Continental Congress, Resolve Retirement of officers, rank, pay etc. D. S. of Charles Thomson. 2 pp. Enclosed in Secretary at War to Washington, 1782, Nov. 20. Published in Genl. Orders Nov. 26.

98, 256

Cf. Resolves of Nov. 20 below.

1782
Nov. 20

W[ashingto]n, G[eorge]. [Newburgh.] To Sir Guy Carleton [New York]. Liberation of Capt. [Charles] Asgill; punishment of murderers [of Huddy]. Draft signed. 1 p. In handwriting of David Humphreys. Enclosed in Washington to the President of Congress, 1782, Dec. 16.

C. C. 152, 11, 45

Printed: Writings of Washington (Ford) N. Y. 1891. 10, 106, note.

1782
Nov. 20

Washington, George. Newburgh. To [Benjamin] Franklin [Passy]. Recommending [John] Wheelock. Draft. 1 p. In handwriting of Tench Tilghman. **A.** VI, pt. II, 407

1782
Nov. 20

Continental Congress, Resolve. Commissions for officers to fill vacancies. D. S. of Charles Thomson. 1 p. Enclosed in Secretary at War to Washington, 1782, Nov. 20. Published in Genl. Orders, Nov. 29. **98,** 258
Cf. Resolves of Nov. 20 below.

[1782]
[Nov. 20]

Continental Congress, Resolves. Explanatory of resolves of Aug. 7, 1782; retirement of officers; filling of vacancies; pay of army etc. Contemporary copy. 2 pp. In handwriting of Nathan Jones. Enclosed in Secretary at War to Washington, 1782, Nov. 20. **98,** 253
Above resolves were then under debate and in forms finally passed are to be found in the Journals of Congress, Nov. 19, 20 and Dec. 2. The explanatory resolve failed of passage.

1782
Nov. 20

Secretary at War. [Philadelphia.] To [George] Washington [Newburgh]. Transmitting resolves; minor matters. L. S. of Benjamin Lincoln. 2 pp. Answered Nov. 27.* **98,** 259

1782
Nov. 21

Washington, George. Newburgh. To the Secretary at War [Philadelphia]. Seizure of rum by Maj. Gen. [Robert] Howe in 1780. Draft. 1 p. In handwriting of David Humphreys. **A.** VI, pt. II, 405

1782
Nov. 22

Washington, George. [Newburgh.] To the Secretary at War [Philadelphia]. Reforming the Invalid Corps. Draft. 1 p. In handwriting of Tench Tilghman. **A.** VI, pt. II, 409

1782
Nov. 22

Secretary at War. [Philadelphia.] To [George] Washington [Newburgh]. Col. [Elias] Dayton; reception of report by Congress; resolve respecting retirements; case of Lt. Col. [Archibald] Lytle. L. S. of Benjamin Lincoln. 4 pp. **98,** 301

1782
Nov. 22

Turner, George. Philadelphia. To Robert Morris [Philadelphia]. Supply of fire-wood for American prisoners at New York; plans for procuring same; exchanges; monetary equivalent proposed. Contemporary copy. 4 pp. Enclosed in Morris to Washington, 1782, Nov. 30. **60,** 212

1782
Nov. 27

Washington, George. [Newburgh.] To the Secretary at War [Philadelphia]. Half pay for officers; clothing for British prisoners; repair of arms etc. Draft. 2 pp. In handwriting of Tench Tilghman and David Humphreys. **A. VI, pt. II, 411**

1782
Nov. 27

Continental Congress, President. Philadelphia. To [George] Washington [Newburgh]. Correspondence; Vermont matters. A. L. S. of Elias Boudinot. 3 pp. Answered Dec. 4.* **98, 262**

1782
Nov. 27

Continental Congress, Resolve. Ordering arrest of Luke Knolton and Samuel Wells of the New Hampshire Grants. A. D. S. of Charles Thomson. 1 p. Enclosed in President of Congress to Washington, 1782, Nov. 27. **98, 261**

1782
Nov. 27

Secretary at War. [Philadelphia.] To [George] Washington [Newburgh]. Lieutenant-colonels Commandant; flags for South Carolinians; Invalid Corps. L. S. of Benjamin Lincoln. 4 pp. Answered Dec. 4.* **98, 266**

1782
Nov. 30

Continental Congress, President. Philadelphia. To [George] Washington [Newburgh]. Indications of approaching evacuation of Charleston. L. S. of Elias Boudinot. 3 pp. Answered Dec. 4.* **98, 264**

1782
Nov. 30

Adye, Stephen P. New York. To Maurice Morgann [New York]. Report on further investigation of execution of [Capt. Joshua] Huddy. Contemporary copy. 1 p. In handwriting of David Humphreys. Enclosed in Washington to the President of Congress, 1782, Dec. 16. **C. C. 152, 11, 51**

1782
Nov. 30

Morris, Robert. [Philadelphia.] To [George] Washington [Newburgh]. Expense incurred at request of Chevalier de la Luzerne. L. S. 1 p. Answered Dec. 11.* **60, 205**

1782
Nov. 30

Morris, Robert. [Philadelphia.] To [George] Washington [Newburgh]. Wood for use of marine prisoners; sale of same to procure clothing; exchanges. L. S. 2 pp. Answered Dec. 11.* **60, 209**

[1782]
[Nov. 30]

Peace. Preliminaries. Fifth and Sixth articles of the Preliminaries signed at Paris. Contemporary copy. 3 pp. Enclosed in Livingston to Washington, 1783, Mar. 12. **62, 68**

1782
DEC. 2

Secretary at War. [Philadelphia.] To [George] Washington [Newburgh]. Resolve of Congress, explanatory of resolve of Aug. 7, 1782; clothing, coats and shirts; German artificers. L. S. of Benjamin Lincoln. 3 pp. Answered Dec. 11.* 98, 270

1782
DEC. 2

Greene, Nathanael. Ashley Hills [South Carolina]. To [the Secretary at War, Philadelphia]. Exchange of prisoners; situation officers, etc. Contemporary copy. 1 p. Transmitted to Washington.
92, 298

1782
DEC. 3

Continental Congress, Resolve. Information given by Christopher Osgood [respecting matters in Vermont]. D. S. of Charles Thomson. 1 p. Enclosed in President of Congress to Washington, 1782, Dec. 11. 98, 273

1782
DEC. 3

Continental Congress, Resolves. Officers' rations and subsistence money; subsistence money for hospital officers. D. S. of Charles Thomson. 3 pp. Enclosed in Secretary at War to Washington, 1782, Dec. 4. Published in Genl. Orders, Dec. 17.
98, 274

1782
DEC. 3

Digby, Robert. New York. To Robert Morris [Philadelphia]. Exchange of marine prisoners; balance in favor of British. Contemporary copy. 3 pp. Enclosed in Morris to Washington, 1782, Dec. 27.
60, 399

1782
DEC. 3

Morris, Robert. [Philadelphia.] To [George] Washington [Newburgh]. Papers respecting marine prisoners. L. S. 2 pp. Answered Dec. 11.* 60, 247

1782
DEC. 4

Washington, George. Newburgh. To [the President of Congress, Philadelphia]. Seizure [of Luke Knolton and Samuel Wells]; British at Gibraltar. L. S. 3 pp. In handwriting of Benjamin Walker and Tench Tilghman. Read in Congress, Dec. 10. C. C. 152, 11, 37

1782
DEC. 4

Washington, George. [Newburgh.] To the Secretary at War [Philadelphia]. Promotion matter; Invalid corps and uniform. Draft. 1 p. In handwriting of Tench Tilghman.
A. VI, pt. II, 415

1782
DEC. 4

Secretary at War. [Philadelphia.] To [George] Washington [Newburgh]. Officers' rations. L. S. of Benjamin Lincoln. 3 pp. Answered Dec. 11.*
98, 276

1782
DEC. 4

Livingston, Robert R. Philadelphia. To [George] Washington [Newburgh]. Resignation of [Lewis R] Morris from army. A. L. S. 2 pp. Answered Dec. 10.*   **60, 251**

1782
DEC. 5

Continental Congress, Resolves. The New Hampshire Grants [Vermont]; interposition of Congress; restitution to Timothy Church and others; exercise of authority in the district etc. Contemporary copy. 2 pp. Enclosed in President of Congress to Washington, 1782, Dec. 11. **98, 280**

1782
DEC. 8

Anonymous. Intelligence of destination of various British regiments at Charleston. Contemporary copy. 1 p. In handwriting of Joseph Carleton. Enclosed in Secretary at War to Washington, 1783, Jan. 22.   **92, 302**

1782
DEC. 10

Washington, George. Newburgh. To R[obert] R. Livingston [Philadelphia]. Minor and personal matters. Draft. 1 p. In handwriting of Benjamin Walker.   **A. VI, pt. II, 417**

1782
DEC. 11

Washington, George. Newburgh. To the Secretary at War [Philadelphia]. Subsistence of officers; troops at Wyoming. Draft. 2 pp. In handwriting of David Humphreys.
A. VI, pt. II, 419

1782
DEC. 11

Washington, George. [Newburgh.] To [Robert] Morris [Philadelphia]. Wood for marine prisoners; exchanges; contractors; supplies at Wyoming. Draft. 3 pp. In handwriting of Tench Tilghman.   **A. VI, pt. II, 421**

1782
DEC. 11

Continental Congress, President. Philadelphia. To [George] Washington [Newburgh]. Intelligence from Charleston; letter and resolves for Thomas Chittenden; embarkation of British at New York. L. S. of Elias Boudinot. 2 pp. **98, 278**

1782
DEC. 11

Carleton, [Sir] Guy. New York. To [George] Washington [Newburgh]. Investigation of death of [Capt. Joshua] Huddy; release of Capt. [Charles] Asgill and Capt. [John] Schaak. Contemporary copy. 3 pp. In handwriting of David Humphreys. Enclosed in Washington to the President of Congress, 1782, Dec. 16.   **C. C. 152, 11, 47**

1782
DEC. 11

Tioguanda. Niagara. Speech before Brig. Gen. [Allan?] Maclean. Complaints of murder of their people and burning of their villages by the Americans;

Newburgh 30th March 1783

Dear Sir

      I have duly received your favors of the 17th and 24th ulto — I rejoice most exceedingly that there is an end to our warfare, and that such a field is opening to our view as will, with wisdom to direct the cultivation of it, make us a great, respectable and happy people; but it must be improved by other means than state politics and unreasonable jealousies — and prejudices; or it requires not the second sight to see that we shall be instruments in the hands of our enemies, & those European powers who may be jealous of our greatness in union, to dissolve the confederation — but to attain this, altho' the way seems extremely plain is not so easy —

      my wish to see the Union of these states established upon liberal & permanent principles — & inclination to contribute my mite in pointing out the defects of the present constitution are equally great — all my private letters have teemed with these sentiments, & whenever this topic has been the subject of conversation, I have endeavoured to diffuse & enforce them, but how far any further essay by me might be productive of the wished for end — or appear to arrogate more than belongs to me — depends so much upon popular opinions, & the temper and dispositions of people, that it is not easy to decide — I shall be obliged to you however for the thoughts which you have promised me on this subject, and

WRITING OF MARTHA WASHINGTON.

intention to dig up the hatchet. Contemporary copy. 2 pp. Enclosed in Washington to the President of Congress, 1783, Apr. 4.

C. C. 152, 11, 203

1782
DEC. 13

Continental Congress, Resolve. Reimbursement of officers for horses lost in service. D. S. of Charles Thomson. 1 p. Transmitted to Washington. 98, 284

[1782]
[DEC. 13]

Greene, Nathanael. [Before Charleston, South Carolina.] To [Brig.] Gen. [Anthony] Wayne [Before Charleston]. Approving arrangements. Contemporary copy. 1 p. In handwriting of Wayne. Enclosed in Wayne to Washington, 1783, Nov. 1.

C. C. 152, 11, 627

1782
DEC. 13

Wayne, Anthony. [Before Charleston, South Carolina.] To Maj. Gen. [Nathanael] Greene [Before Charleston]. Evacuation arrangements. A. L. S. 1 p. Marked by Wayne: "Copy." Enclosed in Wayne to Washington, 1783, Nov. 1. C. C. 152, 11, 623

1782
DEC. 13

Wemyss, J[ames]. [Charleston, South Carolina]. To Morris Simmons [Charleston]. Evacuation of Charleston; proposition to prevent plundering.

Wayne, Anthony. Before Charleston. To Simmons. British propositions. Contemporary copies. 3 pp. In handwriting of Wayne. Enclosed in Wayne to Washington, 1783, Nov. 1.

C. C. 152, 11, 619

1782
DEC. 14

Washington, George. Newburgh. To Joseph Jones [Philadelphia]. Address of Army to Congress; temper of officers; civil and military departments. Auto. draft signed. 3 pp. P. II, 661
Printed: Writings of Washington (Ford) N. Y. 1891. 10, 117.

1782
DEC. 16

Washington, George. Newburgh. To the President of Congress [Philadelphia]. Correspondence with Sir Guy Carleton. Draft. 1 p. In handwriting of David Humphreys. Read in Congress, Dec. 23. A. VI, pt. II, 425

1782
DEC. 16

Washington, George. [Newburgh.] To the Secretary at War [Philadelphia]. Transmitting letter of Sir Guy Carleton respecting prisoners. Draft. 1 p. In handwriting of Benjamin Walker.

A. VI, pt. II, 427

1782
DEC. 16

Washington, George. Newburgh. To Robert Morris [Philadelphia]. Sir Guy Carleton's statement as to condition of marine prisoners. Draft. 2 pp. In handwriting of David Humphreys.

A. VI, pt. II, 429

1782
DEC. 17

Morris, Robert. [Philadelphia.] To George Washington [Newburgh]. Transmitting copy of system for issuing provisions and hospital stores. L. S. 1 p.   60, 317

1782
DEC. 17

Morris, Robert. [Philadelphia.] To [George] Washington [Newburgh].. Transmitting counterpart of provision contract. L. S. 1 p.   60, 319

1782
DEC. 18

Secretary at War. [Philadelphia.] To [George] Washington [Newburgh]. Receipt of papers; post at Wyoming [Pennsylvania]. A. L. S. of William Jackson. 3 pp.   98, 285

1782
DEC. 18

[Morris, Robert.] [Philadelphia.] To [Rear] Adml. [Robert] Digby [New York]. Exchange of marine prisoners; proposition advanced; fire-wood. Contemporary copy. 2 pp. Enclosed in Morris to Washington, 1782, Dec. 27.   60, 401

1782
DEC. 19

Greene, Nathanael. [Charleston.] To the President of Congress [Philadelphia]. The evacuation of Charleston. Contemporary copy. 2 pp. Enclosed in President of Congress to Washington, 1783, Jan. 16.   92, 318

1782
DEC. 19

Morris, Robert. [Philadelphia.] To [George] Washington [Newburgh]. Ration contract; clause dealing with poor quality of supplies; power of inspectors; vinegar; officers' subsistence; economy. L. S. 3 pp. Answered, 1783, Jan. 6.*   60, 336

1782
DEC. 20

Washington, George. [Newburgh.] To R[obert] Morris [Philadelphia]. Payment for engraving cannon presented to Comte de Rochambeau. Draft. 1 p. In handwriting of Benjamin Walker.

A. VI, pt. II, 431

1782
DEC. 22

Secretary at War. Philadelphia. To [George] Washington [Newburgh]. Treatment of Brunswick prisoners at Reading [Pennsylvania]; enlistment in American army. L. S. of Benjamin Lincoln. 2 pp. In handwriting of Benjamin Stoddert. Endorsed: "Copy transmitted to Sir Guy Carleton."

98, 286

1782
DEC. 23

Secretary at War. [Philadelphia.] To [George] Washington [Newburgh]. Receipt of papers; supplies for British prisoners; treatment of Germans; complaints etc. A. L. S. of William Jackson. 4 pp.
98, 289

1782
DEC. 23

Secretary at War. [Newburgh.] To [George] Washington [Newburgh]. Recruiting of infantry in Virginia; artillery and cavalry service. L. S. of Benjamin Lincoln. 2 pp.
98, 291

1782
DEC. 24

[Washington, George.] Newburgh. To the Secretary at War [Philadelphia]. Recruiting New Hampshire and New Jersey regiments; reduction of corps. Auto. draft, partly in handwriting of David Humphreys. 2 pp.
A. VI, pt. II, 433

1782
DEC. 24

Continental Congress, Resolves. Ownership of property, recaptured on land; case submitted by Maj. Gen. [Nathanael] Greene; franking privilege. Contemporary copy, attested by William Jackson. 4 pp. Enclosed in Secretary at War to Washington, 1782, Dec. 28.
98, 315

1782
DEC. 24

Continental Congress, Resolve. Expresses. Contemporary copy, attested by William Jackson. 1 p. Transmitted to Washington.
98, 294

1782
DEC. 25

Washington, George. Newburgh. To R[obert] Morris [Philadelphia]. Scarcity of forage. Draft. 2 pp. In handwriting of David Humphreys.
A. VI, pt. II, 435

1782
DEC. 25

Continental Congress, President. Philadelphia. To [George] Washington [Newburgh]. Britain's acknowledgement of independence of United States in form of [Richard] Oswald's commission; intelligence from Holland; aid to Rev. [James] Caldwell's children. L. S. of Elias Boudinot. 3 pp. Answered, 1783, Jan. 8.*
98, 295

1782
DEC. 26

M[orris], R[obert]. [Philadelphia.] To [George] Washington [Newburgh]. Transmitting bill of exchange; subsistence notes for use of Washington's family. Letter-book copy. **Morris.** E, 14

1782
DEC. 27

Morris, Robert. [Philadelphia.] To [George] Washington [Poughkeepsie]. [Rear] Adml. [Robert] Digby's letter and answer; approval of Congress. L. S. 1 p.
60, 397

1782
DEC. 28

Secretary at War. [Philadelphia.] To [George] Washington [Newburgh]. Franking privilege to certain staff officers; provision return [forms]. A. L. S. of William Jackson. 2 pp. 98, 311

1782
DEC. 28

Chittenden, Thomas. Bennington. Vermont. Certificate of receipt of Act of Congress of Dec. 5, 1782. D. S. 1 p. Enclosed in Washington to the President of Congress, 1783, Jan. 7.
C. C. 152, 11, 57

1782
DEC. 31

Continental Congress, Resolves. Suspension of part of resolution of Aug. 7 [1782] relating to New Hampshire, Rhode Island, New Jersey and Pennsylvania troops; Brig. Gen. [Edward] Hand's continuance as Adjutant General. D. S. of Charles Thomson. 1 p. Transmitted to Washington. 98, 313

1782
DEC. 31

Digby, Robert. H. M. S. *Chatham*, off New York. Passport for sloop *Three Brothers*. Contemporary copy. 1 p. .Enclosed in Washington to the President of Congress, 1783, Feb. 26.
C. C. 152, 11, 91

1782
DEC. 31

Digby, Robert. [H. M. S. *Chatham*, off New York.] Passport to Jacob Cornwell, master of sloop *Three Brothers*. Contemporary copy. 1 p. Enclosed in Washington to the President of Congress 1783, Feb. 26. C. C. 152, 11, 95

1782
DEC. 31

Morris, Robert. [Philadelphia.] To [George] Washington [Newburgh]. Payment for engraving cannon [presented to Comte de Rochambeau]. L. S. 1 p.
60, 416

1783
JAN. 3

Washington, George. [Newburgh.] To the Asst. Secretary at War [Philadelphia]. Post office; complaints of officers at derangement. Draft. 1 p. In handwriting of David Humphreys. A. VII, 1

1783
JAN. 4

W[alker,] B[enjamin.] [Newburgh.] To the Asst. Secretary at War [Philadelphia]. Complaint of Capt. Segord. Auto. draft signed. 1 p. A. VII, 3
Dated in error 1782.

1783
JAN. 6

Washington, George. [Newburgh.] To R[obert] Morris [Philadelphia]. Marine prisoners; necessity of a commissary. Draft. 3 pp. In handwritting of David Humphreys. A. VII, 5

1783 JAN. 6	**Secretary at War.** [Philadelphia.] To [George] Washington [Newburgh]. Settlement of land dispute between Pennsylvania and Connecticut; clothing; Armand's corps at York [Pennsylvania]. A. L. S. of William Jackson, Asst. Secy. 3 pp. Answered Jan. 12.*　　　　　92, 119
1783 JAN. 6	**Moylan,** John. Philadelphia. To [Secretary at War, Philadelphia]. Clothing for Northern Army. Contemporary copy. 1 p. Enclosed in Secretary at War to Washington, 1783, Jan. 6. 92, 118
1783 JAN. 7	**Washington,** George. Newburgh. To Elias Boudinot [Philadelphia]. Subscription toward support of Rev. [James] Caldwell's children. Auto. draft signed. 1 p.　　　　　　P. III, 1
1783 JAN. 7	**Macomber,** Ebenezer. Saratoga [New York]. To Maj. Gen. [William Alexander,] Lord Stirling [Albany]. Report of attempted seizure of Luke Knowlton and Solomon Wells. Contemporary copy. 4 pp. In handwriting of Benjamin Walker. Enclosed in Washington to the President of Congress, 1783, Jan. 30. C. C.　152, 11, 63
1783 JAN. 7	**Continental Congress,** Resolve. Promotion of Cols. John Greaton, Rufus Putnam, and Elias Dayton. D. S. of George Bond. 1 p. Enclosed in Secretary at War to Washington, 1783, Jan. 8. 92, 121
1783 JAN. 8	**Washington,** George. Newburgh. To the President of Congress [Philadelphia]. [Thomas] Chittenden's certificate; negotiations in Europe. L. S. 2 pp. In handwriting of Benjamin Walker. Read in Congress, Jan. 15.　　C. C.　152, 11, 53 <small>Draft, A. VII, 9, is dated Jan. 7.</small>
1783 JAN. 8	**Washington,** George. [Newburgh.] To the Secretary at War, [Philadelphia]. Servants for officers. Draft. 1 p. In handwriting of Benjamin Walker.　　　　　A. VII, 13 <small>Dated in error, 1782.</small>
1783 JAN. 8	**Washington,** George. Newburgh. To Robert Morris [Philadelphia]. Purchase of land in Virginia; money for secret service; ration for women; contractors. Auto. draft signed. 3 pp. P. III, 3 <small>Printed: Writings of Washington (Ford). 1891. 10, 126.</small>

1783
JAN. 8

W[ashingto]n, G[eorge]. Newburgh. To Robert R. Livingston [Philadelphia]. Continuance of war; change of ministry in Great Britain; concessions; treaty with Holland; impost in Virginia; Thomas Jefferson. Auto. draft signed. 2 pp.   **P. III, 7**

1783
JAN. 8

Secretary at War. [Philadelphia.] To [George] Washington [Newburgh]. Transmitting resolves. A. L. S. of William Jackson, Asst. Secy. 1 p. Answered Jan. 29*   **92, 122**

1783
JAN. 12

Washington, George. Newburgh. To the Asst. Secretary at War [Philadelphia]. Shirts for army. Draft. 1 p. In handwriting of David Humphreys.   **A. VII, 15**

1783
JAN. 15

Secretary at War. [Philadelphia.] To [George] Washington [Newburgh]. Subsistence money for cavalry officers; retirement of Brig. Gen. O[tho] H[olland] Williams. A. L. S. of William Jackson, Asst. Secy. 3 pp. Answered Jan. 29.*
     92, 126

1783
JAN. 16

Continental Congress, President. Philadelphia. To [George] Washington [Newburgh]. Donation for Rev. [James] Caldwell's children; evacuation of Charleston. L. S. of Elias Boudinot. 2 pp. Answered Jan. 20.*   **92, 319**

1783
JAN. 16

Continental Congress, President. Philadelphia. To [George] Washington [Newburgh]. [Thomas] Chittenden's receipt for papers; evacuation of Charleston. Letter-book copy.   **C. C. 16, 172**

1783
JAN. 16

Continental Congress, Resolve. Retirement of Brig. Gen. O[tho] H[olland] Williams. Contemporary copy, attested by William Jackson. 1 p. Transmitted to Washington.   **92, 128**

1783
JAN. 20

Washington, George. Newburgh. To the President of Congress [Philadelphia]. Death of Lord Stirling; attempt to secure Luke Knowlton and Solomon Wells. Draft. 3 pp. In handwriting of David Humphreys. Read in Congress, Jan. 27.

     A. VII, 19

1783
JAN. 20

Morris, Robert. [Philadelphia.] To [George] Washington [Newburgh]. Letter to the Paymaster General [John Pierce] and method of payment for supplies. L. S. 1 p. Answered Jan. 29*   **61, 94**

1783
JAN. 20

[**Morris,** Robert.] [Philadelphia.] To [John Pierce, Philadelphia]. Pay of Southern army; subsistence accounts of officers; month's advance pay and payment to privates; instructions. Contemporary copy. 4 pp. Enclosed in Morris to Washington, 1783, Jan. 20.   61, 96

1783
JAN. 21

Morris, Robert. [Philadelphia.] To [George] Washington [Newburgh]. Commissary of marine prisoners; money for secret service; additional ration for women and children. L. S. 3 pp.   61, 104

1783
JAN. 22

Washington, George. [Newburgh.] To R[obert] Morris [Philadelphia]. [Lt.] Col. [Richard] Varick's work. Draft. 2 pp. In handwriting of Benjamin Walker.   **A.** VII, 17

1783
JAN. 22

Secretary at War. [Philadelphia.] To [George] Washington [Newburgh]. Shirts; clothing for Southern Army; exchange of prisoners and retention of troops in South; minor military matters. A. L. S. of William Jackson, Asst. Secy. 7 pp. Answered Jan. 29.*   92, 303

1783
JAN. 24

Morris, Robert. [Philadelphia.] To [the President of Congress, Philadelphia]. Resignation and reasons for same. Contemporary copy. 3 pp. Enclosed in Morris to Washington, 1783, Feb. 27.   61, 351

1783
JAN. 25

Continental Congress, Grand Committee. Report on Memorial of Army respecting arrearages of pay; commutation of half pay; settlement of deficiency in ration accounts. Contemporary copy, attested by Edward Hand. 3 pp. Addressed to: "Col. Humphreys A. D. C. to the Commr. in Chief" Endorsed: "referred to the Financier to take order." "published in Genl. Orders" [Mar. 13.]   92, 135

1783
JAN. 27

Secretary at War. [Philadelphia.] To [George] Washington. [Newburgh.] Blankets from a wreck on the Delaware coast; shirts. A. L. S. of William Jackson, Asst. Secy. 2 pp. Answered Feb. 5*   92, 129

1783
JAN. 28

Continental Congress, Resolve. On death of Maj. Gen. [William Alexander,] Lord Stirling. D. S. of Charles Thomson. 1 p. Enclosed in President of Congress to Washington, 1783, Jan. 29.   92, 131

1783   **Morris, Robert.** [Philadelphia.]   To [George] Washing-
JAN. 28   ton [Newburgh].   Notes for payment to [Lt.] Col.
            [Richard] Varick.   L. S.   1 p.   Answered
            Feb. 4*   **61, 6**

1783   **Washington, George.**   [Newburgh.]   To [the Asst. Secre-
JAN. 29   tary at War, Philadelphia].   Letters to be for-
            warded.   Draft.   1 p.   In handwriting of Ben-
            jamin Walker.   **A.   VII, 23**

1783   **W[ashington], G[eorge].**   Newburgh.   To [Robert Mor-
JAN. 29   ris, Philadelphia].   New ration regulation re-
            specting women; embezzlement through Asst.
            Commissary of Marine Prisoners at Dobbs
            Ferry.   Auto. draft signed.   3 pp.   **P.   III, 35**

1783   **Washington, George.**   Newburgh.   To R[obert] Morris
JAN. 29   [Philadelphia].   Circulation of proposed notes
            among the contractors.   Draft.   1 p.   In hand-
            writing of David Humphreys.   **A.   VII, 25**

1783   **Continental Congress, President.**   Philadelphia.   To
JAN. 29   [George] Washington [Newburgh].   Death and
            character of Lord Stirling; Vermont matters [and
            Jonathan Arnold].   L. S. of Elias Boudinot.   3
            pp.   **92, 133**

1783   **Washington, George.**   Newburgh.   To the President of
JAN. 30   Congress [Philadelphia].   Preparations for next
            campaign; prospect of peace; finances etc.   A.
            L. S.   5 pp.   Read in Congress, Feb. 11.   Re-
            ferred to Hamilton, Peters, Bland, Rutledge and
            Mifflin.   "The returns as well as the contents of
            the letter to be kept secret."   **C. C.   152, 11, 67**
            Printed: Writings of Washington (Ford) N. Y. 1891. 10, 146.

1783   **[Morris, Robert.]**   A state of the receipts and expendi-
JAN. 31   tures of public money upon warrants from the
            Superintendent of Finance from Jan. 1, 1782 to
            Jan. 1, 1783.   Tabular statement from records
            of the Register's Office.   Broadside.   1 p.   En-
            closed in Morris to Washington, 1783, Apr. 7.
                                                     62, 244

1783   **Washington, George.**   Newburgh.   To the President of
FEB. 3   Congress [Philadelphia].   Preparations for future
            operations.   Draft.   8 pp.   In handwriting of
            David Humphreys.   **A.   VII, 27**
            Dated: Jany. 30; redated and endorsed by Varick. Feb. 3.
            Printed: Writings of Washington (Ford) N. Y. 1891. 10, 146.

1783
FEB. 4

Washington, George. [Newburgh.] To [Robert] Morris [Philadelphia]. Money for [Lt.] Col. [Richard] Varick; distress of marine prisoners for subsistence. Draft. 1 p. In handwriting of Benjamin Walker. **A. VII, 35**

1783
FEB. 4

Washington, George. Newburgh. To Jonathan Arnold [Philadelphia]. Capt. [Ebenezer] McComber's report [Arnold's complicity in Vermont affairs]. Draft. 2 pp. In handwriting of David Humphreys. **A. VII, 37**

A copy by Benjamin Walker of McComber's report to Lord Stirling, 1783, Jan. 7, is in C. C. 152, 11, 63.

1783
FEB. 5

Washington, George. [Newburgh.] To [the Secretary at War, Philadelphia]. Appointment of a brigadier for the state of Connecticut; troops in the south. Draft. 2 pp. In handwriting of Benjamin Walker. **A. VII, 39**

1783
FEB. 5

Secretary at War. [Philadelphia.] To [George] Washington [Newburgh]. Forwarding of letters. A. L. S. of William Jackson, Asst. Secy. 1 p. **92, 137**

1783
FEB. 5

Morris, Robert. [Philadelphia.] To [George] Washington [Newburgh]. Extra rations for women; disclaimer of interference. L. S. 2 pp. **61, 200**

1783
FEB. 8

Duane, James. Kingston [New York]. To [George Washington, Newburgh]. Introducing Arent Schuyler; New York's compliance with requisitions of Congress. A. L. S. 1 p. **61, 232**

1783
FEB. 11

W[ashingto]n, G[eorge]. Newburgh. To the President of Congress [Philadelphia]. Printed remonstrance of Vermont against resolution of Congress of Dec. 5, 1782. Auto. draft signed. 1 p. Referred to Carroll, Gorham, A. Lee, Gilman and Wolcott, Feb. 17. Committee renewed as Carroll, Gorham, Lee, White and Mercer, which reported May 26 on the general affairs of Vermont. **A. VII, 41**

1783
FEB. 11

Washington, George. Newburgh. To Joseph Jones [Philadelphia]. Vermont affairs; dependence to be placed on the army. Auto. draft signed. 3 pp. **P. III, 43**

Printed: Writings of Washington (Ford) N. Y. 1891. 10, 153.

1783
FEB. 11

Arnold, Jonathan. Philadelphia. To [George] Washington [Newburgh]. Attack upon his character; Capt. [Ebenezer] McComber; letters sent to Vermont. A. L. S. 2 pp. Answered Mar. 5. *

61, 250

1783   **Arnold**, Jonathan. Philadelphia. Questions to be put to
FEB. 11   Capt. Ebenezer McComber relative to his report
                 implicating Arnold in Vermont affairs. A. D. S.
                 1 p. Enclosed in Arnold to Washington, 1783,
                 Feb. 11.   **61, 252**

1783   **Secretary at War.** [Philadelphia.] To [George] Wash-
FEB. 12   ington [Newburgh]. Arrangement of officers of
                 2d. Pennsylvania regiment; Lt. Col. [William]
                 Hamilton's case. A. L. S. of William Jackson,
                 Asst. Secy. 2 pp.   **92, 300**

1783   **Washington,** George. [Newburgh.] Queries submitted to
FEB. 17   the Secretary of War with the answers thereto.
                 Reduction of regiments; supplies and minor
                 matters. Draft. 3 pp. In handwriting of
                 Benjamin Walker. Signed by Lincoln.
                                                        A. VII, 43

1783   [**Haldimand,** Frederick.] [Quebec.] To [Sir Guy Carle-
FEB. 17   ton, New York]. Outrages by Americans against
                 the Six Nations; retaliatory measures. [Extract
                 of letter.] 3 pp. In handwriting of Benjamin
                 Walker. Enclosed in Washington to the Presi-
                 dent of Congress, 1783, Apr. 4.   **C. C. 152, 11, 207**

1783   **Morris,** Robert. [Philadelphia.] To [George] Washing-
FEB. 17   ton [Newburgh]. Provisions for prisoners.
                 L. S. 2 pp.   **61, 275**

1783   **Secretary at War.** [Philadelphia.] To [George] Wash-
FEB. 19   ington [Newburgh]. Transmitting contracts.
                 A. L. S. of William Jackson, Asst. Secy. 1 p.
                                                             92, 139

1783   **Willett,** Marinus. Fort Herkimer [New York]. To
FEB. 19   [George] Washington [Newburgh]. Report of
                 Oswego expedition; causes of failure etc. Con-
                 temporary copy. 8 pp. In handwriting of
                 Benjamin Walker. Enclosed in Washington to
                 the President of Congress, 1783, Feb. 26.
                                                     C. C. 152, 11, 79

1783   **Continental Congress,** Resolve. Washington's letter of
FEB. 20   Jan. 30; plan of campaign suggested; progress
                 of peace negotiations. D. S. of Charles Thomson.
                 1 p. Enclosed in Livingston to Washington,
                 1783, Feb. 26.   **61, 292**
                 A second D. S. of above resolve, 61, 294, was enclosed in President of
                 Congress to Washington, 1783, Feb. 26.

1783
FEB. 21

Continental Congress, Resolve. Additional pay for Line officers serving on the Staff. D. S. of George Bond. 1 p. Published in Genl. Orders, Mar. 17.
                                              92, 141

1783
FEB. 21

Tallmadge, Benjamin. Greenfield [Connecticut]. To [George] Washington [Newburgh]. Account of taking of British armed vessel in the Sound. Contemporary copy. 2 pp. Enclosed in Washington to the President of Congress, 1783, Feb. 26.   **C. C. 152, 11, 87**

1783
FEB. 24

Washington, George. [Newburgh.] To the Secretary at War [Philadelphia]. Need of overalls and shirts. Draft. 2 pp. In handwriting of Benjamin Walker.   **A. VII, 47**

1783
FEB. 25

Washington, George. [Newburgh.] To [Robert Morris, Philadelphia]. Inspector for beef. Draft. 2 pp. In handwriting of David Humphreys and Washington.   **A. VII, 49**

1783
FEB. 26

Washington, George. Newburgh. To the President of Congress [Philadelphia]. Failure of the Oswego expedition; Maj. [Benjamin] Tallmadge's success; suppression of illicit trade with enemy. Draft. 4 pp. In handwriting of David Humphreys. Read in Congress, Mar. 3.   **A. VII, 51**
       Printed: Writings of Washington (Ford) N. Y. 10, 159.

1783
FEB. 26

Washington, George. [Newburgh.] To the Secretary at War [Philadelphia]. Maj. Villefranche's claim to promotion. Draft. 1 p. In handwriting of David Humphreys.   **A. VII, 55**

1783
FEB. 26

Continental Congress, President. Philadelphia. To [George] Washington [Newburgh]. Resolve of Congress on his proposals for ensuing campaign; news of peace negotiations. L. S. of Elias Boudinot. 2 pp.   **61, 332**

1783
FEB. 26

Secretary at War. [Philadelphia.] To [George] Washington [Newburgh]. Transmitting resolve; blankets. A. L. S. of William Jackson, Asst. Secy. 1 p. Answered Mar. 11.*   **92, 142**

1783
FEB. 26

Livingston, Robert R. Philadelphia. To [George] Washington [Newburgh]. Condition of peace negotiations; attitude of Great Britain. A. L. S. 4 pp.   **61, 344**

1783
FEB. 26

[Morris, Robert.] [Philadelphia.] To the President of Congress [Philadelphia]. Injunction of secrecy in order of Jan. 24; appointment of a successor. Contemporary copy. 1 p. Enclosed in Morris to Washington, 1783, Feb. 27.   61, 351

1783
FEB. 27

Morris, Robert. [Philadelphia.] To [George] Washington [Newburgh]. Transmitting letters; relief of the army; justice of its claims, etc. L. S. 3 pp. Answered Mar. 8.*   61, 349

1783
FEB. 27

Jones, Joseph. Philadelphia. To [George Washington, Newburgh]. Impost duty decided upon by Congress; measures considering for raising of revenue; claims of the army and other public creditors; feeling in the army; rumors of trouble; case of Vermont; her attitude and manœuvers; prospects of peace. A. L. S. 7 pp.   61, 355

1783
MAR. 1

Secretary at War. [Philadelphia.] To [George] Washington [Newburgh]. Arrangement of the Virginia Line; clothes and standards. L. S. of Benjamin Lincoln. Answered Mar. 11.*   92, 144

1783
MAR. 3

Secretary at War. [Philadelphia.] To [George] Washington [Newburgh]. Clothing supply. L. S. of Benjamin Lincoln. 1 p. Answered Mar. 11.*   92, 145

1783
MAR. 3

Morris, Robert. [Philadelphia.] To [George] Washington [Newburgh]. Contract system and Inspectorship; settlement of conflict of contracts. L. S. 7 pp. Answered Mar. 12.*   62, 14

1783
MAR. 4

W[ashingto]n, G[eorge]. Newburgh. To Alexander Hamilton [Philadelphia]. With-holding of information by Congress; non-payment of taxes; danger from the army, its claims etc.; adjournment of Congress. Auto. draft signed. 4 pp.

         P. III, 73

Printed: Writings of Washington (Ford) N. Y. 1891. 10, 163.

1783
MAR. 4

Lincoln, B[enjamin]. Philadelphia. To [George] Washington [Newburgh]. Promotion of Maj. Villefranche; station for Armand's Corps. A. L. S. 3 pp. Answered Mar. 11.*   92, 146

1783
MAR. 5

Washington, George. [Newburgh.] To Jonathan Arnold [Philadelphia]. Capt. [Ebenezer] McComber's replies. Draft. 1 p. In handwriting of Benjamin Walker.   A. VII, 57

1783
MAR. 7

Washington, George. [Newburgh.] To the President of Congress [Philadelphia]. Recommending Col. Armand to Congress. Draft. 1 p. In handwriting of Jonathan Trumbull, jr. Read in Congress, Mar. 11. Referred to Bland, Hamilton and Peters. Reported Mar. 18. A. VII, 61.
Printed: Writings of Washington (Sparks) Boston. 1835. 8, 391.

1783
MAR. 7

Washington, George. Newburgh. To the President of Congress [Philadelphia]. Claim to promotion of Maj. Villefranche and Capt. L'Enfant. Draft. 1 p. In handwriting of Jonathan Trumbull, jr.
A. VII, 59

1783
MAR. 8

Washington, George. [Newburgh.] To Robert Morris [Philadelphia]. His retirement as Superintendent of Finance. Draft. 2 pp. In handwriting of Jonathan Trumbull, jr. A. VII, 63

1783
MAR. 8

Secretary at War. [Philadelphia.] To [George] Washington [Newburgh]. Delaware troops; instruction of officers from the different states. L. S. 2 pp. Answered Mar. 19.* 92, 148

1783
MAR. 10

Washington, George. Newburgh. To Robert R. Livingston [Philadelphia]. Receipt of intelligence; peace negotiations. Auto. draft signed. 1 p.
P. III, 79

[1783]
[MAR. 10]

Anonymous. [Newburgh.] Notification calling for a meeting of General and Field Officers of the Army. Contemporary copy. 1 p. In handwriting of Jonathan Trumbull, jr. Enclosed in Washington to the President of Congress, 1783, Mar. 12.
C. C. 152, 11, 109
Printed: Writings of Washington (Sparks) Boston. 1835. 8, 555.

[1783]
[MAR. 10]

Anonymous. [Newburgh.] Address to the Officers of the Army. Their grievances and redress of same. Contemporary copy. 5 pp. In handwriting of Benjamin Walker. Enclosed in Washington to the President of Congress, 1783, Mar. 12.
C. C. 152, 11, 111
Printed: Writings of Washington (Sparks) Boston. 1835. 8, 555.

1783
MAR. 10

W[alker,] B[enjamin]. [Newburgh.] To the Secretary at War [Philadelphia]. Rations for Canadians. Auto. draft signed. 3 pp. A. VII, 69

1783
MAR. 11

Washington, George. [Newburgh.] To the Secretary at War [Philadelphia]. Clothing; expense of Armand's horse. Draft. 2 pp. In handwriting of Jonathan Trumbull, jr. A. VII, 65

1783
MAR. 11

Washington, George. Newburgh. General Orders. Disapprobation of projected meeting; appointing Mar. 15 for meeting of officers. Extract from Genl. Orders. D. S. Edward Hand's. 1 p. Enclosed in Washington to the President of Congress, 1783, Mar. 12.   C. C. **152, 11, 117**

Printed: Writings of Washington (Sparks) Boston. 1835. 8, 558.

1783
MAR. 12

Washington, George. Newburgh. To the President of Congress [Philadelphia]. Anonymous addresses to the army. Draft. 2 pp. In handwriting of David Humphreys. Read in Congress, Mar. 17. Referred to Gilman, Dyer, Clark, Rutledge, and Mercer [who were discharged Mar. 22 and letter together with one of Mar. 18 referred to Osgood, Bland, Hamilton, Wolcott and Peters. Reported Apr. 1].   **A. VII, 67**

Printed: Writings of Washington (Ford) N. Y. 1891. 10. 168.

1783
MAR. 12

W[ashingto]n, G[eorge]. Newburgh. To Alexander Hamilton [Philadelphia]. Feeling in the army; the anonymous [Newburgh] addresses; the situation. Auto. draft signed. 4 pp.   **P. III, 85**

This letter is the same in substance as the one to Joseph Jones, of this date, many sentences being identical.

1783
MAR. 12

W[ashingto]n, G[eorge]. Newburgh. to Joseph Jones [Philadelphia]. Spirit abroad in the army; rumors etc.; action of officers [Newburgh addresses]; settlement of accounts. Auto. draft signed. 3 pp.   **P. III, 81**

Printed: Writings of Washington (Ford) N. Y. 1891. 10. 174.

1783
MAR. 12

Washington, George. [Newburgh.] To R[obert] Morris [Philadelphia]. Introducing Daniel Parker; proposal for paying army in merchandize. Draft. 3 pp. In handwriting of David Humphreys.

A. VII, 73

1783
MAR. 12

Continental Congress, President. Philadelphia. To [George] Washington [Newburgh]. Substance of the Definitive Treaty of Peace. L. S. of Elias Boudinot. 3 pp. Answered Mar. 19.*

92, 149

[1783]
[MAR. 12]

Anonymous. [Newburgh.] Address to the Officers of the Army. Intention of former address; General Order from the Commander-in-chief; coming meeting. Contemporary copy. 5 pp. In handwriting of Jonathan Trumbull, jr. Enclosed in Washington to the President of Congress, 1783, Mar. 12.   C. C. **152, 11, 119**

Printed. Writings of Washington (Sparks) Boston. 1835. 8, 558.

1783
MAR. 12
Livingston, Robert R. Philadelphia. To [George] Washington [Newburgh]. Brief of articles of the Preliminary treaty of Peace; French negotiations; withdrawal of British troops from America. L. S. 3 pp. **62, 66**

1783
MAR. 13
Lee, A[rthur]. Philadelphia. To [George] Washington [Newburgh]. Prospects of peace; negotiations; refugee outrages; secrecy. A. L. S. 3 pp.

62, 76

1783
MAR. 15
Washington, George. Address to Officers. See following entry.

1783
MAR. 15
Continental Army, Officers. [Newburgh.] Proceedings of meeting. Address of the Commander-in-Chief on the anonymous papers; resolves adopted. Contemporary copy. 16 pp. In handwriting of Benjamin Walker. Enclosed in Washington to the President of Congress, 1783, Mar. 18.

C. C. 152, 11, 137

Printed: Writings of Washington (Sparks) Boston. 1835. 8, 560.
Washington's address printed (Ford) N. Y. 1891. 10, 170.

1783
MAR. 15
[**Laurens,** Henry.] London. To the President of Congress [Philadelphia]. Change of Ministry in England; trade bills in Parliament; attitude of the First Lord of the Treasury [William, Earl of Shelburne] towards America. Contemporary extracts. Enclosed in Boudinot to Washington, 1783, June 9. **63, 203**

1783
MAR. 16
Washington, George. [Newburgh.] To the President of Congress [Philadelphia]. Result of meeting of officers. Draft. 1 p. In handwriting of Jonathan Trumbull, jr. Read in Congress, Mar. 20.

A. VII, 77

Printed: Writings of Washington (Sparks) Boston. 1835. 8, 396.

1783
MAR. 18
Washington, George. Newburgh. To the President of Congress [Philadelphia]. Meeting of officers; grievances of the army. Draft. 8 pp. In handwriting of David Humphreys. Read in Congress, Mar. 22. Referred to Osgood, Bland, Hamilton, Wolcott and Peters. Reported Apr. 1 on above and also on a letter of Mar. 12.

A. VII, 79

Printed: Writings of Washington (Ford) N. Y. 1891. 10, 178.

1783
MAR. 18
W[ashingto]n, G[eorge]. Newburgh. To Joseph Jones [Philadelphia]. Forbearance of army; liquidation of accounts; dangers etc. Auto. draft signed. 3 pp. **P. III, 89**

Printed: Writings of Washington (Ford) N. Y. 1891. 10, 182.

1783
MAR. 18

Continental Congress, Order. Settlement of Army accounts. D. S. of Charles Thomson. 1 p. Enclosed in Secretary at War to Washington, 1783, Mar. 19. Published in Genl. Orders Mar. 25.

          92, 151

1783
MAR. 19

Washington, George. Newburgh. To the President of Congress [Philadelphia]. Prospects of peace. Draft. 1 p. In handwriting of Jonathan Trumbull, jr. Read in Congress, Mar. 24. A. VII, 87
Printed: Writings of Washington (Ford) N. Y. 1895. 10, 184.

1783
MAR. 19

Washington, George. [Newburgh.] To the Secretary at War [Philadelphia]. Arrangement of officers of the Delaware battalion; discipline. Draft. 1 p. In handwriting of Jonathan Trumbull, jr.

          A. VII, 89

1783
MAR. 19

Washington, George. Newburgh. To Robert R. Livingston [Philadelphia]. Peace negotiations; illicit trade with enemy; recent disorder in army. Auto. draft signed. 2 pp.   P. III, 97
Printed: Writings of Washington (Ford) N. Y. 1891. 10, 187.

1783
MAR. 19

W[ashingto]n, G[eorge]. Newburgh. To Robert Morris [Philadelphia]. Household expenses. Auto. draft signed. 1 p.   P. III, 101

1783
MAR. 19

Secretary at War. [Philadelphia.] To [George] Washington [Newburgh]. Transmitting resolve. L. S. of Benjamin Lincoln. 1 p. Answered Apr. 1.*

          92, 152

1783
MAR. 19

Carleton, [Sir] Guy and Robert Digby. New York. To [George] Washington [Newburgh]. Transmitting copy of Treaty of Paris. Contemporary copy. 2 pp. In handwriting of Jonathan Trumbull, jr. Enclosed in Washington to the President of Congress 1783, Mar. 21.

      C. C. 152, 11, 183

1783
MAR. 20

Washington, George. [Newburgh.] To [Robert R. Livingston, Philadelphia]. Exchanges of British officers in Europe. Draft. 1 p. In handwriting of Jonathan Trumbull, jr.

          A. VII, 91

1783
MAR. 21

Washington, George. [Newburgh.] To the President of Congress [Philadelphia]. Transmitting letter of Sir Guy Carleton and Admiral Digby with copy of Treaty of Paris. Draft. 1 p. In handwriting of Jonathan Trumbull, jr. Read in Congress, Mar. 24.   A. VII, 93

1783 MAR. 22	Continental Congress, Resolve. Commutation of half-pay to officers. D. S. of Charles Thomson. 2 pp. Transmitted to Washington. 92, 153
1783 MAR. 22	Bland, Theodorick. Philadelphia. To [George Washington, Newburgh]. Recovery of runaway slaves from British. A. L. S. 1 p. Answered Mar. 31, " & his Letter to Sir Guy Carleton sent into N. York." 62, 138
1783 MAR. 22	Bland, Theodorick. Philadelphia. To [George Washington, Newburgh]. Correspondence; peace negotiations; effect of the preliminary articles; Great Britain's concessions; France; public credit; the army. A. L. S. 4 pp. 62, 139
1783 MAR. 23	Washington, George. Newburgh. To the President of Congress [Philadelphia]. Marquis de Lafayette's request for leave of absence. A. L. S. 1 p. Read in Congress, Apr. 7. Referred to Peters, Dyer and T. Lee. Reported Apr. 8. C. C. 152, 11, 189
1783 MAR. 23	W[ashingto]n, G[eorge]. Newburgh. To the President of Congress [Philadelphia]. Absence of the Marquis de Lafayette. Auto. draft signed. 1 p. P. III, 103
1783 MAR. 24	Livingston, R[obert] R. Philadelphia. To [George Washington, Newburgh]. Arrival of news of peace; Holland and France. A. L. S. 3 pp. 62, 155
1783 MAR. 24	Mathews, John. Philadelphia. To [George] Washington [Newburgh]. Situation of British at Charleston. A. L. S. 2 pp. 92, 155
1783 MAR. 25	Continental Congress, Committee. To [George Washington, Newburgh]. Resolves of officers of the army on the Newburgh addresses; pay and disbanding of army. A. L. S. of Theodorick Bland. 3 pp. 62, 164½

Committee: Osgood, Bland. Hamilton, Walcott and Peters.

[1783] [MAR. 25]	[Continental Congress, Committee.] Tentative resolves for adoption by Congress respecting settlement of pay of the army. A. D. of Theodorick Bland. 1 p. Enclosed in Committee to Washington, 1783, Mar. 25. 62, 166
1783 MAR. 25	Morris, Robert. [Philadelphia.] To [George] Washington [Newburgh]. Additional month's pay to army; Washington's household expense; Morris's resignation. L. S. 2 pp. 62, 158

1783
MAR. 27

South Carolina, Delegates to Continental Congress. Phila-
delphia. To [George] Washington, [Newburgh].
Letter for Sir Guy Carleton. A. L. S. of J[ohn]
Rutledge, signed also by David Ramsay, Ra[lph]
Izard and John Lewis Gervais. 1 p. Answered
Apr. 9.*   **92, 157**

1783
MAR. 29

Washington, George. Newburgh. To Arthur Lee [Phila-
delphia]. Peace; unity of States; Picaroons in
the Chesapeake. Auto. draft. 1 p.
                                   P. III, 121

1783
MAR. 29

[Washington, George.] Newburgh. To R[obert] R. Livingston [Philadelphia]. Peace; Lafayette's wish
to bear ratification to England. Draft. 2 pp.
In handwriting of Benjamin Walker and Washington.   **P. III, 123**
         Printed in part: Writings of Washington (Ford) N. Y. 1891. 10, 198.

1783
MAR. 30

Washington, George. [Newburgh.] To the President of
Congress [Philadelphia]. News of peace; half-
pay for army. Draft. 1 p. In handwriting of
Jonathan Trumbull, jr. Read in Congress, Apr. 7.
                                    A. VII, 95
     Printed. Writings of Washington (Ford) N. Y. 1891 10, 198, note.

1783
MAR. 30

W[ashington,] G[eorge]. Newburgh. To [Elias Bou-
dinot]. Correspondence. Auto. draft signed.
1 p.   **P. III, 127**

1783
MAR. 31

Washington, George. Newburgh. To [Alexander Hamilton, Philadelphia]. End of the war; union of
the States. Draft. 2 pp. In handwriting of
Martha Washington.   **P. III, 129**
         Printed Writings of Washington (Ford) N. Y. 1891. 10, 201.

1783
MAR. 31

Carleton, [Sir] Guy. New York. To George Washington [Newburgh]. Barbarities on the Northern
frontier. Contemporary copy. 2 pp. In hand
writing of Jonathan Trumbull, jr. Enclosed in
Washington to the President of Congress, 1783,
Apr. 4.   **C. C 152, 11, 199**

1783
APR. 1

Washington, George. [Newburgh.] To the Secretary at
War [Philadelphia]. Establishment of regiments;
brevet commissions. Draft. 3 pp. In handwriting of David Humphreys.   **A. VII, 97**

1783
APR. 4

Washington, George. [Newburgh.] To the President of
Congress [Philadelphia]. Complaints by British
of Indians; barbarities. Draft. 1 p. In hand
writing of Jonathan Trumbull, jr. Read in Congress, Apr. 8. Referred to Hamilton, Madison
and Osgood. Reported Apr. 21.   **A. VII, 101**

1783
APR. 4

W[ashingto]n, G[eorge]. Newburgh. To Alexander Hamilton [Philadelphia]. Reply to [Theodorick] Bland's letter; suspicions of army; settlement of accounts and disbandment. Auto. draft signed. 2 pp. P. III, 131

Printed in part: Writings of Washington (Ford) N. Y. 1891. 10, 214.

1783
APR. 4

Washington, George. Newburgh. To [Theodorick Bland, Philadelphia]. Settlement of army accounts; three months pay; committee of Congress; terms of enlistments and peace establishment. Draft. 7 pp. In handwriting of Jonathan Trumbull, jr. P. III, 135

Printed: Writings of Washington (Ford) N. Y. 1891. 10, 206.

1783
APR. 4

W[ashingto]n, G[eorge]. Newburgh. To Theodorick Bland [Philadelphia]. Peace; local prejudices; establishment of a national character; claims of army; military and civil creditors; discriminations. Auto. draft signed. 3 pp. P. III, 145

Printed: Writings of Washington (Ford) N. Y. 1891, 10, 203.

1783
APR. 5

Laurens, [Henry]. London. To [the President of Congress, Philadelphia]. Suggested Parliamentary bill for a provisional establishment; changes in Ministry; interview with [Charles James] Fox on trade reciprocity; David Hartley as Peace Commissioner. Contemporary extract. Enclosed in Boudinot to Washington, 1783, June 9. 63, 203

1783
APR. 6

Carleton, [Sir] Guy. New York. To [George] Washington [Newburgh]. Publication of the peace with the United States, France, Spain and Holland; return of prisoners etc. Contemporary copy. 3 pp. In handwriting of Benjamin Walker. Enclosed in Washington to the President of Congress, 1783, Apr. 9. C. C. 152, 11, 215

Printed: Writings of Washington (Sparks) Boston. 1835. 8, 542.

1783
APR. 6

Carleton, [Sir] Guy. New York. To Robert R. Livingston [Philadelphia]. Proclamation of cessation of hostilities; exchange of prisoners; carrying out the 5th Article of the Preliminaries.

APR. 6

Digby, Robert to Livingston. Cessation of hostilities and exchange of prisoners. Contemporary copies. 3 pp. Enclosed in Livingston to Washington, 1783, Apr. 12. 62, 275

1783
APR. 7

Morris, Robert. [Philadelphia.] To [George] Washington [Newburgh]. Enclosing general accounts of his administration. L. S. 1 p. 62, 241

1783
APR. 9

Washington, George. [Newburgh.] To the President of Congress [Philadelphia]. Forwarding letter from Sir Guy Carleton. Draft. 1 p. In handwriting of Jonathan Trumbull, jr. Read in Congress, Apr. 14. **A. VII, 103**

1783
APR. 9

Washington, George. [Newburgh.] To [South Carolina delegates in Congress, Philadelphia]. Their letter to Sir Guy Carleton. Draft. 1 p. In handwriting of Jonathan Trumbull, jr. **A. VII, 105**
Delegates: Izard, J. Rutledge Ramsay and Gervais.

1783
APR. 9

Washington, George. [Newburgh.] To Robert Morris [Philadelphia]. Proposition of Duer & Parker to advance three months' pay to the army. Draft. 2 pp. In handwriting of David Humphreys.
A. VII, 131

1783
APR. 9

Continental Congress, Committee on the Peace Establishment. To [George] Washington [Newburgh]. Requesting sentiments on a general military establishment. A. L. S. of Alexander Hamilton. 1 p. **62, 292**
Committed: Hamilton, Madison, Osgood, Wilson, and Ellsworth.

1783
APR. 9

Livingston, Robert R. Philadephia. To [George] Washington [Newburgh]. Peace; gratitude due Washington; distresses of the present situation; national honor; desire of the Marquis de Lafayette; question of when hostilities ceased and its importance. A. L. S. 3 pp. **62, 254**

1783
APR. 9

New Jersey, Non-commissioned officers of the line. Jersey Cantonment. To [George Washington, Newburgh]. Petitioning to obtain from Congress an exemption from taxes. 1 p. Enclosed in Washington to the President of Congress, 1783, Apr. 18.
C. C. 152, 11, 227

1783
APR. 11

Livingston, Robert R. Philadelphia. To Sir Guy Carleton [New York]. Actions of Congress respecting cessation of hostilities and exchange of prisoners; restoration of loyalists' estates; evacuation of New York; feeling between the United States and Great Britain. Contemporary copy. 3 pp. Enclosed in Livingston to Washington, 1783, Apr. 12. **62, 277**

1783
APR. 12

Continental Congress, President. Philadelphia. To [George] Washington [Newburgh]. Cessation of hostilities. L. S. of Elias Boudinot. 2 pp.
92, 158

1783
APR. 12

Livingston, Robert R. Philadelphia. To Rear Adml. [Robert] Digby [New York]. Cessation of hostilities; exchange of prisoners; return of captures made since Mar. 3; state of his letter when received. Contemporary copy. 2 pp. Enclosed in Livingston to Washington, 1783, Apr. 15.

62, 278

1783
APR. 12

Livingston, R[obert] R. Philadelphia. To [George] Washington [Newburgh]. Proclamation of cessation of hostilities; exchange of prisoners; [Sir Guy] Carleton's urgence of performance of 5th Article of the Preliminaries; evacuation of New York. A. L. S. 2 pp. Answered Apr. 22.*

62, 262

1783
APR. 14

Carleton, [Sir] Guy. New York. To Robert R. Livingston [Philadelphia]. Inspectors of embarkation of British. Contemporary copy. 1 p. Endorsed by George Bond: "Apr. 24, 1783. Referred to the Commander in Chief. . . . ."   92, 160

1783
APR. 14

Carleton, Sir Guy to Robert R. Livingston. See: Washington to Benson, Smith and Parker, 1783, May 8.

1783
APR. 15

Continental Congress, Resolves. Liberation of marine prisoners; arrangements for receiving posts and property from British. D. S. of Charles Thomson. Enclosed in Secretary at War to Washington, 1783, Apr. 22.   92, 161

1783
APR. 15

Continental Congress, Resolves. Release of marine prisoners; arrangements for taking possession of evacuated posts; delivery of negroes and other property; release of land prisoners. A. D. S. of Charles Thomson. 1 p. Enclosed in Secretary at War to Washington, 1783, Apr. 16. Copy transmitted to Sir Guy Carleton.   92, 293

1783
APR. 15

Livingston, R[obert] R. Philadelphia. To [George] Washington [Newburgh]. Uncertainty of Congress as to the Preliminary Articles; exchange of prisoners; ratification of Preliminaries and evacuation of New York. L. S. with auto. initialed postscript. Answered Apr. 22.*   62, 273

1783
APR. 15

McHenry, James. Philadelphia. To [George Washington, Newburgh]. Invitation to Washington to visit Baltimore; requesting his influence to obtain an appointment. A. L. S. 3 pp.   62, 271

1783
APR. 16

W[ashingto]n, G[eorge]. Newburgh. To Alexander Hamilton [Philadelphia]. Feeling in army as to pay from the Continent or States; committee; embarrassing situation; evasion of articles of treaty. Auto. draft signed. 3 pp.   P. III, 159
Printed: Writings of Washington (Ford) N. Y. 1891. 10, 223.

1783
APR. 16

Washington, George. [Newburgh.] To [Alexander] Hamilton [Philadelphia]. Peace establishment of the army. Draft. 1 p. In handwriting of Jonathan Trumbull, jr.   A. VII, 107

1783
APR. 16

Washington, George. Newburgh. - To [Robert R. Livingston, Philadelphia]. The Marquis de Lafayette's request. Auto. draft signed. 2 pp.
     P. III, 163

1783
APR. 16

Secretary at War. [Philadelphia.] To [George] Washington [Newburgh]. Liberation of prisoners. L. S. of Benjamin Lincoln. 2 pp.   92, 162

1783
APR. 16

Bland, Theodorick. Philadelphia. To [George] Washington, Newburgh. Claims of the army and effort to satisfy them; the national character; depreciation; discharge of debts; personal matter. A. L. S. 6 pp.   62, 341

1783
APR. 16

Irvine, William. Carlisle [Pennsylvania]. To [the Board of War, Philadelphia]. Ravages of Indians; intentions of Congress. Contemporary copy. 3 pp. In handwriting of William Jackson. Enclosed in Secretary at War to Washington, 1783, May 3.   92, 179

1783
APR. 17

Continental Congress, Resolve. Sale of dragoon horses and army supplies. D. S. of Charles Thomson. Enclosed in Secretary at War to Washington, 1783, Apr. 22.   '92, 161

1783
APR. 18

Washington, George. [Newburgh.] To the President of Congress [Philadelphia]. Proclamation of cessation of hostilities; discharge of troops; difficulties. Draft. 4 pp. In handwriting of Jonathan Trumbull, jr. Read in Congress, Apr. 21. Referred to Osgood, Bland, Hamilton, Madison and Peters. Reported Apr. 22. Acted on May 2.
     A. VII, 109
Printed: Writings of Washington (Ford) N. Y. 1891. 10, 225.

1783
APR. 18

Continental Congress, Resolves. Restoration of public credit; import duties; state quotas for discharge of public debt; revocation of portion of Eighth

Article of Confederation. D. S. of Charles Thomson. 4 pp. "Resolved by Nine States" enclosed in Secretary at War to Washington, 1783, Apr. 22. **92, 165**

1783
APR. 19

Welch, Wakelin. London. To Washington. Introducing Alexander Moore. Contemporary copy. 1 p. In handwriting of Benjamin Walker. Enclosed in Washington to Morris, 1783, Aug. 27.

P. III, 293

1783
APR. 21

Washington, George. [Newburgh.] To Sir Guy Carleton [New York]. Cessation of hostilities; return of British prisoners of war; interview etc. Contemporary copy. 4 pp. In handwriting of Jonathan Trumbull, jr. Enclosed in Washington to the President of Congress, 1783, Apr. 30.

C. C. 152, 11, 241

Printed: Writings of Washington (Ford) N. Y. 1891. 10, 231.

1783
APR. 22

Washington, George. [Newburgh.] To [Robert R. Livingston, Philadelphia]. Release of prisoners of war; interview with Sir Guy Carleton. Draft. 1 p. In handwriting of Jonathan Trumbull, jr.

A. VII, 115

1783
APR. 22

W[ashington,] G[eorge]. Newburgh. To [Alexander Hamilton, Philadelphia]. Exchange of prisoners; soldiers' pay; civil and military claims. Draft signed. 4 pp. In handwriting of Martha Washington. **P. III, 173**

Printed: Writings of Washington (Ford) N. Y. 1891. 10, 234.

1783
APR. 22

Washington, George. Newburgh. To [James Madison, jr., Philadelphia]. Recommending James McHenry for appointment as secretary to an U. S. minister abroad. Auto. draft signed. 1 p. **P. III, 171**

1783
APR. 22

Secretary at War. [Philadelphia.] To [George] Washington [Newburgh]. Transmitting resolves. L. S. of Benjamin Lincoln. 1 p. **92, 166**

1783
APR. 23

Washington, George. [Newburgh.] To the President of Congress [Philadelphia]. Baron de L'Estrade's application. L. S. 1 p. In handwriting of Jonathan Trumbull, jr. **C. C. 152, 11, 233**

Draft, A, VII, 117, is dated Apr. 24.

1783
APR. 23

Washington, George. [Newburgh.] To the Secretary at War [Philadelphia]. Case of Mr. Rukless of the Sappers and Miners. Draft. 1 p. In handwriting of Jonathan Trumbull, jr. **A. VII, 119**

1783
APR. 23

Washington, George. [Newburgh.] To [Benjamin Franklin [Passy]. Recommending Baron de L'Estrade. Draft. 1 p. In handwriting of Benjamin Walker. A. VII, 121

1783
APR. 23

Continental Congress, Resolve. Expiration of term of enlistments; furloughs. Contemporary copy, attested by Benjamin Lincoln. 1 p. Enclosed in Secretary at War to Washington, 1783, Apr. 24. Published in Genl. Orders, May 1. 92, 168

1783
APR. 24

Secretary at War. [Philadelphia.] To [George] Washington [Newburgh]. Transmitting papers. A. L. S. of Benjamin Lincoln. 1 p. Answered Apr. 30.* 92, 169

1783
APR. 24

Carleton, [Sir] Guy. New York. To [George] Washington [Newburgh]. Return of British prisoners; interview; advices from England. Contemporary copy. 3 pp. In handwriting of David Cobb. Enclosed in Washington to the President of Congress, 1783, Apr. 30.
C. C. 152, 11, 245

1783
APR. 28

Dickinson, John. Philadelphia. To the Pennsylvania delegates in Congress [Philadelphia]. Notifying Indians of treaty of peace. Contemporary copy. 3 pp. In handwriting of William Jackson. Enclosed in Secretary at War to Washington, 1783, May 3. 92, 177

1783
APR. 29

Madison, J[ames,] jr. Philadelphia. To [George] Washington [Newburgh]. [James] McHenry; delay in appointments. A. L. S. 1 p. 63, 16

1783
APR. 30

Washington, George. [Newburgh.] To the President of Congress [Philadelphia]. Arrangements for interview with Sir Guy Carleton. Draft. 1 p. In handwriting of Jonathan Trumbull, jr. Read in Congress, May 5. A. VII, 123

1783
APR. 30

Washington, George. [Newburgh.] To the Secretary at War [Philadelphia]. Acceptance of commutation by officers; movement toward Western frontier. Draft. 1 p. In handwriting of Jonathan Trumbull, jr. A. VII, 125

1783
MAY 1

Continental Congress, Resolve. Indian tribes to be notified of the peace. D. S. of Charles Thomson. 2 pp. Enclosed in Secretary at War to Washington, 1783, May 3. 92, 171

1783
MAY 1

Connecticut, Sergeants of the Line. West Point. To [George] Washington [Newburgh]. Recital of their case; petition to have it laid before Congress. D. S. by ten sergeants. 4 pp. Enclosed in Washington to the President of Congress, 1783, May 21.

C. C. **152**, 11, 291

1783
MAY 2

Livingston, Robert R. Philadelphia. To [George] Washington [Newburgh]. Maj. James McHenry's merits and ministership at London; [Benjamin] Franklin's grandson at Paris; Lafayette's exertions in Spain. A. L. S. 3 pp. **63**, 34

1783
MAY 2

Livingston, Robert R. Philadelphia. To [George] Washington [Newburgh]. Interview with [Sir Guy] Carleton; evacuation of New York; release of Staten Island, Long Island and other places from British control; attitude of Loyalists. L. S. 2 pp. **63**, 36

1783
MAY 3

Washington, George. [Newburgh.] To the President of Congress [Philadelphia]. Garrisoning of the Western posts. Draft. 2 pp. In handwriting of Jonathan Trumbull, jr. Read in Congress, May 6. Referred to Committee on Peace Arrangements (Hamilton, Madison, Osgood, Ellsworth and Wilson). Reported May 8.

A. VII, 127

Printed: Writings of Washington (Ford) N. Y. 1891. 10, 239.

1783
MAY 3

Secretary at War. [Philadelphia.] To [Maj. Ephraim Douglass? Philadelphia?]. Instructions governing his mission to the Indian tribes. Contemporary copy. 3 pp. In handwriting of Nathan Jones. Enclosed in Secretary at War to Washington, 1783, May 3. **92**, 173

1783
MAY 3

Secretary at War. [Philadelphia.] To [George] Washington [Dobbs Ferry, New York]. Transmitting papers. L. S. of Benjamin Lincoln. 1 p. Answered May 12.* **92**, 175

1783
MAY 3

Henitz, Jean de. Varsovie [Warsaw, Poland]. To [George Washington, Newburgh]. Admission of American officers to the Polish order of Divine Providence. L. S. 4 pp. (In French) Enclosed in Washington to the President of Congress, 1783, Aug. 28. C. C. **152**, 11, 443

1783
MAY 3

Walke, Thomas. Philadelphia. To the Virginia delegates in Congress [Philadelphia]. Complaint of British retention of slaves. Contemporary copy. 3 pp. In handwriting of George Bond. Enclosed in President of Congress to Washington, 1783, May 9. **92, 193**

1783
MAY 6

Washington, George. Orangetown [New York]. To Sir Guy Carleton [Orangetown]. Carrying away of negroes and American property by British; measures for evacuation of New York etc. Contemporary copy. 4 pp. In handwriting of David Cobb. Enclosed in Washington to the President of Congress, 1783, May 8. **C. C. 152, 11, 257**
Printed: Writings of Washington (Ford) N. Y. 1891. **10, 244.**

1783
MAY 6

Washington, George and Sir Guy **Carleton.** [Orangetown.] Conference. Return of British prisoners; carrying away of negroes by the British; evacuation of New York. Contemporary copy. 6 pp. In handwriting of Jonathan Trumbull, jr. Enclosed in Washington to the President of Congress, 1783, May 8. **C. C. 152, 11, 263**
Printed: Writings of Washington (Ford) N. Y. 1891. **10, 241.**

1783
MAY 6

Board of Admiralty. [Philadelphia.] To [George] Washington [Dobb's Ferry]. Forwarding wine. A. L. S. of Francis Lewis. 1 p. Answered May 13.
92, 181

1783
MAY 6

Jones, Joseph. Philadelphia. To [George Washington, Dobb's Ferry]. Plan adopted by Congress [to raise revenue necessary to defray expenses of the war]; payment and disbanding of army; honesty of British intentions; restoration of negroes; confidential communications. A. L. S. 3 pp.
63, 38

1783
MAY 7

Continental Congress, President. Philadelphia. To [George] Washington [Dobb's Ferry]. No intelligence from Europe. A. L. S. of Elias Boudinot. 2 pp. **92, 185**

1783
MAY 7

Continental Congress, Resolve. Indemnification of officers for damages sustained; subsistence accounts of officers who were prisoners when peace was declared. D. S. of Charles Thomson. 1 p. Endorsed by Jonathan Trumbull, jr: "Secty at War to take Order." Transmitted to Washington.
92, 187

1783
MAY 8

Washington, George. Orangetown [New York]. To the President of Congress [Philadelphia]. Results of interview with Sir Guy Carleton; inspectors for embarkation of British at New York. Draft. 2 pp. In handwriting of Jonathan Trumbull, jr. Read in Congress May 12. Referred to Madison, Clark and Hamilton. **A. VII, 129**

1783
MAY 8

[Washington, George.] Orangetown. To Egbert Benson, William S[tephens] Smith and Daniel Parker [Orangetown]. Appointing them commissioners for obtaining delivery of negroes and other property from the British; quotation from Sir Guy Carleton's letter of Apr. 14, 1783 to Robert R. Livingston respecting negroes and other American property in New York City. Contemporary copy. 4 pp. In handwriting of Hodijah Baylies. Enclosed in Washington to the President of Congress, 1783, May 8. **C. C. 152, 11, 271**

1783
MAY 8

Continental Congress, Order. Letter of Thomas Walke to be transmitted to the Commander in chief. D. S. of Charles Thomson. 1 p. Enclosed in Secretary at War to Washington, 1783, May 9. **92, 190**

1783
MAY 9

Continental Congress, President. Philadelphia. To [George] Washington [Dobb's Ferry]. Transmitting Congress' recommendatory system of finance to the States. L. S. of Elias Boudinot. 1 p. Acknowledged May 21.* **92, 188**

1783
MAY 9

Continental Congress, President. Philadelphia. To [George] Washington [Newburgh]. Transmitting papers. L. S. of Elias Boudinot. 1 p. **98, 192**

1783
MAY 10

[Washington, George.] Newburgh. To [Elias Boudinot, Philadelphia]. Friendship; peace and the necessity of union; visit to Jersey. Draft. 3 pp. In handwriting of David Humphreys. **P. III, 201**

1783
MAY 10

Secretary at War. [Philadelphia.] To [George] Washington [Newburgh]. Acknowledging letter. L. S. of Benjamin Lincoln. **92, 195**

1783
MAY 12

Washington, George. [Newburgh.] To the Secretary at War [Philadelphia]. Case of Dr. [James] Craik. Draft. 2 pp. In handwriting of Jonathan Trumbull, jr. **A. VII, 133**

1783
MAY 12

Continental Congress, Resolve. Taking possession of frontier posts. D. S. of Charles Thomson. 1 p. Endorsed by Jonathan Trumbull, jr: "not received till 7th July." Enclosed in Secretary at War to Washington, 1783, July 5.   **92, 196**

1783
MAY 12

Carleton, [Sir] Guy. New York. To [George] Washington [Newburgh]. American Commissioners to superintend embarkation at New York; question of negroes. Contemporary copy. 7 pp. In handwriting of David Cobb. Enclosed in Washington to the President of Congress, 1783, May 14.   **C. C. 152, 11, 279**
Printed: Writings of Washington (Sparks) Boston. 1835. 8, 543.

1783
MAY 13

Washington, George. [Newburgh.] To [Robert R. Livingston, Philadelphia]. Sir Guy Carleton's embarrassments; evacuation of Long and Staten Islands. Draft. 1 p. In handwriting of Jonathan Trumbull, jr.   **A. VII, 135**

1783
MAY 14

Washington, George. [Newburgh.] To the President of Congress [Philadelphia]. Negotiations for evacuation of New York; negroes. Draft. 1 p. In handwriting of Jonathan Trumbull, jr. Read in Congress, May 19.   **A. VII, 137**

1783
MAY 15

Carleton, [Sir] Guy. New York. To Brig. Gen. [Alured] Clarke [New York?] Paroles of American officers. Contemporary copy. 1 p. In handwriting of Nathan Jones. Enclosed in Secretary at War to Washington, 1783, May 21.   **92, 203**

1783
MAY 16

Continental Congress, Resolve. Commutation of half-pay. Contemporary copy. 1 p. In handwriting of Nathan Jones. Enclosed in Secretary at War to Washington, 1783, May 21. Published in Genl. Orders, May 27.   **92, 197**

1783
MAY 16

Secretary at War. [Philadelphia.] To [George] Washington [Newburgh]. Engraving cannon presented to Comte de Grasse. L. S. of Benjamin Lincoln. 3 pp.   **92, 198**

1783
MAY 18

Washington, George. [Newburgh.] To the Secretary at War [Philadelphia]. Evacuation of South by the British. Draft. 1 p. In handwriting of Jonathan Trumbull, jr.   **A. VII, 139**

1783
MAY 18

Washington, George. [Newburgh.] To the Secretary at War [Philadelphia]. Capt. Segord's claim to promotion. Draft. 1 p. In handwriting of Benjamin Walker.   **A. VII, 141**

1783
MAY 19
South Carolina, Delegates to Continental Congress. Phila-
delphia. To [George] Washington [Newburgh].
Commissioners from South Carolina to receive
public and private property carried off by British.
A. L. S. of J[ohn] Rutledge, signed also by
Ra[lph] Izard and John Lewis Gervais. 1 p.
92, 200

1783
MAY 21
Washington, George. [Newburgh.] To the President of
Congress [Philadelphia]. Memorial of sergeants
of the Connecticut Line. Draft. 1 p. In handwriting of Jonathan Trumbull, jr. Read in Congress, May 26. Referred to Bland, Williamson
and Gorham. Reported June 4.   A. VII, 143

1783
MAY 21
Continental Congress, President. Philadelphia. To
[George] Washington [Newburgh]. Transmit-
ting letters. A. L. S. of Elias Boudinot. 1 p.
92, 204

1783
MAY 21
Secretary at War. [Philadelphia.] To [George] Washington [Newburgh]. Letter of Sir Guy Carleton
respecting paroles. L. S. of Benjamin Lincoln.
2 pp.   92, 201

1783
MAY 24
[Benson, Egbert, Daniel Parker and William Stephens
Smith.] [New York.] To Sir Guy Carleton [New
York]. Claim of James Vanderburgh. Tran-
script. Enclosed in Washington to the President
of Congress, 1783, June 23.   C. C. 169, 9, 298

1783
MAY 26
Continental Congress, Resolve. Furloughing of troops.
Explanatory notes respecting same. Contempo-
rary copy. 2 pp. In handwriting of David
Humphreys.   63, 175

1783
MAY 26
Continental Congress, Resolves. Remonstrance against
British carrying off negroes; furloughs to troops;
furloughs in Southern Army. D. S. of Charles
Thomson. 2 pp. Transmitted to Washington.
Furlough resolves published in Genl. Orders,
June 2.   92, 212

1783
MAY 29
Continental Congress, Resolve. Evacuation of New
York. D. S. of Charles Thomson. 1 p. En-
closed in Secretary at War to Washington, 1783,
June 3.   92, 214

1783
MAY 29
Morgann, M[aurice]. New York. To [Egbert Benson,
Daniel Parker and William Stephens Smith, New
York]. James Vanderburgh's horse. Tran-
script. Enclosed in Washington to the President
of Congress, 1783, June 23.   C. C. 169, 9, 298

1783   **Morris,** Robert. [Philadelphia.] To [George] Washing-
MAY 29   ton [Newburgh]. Public misconstruction of
                 his resignation; pay of army; continuance of
                 expense; notes; disapproval of plans proposed
                 for funding the public debt. L. S. 4 pp.
                                                              63, 115

1783   **Benson,** Egbert and William S[tephens] **Smith.** New York.
MAY 30   To [George] Washington [Newburgh]. Embar-
                 rassments of their position; contentions with
                 British authorities; embarkation of negroes and
                 property; loyalists etc. Contemporary copy.
                 7 pp. In handwriting of David Cobb. Enclosed
                 in Washington to the President of Congress,
                 1783, June 23.   C. C. 152, 11, 349

[1783]   **Vanderburgh,** James. Statement regarding horse stolen
[MAY]   from him. Transcript. Enclosed in Washing-
                 ton to the President of Congress, 1783, June 23.
                                                   C. C. 169, 9, 297

1783   **Washington,** George. [Newburgh.] To Sir Guy Carleton
JUNE 2   [New York]. Transmitting a resolution of Con-
                 gress. Contemporary copy. 1 p. Enclosed in
                 Washington to the President of Congress, 1783,
                 June 23.   C. C. 152, 11, 369

1783   **[Washington,** George.] [Newburgh.] To [Egbert Benson,
JUNE 2   William Stephens Smith and Daniel Parker, New
                 York]. Transmitting copy of resolution of Con-
                 gress, of 22d May relating to carrying off of
                 negroes by the British. Contemporary copy.
                 1 p. In handwriting of Jonathan Trumbull, jr.
                 Enclosed in Washington to the President of Con-
                 gress, 1783, June 2.   C. C. 152, 11, 357

1783   **Washington,** George. Newburgh. To R[obert] Morris
JUNE 3   [Philadelphia]. Pay of troops before disbanding;.
                 circular to the States. Draft. 2 pp. In hand-
                 writing of David Humphreys.   A. VII, 145

1783   **Board of Treasury.** [Philadelphia.] To [George] Washing-
JUNE 3   ton [Newburgh]. [Col. Clement?] Biddle's at-
                 tendance on the Board. L. S. of Ezek Forman.
                 1 p.   92, 215

1783   **Secretary at War.** [Philadelphia.] To [George] Washing-
JUNE 3   ton [Newburgh]. Transmitting resolve of Con-
                 gress. A. L. S. of William Jackson, Asst. Secy.
                 1 p.   92, 217

[1783]　　**Heath,** William. [Newburgh.] To [George] Washington
[June 5]　　[Newburgh]. Distress of army; pay due troops
　　　　　etc. Contemporary copy. 4 pp. In handwrit-
　　　　　ing of David Humphreys. Enclosed in Wash-
　　　　　ington to the President of Congress, 1783, June 7.
　　　　　　　　　　　　　　　　C. C.　152, 11, 297

1783　　**Morris,** Robert [Philadelphia.] To [George] Washington
June 5　　[Newburgh]. Signing of bills for payment of
　　　　　army. L. S. 1. p.　　　　　　　　　63, 170

1783　　**Washington,** George. [Newburgh.] To the Secretary at
June 6　　War [Philadelphia]. Maj. Gen. [Henry] Knox's
　　　　　claim to extra allowance. Draft. 2 pp. In hand-
　　　　　writing of Jonathan Trumbull, jr.　A.　VII, 147

1783　　**Washington,** George. [Newburgh.] To the Secretary at
June 6　　War [Philadelphia]. Jonathan Trumbull[jr.]'s
　　　　　claim to a commission in the army. Draft. 1 p.
　　　　　In handwriting of David Humphreys.
　　　　　　　　　　　　　　　　A.　VII, 149

1783　　**Washington,** George. [Newburgh.] To Maj. Gen. [Wil-
June 6　　liam] Heath [Newburgh]. Distress of the army;
　　　　　efforts to obtain pay etc. Contemporary copy.
　　　　　5 pp. In handwriting of Benjamin Walker.
　　　　　Inclosed in Washington to the President of Con-
　　　　　gress, 1783, June 7.　　　C. C.　152, 11, 305
　　　　　Printed: Writings of Washington (Ford) N. Y. 1891. 10, 251.

1783　　**Secretary at War.** [Philadelphia.] To [George] Washing-
June 6　　ton [Newburgh]. Commission of Lt. Col. to
　　　　　[Jonathan] Trumbull, jr.　A. L. S. of Benjamin
　　　　　Lincoln. 2 pp.　　　　　　　　　92, 218

1783　　**Washington,** George. Newburgh. To the President of
June 7　　Congress [Philadelphia]. Complaints of the
　　　　　army; payment of troops. Draft. 2 pp. In
　　　　　handwriting of David Humphreys. Referred to
　　　　　Hamilton, Madison and Bland, June 11. Re-
　　　　　ported June 19.　　　　　　　A.　VII, 155
　　　　　Printed: Writings of Washington (Sparks) Boston. 1835. 8, 438.

1783　　**Washington,** George. Newburgh. To the President of
June 7　　Congress [Philadelphia]. Duportail's plan for
　　　　　establishment of defenses; the Western posts.
　　　　　Draft. 3 pp. In handwriting of David Hum-
　　　　　phreys. Referred to Committee on Peace Ar-
　　　　　rangements (Hamilton, Madison, Ellsworth,
　　　　　Wilson and Holton). Reported June 18.
　　　　　　　　　　　　　　　　A.　VII, 151

1783
JUNE 7

Secretary at War. West Point. To [George] Washington [Newburgh]. Arms for musicians; arsenals for storage of powder etc. A. L. S. of Benjamin Lincoln. 2 pp.   **63,** 188

1783
JUNE 7

Secretary at War. [Newburgh.] To [George] Washington [Newburgh]. Discharge and furlough of troops to save expense. L. S. of Benjamin Lincoln. 3 pp.   **92,** 219

1783
JUNE 8

Izard, Ralph. Philadelphia. To [George] Washington [Newburgh]. Mrs. [Margaret?] De Lancey's complaints. A. L. S. 1 p. Answered June 14.
      63, 191

1783
JUNE 9

Benson, Egbert, William S[tephens] **Smith** and Daniel **Parker.** New York. To Sir Guy Carleton [New York]. Remonstrance in case of negro about to be carried off by British. Transcript.
      C. C. 169, 9, 303

1783
JUNE 9

Boudinot, Elias. Philadelphia. To [George] Washington [Newburgh]. Intelligence from Europe. L. S. 3 pp.   **63,** 201

1783
JUNE 10

[Washington, George.] [Newburgh.] To [Egbert Benson, William S[tephens] Smith and Daniel Parker, New York]. Discussion of their powers; remonstrances to Sir Guy Carleton. Contemporary copy. 4 pp. In handwriting of Jonathan Trumbull, jr. Enclosed in Washington to the President of Congress, 1783, June 23.
      C. C. 152, 10, 377

1783
JUNE 10

Carleton, [Sir] Guy. New York. To [George] Washington [Newburgh]. Complaints of misunderstandings and violations of articles of the treaty of peace. Contemporary copy. 2 pp. In handwriting of Jonathan Trumbull, jr. Enclosed in Washington to the President of Congress, 1783, June 14.   **C. C.** 152, 11, 317

1783
JUNE 12

Washington, George. [Newburgh.] To the Secretary at War [Philadelphia]. Memorials of officers of the Invalid Corps. Draft. 1 p. In handwriting of Jonathan Trumbull, jr.   **A.** VII, 157

1783
JUNE 13

Butler, Richard. [Lancaster, Pennsylvania.] After orders. Furlough option. Contemporary copy. 2 pp. Enclosed in President of Congress to Washington, 1783, June 21.   **92,** 237

1783
JUNE 14

Washington, George. [Newburgh.] To the Secretary at War [Philadelphia]. Capt. [Nathan] Goodale's case. Draft. 1 p. In handwriting of Jonathan Trumbull, jr. **A.** VII, 159

1783
JUNE 14

Washington, George. [Newburgh.] To the President of Congress [Philadelphia]. Transmitting letter of Sir Guy Carleton. Draft. 1 p. In handwriting of Jonathan Trumbull, jr. Read in Congress, June 19. Referred to Mifflin, Mercer and Hamilton. Committee renewed July 16 as Hamilton, McHenry and Peters and letter of July 12 also referred to them. Renewed again July 30 as McHenry, Peters and Duane. **A.** VII, 161

1783
JUNE 14

Continental Congress, President. Philadelphia. To [George] Washington [Newburgh]. Engraving cannon for Comte de Grasse. L. S. of Elias Boudinot. 2 pp. **92, 224**

1783
JUNE 14

Benson, Egbert and Daniel **Parker.** New York. To [George] Washington [Newburgh]. Reception of remonstrances by Sir Guy Carleton; continued embarkation of negroes. Contemporary copy. 3 pp. In handwriting of David Cobb. Enclosed in Washington to the President of Congress, 1783, June 23. **C. C.** **152,** 11, 365

1783
JUNE 16

Continental Army. Officers. [New Windsor.] Petition to Congress. To grant lands on the Ohio. Transcript. Enclosed in Washington to the President of Congress, 1783, June 17.

C. C. **169,** 9, 271

1783
JUNE 16

Putnam, Rufus. New Windsor [New York]. To [George] Washington [Newburgh]. Explanatory of petition of army; establishment of posts on the Western frontier; grants of land to army; settlement of the West etc. Contemporary copy. 14 pp. In handwriting of Benjamin Walker. Enclosed in Washington to the President of Congress, 1783, June 17. **C. C.** **152,** 11, 325

1783
JUNE 17

Washington, George. Newburgh. To the President of Congress [Philadelphia]. Grants of Western lands to discharged soldiers. Draft. 4 pp. In handwriting of David Humphreys. Referred to the Grand Committee of 30th of May.
A. VII, 163

Printed: Writings of Washington (Ford) N. Y. 1891. 10, 267.
Committee: Holton, Arnold, Ellsworth, Hamilton, Clark, Wilson, Bedford, Mercer, Hawkins and Rutledge.

1783
JUNE 17

Benson, Egbert, William S[tephens] Smith and Daniel Parker. New York. To Sir Guy Carleton [New York]. Remonstrance against embarkation of civilians and negroes. Transcript. Enclosed in Washington to the President of Congress, 1783, June 23.   C. C. 169, 9, 310

1783
JUNE 17

Butler, Richard. Lancaster [Pennsylvania]. To the non-commissioned officers and men of 3d Pennsylvania regiment. Argument and advice against their marching to Philadelphia; pay rolls etc. Contemporary copy. 2 pp. Enclosed in President of Congress to Washington, 1783, June 21.   92, 231

1783
JUNE 17

Butler, Richard. Lancaster. To [Prest. John Dickinson, Philadelphia]. Mutiny of troops; measures taken. Contemporary copy. 3 pp. Enclosed in President of Congress to Washington, 1783, June 21.   92, 235

1783
JUNE 17

Henry, William. Lancaster [Pennsylvania]. To [Prest.] John Dickinson [Philadelphia]. Mutiny of troops; their march toward Philadelphia. Contemporary copy. 2 pp. Enclosed in President of Congress, 1783, June 21.   92, 233

1783
JUNE 18

Washington, George. Newburgh. To [Elias Boudinot, Philadelphia]. Negotiations for peace; retirement. Auto. draft signed. 2 pp.   P. III, 235

1783
JUNE 18

Benson, Egbert, William S[tephens] Smith, and Daniel Parker. New York. To [George] Washington [Newburgh]. Representation made to Sir Guy Carleton; British embarkation. Contemporary copy. 1 p. In handwriting of Benjamin Walker. Enclosed in Washington to the President of Congress, 1783, June 23.   C. C. 152, 11, 373

1783
JUNE 21

Continental Congress, President. Philadelphia. To [George] Washington [Newburgh]. Mutiny of troops; occurrences in Philadelphia. L. S. of Elias Boudinot. 4 pp. Answered June 24.*   92, 229

1783
JUNE 21

Continental Congress, President. Philadelphia. To [George] Washington [Newburgh]. Mutiny of troops; resolves of Congress. L. S. of Elias Boudinot. 2 pp. Answered June 25.*   92, 227

1783
JUNE 21

Continental Congress, Resolve. Mutiny of troops; removal of Congress to Trenton or Princeton. A. D. S.

of Charles Thomson. 2 pp. Enclosed in President of Congress to Washington, 1783, June 21.

92, 225

1783
JUNE 23

Washington, George. [Newburgh.] To the President of Congress [Philadelphia]. Embarkation of negroes at New York in violation of treaty. Draft. 2 pp. In handwriting of David Humphreys. Read in Congress, July 1. Referred to Williamson, Madison and Read. Reported July 16.

A. VII, 167

1783
JUNE 23

Washington, George. [Newburgh.] To the President of Congress [Philadelphia]. Services of Reuben Harvey. Draft. 1 p. In handwriting of Benjamin Walker. Read in Congress, July 1. Referred to Read, Ellery and McHenry. Reported July 18.

A. VII, 169

1783
JUNE 24

Washington, George. Newburgh. To the President of Congress [Philadelphia]. Mutiny of Pennsylvania troops; arrangement of the army. Draft. 6 pp. In handwriting of David Humphreys. Read in Congress, June 30.

A. VII, 171

Printed: Writings of Washington (Ford) N. Y. 1891. 10, 271.

1783
JUNE 24

Continental Congress, President. Proclamation. Convening Congress at Princeton, June 26. Broadside, 1 p. Printed by Claypoole. Enclosed in Boudinot, Elias to Washington, 1783, June 26.

92, 243

1783
JUNE 25

Washington, George. Newburgh. To the President of Congress [Philadelphia]. Movement of troops. Draft. 1 p. In handwriting of David Cobb. Read in Congress, June 30.

A. VII, 177

1783
JUNE 26

Boudinot, Elias. Princeton. To [George] Washington [Newburgh]. Inaction of Pennsylvania in furnishing militia guards for Congress; removal of Congress to Princeton; collapse of the mutiny. A. L. S. 2 pp.

92, 241

1783
JUNE 30

Washington, George. [Newburgh.] To the President of Congress [Princeton, New Jersey]. Recommending Baron Steuben to take charge of the Western posts. Draft. 2 pp. In handwriting of David Humphreys. Read in Congress, July 4. Referred to Madison, Ellsworth and Hawkins.

A. VII, 179

1783
JULY 1

Washington, George. [Newburgh.] To the Secretary at War [Princeton]. Release of Brunswick pris-

oners; minor matters. Draft. 1 p. In handwriting of Jonathan Trumbull, jr. **A**. VII, 181

1783   Continental Congress, President. Princeton. To [George]
JULY 1   Washington [Newburgh]. Quelling of the mu-
tiny; Col. [Richard] Humpton. A. L. S. of Elias
Boudinot. 2 pp. Answered July 4.*   92, 249

1783   Continental Congress, Committee Report on Mutiny of the
JULY 1   Pennsylvania Line. Proceedings of committee;
instructions to Maj. [William] Jackson, 1783,
June 19; conference with Pennsylvania council.
D. S. of Charles Thomson. 7 pp. Enclosed in
President of Congress to Washington, 1783,
July 5.   92, 254

1783   Continental Congress, Resolve. Maj. Gen. [Robert] Howe
JULY 1   to march against mutineers. Contemporary
copy. 1 p.   92, 248

1783   [Morris, Robert.] State of receipts and expenditures of
JULY 1   public money on warrants from Superintendent
of Finance from Jan. 1 to June 30, 1783. Tabular statement from Register's Office. D. S. of
Joseph Nourse. Enclosed in Morris to Washington, 1783, July 11.   63, 317

1783   Continental Congress, President. Princeton. To [George]
JULY 3   Washington [Newburgh]. Suggestion as to trial
of mutineer officers. A. L. S. 1 p. Answered
July 16.*   92, 251

1783   Hand, E[dward]. [Newburgh?] To Brig. Gen. [Moses]
JULY 3   Hazen [New Windsor, New York]. Return of
regiment; unauthorized promotions. Contemporary copy. 2 pp. Enclosed in Washington to
the President of Congress, 1783, July 5.
C. C. 152, 11, 401

1783   Hazen, Moses. New Windsor [New York]. To Brig.
JULY. 3   Gen. [Edward] Hand [Newburgh]. Return of
Canadian Regiment; promotions. Contemporary
copy. 1 p. With tabular return in question, on
verso. Enclosed in Washington to the President of
Congress, 1783, July 5.   C. C. 152, 11, 403

1783   Washington, George. Newburgh. To the President of
JULY 4   Congress [Princeton]. Troops under Maj. Gen.
[Robert] Howe ordered to Philadelphia. Draft.
1 p. In handwriting of Jonathan Trumbull, jr.
Read in Congress, July 8.   **A**. VII, 183

1783
JULY 4

Washington, George. [Newburgh.] To [Brig.] Gen. [Edward] Hand [Newburgh]. Promotions in Hazen's regiment. Contemporary copy. 2 pp. In handwriting of Jonathan Trumbull, jr. Enclosed in Washington to the President of Congress 1783, July 5.   C. C. 152, 11, 409

1783
JULY 4

Hand, Edward. [Newburgh?] To [George] Washington [Newburgh]. Return received from Brig. Gen. [Moses] Hazen; promotions noted thereon. Contemporary copy. 1 p. Enclosed in Washington to the President of Congress, 1783, July 5.
          C. C. 152, 11, 405

1783
JULY 5

Washington, George. [Newburgh.] To the President of Congress [Princeton]. Promotions claimed by officers of Hazen's regiment; removal of Congress to Princeton. Draft. 2 pp. In handwriting of David Humphreys. Read in Congress, July 11. Referred to Secy. at War to report.
          A. VII, 185

1783
JULY 5

Continental Congress, President. To [George] Washington [Newburgh]. Action of Congress on mutiny of the Pennsylvania Line. A. L. S. of Elias Boudinot. 2 pp. Answered July 8.   92, 252

1783
JULY 5

Secretary at War. Princeton. To [George] Washington [Newburgh]. Memorial of the surgeon's mates; release of British prisoners; resolve of May 12. A. L. S. of William Jackson, Asst. Secy.   92, 262

1783
JULY 8

Washington, George. [Newburgh.] To the Asst. Secretary at War [Princeton]. Receipt of resolve of Congress. Draft. 1 p. In handwriting of Jonathan Trumbull, jr.   A. VII, 187

1783
JULY 8

Continental Congress, President. Princeton. To [George] Washington [Newburgh]. Baron Steuben's mission [to frontier posts in possession of British]; investigation of the mutiny. A. L. S. of Elias Boudinot. 2 pp. Answered July 16.*   92, 263

1783
JULY 11

Morris, Robert. [Philadelphia.] To [George] Washington [Newburgh]. Transmitting circular letter to the States. L. S. 1 p. Answered Aug. 6.   63, 315

1783
JULY 11

Morris, Robert. [Philadelphia.] Circular letter to the several States. Enclosing state of the public accounts; aid necessary from the states; payment of army; notes and credit; taxes. Contemporary copy. 3 pp. Enclosed in Morris to Washington, 1783, July 11.   63, 318

1783
July 12
W[ashington,] G[eorge]. Newburgh. To Maj. Gen. Baron Steuben [Newburgh]. Instructions governing his visiting the Western posts; surrender of same by British; garrisons, provisions etc. Contemporary copy. 5 pp. In handwriting of Jonathan Trumbull, jr. Referred to Hamilton, McHenry and Peters, July 16, to whom letter of June 14 was also referred. Renewed July 30 as McHenry, Peters and Duane. Enclosed in Washington to the President of Congress, 1783, Aug. 6.
                                   C. C. 152, 11, 423

1783
July 14
Secretary at War. Princeton. To the President of Congress [Princeton]. Promotions in Brig. Gen. [Moses] Hazen's regiment. Contemporary copy. 1 p. Enclosed in President of Congress to Washington, 1783, July 17.   92, 269

1783
July 16
Washington, George. [Newburgh.] To the President of Congress [Princeton]. Aid for Canadians; tour to Northward. Draft. 3 pp. In handwriting of Jonathan Trumbull, jr. Referred to McHenry, Lee and Madison, July 23. Reported July 26.
                                   A. VII, 189

1783
July 16
Continental Congress, Resolve. Recalling Commissioners superintending embarkation of British at New York. A. D. S. of Charles Thomson. 1 p. Enclosed in President of Congress to Washington, 1783, July 17.   92, 268

1783
July 17
Continental Congress, President. Princeton. To [George] Washington [Newburgh]. Promotions in Brig. Gen. [Moses] Hazen's regiment; resolve recalling commissioners superintending British embarkation at New York. Answered Aug. 6.*   92, 267

1783
July 17
[De Peyster, Arent Schuyler.] [Detroit.] To [Brig. Gen. Allan Maclean, Niagara]. Encounter between whites and Indians on the Ohio. [Extract of letter.] Transcipt. Enclosed in Washington to the President of Congress, 1783, Aug. 26.
                                   C. C. 169, 9, 348

1783
July 18
Secretary at War. Princeton. To [George] Washington [Newburgh]. Transmitting resolve. A. L. S. of William Jackson, Asst. Secy. 1 p.   92, 271

1783
JULY 22

Morris, Robert. Philadelphia. To [George] Washington [Newburgh]. Introducing Mr. Darby. A. L. S. 2 pp.   63, 343

1783
JULY 23

T[rumbull,] J[onathan, jr] [Newburgh.] To the Secretary at War [Princeton]. Acceptance of commutation by Delaware officers. Auto. draft signed. 1 p.
A. VII, 193

1783
JULY 24

Continental Congress, President. Princeton. To [George] Washington [on Northern frontier]. Minor matters; arrival of the Definitive Treaty at New York. L. S. of Elias Boudinot. 1 p. Answered Aug. 6.*   92, 272

1783
JULY 28

Continental Congress, Resolve. Attendance of the Commander-in-chief on Congress. D. S. of Charles Thomson. 1 p. Enclosed in President of Congress to Washington, 1783, Aug 1.   92, 278

1783
JULY 31

Continental Congress, President. Princeton. To [George] Washington [on Northern frontier]. His attendance on Congress. L. S. of Elias Boudinot. 2 pp. Answered Aug. 6.*   92,.274

1783
JULY 31

McHenry, James. Princeton [New Jersey]. To [George] Washington [on Northern frontier]. Attendance on Congress; the peace establishment and Rhode Island. A. L. S. 2 pp. Answered Aug. 6.
63, 363

1783
JULY 31

Maclean, Allan. Niagara. To Col. M[arinus] Willett [Albany]. Statement of recent encounter between whites and Indians on the Ohio. Transcript. Enclosed in Washington to the President of Congress, 1788, Aug. 26.   C. C. 169, 9, 349

1783
AUG. 1

Continental Congress, President. Princeton. To [George] Washington [On Northern frontier]. Transmitting resolve. L. S. of Elias Boudinot. 1 p.
92, 276

1783
AUG. 3

Steuben, [Baron von] Chamblee [Canada]. To [Lt.] Gen. [Frederick] Haldimand [Quebec]. Surrender of Western posts by the British. Contemporary copy. 2 pp. In handwriting of David Humphreys. Enclosed in Washington to the President of Congress, 1783, Aug. 30.   C. C. 152, 11, 461

1783
AUG. 6

Washington, George. [Newburgh.] To the President of Congress [Princeton]. Visit to Congress. Draft. 1 p. In handwriting of Jonathan Trumbull, jr.

Read in Congress, Aug. 11. Referred to Holton, Wilson, Carroll, Huntington and Duane. Reported Sep. 10. **A. VII, 195**

Printed: Writings of Washington (Ford), N. Y. 1891. 10, 291.

1783
Aug. 6

Washington, George. Newburgh. To the President of Congress [Princeton]. Provisioning the western posts. Draft. 5 pp. In handwriting of David Humphreys. Read in Congress, Aug. 11. Referred Sep. 10 to Duane, Peters, Carroll, Hawkins and A. Lee. Reported Sep. 19.

A. VII, 197

Printed: Writings of Washington (Ford), N. Y. 1891. 10, 292.

1783
Aug. 6

Haldimand, Frederick. Quebec. To Maj. Gen. Baron Steuben [Chamblee]. Arranging for meeting at Sorel. Contemporary copy. 1 p. In handwriting of David Cobb. Enclosed in Washington to the President of Congress, 1783, Aug. 30.

C. C. 152, 11, 465

1783
Aug. 7

Continental Congress, Resolves. Erection of equestrian statue of Washington; description. D. S. of George Bond. 1 p. Enclosed in Boudinot to Washington, 1783, Aug. 12. **64, 30**

Second D. S. of Charles Thomson, enclosed in Secretary of Congress to Washington, 1783, Aug. 28, 64, 119.

1783
Aug. 11

McHenry, James. Princeton. To [George] Washington [Newburgh]. Reasons for his attendance on Congress; evacuation of New York. A. L. S. 3 pp.

64, 14

1783
Aug. 11

Steuben, [Baron von.] Sorel. To [Lt. Gen. Frederick Haldimand, Sorel]. Surrender of the Western posts; passport to visit same. Contemporary copy. 2 pp. Enclosed in Washington to the President of Congress, 1783, Aug. 30.

C. C. 152, 11, 469

1783
Aug. 12

Washington, George. Newburgh. To Robert Morris, [Princeton]. His personal account with the public and purchases in Philadelphia. Auto. draft signed. 1 p. **P. III, 283**

1783
Aug. 12

Continental Congress, President. Princeton. To [George] Washington. [Newburgh]. Attendance on Congress; peace establishment of army. L. S. of Elias Boudinot. 3 pp. **64, 22**

1783
Aug. 12

Boudinot, Elias. Princeton. To [George] Washington [Newburgh]. Enclosing proposed address of Congress and resolve for erection of statue. A. L. S. 2 pp. Marked: "*private.*" **64. 26**

1783
AUG. 12

Morris, Robert. [Philadelphia.] To [George] Washington [Newburgh]. Demands for money; knowledge of resources. L. S. 1 p. Answered Aug. 25.
64, 20

1783
AUG. 13

Haldimand, Frederick. St. Johns [Canada]. To Maj. Gen. Baron Steuben [Sorel?]. The definitive treaty; harmonious relations between the United States and Great Britain; refusal of passport to visit posts. Contemporary copy. 3 pp. In handwriting of David Cobb. Enclosed in Washington to the President of Congress, 1783, Aug. 30. C. C. 152. 11, 473

1783
AUG. 14

Washington, George. [Newburgh.] To the President of Congress [Princeton]. Reasons for delay in setting out for Princeton. Draft. 1 p. In handwriting of Jonathan Trumbull, jr. Read in Congress, Aug. 22. A. VII, 203
Printed: Writings of Washington (Ford), N. Y. 1891. 10, 297.

1783
AUG. 19

Haldimand, Frederick, to Washington. See: Continental Congress, Order on letter of Haldimand, 1783, Sep. 8.

1783
AUG. 20

Morris, Robert. [Philadelphia.] To [George] Washington [en route to Rocky Hill, New Jersey]. Liquidation of personal account. L. S. 2 pp. 64, 50

1783
AUG. 21

Boudinot, Elias. Princeton. To [George] Washington [en route to Rocky Hill]. Mrs. [Martha] Washington's illness; [Henry] Laurens's report of treaty negotiations in Europe; the reciprocity provision; minor matters. A. L. S. 4 pp. Marked private. 64, 53

1783
AUG. 23

Steuben, [Baron von]. Saratoga [New York]. To [George] Washington [near Rocky Hill]. Report of interview with [Lt.] Gen. [Frederick] Haldimand on subject of evacuation of the Western posts by the British. Contemporary copy. 6 pp. In handwriting of David Cobb. Enclosed in Washington to the President of Congress, 1783, Aug. 30. C. C. 152, 11, 453

1783
AUG. 26

Washington, George. Rocky Hill [New Jersey]. To the President of Congress [Princeton]. Disposition of British officers and savages on the Western frontier. Draft. 1 p. In handwriting of David Humphreys. Read in Congress, Aug. 27. Referred to Duane, Peters, Carroll, Hawkins and A. Lee. Reported Sep. 19. A. VII, 207

1783
AUG. 26

Washington, George. Princeton [New Jersey]. To the President [of Congress, Princeton]. Address on occasion of his reception by Congress. Draft. 2 pp.   A. VII, 205

Printed: Writings of Washington (Ford) N. Y. 1891, 10, 299.

[1783]
[AUG. 26]

Continental Congress President. [Princeton.] Address to George Washington on occasion of his attendance on Congress. Contemporary copy. 2 pp. Enclosed in Boudinot to Washington, 1783, Aug. 12.   64, 28

[1783]
[AUG. 27]

Washington, George. Newburgh. To Robert Morris [Philadelphia]. Introducing Alexander Moore. Auto. draft signed. 1 p.   P. III, 291

1783
AUG. 28

Washington, George. Rocky Hill. To the President of Congress [Princeton]. Admission of American officers to recently established Polish Order [of Divine Providence]. Draft. 1 p. In handwriting of David Humphreys. Read in Congress, Aug. 29. Referred to Ellery, A. Lee, Izard, Peters and McHenry. Reported Sep. 11.   A. VII, 209

1783
AUG. 28

Continental Congress, Secretary. Princeton. To [George] Washington [Princeton]. Erection of statue of Washington; introducing [Joseph] Wright. L. S. of Charles Thomson. 1 p.   64, 117

1783
AUG. 30

W[ashington,] G[eorge]. [Rocky Hill.] To the President of Congress [Princeton]. Arrangements for taking possession of the Western posts; Baron Steuben's report. Auto. draft signed. 1 p. Read in Congress, Sep. 1. Referred to Izard, Hawkins, Duane, A. Lee and Higginson.   A. VII, 211

1783
AUG. 31

Washington, George. Rocky Hill. To the Secretary at War [Princeton]. Capt. Segord's claim. Draft. 2 pp. In handwriting of David Humphreys.   A. VII, 213

1783
SEP. 2

Morris, Robert. [Philadelphia.] To [George] Washington [Rocky Hill]. Garrisons for Western posts; want of an establishment [of army]. L. S. of Robert Morris. 1 p.   64, 128

1783
SEP. 3

W[ashington,] G[eorge]. Rocky Hill. To [Robert Morris, Philadelphia]. Invitation. Auto. draft signed. 1 p.   P. III, 301

1783
SEP. 3

St. Clair, Arthur. Princeton [New Jersey]. To [George] Washington [Rocky Hill]. Pennsylvania officers who wish to be put on the Peace Establishment.

A. L. S. 2 pp. Enclosed in Washington to the President of Congress, 1783, Dec. 21.

C. C. 152, 11, 545

1783
SEP. 4
Washington, George. Rocky Hill. To the President of Congress [Princeton]. Forwarding [Lt.] Gen. [Frederick] Haldimand's letter. Draft. 1 p. In handwriting of David Humphreys. A. VII, 247

1783
SEP. 5
[Washington, George.] Rocky Hill. To James McHenry [Princeton]. Brevet rank. Auto. draft. 3 pp. Partly in handwriting of David Cobb.

A. VII, 215

1783
SEP. 5
Morris, Robert. Philadelphia. To [George] Washington [Rocky Hill]. Exchange of courtesies etc. A. L. S. 3 pp. 64, 143

1783
SEP. 7
Washington, George. Rocky Hill. To James Duane [Princeton]. Settlement of the Indian country. Auto. draft signed. 9 pp. A. VII, 219
Printed: Writings of Washington (Ford) N. Y. 1891. 10, 303.

1783
SEP. 8
Washington, George. Rocky Hill. Observations on the Committee of Congress's intended report on the Peace Establishment. Draft. 8 pp. In handwriting of David Humphreys and David Cobb.

A. VII, 231
Printed: Writings of Washington (Ford) N. Y. 1891. 10, 312.

1783
SEP. 8
Continental Congress. Order on letter of Lt. Gen. Frederick Haldimand to George Washington 1783, Aug. 19, respecting Indians on the Northern frontier. Extract of letter given. Contemporary copy. 1 p. C. C. 152, 11, 481

1783
SEP. 10
[Knox, Henry.] West Point. To [George Washington, Rocky Hill]. Lack of clothing for troops. [Extract of letter.] 2 pp. In handwriting of David Cobb. Enclosed in Washington to the President of Congress, 1783, Sep. 19. C. C. 152, 10, 495

1783
SEP. 10
Morris, Robert. [Philadelphia.] To [George] Washington [Rocky Hill]. Notes for settlement of [Lt.] Col. [Richard] Varick's accounts. L. S. 1 p.

64, 153

1783
SEP. 15
Continental Congress, Resolve. Washington's access to secret papers of Congress. A. D. S. of Charles Thomson. 1 p. Enclosed in President of Congress to Washington, 1783, Sep. 17. 64, 177
Above motion was made by Daniel Carroll and seconded by James McHenry.

1783
SEP. 16

Duportail, [Louis Le Bègue.] Philadelphia. To [George] Washington [Rocky Hill]. Case of officers in the Engineer Department. Contemporary copy. 2 pp. In handwriting of David Cobb. Enclosed in Washington to the President of Congress, 1783, Sep. 19.   C. C.   152, 11, 491

[1783]
[SEP. 17]

Washington, George. [Rocky Hill] To [Maj. Gen. Henry Knox, West Point]. Peace establishment of army; distribution of clothing. [Extract of letter.] 1 p. In handwriting of David Cobb. Enclosed in Washington to the President of Congress, 1783, Sep. 19.   C. C.   152, 11, 497

1783
SEP. 17

Continental Congress, President. Princeton. To [George] Washington [Rocky Hill]. Transmitting resolve. A. L. S. of Elias Boudinot. 1 p.   64, 178

1783
SEP. 18

W[ashingto]n, G[eorge]. Rocky Hill. To the President of Congress [Princeton]. Access to the secret papers of Congress. Auto. draft signed. 1 p. Read in Congress, Sep. 18.   A. VII, 239

1783
SEP. 19

Washington, George. Rocky Hill. To the President of Congress [Princeton]. Duportail's case; clothing for troops on North river; discharge of furloughed troops. Auto. draft signed. 1 p. Read in Congress, Sep. 19. Referred to Huntington, Gerry and Duane. Reported in part, Sep. 29, and finally Oct. 3.   A. VII, 241.

Printed, in part: Writings of Washington (Ford) N. Y. 1891. 10, 317, note.

1783
SEP. 22

Duane, James. Princeton. To George Washington [Rocky Hill]. Foreign despatches. A. L. S. 1 p.
    64, 199

1783
SEP. 22

Continental Congress, Committee. Princeton. To [George] Washington [Rocky Hill]. Desiring conference on subject of Duportail's letter [of Oct. 29]. A. L. S. of Samuel Huntington. 1 p.   64, 201

Committee: Williamson, Osgood and Ellery.

1783
SEP. 24

Continental Congress. "Motion of Mr. S. Huntington 'That the Commander in chief be authorized to discharge such parts of ye federal Army Now in service as he shall deem proper & Expedient and that he direct that necessary Clothing be immediately provided for those that may be longer retained in Service.'" "Commander in Chief. (To take Order)" . . . . . "Secret . . . . ."
    C. C.   186, 126

Above quotation is an entry in the Committee Book, in handwriting of George Bond.

1783
SEP. 25

Washington, George. Rocky Hill. To Samuel Huntington [Princeton]. Wording of the proclamation
disbanding the Army. Auto. draft signed. 2 pp.
A. VII, 243

Printed: Writings of Washington (Ford) N. Y. 1891. 10, 243.

1783
SEP. 25

Continental Congress, President. Princeton. To [George]
Washington [Princeton]. Transmitting resolves.
A. L. S. of Elias Boudinot. 1 p.   **64,** 206

1783
SEP. 26

Washington, George. Rocky Hill. To the President of
Congress [Princeton]. Acknowledging receipt of
resolves respecting [Maj.] Gen. [Robert] Howe
and troops under his command. Draft. 1 p. In
handwriting of Benjamin Walker. **A.** VII, 245

1783
SEP. 26

Kosciusko, Thad[deus]. Philadelphia. To [George]
Washington [Rocky Hill]. Promotion to brigadiership. Contemporary copy. 2 pp. In handwriting of Benjamin Walker. Enclosed in Washington to the President of Congress, 1783, Oct. 2.
C. C. 152, 11, 503

1783
OCT. 2

Washington, George. Rocky Hill. To the President of
Congress [Princeton]. Kosciusko's promotion.
Draft. 1 p. In handwriting of Benjamin Walker.
Read in Congress, Oct. 4. Referred to Read,
Peters and Duane. Reported Oct. 9. Acted on
Oct. 13.   A. VII, 249

Printed: Writings of Washington (Sparks) Boston. 1835. 8, 487.

1783
OCT. 2

Morris, Robert. Philadelphia. To [George] Washington
[Princeton]. Claret. L. S. 1 p.

64, 225

1783
OCT. 2

Williams, O[tho] H[olland]. Baltimore. To [William]
Jackson [Philadelphia]. Recommending Capt.
[Edward?] Dyer for appointment. A. L. S.
2 pp.   C. C. 152, 11, 553

1783
OCT. 3

Washington, George. Rocky Hill. To [Robert Morris,
Philadelphia]. Pay for the dragoon guard.
Draft. 2 pp. In handwriting of Benjamin
Walker.   A. VII, 251

1783
OCT. 3

Carleton, [Sir] Guy. New York. To [George] Washington [Rocky Hill]. Orders for evacuating Penobscot. Contemporary copy. 2 pp. In handwriting of Benjamin Walker. Enclosed in Washington to the President of Congress, 1783, Oct. 7.
C. C. 152, 11, 511

1783   **Washington**, George. Rocky Hill. To the President of
Oct. 7   Congress [Princeton]. Orders for the evacuation
              of Penobscot. Draft. 1 p. In handwriting of
              Benjamin Walker. Read in Congress, Oct. 9.
                                                A. VII, 253

1783   **Morris**, Robert. [Philadelphia.] To [George] Washing-
Oct. 10   ton [Princeton]. Pay [for the dragoon-guard].
              L. S. 1 p.   64, 263

1783   **Greene**, Nathanael. Philadelphia. To [George] Washing-
Oct. 11   ton [Rocky Hill]. Recommending certain officers
              who wish to be placed in the Peace Establish-
              ment. A. L. S. 4 pp. Enclosed in Washington
              to the President of Congress, 1783, Dec. 21.
                                           C. C. 152, 11, 549

1783   **Carroll**, Daniel. Princeton. To [George] Washington
Oct. 14   [Princeton]. Introducing Capt[-lt. James] Bruff.
              Recent copy. 1 p.   63, 277

1783   **Secretary at War**. [Princeton.] To [George] Washington
Oct. 15   [Princeton]. Officers of the Invalid regiment;
              retirement, pensions etc. L. S. of Benjamin Lin-
              coln. 3 pp. In handwriting of Samuel Shaw.
                                                        64, 286

1783   **Washington**, George. Rocky Hill. To [the Secretary at
Oct. 18   War, Princeton]. Disposition of the invalids.
              Draft. 1 p. In handwriting of Benjamin
              Walker.   A. VII, 255

1783   **Morris**, Robert. Philadelphia. To [George] Washington
Oct. 20   [Rocky Hill]. Introducing Arthur Noble; emi-
              gration from Ireland.   A. L. S. 1 p. 64, 298

1783   **Washington**, George. Rocky Hill. To Robert Morris
Oct. 28   [Philadelphia]. Invitation. Auto. draft signed.
              1 p.   P. III, 339

1783   **Lincoln**, B[enjamin]. Princeton. To [George] Washing-
Oct. 30   ton [Princeton]. Letter of introduction for Wil-
              liam Jackson. A. L. S. 1 p.   64, 322

1783   **Secretary at War**. [Princeton.] To [George] Washington
Nov. 1   [Rocky Hill]. Subsistence roll of Hospital De-
              partment. A. L. S. of Benjamin Lincoln. 1 p.
                                                        64, 330

1783   **Wayne**, Anthony. Philadelphia. To [George] Washing-
Nov. 1   ton [Rocky Hill]. Report of operations of troops
              under his command in Georgia from Jan. 19,
              1782, to Dec. 9. Victories over British and In-

dians; speeches, correspondence etc. A. L. S. 12 pp. Transmitted to Congress.

C. C. 152, 11, 555

1783
Nov. 4
Washington, George. R[ocky] Hill. To the Secretary at War [Princeton]. Continuance of officers of the Hospital Department. Draft. 1 p. In handwriting of Benjamin Walker. A. VII, 257

1783
Nov. 4
Washington, George. Rocky Hill. To the Board of War [Philadelphia]. Certificate of Maj. Allen McLane's services and right to pension.

McLane, Allen. History of above claim and later services to the country during war of 1812. Recent copies. 3 pp. C. C. 152, 11, 647

1783
Nov. 4
Lincoln, B[enjamin]. [Princeton.] To [George] Washington [Rocky Hill]. Motion in Congress to reduce army to 500 men; vote on same; adjournment to Annapolis. A. L. S. 3 pp. 64, 335

1783
Nov. 6
Washington, George. Rocky Hill. To the Secretary at War. Pay for the members of his military family. Auto. draft signed. 1 p.

P. III, 361

1783
Nov. 6
Washington, George. Rocky Hill. To [Alexander Hamilton, Princeton]. His retention of rank. Auto. draft signed. 2 pp. P. III, 363

1783
Nov. 8
Washington, George. Rocky Hill. To [the Secretary at War, Princeton] [Capt-lt. Peter] Taulman's claim to promotion; discharge of invalids. Draft. 3 pp. In handwriting of Benjamin Walker.

A. VII, 259

1783
Nov. 8
Secretary at War. [Princeton.] To [George] Washington [Rocky Hill]. Invalids to go to West Point; journey to Boston. A. L. S. of Benjamin Lincoln. 2 pp. 64, 347

1783
Nov. 12
Secretary at War. [Princeton.] To [George] Washington [West Point]. Returns for subsistence estimate. A. L. S. of Joseph Carleton. 1 p.

65, 29

1783
Nov. 12
Carleton, [Sir] Guy. New York. To [George] Washington [Orangetown]. Arrangements for evacuating New York. Contemporary copy. In handwriting of Benjamin Walker. Enclosed in Washington to the President of Congress, 1783, Nov. 18. C. C. 152, 11, 519

See: Writings of Washington (Ford) N. Y. 1891. 10, 334, note.

1783	**Continental Congress,** Secretary. Princeton. To [George] Washington [en route to West Point]. Election of Thomas Mifflin, President of Congress; adjournment to Princeton. L. S. of Charles Thomson. 1 p. **64**, 357

1783
Nov. 13

1783
Nov. 14

Washington, George. West Point. To [Sir] Guy Carleton [New York]. Arrangements for evacuation of New York. Contemporary copy. In handwriting of Benjamin Walker. Enclosed in Washington to the President of Congress, 1783, Nov. 18. C. C. **152**, 11, 519

See: Writings of Washington (Ford) N. Y. 1891. 10, 334, note.

1783
Nov. 15

[Washington, George.] West Point. To [Philip John Schuyler, Robert R. Livingston and James Duane]. Announcement of date of intended evacuation of New York by the British. Draft. 1 p. In handwriting of Benjamin Walker.

P. III, 365

1783
Nov. 18

Washington, George. West Point. To the President of Congress [Princeton]. Time fixed for evacuation of New York. Draft. 1 p. In handwriting of David Humphreys. Read in Congress, Dec. 13.

A. VII, 267

Printed: Writings of Washington (Ford) N. Y. 1891. 10, 334.

1783
Nov. 18

Washington, George. [West Point.] To the War Office [Princeton]. Discharge of troops. Draft. 1 p. In handwriting of Benjamin Walker.

A. VII, 265

1783
Nov. 18

Washington, George. West Point [New York.] To Robert Morris [Princeton?]. Approaching evacuation of New York; pay of officers. Draft. 2 pp. In handwriting of David Humphreys.

A. VII, 263

1783
Nov. 19

Jackson, M[ichael]. West Point [New York]. To George Washington [West Point]. Enclosing memorial to Congress. L. S. 1 p. Enclosed in Washington to the President of Congress, 1784, Jan. 19. C. C. **152**, 11, 639

1783
Nov. 25

Morris, Robert. [Philadelphia.] To [George] Washington [New York]. Introducing Baron Poellnitz. L. S. 1 p. **65**, 35

1783
Nov. 26

Morris, Robert. [Philadelphia.] To [George] Washington [New York]. Inability to comply with memorial officers or relieve distress of army as to pay; disagreeableness of his situation; backwardness of states. L. S. 2 pp. **63, 37**

1783
DEC. 1

Carleton, [Sir] Guy. H. M. S. *Ceres*, off Staten Island. To [George] Washington [New York]. Final departure of British. Contemporary copy. 1 p. In handwriting of Richard Varick. Enclosed in Washington to the President of Congress, 1783, Dec. 3. **C. C. 152, 11, 527**

1783
DEC. 3

Washington, George. New York. To [the President of Congress, Princeton]. Announcing departure of British from New York. Draft. 1 p. In handwriting of Benjamin Walker. Read in Congress, Dec. 18. **A. VII, 269**

Printed: Writings of Washington (Sparks) Boston. 1835. 8, 500.

1783
DEC. 15

Washington, George. Philadelphia. To [Col. Charles Armand-Tufin,] Marquis de la Rouerie [Philadelphia]. His merit as an officer and services to America. Contemporary copy. 3 pp. Endorsed: "Mar. 1, 1784. Original returned to Genl. Armand." **C. C. 152, 11, 643**

1783
DEC. 20

Washington, George. Annapolis [Maryland].. To the President of Congress [Annapolis]. Arrangements for resigning his commission. Draft. 1 p. In handwriting of Benjamin Walker.

A. VII, 271

1783
DEC. 21

Washington, George. Annapolis. To [the President of Congress, Annapolis]. Reduction of the army; recommending Brig. Gen. Michael Jackson and Col. Richard Butler; other miscellaneous military matters. Draft. 5 pp. In handwriting of Benjamin Walker. Read in Congress, Dec. 22.

A. VII, 273

Printed, in part: Writings of Washington (Sparks) Boston. 1835 8, 502.

[1783]
[DEC. 21]

Continental Army. Officers desiring to be placed in the Peace Establishment of the Army. List of names by states. 1 p. In handwriting of Benjamin Walker. Enclosed in Washington to the President of Congress, 1783, Dec. 21.

C. C. 152, 11, 541

1783
DEC. 22

Continental Congress, Annapolis. Resolve establishing order of the public audience of Gen. George Washington. Draft. 1 p. In handwriting of Charles Thomson. **A. VII, 279**

Printed: Writings of Washington (Ford) N. Y. 1891. 10, 377, note.

1783
DEC. 23

W[ashingto]n, G[eorge]. Annapolis. To the President of Congress [Annapolis]. Address resigning his commission. Draft signed. 2 pp. In handwriting of David Humphreys.   **A. VII, 281**

Printed: Writings of Washington (Ford) N.Y. 1891. 10, 338.

1783
DEC. 23

Continental Congress. [Annapolis]. To George Washington [Annapolis]. Address of the President of Congress on resigning his commission. 2 pp. In handwriting of and attested by Charles Thomson.   **A. VII, 283**

Printed: Journals of Congress of given date.

1784
JAN. 5

Continental Congress, Resolve. Declining to nominate persons to be created Knights of the Order of Divine Providence. Contemporary copy. 2 pp. Enclosed in President of Congress to Washington, 1784, Jan. 9.   **65, 175**

1784
JAN. 9

Continental Congress, President. Annapolis To "General" George Washington [Mt. Vernon]. Transmitting resolves relative to Polish Order of Knights of Divine Providence. A. L. S. of Thomas Mifflin. 1 p.   **65, 174**

1784
JAN. 14

Washington, George. Mount Vernon [Virginia]. To the President of Congress [Annapolis]. Recommending [Lt.] Col. [David] Humphreys for office. A. L. S. 3 pp. Read in Congress, Jan. 29.
   C. C. 152, 11, 631

Printed: Writings of Washington (Sparks) Boston. 1835. 9, 7.

1784
JAN. 19

Washington, George. Mount Vernon. To the President of Congress [Annapolis]. Submitting papers in case of Brig. Gen. Michael Jackson; recommending Capt. [Michael Gabriel] Houdin for commission in Peace Establishment of the Army. L. S. 2 pp. In handwriting of David Humphreys. Read in Congress, Jan. 29.   **C. C. 152, 11, 635**

1784
MAR. 19

Steuben, [Baron von]. Annapolis [Maryland]. To the President of Congress [Annapolis]. Appointment of Major [William] North to Inspectorship of the army. L. S. 1 p. Read in Congress, Mar. 22. Mar. 23 referred to Howell, Gerry and Williamson.   **C. C. 152, 11, 477**

[1789]
[APR. 14]

[Thomson, Charles.] [Mt Vernon.] To [George Washington, Mt Vernon]. Address informing him of his election as President of the United States. Auto. draft. 1 p.   **115, 125**

ERRATA.

p. 40, item 90, 104, for 1776 *read* 1777.

p. 79, item 152, 3, 137, for D'Emory *read* D'Emery.

p. 153, item 93, 201, for 1777 *read* 1779.

p. 160, item 91, 227, for 1777 *read* 1778.

p. 161, item 152, 4, 359, for Robert *read* Richard.

p. 162, item 152, 4, 391,   same.

p. 169, item 90, 262,   same.

p. 207, item W, *read* Navy Board to George Washington.

p. 232, item 93, 110, for 1778 *read* 1779.

p. 319, item 93, 146, for Johnston *read* Johnson.

p. 321, item 93, 143,   same.

p. 339, item 93, 237, for Hancock *read* Jay.

p. 353, item 152, 7, 477, for New York *read* New Jersey.

p. 361, item 34, 43, for Spooner *read* Spencer.

p. 365, item 34, 93, for Richard *read* Robert.

p. 373, item 152, 8, 151, after Fort Herkimer, New York, **read** To [Brig.] Gen. [Abraham] Ten Broeck.

p. 403, item 94, 203, for 1780 *read* 1777.

p. 455, item A. V. pt. II, 233, for Walter *read* Walton.

p. 465, A. V. pt. II, 281, for Walker *read* Walton.

p. 487, item 95, 93, for North *read* South Carolina.

p. 497, item Miscel., for 1781 *read* 1782.

p. 523, item A. VI, pt. I, 127, for Charles Carroll *read* Daniel.

p. 581, item 152, 10, 555, for death of Aaron White *read* Philip.

p. 629, item 152, 11, 37, for Samuel *read* Solomon.

p. 674, item 64, 201, for Williamson *read* Huntington.

p. 678, item 64, 357, for Princeton *read* Annapolis.

p. 678, item 152, 11, 519, for West Point *read* New York.

LIST OF PRESIDENTS OF THE CONTINENTAL CONGRESS.

Peyton Randolph, of Virginia_____Sept. 5, 1774
Henry Middleton, of South Carolina_____Oct. 22, 1774
Peyton Randolph_____May 10, 1775
John Hancock, of Massachusetts_____May 24, 1775
Henry Laurens, of South Carolina_____Nov. 1, 1777
John Jay, of New York_____Dec. 10, 1778
Samuel Huntington, of Connecticut_____Sept. 28, 1779
Thomas McKean, of Delaware_____July 10, 1781
John Hanson, of Maryland_____Nov. 5, 1781
Elias Boudinot, of New Jersey _____Nov. 4, 1782
Thomas Mifflin, of Pennsylvania_____Nov. 3, 1783
Richard Henry Lee, of Virginia_____Nov. 30, 1784
John Hancock_____Nov. 23, 1785
Nathaniel Gorham, of Massachusetts_____June 6, 1786
Arthur St. Clair, of Pennsylvania_____Feb. 2, 1787
Cyrus Griffin, of Virginia_____Jan. 22, 1788

INDEX.

A.

Holtzendorf, Baron, 502.

Homans, John, 281.

Hondgson, Robert, 469.

Honor, National, 650.

Hooper, Robert Lettis, jr., 215, 378.

Hoops, Robert, 158.

Hopkins, David, 180, 350.

Hopkins, Esek, 56, 57, 130.

Hopkinson, Francis, 170, 181, 199, 204, 206, 207, 217, 221, 223, 224.

Horse Neck (Connecticut), British at, 294; skirmish, 296.

Horses, 119, 172, 394, 499; for Armand's corps, 387, 602; for Baylor's dragoons, 329, 330, 382, 383; difficulty in obtaining, 170; kept at public expense, 410; officers' lost in service, 392, 474, 631; pasturage, 411; purchase, 296, 470; prisoners', 590; reduction of number in camp, 470; sale of, 652; seized by Hessians, 170; for Sheldon's dragoons, 387; surrendered at Yorktown and Gloucester, 555.

Hosmer, Titus, 251.

Hospital, 30, 49, 97, 100, 116, 118, 127, 128, 132, 134, 135, 456, 584, 586; appointments, 533, 545, 547; arrangement, 284, 445; at Bethlehem, Pa., 342; in Canada, 48; director, 22, 486; Eastern department, 330; establishment, 14, 124, 133, 134, 199; inquiry, 106; inspection, 139; instruments, 77; management, 70; needs, 548, 603; for Northern army, 106; officers, 70, 135, 468, 469, 486, 566, 604, 606, 629, 677; pay, 468, 469, 486, 524; plan, 124, 199, 465, 537, 539; promotions, 533, 534, 547; regulations, 77, 133, 134, 486, 599; subsistence, 629, 676; sick, 89; supplies, 70, 71, 77, 439, 537, 553, 603, 604, 632; vacancies, 525; in Virginia, 585, 588.

Hospital mates, 547.

Hostages, 403, 406, 517, 541.

Hostilities, suspension of, 612, 613; cessation of, 649, 650, 651, 652, 653.

Houdin, Michael Gabriel, 680.

Houston, William Churchill, 373, 379, 413; commissaries, 156; drafts and

Houston—Continued.

copies by, 120, 149, 158, 159, 167, 168, 169, 178, 179, 181, 394.

Howe, Richard, Viscount, 203, 243; letters, 84, 90; approach to New York, 63; commission, 226; committee of Congress, 87; Congress reply to, 242; peace conference, 87, 88, 89; prisoner matters, 83, 84, 134; refusal of letter to Washington, 69, 70.

Howe, Robert, 433, 454, 675; letters, 353, 359, 454, 488; acquittal of, 567; charge against, 465; conduct of, 395; court-martial, 566; inquiry into conduct of, 544; ordered against Pennsylvania mutineers, 666; seizure of rum, 627.

Howe, Sir William, 36, 82, 152, 174, 200, 203, 205, 208, 209, 211, 212, 213, 214, 217, 220, 224; letters, 31, 37, 77, 81, 84, 91, 95, 102, 103, 121, 127, 138, 147, 148, 152, 201, 209, 210, 211, 213, 215, 216, 217, 220, 223, 236, 239; commissions, 218, 226; conciliatory acts of Parliament, 239; declaration of King's intention, 90; designs, 110; expressions of, 222; junction with Burgoyne, 159, 167; prisoner matters, 37, 76, 77, 84, 91, 92, 94, 95, 102, 103, 121, 127, 138, 147, 148, 149, 151, 154, 155, 201, 202, 210, 211, 213, 215, 216, 217, 220, 223, 236; proclamation, 108; refusal of letter to Washington, 73; resolves of Congress, 69.

Howell, David, 680.

Howell, Ebenezer, 96.

Howell, Richard, 390, 615, 618.

Howley, Richard, 468, 538, 539.

Hubley, Adam, 320, 331.

Hubley, Adam, jr., 342.

Huddy, Joshua, capture, 577; case of, 580, 584, 617; demand for murderers of, 578; investigation of death, 630; placard pinned to body of, 576; murder of, 576, 577, 578; murderers of, 625; punishment of murderers, 626; papers relative to murder, 610; retaliation for, 576, 578, 581, 583.

Hudson Bay Company, 623.

Stores—Continued.

oming, 347; at West Point, 398, 434; at Yorktown, 553, 558. *See also* Commissary-General of Military Stores.

Stores, Department of Military, 496.

Store-ship, British, 106; loss of, 120.

Storrs, Experience, 23.

Strauben, Philip, 536, 539.

Stringer, Samuel, 48, 116, 117.

Subalterns, 20.

Subsistence, 19, 22, 70, 191, 269, 318, 367, 369, 371, 372, 377, 385, 388, 561, 580; estimate, 677; for general officers, 372; roll of hospital department, 676; of hospital officers, 629; money, 356; notes for Washington's family, 633; of officers, 441, 447, 629, 630, 632, 636, 637, 656; of prisoners, 448, 497, 612, 613, 619, 621, 639; for recruits, 120.

Substitutes, 202.

Suffolk County. (*See* New York, Suffolk County.)

Sullivan, Daniel, 307.

Sullivan, Ebenezer, 221.

Sullivan, John, 52, 53, 56, 57, 253, 255, 313, 320, 324, 327, 330, 331, 334, 335, 338, 341, 342, 345, 350, 351, 352, 357, 413, 460, 461, 465, 466, 469, 471, 472, 474, 475, 482, 483, 484, 485, 486, 490, 495, 496, 501, 502, 512, 513, 514, 532, 535; letters, 53, 54, 61, 85, 110, 150, 158, 195, 218, 231, 252, 253, 256, 258, 272, 307, 319, 325, 327, 329, 332, 333, 336, 339, 340, 341, 344, 354, 360, 367, 470, 472, 475, 478, 483, 484, 488, 496, 503, 511, 515, 519, 521, 524, 530, 535, 620; abilities of, 58; address to troops, 360; arms for, 248; command of expedition against Six Nations, 295, 296; commissions to officers in Canada, 59; complaints, 352, 357; controversy with Board of War, 360; court of inquiry on, 180, 195, 198; exchange of, 88; failure against Staten Island, 181; general orders of, 356; impropriety of letter, 159, 160; instructions for Western expedition, 331; misstatements of, 354; Oneida addresses, 361, 368;

Sullivan—Continued.

papers sent to Congress, 347; questions to General officers in Rhode Island, 256; recall from army, 185, 186, 187; request for Stark, 234, 238; resignation of, 158, 382; services to Army in Congress, 531; success of, 370; supplies for, 352; victories of, 363; terms with Indians, 333, 334.

Sumner, Job, 304.

Sumter, Thomas, 450, 500.

Superintendent of Finance. (*See* Finance, Superintendent of.)

Supplies, 18, 20, 22, 23, 54, 68, 91, 94, 100, 110, 112, 155, 186, 205, 280, 317, 354, 377, 379, 388, 391, 399, 405, 409, 411, 412, 414, 422, 424, 429, 431, 433, 434, 435, 441, 448, 449, 450, 455, 477, 479, 480, 484, 489, 507, 510, 520, 526, 530, 532, 567, 640; at Albany, 272; articles of agreement for, 575; from Bermuda, 309; British, 139; called for, 427; captured on high seas, 77; collection of, 206, 485; contract matters, 516, 523, 575, 582, 586, 588; for Convention troops, 518; curtailment of, 282; from Delaware, 432; difficulties, 592; distribution of, 161; estimates, 387, 441; from Europe, 63; for Fort Pitt, 406, 408, 417, 603; at Fort Schuyler, 330, 456; from France, 404, 406; for the French, 323, 362, 512; furnished British, 71, 74, 469, 624; furnished by James White, 447; Hollingsworth's report on, 408; hospital, 537, 603, 604; for Indians, 494, 604; lack of, 330, 344, 350, 378, 410, 411, 420, 425, 431, 432, 440, 449, 450, 451, 462, 470, 474, 505, 509, 512, 576; for march of army to south, 542; from Maryland, 407; energy of New Jersey in furnishing, 396, 398; for New Jersey troops, 572; New York's inability to furnish, 482; for operation against New York City, 492; in North, 469; for Northern army, 118, 160, 162, 164, 275; payment for, 279, 298, 493, 636; for partisan corps, 469; from Pennsylvania,